THE SOVIET EXPERIMENT

THE SOVIET EXPERIMENT

Russia, the USSR, and the Successor States

Ronald Grigor Suny

New York   Oxford
OXFORD UNIVERSITY PRESS
1998

Oxford University Press

Oxford   New York
Athens   Auckland   Bangkok   Bogota   Bombay   Buenos Aires
Calcutta   Cape Town   Dar es Salaam   Delhi   Florence   Hong Kong
Istanbul   Karachi   Kuala Lampur   Madras   Madrid   Melbourne
Mexico City   Nairobi   Paris   Singapore   Taipei   Tokyo   Toronto   Warsaw

and associated companies in
Berlin   Ibadan

Copyright © 1998 by Oxford University Press, Inc.

Published by Oxford University Press, Inc.
198 Madison Avenue, New York, New York 10016

Oxford is a registered trademark of Oxford University Press

Library of Congress Cataloging-in-Publication Data

Suny, Ronald Grigor.
    The Soviet experiment : Russia, the USSR, and the successor states
/ Ronald Grigor Suny.
        p.   cm.
    Includes bibliographical references and index.
    ISBN 0-19-508104-8 (acid-free paper). — ISBN 0-19-508105-6 (pbk.
:   acid-free paper)
    1. Soviet Union—History.   I. Title.
DK266.S94
1998
    947-dc21   97-19996
                                                                    CIP

Printing (last digit): 1 3 5 7 9 8 6 4 2
Printed in the United States of America
on acid-free paper

For My Father,

Gourgen "George" Suny

(1910–1995)

who started me up the road that led to this book.

Contents

INTRODUCTION: Utopia and Its Discontents

Trying to understand Russia or the Soviet Union has preoccupied serious Western observers at least since the fifteenth century, probably much earlier. A society closed to easy penetration and comprehension, Russia has fascinated many precisely because it is so difficult to know. Winston Churchill spoke of Russia as a "riddle wrapped in a mystery inside an enigma." Journalists and political leaders, Kremlin watchers and scholars have written so many contradictory things about the USSR that they confirm what the American humorist Will Rogers said: "Russia is a country that no matter what you say about it, it's true."

The last years of the twentieth century seem to be the right moment to tell the story of the Soviet Union as a whole. That turbulent tale now has a beginning, a middle, and an end. So traumatic and painful have been this century's transformations of Russia and the Soviet republics, so controversial their motivations and effects, and so filled with political passion have the observers and participants been that no single historian's view can be convincing to all. The Soviet Union may be gone but its effects remain. Understanding that experience, giving it meaning and making judgments about it, will continue for a long time to engage present and future generations of social scientists and students. This book is an attempt to deal fairly and dispassionately with a complex history that has divided friend from foe, East from West, Left from Right—not with the vain hope of reconciling irreconcilable differences, but with the expectation that an analytic and interpretative narrative will add to our understanding.

In overall design this history of the Soviet Union is conceived as the story of three revolutions, each identified with a single individual: the revolution of 1917, in which Vladimir Lenin played a key role and that founded the Soviet political order; Joseph Stalin's revolution of the 1930s, which forged the statist economic system that the West would call "totalitarian" and the Soviet leaders would identify as "socialism"; and Mikhail Gorbachev's revolution (1985–91), which tried to dismantle the Stalinist legacy and ended by undermining the Leninist heritage as well. Two major periods of reform separated these revolutionary episodes: the New Economic Policy (1921–28), with its confusion about the transition from capitalism to socialism and the power struggle among the leading Communists for leadership, and the post-Stalin years divided between Nikita Khrushchev's erratic and incomplete reforms and the nearly two decades of Leonid Brezhnev's conservative retrenchment.

The Soviet Union, its leaders, and its mission to build socialism have often been characterized as utopian. The word *utopia* means "no place," something that does not exist in the real world but, like Thomas More's peaceful and harmonious island society, only in the imagination. The word stirs up notions of perfection and perfectability, of a possible resolution of the mundane problems of human existence, but also brings to mind an impossible ideal, a lack of realism, or an impractical scheme for social improvement. In the present "post-utopian" world, utopia is most often associated with senseless dreams that can lead to social disaster, and much futuristic fiction, from George Orwell's *1984* to Aldous Huxley's *Brave New World*, warns readers away from zealous tampering with the delicate mechanisms and achieved compromises of the societies in which they live.

But utopia can also be understood to be an ideal, a goal toward which people aspire. In this sense of utopia are contained the political hopes and ends for which people are prepared to work, die, even kill. In a sense, every political movement seeking change contains within it a utopia, a place where if all were possible people would like to end up. The early Soviet leaders traced their political heritage back to the revolutionary Left that emerged in the French Revolution. Its goals were admittedly utopian in the sense that they sought to change and reconstruct society in line with their ideals of equality, social justice, and popular participation in the political world. From the early nineteenth century, socialism, in its variety of specific meanings, has referred to the principal set of ideas and the principal social movement opposed to capitalism, the form of human organization that arose to become the dominant system of production throughout the world. From its origins, socialism had the goal of broadening the power of ordinary people, that is, of extending as far as possible the limits of democracy, not only in the realm of politics (which was the goal of democratic radicals and leftist liberals) but in the economy as well. Indeed, socialists were always convinced that the ideal of liberal democrats of a representative political order coexisting with the private ownership of the means of production and the potential accumulation of enormous wealth was fundamentally contradictory. The power implicit in property and wealth, they believed, would inevitably distort and corrupt the democratic political sphere. Therefore, socialists searched for mechanisms of social control or social ownership of the means of production.

Devoted to Karl Marx's vision of socialism, in which the working class would control the machines, factories, and other sources of wealth production, the Communists led by Lenin believed that the future social order would be based on the abolition of unearned social privilege, the end of racism and colonial oppression, the secularization of society, and the empowerment of working people. Yet within a generation Stalin and his closest comrades had created one of the most vicious and oppressive states in modern history.

Soviet-style "state socialism" ended up as a perverse imitation of authentic social ownership, in which a ruling elite of party chieftains and bureaucratic managers ran the country in the name of—and ostensibly in the interests of—the mass of the people. Unless one believes that any attempt at social engineering or revolutionary transformation, any tampering with the delicate mechanisms of existing societies, must inevitably end up in authoritarianism, historians must attempt to explain the rapid fall from democracy and egalitarianism into the terror and totalitarianism of Stalinism.

Soviet history has been used to tell many stories. Its sympathizers have lauded its virtues as evidence of what a socialist system can achieve, from high levels of industrial growth to championship Olympic teams; its opponents have depicted its history as the proof of the evils (indeed, the impossibility) of a non-market road to modernity. Gorbachev's efforts to create a more democratic evolution of the system, to restrain the power of the Communist party, to awaken public opinion and political participation through glasnost, and to allow greater freedom to the non-Russian peoples of the Soviet borderlands seemed to confirm the optimism of those who believed in the democratic potential of Soviet socialism. But the collapse of communism in 1989–91 dragged down with it not only the hard-line Communists but also more democratic socialists who had banked on gradual reform toward social democracy or some moderate form of market economy. In its wake came the widely touted belief that Gorbachev's failure had finally proven the infeasibility of a socialist state and the exclusive possibility of a rapid move toward capitalism. Many liberal and conservative analysts believe that freedom, democracy, and the market are inextricably tied together; property rights and personal rights are not only not in opposition but necessary for one another. And the bankruptcy of Soviet-style socialism, the exposure of the vastness of Stalin's crimes, the rapid conversion of many former Communists, like Boris Yeltsin, to the ideas of market economics—all came together in a powerful perception that the Soviet experiment had been doomed from the beginning and that there is no real alternative to capitalism, which remains, as it has always been, the one great economic system that best fits human nature. We have reached, proclaimed the writer Francis Fukuyama, the end of history, and the West has won!

This book is an attempt to recover the complexities and contradictions of the seventy years of Soviet power, its real achievements as well as its grotesque failings. Rather than see all of Soviet history as moving toward a preordained end, made inexorable because of the impossibility of realizing the original utopian vision, this history of the Soviet Union seeks to show the false starts and unintended results of the Soviet experience, as well as the ways in which human will and effort are able to transform society. If there is an overall thesis, it is that Soviet achievements produced the factors that eventually led to its decline and collapse. One of the recurrent ironies of the twentieth century has been that Marxist governments have come to power, not where they were supposed to in theory, in the highest developed capitalisms, but in backward, semicolonial states. And their greatest achievements have been to reproduce in many ways the great transformation that the Western middle classes accomplished in their capitalist industrializations. That is, the actual project of

Leninist states has been to modernize, but under noncapitalist conditions. And in crude terms they were extraordinarily successful, transforming agrarian societies into urban, industrial ones in far shorter time than in most Western countries. But even as they did so these actually existing socialisms abandoned much of the original socialist utopia.

Social revolution is always a compromise between the historical material available and the visions of the revolutionaries. Russia was one of the most inhospitable places on the globe for social experimentation either socialist or capitalist. A country 85 percent peasant, the least likely candidate in Europe to create a society modeled on Marx's ideas of proletarian democracy, Russia suffered years of war, revolution, civil war, economic collapse, and famine before the Communists were securely in power. Even Lenin argued, until his death, that socialism could not be built in one country, certainly not in Russia, without an international proletarian revolution to come to the aid of more backward nations. But that revolution never came, and the Soviet Union was left isolated and backward at the edge of Europe. If the country was to become modern, it would have to do it on its own.

Marxism's intellectual roots ran deep in the industrial revolution, and along with its aspirations to end exploitation and fully realize human potential, it also shared certain logics with capitalism and the whole Western project to achieve a particular kind of industrial modernization. The Communist Party committed itself to the enormous task of transforming the people from peasants to workers and the country from basically agrarian to industrial. But as it used the instruments of its power to force change on a reluctant people, the party moved rapidly away from any conceivably democratic concept of popular participation. In many ways, the story of the twentieth century can be told as the erosion of the emancipatory, moral, humanistic side of Marxism, indeed socialism in general, and the elevation of the economistic, productivist, statist elements—to the point that its utopia became, in the USSR, the dystopia of Stalinism, and in the West the compromise with capitalism embodied in Western Social Democracy.

Though what the Communists eventually created was a distorted version of what the early revolutionaries had intended, their efforts had profound and lasting effects. A self-perpetuating class of Communist bosses ran a colossal state-driven, nonmarket economy and a gargantuan state apparatus that crushed any opposition to its rule, stifled free expression outside its own strict limits, and constantly forced the population to display its loyalty to the system. Arbitrariness and personal power overruled the rule of law. In the economy command and obedience replaced enterprise, innovation, and initiative. When the gears of the Soviet system began to grind more slowly in the 1980s, Gorbachev tried first lubrication, then major repairs, but the machine fell apart. In the ruined landscape left by the Soviets, new leaders are attempting another great experiment, this time embracing capitalism and democracy. Whatever its chances for success, whatever its outcome, the shape of the post-Soviet world will be indelibly marked by the Soviet experience that preceded it. This book is about that experience.

This history of the USSR, its origins, evolutions, and collapse, is the product of more than twenty-five years of teaching, reading, and writing on the subject. An enormous debt is owed to my own teachers but an even greater one to colleagues and students who have continued to contribute to my understanding. I especially want to thank David Kerans, Valerie Kivelson, Daniel Orlovsky, Lewis H. Siegelbaum, Peter Martinson, Thomas Noonan, Amir Weiner, Sheila Fitzpatrick, and Steven Zipperstein for reading parts or the whole of earlier drafts; James Reische for his diligence, care, and intelligence in compiling the index; my editor James Miller for numerous suggestions on how to improve the manuscript; and especially Nancy Lane, who first conceived of the project, convinced me to undertake it, and kept me at it through times of discouragement. Though some historians are mentioned in the text, many more would have had footnotes to their work in a conventional scholarly work. I have made an effort to list all those who have contributed to this history in the suggested readings. Finally, as always, I must mention with gratitude the patience and tolerance of my wife, Armena Marderosian, and my daughters, Sevan and Anoush Suni. We all live with the loss of the time taken from our lives together to tell this story.

Two technical points are in order. First, the calendar used in Russia was twelve days behind the Western calendar in the nineteenth century and thirteen days in the twentieth. I have used the Russian ("old style") dating up to the Soviet adoption of the Western calendar in February 1918 and indicated the equivalent Western "new style" (n.s.) date in parentheses. Second, the spelling of Russian names and terms follows the Library of Congress usage with a few modifications for clarity (e.g., no marks for soft or hard signs). Names familiar to Western readers are given in the generally accepted form. The word *soviet* refers to the council of deputies, as in Petrograd soviet; when capitalized, *Soviet* refers to the state or government (e.g., the Soviet Union or Soviet people).

THE SOVIET EXPERIMENT

PART I

CRISIS
AND
REVOLUTION

CHAPTER 1
The Imperial Legacy

Land and People

The first impression of a traveler moving across Russia at the turn of the twentieth century was the vast size of the country. Stretching nine thousand miles from Central Europe to the Pacific Ocean, Russia was the largest country in the world. Finland and most of Poland, with its historic capital, Warsaw, were within its borders, as were the ancient Christian kingdoms of Armenia and Georgia and the Muslim emirates of Bukhara and Khiva. Traveling from west to east, one moved across an enormous plain without any significant natural barriers. Even the Ural Mountains, which mapmakers established as the border between Europe and Asia, were no obstacle to nomads or invaders. Only in the south were there major mountain chains, like the Caucasus in European Russia and the Pamir, Tien Shan, and Altai at the edge of Central Asia and China. A lesser range, the Carpathians, marked the border between Ukraine and the countries of Central Europe. Moving from north to south was as easy as east to west, facilitated by the great river systems of the Dnieper, Don, Volga, Ob, Enisei, and Lena.

Russia began as a landlocked cluster of small states that grew first to the north and west, later to the east and south, until it bordered on the Baltic Sea and the Arctic Ocean, the Black and Caspian Seas, and, by the seventeenth century, the Pacific Ocean. Russia lay to the north of most of the other major powers in the world. Two-thirds of the empire was above the 50th parallel. One of its southernmost towns, Erevan, later to be the capital of Armenia, was on a parallel with Philadelphia. The harsh continental climate of Russia proper was alleviated only in the empire's peripheries—on the Baltic and Black Sea coasts, in Transcaucasia, Central Asia, and the Far Eastern maritime regions. Much of northern Russia and Siberia is permanently frozen tundra, a wasteland of scrubby vegetation. To its south are the massive coniferous forests of the taiga, followed by the mixed-forest zone and the great plains, or steppe. Still farther south, especially in Central Asia, are the arid deserts that make up another 20 percent of the country's territory.

Russia's unfortunate position on the earth's surface determined both the limits of development and the burdens that ordinary Russians bore as their rulers attempted to compete with more industrialized and technologically more sophisticated countries to the west. Despite its abundant mineral resources, often forbiddingly difficult to recover, Russia was a relatively backward, underdeveloped country as it entered the twentieth century. In the words of one economist, prerevolutionary Russia was "the poorest of the civilized nations." It was the great power least transformed by the industrial revolution of the nineteenth century. In 1913 Great Britain was almost five times richer per capita than Russia; the United States was more than eight times richer. Indeed, Russia was poorer per capita than Italy and Spain. And the gap between Russia and the richer nations of Europe widened between 1861 and 1931. Both tsarist and Soviet elites were motivated by the drive to overcome their inferior position and rival the greatest powers on the globe. A sense of backwardness and the need to catch up stimulated, inspired, and sometimes brought Russian leaders to despair.

Just over 43 percent of the people of the Russian Empire in 1900 were ethnic Russians, sometimes called Great Russians, speakers of a Slavic language, usually members of the Orthodox Church, and primarily peasant farmers. They were closely related linguistically, socially, and religiously to the two other major Eastern Slavic groups, the Ukrainians and Belorussians. These three peoples, along with the Poles, made up the Slavic core of the empire, about 72 percent of the population. But since the conquest of the Tatar Khanate of Kazan on the Volga in 1552, Russia had been a multinational empire, and in the early twentieth century it ruled over millions of Jews (4 percent of the population), Kazaks (3 percent), Finns (2 percent), Tatars, Germans, Armenians, Georgians, Muslims of the Volga region, Caucasia, and Central Asia, and the so-called small peoples of the north. The dominant language, used by officials and higher education, was Russian, but over a hundred other languages, from the Turkic tongues of the Central Asian nomads to the Baltic languages of the Latvians and Lithuanians, coexisted uneasily with Slavic. The empire proclaimed itself religiously Orthodox, the heir to the heritage of Byzantium, but many of its subjects followed other Christian churches, like that of the Armenians, as well as Islam, Judaism, Shamanism, and Buddhism. Russia was a great state, a multinational empire, but not a single nation with a single culture and sense of collective identity.

The first Russian state was founded on the Dneiper, in what is now Ukraine, in the late ninth century (traditional date, 882). The princes of Kievan Rus adopted Christianity as their official religion around 988, establishing a relationship with the Byzantine Empire and what became Orthodoxy, which had enormous influence on the future ideology of tsarism. The imperial two-headed eagle, symbolizing the close relationship of state and church, with the latter headed by the tsar, the separation from the Catholic West and its Renaissance, and a sense of religious mission—all came from Byzantium and influenced the shape of the Russian world. With the decline and fall of Kiev in the twelfth and thirteen centuries, the Russian lands were fractured into smaller, competing states, which were subjugated by the Mongols in 1237–40. For nearly two hundred years Russia and much of Eurasia were ruled by a great empire with its center far to the east in the steppes of Mongolia. Paying tribute to the Great Khans like the other Russian states, one of the least prominent of the principalities, Moscow, emerged eventually as the center of resistance to the Mongols and effectively "gathered the Russian lands" into a single state. In the reign of Ivan III, "the Great" (1462–1505), Moscow conquered Novgorod and Tver, and its particular system of absolutist rule replaced the more oligarchic forms in other states. Muscovite Russia was autocratic, with absolute power in the hands of the grand duke (later the tsar), highly centralized (eventually bureaucratic), and militaristic, with its warrior nobles having little independent authority and serving only at the pleasure of the prince.

Muscovy expanded steadily in the sixteenth and seventeenth centuries, and in the reign of Ivan IV, "the Terrible" (1533–84), it moved beyond the Volga and south to Astrakhan on the Caspian. Ivan IV was the first Russian ruler to call himself "tsar," the Russian word for emperor borrowed from the Latin *caesar*. After his death, the empire suffered a "Time of Troubles," civil strife and foreign invasions by the Poles. But with the founding of the Romanov dynasty in 1613, greater stability led to renewed growth, first to the west with the incorporation of Ukraine (the union of Pereiaslavl, 1654), then to the east with the steady migration into Siberia. Russians crossed the Bering Strait and the Pacific and briefly established colonies in California. In the eighteenth century dynamic emperors pushed Russia's frontiers to the Baltic and Black Seas, bringing Latvians, Lithuanians, Estonians, Baltic Germans, and Tatars into the empire. In the first half of the nineteenth century Russians crossed the Caucasus and annexed the lands of Georgians, Armenians, and Azerbaijanis, after which they had to fight for decades to "pacify" the peoples of the mountainous North Caucasus. The final phases of Russia's expansion came in the second half of the century with the drive into Central Asia and the ultimately futile effort to extend Russian power in the Far East. Russia reached its greatest size in the decades before the revolution of 1917. Though Soviet influence and power would at times reach far beyond the borders of the Soviet state, the trend in the twentieth century was no longer expansion of the empire's borders but "downsizing" of the Russian realm, until by the last decade of the century Russia shrank back to the contours of Muscovy and Siberia.

In the late sixteenth and early seventeen centuries the Muscovite state steadily limited the movement of Russian peasants, who had enjoyed relative freedom to pursue their own economic lives, gradually turning them into serfs of the landholding nobles. A vast gulf developed between the top and bottom of society. Peasants lived as a separate class, isolated from the larger towns in village communes, holding on to their traditions, superstitions, and religion. The tsars and nobles adopted the ways of the West, particularly after the reign of Peter I, "the Great" (1682–1725), who forced the elites of Russia to study Europe in order to better serve the imperial state. Peter built up his army, levied new taxes, increased service obligations on the nobles, gave greater emphasis to European education, and introduced new industries and technologies borrowed from the West. Peter began a pattern of economic and political reform from above, in response to foreign challenge and domestic pretensions to greatness, that would be repeated throughout the next three hundred years. In the eighteenth century the educated elite of Russia took on the manners, and even the French language, of the European nobility, and in the reign of Catherine II, "the Great" (1762–96), the empress and her courtiers saw themselves as participants in the cultural and literary Enlightenment. While the upper layers of Russian society were marked by the more secular and cosmopolitan culture of the West, the great mass of the Russian people remained imbedded in the traditional religious culture that was wary of, even hostile to, foreign influences.

The vastness of the Russian Empire was a mixed blessing for its people. The very size of the country meant that the distances to market were extremely great. The riches that lay under the ground and might have contributed to industrialization were far from centers of population. Roads, railroads, and transportation networks in general were poorly developed, though they slowly improved in the century before the revolution. Yet in earlier centuries the frontier was a place to which peasant serfs might flee, and later Siberia attracted migrants from European Russia. Open lands, often quite rich, as in the southeast of central Russia, supported the peasants of the peripheries, though they were faced by unreliable precipitation and fewer sources of water. For the native peoples of the south, the mountains of Caucasia and the great deserts of Central Asia were refuges where the arm of the state could only weakly reach.

Life for most subjects of the tsar was as harsh as the climate. Life expectancy in 1887 was on average only thirty-two years. Russia's infant mortality rates were the highest in Europe. On the eve of World War I, 245 infants per 1,000 died before completing their first year of life (compared to 76 per 1,000 in Sweden). It was estimated that half of all peasant children did not live until their fifth birthday. Still, Russia's birthrate, one of the highest in Europe, more than made up for high mortality. The population grew rapidly, even after birthrates began to decline just before 1900. As nutrition improved, and famine and other catastrophes occurred less frequently in the early twentieth century, death rates also began to decline.

Dependent on peasant agriculture for the creation of wealth, Russians were able to cultivate only a small percentage of their land (about 11 percent). Huge territories lay in permafrost, and the unpredictable rainfall, poor soil, brief growing season (four to five months instead of the eight to nine months average in Western Europe), and the low level of agricultural technology conspired to make the Russian peasant one of the least productive farmers in the world. The antiquated agricultural methods resulted in the lowest yields in Europe. In Russia peasants averaged 8.8 bushels of grain per acre, while in Britain farmers produced 35.4 bushels. Widespread poverty was made worse by the great social inequality among Russians. In 1905, 1 percent of families accounted for 15 percent of the total income of the empire.

Russia was a society divided into legally constituted social categories called "estates" (sosloviia). In 1897, the year of the first all-Russian census, the empire's population numbered 124,649,000. Of these only 18,436,000 people lived in towns and cities, making up less than 14 percent of the population. They included artisans, industrial workers, clergy, nobles, bureaucrats, merchants, and a variety of other townspeople. The most powerful and influential people in the empire, the hereditary and personal nobility, numbered less than 1.5 percent of the population. Over three-quarters of the empire's population were peasants.

Generalizing about the more than 100 million people living in rural areas scattered across Eurasia and divided into dozens of different nationalities is impossible. Enormous differences divided nomads and seminomads in Central Asia from fur trappers and hunters of northeastern Siberia or the farmers of southern Ukraine. Rather than attempt here to characterize the variety of ways of life and mentalities of villagers throughout the country, we can make a few points about the peasants of European Russia.

Throughout Russia's history, the peasants paid for the rest of society, for the state, for industry, for the civilization of the towns and cities, which they despised and admired simultaneously. Particularly in the last half century of tsarist rule the government forced the peasants to "underconsume," as it has been euphemistically put, in order to tax their output and export grain abroad so that purchases and payments on the foreign loans that financed Russia's industrialization could be made. Living at the bottom of the social ladder, peasants were considered socially inferior to the rest of society and had little effect on the state's actions. Rather, they were acted upon by the state in the guise of its agents—the tax collector, the police officer, and the military recruiter. To the villagers, the government was foreign, far away, and appeared only as an intruder.

Yet this mass of people by its very size and importance in the economy of Russia was quite powerful, if in no other way because of what it could prevent from happening. During the imperial period the government and intellectuals at times saw the peasantry as the major obstacle to progress and development, at other times as the principal dike against the threat of revolution. Indeed, what the peasantry did or did not do would determine whether Russia would grow economically, stagnate, or even slide backward. The general poverty of the peasants limited the growth of markets—they had little money to buy very much—and restricted the formation of capital with which to industrialize the country. Many intellectuals saw the peasantry as the major obstacle to economic and social development. Some argued that the poverty of the peasants prevented the rise of a consumer market and that their lack of skills retarded the formation of a industrial working class.

Peasants were basically grain producers. On the eve of World War I over 90 percent of the sown land area was in grain. Not only were wheat and rye what the peasants ate and sold, but grain was the major export of the Russian Empire. The central economic struggle was over how much grain the peasants could keep or control and how much landlords and the state could take from them through rents, collection of debts, and taxation. Most peasants had very little disposable grain. Poverty, disease, death, and ignorance were their constant companions. They were poor in livestock and draft animals, and a cruel image from peasant life was that of a peasant pulling his own plow. The number of horses, cattle, and pigs per capita fell in the late nineteenth and early twentieth centuries, and the rapid growth of the population in the second half of the nineteenth century (25 million more peasants) meant less land for individual peasant families, higher prices for land, and forced migration either to Siberia or into cities.

Just after the Emancipation of the peasant serfs in 1861, slightly more than a quarter of Russia's peasants were unable to support themselves through agriculture alone. By 1900 just over half of the peasants could no longer make a living without outside earnings. For generations peasants lived on the edge of starvation, threatened by unpredictable natural forces. A drought or an epidemic could produce widespread famine, as in 1891. Outside the villages wolves roamed, killing upward of a million head of livestock a year. Movement from the village was difficult, even after Emancipation, for laws and economic ties bound people to the peasant commune. Peasant males might leave the village if drafted into the army or sent into Siberian exile or for seasonal work on other farms or in factories. Many peasants were so desperate for improvement in their material conditions that in the last twenty years of the empire 4.5 million Russians migrated to western Siberia and Central Asia.

Nevertheless, peasants managed to cope with the shortage of land and the backwardness of their technology. For all the uncertainty and brutality of peasant life, their conditions may have improved somewhat in the decades before World War I. Overall per-capita grain production actually increased between Emancipation and World War I. In many regions peasant income grew, especially after 1900, and peasants were able to keep more grain in their villages for their own consumption. After the peasant revolts of 1905–7, the government canceled many peasant debts (the payments to redeem the land given peasants after the Emancipation), and their incomes rose even more because of higher prices for grain. Peasant farmers may have felt poor and exploited, overtaxed and abused by the noble landlords in their midst, but in fact they produced on their own fields 86 percent of the total cereal output of the empire and 75 percent of the grain that reached market.

In the ethnically Russian center of the empire, peasant life and work was organized by a unique institution, the commune (in Russian, *obshchina* or *mir*). The commune's boundaries were those of the village, and it was at one and the same time the local administration, police, and enforcer of custom and tradition. A typical agricultural commune was made up of anywhere from four to eighty peasant households, with a mean in the late nineteenth century of roughly fifty-four households and 290 people. But in those provinces where water sources were more sparse, toward the south and east of European Russia, villages often included up to one thousand families. The commune ran the lives of the peasants and stood between them and the state. It collected taxes for the government, recruited young men for military service, and kept order in the village. While urban and upper-class Russians lived under written laws, tempered by the will of the autocrat, the peasants lived largely under the customary laws of their region. As a peasant saying declared, "God is invisible and the tsar is far away." But the state, represented by the police or local officials like the justice of the peace, could make itself felt when it needed to. After 1889 a new official, the land captain, appointed from the local nobility, enjoyed broad administrative and judicial powers over peasants.

Whereas state law was based on individual responsibility, peasant law recognized the collective responsibility of the village commune. The village as a whole was responsible for all taxes and obligations assured on the villagers.

Whereas private property was the norm in towns and cities, family-held or communal forms of property were dominant in the villages. Townspeople might accumulate wealth and rise far above their neighbors socially, but village folk remained generally equal in material terms to one another, and the commune periodically redistributed the village lands to keep households relatively equal. Peasant society was egalitarian and collective, in distinction to the world of the middle and upper classes, which was more individualistic and hierarchical. Instead of individual autonomy being highly praised, conformity to the ways of the village was enforced by the favorable or unfavorable opinion of others. Peasants were hard on those who deviated from social norms. Besides ridiculing them or gossiping about them, peasants controlled their fellow villagers more harshly by beating them, expelling them from the commune, turning them over to the military recruiter, or even, in the case of thieves or arsonists, killing them.

Peasants largely ran their own local affairs through a village assembly and their elected leaders, the elder and the tax collector. While the state tried to impose its authority through these officials, in practice they governed with the consent of the village assembly. The assembly had the greater authority among the peasants, who would obey government directives only after they had been adopted by the assembly. Male heads of household participated and voted in the assembly, which was dominated by older and better-off peasants and excluded women, youths, and men who did not have their own independent household.

Everything in peasant life was geared to the survival of the household and its meager economy. Marriage, for example, was based not so much on fulfilling emotional needs as on maintaining the supply of labor for the fields. The family usually worked together and produced for themselves. Little was left over for the market or the tax collector. In this way, they may be said to differ from what we usually understand as farmers, those who produce surpluses for the market and are, therefore, intimately involved in the capitalist system. Russian peasant society was far from what Marxists call "bourgeois" society, in which social improvement and position based on accumulated wealth, profit, and saving is both a goal and an incentive to work more than one needs to satisfy basic needs. Traditional in their work habits and ambitions, peasants were not guided by ideas of profit, maximizing their wealth, or efficiency, as capitalist farmers might be. Peasants suspected those with wealth and believed that it was accumulated at someone else's expense. They valued a rough equality, and anyone better off than another was expected to help the less fortunate, at least ideally. Peasants bought and sold in the markets when they could, but in times of great need they could withdraw, lower the amounts that they ate and used, tighten their belts, and wait for better times.

Their ideas of time were also different from those of people in modern industrial societies. Rather than being "spent" or "wasted" as in capitalist economies or regulated by clocks as in the modern world, peasant time responded to the natural rhythms of the sun and the seasons. Peasants might work from dawn till dark or for just a few hours, depending on what tasks or needs faced the family. When sowing or harvesting had to be done, peasants worked long, hard hours, but in winter they might spend most of the day asleep on the stove. Peasants worked as long as they had to to finish a job, not as long as a boss or a time clock told them to work. In this way, peasant work was task-oriented, not time-oriented. In addition, the work year was punctuated by religious holidays and feast days, which when added to Sundays made up over one hundred free days a year. The feasts were marked by huge consumption of food and alcohol, toasts, singing, and fistfights that helped alleviate the petty hostilities and tensions of village life.

Though the Russian villagers lived in a world apart from that of the urban classes, many peasants moved back and forth to towns to find work. The circumscribed cultural horizons of most peasants were broadened by such movements, as well as by schooling, which peasants sought as a means to improving their lives. In 1900 almost three-quarters of them were illiterate. More men than women could read, many of them learning their letters while serving in the army. The rate of literacy rose dramatically in the last decades of the tsarist empire, from 21 percent of the population in 1897 to about 40 percent on the eve of World War I. Though it is difficult to generalize about the mentality and beliefs of millions of peasants, historians have argued that they basically accepted the legitimacy of the existing social and political order. The "Little Father Tsar" was a revered and holy figure whom, it was thought, cared for his children, the peasants, and would redress their grievances if only nobles and bureaucratic officials did not prevent their cries from reaching his ears. Loyal primarily to family and village, and perhaps their region, tsar, and the Church, peasants did not have a very clear notion of allegiance to a broader Russian nation.

The existing order was sanctioned by God, and peasants were wary of change. They resisted innovation with the declaration that "our fathers and grandfathers didn't do that and they lived better than we do." They opposed experiments with new tools and were suspicious of the agronomists who tried to teach them new techniques. One provincial administrator in Tambov went so far as to claim that "fear of ridicule is deeply entrenched among the people. They fear evil much less than being laughed at." The world was highly unpredictable and full of dangers. Nature was populated by spirits and demons, water nymphs and devils who might be cruel or kind. Popular religion included belief in sorcerers and witches, spells and curses, the evil eye, and the power of magic. Natural signs were used to tell the peasants when to sow—"when the trees get dressed," for example, or when a certain bird would arrive in the village.

The household, like the commune, was patriarchal in structure, with the older men in charge and women subordinate and under their authority. As a Russian peasant saying proclaimed, "A crab is not a fish, a woman is not a person." Often the victims of beatings or the violent justice of the village, peasant women had little choice but to accept male dominance, which was enhanced by their own belief that they inhabited unclean bodies. "The more you beat the old woman," another proverb stated, "the tastier the soup will be." Though they were in most things dependent on men and far less socially mobile, peasant women were allowed to retain their dowries and their earnings from certain kinds of work, such as selling eggs or feathers. Women maintained the home and the children, reproducing the relations of power in the household and the commune. They socialized the children and taught them the values of the village world. The children grew up nurtured by mother's love ("There is no other friend like your mother," a proverb proclaimed) and disciplined by the blows of an authoritarian father ("Parental blows give health," claimed another).

Peasants lived in simple, small cottages that outsiders experienced as dark, dank, smelly, and smoky. A frequent visitor to Russian villages, the journalist Maurice Hindus, put together a vivid composite picture of what it was like entering a peasant house:

> There is no door from the street. To enter it you must go into the courtyard, which is always thickly strewn with rags, egg-shells, bones, garbage, and all manner of filth, for the peasant housewife dumps her refuse into the yard. In spring and fall and at other times after a heavy rain, the yard, especially if it is on low ground, turns into a puddle of slush.... The first room you enter is the *seny*—a sort of vestibule with no windows and no light, excepting what dribbles in through the crannies in the walls or the thatch overhead. In this room certain agricultural and house implements are kept and provisions are stored. It is always cold and damp, and smells of rotting wood and musty bread.... In front of the *seny* are the living quarters, usually only one room, fair-sized, dark, damp, fetid, smoky, with bare walls, a floor of earth or rough boards—always, excepting at Easter or Christmas, in sad need of scrubbing. In the place of honor in the corner, directly beneath the ikons, stands a big bare polished table; near or around it, crude backless benches, often also a few chairs, and heavy planks around the walls. Then there is the *polati*, a wide spacious platform, resting against the back wall, which serves as a sleeping place. There is no mattress on it, no pillow, no sheets, no blankets, no semblance of bedding, excepting loose straw or sacks stuffed with straw and covered with a home-woven hemp cloth. When bedtime comes, the peasant pulls off his boots, if he has any on, and drops on the *polati*, usually in his clothes.... If the family happens to be very large every available inch of space on the *polati* is occupied.

No glass on the windows, the wind and rain were kept out by stuffing rags or hay into the openings. What warmth there was came from the large brick oven, where cooking and laundry were done, where peasants bathed, and on top of which in cold weather older folks or visitors slept. Under the stove lived the hens. The whole hut was filled with dense smoke. "Whenever it comes to a choice between smoke and warmth on the one hand and cold on the other," writes Hindus, "the *mouzhik* [peasant] always prefers the first."

Autocracy, Nobility, Bureaucracy, and the Church

In 1900 the head of the Russian state was Nicholas II (1894–1917). Though himself a weak and indecisive man, he sat atop an unwieldy, overly bureaucratic political structure that endowed him with enormous power. The Russian political system was an autocracy, that is, a system in which the emperor or tsar's will was unlimited. In Muscovite times, the whole of Russia was conceived of as the tsar's own patrimony, though from at least the sixteenth century a distinction was made between the tsar's person and the state. From the time of Peter the Great, the law declared that the monarch was "not obliged to answer for his actions to anyone in the world." The emperor or empress was both legislator and executive, final judge and arbiter of the fate of millions of his or her subjects.

Autocracy was the opposite of constitutionalism or limited government. Unlike in Western monarchies, where the powers of rulers were constrained by parliaments or noble councils, through charters or feudal rights invested in landed elites, in Russia the nobility was not entitled to implement its interests or its will through state insitutitions. Nobles had no independent claims to authority in the state but were seen as the chosen servants of the tsar. Their land had originally been granted to them by the grand dukes of Moscow, and later the tsars, and in earlier centuries could have been taken from them at the will of the sovereign. The Russian aristocracy made few attempts to limit the tsar's power, and none were successful. The bulk of the nobility preferred continuance of the autocracy, rather than any aristocratic oligarchy or European representational institution, at least until the early twentieth century. Tsar and noble supported each other, maintaining a stable political regime that could defend the realm against foreign threats, keep the various nobles from fighting each other, collect taxes and keep order over the immense spread of the Russian lands, and preserve the nobles' hold over their peasant serfs.

While not a ruling class, the landed nobility was in actuality the dominant class in Russian society and remained so until the revolution swept them into oblivion. Their very way of life—their wealth, style, behavior, and distance from ordinary people, all of which stemmed from their birth—gave them a sense of their own right to rule and to be obeyed. The tsar and his state were the ultimate guarantor and protector of the nobility and the landlord's relationship to the peasantry. It was the tsarist government that enserfed the Russian peasantry in the late sixteenth and seventeenth centuries, the state that crushed peasant rebellions, and the Tsar-Liberator, Alexander II (1855–81), who handsomely rewarded the landed gentry when he freed the serfs from bondage.

On the other hand, landed nobles thought of themselves as the proper governing class of the empire, particularly in the provinces, even though those nobles who stayed in the countryside lost much of their influence to the highest hereditary nobles nearer to court and to a less prestigious personal nobility within the civil bureaucracy and the military. After the tsar gave legal freedom to the serfs, the noble landlords lost their unpaid serf labor, and the amount of land held by the nobility steadily dropped after 1861. The amount held by peasants increased until by 1905 peasants owned about two-thirds of the arable land.

The monarchy made a strong effort to improve the position of the nobility during the reign of Alexander III (1881–94), often viewed as a period of reactionary policies and social repression. The emperor himself was an avowed anti-Semite, who once said, "In the depth of my soul I am happy when the

Jews are beaten up." His policies increased the influence and power of the landed nobility, among the most conservative groups in the empire, and tied the peasants even more securely to the village communes. He rejected the suggestion that courts and other state institutions be open equally to all his subjects regardless of estate. Prepared to quash any resistance or opposition to the smooth functioning of his state, he sought to surround himself with "true Russians" as advisors. His ministers initiated severe censorship of the press and in universities and carried out discriminatory policies toward non-Russians. By the turn of the century the nobles' economic and political decline was reversed, largely because of global economic trends . Like the peasants, those nobles who held onto their land benefited from the rise of cereal prices after 1900 and enjoyed a period of considerable prosperity on the eve of World War I.

Noble attitudes on the autocracy varied from the reverent to the rebellious. The Grand Duke Nikolai Nikolaevich, the uncle of Nicholas II, asked Sergei Witte, a key advisor to the tsar, whether he thought the emperor was "merely a human being or is he more?" Witte answered, "Well, the Emperor is my master and I am his faithful servant, but though he is an autocratic ruler, given to us by God and Nature, he is nevertheless a human being with all the peculiarities of one." The grand duke disagreed. "To my mind," he said, "the Emperor is not a mere human being, but rather a being intermediate between man and God." A conservative newspaper editor was more cynical when he confided to his diary in February 1900:

> Autocracy is far superior to parliamentarism because under parliamentarism people rule, while under autocracy—God rules. . . . The Sovereign listens only to God, and only from God does he take advice, and because God is invisible, he takes advice from everyone he meets: from his wife, from his mother, from his stomach . . . and he accepts all this as an order from God.

One of Alexander III's ministers, fearful of Western-style innovations that would tamper with the divinely sanctioned autocratic system, warned:

> Every attempt to introduce West European parliamentary forms of government into Russia is doomed to failure. If the tsarist regime is overthrown, its place will be taken by pure undisguised communism, the communism of Mr. Karl Marx who has just died in London and whose theories I have studied with attention and interest.

The constitution granted by the last tsar, Nicholas II, in 1905 helped to revive noble power by giving them influence in the upper house of parliament, the State Council, and in the lower house, the Duma, thanks to property qualifications for enfranchisement, and within high state institutions. The semiconstitutional, semiautocratic regime created after 1905 gave unexpected clout to a small number of landed nobles, who in the last decades of the tsarist regime were able to make political and land reform difficult, if not impossible. Their recalcitrance and shortsightedness contributed directly to the final crisis of the imperial state. So closely tied to the tsarist regime was the nobility that its demise quickly followed the fall of tsarism.

In stark contrast to the fate of the nobility, another institution of the tsarist period, the bureaucracy, not only survived the revolution but after some major surgery transformed itself into the central nervous system of the new Soviet system. From its modest origins in the Muscovite state the Russian state bureaucracy grew steadily as an instrument of westernization, expanding from about 15,000 to 16,000 officials in the late eighteenth century to more than 74,000 by the mid-nineteenth century and on to about 385,000 in the early twentieth. During the nineteenth century the number of officials rose seven times as rapidly as did Russia's population. Though the very highest officials and officers were often men of great property and wealth, family ties became far less important for a state or military career as time went on. Increasingly nonnoble in origin, the bureaucrats were people whose status depended less on birth and more on education and achievement.

As members of the bureaucracy became more professional in their outlook and work habits, particularly in the nineteenth century, many attempted to promote regular procedures and an adherence to law in order to combat the corruption and disarray within the ministries and the influence of court favorites. They were ultimately thwarted by the autocratic nature of the tsarist system, which allowed the tsar to act in arbitrary and contradictory ways, making a decree on a Tuesday and changing his mind on a Thursday. The autocrat's ability to act on whim precluded the establishment of a general rule of law in Russia. The country was a land of regulations and personal favoritism rather than a land of impersonal rules, predictable laws, and rational bureaucracy. Russian officials were often petty men of little talent who did not have clearly defined functions and procedures within the bureaucracy. Moreover, there were no effective channels of communication through which influential people in society could express their interests to the bureaucratic state.

Closely allied to the state was the Russian Orthodox church. The tsar was head of both church and state, and from the time of Peter the Great, the Holy Synod, a state institution, replaced the Muscovite patriarchs as the highest authority within the church. Steadily from the early eighteenth century, the church lost influence and power within the ruling groups, even as it retained the loyalty of the vast peasant population. Catherine the Great secularized the church's enormous land holdings and deprived it of its serfs and much of its revenues. The church became dependent on state subsidies, while ordinary parish clergy grew ever poorer, living off contributions from their parishioners. As Russian elite culture became more Western and secular, the role of religion in life diminished, and much of the intelligentsia saw the church as a reactionary ideological pillar of the autocracy. The church retained control over marriage and divorce, however, and much of education was in its hands. At times conservative tsars, like Nicholas I (1825–55) or Alexander III, turned to the church to reinstate old Russian values and religion in the minds of the young. On occasion missionaries attempted to convert pagans and Muslims among the non-Russian population to Orthodoxy but with limited success.

Russia's Orthodox church was highly traditional, seldom innovative theologically, and never experienced anything like the Reformation. Indeed, its greatest challenge came from an antireformationist movement, known as Old Belief, that beginning in the seventeenth century resisted any changes in liturgy or ritual. Ironically, the ultratraditionalist schismatics, particularly those who chose to live without priests of any kind, brought a spiritual vigor and even radicalism to their religious practices. They resisted the church hierarchy's injunction to cross oneself with three rather than the traditional two fingers, and thousands of schismatics burned themselves to death rather than succumb to alien authority. For millions of Russians religion was deeply felt, though very often its most passionate practice, whether among sectarians or peasants, who mixed Orthodoxy with superstition and remnants of paganism, occurred outside the church.

The ponderous bulk of the tsarist state weighed heavily on the Russian landscape, crushing the weak institutions of civil society that budded outside of the state. The tsar and his ministers remained suspicious of all autonomous organizations and activities of his subjects that in any way might compromise their absolute power. Censors and the police patrolled the society, restricting intellectuals to private discussions, preventing workers from forming unions (up to 1906), and restraining efforts by professionals and even nobles to form organizations to express their own views and interests. What did develop was a public sphere of educated people who were able in a limited way to express their ideas, largely through literature and art, but the regime stifled a broad civil society of autonomous organizations and interest groups. Only in the last decade of the regime, after the constitutional reforms of 1905, was the realm of rights briefly and hesitantly extended to the population. Between society and the state emerged the alienated intelligentsia of liberals, radicals, and revolutionaries, which became a rival society with oppositional ideologies that seriously threatened the defenders of tsarism. In Russia, as the Italian Marxist theorist Antonio Gramsci put it, "the state was everything, civil society was primordial and gelatinous."

The Coming of Capitalism

As Russia entered the last quarter of the nineteenth century, its economy was still dominated by peasant agricultural production, much of which never reached the market. Trade and commerce were poorly developed, and for nearly a century influential Russian economists had been advocating that the country follow Western Europe and America in the direction of market capitalism. The European and American economies were based on private ownership of enterprises, hired rather than compulsory labor, and production of goods for sale on the market. Moreover, England, the first capitalist economy, had led the world into industrialization and mass production. Though in many ways the 1880s and early 1890s were the height of tsarist patriarchy or patrimonialism, those decades were also the moment of the first great takeoff of

Russian industrialization and began a radical transformation of the economy. As his minister of finance Sergei Witte wrote in his memoirs, "Alexander III recognized that Russia could be made great only when it ceased being an exclusively agricultural country. A country without strongly developed industry could not be great."

Serfdom had inhibited the formation of an industrial workforce by keeping peasants tied to the land, and the great power of the landed nobility, the estate most opposed to capitalist development, inhibited the shift to a market economy. Once the serfs were freed, however, and noble power suffered a decline, the road to capitalism was somewhat smoother. By requiring redemption payments for their land from the peasants, nobles contributed to the circulation of money. Those nobles able to adjust to the new economic environment consolidated considerable estates and successfully engaged in commercial agriculture. The increased flow of grain to market and the greater (though still restricted) mobility of peasants aided the growth of cities and the emergence of a working class.

Russia was capital-poor and had only a small entrepreneurial class of industrialists and merchants. The least "bourgeois" of any major European state, Russia had few traditions that encouraged enterprise. Almost all social groups were suspicious of middle-class virtues, such as thrift, delayed gratification, and investment for the future, and considered the accumulation of wealth obscene. Intellectuals from the conservative novelist Fedor Dostoevsky to the Marxists shared with nobles and peasants a contempt for the "bourgeoisie," the propertied middle class of the West. Standards of honesty were low; arbitrariness, cheating, bribery, and the currying of favor with officials marked economic and social interchanges. In a society where obedience to law was not internalized but required a firm authority to enforce it, personal relationships often took precedence over legal norms.

Yet a small group of entrepreneurs, some of them former serfs, many members of dissident religious sects like the Old Believers, emerged in the nineteenth century to plant the seeds of a market economy. Over time the merchants developed respect for hard work, thrift, temperance, and modest living. Russian business operators tended to be patriotic and devoted to autocracy, probably because they were dependent on the state for support. They did not develop oppositional ideologies, like liberalism, as was common in Western Europe, but were instead nationalistic, anti-Western, and supportive of Russian imperialism in Central Asia and Eastern Europe. Merchants were hostile to nobles, whom they considered lazy and undeservedly privileged, and nobles reciprocated by looking upon businesspeople as "dirty-faced" and "fat-bellied."

The weakness of the Russian middle class meant that other sources of capital formation had to be found. Some economic growth resulted from private industries, such as cotton textiles and sugar refining, that found domestic markets. But the weakness of the internal market and the lack of purchasing power among the peasants constricted rapid development. Beginning in the 1880s the tsarist state became a major initiator of industrial development. Taxing the peasants, exporting grain abroad, and borrowing from foreign investors, the government established a program of public works, such as the building of the Trans-Siberian railroad, that stimulated other enterprises, among them the iron and steel industry. In 1891 the Mendeleev Tariff, favored by the merchants, placed high duties on imported European goods and created a protected area in which native industry could develop. The government acted in the role of the largely absent Russian bourgeoisie through a system of state capitalism, which was an early version of deficit financing. Long before Communists took power, Russia had the largest state-financed industrial sector of any major power.

The results were spectacular. Gross factory output increased more than 5 percent per year from 1883 to 1913, sustaining an annual rate of overall industrial growth of 8 percent per year in the 1890s. The labor force grew about 3 percent per year, and labor productivity in industry increased 1.8 percent annually. The older industrial regions of Russia, like the Urals, were soon eclipsed by the newly industrialized Ukraine. Coal from the Donets region provided fuel for locomotives as well as coke for the iron and steel works that made rails for the new railroads. Iron ore from Krivoi Rog created a new industrial landscape around Kharkov and Ekaterinoslav. At the same time, Moscow and Vladimir took the lead in textile production away from Saint Petersburg, which remained, however, both a textile and metallurgical center. Industrial production in Russian Poland increased ten times between 1870 and 1890, doubling between 1887 and 1893.

The Russian Intelligentsia

Education was a privilege in tsarist Russia reserved for the few. From the early nineteenth century those distinguished from the rest of society by education and their reformist attitudes were known collectively as the intelligentsia. As a social group, the intelligentsia was marked by its sense of being apart from the people around them and its distance from the tsarist state. One of its earliest representatives, Aleksandr Herzen, defined his fellow Moscow intellectuals as possessed of "a strong feeling of alienation from official Russia and from their surroundings." The historian Marc Raeff sees as "the characteristic trait of the intelligentsia" its conception of "its role as one of service to the people." Less generously, Dostoevsky criticized the intelligentsia for being "historically alienated from the soil" and for "raising itself above the people." While liberals in Russian society saw the intelligentsia as social reformers engaged in enlightened activity, conservatives thought of it as pathological and ultimately harmful.

The intelligentsia was not a social class, that is, a group of people of similar social position or engaged in related work; rather it was a group of men and women of different social origins united by vague feelings of alienation from society and dedicated to changing Russian society and politics. At first most intellectuals were nobles, but increasingly a number of people from no definite social estate, the so-called *raznochintsy*, joined their ranks. Idealist in both the philosophical and political sense, the early intellectuals gathered in discussion circles where they debated questions of art and philosophy. After the December 1825 conspiracy by Western-oriented nobles to overthrow the autocrat was crushed, the new emperor, Nicholas I, became deeply suspicious of intellectuals and reformers. As police surveillance increased, real politics became too dangerous, and discussions about the perfectability of human beings and society became a kind of surrogate.

The first generation were liberals either enamoured of the West (the Westernizers) or who looked backwards to an idealized collectivist Russia (the Slavophiles). Herzen and his friend Nikolai Ogarev became interested in the fledgling socialist movements in France, but their innocent search for political alternatives ended with their arrest in 1834. In the next decade a few intellectuals became more radical, more critical of religion, and more directly involved in politics. Slavophiles and Westernizers no longer frequented each other's circles, and among Westernizers socialists broke with the more moderate liberals. The Slavophiles celebrated the imagined harmony and collectivity of the peasant commune and feared that western capitalism combined with Russian bureaucratic absolutism would eventually destroy the unique values of traditional Russian life. The liberal Westernizers believed that Russia had to abandon its backward ways and become more like Europe—industrial, urban, and constitutional. Reform had to come from above, from the state, and be gradual and moderate. The socialists combined elements from both Slavophilism and Westernism. They called for a leap beyond capitalism into a social order based on the peasant commune. For men like Herzen socialism meant a fusion of what they took to be democratic and egalitarian elements of the commune with the guarantees of individual dignity and rights found in the most advanced Western states. But they fervently wanted to avoid the West's capitalism, private property, a proletariat, and an urban industrial system as Russia moved along its own unique road into the future. If reform did not work, they were prepared to advocate revolutionary change.

With the outbreak of revolutions in western Europe in 1848, the tsar cracked down hard on dissident politics within his empire. The liberal writer Ivan Turgenev was sent into exile for writing a laudatory obituary for his fellow writer Nikolai Gogol. Dostoevsky was arrested and sentenced to death for belonging to a socialist circle. At the last moment, with the novelist standing before a mock firing squad, the sentence was changed to exile in Siberia. This dark period culminated in Russia's hapless drift into war over Crimea (1853–56) and its defeat at the hands of the European powers. With the ascension of Alexander II, a new era of somewhat freer expression and reform began. New journals and newspapers, discussion circles, and underground political movements blossomed. Poetry, short stories, and novels, which had appeared for the first time in Russia in significant quantity and quality only in the first decades of the century, now became a major medium through which powerful thoughts about society, personality, and morality were expressed. Even when hobbled by the censors, Russia's writers, from Pushkin and Mikhail Lermontov to Turgenev, Lev Tolstoi, Dostoevskii, and on to Anton Chekhov and Maksim Gorkii, managed to produce a literature that in its profound explorations of human existence exposed the pettiness and brutality of Russian life.

The 1860s was an age of radical, even revolutionary, politics, but the young radicals denigrated the elitism of Russia's westernized culture. They considered literature and art to be products of upper-class sensibilities, and thus cut off from the great majority of the people. Rather than poetry and romantic intuition, the radicals called for a commitment to science, reason, and useful art. The acknowledged leader of the "men of the sixties" was Nikolai Chernyshevskii (1828–89), a philosopher and the editor of a leading intellectual journal, who boldly identified beauty with the morally and socially desirable. Art was to show life as it is and ought to be. Turgenev called Chernyshevskii a "literary Robespierre," and in his famous short novel *Fathers and Sons* he drew a sharp portrait of the rival political generations. From his jail cell Chernyshevskii answered with his own novel, *What Is to Be Done?*, in which he portrayed a model revolutionary that inspired many young men and women to turn to revolutionary activity.

Alexander II's early reign was also a time in which non-Russian peoples of the empire enjoyed relatively benign treatment by the tsarist government. Some ethnic leaders, as well as tsarist officials, advocated assimilation into the dominant Russian culture. Urban Armenians russified the endings of their names, and influential Jewish intellectuals pushed for secular reform of their community. At the same time poets and patriotic writers in Ukraine, the Baltic, and the Caucasus elaborated ideas of national culture and history that laid the foundation for future claims to nationhood. But when Poles rebelled against the empire in 1863, Alexander brutally suppressed the movement and moved away from his earlier reformist efforts. The government was particularly determined to deny separate nationality to the Slavic peoples of the empire. Petr Valuev, Alexander II's minister of the interior, declared that "a special Little Russian language [Ukrainian] has not existed, does not exist, and cannot exist." Later, just as Ukrainian writers were developing their own literary language, the state forbade all printing and performances in Ukrainian.

In 1866 an attempt was made on the life of the tsar, and the era of tolerance came to an abrupt end. Liberals bided their time, hoping that the emperor would renew his program of reform. Radicals went underground, and in the 1870s several thousand dedicated young people organized a movement "to the people," to try both to teach the peasants as well as to learn from them. These propeasant activists made up the political movement known as populism, which sought to create a Russian socialist society based on the peasant commune. When their efforts at propaganda met little positive response from the peasants, one wing of the populist movement turned to terrorism to weaken the government and inspire peasant rebellion.

Marx, Lenin, and the Case of Russia

The writings of the German philospher and historian Karl Marx (1818–83) were known to a small segment of the Russian reading public from about 1848, when the government censor permitted translations to enter Russia. The state's guardian of proper information was convinced that Marx's work in no way threatened the regime but rather was "an abstract speculation" with no relevance to Russia. In 1872 the first volume of Marx's major economic treatise, *Capital*, was translated into Russian, and Marx himself was surprised by its reception. "By some irony of fate," he wrote, "it is just the Russians whom for twenty years I have incessantly attacked [who] have always been my well-wishers."

Marxism was first taken up in Russia by the young populist revolutionaries, who, impressed by his analysis of capitalism and appalled by the rise of "bourgeois society" in the West, resolved to prevent such a social evolution in Russia. Both Marx and his closest associate, Friedrich Engels, admired the revolutionary zeal of the populists and argued that Russia would be an exception to the general European development of capitalism. If it acted soon enough, Russia would be able to avoid capitalism and build its socialism on the commune, but only "if the Russian Revolution becomes the signal for a proletarian revolution in the West, so that both complement each other." But Marx's most fervent followers came, not from the radical, but from the moderate wing of populism. Led by Georgii Plekhanov (1856–1918), a number of young socialists gradually lost faith in the commune, which they saw as already infected by the polarizing effects of the market economy, and declared themselves "Marxists." Rather than concede that Russia might build a peasant-based socialism, Plekhanov concluded that Russia could not avoid a bourgeois-capitalist stage. A "bourgeois revolution," like that in North America in 1776 or France in 1789, was inevitable in Russia and was necessary to create the conditions for the full development of capitalism and democracy. The task of socialists and workers, wrote Plekhanov, was to aid the Russian bourgeoisie to make its revolution and once that revolution was victorious to demand the political rights necessary for the working class to create the conditions for the next, the socialist, revolution.

With Plekhanov, Russian Marxism began its own drift away from the complex and often contradictory writings of Marx himself into a more deterministic, rigid, and dogmatic philosophy. For Plekhanov economic forces were decisive in determining social structures and ideological superstructures, that is ideas, laws, and culture. Changes in the material basis of society provided the initial impetus for institutional and ideological change. The coming of capitalism to Russia meant that the peasant commune was a relic of history and should not be preserved. Objective economic trends and experience in the factories would create a proletarian-socialist consciousness among workers. "Let our intellectuals go to the workers," wrote Plekhanov. "Life itself will make them revolutionaries."

Plekhanov and his comrades formed the first Russian Marxist organization, the Liberation of Labor Group, in Geneva in 1883. At first only a few isolated intellectuals and workers read their pamphlets, but by the mid-1890s Marxist ideas became increasingly popular among students, the broader intelligentsia, and the new working class. The extraordinary reception for a body of ideas that to many seemed inappropriate for a largely peasant, primarily agricultural country with an insignificantly small proletariat was the result of the conjuncture of several developments. First, history seemed to be on the side of the Marxists. The Russian industrialization, producing in its wake a class of factory workers and a new urban environment, conformed to the predictions of the Marxists that the future lay with industry and capitalism, rather than with the peasant commune. Second, the famine of 1891 demonstrated the helplessness and passivity of many peasants and turned many young intellectuals toward the workers as an alternative revolutionary force. Third, Marxism itself had a number of internal appeals. It was both a sociological tool of analysis of the present and a philosophy of history that anticipated a classless society at the end of a long struggle. Marxism contained both an appreciation of the power of industrial capitalism to create the modern world and a powerful critique of the new economic order that promised transcendence into a more just, egalitarian, and harmonious realm. And finally, Marxism was a doctrine from the West identified with the most progressive social movements of the age, the Social Democratic parties of Germany, Austria, and other European countries. Rather than isolating Russia and making its development peculiar, Marxism linked Russia's future to that of the rest of the continent.

One of the precocious young Marxists of the 1890s was a brilliant and self-assured law student from the Volga city of Simbirsk, Vladimir Ulianov (1870–1924), soon to be known by his revolutionary nom de guerre Lenin. Born April 10 (22 n.s.), 1870, the son of a dedicated civil servant who was an inspector of schools and a mother who raised five children, Vladimir Ulianov had a happy childhood and excelled at school. Ironically, his father reached the rank of hereditary noble shortly after little "Volodya" was born. His older brother, Aleksandr, joined a revolutionary conspiracy and was executed when Volodya was seventeen—an event that had a profound effect on the younger boy. Vladimir Ulianov entered Kazan University but was expelled within a few months for participation in a student protest. He completed his law degree as a correspondence student, but by the early 1890s he was already studying Marxism. After moving to St. Petersburg in 1893, he met his future wife and party comrade, Nadezhda Krupskaia. From his earliest days in the Marxist movement, Lenin was respected for his militance and leadership qualities. For these reasons as well as his premature baldness, his fellow Marxists nicknamed him "Old Man."

Lenin was by nature and training an intellectual, a scholar of politics whose published works would fill fifty-five volumes. He was a rationalist who proposed the application of reason and science to political and social problems, which he believed could be solved through the institution of socialism. As a scientist of insurrection, he worked hard to discipline his emotions, overcome his irritations, and direct all his knowledge and energies to the revolution. Gorky remembered Lenin's musings as they listened to Beethoven's "Apassionata" Sonata in the writer's home on Capri sometime before the revolution:

> I know nothing greater than the "Apassionata." . . . I always think with pride: what marvellous things human beings can do! But I can't listen to music too often. It affects your nerves, makes you want to say stupid, nice things, and stroke the heads of people who could create such beauty while living in this vile hell. And you mustn't stroke anyone's head—you might

get your hand bitten off. You have to hit them over the head, without any mercy, although our ideal is not to use force against anyone. Hm, hm, our duty is infernally hard

Supremely self-confident, often aggressive, even ruthless, in his polemics with opponents and comrades, Lenin could be personally charming, had a good sense of humor, and was modest and unassuming. A man without personal pretensions and ascetic in his personal life, Lenin was coldly practical about the struggle for the international revolution. Power was the means of achieving socialism, and nothing in his view could be allowed to stand in the way of its victory. "The scientific concept of a dictatorship," he wrote, "signifies nothing other than a power which, unrestricted by any laws, uninhibited by any absolute rules, resorts freely to the use of violence." While his ultimate vision was to create a society in which the simplest people would rule themselves, he argued that dictatorship and violence, civil war and repression of the enemy, were the only practical means to that end.

Like many of the younger recruits to the Social Democratic movement in the 1890s, Lenin shifted his attention from the economic struggle, agitating for improved wages and working conditions for workers, to a more political strategy aimed at overthrowing the autocracy. After the first attempt to unite Russian Marxists in a Russian Social Democratic Labor Party failed in 1898, Lenin and his associates began publishing a newspaper, *Iskra* (The Spark), around which politically minded revolutionaries could coalesce. The number of small circles of workers and socialist intellectuals loosely affiliated with social democracy mushroomed in the next few years.

In the spring of 1902 Lenin published *What Is to Be Done?* a comprehensive statement of his thoughts on the role of a revolutionary Social Democratic party. Here he called for a "party of the new type," a centralized, disciplined army of Social Democratic professionals, rather than a broad-based party of simple adherents. Lenin broke with those Marxists who believed that class consciousness generated by actually living and working under capitalism was sufficient for workers. "The history of all countries shows," he wrote in one of his most revealing phrases, "that the working class, exclusively by its own effort, is able to develop only trade-union consciousness." Raising workers' wages and shortening hours was not enough for Lenin. Workers must become aware of the need for the political overthrow of autocracy. That awareness could be acquired by workers only from outside the economic struggle, from the Social Democratic intelligentsia. The party of revolutionary Social Democrats was to act as the tribune of the whole people, expounding the need for democracy, and not as a "trade union secretary" advocating the immediate material interests of workers alone. Under Russian conditions the party was to be made up "first and foremost of people who make revolutionary activity their profession. . . . All distinctions between workers and intellectuals . . . must be effaced." Such an organization was to be small, as secret as possible, and willing to push the workers beyond their immediate desires.

The issues laid out in *What Is to Be Done?* had been widely discussed in Social Democratic circles, but they had never before been exposed so starkly.

Lenin's personal political style, which was to have a decisive influence on the Bolshevik wing of Russian social democracy, was expressively demonstrated in this book. Here he promoted sharp ideological distinctions, principled divisions, and purity of position and threw aside accomodation, compromise, and moderation in favor of an impatient commitment to action. For a militant revolutionary like Lenin conciliation was a negative quality. Discipline, sobriety, toughness, and subordination to the dictates of the party leaders became the new virtues.

Though Leninism was not yet a fully formed political tendency, Lenin's language and proposed practice had an immediate appeal for certain Social Democratic activists. In the summer of 1903, Lenin's plans for a "party of a new type" seemed about to bear fruit, as Social Democrats from all over Russia made their way to Brussels for the Second Congress of the Russian Social Democratic Labor Party (RSDLP). But on the crucial question of who should be allowed to join the party, the delegates split into rival factions. Lenin wanted only people who actively participated in one of the party organizations to be members. On this issue he lost to his friend Iulii Martov, who favored including anyone who rendered regular personal assistance to the party under the guidance of one of its organizations. Though to many outsiders the matter of defining membership seemed trivial, in fact two different visions of the political party—one an army of professional revolutionaries, the other a mass party of supporters—divided the Russian Social Democrats irrevocably. After other divisive debates and walkouts by dissidents, Lenin soon gained a majority in the congress, and his faction came to be known as Bolsheviks (the majority) and those who followed Martov and others were labeled Mensheviks (the minority). The split between those Marxists who emphasized leadership and direction over the workers' movement (the Bolsheviks) and those who promoted more democratic participation of the rank and file in the movement (the Mensheviks) would eventually divide the political Left throughout the world. After World War I, those who preferred Lenin's vanguardist model would be known as Communists and those who favored a more moderate, democratic approach would be known as Social Democrats.

The Final Crisis of Tsarism

In the first decade of the twentieth century Russians frequently debated with one another the causes of the current social and political crisis. The young monarch Nicholas II seemed particularly ineffectual, unwilling either to make significant concessions to the growing sentiment for reform in educated society or to crack down hard enough on the growing opposition movements among all classes of the population. On ascending the throne at age 26, Nicholas silenced those "voices of persons who have been carried away by senseless dreams" of participation by representatives of various classes in state administration. He declared firmly that "I, while devoting all my energies to the good of the people, shall maintain the principle of autocracy just as firmly and unflinchingly as did my unforgettable father." Educated society was shocked by the tsar's speech on "senseless dreams," and a leading political activist, Petr Struve, who was then a Marxist and would soon become a liberal, spoke for much of society when he replied to the speech with an "Open Letter." Russia, he wrote, was only asking for the removal of "that wall of bureaucracy and court that separates the tsar from Russia." And he concluded, "You have begun the struggle, and the struggle will not be long in coming."

Sensitive to the weakness of civil society and the rule of law in Russia, a small but vocal group of Russian liberals attempted to influence the government either to allow some form of representative institutions to register public opinion or to move toward a more law-regulated state (in German, *Rechtsstaat*). Just as Russian Marxism differed from Western European Marxism, so Russian liberalism was different from that of the West. Instead of being the expression of a confident industrial and commercial middle class, Russian liberalism reflected the views of democratic intellectuals and a few enlightened landed nobles. Liberals believed that they defended, not the interests of specific classes, as claimed by the populists and Marxists, but those of the whole people regardless of class. Their model of a good society was an idealized version of Western capitalist democracy, and their hope was to promote free enterprise and guarantee civil rights and some representation of public opinion in government. Until 1905, however, very few among the liberals moved as far as to call for constitutional limitations on the tsar's powers. Willing to pressure the government for reforms, most liberals stopped far short of advocating revolution, which they feared would degenerate into massive violence. Here was the liberals' dilemma: If the government did not concede reforms, they had no recourse but to accept the status quo.

Russia's first industrial revolution, in the 1880s and 1890s, was a mammoth change for the agricultural empire, but it stopped short of transforming the whole of Russian society. Capitalist industry existed in pockets, around key cities in certain regions, while much of the country lived in the old way, even though they now experienced the effects of the booms and busts of the industrial economy. Around 1900 industrial growth slowed down. As railroad construction tapered off, the demand for goods that it had stimulated dried up. The fall in government orders led to a crisis of overproduction in metals and other industries; ninety thousand workers were unemployed in the Ukrainian metal industry alone. Other markets were insufficient for Russian industry's greater capacity to produce. Three thousand firms closed in Russia in the first few years of the new century.

The industrial crisis of 1901–3 hit at the same time that peasants suffered from low grain prices. Peasant uprisings broke out in Poltava, Kharkov, and western Georgia. The number of strikes and protests by workers rose each year. Red flags were unfurled, revolutionary songs were sung, and workers took on the police and Cossacks. University students protested being drafted into the army and the government's abuse of fellow students. Terrorists killed the minister of education in 1901 and the minister of the interior the following year.

The economic and social crisis was exacerbated by the government's Far Eastern policy, which led it into a disastrous war with Japan in 1904. Defeated at Port Arthur in China, its fleet sunk by Japanese warships in the Straits of

Tushima, Russia was the first European state to be humiliated by an Asian power. Unrest and disaffection from the regime grew. One of the pillars upon which tsarism rested was the widely accepted sense that the tsar was the father of his people, that his state had a paternal role to play in the great Russian family, and that even if bureaucrats and nobles oppressed the people, the tsar would hear their pleas and redress their grievances. Yet this "naive monarchism" was severely shaken when the tsar's troops fired upon a crowd of petitioners that marched reverently to the Winter Palace on January 9 (22 n.s.), 1905 to ask for improvement of their material lot and the establishment of legal rights. About 130 demonstrators were killed and several hundred wounded on "Bloody Sunday." The shootings galvanized the country and gave credence to the message brought by Marxist revolutionaries and liberal intellectuals that the cause of Russia's problems was autocracy and the regime of arbitrary power. Growing numbers of ordinary people came to believe that the state was the source of their oppression.

The years 1905–7 are referrred to as the "first Russian Revolution," though in fact the regime merely tottered and did not fall. At times, however, during the first year of the revolution the government lost control of certain towns, cities, and regions as industrial workers struck in massive work stoppages. Mutinies in the army and navy broke out repeatedly, the most famous on the battleship *Potemkin* in the Black Sea. A nationwide general strike in October brought the country to a near standstill. Workers formed their own councils, called soviets, in industrial towns. In St. Petersburg the soviet was led briefly by a young Marxist, Lev Trotsky (1879–1940), whose oratory and pen made him an instant revolutionary celebrity. Attempts to stem the revolutionary tide with piecemeal reforms failed time and again, until the war with Japan was brought to an end in the summer and the tsar answered the popular protests with his October Manifesto, which established a limited constitutional regime. Rights of assembly and speech were guaranteed, though often abrogated in practice, and an elected parliament with two houses, the State Council and the Duma, was established. For the first time in Russian history political parties and trade unions were allowed to exist legally. Though revolutionary violence continued for another year and a half, the tsar's concessions broke the unity of the opposition and gave him the breathing space to use his army to bring a harsh order back to the country. Soldiers crushed an insurrection of workers in Moscow in December 1905, disbanded the Petersburg soviet, and arrested Trotsky. Punitive expeditions stomped out the autonomous peasant "republic" in western Georgia, and military units "pacified" and patrolled regions placed under martial law.

The most perplexing question about the final years of the three-hundred-year-old Romanov monarchy is, how did the social and political and ideological support for tsarism erode so quickly in the last two decades of its existence. Historians are divided into two camps on this issue. Optimists argue that tsarism was dealing effectively with the crises in the economy and society and responded to the revolution with significant reforms that included a constitutional regime complete with a parliament, legal trade unions, and land reform. The last years of tsarism were marked by rapid economic growth, and the final crisis came when imperial Germany forced tsarist Russia to enter World War I, a war for which it was not yet adequately prepared. Pessimists, on the other hand, believe that Russia was in a deep and chronic crisis that would have led to revolution even without the war. Industrialization, for all its rapidity and considerable success, both in the 1890s and between 1910 and 1914, had created a new and volatile working class that increasingly felt itself separate from the rest of society. Moreover, another split was taking place between the monarchy and educated society, which was growing more alienated from the tsar, more disillusioned, even despairing.

While the optimists are correct to emphasize the importance of the war as the last straw that cracked the back of tsarism, the pessimists are right that a rising crescendo of social and ethnic conflict intensified in the last ten years before World War I. The semiconstitutional regime created in 1905, which was far from democratic, only increased the appetites of liberals, socialists, peasants, and workers for further reforms. Though there was universal manhood suffrage, representation in the Duma was heavily weighted toward people of property, namely, the nobility and the commercial-industrial class, the last supporters of tsarism. Yet even they became less enthusiastic about Nicholas II and autocracy after 1910. The middle class wanted greater participation in both politics and the economic direction of the country and resented state intervention, although the nobility grew more conservative and rejected any further political or social reforms. Politicians in the Duma wanted a greater role in foreign policy, but here the tsar and the government refused to compromise their powers.

After its defeat at the hands of Japan, Russia was much more tentative in its foreign policy. The government's first task was to restore domestic order, and the able prime minister Petr Stolypin (1906–11) clamped down hard on radicals and revolutionaries, executing over a thousand, closing oppositional newspapers, and harassing trade unions. Stolypin hoped to create a "Great Russia" through a careful program of internal reforms and believed that for this he required "twenty years of peace." His most significant reform was to encourage peasants to leave the commune and become independent farmers on their own privatized land. Altogether, somewhere between a quarter and a third of the peasant households left the communes and formed enclosed farms by 1916, though such separations from the collective were resented by those who remained in the commune. As long as Stolypin was able to manipulate the Duma parties and repress the revolutionaries, Russia was domestically stable. He pursued a pacific foreign policy, signing an entente with England in 1907, making concessions in Persia and Afghanistan, and solidifying Russia's relations with Germany. But more aggressive politicians, like Foreign Minister Aleksandr Izvolskii and his successor Sergei Sazonov, did not hesitate to stir up latent nationalist feeling in society when Austria-Hungary asserted its power over Bosnia-Herzegovina in 1908. Educated Russian public opinion was pro-Slav and responded to talk of "Russia's historic mission" as "defender of the Slavonic nation."

In 1911, while attending an opera in Kiev and in the presence of the tsar, Stolypin was assassinated by someone associated with the secret police. With his demise, effective government in Russia ceased. The meddling empress, Aleksandra, told his successor, "We hope that you will never go along with those terrible political parties, which dream only of seizing power or of subjecting the government to their will. . . . Remain yourself: do not seek support in political parties. They are so insignificant in Russia. Rely upon the confidence of the Emperor." The new prime minister found himself isolated, unable to deal with the Duma nor with the influential figures, such as the dissolute "holy man" Grigorii Rasputin, who surrounded the tsar.

For the last three years before World War I Russia's government drifted and became cut off from the very social groups that had supported it earlier. Lenin later referred to the stagnation and impotence in the state and among the ruling elites as a "crisis at the top" of society. At the same time a "crisis at the bottom" of society also developed rapidly. The militant phase of the labor movement had ended abruptly with the defeat of the Moscow insurrection of December 1905, and in the coming years, even as trade unions were legalized and the labor press could operate relatively freely, the government came down hard on strikes (which remained illegal) and worker protests. Thousands of activists were arrested and exiled to Siberia. Employers fired "undesirable elements," and the stagnating economy led to layoffs and growing unemployment. Labor was largely impotent until the eve of the war, trade unions withered, and the radical parties languished as their rank-and-file members deserted.

Not until 1909 did Russia emerge from the deep economic depression that had halted the industrialization of the 1890s. The four years before World War I were a period of renewed growth. But unlike the earlier industrialization this growth was stimulated not so much by state contracts but by a new market provided by the peasantry and the urban population. The rise in world wheat prices between 1906 and 1912 put money into the pockets of peasants, as well as the noble landlords, improving their standard of living and purchasing power. Here was the home market that the populists had said could not develop in Russia, the one the Marxists in the early 1890s had predicted would soon appear. So great was demand that industrial output could not keep up.

The new working class in Russia was becoming increasingly urban and less tied to the countryside. Older workers, who had come into the working class between 1890 and 1900, were now joined by younger workers (about 25 percent of the industrial labor force), who entered factories and plants after 1910. Two different generations of workers coexisted. These workers lived in a new world, distant from and less stable than the villages in which they had been born, and their attitudes differed from the ones of those left at home. Whereas peasants lived in a world close to nature and with a sense that God ordained the lives they lived, workers experienced a much more chaotic world in which rules and timetables were imposed by men, managers and foremen, who were not sanctioned by the divine. The abuses of the shopfloor and poverty of the tenements were much harder to take than the customary hardships endured back in the village.

In 1910 the great Russian novelist Lev Tolstoy died. The Orthodox Church, which considered Tolstoy to be a heretic, refused to give him a church burial.

His funeral became a massive demonstration against the authorities. Students boycotted classes and called for an end to the death penalty (something long desired by Tolstoy). This was the first sign of a new awakening of society. In February 1911 students organized a general strike, and the minister of education answered them with arrests and expulsions. The next year the expression of discontent took on massive dimensions when on April 4, 1912, government troops fired upon a peaceful demonstration of some three thousand workers at the Lena gold fields in Siberia. One hundred seventy people were killed, and another 202 wounded. Spontaneous strikes in support of the Lena workers broke out throughout the country. The massacre shocked Russian society, and the press reported the angry Duma debates on the government's responsibility for the killings, which only increased workers' fury at the government. The minister of the interior insensitively commented on the Lena events, "That's the way it's always been, and that's the way it will be in the future." With the intelligentsia and politicians debating the future of the country, many workers sensed that the authority of the state could be challenged, that they might act to change the rules of the game of their own society.

By the first half of 1914 the number of striking workers was ten times what it had been for the whole year of 1911, and strikes with political demands outnumbered those in the revolutionary year, 1905. Angry at the intransigence of the industrialists, who consistently refused to concede on wages, hours, and conditions of work, many workers perceived the state as allied with the factory owners. Those who thought little was to be gained within the confines of the existing system, like the metalworkers of St. Petersburg and the oil workers of Baku, became even more militant. The voices of the dissenters in educated society were reaching the factory floor. And among the most resonant voices were those of the most radical socialists, the Bolsheviks, who argued that accommodating attitudes had gotten the workers nowhere and that more radical approaches should now be on the agenda. The more moderate Mensheviks despaired of the new successes of the Bolsheviks, blaming the "romantic rebelliousness" of the workers, their youth, and the peasant outlook of the newer workers. On the eve of World War I thousands of Russia's workers took to the streets to protest their condition and the irresponsibility of those in charge.

The autocracy, which appeared to many foreigners to be a strong and stable government, in fact had feet of clay. Over time tsarism had prevented the development of an autonomous civil society, repressed the emergence of independent institutions and channels of communication from society to the state. Instead, an inefficient, unruly bureaucracy stood between educated society and the monarchy, and even as some energetic ministers tried to reform the system, the inertia of inherited practices and the active resistance of powerful nobles stifled meaningful change. At the same time industrialization had transformed the economy of much of Russia and introduced new social elements, workers and the commercial–industrial groups, that coexisted quite uneasily with the landed nobility and entrenched bureaucrats. Yet even as the state became less effective domestically, Russian leaders remained convinced that Russia must act internationally like a Great Power.

The Tsar's Last War

On Russia's western border lay imperial Germany, a burgeoning industrial and military power, and Austria-Hungary, a disparate multinational state that by contrast was the weakest of the major European powers. In Germany advisors to the kaiser believed that it would be to Germany's advantage to fight a preventive war with Russia before the tsarist empire became any stronger. Aware of Russia's enormous potential strength in the future and its weakness at present, German leaders feared that Russia's "crude physical manpower" and its "expansive and gigantic industrial power" might one day crush Germany. In the summer of 1914 Austria responded to the killing of the Austrian heir apparent, Franz Ferdinand, in the Bosnian capital of Sarajevo, by issuing an ultimatum to tiny Serbia. Pro-Serbian sentiment was high in Russia, particularly among liberal politicians in the Duma. The emperor and his government decided it was time for Russia to take a "firmer and more energetic attitude." Once Russia determined to back Serbian independence against Austria, and Germany gave its "blank check" to Austria, war was inevitable. On July 30, 1914, Nicholas I ordered the general mobilization of the Russian army. The next day Germany demanded that Russia cease her preparations along the German frontier. On the afternoon of August 1, France ordered mobilization against Germany, and Germany responded five minutes later with its own mobilization. At seven that evening Germany, having heard no reply to its ultimatum, declared war on the Russian Empire. The tsar and his ministers ignored cautious advisors, like the Caucasian viceroy, who warned that "war must not be allowed . . . general dissatisfaction is growing . . . the question of a war could become 'dynastic.' "

Russia entered World War I with enormous liabilities. Though the economy was growing rapidly, the country lagged far behind Germany in industrial output. Russia's population was still fettered by illiteracy. Just over a third of the population could read and write, a figure that matched the level of literacy in Great Britain in 1750. Yet victory, even survival, in modern warfare depended on the overall industrial might of a country and the skills of its population, and here Russia was at a considerable disadvantage. A huge share of Russia's net national product, more than 10 percent, was spent on the military, which received five times as much money from the state as did education. An amount equivalent to half of the average Russian's income in 1913 went to current defense spending. And this in a country of widespread poverty! The average per-capita income of a Russian in 1913 was $57, just over a quarter of the per-capita income of the average English citizen subject at the time. Russia's backwardness meant not only that a larger part of the nation's output went to arming the country but that each ship and gun cost more to produce because of low labor productivity and high material costs.

At the outbreak of the war the Russian army was the largest in Europe, some 1.4 million men. Russia's Western allies, Britain and France, were counting on the effectiveness of the famous "Russian steamroller," its millions of mobilized men, to exhaust the Germans on the eastern front. In their plans Russia was to draw off a large portion of the German forces to allow an Anglo-

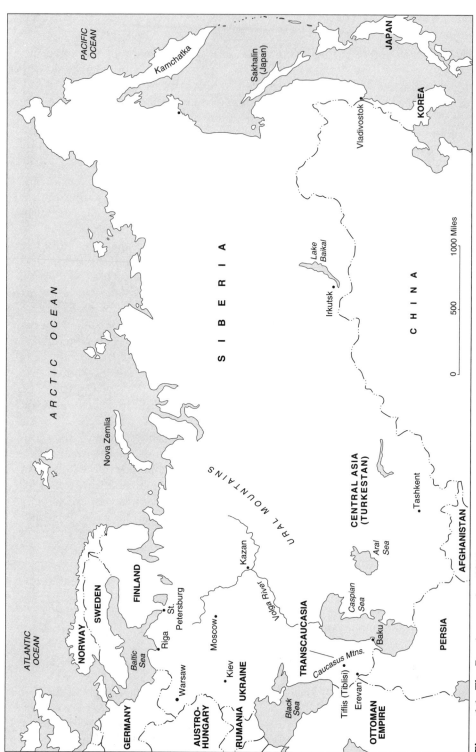

Figure 1.1. The Russian empire, 1914.

French breakthrough in the west. A two-front war was the only hope that the Entente—Russia, France, and Britain—had for victory over the Central Powers—Germany, Austria-Hungary, and the Ottoman Empire. Russia did manage to mobilize more than 15 million men into the armed forces in its two and a half years in the war. In 1914 alone 5.1 million men were drafted, or 15 percent of the male population. But the draft was indiscriminate, calling up skilled industrial workers along with illiterate peasants.

Russians suffered from low military morale in the early twentieth century. Their memories extended back to the defeats of the Crimean War, the humiliating peace treaty imposed on Russia after their victory in the Russo-Turkish War of 1877–78, and the disasters of the Russo-Japanese War (1904–5). The ruling elites reflected the pessimism and bitterness of men like General A. A. Kireev, who wrote in 1909 in his diary, that "we have become a second-rate power." This was the same Pan-Slav who nine years earlier had written: 'Of course, we, like any powerful nation, strive to expand our territory, our 'legitimate' moral, economic, and political influence. This is the order of things." The fat, old minister of war, General Vladimir Sukhomlinov, held quite definite and antiquated ideas about how war should be fought. He had learned nothing new since the victorious campaigns against the Turks at the end of the 1870s. 'Look at me," he said proudly. "I have not read a military manual for the last twenty-five years." For Sukhomlinov all the talk of fire tactics was annoying; the saber, lance, and bayonet charge were the essence of manly fighting in his opinion. He personally despised the commander in chief of the army, Grand Duke Nikolai Nikolaevich, an advocate of military reforms, and kept his post because of his personal closeness to the imperial family and Rasputin and his talent for telling funny stories.

In the first months of the war the Russian armies did well against the Austrians, but in late August the Germans, under Hindenburg and Ludendorff, soundly defeated the Russian army of General Samsonov at the Battle of Tannenberg. The Germans took one hundred thousand prisoners and stopped the Russian advance into East Prussia. In despair Samsonov shot himself. The Germans advanced through Russian Poland in the next few months, and only at the end of the year were the Russians able to hold the line against further German or Austrian penetration. In two great campaigns in the spring and summer of 1915, the Germans took all of Poland, Lithuania, and Courland in the Baltic region, inflicting losses on the Russians of 1 million dead soldiers. The tsar responded by relieving his uncle and taking command of the army himself.

The failures in the military reflected widespread failures throughout the state and the economy. The tsarist state failed to organize an effective war economy. In the first month of the war the government prohibited the sale of intoxicating beverages for the duration of the war, thus making Russia the first country ever to attempt prohibition on a national scale. But this led to a sharp drop in state revenues from the loss of alcohol taxes. With soldiers using the railroads, state revenues fell off here as well. For all its vastness Russia had only 42,400 miles of railroad in 1914, and the inadequate transport system broke down under the strain of war. Taxes proved more difficult to collect during the war, and the government was forced both to float loans domestically and abroad and to print more paper money, which led to inflation. Though grain was plentiful in the countryside, and there was enough to satisfy the population's needs, it was not effectively distributed to the towns. The government fixed prices for grain in order to stem inflation, but with industry turning out war material, farmers were denied the manufactured goods from the towns for which they had exchanged grain. Their paper rubles quickly depreciated, and they grew reluctant to part with their grain.

The war brought millions out of the countryside into the army and into new jobs in the cities. Industry and agriculture both suffered the loss of skilled hands, though farming was hurt less because of the chronic excess of labor on the land. But by the fall of 1915 all nonbreadwinners had been recruited, and "first breadwinners," the last males in the villages, were being called up. Military experience had a profound effect on the lives of country folk, as they were thrown together with people of other social classes and different political views. Mobilized peasants were quite receptive to the ideas of their city brothers and the radical intellectuals who interpreted the wider world for them. While peasants gave in to the enthusiasm of the educated classes for the war at first, as the war went badly—4 million casualties in the first year, 1 million of them fatalities—a sullen resentment against the war grew. When supplies of ammunition began to run out at the end of 1914 and casualty rates rose rapidly, morale fell precipitously. By 1915 Russian industry could not fulfill the supply needs of the army. Few peasant soldiers felt a genuine patriotism or identification with Russia; their loyalties remained local, and they did not think of the war as their war. They had little affection for their officers, whom they identified with the landlord class, and many believed that the war threatened the peasant way of life. Unrest started with the older soldiers, family men who had served before the war. Rumors about pro-German sympathy among the aristocracy spread through the army and led to a number of mutinies at the front. In 1915–16 riots broke out in the rear against recruitment, and at the front a general fatigue and disgust with the war spread among the soldiers.

Though the autocracy had seldom involved society in tasks thought to be in the competence of the state, the burdens of the war forced the government to deal with various social groups, particularly in towns. Still suspicious of the political parties, the tsar chose to suspend the parliament and rule through his emergency powers. The Duma met only twice in 1915. The government turned to so-called voluntary organizations, local district and provincial bodies and the municipal dumas, to help organize supplies for the army. In May 1915 industrialists met in Petrograd to form the war-industry committees and invited workers to elect representatives to serve in labor groups attached to the committees. These elections, held in September 1915, helped to revive labor activity that had been quiescent since the outbreak of the war. Though still bitterly divided, both from society in general and within its own ranks, many workers encouraged by the Mensheviks, participated in this movement.

The military and political situation reached a crisis point in the summer of 1915. Scandals brought down the minister of war, Sukhomlinov, and other ministers. As the Germans advanced relentlessly, the new war minister told the cabinet, "I rely on impassable spaces, on impenetrable mud, and on the mercy of Saint Nicholas, the patron of Holy Russia." Each military setback helped the liberals in the Duma, as defeats were blamed on governmental mismanagement and incompetence. Pavl Miliukov, the leader of the most important liberal party, the Kadets, called for the appointment of a government of liberals that would enjoy the confidence of the educated people of Russia. Miliukov brought together the three leading parties in the Duma—the Kadets, Octobrists, and Progressists—to form a political coalition known as the Progressive Bloc to pressure the tsar to bring the liberals to power. The tsar answered by again suspending the Duma on September 3, 1915, and moving to the front to be nearer his troops.

Government was now largely in the hands of the empress and her confidant, Rasputin. Her advice to her husband was "Be more autocratic!" When Nicholas received his ministers at headquarters, Aleksandra suggested that he steel himself by combing his hair with Rasputin's comb. The monarchy's association with this debauched man of the people ate away at the residue of charisma attached to the Romanovs and presented an image to the public of moral emptiness at the heart of the state. Completely shut out of decision-making, the leaders of the Duma met secretly to discuss what seemed to them to be the pro-German sentiments of the empress and her coterie. A few, like Aleksandr Guchkov, the leader of the conservative Octobrists, plotted to overthrow the monarchy. On November 1, 1916, Miliukov rose in the reconvened Duma to denounce the government where, he claimed, there was "treason in high places."

The disaffection with the government spread from the Duma liberals to aristocrats and military officers close to the tsar. On the evening of December 16, Prince Feliks Iusupov lured Rasputin to his palace in Petrograd where he and several co-conspirators poisoned, shot, and finally drowned him in a canal. When the news reached her the following morning, the empress wrote to the tsar, "Our friend has disappeared. Such utter anguish. Am calm and cannot believe it." With thousands dying at the front and pathetic incompetents dithering away their power, the three-hundred-year history of the Romanov dynasty was rapidly coming to a close.

Suggestions for Further Reading

For a synthetic overview of prerevolutionary Russian history, the best work is Nicholas V. Riasanovsky, *A History of Russia* (New York, 1984). On the years of industrial formation and revolutionary upheaval, see Theodore von Laue's *Sergei Witte and the Industrialization of Russia* (New York, 1963); Abraham Ascher, *The Revolution of 1905*, 2 vols. (Stanford, Calif., 1988–93); Andrew Verner, *The Crisis of Russian Autocracy: Nicholas II and the 1905 Revolution* (Princeton, N.J., 1990); Geoffrey Hosking, *The Russian Constitutional Experiment: Government and Duma, 1907–1914* (Cambridge, 1973); Roberta T. Manning, *The Crisis of the Old Order in Russia: Government and Gentry* (Princeton, N.J., 1982); Tim Mc Daniel, *Autocracy, Capitalism, and Revolution in Russia* (Berkeley, Calif., 1988); and Leopold H. Haimson (ed.), *The Politics of Rural Russia, 1905–1914* (Bloomington, Ind., 1979).

The literature on the workers and the Social Democratic movement is varied and rich, and among the most interesting works are: Reginald E. Zelnik (ed.), *A Radical Worker in Tsarist Russia: The Autobiography of Semen Ivanovich Kanatchikov* (Stanford, Calif., 1986); Charters Wynn, *Workers, Strikes, and Pogroms: The Donbass-Dnepr Bend in Late Imperial Russia, 1870–1905* (Princeton, N.J., 1992); Victoria E. Bonnel, *Roots of Rebellion: Workers' Politics and Organizations in St. Petersburg and Moscow, 1900–1914* (Berkeley, Calif., 1984); Heather Hogan, *Forging Revolution: Metalworkers, Managers, and the State in St. Petersburg, 1890–1914* ((Bloomington, Ind., 1993); Samuel H. Baron, *Plekhanov: The Father of Russian Marxism* (Stanford, Calif., 1963); Allan K. Wildman, *The Making of a Workers' Revolution: Russian Social Democracy, 1891–1903* (Chicago, 1967); Leopold H. Haimson, *The Russian Marxists and the Origins of Bolshevism* (Cambridge, Mass., 1955); and J. L. H. Keep, *The Rise of Social Democracy in Russia* (Oxford, 1963).

Though there is less written on other social groups, some splendid works are available: Alfred Rieber, *Merchants and Entrepreneurs in Imperial Russia* (Chapel Hill, N.C., 1982); Esther Kingston-Mann and Timothy Mixter (eds.), *Peasant Economy, Culture, and Politics of European Russia* (Princeton, N.J., 1991); Ben Ekloff, *Russian Peasant Schools: Officialdom, Village Culture, and Popular Pedagogy, 1861–1914* (Berkeley, Calif., 1986); Christine D. Worobec, *Peasant Russia: Family and Community in the Post-Emancipation Period* (Princeton, N.J., 1991); Stephen P. Frank and Mark D. Steinberg (eds.), *Cultures in Flux: Lower-Class Values, Practices, and Resistance in Late Imperial Russia* (Princeton, N.J., 1994); Joan Neuberger, *Hooliganism: Crime, Culture, and Power in St. Petersburg, 1900–1914* (Berkeley, Calif., 1993); and Nancy Mandelker Frieden, *Russian Physicians in an Era of Reform and Revolution, 1856–1905* (Princeton, N.J., 1981).

A book in a category of its own, exploring the discourses around gender and sexuality, is Laura Engelstein, *The Keys to Happiness: Sex and the Search for Modernity in Fin-de-Siècle Russia* (Ithaca, N.Y., 1992). On foreign policy the single best work is David M. McDonald, *United Government and Foreign Policy in Russia, 1900–1914* (Cambridge, 1992).

CHAPTER 2
The Double Revolution

The February Revolution and the End of Romanov Rule

On January 22, 1917, just a month before the outbreak of the revolution in Russia, Vladimir Lenin, in exile in Zurich, addressed a meeting of young Swiss workers in German. His topic was the Russian revolution of 1905, and his aim was to counteract the despair that many revolutionaries felt in the third year of World War I. "We should not be deceived by the present graveyard silence in Europe," he stated soberly.

> Europe is pregnant with revolution. The monstrous horror of the imperial-ist war and the suffering caused by the rise in the cost of living engender a revolutionary spirit, and the ruling classes, the bourgeoisie and their lack-eys, the governments, are moving deeper and deeper into a blind alley from which they will never be able to extricate themselves without tremendous upheavals. . . .

He confidently told his audience that the coming revolution would be a "pro-letarian, socialist revolution," but he was more pessimistic about its timing. "We of the older generation may not live to see the decisive battles of this com-ing revolution."

Lenin proved to be a better revolutionary than a prophet of revolution. The brief wave of patriotism at the beginning of the war had only temporarily ame-liorated the political crisis of tsarism. By the spring of 1915, the chasm between the government and educated society had opened up again, as the majority of Duma members, the Progressive Bloc, called for a cabinet that had the support of the Duma. But the tsar had steadily refused to grant such a government and instead threatened to dissolve the Duma. Disenchantment with the emperor and empress reached into the royal family itself. High officials, even the tsar's uncle, Grand Duke Nicholas, knew of plots to overthrow the tsar and did not report them. Defeats and economic disarray turned more and more people against the regime. The Romanov dynasty existed almost without support, held in place by the inertia of three centuries and fear of the alternatives.

Revolutions, at least in their initial phases, are often affairs of a single city, and 1917 was no exception to this general rule. With the outbreak of World War I tsarist officials decided to change St. Petersburg's German-sounding name (Sankt Peterburg was from the Dutch!) to the Russian Petrograd. The largest city in Russia at the time, Petrograd was the creation of Peter the Great, who founded the town in 1703 on the swampy ground where the Neva River meets the Gulf of Finland and made it his capital. Peter's "window on the West" was a showpiece of classical and Baroque architecture, with the grand Winter Palace facing the Neva and a string of lesser palaces lining the main boulevard, the Nevskii Prospekt. The city center, with its official buildings and elegant residences along the canals, gave the city the aspect of a "Venice of the North." The very geography of the city reproduced the class distinctions and separations of the population. Outside the eighteenth- and nineteenth-century core lay grim factory and worker districts, some of them across the river on islands such as Vyborg and Petrograd. Bridges that could be raised at night separated the poorer sections of the city from the fashionable center. In some ways the imperial center was the symbolic heart of the empire, brilliantly painted in pastels, evoking in stone and gild the distance of the monarchy and aristocracy from the simple people. The peasants who had become workers were strangers in certain parts of the city, and those who had more recently become soldiers and now were housed in barracks awaiting transfer to the front were even more alien. In the winter of 1917, in the bone-chilling cold and dark of the Baltic north, where the sun shone without heat for only a few hours of the day, the mood of workers and soldiers matched the weather.

No one suspected in February 1917 that they were about to experience events that would alter world history. After some preparation by Social Democrats, women workers, hungry and embittered, met illegally in several textile mills in the Vyborg district on February 23 (March 8 n.s.), which in the socialist calendar was celebrated as International Women's Day. In many ways more radical than the socialist intellectuals who sought to guide them, the women decided to go on strike and marched to other factories shouting for bread. Even Bolshevik activists were at first wary about this unplanned strike, though they soon decided to support it. By noon twenty-one factories and fifty thousand workers had joined the strike. They marched on the Arsenal, the large state armaments plant, but were met there with a largely negative response from the well-paid munitions workers. The strikers forced the plant to close and moved on until the strike spread throughout the Vyborg and Petrograd districts of the city. The workers were determined to stage a demonstration on Nevskii Prospekt, the main street of the capital. The police guarded the bridges, but the strikers simply crossed the ice covering the river. Bread shortages inflamed those in bread lines, and they joined the strikers. The angry crowds beat up several police officers, and the Cossacks, usually the troops most loyal to the tsar, made little effort to restore order. An eyewitness, historian Nikolai Sukhanov, wrote, "The mass street movement in the February Days revealed no sort of purposefulness, nor was it possible to discern in it any kind of proper leadership."

By the second day, February 24, two hundred thousand people, one half the industrial workers of Petrograd, were on strike. As factories closed down around the city, the metal workers joined the strike. The police tried to stop demonstrations, but the Cossacks refused to shoot down the workers. In the Duma the liberals now called for a government responsible to the Duma. A Duma leader, F. I. Rodichev, appealed to the tsar: "Give us those people whom all Russia can believe. We demand above all the expulsion from [the government] of persons whom all Russia despises." But more radical voices were also heard. The Menshevik Nikolai Chkheidze argued that compromise with the government was impossible and that contact with the streets was essential.

In Chinese the characters for the word *crisis* can be translated "dangerous opportunity." In this sense the various political parties that had opposed tsarism for decades were now faced by their greatest political crisis. Liberals in the Duma were fearful that the spontaneous rebelliousness of the masses was already breaking loose of state control. Miliukov, the leader of the liberal Constitutional Democratic Party, or Kadets, later admitted, "We did not want this revolution. We did not wish particularly that it would come at the time of the war. And we had desperately struggled so that this would not happen." Miliukov tried in vain to save the monarchy, but as the revolution sped forward the masses in the street would not sanction preservation of the Romanov dynasty.

The socialist parties were divided between the propeasant Socialist Revolutionaries, or SRs, and the worker-oriented Social Democrats, or SDs. The Social Democrats entered the revolution divided between the moderate Mensheviks and the more militant Bolsheviks, and even these broad factions had further fractures within them. Both SDs and SRs had been traumatized by the outbreak of World War I. The more conservative elements in each party had come out in support of the war, taking a position called "defensism," while the Left took what was known as the "internationalist" position and either opposed the war or called for Russia's defeat ("defeatism"). Among the SDs Lenin led the Defeatists; Martov headed the Menshevik Internationalists; and Chkheidze and Iraklii Tsereteli, both from Georgia, were among the leading Menshevik Defensists. Tsereteli, who has been largely forgotten except by historians, was a dynamic, charismatic young man who had been elected to the Second Duma only to be arrested and exiled to Siberia by the tsarist government. On his return to European Russia in March 1917, he soon emerged as the principal theoretician of the Menshevik-Defensist position and a major force in the Petrograd soviet. The leaders of the SRs were unable to unify their ranks, which were divided among a militant, internationalist Left, which would gravitate toward the Bolsheviks; an accommodating Center, led by Viktor Chernov; and a Right that wanted victory in the war and a strong and stable government. As serious as the differences between and within the left parties were, the euphoria of the unfolding revolution momentarily pulled them together, and in February and March Mensheviks, Bolsheviks, SRs, and nonparty workers fought together against the monarchy.

On February 25, three hundred thousand workers left work in a general strike that spread throughout the city of Petrograd. Streetcars and cabs stopped running; newspapers ceased publication; and the banks closed. Crowds of workers, students, and others surged through the streets, and the soldiers did not stop them. In Znamenskaia Square in front of the main railroad station, thousands of demonstrators heard revolutionary speeches. When a police officer led a charge to break up the demonstration, he was cut down, either by workers or Cossacks. By the next day workers knew that they might be fired upon by the police or even the army, but they came out anyway. Workers were more militant than their socialist, even Bolshevik, leaders. In the throes of the revolution, the Bolsheviks were divided into factions and hardly resembled the monolithic disciplined party of later Communist mythology or Cold War–era Western fears. Some party committees called for an armed uprising, while the more moderate Russian Bureau of the Bolshevik Central Committee, the highest ranking Bolshevik committee in the city, opposed that demand.

On the fourth day of the revolution the government went on the offensive. The emperor ordered the Duma to dissolve, but though its members dispersed, they remained in the city. Duma leaders tried to mediate between the government and the streets, but the tsar did not reply to their chairman's call for a government with the confidence of the Duma. The police arrested one hundred people they believed to be important leaders of the rebellion. Soldiers fired into the crowds, machine-gun fire rained from rooftops, and the fraternization of the crowds with the soldiers briefly ceased.

Despite the danger, the crowds in the streets continued to march, becoming angrier by the hour. Suddenly, unpredictably, some members of the fourth company of the prestigious Pavlovskii Guards Regiment mutinied and joined the crowds. This soldiers' mutiny was the turning point in the insurrection. The workers' rebellion of the first days of the revolution would have failed had the soldiers not decided to join them. On the next day, February 27, more guards regiments mutinied. By evening, sixty-six thousand soldiers in Petrograd had come over to the insurrection. That day a group of influential members of the Duma formed the Provisional Committee of the Duma. In the other wing of the same building, the Tauride Palace, deputies elected by workers around the city met to form their own representative institution, the Soviet (Council) of Workers' Deputies. The capital of the Russian Empire was now in the hands of the revolutionaries, and no major social groups or significant military units were any longer prepared to fight and die for the emperor. A few days later, on March 2 (15 n.s.), the last tsar of Russia, Nicholas II, isolated on a railroad siding in Pskov, about two hundred miles from Petrograd, abandoned by his generals and closest advisors, abdicated. Russia, which had been a monarchy for a thousand years, became a republic.

The Romanov dynasty fell with stunning speed, after just five days of rebellion in the capital. But the February Days were only the proximate cause of the collapse of the tsarist regime. The revolution was the result as well of a long and deep social crisis that tsarism was unable to overcome. The monarchy had proven incapable of resolving the growing contradiction between capitalist industrialization, with its newly empowered middle and working classes, and the maintenance of an autocratic government and an antiquated social hierarchy of noble privilege that closed itself off from a mobilizing society. The tsar's attempt at limited constitutionalism after 1905 brought the subterranean tensions in society into a public arena, as the government vacillated between repression and concession. Nicholas II was intransigent on the question of forming a government of ministers who enjoyed the confidence of the Duma. Once the war broke out, the government appeared to more and more people to be incompetent to govern or win the war, and the authority of the ruling elites eroded rapidly. The failures at the front and the resultant economic shortages, which led to a sharp rise in the cost of living, intensified the social discontents of the prewar era and added a new and potent element, the armed peasantry in uniform. In the context of material hardship and foreign danger the messages of liberals and socialists that linked the people's misery with the autocracy resonated loudly. When the revolution broke out, the attempts by liberals to contain the fury of ordinary people and mediate between the tottering state and the crowds in the streets failed, and new political actors—the workers and the soldiers—pushed the dynasty off the stage altogether. Though the imperial government limply fought one last battle in the streets of Petrograd, its authority and support had seeped away years before.

Overlapping Revolutions, Dual Power

The revolution of 1917 was actually a series of overlapping revolutions. The first was the workers' rebellion, followed by the soldiers' mutiny, that ended with the establishment of two centers of authority. The revolutionary lower classes, or *demokratiia*, as they were styled by the socialists, elected their own organs of power, the soviets, while the middle and upper classes, the military officers, much of the state bureaucracy, and educated society identified with the Provisional Government self-selected by leading members of the Duma. Much of the period from early March until October 1917 can be seen as a second, liberal revolution, led by middle-class politicians and part of the intelligentsia, that attempted to create a new constitutional order amid conditions of ever-deepening social and political disorder. In October the workers' revolution was renewed with the establishment of "soviet power," but this time it was led by the Bolshevik party. Simultaneous, and gaining momentum, was the peasant revolution that culminated in the seizure of land, the expropriation of the nobility, and the leveling of landholding in 1918. Finally, the multiple revolt of the non-Russian peoples of the empire splintered the unitary empire and gave rise to the establishment of national states along the peripheries of Russia.

As calm returned to Petrograd after the battles of the revolutionary days in February, workers turned to the Duma, shouting, "Give us leaders; we need leaders." Suspicious of the Duma and the upper classes in general, the mobilized workers and soldiers were not yet prepared to take power into their own hands. Nor were their socialist leaders. With the war raging and the economy in rapid decline, those who had made the revolution in the streets were prepared to recognize their social "betters" as the legitimate new leaders of the country. But when Duma leaders formed a government, headed by Prince

Georgii Lvov, workers and soldiers elected their own soviets to represent their interests and keep a watchful eye on the Duma and the new government. The leaders of the Petrograd soviet turned out to be primarily moderate Mensheviks and SRs, who had been prominent among workers in the city during the war years. The major Bolshevik leaders were in exile, either in Europe or Siberia, and would return to the capital only weeks later.

Almost immediately the differences and distance between the two new governing institutions became apparent. The Duma wanted to restore immediately the command over the army of the military officers, but rank-and-file soldiers were opposed to giving up their new power. On March 1, the soviet met with representatives of the soldiers and adopted the famous "Order No. 1," which stated that soldiers should obey no order unless it was sanctioned by the soviet. Soldiers mistrusted their officers and quickly rallied to the soviet. With this order the soviet gained authority over the soldiers, and though the Provisional Government would have formal power and be recognized as the government of Russia by its allies, the Petrograd soviet had the real power. It alone could issue orders, bring out the troops, and order the factories to operate. The soviet, however, decided not to seize official power in its own name but to recognize the new government and maintain a watchful eye over its activities. Its resolution of March 2 (15 n.s.) reflected the soviet's suspicion of the government:

> The Provisional Government that emerged from the revolution speaks for the interests of the bourgeoisie and, therefore, the working class can support this government only in so far as its policy will not turn against the interests of the broad laboring masses; at the same time the working class must organize itself for the defense of its class interests and the consolidation of all the achievements of the revolution.

This dual power (*dvoevlastie*) reproduced and reinforced the real balance of power in the city. On one side stood a suspicious working class and its allies, the soldiers; on the other were the people of property—the liberal and conservative politicians, officers, and nobles—who feared the potential wrath of an aroused people. Later a liberal politician remembered:

> Officially we celebrated, we praised the revolution, shouted "hurrah" to the fighters for freedom, wrapped ourselves with red bunting and marched under red flags. . . . We all said "we," "our" revolution, "our" victory, and "our" freedom. But inside, in our solitary discussions, we were horrified, we shuddered, and felt ourselves to be prisoners of inimical elements moving along some sort of uncharted path.

In the early months of the revolution workers were not interested in ruling the country but merely in gaining greater control over their own lives. Though they were wary of the government, they hoped that the new political leaders of the country would work in the interests of the poor as well as the well-off. In their factories they loaded hated foremen or known police spies into wheelbarrows and carted them out of the plants. They elected their own factory committees to look after their interests and to maintain discipline within the factory. Extremely popular was the Social Democratic program of an eight-hour workday, the confiscation of landlords' land, and the formation of a democratic republic.

The polarization of urban society that had been evident before the war was far less extreme in the first month of the revolution. Industrialists made significant concessions to workers in many cities in order to enhance social peace and aid the war effort. They accepted with little resistance the reduction of the workday from ten or twelve hours to eight. Factory owners also agreed to pay raises, which pleased the workers but also raised expectations. When inflation wiped out the wage gains in the next few months and industrialists proved less willing to offer another round of pay increases, bitterness set in among the workers.

Peasants joined the revolution later than people in the cities. Their interests centered on gaining control of the land, and they were generally in favor of distributing the land to those who worked it. Their gradual radicalization came from impatience with the government, which vacillated between the radical rhetoric of the Socialist Revolutionaries and the hesitancy of the representatives of the landlords. A peasant from Riazan wrote of his discontent, "Well, nothing has changed yet, and the revolution is already six weeks old."

The most politically active peasants were the more than 4 million in uniform. Like their brethren back in the villages, soldiers looked at the revolution as a means to achieve land and peace. With red ribbons pinned to their uniforms, they became insubordinate to their officers, organized constant rounds of meetings, and took out their hostility on officers they felt were opposed to the revolution. At first the soldiers were willing to continue fighting, but as winter turned to spring they balked at launching another offensive against the Germans. Revolutionaries met with the soldiers and urged that they support the workers and the soviets. By April soldiers had grown suspicious of the Provisional Government and had become reliable allies of the workers and their elected councils. Daily reports of units refusing to obey orders alarmed the government, as did news of Russian soldiers fraternizing with their purported enemies, the Germans and Austrians, across the lines. At Easter time Germans served rum to the Russians, brought out their orchestras, took pictures of the enemy, and talked to the Russian soldiers about the futility of war. Desertions rose as Bolsheviks agitated against any offensive military operations.

At first most ordinary people did not distinguish between political parties. With the Bolsheviks, Mensheviks, and Socialist Revolutionaries cooperating in the early days of the revolution, few people understood the differences among them. Bolsheviks presented themselves as the most radical of the socialist parties, the most fervently opposed to the war, and the most suspicious of the Provisional Government. Yet until Lenin returned from exile, most Bolsheviks were willing to support the new government and the policies of the soviet. In Petrograd two of Lenin's followers, Joseph Stalin and Lev Kamenev, led the party toward cooperation with the Provisional Government. Traveling by closed train across Germany, Lenin arrived at the Finland Station in Petrograd on April 3

(16 n.s.). As Trotsky, who was soon to join the Bolsheviks, later remarked, "The party was as unprepared for Lenin as it had been for the February Revolution." Lenin exploded in anger at the party's soft line toward the government and insisted that it support the "conquest of power by the soviets of workers' deputies." Lenin believed that Russia was in transition from the bourgeois to the proletarian stage of revolution and that only a republic of soviets could bring the war to an end and spark the international socialist revolution for which he had worked his entire adult life. Party leaders were stunned by Lenin's militance, but they eventually adopted his "April Theses," which rejected support for the Provisional Government. By this resolution the Bolsheviks emerged as the clear alternative to the Menshevik and SR policy of cooperation with a government that over time became identified in the minds of many with the upper and middle classes.

Russia's middle class, insofar as it acted as a coherent social group, was led by powerful industrialists, who had begun to see themselves as the harbingers of a new economic and social order. They wanted full economic freedom, the end of governmental regulation of corporations and banks, and an enhanced role for themselves in political decision-making. With the autocracy out of the way and bourgeois parties leading the new government, Russia's merchants and industrialists entertained high hopes that the new order would usher in an age of enterprise free of the heavy hand of the state.

The leading parties in the Provisional Government were the liberal Kadets, headed by Foreign Minister Miliukov, a more conservative party, the Octobrists, led by Minister of War Guchkov, and the self-styled representatives of the bourgeoisie, the Progressists, headed by Minister of Trade and Industry Aleksandr Konovalov. No socialists joined the government, except the impulsive Aleksandr Kerensky, a well-known lawyer who had been a secret member of the SR party and now became minister of justice. A flamboyant personality and a dynamic public speaker, he enhanced his considerable reputation and gained immediate popularity by issuing an amnesty to all political prisoners. But despite the fact that the government was recognized by other states and held legal authority, despite all the formality and even pomp that surrounded it, the Provisional Government soon realized that it was dependent on the good will of the soviet. Guchkov wrote to General Mikhail Alekseev in mid-March:

> The Provisional Government does not possess any real power, and its directives are carried out only to the extent that is permitted by the Soviet of Workers' and Soldiers' Deputies, which enjoys all the essential elements of real power, since the troops, the railroads, the post and telegraph are all in its hands. One can say flatly that the Provisional Government exists only so long as it is permitted by the Soviet.

The imbalance of power between soviet and government was dramatically illustrated in a dispute over Russia's foreign policy. At the end of March the Petrograd soviet, under the guidance of the influential Menshevik Iraklii Tsereteli, adopted its own position on the war, called "revolutionary de-

Figure 2.1. Lenin addressing a mass meeting in Petrograd in 1917 (Stock Montage, Inc.).

fensism." Russia should fight the war in order to defend the revolution, Tsereteli argued, but it should also carry on a campaign for peace. The soviet favored a "democratic peace" with no imperialist seizures of territory or reparations paid by one side to the other. The leaders of the government, on the other hand, wanted to fight the war "to a victorious conclusion" and to "sacredly observe the alliances that bind us to other powers." Foreign Minister Miliukov disregarded the soviet's policy of "no annexations or contributions" and continued to articulate the war aims of the deposed tsarist government, which included Russian control of Constantinople and the Dardanelles. When the public heard about Miliukov's note to the Allies retaining the old imperial policy, thousands of workers and soldiers poured into the streets, marched to the residence of the government, and called for the removal of the "capitalist ministers" and "Miliukov-Dardanelskii" (Miliukov of the Dardanelles). One woman who joined the demonstration was confused by the issues involved and questioned who were these terrible women, Anneksiia (annexation) and Kontributsiia (contribution), who wanted to continue the war!

The weakness of the Provisional Government and its dependence on the soviet were now readily apparent. From the Left the Bolsheviks called for the abolition of the government and "all power to the soviets," but there was still relatively little support for this idea. From the Right Miliukov and some of the conservative forces wanted to strengthen the government and remove soviet influence over it, but that would have required strong military backing, which they did not have. In the middle some liberals called for a coalition government, which would include representatives of the soviet. But their potential allies, the moderate Mensheviks and SRs who led the soviet, were reluctant either to take power on their own or to enter a coalition government with the "bourgeois ministers." The soviet leaders wanted above all to preserve the unity of the alliances that had brought about the February Revolution and to keep the country from disintegrating along class or ethnic lines. When Minister of War Guchkov resigned his post, the soviet leaders suspected that conservatives might be planning a military move against them. Only then did the soviet vote for coalition on May 1. Two days later Miliukov resigned, and on May 5 a coalition government with a minority of socialists was formed.

The Revolution Deepens

By 1917 Russia was too weak and weary to carry on the war against the Central Powers with any real effect. The army was sullen and demoralized and no longer interested in fighting. Yet the war went on, and the Provisional Government remained enthusiastically committed to victory. After he became minister of war in May, Kerensky pushed for a major new campaign against the Germans. On June 18 the so-called Kerensky Offensive was launched, with disastrous results. Fighting a war that was beyond the means of the country was like running an engine that was overheating. The demands of supplying a massive army and large cities with food and fuel proved too great for the inadequate transportation network and the organizational skills of the government. Though supplies to the cities had improved briefly just after the February Revolution, the movement of foodstuffs fell off by 40 percent in April and May. Shortages led to rising prices, and the inflation wiped out wage gains. Factories closed because of the high fuel costs and inadequate supplies of raw materials. Unemployment increased. The number of strikes rose, almost doubling in May. Industrialists responded to worker pressure by closing factories, only compounding the problem and sharpening worker hostility. Outside government the voices of the militant Left became louder and more convincing to workers and soldiers.

Figure 2.2. Alexander Kerensky reviewing his troops, 1917 (Brown Brothers).

The revolution of 1917 largely took place in the capital, and here the workers and soldiers were far more hostile to carrying on the war or working with the bourgeoisie than people outside the capital. Besides Petrograd volatile workers were concentrated in a dozen large cities: in Moscow and Ivanovo-Voznesensk in central Russia, in Saratov and Nizhnyi Novgorod on the Volga, in Ekaterinburg in the Urals, in the Don Region, in Kharkov, Odessa, and Kiev in Ukraine, and in Baku. Though there was adequate grain available in the countryside for both civilians and soldiers, it was not delivered on time and in the necessary quantities to the cities. Shortages in the industrial areas had immediate and catastrophic effects both on the productivity of the whole country and on the political attitudes of the workers.

From May until October the Mensheviks and Socialist Revolutionaries sat in the government. As the government proved unable to solve the problems of the economy or end the war, its popularity withered and the lower classes began to perceive the moderate socialists in the government as collaborating with the enemy. Beginning in late spring and continuing through the fall, the social distance between the top and the bottom of society widened, and the attempts by moderates to hold together an alliance of all social classes proved impossible. Workers moved leftward; the middle and upper classes moved to the right and both became more resistant to the interests of the other. There was no broad consensus, either in government or society, on the future economic order in Russia. Was the economy to be free-market capitalism, with a minimum of state intervention, or some form of socialism, with considerable regulation by the state? The Mensheviks in government, working through the newly formed Ministry of Labor, favored state control of the economy, which meant that the government would regulate and supervise economic relations in a basically capitalist economy. But the business community and its spokesmen in the Ministry of Trade and Industry opposed state regulation and called for a rejection of socialism. The government was unable to resolve this key question, and few measures could be taken to stimulate the industrial sector.

Outside the government workers saw the "capitalist ministers" as saboteurs of the revolution, and industrialists saw workers as the cause of industry's decline. On the last day of May the workers' section of the Petrograd soviet voted for a Bolshevik resolution in favor of "All power to the soviets!" From the first days of the revolution, workers had elected their own committees within factories, and these factory committees soon became more responsive to the changing mood of workers and more radical than the soviets. The government's failure to implement state control convinced many workers to push for a more radical solution, "workers' control," which involved factory committees keeping an eye on the running of the factories. As promoted by the Bolsheviks, workers' control meant supervision of the managers by worker representatives and not, as it was often interpreted, the actual seizure of the factories by workers. In early June the First Conference of Petrograd Factory Committees, which was dominated by the Bolsheviks, voted in favor of workers' control. The Mensheviks called on the workers to restrain their demands, but faced by falling real wages, workers stepped up the number of strikes. As early as mid-May, the Menshevik Vladimir Voitinskii noted, "In the workers' quarters the ground was slipping out from under our feet, and the same observation held true for the barracks."

Insofar as they expressed themselves politically, peasants voted for the large, loosely organized Socialist Revolutionary Party, the one major political party that saw itself as expressing the peasants' interests. The SR Party was potentially the strongest party in Russia, with activists scattered throughout the country and a commitment to further the interests of the peasant majority. SRs consolidated their support in the countryside in the early months of the revolution by organizing peasant soviets in the villages and promoting the nationalization of the land. Especially strong in the Volga region and Siberia, the SRs also had support in the cities, especially among soldiers. But the party was deeply divided into a right wing that supported the coalition government and the war effort, a vacillating center, and a left wing that drew ever closer to the Bolsheviks. At the First All-Russian Congress of Peasants' Soviets, which met early in May, the right-wing SRs, who dominated the meeting, pushed through a resolution that all agricultural land be handed over to land committees, which could then decide on its equitable distribution. The congress opposed all buying and selling of land, fearing that landlords would sell out to rich peasants or others. Land was, thus, to be nationalized without reimbursement to the landlords and redistributed on the basis of equality. The minister of agriculture in the coalition government, SR party leader Viktor Chernov, began elaborating a series of agrarian laws to implement these policies. But he met resistance from the chairman of the government, the liberal landlord Prince Georgii Lvov, who opposed any restrictions on the rights of private property. Chernov followed his party's strictures on the sale of land, but the nonsocialist ministers refused to sanction the land committees or prevent the sale of land. Thus, on the land question, as on the question of state regulation of the economy, the government arrived at an impasse. After enduring personal and political attacks, Chernov resigned from the government on July 20. The strategy of working through the government had clearly failed.

Like the workers and the soldiers, the peasants became more active in running their own lives as a result of the revolution. At first peasant assemblies expressed support for the Provisional Government and drafted proclamations on the land question that were influenced by SR intellectuals. But when peasants gained little satisfaction from the government, they took matters in their own hands, forming "committees of people's power" that endorsed peasant seizures of uncultivated land. Local land committees simply disregarded the decisions taken in Petrograd with which they disagreed, and month after month the number of peasant seizures of landlord estates rose. How they treated the nobles often depended on the past behavior of the lords. Sometimes they burnt his house and stole his livestock; other times they left the lord a parcel of land for his family. Occasionally peasants killed landlords and burnt down their houses, but more often crowds ransacked the manors and simply took over the land. In Riazan province peasants soberly considered whether they should turn the lord's home into a school. "What sort of a school would this make?" one peasant asked. "Our children would get lost in it." The next day they chopped out the doors and windows, smashed the mirrors, poured kerosene over the wooden structure, and set it ablaze.

By the end of the summer, peasants had entered the revolution in large numbers, and the countryside was no longer under the control of the weakened Russian state. The single country of Russia fragmented into village and regional governments; these republics of peasants with their own laws took little account of what Petrograd ordered. What looked like anarchy to liberals and the government was celebrated by the Bolsheviks as manifestations of the people's will. As spring turned into summer, the unity of the soviet forces began to fray. Bolshevik strength grew steadily among workers and, after the June military offensive, among soldiers as well. The moderate socialist leaders of the soviet remained confident that they represented the most responsible elements in the "democracy." At the opening of the First All-Russian Congress of Soviets in early June, Tsereteli announced, "At the present moment, there is not a political party in Russia that would say: Hand the power over to us, resign, and we will take your place. Such a party does not exist in Russia." He was interrupted by a voice from the audience: "It does exist!" Lenin later rose to defend his position, sarcastically referring to Tsereteli as "Citizen-Minister of Post and Telegraphs": "I say: Such a party exists! No party has a right to refuse power, and our party does not refuse it. Our party is ready at any moment to take all power in its hands." He was greeted by applause from his supporters and laughter from his opponents, to whom the Bolshevik's audacious claim appeared ridiculous.

The Congress reflected more the mood of Russia outside the capital than the more militant voices in Petrograd. Led by the Mensheviks and SRs, the delegates voted to support the coalition government and the military offensive against the Germans. Always ready to address a large audience, Kerensky defended the democratic program of the government that would prevent the Russian Revolution from following the pattern of other revolutions:

> The problem of the Russian socialist parties and of the Russian democracy is to prevent such an outcome as occurred in France [the fall of the republic and the rise of a dictator]—to hold on to the revolutionary conquests already made; to see to it that comrades who have been released from prison do not return there; that Comrade Lenin, who has been abroad, may have the opportunity to speak here again, and not be obliged to flee back to Switzerland.

But when the Bolsheviks tried to hold a demonstration in the streets of Petrograd calling for the removal of the nonsocialist ministers, the Congress voted unanimously (even the Bolshevik faction, unaware of the leadership's decision) to prohibit street demonstrations. Tsereteli, who had emerged as the most decisive leader of the soviet, charged that the Bolsheviks were plotting to seize power and called for drastic measures to "kill the counter-revolution." But the Congress stopped short of repressing the Bolsheviks and decided to hold its own demonstration. On June 18, four hundred thousand people marched down the Nevskii Prospekt. To the dismay and embarrassment of the soviet leaders reviewing the parade, the great majority of the marchers carried Bolshevik slogans: "All power to the soviets!" and "Down with the ten capitalist ministers."

On the same day as the Petrograd demonstration, hundreds of miles south and west of the capital, the Russian army advanced against the enemy. The Kerensky Offensive had begun. The middle and upper classes greeted the news from the front with patriotic sighs of relief. At last the army, which seemed to be falling apart through inactivity, would be revitalized by engaging the enemy. Perhaps the volatile soldiers in Petrograd could also be sent to the front. Workers greeted the news of the offensive either with apathy or powerful opposition. Many soldiers mutinied against mobilization for the front. Others yielded to patriotic appeals only to waver under fire. "What good is the land and freedom to me," a peasant soldier complained, "if I am dead?" Bolsheviks urged the soldiers not to participate in the offensive, while Kerensky and soviet representatives tried to convince them to fight. The mood of the soldiers darkened against both the government and the soviet, and "trench Bolshevism" grew rampantly at the front. Soldiers beat up emissaries from the soviet. With demoralization undermining the will to fight, the offensive faltered soon after it began.

As news trickled into Petrograd of the losses at the front, a major political crisis erupted. Late in June delegates from the government conferred in Kiev with representatives of the Ukrainian Rada, a locally elected parliament. The Rada had issued its First Universal declaring autonomy for Ukraine and itself the supreme political authority. After heated discussions, the Petrograd delegation reluctantly decided to recognize the Rada's competence to work out reforms in Ukraine and run the region until the convocation of the Constituent

Assembly. On July 2 several members of the Kadet party resigned from the government in protest over the concessions made in favor of autonomy for Ukraine. The next day, with the government disintegrating, a machine-gun regiment in Petrograd took to the streets on its own initiative to stir up a movement for the overthrow of the government. In the workers' section of the Petrograd soviet, Bolsheviks convinced the deputies to back the street demonstrations and call once again for soviet power. Twenty thousand sailors from the Kronstadt naval base joined the workers in a march to Bolshevik headquarters, where a hesitant and reluctant Lenin, who was not in favor of violent action at this time, called for caution and a peaceful demonstration. The crowd moved to the Tauride Palace, seat of the soviet. Chernov tried to calm the crowd, but he was surrounded and someone yelled at him, "Take power, you son-of-a-bitch, when it is given to you." After several hours in which power had fallen into the streets, the government brought loyal troops from the front to quell the demonstrators. Newspapers reported, falsely, that Lenin was a German agent, and the mood of the city changed immediately. Neutral troops rallied to the government, and the pro-Bolshevik soldiers slipped back to Kronstadt. That very evening Lenin and his close comrade, Grigorii Zinoviev, went into hiding. Other Bolshevik leaders, Lev Trotsky among them, were thrown into jail, and the Bolsheviks suffered an immediate, but temporary, political eclipse. An obscure party functionary, Joseph Stalin, became briefly the most important Central Committee member at large. Discouraged by the actions of the soviet, Lenin abandoned the idea of soviet power and called for a new slogan—"All power to the working class led by its revolutionary party, the Bolshevik-Communists!" Four hundred people lay dead after the armed clashes of the "July Days." The revolution's leftward drift came to a sudden, bloody halt, at least for another month.

On the Road to October

The government reeled in confusion after the July Days. Lvov resigned as prime minister and was replaced by Kerensky. Popular with the crowds, the new head of government was seen by his rivals as overly ambitious and lacking the character to lead the revolution. "It is a curious fact," wrote Tsereteli later, "that this man, whose name became the synonym of a weak, spineless government, had a pronounced personal predilection for the exercise of strong, commanding power. Had this tendency been combined with strength of character and organizing ability, he might have played a much more substantial and constructive part in the revolution than the one he actually performed." Almost three weeks passed before a new government could be put together, now with moderate Kadets and socialists attempting to work together. The soviet leaders agreed to empower the government to "save the revolution" by restoring discipline in the army. Kerensky appointed General Lavr Kornilov, an officer known to be hostile to the revolution, as supreme commander of the army. About Kornilov General Alekseev reportedly commented that he had "the heart of a lion and the brain of a sheep." Under pressure from the socialists, the government declared a program of reforms to democratize Russian society, abolish *sosloviia* (social estates), support the land committees, and regulate industry. The program drove the more conservative Kadets into opposition. Miliukov pledged to fight the Left to save the motherland, and an alliance of gentry landowners, military officers, the church, the Cossacks of the Don, and Russian nationalists formed to struggle against socialism. Adopting the language of the Marxists, the wealthy Moscow entrepreneur Pavl Riabushinskii expressed the view of the liberal-conservative opposition most militantly when he told the conference of industrialists in August:

> We ought to say ... that the present revolution is a bourgeois revolution, that the bourgeois order that exists at the present time is inevitable, and since it is inevitable, one must draw the completely logical conclusion and insist that those who rule the state think in a bourgeois manner and act in a bourgeois manner.

In the belief that the government was increasingly helpless before the soviet, the business and industrial elite rallied around General Kornilov as their best hope to bring the radicalization of the revolution to an end. On August 3 Kornilov presented the government with demands that he wanted the government to fulfill: restoration of the death penalty throughout Russia for civilians and military personnel, restoration of the authority of the officers over the soldiers, the abolition of soldiers' assemblies and the introduction of censorship at the front, and the disbanding of revolutionary-minded regiments. Kerensky understood that accepting such demands would have meant a declaration of war on the soviet, but in the end he accepted some of his demands.

By midsummer the country was irreconcilably divided. Bolsheviks quickly rebounded from their slump, reaping the harvest of the continuing economic decline, rising unemployment, and falling real wages. They shaped the anger and frustration in the factories and the garrison, explaining in their own way the causes of the crisis. Among workers and soldiers anger mixed with physical misery and fear. A leading Kadet tried to address a mass meeting and spoke of defense of the fatherland but was shouted down: "A worker has no fatherland; he has a fist!" Such words, replied the speaker, would lead to people chopping off each other's heads, just as in the French Revolution. A sailor yelled out, "And your head should be chopped off too."

When two thousand delegates gathered in Moscow on August 14 for a state conference to rally support for the government, the Left and Right cheered their own and jeered their opponents. Tsereteli called once again for unity behind the government, symbolically embracing a prominent industrialist. But the most tumultuous welcome was reserved for Kornilov, who spoke of "a ruthless struggle against anarchy." The wild reception convinced the commander in chief to take matters into his own hands. Kornilov believed that he had an agreement with Kerensky to back his decision to send troops to Petrograd to establish a military dictatorship, but in the eleventh hour the prime minister refused to back Kornilov and announced that a mutiny was taking place. The soviet rallied to the government's defense, Kerensky opened up the arsenals to arm the workers of Petrograd; and soldiers and workers along the route to the capital prevented Kornilov's troops from reaching the city. The supreme commander was dismissed and placed under arrest.

The failure of the Kornilov revolt had profound effects on the Russian political scene. Workers and soldiers all over the country were now convinced that Bolshevik warnings of counterrevolution were correct, that the government of Kerensky was somehow involved in the attempted coup d'etat, and that the leading liberal party, the Kadets, was part of an antiworker conspiracy. All the latent and overt suspicions and hostilities of the lower classes toward the middle and upper classes now intensified. At the very end of August Lenin wrote to the Bolshevik Central Committee:

> Events are developing with a speed that is sometimes dizzying.... Kornilov's revolt is an altogether unexpected ... and almost unbelievably sharp turn in the course of events.... An active and most energetic, really revolutionary war against Kornilov ... by itself may lead us to power, though we must speak of this as little as possible in our propaganda (remembering very well that even tomorrow events may put power in our hands, and then we shall not relinquish it).

The very next day, August 31, the Bolsheviks won an absolute majority in the Petrograd soviet (workers and soldiers' sections voting together) for the first time. Their resolution called for a government "of representatives of the revolutionary proletariat and peasantry." In early September Bolsheviks became the most popular party in the Moscow soviet as well.

As the Russian political crisis reached its climax, parties and politicians groped for a way out. They divided around four possible solutions to the question of power. First, Kornilov had tried and failed to establish a dictatorship of the Right. That path was now blocked, though the so-called White forces would make other attempts during the coming civil war. Second, some moderate Kadets, the Menshevik-Defensists, and the moderate SRs continued to support coalition and call for an immediate peace "in the spirit of democratic principles." But they were opposed by other influential liberals, including Miliukov, who wanted no further collaboration with the socialists. Eventually, in late September, a third coalition government was formed by Kerensky, but its power did not extend far outside the Winter Palace where it met.

Some leaders on the Left, like Martov and the Menshevik-Internationalists, proposed a third possible solution, a government made up of all the socialist parties. This seemed the only possible alternative to the fourth solution, a Bolshevik takeover. The idea of a broad-based government of the Left was popular among workers and soldiers, particularly in the larger cities and on the northern front, and was often conflated with the idea of soviet power. The real choice in the fall of 1917 was between such a multiparty democratic socialist government or a one-party government by the Bolsheviks.

The October Insurrection

The rapid radicalization of the largest cities became clear in late September when Muscovites elected a Bolshevik majority to their city Duma, with the Kadets coming in second. Bolsheviks also won big in Samara and Tomsk at the expense of the moderate socialist parties. The center was eroding, and the electorate polarizing. By the second week of September Bolsheviks were a majority in the Petrograd soviet, and Trotsky, who had joined the Bolsheviks after his arrival back in Russia in May, was elected its chairman. Lenin was anxious to take power in the name of the soviets and revived his old slogan, "All power to the soviets!" Still in hiding, he suggested in an article, "On Compromises," written in the first days of September, that though "our party, like all political parties, strives for political power *for itself*," it would support a government of the Mensheviks and SRs based on the soviets. Quickly disillusioned by the refusal of the moderate socialists to push for a soviet government, Lenin abruptly withdrew his compromise and simply advocated soviet power, which in his mind now required a leading or exclusive role for the Bolsheviks. He wrote to his comrades in Petrograd:

> The Mensheviks and Socialist Revolutionaries, even after the Kornilov revolt, refused to accept our compromise of peacefully transferring power to the soviets. . . . They have again sunk into the morass of mean and filthy bargaining with the Kadets. Down with the Mensheviks and SRs! . . . Ruthlessly expel them from all revolutionary organizations. No negotiations, no communications with these friends of the . . . Kornilovite landlords and capitalists.

Convinced that an armed insurrection was necessary to overthrow the Provisional Government, Lenin urged his comrades in the capital to prepare the uprising while they still had a majority in the soviets and before Kerensky surrendered the city to the Germans. But other Bolsheviks were hesitant to seize power. Some, like Trotsky, suggested waiting for the opening of the Second Congress of Soviets, which would "legitimize" the seizure of power. Workers too were more cautious about militant action in October than they had been in July, though they were willing to respond to a first move by the government against the Bolsheviks or soviets. Lenin, fearing that Kerensky would act first and attack the Bolsheviks, called such delays idiotic and even tried to resign from the Central Committee when the majority refused to take immediate action.

On October 7 Lenin returned secretly to Petrograd, and three days later in a historic session he convinced the Bolshevik Central Committee to "place the armed uprising on the agenda." Moderate Bolsheviks were upset by the decision to move toward an armed uprising, and two of Lenin's closest comrades, Kamenev and Zinoviev, broke ranks and issued a handwritten declaration against the seizure of power that soon appeared in the press. The Bolsheviks' plans were hardly a secret. On October 16 the government decided to deploy troops to meet the expected Bolshevik move. Lenin spoke the same day to the Central Committee:

> The masses have given the Bolsheviks their trust and demand from them not words but deeds, decisive policies both in the fight against the war and in the struggle with economic dislocation. . . . Acting now we will have the entire European proletariat on our side. . . . The bourgeoisie is intent on surrendering Petrograd as a means of crushing the revolution, and the only way of avoiding this is by taking the defense of the capital into our own hands. . . . It follows that the most decisive political action possible is now required—which can only mean an armed uprising. . . . Power must be seized immediately, at once. Every day lost could be fatal. History will not forgive us if we do not take power now!

The soldiers of the capital agreed to follow the orders of the soviet's Military Revolutionary Committee, which was controlled by the Bolsheviks and their allies, the Left SRs, and headed by Trotsky. With the garrison on their side, the Bolsheviks had won the struggle for soviet power even before the armed seizure was launched. In a futile attempt to prevent a Bolshevik victory, Kerensky made the first move and tried to arrest the Military-Revolutionary Committee and close the Bolshevik newspapers. The battle was joined on October 24, as Lenin made his way secretly to Bolshevik and soviet headquarters at the Smolny Institute. Within a few hours the city was in the hands of soviet forces, under the direction of the Bolsheviks. There was little fighting, and little active participation by workers. The Military-Revolutionary Committee demanded the surrender of the ministers of the Provisional Government, who were isolated within the Winter Palace, defended only by the Women's Battalion of Death and a few teenage cadets. At 9 P.M. the cruiser *Aurora* fired a blank salvo as a warning, and a few hours later sailors and Red Guards entered the palace and arrested the ministers. Kerensky had escaped earlier to rally troops.

Early in the morning of October 25, 1917 (November 7 n.s.), the Second All-Russian Congress of Soviets declared all power to belong to the soviets. Lenin had won his gamble, but history would be unforgiving in ways he had not suspected. By launching the insurrection before the Congress of Soviets officially took power, the Bolsheviks threw down the gauntlet to the rest of Russia, including the other socialist parties. Instead of a multiparty socialist government, the likely outcome of the struggle for power now seemed to be dictatorship and civil war.

Historians are divided between those who explain the October Revolution as a Bolshevik conspiracy or coup d'etat and those who emphasize the deeper social conflicts that propelled the Bolsheviks into a dominant position. Certainly Lenin's will to power and the effective organization of the Bolsheviks contributed to their victory, and their policies and proclamations appealed to workers and soldiers driven to desperation. But of all the major political parties in revolutionary Russia, Lenin's followers were unique in opposing the coalition government that attempted to link the top and bottom of society in a common political effort. The Bolsheviks committed themselves to the idea of class government, of rule by the lower orders of society and the elimination from political power of people of property. As workers grew increasingly discontent with industrialists through the summer and fall of 1917, because of the

rising cost of living and the refusal of industrialists to make further concessions to labor, the industrialists in turn became ever more alienated from the
revolution. Liberals turned more conservative and sought assistance from the
army in putting down the lower classes. At the same time ordinary rank-and-
file soldiers grew suspicious of the Provisional Government, which seemed incapable of or uninterested in ending the war; officers, on the other hand, drew
away from the government because of its indecision and inability to discipline
the soviets. Society was polarizing as it had in 1914, but now that polarization
was leading toward civil war, with the lower classes on one side and the upper and middle classes on the other. The moderate parties, like the Mensheviks and SRs, which tried to reconcile the interests of the antagonistic extremes
in Russian society lost the backing of key groups like the workers and soldiers,
while the Bolsheviks confidently rode the wave of popular radicalization to
power.

Suggestions for Further Reading

The historiography of the Russian Revolution solidified in the years before and during
the Cold War into an "orthodox" interpretation, which sees Lenin and the Bolsheviks
as unscrupulous and power-hungry conspirators who seized power in a coup d'etat
with relatively little popular support behind them. One of the classic works that ex-
presses this point of view is Leonard Schapiro, *The Origins of the Communist Autocracy*
(1955). Robert V. Daniels, *Red October* (New York, 1967), emphasizes the role of accident and chance in 1917, and George Katkov, *Russia 1917: The February Revolution* (New
York, 1967), extends the theory of conspiracy to the events of February. Beginning in
the 1970s a new generation of "social historians" broadened the more political and bi-
ographical studies of earlier years to include the history of workers, soldiers, and peasants. With a few exceptions, such as John H. L. Keep, *The Russian Revolution: A Study
in Mass Mobilization* (New York and Toronto, 1976), social historians in the last years of
the Cold War developed a "revisionist" interpretation, which argues that the Bolsheviks rode a wave of popular discontent and enthusiasm for Soviet power, particularly
in the large cities and among soldiers. Among the revisionist works are: Tsuyoshi
Hasegawa, *The February Revolution: Petrograd 1917* (Seattle, 1981); Steve A. Smith, *Red
Petrograd: Revolution in the Factories, 1917–1918* (Cambridge, 1983); Allan K. Wildman,
The End of the Russian Imperial Army, 2 vols. (Princeton, N.J., 1983–87); Ziva Galili, *The
Menshevik Leaders in the Russian Revolution: Social Realities and Political Strategies* (Princeton, N.J., 1989); William G. Rosenberg, *Liberals in the Russian Revolution: The Constitutional Democratic Party, 1917–1921* (Princeton, N.J., 1974); Alexander Rabinowitch, *Prelude to Revolution: The Petrograd Bolsheviks and the July 1917 Uprising* (Bloomington, Ind.,
1968) and *The Bolsheviks Come to Power: The Revolution of 1917 in Petrograd* (New York,
1976); Diane Koenker, *Moscow Workers and the 1917 Revolution* (Princeton, N.J., 1981);
and Daniel H. Kaiser (ed.), *The Workers' Revolution in Russia, 1917: The View from Below*
(Cambridge, 1987). Two earlier works on the Socialist Revolutionary Party remain the
standard texts: Oliver H. Radkey, *The Agrarian Foes of Bolshevism* (New York, 1958) and
The Sickle under the Hammer (New York, 1963).

   More recently an "antirevisionist" turn has been reflected in a number of works:
Richard Pipes, *The Russian Revolution* (New York, 1990) and *Russia under the Bolshevik
Regime* (New York, 1993); and Martin Malia, *The Soviet Tragedy: A History of Socialism in*

Russia, 1917–1991 (New York, 1994). For discussions of the changing approaches to the Russian Revolution, see the historiographical reviews by Ronald Grigor Suny, "Toward a Social History of the October Revolution," *American Historical Review* 81, no. 1 (February 1983): 31–52; "Revision and Retreat in the Historiography of 1917: Social History and Its Critics," *The Russian Review* 53, no. 2 (April 1994): 165–82; and Ronald Grigor Suny and Arthur Adams (eds.), *The Russian Revolution and Bolshevik Victory: Visions and Revisions* (Lexington, Mass., 1990). Finally, one should consult Orlando Figes, *A People's Tragedy: the Russian Revolution, 1891–1924* (New York, 1997), for a broad overview of the revolutionary period.

CHAPTER 3
Socialism and Civil War

On the Road from Democracy to Dictatorship

Many historians have viewed Russia as condemned to authoritarianism. Russia's fate, they argue, was essentially preordained by its history under tsarism, perhaps by its physical vastness and the lack of natural borders, and perhaps by the Russian national character or what was sometimes referred to as "the Russian soul." In this view, Russia could not be like the West, for there was no tradition of democratic government. These historians who emphasize continuity note that the basic contours of the Soviet regime were strikingly similar to those of autocratic Russia: authoritarian rule, an elite in control of the fate of millions, political repression, immobility, and backwardness. For the "continuity theorists," communism was in a sense tsarism in modern dress.

Other analysts explain the evolution of the Soviet system from revolutionary democracy to Stalinist dictatorship as the understandable outcome of Marxist or Leninist theory. The nature of the Soviet system is largely seen as the product of the special nature of the Russian intelligentsia and of views that it generated, particularly the views of Lenin as expressed in *What Is to Be Done?* The Soviet Union was an ideocracy, a state ruled by an ideology, and the elitism of the party of the new type led to a tutelary relationship to the population and a dictatorship of the party over the people.

Most historians, however, shy away from deductions from ideology and emphasize the particular historical context in which the Bolsheviks found themselves after the revolution. The isolation and backwardness of the country, they claim, was the most powerful influence in the degeneration into dictatorship, but social context, political experience, and the dominant ideas of key players should all be woven into a synthetic and more complete explanation. Incontestably, when compared with the other Great Powers in Europe or with the United States or Japan, Russia was a backward society. Its economy was still in the early stages of developing capitalist industry, and the great bulk of the population still worked in an inefficient agriculture. The state was autocratic and inhibited the growth of social and political institutions outside the state.

Society remained weak and dependent on the state. Russia never experienced anything like the socialists' idea of a bourgeois-democratic revolution, no equivalent of the American or French revolutions of the eighteenth century. The long and deep crisis that predated the war worsened during World War I, the revolution, and the civil war, and Russia fell behind even where it had been in 1914. In the decade from 1912 to 1922, in a context of extraordinary social deprivation and constant warfare, the fragile flower of representative democracy, which had hardly been able to root itself, withered. Faced by civil war and economic collapse, the Bolsheviks successfully built a new state apparatus, suspended above the roiling sea of peasants. But that state, created in and for war, was of a particular type: authoritarian, centralized, and prepared to use its full repressive apparatus against its foes.

Yet the Soviet state was not only a product of backwardness and civil war but also of Bolshevik ideology and political culture, which rejected liberal parliamentary forms, a "free market of ideas," and capitalism. That state depended on the dedication, idealism, and sacrifice of hundreds of thousands of Bolshevik cadres and Red Army soldiers, who entered the fray with enormous confidence in history's outcome and a conviction that they had a moral right to use force and terror against their opponents in order to build a socialist society. Even though the conditions for the rule of a proletarian party did not exist in Russia, Bolsheviks' commitment to their own vision of history made it impossible for them to contemplate giving up power. When no international revolution came to rescue them, Lenin and his comrades were forced to rely on Russia's own meager resources. As a minority touting itself as the vanguard of a minuscule working class in an overwhelmingly peasant country, they could not both stay in power and institute a democracy based on the will of the majority.

The Bolsheviks had no a priori blueprint for socialism or dictatorship. Much of what would become the Soviet system was influenced by the Bolsheviks' understanding of Marxist theory, but at the same time the new political order was shaped and refined in response to historical events that the Bolsheviks could neither predict nor control. Both ideology and circumstances played a role, not to mention the particular personalities that emerged to head the Communist Party. Neither Marxism nor Lenin's writings provided a recipe book from which Bolsheviks could pick the right formula to solve a particular political problem. Rather than a tightly conceived dogma, what came to be called Leninism was an incoherent mixture of tactics and programs formed at different times for different purposes. The form of Soviet rule was improvised, but within a general script that the Bolsheviks culled from Marx and their own reading of (largely French) history. Ideology served as a source of ideas, a prism through which the world was viewed, a rationalization of actions taken, and a mobilizing force that could motivate people to make sacrifices for something larger than immediate personal interests.

After October

It was nearly midnight on October 25, 1917, when the Second Congress of Soviets began its first session. Of the over five hundred delegates almost half were

Bolshevik, and with their Left SR allies Lenin's party was assured of a majority. The Menshevik-Internationalist Martov rose and made a motion to form an all-socialist, multiparty government. The resolution passed unanimously, but the Right SRs and the Menshevik-Defensists declared that they were walking out of the Congress in protest against the attack on the Provisional Government. Trotsky, who was chairing the meeting, scorned the departing delegates: "To those who have left us and to those proposing negotiations [with the government], we must say: You are a mere handful, miserable, bankrupt; your role is finished, and you may go where you belong—to the garbage heap of history."

A few hours later the news came of the fall of the Winter Palace, and the Congress voted to transfer all power to the soviets. At that point the Menshevik-Internationalists also left the Congress. With only the most radical elements left in the Congress, Lenin proposed a declaration on peace, with a call for an immediate armistice. The motion passed unanimously. He followed with a decree on land, basically appropriating the SR policy of nationalization of agricultural land. But instead of waiting for the government to enact the land reform, he proclaimed, "Let the peasants from their end proceed to solve that question." Only one vote was cast against it.

At two in the morning the new government was formed, the Council of People's Commissars (Sovnarkom), made up entirely of Bolsheviks. Its chairman was Lenin. Trotsky was the people's commissar of foreign affairs. Aleksei Rykov headed internal affairs; Aleksandr Shliapnikov, labor; Anatolii Lunacharskii, education; and Joseph Stalin, nationalities. The Sovnarkom was supposed to be subordinate to the All-Russian Central Executive Committee of Soviets (VTsIK), which in turn was elected by and responsible to the Congress of Soviets. But almost immediately after its creation, the Sovnarkom became the principal decision-making body and only occasionally consulted with VTsIK.

The new government was on shaky legs in its first month. Kerensky rallied troops outside the capital to retake the city. Military cadets and some Right SRs joined the effort. In the south of Russia Cossacks under Generals Kaledin and Kornilov, who had escaped from Petrograd, organized resistance to the Bolsheviks. But within the first week fierce fighting in Moscow ended in a Bolshevik victory, and the armed opposition to the Bolsheviks in and around Petrograd collapsed. The most militant elements among the workers and soldiers defended Soviet power, but outside the two capitals, Petrograd and Moscow, whole regions of the country awaited with suspicion the outcome of the political struggles in the center. Almost all the workers in Petrograd, except for the printers and some railroad workers, as well as most soldiers enthusiastically supported an all-socialist, multiparty government, rather than the purely Bolshevik government favored by Lenin. Throughout the country local soviets were taking power but usually as multiparty governments. Lenin opposed a socialist coalition government, especially with those who had walked out of the congress. Only under pressure from the railroad workers' union and after thirteen leading Bolsheviks, led by Kamenev and Zinoviev, resigned from the Central Committee and the Sovnarkom did he finally agree to look for coalition partners. The Left SRs received six commissariats, including agriculture, justice, and post and telegraphs, and for the next four months Soviet Russia had a two-party socialist government.

In its first months in power the Soviet government tried to legislate a new egalitarian legal and political order into existence pell-mell. All civil ranks, special social privileges, and class distinctions that had marked off nobles from merchants, peasants from townspeople were abolished. Everyone was now simply a citizen of Russia. The state set limits on the salaries of state officials, even people's commissars, and prohibited public officials and bureaucrats, many of whom were hostile to the new regime, from striking. The Sovnarkom swept away the old system of courts and set up new local courts and revolutionary tribunals in which professional judges were to sit side by side with laypersons acting as the people's instruments of justice. Church and state were separated. All ethnic groups and religions were declared equal, as were men and women. The authorities took away the property rights of owners of large houses and divided the dwellings among needy families or people with the right connections. Ranks, epaulettes, saluting, and decorations were eliminated in the army, and soldiers elected their own officers. The final word in each military unit lay with the elected soldiers' committees.

In mid-November people across the country went to the polls to elect the Constituent Assembly, a founding constitutional congress to decide the fundamental questions of the form of government, land reform, social welfare and economy of the future Russian state. The Assembly had long been a dream of liberals and the Left, but the Provisional Government, which had not implemented many reforms so as not to predetermine the decisions of the Assembly, had continually delayed the elections because of the war. Reluctantly the Bolsheviks went on with the elections only to be bitterly disappointed in the results. The Socialist Revolutionaries won the largest number of votes, 40 percent; the Bolsheviks were second with 24 percent, with the other parties far behind. The SRs won absolute majorities in nineteen provinces, though they did not win more than a quarter of the vote in any major Russian city or provincial capital. The Bolsheviks, on the other hand, outpolled the other parties in most of the major cities of Russia, including Moscow and Petrograd, and among the soldiers at various fronts, where they won 40 to 64 percent of the vote.

On January 5, 1918, four hundred delegates met in the White Hall of the Tauride Palace to open the first, and only, session of the Constituent Assembly. Though he had allowed the elections to the Assembly in November, Lenin was frank about his hostility to a rival authority. The Bolsheviks demanded that the Assembly recognize the Soviet government, but the majority, led by SR leader Chernov, decided to deal with questions of land and peace first. The Assembly passed laws, discussed negotiations with foreign powers, all as if Soviet power did not exist. On one side sat the supporters of the Assembly with its authority legitimized by the elections; on the other sat those who favored the soviets, which had real power backed by armed men in the towns. The Bolsheviks stayed in the hall until midnight; the Left SRs until four in the morning. About forty minutes later a sailor told chairman Chernov that the guard was tired and everyone must leave the hall. When the delegates tried to return the next day, they found the doors bolted. Lenin had signed a decree dissolving the Constituent Assembly. A few people protested the dissolution and were easily dispersed by Red Guards.

The next morning Lenin wrote:

> The transfer of all power to the Constituent Assembly is nothing but the old policy of "conciliation" with the malevolent bourgeoisie. . . . As long as Kaledin exists, and as long as the slogan, "All Power to the Constituent Assembly" is used as a cloak to the slogan "Down with Soviet Power," so long will there be no escape from civil war, for we will not give up Soviet power for anything in the world. . . . The Constituent Assembly, which failed to recognize the power of the people, is now dispersed by the will of Soviet power. . . . The Soviet republic will triumph, no matter what happens.

As in October, so in January, Lenin displayed his understanding of revolution. Revolution was not like an election campaign in which the party that gains a majority gains the upper hand; rather it was like a military campaign in which the side that can mobilize the greatest physical strength in the most sensitive places wins the day. In a very real sense, by dispersing the Constituent Assembly, Lenin closed the door on the February Revolution and declared war on that part of the country unwilling to accept Soviet power and the socialist revolution. With little hesitation the Bolsheviks set out on the road to civil war.

Socialism: What's in a Name?

A few days after the dispersion of the Constituent Assembly, Lenin proudly announced to the Third Congress of Soviets that the Soviet government had lasted five days longer than the Paris Commune. He emphasized the importance of the workers' alliance with the peasantry:

> Alone the proletariat could not maintain itself in power. . . . Only by forming . . . a union of the proletariat and the poor peasants can a government maintain itself in power. . . . This we succeeded in accomplishing immediately after October 25, and we organized a government on the basis of such a union. . . .

He went on to caution that the victory of socialism required patience and ultimately depended on workers' abroad:

> We never flattered ourselves with the hope that we could reach the end without the aid of the international proletariat. . . . Of course, the socialist idea cannot be attained in one country alone. . . . [Yet] we can see how the socialist revolution is ripening in every country of the world by hours and not by days. . . .

Lenin had long believed that history was moving beyond the bourgeois stage, beyond parliamentarianism and capitalism, toward socialism and socialist democracy on a world scale. Though Russia was backward and unable to build socialism on its own, Bolsheviks were convinced that the international proletarian revolution would soon break out and come to the aid of Russia.

The Bolsheviks formed the first government in world history to call itself socialist. Coming to power in the midst of a world war, with the capitalist economy of Russia in collapse and incipient civil war on the horizon, they quickly improvised measures to keep the economy running. They had little guidance in their tasks from the classics of Marxism. Karl Marx himself had had little to say about the eventual contours of socialism and had devoted most of his intellectual work to dissecting the nature of capitalism. He and Engels had seen socialism as a social system that would eliminate the market and redirect production away from what could be sold ("exchange value") toward what society needed ("use value"). Nothing, however, was written about how economic decisions were to be made under socialism. Their Russian disciples attempted to cull some wisdom from his writings, particularly from the *Communist Manifesto*, in which Marx and Engels had called for nationalization of the banking system and the basic means of production. In his *Critique of the Gotha Program* Marx had spoken of new distribution criteria: each producer could draw products from a common consumption fund equivalent to the amount of labor expended in production.

Marxists distinguished themselves from anarchists by their emphasis on the importance of the state in the construction of socialism. Though their ultimate goal, like that of the anarchists, was the "withering away of the state," they believed that the only means to defeat socialism's enemies and build the infrastructure for the new society was through the state. For many Marxists of the Second International (1889–1914), large-scale capitalism, with the burgeoning role of the state, was growing closer to what they envisioned as socialism. Lenin even more vigorously emphasized the importance of state power: "The proletariat needs state power, a centralized organization of force, an organization of violence, both to crush the resistance of the exploiters and to lead the enormous mass of the population—the peasantry, the petty-bourgeoisie and the semi-proletarians—in the work of organizing a socialist economy."

Yet the form of the future socialist state was not very clear. In the pamphlet *State and Revolution*, written in the summer of 1917, Lenin proposed a radically democratic commune state in which society would be administered by ordinary people. Following Marx's thoughts on the Paris Commune of 1871, Lenin argued that the first requirement to win the battle for democracy was that the working class seize political power and eliminate all instruments of power from the hands of the bourgeoisie. Unlike the moderate socialists, who were prepared to work with the bourgeois state, and the anarchists, who wanted the entire state demolished immediately, Lenin spoke of smashing only the repressive aspects of the old state, including the bureaucracy, army, and police. "It is still necessary to suppress the bourgeoisie and crush its resistance," Lenin wrote.

> But the organ of suppression is now the majority of the population, and not a minority as was always the case under slavery, serfdom, and wage labor.

And, once the majority of the people *itself* suppresses its oppressors, a "special force" for suppression *is no longer necessary.* In this sense the state *begins to wither away.*

The task of the Russian socialists was to hold power until the revolution from abroad came to their assistance. But Lenin's wager on the West did not pay off, and as civil war tore Russia apart, he shifted his views. It was no longer possible to build immediately a socialist commune state, he believed, but it was necessary to establish a dictatorship of the proletariat as a transition to socialism. The soviets would be the nucleus of a proletarian and peasant state, and they in turn would control the economic functions of the state. Repeatedly Lenin claimed that this proletarian state would be truly democratic because it would be subordinated to the majority in society. Yet as a state it would employ coercion, even terror, to enforce its will on its opponents.

For much of the early years of Soviet power, the Bolsheviks improvised their economic policies, changing them after trial and error. They engaged in intense debate about whether they were building socialism or state capitalism. The shifts in their ideas and practices in the first decade can be conveniently divided into three periods:

October 1917 to July 1918—the period before the civil war broke out in earnest when the Soviet government attempted to maintain economic production through a policy of "state capitalism."

July 1918 to March 1921—the period of the civil war during which the Soviet state expanded its role in the economy, nationalizing industry, requisitioning grain from the peasantry, suppressing markets, and conscripting labor, in order to win the war. This period would later be known as "War Communism."

March 1921 to the end of the 1920s—the period following the Civil War, when the Communists made a strategic retreat back to "state capitalism" in what they called the New Economic Policy, or NEP. While the "commanding heights" of the economy—large-scale industry, the railroads, and banks— were held by the state, markets were reintroduced; much industry was denationalized; peasants were allowed to sell their grain in the market after paying a set tax-in-kind; and workers were free to move from job to job.

Building State Capitalism

The war and the first year of the revolution caused havoc in Russian industry. Real wages collapsed and production fell. Between March and August 1917, 568 enterprises employing over 100,000 workers were closed, and the number increased each month. The decline in production only worsened after the October Revolution. Important sectors, like metals and chemicals, which had been closely tied to the war effort since 1914 and depended on state orders, collapsed with the armistice and demobilization of troops. Unemployment grew, and food supplies worsened. Since the capital, Petrograd, was the center of war production, it suffered most, and by the spring of 1918 three-quarters of metal and chemical workers were out of work. Labor protest mounted, and many workers left the cities to find food and shelter among relatives in the villages.

Within weeks of seizing power, the Bolshevik government passed a decree on workers' control. Though private ownership of factories was retained, the prerogatives of owners were limited by the factory committees. Owners of factories were no longer allowed to dispose of their property as they wished. The government tried to make it clear that workers' control meant supervision from below of the activities of the bosses, not workers' management of the enterprises. In some instances, however, workers adopted the more radical version of workers' control favored by anarchists and actually took over the running of the factory. Factory owners, as well as engineers, technicians, and the clerical staff, resisted workers' control by closing the factory or simply walking out. Workers would sometimes take over the factory in order to prevent its closure or "sabotage."

The Soviet government wanted to preserve what it could of the existing economy and at first held back from nationalizing industry, except for former state enterprises, which were immediately nationalized. The state had neither the personnel nor the expertise to run a complex and disintegrating economy. While radicals in the party, the so-called Left Communists, called for rapid nationalization and an immediate move toward "state socialism," Lenin and the majority of Bolsheviks favored making deals with capitalists, employing those they called "bourgeois specialists," and regulating private enterprises by the state in order to restore the economy as rapidly as possible. But with industry collapsing around them, the Soviet government gradually increased state intervention, and on December 1 it created a new state institution to supervise the economy—the Supreme Council of National Economy (Sovnarkhoz, or VSNKh).

From below, factory committees pressured the government to nationalize industry, and many Communists argued that the state might fare better in the economy than the anarchic market. In mid-December, Bolsheviks occupied and nationalized the banks. Early in the new year the merchant fleet was nationalized, followed by mines and factories in the Urals and Donbass. In late January 1918, the Conference of Factory-Plant Committees in Petrograd demanded the transfer of "all means of production, factories and workshops" into the hands of the state. In May the state took control of the sugar industry, and a month later, after the local soviet in Baku nationalized the oil industry, Moscow begrudgingly approved the move. By the spring of 1918, nearly five hundred enterprises had been transferred to state management. As the country drifted into civil war, not much was left of the free-market capitalist economy. On June 28, 1918, the Soviet government decreed the nationalization of almost all large industry.

In a major statement in April 1918, Lenin clarified his economic preferences. He told his comrades: "Keep regular and honest accounts of money; manage economically; do not be lazy; do not steal; observe the strictest labor discipline." Do not fear using "bourgeois specialists." "Without the guidance of experts in various fields of knowledge, technology, and experience, the transition to socialism will be impossible, because socialism calls for a conscious mass advance to greater productivity of labor compared with capitalism and on the basis achieved by capitalism." He called for paying these specialists more than the average worker, thus departing from the ideal of the Paris Commune in which workers and state officials were paid equally.

The very economic backwardness of Russia, which had made the political triumph of the revolution possible, Lenin wrote, made the construction of socialism very difficult. He looked at the future socialist state "as a network of producers' and consumers' communes, which conscientiously keep account of their production and consumption, economize on labor, and steadily raise the productivity of labor, thus making it possible to reduce the working day to seven, six, and even fewer hours." Yet as benign as his vision of the future was, Lenin believed that "it would be extremely stupid and absurdly utopian to assume that the transition from capitalist to socialism is possible without coercion and without dictatorship." "Our government," he complained, "is excessively mild; very often it resembles jelly more than iron."

Founding the New State: War, Peace, and Terror

The new Soviet state was notoriously weak. The government faced two principal tasks: to prevent its overthrow at the hands of its domestic enemies and to withdraw Russia from the world war and give the new state time to consolidate itself. In its first months the Bolsheviks used what power they had to harass and suppress its opponents, but until the summer of 1918 they did not launch indiscriminate terror against their enemies. During the October Revolution the Bolsheviks had arrested the ministers of the Provisional Government and a number of anti-Bolshevik generals, but most were later released. In December they imprisoned several Right SRs who were actively fighting the new government, but the police spent most of their energy fighting the crime rampant in the cities. The government even abolished the death penalty, though many Bolsheviks, Lenin among them, believed that the death penalty and terror were essential to achieve revolutionary success. Trotsky was perhaps the most eloquent defender of terror and later, as commissar of war, would use it to discipline his troops and officers. "We shall not enter into the kingdom of socialism," he is purported to have said, "in white gloves on a polished floor." Less eloquently, people repeated clichés like "When you chop wood, the chips will fly" or "You must break eggs to make an omelet." Less often did they consider that in order to make omelets properly eggs must be carefully handled, not smashed so that yokes and whites end up mixed inextricably with broken bits of shell.

When Sovnarkom abolished the Military-Revolutionary Committee in early December, it created a new organ for keeping order, the Extraordinary Commission to Combat Counterrevolution and Sabotage (Cheka), under the chairmanship of the Polish socialist, Feliks Dzerzhinski. This commission was the first of the infamous Soviet secret police organizations that, like the OGPU, NKVD, and KGB, became essential parts of the Soviet system. But even the

Cheka did not use systematic violence against its enemies in its first nine months. The government did not so much promote violence in the early months as allow spontaneous social retribution and hostilities to take their course. When a few sailors murdered two prominent Kadets in their hospital beds, Lenin reacted with shock, but when the culprits were protected by their mates, he decided not to pursue the case. Far from Petrograd, however, local Bolshevik officials often dealt much more brutally with capitalists and aristocrats.

The issue of repression strained the political alliance that ruled the country. The Left SRs were definitely the junior partners in the socialist coalition, though they controlled the important commissariats of agriculture and justice. In their revolutionary past they had themselves used individual terrorism, assassinating tsarist officials, but the Left SRs opposed the use of terror by the revolutionary government. The people's commissar of justice, Isak Steinberg, warned that beginning a campaign of terror was easier than stopping one and tried in vain to convince the Soviet leaders of the importance of observing legal procedures.

Though a number of issues divided the coalition partners, the final break of the Left SRs with the Bolsheviks came over the question of Russia leaving the world war. The October insurrection not only brought the most radical socialist party in Russia to power but marked the victory of an internationalist party interested in world revolution. As Lenin put it, "The Russian Revolution, having overthrown tsarism, could not stop at the stage of a bourgeois revolution. It had to go further because the war with its resulting unheard-of suffering of the exhausted nations produced the soil for the outbreak of the social revolution." The Left SRs shared this vision with the Bolsheviks. Indeed, as it turned out, they were more militantly in favor of revolutionary war against the imperialists than was Lenin. In the first months of the new regime, roughly October 1917 to March 1918, the Bolsheviks' primary foreign policy interests were to take Russia out of the war, end the hostilities with the Germans, who were occupying much of the western portion of the old Russian Empire, and to gain breathing space as they waited for the expected proletarian revolution in Europe.

Supremely confident that the international proletarian revolution would soon break out and make interstate relations irrelevant, Commissar of Foreign Affairs Trotsky declared shortly after taking office, "What diplomatic work are we apt to have now? I will issue a few revolutionary proclamations to the peoples of the world and then shut up shop." The very first act of the new Soviet government in October 1917 was the Decree on Peace, drafted by Lenin. It called on "all belligerent peoples and their governments . . . to open immediate negotiations for a just and democratic peace" without territorial annexations or reparations. The Decree was a new form of international diplomacy; it appealed both to governments of England, France, and Germany and to "the class-conscious workers of the three most advanced nations." Thus, from its first day Soviet foreign policy was dualistic: directed at legitimate governments *and* over the heads of those governments to the people. This duality would soon be expressed in the division of labor between the People's Commissariat of Foreign Affairs and the Communist International (Comintern).

The Allies were deeply suspicious of the Bolshevik regime, which they considered to be extremely pro-German, if not led by secret German agents. They argued about whether to work with the Bolsheviks in order to keep Russia in the war or to aid the anti-Bolshevik forces. But they refused formally to recognize the new government, and official diplomatic relations lapsed. Within weeks after the October Revolution, the French and British, fearing that the Bolsheviks would take Russia out of the war, began to make contact with anti-Bolsheviks within Russia. Even before the Soviet armistice with the Germans, the British Cabinet decided to offer financial aid to the Don Cossacks under General Kaledin, who were already grouping in southern Russia to resist the Bolsheviks. As if to antagonize the Allies further, the Bolsheviks published the secret treaties that the tsarist government had concluded with Britain and France, convinced that exposing these treaties, which promised Russia the city of Constantinople and parts of historic Armenia, would reveal the real nature of the war and imperialism. Employees of the old Foreign Affairs Ministry at first refused to show the Bolsheviks where the treaties were stored, but they complied when a commissar showed his Mauser pistol and threatened to arrest them. The Western powers were incensed by publication of the secret diplomatic documents.

Germany wanted an armistice on the eastern front to strengthen its hand in the west against the British, French, and Americans. The Bolsheviks, who had expressed opposition to a separate peace with Germany before they had come to power, were now left with an unenviable choice: either continue the war with Germany, which had become physically and materially impossible, or sign a separate peace. The Russian army did not want to fight any more. The ranks refused to obey their officers. When their commander tried to slow down negotiations with the Germans and released antirevolutionary officers, like Generals Kornilov and Denikin, enraged soldiers lynched him. With the Allies silent, the Soviet government signed an armistice with Germany on December 2 (15 n.s.), 1917. Hardly the general peace they sought, nevertheless, the Bolsheviks had achieved one of their aims and brought the war on the eastern front to an end. Many in Russia were grateful, particularly soldiers, and the armistice gave the new Soviet government both a degree of popular support and time to push the revolution forward.

With the Allies unwilling to deal with the Bolsheviks, a Soviet delegation met the Germans, Austrians, Bulgarians, and Turks at the border town of Brest-Litovsk, armed with an outline for peace written up by Lenin in which the Bolshevik leader called for full self-determination of nations. Any territory annexed by another state since the mid-nineteenth century was to be allowed to express its political will through a referendum and, if its people desired, move toward independence. To the surprise of the Bolsheviks, the Central Powers accepted the Soviet peace proposal, but they refused to raise the question of national self-determination outside the territory of the former Russian Empire. Germany was prepared to recognize the independence only of Poland, Ukraine, Lithuania, and the other Baltic territories, which at the time were occupied by the Germans. The German diplomats had outfoxed the Soviets and turned the principle of national self-determination into a cover for German expansion.

General Ludendorff, the strong-willed architect of German policy in the east, envisioned increasing German power by creating new buffer states between Russia and Germany that would be dependent on German power. The Soviets were at a serious disadvantage, unwilling to accept German terms but unable to fight effectively against them. The chief German negotiator told his Austrian counterpart, "The only choice they have is as to what sort of sauce they will be eaten with."

In January 1918 the Bolsheviks faced their first international diplomatic crisis. Many Bolsheviks, most importantly the young Nikolai Bukharin, were so angered at the audacity and cynicism of the Germans that they called for revolutionary war against the imperialists. Trotsky, however, argued that Soviet Russia should simply declare the war over and refuse to accept the German terms, in other words, no war, no peace. But Lenin remained convinced that Soviet Russia was too weak to do anything but conclude a separate peace with the Germans. "For the success of socialism in Russia," he said, "a certain amount of time, several months at least, will be necessary, during which the hands of the socialist government must be absolutely free for achieving victory over the bourgeoisie in our own country first, and for launching on a wide scale far-reaching mass organization work." The party's Central Committee decided to continue the negotiations, and Trotsky returned to Brest-Litovsk. The Germans tried to outflank the Soviets by announcing that they had signed a separate treaty with the Rada, the government of Ukraine. Unimpressed, the Soviets displayed their own Ukrainian government and were soon able to announce that the Red Army had taken the Ukrainian capital, Kiev. Trotsky then declared unilaterally that the war was over and left the conference. The Germans were furious. General Hoffman wrote in his diary:

> Tomorrow we are going to start hostilities against the Bolsheviks. No other way out is possible; otherwise these brutes will wipe up the Ukrainians, the Finns, and the Balts, and then quietly get together a new revolutionary army and turn the whole of Europe into a pig-sty. . . . The whole of Russia is nothing more than a vast heap of maggots, a squalid, swarming mass.

On February 18 (n.s.), the German army began marching eastward.

Lenin again insisted on acceptance of the German terms. He threatened to resign from his party and government positions if the treaty was not signed. "The politics of revolutionary phrasemongering," he said, "have come to an end." The Left Communists around Bukharin and the Left SRs still pushed for revolutionary war, but this time Trotsky sided with Lenin. On March 3, 1918, Soviet Russia signed the onerous Treaty of Brest-Litovsk. Germany became the dominant power in the Baltic region and in Ukraine, Turkey was given a free hand in Transcaucasia, and Soviet Russia lost the western areas of the old Russian Empire. "We have signed a Tilsit Peace," Lenin wrote in the party newspaper *Pravda*,

> just as the Germans did [in 1807], and just as the Germans freed themselves from Napoleon, so we shall get our freedom. It will probably not take so

long, for history moves more rapidly now than then. Let us cease the blowing of trumpets and get down to serious work.

Keenly aware that the Germans still posed an enormous threat to their weak state, the Communists decided in March to move the capital from Petrograd to Moscow where they could await the international revolution at a safer distance.

The temporary resolution of the international crisis, however, led directly into a major internal crisis. On March 19, the Left SRs resigned from the Sovnarkom in protest against the treaty signed at Brest-Litovsk. Like the Left Communists within the Bolshevik party, they opposed any dealings with German imperialism and even hoped for a German invasion which, they believed, would be met by a spontaneous peasant uprising. The Left socialist coalition dissolved, and for the next seventy-three years, from March 1918 until August 1991, Soviet Russia was ruled by a single party, the Russian Social Democratic Workers' Party (Bolsheviks), soon to be known as the Communist Party.

Even without political allies among the other parties, the Bolsheviks never seriously contemplated giving up power. But the deteriorating economic situation and the inability of the Bolsheviks to improve conditions soon eroded their base of support among their most loyal constituents, the Petrograd workers. On March 13, 1918, workers met in an Assembly of Factory and Plant Representatives in Petrograd and expressed their suspicion of all parties. They feared that Bolsheviks were undermining soviet democracy and felt that Soviet leaders were no longer responsive to the workers. They called for freedom of the press. Labor discontent increased in the spring of 1918, and the Soviet government used its state powers to repress real and potential opposition. In early April the Cheka raided twenty-six anarchist centers in Moscow, and in the process of closing them down one hundred people were killed. On May 9 workers in Kolpino, outside Petrograd, protested when a bread shipment failed to arrive. In panic a soldier fired into the crowd; one man died and several others were hurt. This was the first clear instance of the Soviet state attacking a demonstration by workers. On June 16, the government that eight months earlier had abolished the death penalty reintroduced it.

In the eyes of many politically active workers in the largest cities, the Bolsheviks stood most firmly for the workers' government, but others followed the call of the Mensheviks to participate in an Assembly of Representatives in Petrograd in May and early June 1918. The conference came out in favor of restoring the Constituent Assembly. One Menshevik even proclaimed, "Long live capitalism!" though that message had few supporters among the workers. The Bolsheviks had clearly lost the hegemony over workers in the old capital that they had held securely in the fall of 1917, though they still could rally significant support. In June the Bolsheviks won the elections to the soviets in Petrograd with the slogan "Support Soviet Power!" and used their mandate to dissolve the Menshevik-led Assembly of Representatives. Increasingly the Bolsheviks had to rely on their most loyal supporters, those workers organized in Red Guards units, soldiers, and party members.

As the battlelines were drawn for the coming civil war, the two principal sides borrowed the labels that had come down from the French Revolution: the Bolsheviks and their supporters were known as the Reds, and the opponents of Soviet power, who ranged from monarchists to liberals, were known as the Whites. The moderate socialists, the Mensheviks and SRs, who hoped for a constitutional order, with a gradual transition to some kind of democratic socialism, were caught between the Reds and the Whites. The Right SRs decided in May 1918 to call for the overthrow of the Bolshevik government and to work with the Allies to that end. The Mensheviks, however, refused to ally either with the Allies or the Germans and opted for a political, rather than an armed struggle, against Lenin's authority. The Bolsheviks, however, made little distinction between "those who are not with us" and treated them all as if they "are against us." They manipulated local soviet elections, closed newspapers of opposition parties, and arrested their rivals. On June 14, 1918, the Bolshevik majority expelled the Mensheviks along with the Right SRs from the All-Russian Central Executive Committee of Soviets (VTsIK), the legislature chosen by the congress of soviets. An eyewitness remembered:

> Martov, shouting curses against dictators and Bonapartist usurpers in his sickly, tubercular voice, grabbed his coat and tried to put it on, but his shaking hands could not find the sleeves. Lenin, very pale, stood looking at Martov. What was he thinking at that moment? Was he remembering how, more than two decades ago, he and Martov—friends, comrades-in-arms, comrades in the party—had set out together on the road to revolution? . . . Pointing to Martov . . . a Left SR burst into laughter. . . . "You have no reason to be so jolly, young man," croaked Martov, turning to him. "Before three months are out, you will follow us. . . ." With a trembling hand Martov opened the door and went out.

The Left SRs, still a very popular party among the peasants, became more hostile to the Bolsheviks in the summer of 1918 over the peace with Germany and Lenin's policy of backing poor peasants against richer peasants. Secretly they organized a mutiny against the government. This comic-opera rebellion was aimed, not at overthrowing the Bolsheviks, but at disrupting the alliance with the Germans. At 2:30 in the afternoon on July 6, two Left SRs entered the German embassy in Moscow with a forged document from the Cheka. When they were ushered into the office of the German ambassador, Count Wilhelm von Mirbach, they opened fire on him and finally dispatched him with a bomb. When "Iron Feliks" Dzerzhinski, the Cheka chief, heard what had happened, he drove to the headquarters of the 600-man Left-SR Cheka detachment to arrest the assassins, but he failed to bring any armed men with him and was himself arrested. The Left SRs managed to seize the main post-and-telegraph in central Moscow, but within a day the mutiny was over. The Bolsheviks purged them from the Congress of Soviets, and the Cheka arrested members of the party. Other revolts along the Volga, most notably one in Yaroslavl' led by the SR terrorist Boris Savinkov, also failed, and by the end of July all the rebellions had been bloodily suppressed.

When in late June an SR assassin killed a local Petrograd commissar, Lenin told the Petrograd party leaders that the time had come for mass terror against the enemies of the Soviet government. But many Soviet officials, like the head of the Petrograd Cheka, Mikhail Uritskii, opposed the use of the death penalty against political opponents. Lenin was prepared to "hang (hang without fail, so *the people see*) *no fewer than one hundred* known kulaks, rich men, blood suckers, "but to implement such orders he had to "find some truly hard people." The first instances of terror occurred, not in the capitals, but in the provinces where local authorities used armed force against real and suspected opponents. Instances of violence produced a habit of violence. At first isolated acts of revenge were taken by armed groups, against criminals, "speculators" (traders who overcharged their customers), and people identified as *burzhui* (bourgeois), but in general there were few pogroms against the better-off or other ethnic groups. Once active fighting broke out between Soviet and anti-Soviet forces, however, violence against civilians escalated. The most prominent victims of Red violence in the early days of the civil war were the last tsar, Nicholas II, his wife, Aleksandra, and their children and servants. They had been under house arrest in the Urals city of Ekaterinburg, when on the night of July 16, 1918, local Bolsheviks, afraid that the imperial family would fall into the hands of advancing anti-Soviet forces, and with the sanction of top party leaders in Moscow, took the family and their servants into the basement of the Ipatev house and shot them to death. In the fusillade bullets ricocheted off the dresses of the women, who had sewn their jewels into their clothes. The executioners then hacked the bodies with swords and threw them into a pit.

The reluctance to use violence by some high Communist leaders was overcome on August 30. That day Uritskii was shot. The same evening Lenin spoke to Moscow workers, ending his speech with the words "For us there is one alternative: victory or death." As he was leaving the hall, he was shot twice, allegedly by the Right SR Fanny Kaplan. Zinoviev, the head of the Petrograd Soviet, hysterically proposed terror:

> Comrades, beat the Right SRs mercilessly, without pity; neither courts nor tribunals are necessary. Let the workers exact revenge. Let the blood of Right SRs and White Guards flow. Exterminate the enemies physically!

The other leaders rejected the proposal, but from Moscow, Iakov Sverdlov, the chairman of the All-Russian Central Executive Committee of the Soviets, called for a "massive red terror against the bourgeoisie and its agents." On September 2, the anniversary of the Terror of the French Jacobins, the hesitation ended and systematic terror began in Soviet Russia. Between 500 and 1,300 people were shot in Petrograd and 6,000 arrested in reprisal for the murder of Uritskii. The terrorist campaign fell heaviest on officials of the tsarist regime and wealthy people. Among those killed were four former tsarist ministers, but few SRs, members of the party that had initiated assassinations of Soviet officials, were killed.

Massive violence against civilians had become part of war since 1914, and politics quickly descended into a new barbarism that would mark the rest of the twentieth century. Once the green light was given by the authorities in Russia, violence and retribution moved from the exceptional to the general and became ordinary behavior on both sides of the civil war. Both Reds and Whites engaged in terror, though each targeted different victims as the terror took on a class character. The Reds often shot captured officers or turned on the upper classes; the Whites took vengeance on ordinary soldiers, Communist Party members, and Jews. Red Army men were instructed to treat the ordinary population well, but such orders were often not obeyed. While some Bolsheviks tried to limit terror to "the leading actors of the White guard camp," they were often overruled by their superiors. In January 1919 one of the most powerful party institutions in Moscow, the Orgburo, instructed its agents in the Don Cossack region to "conduct *mass terror* against wealthy Cossacks, extirpating them totally; to conduct merciless mass terror against all Cossacks who participated, directly or indirectly, in the struggle against Soviet power." As a result of Moscow's intervention, local Bolsheviks executed thousands of Cossacks in the next few months before the center called a halt. In September of that year, with the Whites closing in from several directions, the Cheka arrested about a thousand Kadets and their supporters, accusing them of belonging to a National Center that was planning an uprising against the Soviets. At the end of the month the Cheka executed sixty-seven of the imprisoned leaders, and after a bomb attack by anarchists and Left SRs on Moscow party headquarters Dzerzhinski unleashed a massive terror on Kadets, aristocrats, and former tsarist officials, executing prisoners and hostages. In this same years, 1918–19, the Cheka set up forced labor and concentration camps for opponents of the regime, the first islands in what would be known as the GULag archipelago.

The Whites and their sympathizers also engaged in mass violence against civilians and cold-blooded executions of Communists and workers. As early as December 1917, when White forces put down a pro-Bolshevik uprising in Rostov, they turned their guns on the defeated workers. Kornilov and other White generals told their men, "Take no prisoners! The more terrible the terror, the more victories." A certain Colonel Drozdovskii regretted that "we live in a terrible time, when man is becoming an animal," but the Bolsheviks, "these unbridled hooligans understand only one law: an eye for an eye, a tooth for a tooth. But I would propose two eyes for one, and all teeth for one." Eventually anyone associated with the Communist party or participating in a local soviet was subject to the death penalty. General Wrangel formed a regiment of Red Army prisoners after ordering their 370 commanders to be shot. Though army units were somewhat more selective in their killing, popular movements allied to the Whites engaged in far more indiscriminate violence. In the summer of 1918, after three months in power a Bolshevik-led government in the oil-producing city of Baku, which had not exercised any terror during their brief exercise of power, peacefully left office after losing a crucial vote in the soviet. Later when the famous Twenty-Six Baku Commissars fled the city as the Turkish army approached, they were captured by anti-Communists in Turkestan, brutally cut down, and hastily buried in the desert. In Ukraine in 1919 bands of Cossacks or peasants broke into houses, raped, robbed, and killed thousands of Jews, whom they identified with the hated Soviet regime.

Though full figures for the extent of Red or White terror in the early years of Soviet power are elusive, historians have given various estimates. Official Soviet accounts claim only about 13,000 killed by the Red terror from 1918 to 1920, but Western historians have estimated between 50,000 and 140,000. Figures for the White terror are even more difficult to come by because the White forces fell under different administrations, and much of the violence on the anti-Bolshevik side was carried out by undisciplined forces operating independently of the more disciplined White forces. According to the best estimates, bands allied with Simon Petliura, who emerged as a major leader of independent Ukraine in 1918–19, committed 40 percent of anti-Jewish atrocities during the civil war; another 25 percent were carried out by other Ukrainian forces; non-Ukrainian White armies, primarily Cossacks, were responsible for 17 percent; while units of the Red Army accounted for 8.5 percent. If by terror one means only the violence outside of armed conflict turned against civilians and prisoners by state or military authorities, then Red terror probably exceeded White terror. But if one includes the violence by anti-Soviet popular movements and the pogroms against Jews, the numbers killed by the opponents of the Bolsheviks reach and surpass those cut down by the Reds.

The fronts in the civil war fluctuated back and forth, and people found themselves under Red rule one day and White the next. Political institutions were fragile, if not nonexistent, and terror was used to pacify or purify populations that were thought to be unreliable or disloyal. But, ironically, terror proved to be counterproductive, for in trying to eliminate enemies it created more enemies, not supporters, and stirred up opposition and resistance rather than quieting the population. The Bolsheviks' arbitrary use of terror against the Cossacks, whom they branded counterrevolutionary, made them very unpopular in the Don and Kuban regions, and their cavalier treatment of peasants, from whom they forcibly requisitioned grain, bred sullen opponents in the villages. Both Reds and Whites were crude and clumsy amateurs at winning over the hearts and minds of the people, but over time the Reds learned the lesson better and gradually broadened their base of support.

Intervention and the Civil War in the South

Five distinct groups lined up to fight the Soviet government. The first were the supporters of the *ancien régime*: former army officers, people of great property, aristocrats, and some disenchanted liberals who hoped to restore the monarchy. These groups would soon become the core of the Whites. The second group were the supporters of the February Revolution and the Constituent Assembly and included some liberals, the Right SRs, various nationalist groups, and the Menshevik-Defensists. The third group was made up of foreign interventionists: Germans, who wanted to create a German sphere of influence in the East; the Allies, who wanted to reestablish the eastern front and prevent the spread of Bolshevism; and the Japanese, who occupied parts of the Russian Far East. At the same time peasants in various parts of Russia staked out claims to an independent way of life free from the interfering state. Bands of "Greens" roamed the Volga region, Ukraine, and Siberia as they resisted the encroachments of the Bolsheviks and the Red Army. Finally, in the borderlands of the old empire nationalist politicians and their ethnic constituents formed their own independent states and looked to the West for support against the new centralizing forces from Moscow.

The civil war was fought all over the huge Eurasian landmass, from the Baltic to the Pacific, but the three major areas of struggle were in the south (the Don region, Kuban, the North Caucasus, and Ukraine), the east (the Volga region, Urals, and Siberia), and the northwest (the Baltic region and Poland). The civil war can be divided into three distinct periods. The first, from November 1917 until the end of World War I in November 1918, was one of initial organization of the hostile camps, the first wave of foreign intervention, and loosely formed armies engaged in both partisan and regular warfare. The second period ran from the end of World War I to November 1919, when Denikin in the south, Kolchak in Siberia, and Iudenich in the Baltic threatened the survival of the Soviet state. But by mid-November 1919 the White forces had been broken. The third period is marked by a long year of mopping up the remnants of the anti-Bolshevik forces and the advance of the Soviets beyond ethnic Russia into the non-Russian peripheries. The last White armies left, along with the British and the French, late in 1920, and the civil war ended early in 1921 with the conquest of Georgia and the peace treaty with Poland.

The intervention into the Russian civil war grew out of, and for a time was part of, the last stages of World War I. By the beginning of 1917 Europe was tired of the war. Yet neither the Central Powers nor the Allies could deliver the final blow that would result in victory. That year two important changes shifted the balance between the belligerents: the United States entered the war on the Allied side, and Russia, after the Bolshevik Revolution, left the war and signed an armistice with the Germans. Determined to reestablish the eastern front and bring the Russians back into the war, the Allies began to consider, first, material aid and, later, active military intervention into the nascent civil war. The prime ministers of Great Britain (David Lloyd-George), France (Georges Clemenceau), and Italy (Vittorio Emanuele Orlando) were the strongest supporters of armed intervention in Russia to recreate the eastern front. More wary of intervention was the American president, Woodrow Wilson, who favored a "soft peace," with concessions to the defeated, and hoped to inspire a new world order that would end the balance-of-power politics that, in his view, had led to war. Wilson's vision of expanded democracy, free trade, and a League of Nations was shared by Europe's moderate socialists, who favored a democratic road to socialism and containment of Bolshevism. From late 1917 the Allies faced, not only the Germans, with their grand but increasingly elusive plans for German dominance of Central Europe, but also the Bolsheviks, prepared to push ahead for an international socialist revolution and an end to liberalism, capitalism, and imperialism.

Until the Soviets signed the Treaty of Brest-Litovsk, the Allies restrained their intervention in Russia to monetary support for the counterrevolutionaries. In January 1918 Rumanian troops took advantage of Russian weakness and occupied Bessarabia (now Moldova), an area inhabited by Rumanian-speaking

Figure 3.1. European Russia during the civil war, 1918–21.

peasants that the Russians had seized in the nineteenth century. On March 6, 1918, British troops, invited by the local soviet, landed in Murmansk with Lenin's approval. He hoped to prevent a German seizure of the port. A month later (April 5) Japanese and British marines landed at Vladivostok, despite the misgivings of the American president. Though not sympathetic to the Bolsheviks, Wilson opposed the use of the military to overthrow them. Eventually the president agreed to American intervention aimed at guarding supplies in the north, rescuing stranded Czech military forces, and restraining Japanese expansion into Siberia.

In 1918 the principal internal threat to the Bolsheviks came from the south of Russia. There General Alekseev had formed the Volunteer Army of about four thousand men largely made up of former tsarist officers and heavily dependent on the local Don Cossacks. He was joined by Generals Kornilov and

Anton Denikin and loosely affiliated with the ataman of the Don Cossacks, General Kaledin. Here the ebb and flow of Soviet and White fortunes was typical of what followed elsewhere in the civil war. At the end of November 1917 a revolt aided by Black Sea sailors established Soviet power in Rostov-on-Don, but within a few days the Volunteer Army retook the city and took retribution on the rebels. In February 1918 the Bolsheviks then successfully pushed the Whites back from Rostov to the Kuban steppes and took Ekaterinodar, the capital of the Kuban Cossacks. In despair General Kaledin committed suicide. When General Kornilov tried to dislodge the Bolsheviks from the town, he was killed by a Bolshevik shell (April 13). The Cossack counterrevolution might have been mopped up had the Germans not come to its rescue, occupying Rostov in early May. General Krasnov, the newly elected ataman of the Don Cossacks, allied himself with the Germans, declared "an independent democratic republic" in the Don region, abolished all institutions and laws of the revolution, and restored the *ancien régime* as much as possible.

To the west, in the spring of 1918, the Germans forced the Bolsheviks to abandon Ukraine, the breadbasket of tsarist Russia. A group of Ukrainian nationalists, gathered around a parliament called the Rada, had in January 1918 declared Ukraine independent. At the same time a Soviet government existed in Kharkov, an industrial town within Ukraine largely inhabited by Russians. The Bolsheviks managed to occupy Kiev in February and drive the Rada out, but once the Brest-Litovsk peace was signed, the Germans returned and essentially made Ukraine their protectorate. By April the Germans overthrew the Rada, which was too radical for them, and installed General Pavlo Skorapadsky as Hetman. Here again, as in the Don region, the counterrevolution, backed by the Germans, tried to restore the old order. Skorapadsky was supported primarily by the large landlords who opposed a land reform, such as had been proposed by the Rada. He appointed a cabinet made up of Kadets, the liberal party that had formerly been so anti-German. For the liberals order and an end to radical social reform was preferable to the kind of democracy that had led to anarchy and the collapse of the nation. Ukrainian peasants were disappointed by the anti-Soviets' failure to break up the noble estates, and many drifted over to the Bolsheviks or joined anarchist bands.

A major campaign in the summer of 1918 swept the Reds out of southern Russia that lay between the Black and Caspian seas. In August Ekaterinodar fell to General Anton Denikin, Kornilov's replacement, and the Whites moved on to take the port of Novorossiisk, through which they could receive British supplies. Where they conquered, the Whites established a military dictatorship, though they were also assisted by liberal politicians who acted as administrators. Fortunately for the Bolsheviks, the Whites could not depend on their allies, the Cossacks. Krasnov refused to subordinate himself to Denikin, and Denikin could not accept Krasnov's pro-German attitude. When Denikin decided to campaign in the North Caucasus, Krasnov acted on his own and attempted, unsuccessfully, to take Tsaritsyn on the Volga. Had he succeeded, the anti-Bolsheviks in the south would have been able to link up with those in the east.

By October 1918 Denikin's forces numbered forty thousand. From their secure base in the Kuban, they cleared the North Caucasus of Bolsheviks and moved to launch an offensive to the north. Denikin was somewhat unusual among the White generals. Born a peasant, he was more sensitive to the social discontents that had led to the revolution. But like his fellow officers, Denikin was highly suspicious of the liberals and moderate socialists who had failed in 1917 to contain the radical impulses from below. More typically, White generals saw the revolution simply as a conspiracy of the Jews, the perennial scapegoat for reactionary Russian politicians. Prepared to rely on their own men, the remnants of the nobility and some of the urban middle classes, and foreign assistance, they made few concessions to the interests of the peasants and did little to prevent their men from plundering villages or committing anti-Semitic outrages. Not interested in seeking social support among the lower classes, they wavered between a program of restoring the old order and backing the political changes after the February Revolution. When General Wrangel beat back the Reds in the Crimea, he treated the region as captured enemy territory, pillaging, raping women, and even murdering children. Once the area was secured, the new governor issued a decree reinstating all the laws of Russia before February 1917. This White counterrevolution shared few values with the anti-Bolsheviks on the Volga and in Siberia, who were promoting the Constituent Assembly.

Civil War in Siberia and the Volga

The full-scale Allied intervention came in the late spring of 1918 after a peculiar incident. Former prisoners of war and deserters from the Austro-Hungarian Army who wanted to fight on the side of the Allies formed a Czechoslovak army inside Russia. By March they numbered forty thousand, and the Bolsheviks perceived their growing numbers as a potential threat. Lenin ordered the Czechoslovaks to be evacuated along the trans-Siberian railroad to Vladivostok on the Pacific. As they moved eastward, some units met up with a group of Hungarian POWs, who favored the Central Powers, near Cheliabinsk in the Urals. When a Hungarian threw a piece of iron and wounded a Czech, a fight broke out. The local Soviet authorities arrested the Czechs. Their comrades revolted, seized the city, and began traveling along the railroad, overthrowing local soviets as they continued east through Siberia. Moscow ordered that the Czechs be disarmed, and People's Commissar of War Trotsky declared that "every armed Czechoslovak on the railway be shot on the spot." When the Czechoslovak troops reached Omsk, the "capital" of western Siberia, anti-Bolshevik groups joined them and formed a West Siberian Commissariat, headed by a Right SR, as an anti-Soviet government. Here was a new center of opposition, one identified, not with the reactionary Cossack generals of the Don, but with more democratic elements.

Along the Volga as well, other Czechoslovak units overthrew local soviet authorities and installed Right SR governments. In Samara a government, called Komuch (Committee for the Constituent Assembly), was established with the purpose of restoring Russia's elected parliament. Opposed by factory workers and with little enthusiasm from the surrounding peasantry, Komuch depended on the Czech forces, who expanded their authority to Simbirsk, Kazan, and Ufa. Given its fragility, the SR government resorted to repression and arrests to hold power. Here the Czechoslovaks, accidental actors caught in the midst of civil war, played the same role as the Germans and Allies elsewhere in Russia. Though they were never strong enough to destroy the Soviet regime and create an unchallenged anti-Bolshevik authority, their aid was enough to prop up the SRs and the Whites for a time and establish several independent power centers throughout the former Russian empire.

By fall 1918 Britain, France, the United States, Japan, Germany, France, Rumania, and Ottoman Turkey all had troops in Russia, along with Finnish, Polish, and Serbian soldiers. The Germans created and backed anti-Soviet governments in Belorussia, Ukraine, Lithuania, Latvia, Estonia, and Finland. Imperial Germany was on its way to realizing its goal of a *Mitteleuropa*, German dominance in the center of Europe with parts of the old Russian Empire as client states. Germans not only advanced into the Don region, where they aided the Cossacks to drive out the Soviet troops, but also occupied the Crimean peninsula and sent an expeditionary force to Georgia, which declared its independence on May 26. The British secured a base at Arkhangelsk in the north, and in August they briefly occupied Baku in the south. In September the Turks took Baku, overthrowing the local socialists, and eventually installing a dependent Azerbaijani government. Americans joined British, French, and Serb troops at Murmansk, and the Japanese sat in Vladivostok. Fortunately for Soviet Russia, the imperial powers were not united but still engaged in the mortal combat of the world war. Lenin told his beleaguered comrades that "the final solution depends on the outcome of the vacillations of the two hostile groups of imperialist countries—the American[-Japanese] conflict in the Far East and the Anglo-German in Western Europe." Caution and patience was essential to a successful outcome. "We must remain at our post until the arrival of our ally, the international proletariat, for this ally," he assured his readers, "is sure to arrive."

The civil war was not only a war of armies but of ordinary people who had to chose in whose ranks to serve and whether to hold their positions under fire or desert. In the flush of the October Revolution the Soviet government had replaced the old army with a socialist militia, abolishing all ranks and titles and forming a volunteer army with elections of officers by the rank and file. Just over one hundred thousand men joined the new army. When Trotsky took over as commissar of war in March 1918, the only battle-ready military units on which the Soviet government could rely were the thirty-five thousand Latvian riflemen commanded by Colonel Vatsetis. A few units of the former tsarist army backed the Bolsheviks in the first armed clashes with the Whites, but the old army was rapidly disintegrating, as hundreds of thousands of soldiers voted with their feet and left the front for home. The few Red Guards that had distinguished themselves in October 1917 numbered only four thousand in Petrograd and another three thousand in Moscow. From these meager forces, Trotsky began the hard work of fashioning a Red Army of 5 million men over the next two and a half years. As the army ranks expanded, the class composition of the army changed, as the bulk of the fighting men no longer came from the workers but from the peasantry.

Figure 3.2. Commissar of War Lev Trotsky during the civil war (Culver Pictures).

Trotsky's slogan was "Work, discipline, and order will save the Soviet Republic!" At first he relied on the voluntary army, filled with revolutionary enthusiasts, but by the summer of 1918 he began drafting industrial workers into the army. He soon began to reverse the radical democratization of the army that had taken place after the October insurrection, ending the election of officers and instilling iron discipline in the ranks and among officers by the liberal use of threats and capital punishment. He ordered deserters, if caught, to be shot. Trotsky recruited former tsarist officers, and as early as April 1918 he introduced "political commissars" into the army to keep an eye on the officers. Within the Bolshevik Party a military opposition to Trotsky's reforms and use of tsarist officers came to a head in March 1919 at the Eighth Congress of the party. Even Lenin was wary of the so-called military specialists, until Trotsky informed him that the Red Army had no less than thirty thousand former tsarist officers. Over three-quarters of the whole command and administration of the Red Army was made up of such specialists in the early years, though that percentage would fall to a third by the end of the civil war. Backed by Lenin, Trotsky easily overcame the resistance of his opponents.

Russia on Its Own

In November the world war ended with the defeat of the Central Powers. Revolution broke out in Germany, and the Kaiser fled to the Netherlands. Moderate Social Democrats came to power in Berlin, and the German army pulled out of Ukraine and southern Russia. The Ottoman Turks abandoned Transcaucasia. The collapse of Germany and Turkey boosted Bolshevik fortunes and weakened those governments in Ukraine, the Baltic region, Georgia, and Azerbaijan that had been dependent on aid from the Central Powers. The Allies quickly replaced the Germans: the British reoccupied Baku, and the French landed on the Black Sea coast of Ukraine. The Soviet government declared the Brest-Litovsk Treaty null and void, and in January 1919 the Red Army advanced westward, taking Riga on the Baltic, the Polish-Lithuanian city of Vilno, and Kharkov in Ukraine. Aided by peasant partisans under Nikifor Grigoriev and the anarchist Nestor Makhno, the Bolsheviks took the Ukrainian capital, Kiev, driving back the pro-German government, and Grigoriev moved south and drove the French and Greeks from Kherson.

The Allied intervention had begun as an effort to keep Russia in the war against the Germans, but with the defeat of the Central Powers the fear of the little-known Bolshevik menace rose in importance. To many in government throughout Europe and the United States, Bolshevism looked like a new "specter haunting Europe." "Bolshevism must be suppressed," said American Secretary of State Robert Lansing. "It is the worst form of anarchism . . . , worse than any autocracy, a greater enemy of individual liberty. . . . America is sound to the core, but Europe is not." The spread of Bolshevism was seen to be connected to human misery, to hunger and hopelessness. The *Wall Street Journal* declared in November 1918 that "hunger breeds anarchy, and . . . the most effective weapon against Bolshevism is a loaf of bread." Wilson sent food and fuel to Europe and placed Herbert Hoover in charge of the first major American peacetime relief program. Yet with the war over, military intervention was more difficult to sustain. Lloyd-George and Wilson wondered if the West should just let the Russians fight it out among themselves. The victorious Allies organized an economic blockade of Russia and requested that the Germans remain in Lithuania and Latvia to prevent a Soviet takeover in the Baltic region. Even though the world war had ended, Soviet Russia was surrounded by foreign forces and faced a renewed danger from the White armies.

Whenever the White forces were advancing, the Allies grew less interested in a political resolution with the Soviets and the Communists became more interested in a peaceful settlement. Conversely, when the Red forces were advancing, the Allies grew doubtful about military solutions and looked toward diplomacy, while the Communists grew cool toward a political resolution. In late December 1918 the Soviet government, uncertain about its ability to hold out against all its enemies, tried to interest the Allies in "a peaceful settlement of all outstanding questions," and plans were made for a conference on the Turkish island of Prinkipo. But the recalcitrant French convinced the Whites to reject the invitation, and the conference was never held. A young American journalist, William Bullitt, sent by Wilson on an unofficial mission to Moscow to assess the situation, reported back that the Soviet government had considerable popular support, that the Whites were completely dependent on the West, and that Lenin was willing to compromise with his domestic enemies in order to end the civil war. But Allied leaders, who were faced by conservative opposition to any compromise with Bolshevism, suspected Lenin's sincerity and disregarded Bullitt's report. When diplomatic channels failed, the Communists turned toward extragovernmental appeals, using revolutionary propaganda to go over the heads of governments directly to the people.

The Allies were unable to enforce any unity among the quarreling anti-Bolshevik governments in the Volga and western Siberia. Various representatives of the Right SR Komuch, the conservative Omsk government, and others formed an All-Russian Directorate in Ufa in September, but more radical SRs, led by Victor Chernov, in Samara opposed them. By November the Directorate was sitting in a railroad car near Omsk, when military conspirators overthrew it and installed Admiral Aleksandr Kolchak as the ostensible "Supreme Ruler" of all Russia. The SR party was in disarray. Some fled abroad; others, willing to give up armed resistance in exchange for amnesty, opened negotiations with the Soviet government. Still others tried to overthrow Kolchak, but Cossacks and Czechs suppressed their coup in December 1918, and Kolchak's men executed hundreds of them. In the belief that Bolshevism was the lesser danger to the revolution, the SR party decided in February 1919 to give up its efforts to overthrow the Bolsheviks and to concentrate its energies on fighting the counterrevolution of Denikin and Kolchak. That same month the Bolsheviks arrested two hundred of their former Left SR comrades. With Kolchak's coup the moderate "democratic" phase of the civil war came to an end, and the lines of the civil war hardened between the Red dictatorship on one side and the White counterrevolution on the other.

The new "Supreme Ruler," Admiral Kolchak, had never won a victory at sea and was best known for throwing his ceremonial sword into the Black Sea during the revolution rather than surrender it to the sailors. Now beached in the middle of Siberia, Kolchak received material support from the British and administrative assistance from Kadet advisors, who had become disillusioned with democratic forms of rule. He faced, not only large Red armies, but the Japanese in eastern Siberia and well-armed gangs of bandits along the trans-Siberian railroad. Though Kolchak considered adopting a land reform that might have gained him support among the peasants, his Kadet ministers warned him that such a reform would cost him the support of the landlords, who held important positions in his army. One prominent Kadet, Ariadna Tyrkova-Williams, wrote at the time:

> We must support the army first and place the democratic programs in the background. We must create a ruling class and not a dictatorship of the majority. The universal hegemony of Western democracy is a fraud, which politicians have foisted upon us. We must have the courage to look directly into the eye of the wild beast—which is called the people.

Instead of reform, the admiral turned to terror, which in turn drove potential supporters over to the Bolsheviks. Kolchak launched a spring offensive and took Ufa in March 1919, but the Red Army under Mikhail Frunze counterattacked, preventing the admiral from reaching the Volga and linking up with Denikin.

White defeats in Siberia were offset in 1919 by Denikin's successes in southern Russia and General Nikolai Iudenich's advances in the Baltic region. In January the Volunteer Army destroyed the Red Army in the North Caucasus, and in late spring Denikin moved steadily northward, aiming at Moscow. His army grew to one hundred fifty thousand men as he took Tsaritsyn on the Volga. In Ukraine the partisan leader Grigoriev broke with the Reds, turned his anger on the Jews of Elizavetgrad in a massive pogrom, and opened the Ukrainian front to Denikin, who occupied Kharkov and Kiev. The one great chance the Whites had to win the war was at hand. In May Iudenich launched his twenty-five thousand-man army from his base in Estonia toward Petrograd. At the same time fifty-thousand men, equipped with British arms and tanks, participated in Denikin's spring offensive. The British also helped by disabling several Soviet ships in the Baltic and organizing a blockade of Soviet Russia. Some of Denikin's forces managed to reach into western Siberia in August and September, and his main force moved as far north as Orel, two hundred miles from Moscow. Iudenich in the north closed in on Petrograd, taking the Pulkovo heights less than twenty miles from the old capital. Many in the West predicted the end of the Communist regime in a few weeks.

Yet the White armies had only as much power as they could muster at the point of a gun. Peasants and townspeople might cheer the Whites as they entered their villages and towns, but they soon turned away and refrained from actively supporting them. Many Ukrainians and other non-Russians feared Denikin, who promised to restore a single, united "Great Russia," more than the Reds, who promoted a program of "national self-determination." The turning point in the war came suddenly. The Red Army dispatched a shock detachment against Orel in October and sent the Whites reeling backwards. Trotsky rushed north, rallied troops outside Petrograd, and beat Iudenich back into Estonia, just as the Red Army took Omsk in Siberia. By the end of 1919 Ukraine was in the hands of the Reds, and their army reached Rostov at the mouth of the Don River.

After the great counterattacks by the Reds in late 1919, the civil war steadily wound down. Most of the interventionists began pulling out. The last British troops left Arkhangelsk at the end of September, Murmansk and the Caucasus in mid-October, and abandoned Kolchak in Siberia in November. The Americans left northern Russia in July 1919 and Vladivostok in April 1920; Kolchak abdicated early in January 1920 in favor of Denikin, who in turn gave up his post to General Baron Petr Wrangel and sailed for Constantinople. Wrangel's army, crowded into Crimea, with its back to the Black Sea, was finally evacuated in November 1920. Kolchak was not so lucky. Captured by the Reds, he was interrogated and executed in Irkutsk by the local revolutionary committee. The Red Army and the Czechoslovak Army signed an armistice that permitted the Czechoslovaks to leave Russia. Yet even with its major enemies gone, Soviet power was not completely secure in Siberia until it was able to defeat independent peasant armies and pressure the last Japanese troops to leave more than two years later.

Soviet troops took the ports of northern Russia, Arkhangelsk and Murmansk, where pro-Allies governments had existed, in February 1920 and shot thousands of suspected collaborators. The final campaigns in 1920–21 were in the non-Russian borderlands. The Red Army marched into Baku (Azerbaijan) in April 1920, into Erevan (Armenia) in December, and into Tiflis (Tbilisi, Georgia) in February 1921. In the west Soviet Russia fought a brief war with the Poles, losing the western parts of Belorussia and Ukraine but keeping Minsk and Kiev. Campaigns in 1921 drove the emir of Bukhara into Afghanistan and subdued Dagestani rebels in the high mountains of the Caucasus. The last hurrah of Islamic resistance to Soviet rule was the Basmachi movement, led by the former minister of war of the Ottoman Empire, Enver Pasha, a flamboyant and daring soldier whose career included organization of the Armenian genocide in Turkey in 1915 and a brief alliance with Soviet Russia. In November 1920 he arrived in Central Asia and proclaimed himself "commander-in-chief of all the armed forces of Islam." On August 4, 1922, the Red cavalry tracked him down and killed him near the Afghan frontier. That date serves as well as any other to mark the final whiff of smoke in the civil war.

Waiting for the International Revolution

The unprecedented destructiveness of World War I, in which tens of millions of people were crippled or killed, convinced radical socialists that the horrors of war would lead to a revolutionary termination of the bloodshed and of the society that had created it. Trotsky declared that the war had "transformed the whole of Europe into a powder magazine of social revolution." Indeed, beginning in 1917 and running through 1921, Europe experienced a new age of revolution, the like of which had not occurred since 1789–1815. Several imperial states (Russia, Austria-Hungary, the Ottoman Empire) collapsed; existing governments fell; new states (Czechoslovakia, Yugoslavia, Poland, Estonia, Latvia, Lithuania, Finland, Hungary, Austria) were created; and a series of radical revolutions (in Russia, Germany, Hungary) shook the foundations of the old order.

From the moment of their seizure of power, leading Bolsheviks argued that protection of the infant Soviet state went hand in hand with Communist ambitions to stimulate revolutions in other countries. The Bolsheviks saw themselves as liberators, not only of Russia and its empire, but of colonized peoples everywhere. They appealed almost immediately to "all Muslim toilers of Russia and the East" to overthrow their oppressors. Soviet Russia proclaimed itself the first anticolonial, anti-imperialist power ready to combat the European empires, which controlled 80 percent of the world's surface. To the Bolsheviks Soviet Russia was not an ordinary nation-state but the harbinger of the future stateless society. Soviet Russia had to show other countries and peoples by example that it harbored no imperialist desires but was prepared to fight for the liberation of the colonized. Lenin extended his anti-imperialism to parts of the former tsarist empire, which, he declared, were free to leave and form separate states if they desired. He believed that if Soviet Russia gave the non-Russians full rights of national self-determination, even to the point of separation from Russia, that they would eventually come back into the socialist fold.

The years 1919–20 have been called "the Red Years" in European history. Ordinary people throughout Europe expressed a tremendous revulsion against militarism and an enthusiasm for the liberal Woodrow Wilson and for the Russian Revolution. In March 1919 a socialist-communist government came to power in the newly independent state of Hungary. A soviet republic was declared in Bavaria, in southern Germany. Strikers were in the streets of northern Italy, and in Britain workers marched in a "Hands Off Russia" campaign against the intervention. Even the United States was shaken by a "Red Scare," and the attorney general rounded up, quite unconstitutionally, hundreds of suspected subversives and deported them to Russia on the SS *Buford*, known as the "Red Ark."

Lenin and the Bolsheviks had broken with the majority of European socialists at the beginning of World War I, when the leading parties of the Second International supported their governments' entry into the war. In March 1918 the Bolsheviks changed the name of their party from Russian Social Democratic Workers' Party (Bolsheviks) to Russian Communist Party (Bolsheviks), or RKP (b), signifying the definitive break with the more moderate Social Democrats of Russia and the West and the return to the militant traditions of the Communist League of the young Marx and Engels. Other radical socialists were invited to emulate the Bolsheviks, break with their old parties, and form new, Communist parties. In August 1918, the first Communist parties were formed in Latvia and Finland, followed months later by Communists in Hungary, Austria, Poland, and Germany. The international socialist movement was irrevocably split between social democracy in the West and Bolshevism and its allies.

The majority of socialists in Europe and America opposed the Bolshevik takeover in Russia, because it was dictatorial and used terror against its enemies. The social democrats of Europe declared in 1919, "Socialism will not base its political organization upon dictatorship. It cannot seek to suppress democracy; its historic mission, on the contrary, is to carry democracy to completion." As Lenin began to implement his plan for a rival international socialist organization, he met opposition from one of the most eminent and respected radical socialists, the Polish-born leader of the German Left, Rosa Luxemburg. Luxemburg argued that an international organization in which only one party, the RKP (b), had a mass following would inevitably be dominated by that party. But her prophetic words were not heeded, and in January 1919, her comrades launched an uprising in Berlin. Right-wing soldiers crushed the rebellion, and Luxemburg became their most prominent victim. Captured and brutally murdered by reactionary fanatics, her body was dumped into a canal. Two months later, on March 2, 1919, forty-four delegates, most of them from parts of the former Russian empire, gathered in Moscow and founded the Communist International, or Comintern. Its chairman, Grigorii Zinoviev called for a "communist workers' revolution that must destroy and break up the bourgeois state machine and organize a new power, the dictatorship of the proletariat." Europe and America must move beyond "bourgeois democracy" toward a Soviet republic. Communists everywhere should use existing parliaments "as tribunes for revolutionary agitation" but at the same time form secret, underground parties for revolutionary action.

Enthusiasm and organization were not enough to sustain the wave of revolution in early 1919, and it began to recede later in the year. By fall both the soviet government in Bavaria and Bela Kun's Communist government in Hungary had fallen before local opposition and foreign intervention. To most observers it was clear that postwar Europe would be shaped, not by revolutionary socialists, but by the "forces of order," the Great Powers, that had signed the Treaty of Versailles at the beginning of the year. By the time of the Second Congress of the Comintern, in the summer of 1920, Communist parties could show little improvement in their political prospects. In Germany, where Bolsheviks had misplaced their hopes for the rescuing revolution, elections brought the moderate Social Democrats to power with ten times the vote that the fledgling Communist Party could muster. The weakness of all Communist parties, except for the Russian, confirmed Luxemburg's prediction of Russian dominance of the International. At the insistence of the Bolsheviks the Second Congress adopted "Twenty-One Conditions" that parties had to accept before admission to the Comintern. One of those conditions required that Communists everywhere "give every possible support to the Soviet republics in their struggle against all counter-revolutionary forces." In time this proviso came to mean that the primary duty of Communists in all countries was to the "first socialist state" even before their home country.

With the end of civil war and the ebbing of the revolutionary tide, some important state officials in Soviet Russia argued that Russia must begin to act more like any other state, in state-to-state relations at least, and constrain its revolutionary ambitions. The Commissariat of Foreign Affairs, headed by Georgii Chicherin, promoted normalization of relations with other states, but its goals were often thwarted by those Bolsheviks who had not abandoned their hopes for an international revolution. With their White allies defeated, several Western governments shifted their Russian policy, lifting the blockade of Russia in January 1920 and opening trade with the former enemy state. An uneasy truce was established between West and East. The Western powers recognized the surviving independent states of the Russian borderlands in order to maintain a buffer between the Soviets and Europe. Wary about the Comintern and the revolutionary virus that the Bolsheviks had unleashed on Europe, the European states could be content, at least for a time, that they faced a significantly smaller Russia that was less of a military threat to the West than the old empire.

Where Have All the Workers Gone?

Workers suffered enormously during the civil war. The shortages of food and fuel forced factories to close and workers to migrate to the countryside in order to survive. Of the 3.5 million workers in middle and large industries just before the revolution, only about 1.5 million were still working in industry by the end of 1920. About the same number were working as artisans and handicraft workers. The "Red proletariat" of Petrograd, the very class of nearly 400,000 that had made the Bolshevik victory in October 1917 possible, evaporated to 123,000 in mid-1920. Moscow's population fell by half, Kiev's by a quarter. As a result, the class of "proletarians" on which the Bolsheviks based their regime grew weaker. Civil war and socialist ideology had conspired to create a particular kind of wartime economy with highly centralized state control over nationalized industry. Trade unions and cooperatives became instruments of the state, and collective forms of running industry gave way to one-person management. Compulsory labor, fixed prices and wages, forced requisitioning of grain, and the elimination of money payments and legal markets became the rule as the state took up where the market had been. Despite (or perhaps because of) these draconian methods, as well as the devastating effects of the war, production continued to fall.

From the beginning of the civil war, as the economy ground to a halt, workers produced very little but still had to be fed, kept warm, and housed. They became, in effect, state dependents. One disgruntled Communist, Aleksei Gastev, complained in May 1918:

> At the present time the laboring masses function in the capacity of consumers and not as producers. . . . I find it ridiculous to hear people talk about sabotage by the bourgeoisie, when the frightened bourgeois is picked as one engaged in sabotage. What we really have is sabotage on a nationwide scale, by the whole people, by the proletariat. We encounter opposition on the part of working masses whenever we attempt to establish output norms. . . .

All Communists wanted greater productivity, but they disagreed greatly on how to achieve it. The Left Communists believed that there must be state control of industry but greater participation in the running of factories by workers. They wanted unionized workers to elect factory managers. Trade unions and soviets favored collegial management, but Lenin favored one-person management, a single boss chosen by the state. In early June 1918, the First Congress of Sovnarkhozy (the Councils of People's Economy) adopted a compromise policy—a team of managers, instead of one, which was partially elected from below and partially appointed from above. In the next few years these collegial management boards included both "bourgeois experts" and workers, some elected, some appointed. As time passed, however, the weight of the state economic authorities, like the sovnarkhozes, grew, and factory committees became local agents or cells of the unions. As their formal organizations lost power, however, workers were still represented on management boards and often were administrators, along with the specialists.

Russia was the least appropriate country in Europe in which to try to build Marxist socialism. Capitalism had only partially transformed the Russian economy, the working class was a pitiful minority of the population, and most Russians were peasants hostile to a political and economic order that privileged the cities and the industrial proletariat. Lenin himself wavered in his estimation of the potential of the Russian working class. Never very optimistic about workers developing socialist consciousness on their own, Lenin was nevertheless often enthusiastic about their raw energy and toughness. In November

1918 he revealed his hesitation about introducing socialism into Russia because of the backwardness of the workers:

> We did not decree socialism immediately throughout industry because socialism can be established and consolidated only when the working class has learned how to administer, when the authority of the working masses has been firmly established. Without that, socialism is mere wishful thinking.

But, he went on to argue, worker control of industry and later worker participation on management boards were the first steps toward socialism. In January 1919 Lenin complained that Russia's workers had "retained much of the traditional psychology of capitalist society. The workers are building a new society without having transformed themselves into new human beings by cleansing themselves of the filth of the old world." The Congress decided that trade unions should take a more active role in government, gradually fusing with state organs. The unions were to prepare and train workers "for the management, not only of production, but also of the entire state machinery." Two months later Lenin elaborated his position about the need to involve workers in state administration and production, though he retained his skepticism about their readiness for such a role:

> We now have passed, or are about to pass, from workers' control to workers' management of industry. . . . [But] the idea that we can build communism by the hands of pure Communists, without the assistance of bourgeois experts, is a childish idea. . . . Socialism cannot be built unless advantage is taken of the heritage of capitalist culture. There is nothing communism can be built from except what has been left us by capitalism. . . . We must create the communist society with the hands of our enemies.

Among workers and the soviets there was widespread support for "economic equality for all true workers," but the government's policy shifted toward paying specialists at a higher rate. Workers opposed the reintroduction of piecework, payment pegged to the number of pieces produced, but union and government leaders believed that a piecework system would increase productivity. Workers gave in, though not without resistance, and the workers' own government reintroduced this most resented form of "capitalist exploitation." All agreed that this was a temporary measure, necessary under current conditions of war and poverty.

The state had no material incentives to offer its workers, only an inadequate ration. Desperate to stem the rapid collapse of industry and the evaporation of the working class, the Soviet government introduced a compulsory labor obligation for all workers. On October 31, 1918, all able-bodied citizens between sixteen and fifty years of age became subject to compulsory labor. "He who does not work does not eat" was the slogan of the day. A few months later, in April 1919, the first labor camp for deserters and shirkers was established under the Cheka. In June the government decreed that every worker would be issued a labor book as a record of employment, and in November disciplinary courts were set up under trade unions to punish workers for minor offenses. But nothing helped. The stream of workers to the countryside never abated. Workers complained about the inadequate rations and the failures of the soviets to improve them. They went out on strike to pressure party leaders. Angry workers shouted, "Down with Lenin and horsemeat. Give us the tsar and pork!"

At the end of 1919 more drastic methods were suggested by Trotsky. With the civil war winding down and millions of soldiers soon to be demobilized, Trotsky proposed treating workers as if they were mobilized for war. Workers in vital industries would be forbidden to leave the factory without permission. Groups of idle workers would be rounded up for odd jobs. The economy would be run as if for war, and the state would form labor armies to send wherever needed. The idea was very unpopular both within and outside Bolshevik circles, but one of its strongest advocates was none other than Lenin himself. He publicly repudiated the "liberal capitalist principle of 'freedom of labor,' " and helped push Trotsky's theses through the Central Committee of the party in January 1920. Dzerzhinski, head of the Cheka, was named chairman of the Principal Committee for the General Labor Obligation. Black markets were shut down and the traders swept into the labor armies, which operated under military discipline. But like the other efforts to prod workers into higher productivity, militarization largely failed.

Marxism was a promise of liberation. To its adherents and advocates it meant the end of oppression and the beginning of a new humane life. Yet even when an American visitor, Lincoln Steffens, might tell his compatriots that he "had seen the future and it works," the dismal everyday reality of Russian life resembled in few ways the utopian visions of revolutionary thinkers. To overcome the indolence, drunkenness, and clumsiness that appeared to many intellectuals to characterize Russian peasants and workers, Soviet leaders turned to Western technology and American know-how. A number of Bolsheviks, with Lenin prominently among them, favored using the techniques of scientific management (which they renamed "the scientific organization of labor") that had been developed in the United States. The American engineer Frederick Winslow Taylor had studied how production could be raised if managers broke down the work process, estimating how much time it took for each task. Workers would then be compelled to work at the most efficient rates. From its introduction into American, and later European, factories, Taylor's time-motion methods had engendered opposition from workers who resented being reduced to machines and losing their own power to make decisions on the job. Though the methods were tried early on in some Russian factories, Taylorism made little headway in the civil-war years, for tired, hungry workers could barely make it through the day. Some prominent Bolsheviks opposed Taylorism as the "scientific exploitation of labor," condemning its antiegalitarianism and its reduction of human beings to cogs in the production machine.

Most Communists, however, remained fascinated with machines and technology. Lenin and his comrades aspired to reproduce the mass production methods introduced by Henry Ford into the American automobile industry. "Fordism" and "Americanism" were the signs of modernity and the promise of a more productive future. The left-leaning American businessman Armand Hammer made a deal with Ford to supply Soviet Russia with Ford tractors and other equipment, and the name Ford was so revered that peasants named their children after the American capitalist. Perhaps the most enthusiastic disciple of Ford and Taylor was Gastev, who founded the Central Institute of Labor in 1920 as a training center to turn out workers of the future. Here hundreds of workers in identical uniforms sitting at identical benches operated machines in unison. Humans had become machines. But for most workers in Soviet Russia outside the reach of the dreamers, life was a bitter struggle for survival. With the pressure for productivity and compulsory labor, workers grew demoralized. And the vision of a "socialist factory," in which the workers themselves would have greater power and influence, faded further into the distance.

The Peasant Revolution

The ultimate success of the Communists in the civil war depended on their ability to win over or at least neutralize the peasantry. But they began with great disadvantages. The visceral hostility of many Marxists to peasants and to nationalism led to cavalier attitudes toward the people of the countryside, and the policy of forced requisitioning of grain that they initiated in 1918 deeply alienated the peasants. Yet through the course of the civil war, as they faced the possibility of a White victory and the restoration of the old landlords, the peasants turned to the Communists as the lesser of two evils.

On October 26, 1917, the first day of the new regime, the Second Congress of Soviets passed a decree abolishing all private property in land and placing all land held by landlords, the church, and the state, as well as peasant allotments, at the disposal of rural land committees and peasant soviets until the convening of the Constituent Assembly. No compensation was given to nobles whose lands were seized. The decree forbade the hiring of labor and the buying, selling, mortgaging, or renting of land. On January 18, 1918, the Third Congress of Soviets adopted a law on "the socialization of the land," which stated that "the right to use the land belongs to him who cultivates it with his own labor" and referred to developing a "collective system of agriculture" as a higher stage of agrarian economy. Most importantly, this law empowered the rural soviets to carry out the redistribution of the land, rather than the old land committees set up under the Provisional Government and still dominated by the Right SRs.

Encouraged by Bolshevik policy and the chaos in the countryside, peasants all over Russia seized land and expropriated landlords. In areas where agriculture was most oriented toward sale on the market or most capitalistic (as in beet cultivation, where large farms used hired labor and produced for export), the seizures were fairly orderly and well organized. These areas, which included western Ukraine, Podolia, and the Central Agricultural Region, lay behind the Red lines in the civil war. But in the Black Earth district of Ukraine, the Middle Volga, and areas where land hunger was most acute, seizures were violent, anarchic, and carried out with little help from the authorities. Several of these regions later fell behind White lines.

In many ways the peasants' own revolution confirmed the workers' and soldiers' revolutions in the towns and made impossible a restoration of the old regime. They destroyed the whole structure of governance in the countryside, replacing the old local administrations with ad hoc peasant committees and later soviets. The village communes organized the seizures, which were directed not only against noble landlords but also at the "separators," who had left the commune during the Stolypin land reform (1906–14). Most peasants generally opposed private property and the buying and selling of land, with the notable exception of those who had benefited from Stolypin's consolidation of private farms. Ironically, Bolshevik policy actually increased the power of the communes, which had organized the land seizures and received much of the land.

The assemblies of the Volga region were particularly radical already by the early summer, and there peasants expressed frustration with the socialist parties, which did not enthusiastically back their activities. This region was particularly important to the Soviet government, which held much of the Volga for most of the civil war. The bulk of the food that fed the armies and cities of the besieged republic came from the region, and some historians claim that in large part the fate of the revolution was decided on the Volga.

The agrarian revolution eliminated the nobility and the richer peasants in the countryside and created a relatively equal peasantry. By the spring of 1918 most of the confiscations had been completed, and by fall resistance by better-off peasants to redistribution had collapsed. By early 1919, 81 million acres had been transferred from the gentry, the state, or the church to peasants. Three million landless peasants received land, and gentry land was virtually eliminated. By 1919, 96.8 percent of all agricultural land was in the hands of the peasants. The overwhelming majority of peasants (86 percent) held middle-size plots, roughly eleven to twenty-one acres of land. Less than 6 percent of the peasants had less than eleven acres, and less than 2 percent had more than twenty-one. As a result of the peasant revolution in the countryside, two important political benefits fell to the Soviets: the economic base of the opposition to Bolshevism was destroyed, and active and passive support among the peasants for the new government had been established (however temporarily).

Like the tsarist regime and the Provisional Government, the Soviets faced a crisis of food supply. Worker delegations sent from individual factories tried to buy grain from the peasants, but the state opposed such activities. In May 1918 food shortages in the towns led to the creation of a "food supply dictatorship" by the Commissariat of Food Supply. The Bolsheviks argued that rich peasants, known as kulaks, were responsible for the food crisis and that the state had to wage a "struggle against the rural bourgeoisie concealing and speculating in grain." Kulaks were a category known in popular language, but no precise definition existed, then or now, for what constituted a kulak (from the Russian word meaning "fist"). The term referred to a "rich peasant," but few peasants in Russia were really rich. Kulaks were those who were productive enough to grow for the market as well as for their own families and sometimes used hired labor. Bolsheviks hardened the term and gave it the meaning of a peasant hostile to Soviet power.

The regime was friendly to those it considered "middle peasants," those who had little surplus to sell, did not hire labor, but managed to support their families through their own production. It was even friendlier to "poor peasants," those who either had too little land to support his family or were landless and forced to hire themselves or family members out for wages. Soviet leaders tried to sow dissension or class warfare within peasant ranks. On June 11, 1918, they set up Committees of the Poor Peasantry to help local procurement agencies take grain "surpluses" from the kulaks. Lenin wanted to turn the poorer peasants against the richer peasants. The Left SRs opposed creating class division within the peasantry. The peasants themselves considered all peasants to be members of one social group or family and were unenthusiastic about these committees created by outsiders. Soon the Bolsheviks themselves realized the futility of this approach, and by the fall of 1918 the Communists abolished the Committees of the Poor and fused them with the soviets.

Experimenting with a new approach, the government tried "neutralization of the middle peasants," relaxing its control over the grain trade and allowing individual purchases. The attempt to woo the middle peasants coincided with a turn by Soviet leaders toward a softer, more tolerant policy toward its opponents. At the end of 1918 Bolsheviks made an effort to convince Mensheviks and SRs to support their regime and appealed to middle-class intellectuals and technicians ("bourgeois specialists") to work with the Soviet government. They even briefly limited the activities of the Cheka. Mikhail Kalinin, a Bolshevik who was considered sympathetic to the peasantry, was appointed to the presidency of the Central Executive Committee of the Soviets on the death of Iakov Sverdlov early in 1919.

But the softer policy did not improve production in agriculture and industry. War took a toll on livestock, and tools and fertilizers were in short supply. The army called up many young men, reducing further the number of hands down on the farm. Large-scale farms, which had always been more productive, had been eliminated, and subsistence farming became the norm. Grain was cultivated but specialized crops like cotton were not. Peasants reduced the area they sowed, consumed what they could, and sent as little as possible to the towns.

By the fall of 1918 the Soviets adopted a more coercive policy, the forced requisition of grain. The state simply estimated what it needed, assessed the peasants, took what they could in exchange for whatever industrial goods they had on hand. The remainder of the grain stayed with the peasantry. Once again no grain was allowed to be privately traded. The Bolsheviks believed that the food supply crisis and the imperatives of fighting the civil war required "squeezing out" the market economy and replacing it with state distribution of goods and state-organized trade. Pragmatism and their commitment to a nonmarket socialism reinforced their emphasis on state solutions to economic problems. "If you want freedom to trade in grain in a devastated country," Lenin warned those who opposed the forced seizures of grain, "then go back, try Kolchak, try Denikin! We will fight against this to our last drop of blood. Here there will be no concessions."

Military food brigades, first formed in August 1918, now began roaming the countryside in search of food. One hundred fifty thousand Bolsheviks and their sympathizers were mobilized for the "grain front" during the civil war to seize grain by force from the peasants. The government and its agents saw the peasantry, at least its better-off members, as a dangerous enemy. When the food brigades entered the villages, they were often brutally violent. They took so much grain that peasants could not feed their families and sometimes were left with no seed grain for the coming year. Peasants resisted fiercely, and in 1918 alone they killed twenty thousand on the Soviet side. Hostility toward the Soviet authorities grew. Peasants remembered fondly that the Bolsheviks had given them the land in 1917–18; now the Communists (the new name adopted by the Bolsheviks in March 1918) were forcibly taking the grain from them. Force replaced any notion of negotiation with the peasantry. Even peasants who favored the Reds over the Whites concealed stocks and often refused to sow more land than necessary for feeding their own families. At the same time a huge underground, illegal market in grain operated. The peasants said, "He who does not speculate neither shall he eat."

Only later, after the civil war subsided, did Lenin and other Bolsheviks reevaluate their policies toward the peasantry. They later referred to forced requisitioning of grain, along with nationalization of industry, attacks on the free market and the closing of bazaars, and the attempts to militarize labor as "War Communism." A bitter necessity of war, they argued, forgetting that many in their enthusiasm for state control of the economy had seen the civil war economy as a progressive step toward socialism. After the policy was abandoned (in 1921), Lenin tried to justify this harsh approach.

> The peculiarity of War Communism consisted in the fact that we really took from the peasants all their surpluses, and sometimes even what was not surplus, but part of what was necessary to feed the peasant, took it to cover the costs of the army and to maintain the workers. We took it for the most part on credit, for paper money. Otherwise we could not beat the landlords and capitalists in a ravaged small-peasant country.

Though Bolshevik policy toward the peasantry in the first Soviet years was pragmatic rather than driven primarily by socialist goals, Soviet leaders made halfhearted attempts during the civil war to encourage the formation of large-scale collective farms. They promoted three types of large-scale farms with varying degrees of collective ownership. The *sovkhozy*, or state farms, hired labor and paid them wages. The *kommuny*, or communes (not to be confused with the *obshchiny*, the peasant village communes), were worked by peasants collectively and shared the proceeds. Here, as in the state farms, the land belonged to the state. Finally, in the *arteli*, or collectives, the land belonged to the peasants, but they pooled their resources and labor and marketed their products together. Ten years later the *artel* would be the basic form on which the collective farms (the *kolkhozy*) of Stalin's revolution would be created. Except for a small minority, the land-hungry peasants were not interested in such collective forms of farming, and those that existed were usually set up by the government or by workers who had left the towns for the countryside in 1918–19.

Peasants fought on both sides in the civil war but preferred to fight in their own districts and not to leave home and fight on some distant front. Increasingly they saw the war as the struggle of the townspeople and not their fight. Those peasants who fell behind White lines experienced the same kind of grain seizures as those behind Red lines. Treated particularly badly by the Whites in 1918–19, they turned in greater numbers toward the Reds during 1919–20. The Volga peasants were among the most enthusiastic Red Army recruits. But desertion was very high, especially when the front moved far from the farm. It is estimated that by late 1919 there were 1.5 million deserters in Russia. Many left to return home to help with the harvest, while others were concerned about their families, while others were upset at the shortages of supplies in the army.

While Reds and Whites were fighting each other, hundreds of peasant wars were being waged behind the lines. Peasants in the Volga region resisted the efforts of Soviet authorities to establish themselves in the villages and longed for a return of the village democracy that they had enjoyed in 1917–18. In the south of Russia a huge peasant war, involving one hundred fifty thousand people, resisted the taking of peasant grain. The rebels called for soviets without Communists; their slogans were "Long live the power of the Soviets on the Platform of the October Revolution!" and "Down with the Communists, long live the Bolsheviks!" Peasants purged the soviets of Communists and reelected them more democratically. Peasant rebels usually had only local interests and were opposed to central government in any form. The Left SRs supported the peasant uprisings, but could not guide them along their own political lines. The Soviet government arrested their leaders, Maria Spiridonova and Isak Steinberg, in February 1919 because they wanted to replace the Bolshevik regime in Moscow with an all-socialist alliance. Ultimately, the massive peasant wars in Tambov province and Ukraine convinced the Communists that their policies toward the countryside had to change.

The hard blows from recruiters and tax collectors only reinforced the peasants' desire to be left alone. In the first six months of Soviet rule, the state was still far away, and peasants simply ran their own economy and social life. But once the food supply crisis in the cities became acute, the Bolsheviks intensified efforts to gain some control over the countryside. Returning peasant soldiers, most of whom were either Bolsheviks or Left SRs, were key to establishing the power of the soviets in the villages. They set themselves up as leaders of the revolution in the countryside, challenging the traditional hierarchies. and called for "stealing back what has been stolen." Some became Soviet officials; others turned to banditry. Red Army men also established themselves as local authorities in the district towns. By 1922, for example, 62.5 percent of village soviet chairmen in Tsaritsyn province (on the Volga) were Red Army exservicemen. The Communist Party as well grew in the countryside during the civil war, even though many of its members were pulled into the Red Army, and the percentage of peasants in the party increased steadily, from 14.5 percent in 1918 to 28.2 percent in 1921.

Nevertheless, Soviet power remained weak in the countryside from the revolution until Stalin's collectivization of the early 1930s. The Communists were faced by an extremely difficult problem of governing the vast country over which they reigned. Though former peasants, now soldiers, became the representatives of Soviet power in the countryside, most ordinary peasants drifted away from soviet institutions back into the commune. A dual power structure reemerged in the countryside, soviets in towns, communes in the villages. Bolsheviks sat on district executive committees with little real influence among the peasants. Peasant patriarchs and respected local leaders possessed far greater authority at the grassroots than any outsider. Tensions developed between representatives of the Soviet government and the local parish priests. After the Soviet government legislated the separation of church and state on January 23, 1918, the state took over education, most of which had been in church hands. The clergy resisted, and in some villages peasants defended the church when the Bolsheviks attacked it. The villages remained in many ways free of the urban-based authority of the state, and after 1921 much of the economic power over the production and sale of grain would also fall into the hands of the peasants.

Why the Bolsheviks Won the Civil War

At least 1 million people died in combat or from White or Red acts of terror during the Russian civil war. Several million more died from disease, hunger, and the cold. About a million people left the country and never returned. The Red victory had been earned with enormous sacrifice and pain on all sides. From a strategic point of view the Bolsheviks had had several advantages. They held the center of Russia, the most densely populated parts, including the industrial heartland and the two major cities, Petrograd and Moscow, throughout the war. Soviet-held Russia had a population of about 60 million, while the most reliable territories held by the Whites held only 8 or 9 million. The Bolsheviks were able to mobilize more people more easily than the Whites. Their lines of supply and communication were shorter than those of the Whites, who were scattered on several fronts hundreds or even thousands of miles apart. The Reds also benefited from the war materiel left by the tsarist army, while the Whites depended on military supplies they received from the Allies or the enemy.

The Bolsheviks also enjoyed the prestige of ruling from the traditional capital of Russia. To many in the provinces they occupied the symbolic center of Russian authority, the Kremlin, and though as internationalists the Bolsheviks refrained from using the rhetoric or rituals of Russian nationalism, they reaped some support from former tsarist officers and others with feelings of patriotism. More than the Whites and even more than other Bolsheviks, Lenin was sensitive to the multiethnic character of the Russian and Soviet states, and he promised non-Russians self-determination and equal rights in a new socialist federation. On the other hand, the Whites, who employed symbols of the Russian "nation," found that the strength of grassroots Russian nationalism was not very great. Their slogan, "Russia, one and indivisible," had little appeal either to the lower classes or to non-Russians. Localism, identification with the village or region, was far stronger for most peasants than was loyalty to any idea of a Russian nation or, indeed, the Soviet state.

Rather than nationalism the Soviet forces benefited from the promise of revolutionary social change—the abolition of the old landed nobility and the partition of the land among the peasant masses. The peasants were very suspicious of the *burzhui* (bourgeoisie), the propertied classes, and severely damaged Kolchak and Denikin's efforts in debilitating peasant uprisings behind their lines. Though the Reds too faced peasant revolts, at the critical moments the rural areas behind the Red lines remained quiet. However much the peasants hated the Communists, who took their grain by force, their hatred of the old regime, which would restore the land to the landlords, ran far deeper. Extremely important was the support that the Bolsheviks were able to secure from workers in the towns, who usually proved to be their most reliable soldiers. In Bolshevik eyes workers were a breed apart, the raison d'être for their revolution, and predictable, dependable comrades-in-arms. In the new social order, where class origin was believed to be a key determinant of consciousness and behavior, Bolsheviks expected workers to be their natural allies, and recruiters favored them in the army and the party.

The White forces were unable to find a social base for their movement. They remained an army without a loyal population. Their unwillingness to consider social reforms and their reliance on a purely military solution alienated significant groups in the population. The Whites suffered from their inability to unite all the anti-Bolsheviks into a single movement. Monarchist officers hated the moderate socialists almost as much as they hated the Bolsheviks, and liberal politicians remained under suspicion by more conservative elements. Some Whites favored the Germans, others the Allies, and their program for a single, united Russia alienated the non-Russians.

The Bolsheviks proved to be successful state-builders able to create an effective bureaucracy and army. Political skills and confidence in their vision aided the Bolsheviks in organizing the Red Army and forging a disciplined party apparatus. Propaganda was supplemented by terror and violence, and the Bolsheviks were prepared to be ruthless to advance their cause. Though Whites too could be ruthless, in the deadly competition for the loyalty of ordinary people they were far less effective than their opponents.

The Bolsheviks won the war, but at an extraordinarily high price. After the fighting died down, the Soviets were left with a devastated country of war-weary veterans, disgruntled and hungry peasants, and hundreds of thousands of orphans. A Red Guardsman who had served through the war mused at its end, could it be "that without a world revolution we had given birth to a classless, starving collection of people, with silent factories and mills?"

Suggestions for Further Reading

For a survey of scholarship on the social history of the civil war years, see Diane Koenker, William G. Rosenberg, and Ronald Grigor Suny (eds.), *Party, State, and Society in the Russian Civil War: Explorations in Social History* (Bloomington, Ind., 1989). Perhaps the most important social history of the civil war is Orlando Figes, *Peasant Russia, Civil War: The Volga Countryside in Revolution, 1917–1921* (Oxford, 1989). The economy is dealt with in Sylvana Malle, *The Economic Organization of War Communism, 1918–1921* (Cambridge, 1985). On the military aspects, there are useful accounts by Evan Mawdsley, *The Russ-*

ian Civil War (Boston, 1987); and John F. Bradley, *The Civil War in Russia, 1917–1920* (London, 1975). For discussions of the politics of the war, several works should be consulted: Peter Kenez, *Civil War in South Russia*, 2 vols. (Berkeley, Calif., 1971–77); William G. Rosenberg, *Liberals in the Russian Revolution* (Princeton, N.J., 1974); and Vladimir Brovkin, *The Mensheviks after October: Socialist Opposition and the Rise of the Bolshevik Dictatorship* (Ithaca, N.Y., 1987); (ed.), *Dear Comrades: Menshevik Reports on the Bolshevik Revolution and the Civil War* (Stanford, Calif., 1991); and *Behind the Front Lines of the Civil War: Political Parties and Social Movements in Russia, 1918–1922* (Princeton, N.J., 1994). On the intellectuals' opposition to the Bolsheviks, see Jane Burbank, *Intelligentsia and Revolution: Russian Views of Bolshevism, 1917–1922* (New York and Oxford, 1986). A fascinating memoir of the period is by Isak Steinberg, *In the Workshop of the Revolution* (New York, 1953), which should be supplemented with the collection of documents in James Bunyan, *The Origin of Forced Labor in the Soviet State, 1917–1921* (Baltimore, Mar., 1967). One of the most thoroughly explored topics is foreign intervention in Russia, as found in George Kennan, *Soviet-American Relations, 1917–1920*, 2 vols. (Princeton, N.J., 1956–58); Richard H. Ullman, *Anglo-Soviet Relations, 1917–1921*, 3 vols. (Princeton, N.J., 1961–72); John A. White, *The Siberian Intervention* (Princeton, N.J., 1950); Betty Unterberger, *America's Siberian Expedition, 1918–1920* (Durham, N.C., 1956); John M. Thompson, *Russia, Bolshevism, and the Versailles Peace* (Princeton, N.J., 1966).

CHAPTER 4
Nationalism and Revolution

The Russian Empire had formed over hundreds of years, with a largely Russian population at its core and dozens of other ethnicities on its peripheries. The largest contiguous land empire in the world, tsarist Russia was content for much of its history to rule its non-Russian peoples in a mixed, contradictory system. In some places direct military government was applied, in others local elites that had assimilated into the Russian administrative system held sway, and in still others people were granted various forms of constitutionalism, for example, in the Grand Duchy of Finland and the Kingdom of Poland. For the grand dukes of Muscovy and the early tsars, empire building was merely the extension of the tsar's sovereignty, through the institutions of his household and court, over the adjacent borderlands. The "gathering of Russian lands" meant at first absorbing territories populated by Great Russians, later incorporating the Volga regions held by the Kazan Tatars, and still later annexing the Baltic littoral settled by Finnic peoples, Germans, and others. The rulers of the empire understood that they governed a multinational state, and they referred to the empire as *rossiiskaia* (of Russia) rather than with the ethnic term *russkaia* (Russian). Russia's emperors saw themselves as foreigners who had come to this chaotic land to bring order. Separate from the people, they brought the benefits of civilization to ethnic Russians and non-Russians alike. Only in the nineteenth century, when challenged by the rising nationalism prevalent in Europe, did Russian tsars tentatively begin to identify themselves with their own people. That nationalizing of the monarchy, in turn, distanced the rulers from the non-Russians, who themselves were gaining a sense of their own cultural distinctiveness.

At times the regime was extraordinarily tolerant of differences; at others it was callously repressive. In the eighteenth and early nineteenth century Russification was limited to the extension of bureaucratic absolutism and serfdom over selected non-Russian peoples. Besides this administrative Russification, non-Russians engaged in spontaneous self-Russification—learning Russian, dressing like Europeans, chancing the endings of their names, even converting to Orthodoxy—to improve their chances for advancement in society. But after 1881 these relatively benign forms of acculturation were supplemented by an intermittent state policy of forced cultural homogenization. Tsarist officials considered the Slavic peoples, the Belorussians and Ukrainians, to be part of a greater Russian nation and forcefully discouraged the use of the Slavic languages in the western provinces. Though confronted with a compact population of tens of millions of Poles in the formerly abolished Kingdom of Poland (1815–31), the government suppressed education in the Polish language, turned Warsaw University into an institution of Russification, restricted Polish ownership of land, and even forced shopkeepers to hang signs with Russian above or larger than the Polish. Driven from education and employment in the bureaucracy, Poles, like the Jews, faced lives of permanent disability. No matter how loyal they might in fact be, the regime regarded them—and after 1881 most other non-Russians—as alien and suspicious, inferior and unworthy of full inclusion in imperial society unless they fully assimilated by using Russian and converting to Orthodoxy. Meeting obstacles to advancement in a discriminatory society drove many of the frustrated non-Russians into active opposition.

Most of the non-Russian peoples of the tsarist empire were overwhelmingly peasant. Though they spoke different languages and often experienced discrimination from Russian officials or landlords of a different nationality, they did not automatically translate their social grievances into nationalism. The most powerful identification of the common people was with their religion, but also with their locality and their peasant status. Non-Russian peasants identified with their nearby ethnic compatriots but not with the abstract concept of nation. Like socialism, nationalism was an ideology brought in by intellectuals and activists, and those nationalities that were more directly affected by industrial capitalism and had a working class of their own, such as the Georgians, Latvians, Estonians, Jews, and to an extent, the Armenians, came into more immediate contact with their own radical intelligentsia and developed political movements of great power. Peoples who had little presence in the towns, like Lithuanians, Ukrainians, and Belorussians, were slower to develop national consciousness than those more directly affected by urbanization, education, and their own intelligentsia. Furthest removed from the social revolution of industrialism were the Muslim peoples of the empire. Some Muslims, such as the Azerbaijanis and the Volga Tatars, had a significant if small urban presence, but the vast majority of Central Asians, many of whom were nomadic or seminomadic, had relatively little urban experience and almost no contact with the socialist or nationalist intelligentsia. Here conservative clerics dominated the public sphere, and Islamic reformism and an embryonic nationalism were found only among a small group of intellectuals and activists. The Russians, even the radical intellectuals among them, considered Muslims to be a dark, unenlightened mass, and in Baku and Tashkent they devoted most of their educational and organizational efforts to local Christians rather than to the Muslims to whom they could not speak.

Transcaucasia

To the south of Muscovy, across the Caucasus Mountains, between the Black Sea and the Caspian Sea lay the mountainous isthmus that Russians called

Transcaucasia. In the medieval principalities, kingdoms, and emirates of the Georgians, Armenians, and Islamic peoples, politics was a local affair, infused with dynastic and religious conflicts and absent a generalized, secular, ultimately territorial or ethnocultural sense of homeland or nation. For medieval Georgians or Armenians, the primary identity was with religion and the church, the primary loyalty to the local dynast. After the eleventh century, when the invasions of the Seljuk Turks pushed back the power of Byzantium and subdued the Armenians, the Georgians alone remained precariously independent. After almost two thousand years of political presence, no Armenian state existed between 1375 and 1918. Only with the coming of the Russians at the beginning of the nineteenth century did the last Georgian monarchs lose their thrones and the bulk of the Georgian lands come once again under a single political authority.

Georgians, who lived compactly in their historic territory, were largely a peasant people with a dominant noble elite that within a generation after the Russian conquest was successfully integrated into the tsarist civil and military service. Armenians, by the nineteenth century scattered and divided between three empires (Russian, Ottoman, and Persian), were almost nowhere a compact majority, except in Erevan province. Their dominant elite was the Armenian merchants and manufacturers who developed industry and trade in both Turkey and Caucasia, pioneering the development of Baku oil and constituting the entrepreneurial middle class of Tiflis, the ancient Georgian capital.

In the course of the nineteenth century, three related processes initiated a long transformation of the ethnoreligious communities of Transcaucasia into more politically conscious and mobilized nationalities. First, the imposition of tsarist rule eliminated barriers between Georgian principalities, brought Armenians of Russia and those who lived in formerly Persian provinces under a single legal order, and imposed uniform laws and taxation systems on the Muslims of Transcaucasia. Second, tsarist imperial rule brought relative peace and security and fostered a rise in commerce and industry, the growth of towns, the building of railroads, and the slow end to the isolation of many villages. Third, the imposition of bureaucratic absolutism on the looser political structures of Transcaucasia and the initial undermining of local elites gave rise to resistance both by the gentry and the peasants. A new educational system became the crucible of a secular intelligentsia inspired by Western humanism and science. Educated Caucasians were torn between the benefits and burdens of Russian autocratic rule. Some became loyal servants of the tsar, even members of the nobility; others turned toward the revolutionary movement.

The three major peoples of Transcaucasia developed unevenly and at different rates. Armenians were the most urban, Azerbaijanis the least. Georgians and Azerbaijanis were the more compact populations, living in coherent territories, whereas Armenians were dispersed. Clerics dominated Azerbaijani society, the old national nobility held sway among Georgians, and a merchant middle class was the dominant social group among the Armenians. Intellectuals of all three peoples were deeply influenced by the debates in Russia and shared an appreciation for the insights of Western Marxists. But the national-

ist movements among the three peoples were distinct: among Armenians nationalism overwhelmed socialism as the leading ideology; for most politically
active Georgians Marxism predominated over nationalism; and among Azerbaijanis the influence of either socialism or nationalism was quite limited and
loyalty to Islam overwhelmed secular ideologies.

The demographically dominant people in eastern Transcaucasia were
known in the nineteenth century as Tatars, but by the late 1930s the term "Azerbaijani," favored by the national leaders, was universally adopted. Linguistically related to the Ottoman Turks who came to dominate Anatolia, the Caucasian Muslims of Azerbaijan were for centuries under Persian social and
cultural influence and became Shi'i, rather than Sunni Muslims. No specifically
Azerbaijani state existed before 1918, and rather than imagining themselves as
part of a continuous national tradition, like the Georgians and Armenians, the
Muslims of Transcaucasia saw themselves as part of the larger Muslim world.
Annexation to the Russian Empire early in the nineteenth century separated
the Azerbaijani Turks of Caucasia from the majority of Azerbaijanis, who remained in Iran.

On both sides of the border the Azerbaijanis were a largely rural population, though small merchant and working classes grew up in Russia and Iran.
As the city of Baku on the Caspian became the major source of oil for Russia,
tens of thousands of Iranian workers streamed across the border. But they were
given the dirtiest jobs and the lowest pay of any workers. With Armenians and
Russians in the middle of the social and economic hierarchy, and local Christians and Europeans at the top, poor Muslim workers developed resentment
against skilled workers and employers, most of whom were Christians. Russians and Armenians lived in the segregated central part of the town, and Muslims clustered in poorer outer districts. Ethnic and religious differences, enhanced by feelings of inferiority and superiority, defined the battlelines in
bloody clashes between Azerbaijanis and local Armenians in 1905 and 1918.
No single, coherent ideology or movement dominated Azerbaijani intellectuals, though by 1905 a growing number had adopted the program "Turkify, Is-
lamicize, Europeanize." At the same time, however, anxiety about the perceived
Armenian threat, distance from and hostility to this privileged element within
their midst, and a feeling of connection to other Muslims, particularly Turks
became part of an Azerbaijani sense of self.

Though Azerbaijani political activists participated in the revival of Muslim organizations in the first year of the revolution, traveling to congresses and
issuing manifestos, in Baku the political center was held by Russian Social Democrats and Armenian nationalists. The Azerbaijanis identified Soviet power
in 1917–18 with the Christians, and in March 1918 the city soviet in Baku put
down a revolt by Muslims with the help of Armenian nationalists. The Baku
Commune, a Soviet government that ruled Baku from April to late July 1918,
failed in its attempt to rally the peoples of Transcaucasia around Soviet power.
The Bolsheviks met indifference or active resistance when they attempted to
extend their sway over the surrounding countryside and the Azerbaijani town
of Gandja (Elisavetpol). Though the Azerbaijani nationalist leaders, located in
Gandja, had been largely pro-Russian in the prewar years, they welcomed the

leverage and support offered by the advancing Ottoman Turkish army, and they entered Baku with those Ottoman troops. In September 1918 Azerbaijanis took their revenge for the "March Days," killing between nine and thirty thousand local Armenians.

Azerbaijani nationalists had declared Azerbaijan an independent state on May 28, 1918, but even after they secured control over Baku, they faced a mixed population of Russian, Armenian, and Muslim workers who had undergone a long socialist and trade unionist education. Never fully secure in their own capital, where Bolshevism had deep roots, the nationalists relied on foreigners, first the Turks and later the British, to back them against the Reds. Among the peasantry, whom they claimed to represent, national consciousness was still largely absent. Once the British left, independent Azerbaijan's days were numbered. When the Red Army marched into Baku in April 1920, there was little resistance.

For two millennia, if not longer, Armenians and Georgians have had recognizable identities, first mentioned in the inscriptions and manuscripts of their Iranian and Greek neighbors and later (from the fifth century A.D.) in texts in their own languages. Since the fourth century A.D. they have been Christian peoples, yet distinct from one another. The Georgians became part of the Orthodox church, to which the Greeks and Russians adhered, while the Armenians remained in a unique national church with its own Christology. Largely a rural people, Georgians were divided into a peasant majority and a declining nobility that failed to make a successful adjustment to the post-emancipation economy (after 1861). Through the nineteenth century the Georgian nobility steadily lost its dominant economic and political position to Armenian merchants and artisans who had formed the Caucasian middle class since the Middle Ages. The Georgian intelligentsia, themselves the offspring of the déclassé nobility, turned to a radical analysis of Georgia's condition and in the 1890s adopted a specifically Marxist worldview that saw both the bourgeoisie (which in this case was largely Armenian) and the autocracy (which was Russian) as enemies of Georgian social and political freedom. Instead of uniting around a conservative nationalism, the social and national struggles were successfully merged under a Marxist leadership ready to link up with all-Russian social democracy.

The natural constituency for Georgian Social Democrats, the workers, was supplemented by 1905 by broad support (almost unique in the Russian empire) among the peasantry. Georgian Marxist intellectuals had joined the more moderate wing of the Russian Social Democratic Party, the Mensheviks, and in the first years of the twentieth century found themselves at the head of a genuinely supraclass national liberation movement. The Mensheviks easily won the elections to the four state dumas from 1906–12, controlled soviets and councils in the towns and countryside in 1917, and were the overwhelming choice of Georgians in the elections to the Constituent Assembly. In Georgia a mass national movement had been achieved in the first decade of the twentieth century, but instead of adopting an ideology of exclusivist nationalism, Georgians adopted an expressly nonnationalist and democratic socialism.

With the October Revolution, the Georgian Mensheviks acted swiftly to disarm the Russian garrison in Tiflis and establish local soviet power. Refusing to recognize the Bolshevik government in Petrograd, the Transcaucasian socialist parties (with the exception of the local Bolsheviks) gradually separated the region from the rest of Russia by first declaring autonomy and later independence for the whole of Transcaucasia and finally establishing three separate independent republics. Certainly the most viable and stable state in Transcaucasia was Georgia. Here social democracy was well grounded in both the working class and the peasantry. When the Georgian government invited the Germans to send troops to Georgia, it was not for the purpose of shoring up their regime internally but to discourage attack from outside by the Bolsheviks or the Turks.

Ironically, the Georgian nation-state was formed and led by Marxists who expected a democratic revolution in Russia that would solve in one sweep the people's ethnic and social oppression. Instead, the Marxists found themselves at the head of an independent "bourgeois" state, the managers of the "democratic revolution" in one small country. Unquestionably Georgia had an excellent chance for political survival. Not only did the Mensheviks have the support of the great majority of the Georgian people, but they managed to establish a stable multiparty democracy and begin a program of social and economic reform. The central Soviet government in Moscow, however, did not permit them to demonstrate the potential for democratic socialism in a postrevolutionary state. By 1920 a powerful group within the Bolshevik party pushed for an uprising within Georgia, to be followed by an invasion by the Red Army. Though Lenin initially opposed this cynical disregard for the evident influence of the Georgian Social Democrats, he backed down in face of the fait accompli engineered by Stalin and his close collaborator, Sergo Orjonikidze. In February 1921 the Red Army marched into Georgia and the Mensheviks fled to Europe. Three years later the Social Democrats organized an uprising, but the local Communist government brutally suppressed the rebels and executed many of their leaders. The national revolution led by democratic socialists was over.

Within the Russian empire, Armenians were scattered in urban centers with a relatively compact peasantry in Erevan province. At the same time, an influential diaspora connected the educated and business people of Anatolia and Transcaucasia with Europe, the Middle East, and even India. Despite the increase in the number of Armenians in the nineteenth and early twentieth centuries and their economic and political dominion over the largest cities of the Caucasus, Armenians increasingly perceived themselves to be in a vulnerable demographic and political position. The relative status of the largest Armenian community, on the Armenian plateau of eastern Anatolia (present-day Turkey), worsened with the rapid growth of the Kurdish population, the inmigration of Circassians and other Balkan and Caucasian Muslims, and the out-migration of Armenians, particularly after the massacres of 1894–96.

Within Russia Armenian clerics and intellectuals developed schools, published newspapers, and expanded popular literature and drama, all as part of a "national revival." In contrast to the Georgians, the Armenian revolutionary parties, founded at the end of the 1880s and the beginning of the 1890s, chose not to work with other parties of the Russian Empire and sent their young militants to organize in Turkey. The leading Armenian political party by the early twentieth century was the Armenian Revolutionary Federation, or Dashnaktsutiun. When the tsarist government requisitioned Armenian church properties in 1903, the Dashnaks organized resistance and gained wide support among city dwellers and peasants in the Caucasus as the principal defender of the Armenian church.

In the spring of 1915, with Turkey at war with Russia and Armenians living on both sides of the border, missionaries, diplomats, travelers, and victims reported that the Turkish military was systematically murdering adult male Armenians and forcibly deporting hundreds of thousands of others. Though the exact number of those killed or deported may never be known, estimates run from 600,000 to 2.5 million Armenian deaths in the years 1915–22. Tens of thousands of refugees fled to the Caucasus with the retreating Russian armies, and the cities of Baku and Tiflis filled with Armenians from Turkey. Driven from their historic homeland in Anatolia, the bulk of the Armenians were now confined to the small territory of Russian Armenia.

Each nationality in Transcaucasia had to choose between Soviet Russia, the Entente, or the Germans, and each national leadership chose a different path. The central political issue became self-defense, and in the context of Russian retreat and Turkish-German advance it quickly took on an ethnic dimension. By late May 1918 the Georgians opted for the Germans rather than the Bolsheviks; the Azerbaijanis turned expectantly toward the Turks, the multinational city of Baku came under local soviet power; and the Armenians turned toward the Entente. The principal threats to the Armenians came from the Ottoman Turks and the Azerbaijanis, and Caucasian Armenians rallied around the Dashnaktsutiun, which became the de facto leader of the nation.

The only realistic hope for an ethnic Armenian homeland in the postgenocide period was the small enclave around Erevan, which in May 1918 became the center of a fragile independent republic. The first Republic of Armenia lasted only two and a half years, from May 28, 1918, until December 2, 1920. A land of sick and hungry refugees, threatened by Turkish invasion and armed clashes with both Georgia and Azerbaijan, tiny Armenia managed to maintain a relatively democratic government. American aid sustained the starving population, but the claims of the Armenian government to territory that the Turks refused to give up led to the final crisis of the fledgling state. As the armies of the Turkish nationalist Kemal Ataturk pushed into Armenia, the Dashnak government concluded an agreement with Soviet Russia to establish a Soviet government in Armenia. After a few months of Soviet power, Dashnak-led rebels overthrew the new government, but the Red Army returned from Georgia to reestablish Soviet authority that would last for the next seventy years.

Ukrainians and Belorussians

Except for a small intelligentsia, Ukrainians were almost entirely peasants. Unlike most Russian peasants, they were not organized into village communes but held individual farmsteads. Landowners and officials in the region were Poles or Russians, whereas the commercial bourgeoisie was largely Jewish. Ukraine had developed a distinct ethnic culture and language in the long period from the fall of Kiev to the Mongols (1240) through the Polish dominion (1569) to the union with Russia (1654). Early in the nineteenth century nationalist intellectuals promoted the notion of Ukrainian distinctiveness, and the romantics Taras Shevchenko and Panko Kulish formed a Ukrainian literary language from the vernacular of the southeast. The brief flourishing of Ukrainian intellectual culture in the tsarist empire in the first two thirds of the nineteenth century was curtailed after the Polish insurrection of 1863, however, particularly in 1876, when the tsarist state prohibited public expression in Ukrainian. With the restrictions on Ukrainian culture in the Russian Empire, Galicia, the western Ukrainian regions under Austrian rule, became the center for literary expression and a popular nationalism. In contrast, the movement of Ukrainian peasants in the Russian Empire in 1905–7 had only superficial nationalistic characteristics. Russian Ukraine, a vast territory with non-Ukrainians dominating urban centers and state-imposed constraints on ethnic intellectual life, developed neither a coherent mass-based national movement nor even a widely shared sense of a Ukrainian nation in the decades before the twentieth-century revolutions.

With the outbreak of the February Revolution in 1917, an articulate and active nationalist elite in Ukraine, made up of middle-class professionals, confronted both the Provisional Government in Petrograd and later the Sovnarkom in Moscow with its demand for autonomy and self-rule. At first the local national council, or Rada, was committed to finding a democratic solution to the political crisis; its leaders wanted to remain within a federated Russian state and launch a radical program of land reform. Ukrainian politicians managed in June 1917 to extract from Petrograd some recognition of Ukrainian autonomy. As central control weakened over Ukraine, the idea of a unique Ukraine gained strength. In the November elections to the Constituent Assembly, the peasantry overwhelmingly supported Ukrainian parties, particularly Ukrainian peasant parties. The peasants in Ukraine preferred parties and leaders of their own ethnicity, people who spoke to them in their own language and promised to secure their local interests. They were ethnically aware, preferring their own kind to strangers, though not yet moved by a passion for an abstract nation, and certainly not willing to sacrifice their lives for anything beyond the village. Yet the revolution, which toppled old authorities and allegiances, mobilized and politicized formerly passive peasants and accelerated the protracted process of nationality formation.

Ukrainian peasants were most concerned about the agrarian question and their own suffering in the years of war and scarcity. They thought of themselves as peasants first, which for them was the same as being Ukrainian (or whatever they might have called themselves locally). Their principal hope was for agrarian reform and the end of the oppression identified with the state and the city. Russians, Jews, and Poles were the sources of that oppression, and it is conceivable that for many peasants the promise of autonomy was seen as the means to ending the onerous and arbitrary power of these groups.

The years of civil war in Ukraine were volatile, with nationalists fighting Bolsheviks, Bolsheviks allying with and then breaking with anarchists and "Green" peasant movements. The bid by Ukrainian nationalists for autonomy, and then for independence at the end of 1917, was unacceptable to most Bolsheviks, particularly those in Ukraine. Even when Lenin advocated a more conciliatory line toward Ukraine, his followers refused to concede to the nationalists. When the nationalist Rada was unable effectively to resist the Bolshevik advance in January 1918, it turned as a last resort to the Germans. But the Germans soon began requisitioning grain and terrorizing the peasants. When the nationalists failed to back up their own agrarian reform, support among the peasants rapidly evaporated. The nationalist cause was linked by many to foreign intervention. To antinationalist elements, particularly in towns, the only viable alternative to social chaos, foreign dependence, and Ukrainian chauvinism appeared to be the Bolsheviks. But like the German-backed nationalists, the Bolsheviks squandered their potential peasant support. Where and when they were in charge, they effectively disenfranchised the middle and wealthier peasantry and instituted a new round of requisitioning. Formerly sympathetic villagers turned against the Soviets, and the final Bolshevik victory depended on support from the workers, Russian and Russified, of the cities as well as the Donbass and the Red Army. Here the Bolsheviks were stronger than any of their rivals.

Among the most peasant of the peoples of the Russian Empire were the Belorussians, those eastern Slavs who had succumbed neither to Polish culture and language (as had much of the local nobility) nor to the Russian language and culture of the towns. Nearly three-quarters of the people of the Belorussian provinces were illiterate. They spoke up to twenty local dialects that fell between Russian, Polish, and Ukrainian. The towns and cities of the region were predominantly inhabited by Russians, Poles, and most numerously Jews. Belorussian nationalism was never very influential in the multiethnic towns, or among the mass of peasants primarily concerned with local social problems. The peasants made little distinction between a generalized Russian culture and a specifically Belorussian nationality. The closeness of the Belorussian language to Russian and other Slavic languages of the area permitted easy access to related cultures and blurred ethnic boundaries. Only in the last decades of the nineteenth century did a Belorussian ethnic nationalism find its voice, and even then it was part of the broader discourse of the Russian revolutionary movement. In 1902 Belorussian students in the Russian capital, with the help of Polish socialists, founded the Belorussian Revolutionary Hramada (party or association), which proposed the formation of a Belorussian state as a first step toward the solution of social problems.

The progress of the revolution in Belorussia was fundamentally influenced by the Russo-German battle lines that ran through the region. Russian soldiers, increasingly influenced by Bolshevism, played a key role in the formation of the first soviets and the establishment of a Soviet government in Minsk just after the October Revolution. The peasants remained outside the political struggle in the towns and gave little encouragement to either the socialists or the nationalists. In the elections to the Constituent Assembly in November, the Bolsheviks secured over 60 percent of the vote (in large part thanks to soldiers), while the Hramada failed to elect a single delegate. As winter approached, the uneven struggle in the towns pitted the nationalists and moderate socialists against the Bolsheviks with their supporters in the Russian Army. In December the Hramada called a Belorussian National Congress, which refused to recognize the local Council of Peoples Commissars. When on December 17–18 the congress declared Belorussia independent, the Bolsheviks used their military muscle to disperse the delegates. Soviet power in Belorussia lasted only until the Brest-Litovsk Treaty forced the Russians to retreat, and the Germans backed the nationalists' declaration of independence (March 25, 1918). The peasants, who had been taking what land they could since late 1917, resisted the German occupation and gravitated toward the Communists. When the Germans retreated at the end of the war, the Russian Communists formed a Belorussian Communist party, which in turn established a Belorussian Soviet Socialist Republic (BSSR) and then a joint Lithuanian-Belorussian Soviet Republic (Litbel). But in the future both Belorussia and Ukraine would become pawns in the larger struggle between Soviet Russia and newly independent Poland.

Poland and the Russo-Polish War

One of the victors in World War I was a state that had not existed as an independent country at the outbreak of the war—Poland. A great east European power in the seventeenth century and the major rival of Muscovy, Poland disappeared as a state in the late eighteenth century when Russia, Prussia, and Austria partitioned Poland among them. After the Napoleonic wars of the early nineteenth century, Russia dominated most of Poland, first as an autonomous kingdom within the empire and later, after failed Polish rebellions, as a province. Polish nobles and intellectuals harbored the dream of restoring Polish independence for over a century, and European intellectuals, including Karl Marx, took up their cause. In June 1918 the Allies, led by President Wilson, decided that one of their war aims would be the creation of an independent Poland with access to the sea.

Polish nationalists were interested in recreating a large state that included all the territory held by Poland in 1772, before the partitions. However, a disagreement in principle arose: should states be based on self-determination for the ethnic group(s) now living in a territory or on the historical claims of those who once occupied and held the territory? The principal problem was that large German, Ukrainian, and Belorussian populations were contained within regions claimed by the Polish nationalists. The victorious Allies recognized a recreated, large Polish state, but the eastern border with the Soviet republics remained disputed. The leader of the newly independent Polish state, Marshal Jozef Pilsudski, had dreams of a grand eastern European federation that included Russian borderlands. To the Soviets Poland, which seized Vilna in April 1919 from the Communist Litbel Soviet Republic, appeared to be an aggressive and expansionist state.

At first Poland remained neutral in the Russian civil war, afraid of a victory by the Whites who might want to retake Poland for Russia. But Pilsudski was convinced that war with Russia was inevitable, and in April 1920 he issued orders to prepare for "a definitive settlement of the Russian question." He wanted an independent Ukraine as a buffer between Soviet Russia and Poland, but the Soviet government rejected the idea. Pilsudski then made a secret agreement with Simon Petliura, an anti-Soviet Ukrainian leader, pledging support for an independent Ukraine if Petliura recognized Polish claims to areas of eastern Galicia. On April 25, 1920, the Poles, allied with Petliura, began a "liberation drive" into Ukraine and took Kiev in early May. Though they met little resistance in their campaign, the Polish army was suspect in the eyes of the Ukrainian peasantry, which by this time was both anti-Bolshevik and anti-Polish. Petliura's alliance with Poland only served to compromise his movement among the peasants.

The Soviet government had no plans to conquer Poland, though some Bolsheviks had advocated a tactic of "revolution from without" in the Baltic and in Finland. But with the invasion of Ukraine, the Communists now saw "capitalist" Poland as a threat to Moscow, and mass rallies were held to protest the Polish advance. Polish Communists, like Dzerzhinski and Karl Radek, warned against trying to "liberate" Poland with the Red Army, for Russophobia was very strong in Poland. But Red Army leaders, like future Marshall Mikhail Tukhachevskii, wanted to launch an attack, and Lenin, Zinoviev, and Kamenev saw the war as an opportunity to turn the revolution westward. In June 1920 the Red Army counterattacked. The Poles retreated, and the retreat turned into a rout. Lord Curzon, the British foreign secretary, warned the Red Army not to cross the ethnic boundary (the Curzon Line) into Polish territory. Radek attempted to caution Lenin but failed, and on July 24, the Red Army crossed the Curzon Line and took Bialystok.

The Soviets set up a Polish Provisional Revolutionary Committee (Revkom), which was greeted enthusiastically in Bialystok, a city in which three-quarters of the population were Jews who were not happy about Polish independence. In August the Red Army neared Warsaw. But the Revkom and the Red Army found little support among the Polish population, which saw them (as Lenin was forced to concede) "not as brothers and liberators" but as enemies. The Poles counterattacked and routed the Reds. An armistice was signed in October, and in March 1921 the Treaty of Riga established a large Poland with Ukrainian and Belorussian areas within the state. Those areas would remain in Poland until 1939 when another partition, between Nazi Germany and Stalin's USSR, eliminated the Polish state once more and annexed western Belorussia and western Ukraine to their respective Soviet republics. The volatile border between Russia and Poland was not only contested in 1920 and 1939 but again in 1945 in the opening days of the Cold War.

Lenin apparently learned a bitter lesson from the Polish adventure, and it would be nearly twenty years before the Soviets would again send their armies abroad to "make revolution." From this point on, caution rather than heroic gestures characterized Lenin's foreign policy. But he remained keenly suspicious of the possibility of coexistence with the bourgeois world. "We live not only in a state," he wrote, "but in a system of states, and the existence of the Soviet Republic side by side with the imperialist states for a long time is unthinkable. In the end either one or the other will conquer. And until that end comes, a series of the most terrible collisions between the Soviet Republic and the bourgeois states is inevitable." Political pragmatism in the short run, however, forced his government to recognize the independence of several "bourgeois" states along the Soviet border, most notably those in the Baltic.

The Baltic Peoples

The only states to end up independent after the civil war were in the northwest of Russia along the Baltic: Poland, Finland, Estonia, Latvia, and Lithuania. As in Georgia, Ukraine, and Belorussia, the numerically dominant peasant classes in the Baltic region were of one nationality while the middle and upper classes were of another. Along the eastern Baltic coast, German nobles dominated rural life in areas of predominantly Estonian and Latvian peasantry. Polish and Jewish city dwellers almost exclusively ran Vilnius, which was surrounded by Belorussian and Lithuanian villages. In Tallinn (Reval) and Riga the German bourgeoisie and nobles dominated local governing institutions, but the number of Estonians and Latvians in the towns grew rapidly until the local peoples became the most numerous nationalities in their respective capitals. Latvian and Estonian working classes and a small bourgeoisie had developed by the early twentieth century.

A small but distinct people speaking a language related to Finnish, the Estonians developed their nationalism relatively late. Influenced by the West and Central European Enlightenment, German pastors and writers first explored the culture of the Estonian peasantry. They were joined by native Estonian intellectuals in the 1820s. Four decades later village schoolteachers joined the university-trained intellectuals, and together they set up schools for peasants and organized choruses and patriotic clubs. In Estonia music and group singing was one of the most important vehicles for the spread of nationalist feeling. But most Estonian nationalists spoke of their people as a "cultural nation," not as a nation destined for modern statehood. Until the revolution, probably in a realistic appreciation of what was possible in Russia, they looked forward to autonomy within the empire rather than independence.

The patriotic intelligentsia faced serious difficulties as it tried to penetrate the largely peasant population. Estonians had no political past with which to identify, no written language, and no national literature. They were kept out of educational, religious, and political institutions by the ruling Germans. Gradually the social hostility of Estonians toward the ruling Germans fed into a feeling of group solidarity among Estonian speakers and laid the basis for nationalism. National consciousness was further promoted in the last decades of the nineteenth century when Estonians entered the towns, gained more education, and, along with the Latvians, achieved the highest level of literacy in the Russian Empire. The tsarist campaign of Russification in the Baltic in the last decades of the nineteenth century further helped to stimulate national awareness among the broad population of Estonians, Latvians, and Finns.

Despite the stirring of cultural nationalism, Estonians nevertheless gravitated toward the Bolsheviks through much of 1917. In the summer the Bolsheviks, whose greatest strength was in the larger industrial towns of Tallinn and Narva, won almost a third of the vote in municipal council elections. They were backed by Russian soldiers in the towns and did less well in purely Estonian areas. Still, in the November elections to the Constituent Assembly, socialists as a whole won just over 50 percent and the nonsocialists nearly matched them. The Bolsheviks won more votes than any other party. After the October Revolution, Bolshevized soviets ran many of the towns in Estonia, but support for the soviets began to erode rapidly. The Bolsheviks were unenthusiastic about Estonian independence, failed to expropriate the estates of the Baltic barons, and tried to suppress oppositional parties. When the Germans advanced in late February 1918, the nationalists used the opportunity to declare Estonia independent of Russia.

A small, compact ethnic community clearly demarcated from their German and Russian overlords and Latvian neighbors, the Estonians were nevertheless divided politically. Socialist sentiments were strong, and anti-Russian feeling was far less apparent than anti-German. Yet Bolshevik ineptitude eroded support for linking up with Soviet Russia and helped the nationalists achieve their new goal of national independence. The small nationalist elite was able to mobilize Estonians when the Bolsheviks overplayed their hand after October and the Germans provided the nationalists with an irresistible opportunity by backing them with force of arms.

To the south of the Estonians lived a people who spoke Latvian, the language, which belongs to the Baltic branch of Indo-European languages (along with Lithuanian and Old Prussian). The ancestors of the Latvians inhabited the Baltic littoral in the ninth century. German merchants and missionaries arrived in the mid-twelfth century, and soon after, the "treacherous Livs" were converted to Christianity. The establishment of German rule obliterated the tribal structure of the indigenous peoples, and Latvians existed as a subject peasant population until the tsarist period. Here too, as with the Estonians, the German clergy dominated learning in the region and initiated scholarly interest in Latvian folk culture. A national awakening, that is, the development of significant secular writing by Latvians, dates from the mid-nineteenth century.

By the last decade of the nineteenth century young Latvians were joining the Russian revolutionary movement, first the populists and after 1893 the fledgling Marxist circles. With high levels of literacy and urbanization (in 1897, 79.4 percent of the people of what would become Latvia lived in cities), as well as growing labor discontent, the Social Democrats found a ready response among both radical intellectuals and workers. Latvian parishioners resented the protectorate of the German barons over local churches and allowed the churches to be used for political agitation. Social Democrats distributed socialist appeals in rural churches and developed strong ties with agricultural workers. By 1905, the Latvian Social Democratic Labor Party (LSDLP) boasted ten thousand members. The national struggle against the German lords combined with a broad political movement, led by Marxists, against autocracy.

Whereas Estonians and Ukrainians vacillated between nationalism and other social movements, Latvians, like Georgians, combined their ethnic and social grievances in a single, dominant socialist national movement. Social democracy, particularly Bolshevism, had exceptionally strong support in 1917 among Latvian and other workers and among the famous Latvian riflemen. Many Latvians in 1917 saw the solution to their national future in a Russian federation, but one that had moved beyond the bourgeois revolution. The extraordinary success of Bolshevism among Latvians stemmed from a number of factors. Latvians hated the Germans much more than they did the Russians. They had a high proportion of landless peasants (more than 1 million in 1897) that favored social democracy and opposed the "gray barons" (Latvian small-holders) almost as much as they did the German nobles. Social democracy had solid support among workers and among many intellectuals, schoolteachers, and students. Also important in shaping the pro-Bolshevik attitude of Latvians was the particularly devastating experience of the world war, which had brought the fighting deep into Latvia, dividing the country, causing great hardship, and radicalizing the population. Finally, the Latvian Bolsheviks were able to develop and propagate a program that attempted to deal with both social and ethnic grievances. Yet the brief experiment in Bolshevik rule after October, the Iskolat, collapsed when the Germans moved into unoccupied Latvia in February 1918. In all likelihood, Bolshevism would have been the eventual victor in Latvia save for the German intervention, which gave the nationalists a chance to create their own independent republic.

The Lithuanians, like their neighbors, the Belorussians, had no urban presence to speak of, and nationalist sentiments did not reach much beyond the relatively insignificant intelligentsia because of the large Lithuanian diaspora. The upper class in the region was Polonized, and the Lithuanian peasantry was mixed with Belorussian speakers (who made up 56 percent of Vilnius [Wilno in Polish, Vilna in Russian] province). Towns were either Jewish or Polish in culture; Vilnius was 40 percent Jewish, 31 percent Polish. Yet here the very differentness of the Lithuanian language from the neighboring Slavic tongues kept Lithuanian-speaking peasants separate from the other peoples around them.

Lithuanians speak an Indo-European language (classified along with Latvian as Eastern Baltic) and have been present in the Baltic region since classical times. Lithuanian tribes united briefly in the thirteenth century to resist German incursions, but the great medieval state around Vilnius was a multiethnic commonwealth that used Belorussian and later Latin in its official communications. In the first half of the nineteenth century, some Polish and German intellectuals and clergy began collecting and publishing Lithuanian folk songs and popular art, but only in the 1870s did Lithuanian students begin to distance themselves from Polish culture. Yet nationalist agitation had almost no effect on the towns. Even the Catholic church did not support a separate Lithuanian identity, but encouraged ties to Poland and antagonism to Russia. Before 1905 the tsarist authorities allowed only one newspaper in Lithuanian, an official gazette, to be published; other periodicals had to be smuggled from abroad.

With Lithuania occupied by the Germans through much of the early revolutionary period, Lithuanian political activity began at a congress of Lithuanians held in the Russian capital in early June. Nationalists passed a resolution in favor of Lithuanian independence, but the center and left, unwilling to antagonize "democratic Russia," called instead for a recognition of Lithuania's right to self-determination. Later the creation of a Lithuanian National Council, the Taryba, in September 1917 and the declaration of independence in December were both carried out under German supervision. The nationalists antagonized local Poles by rejecting any form of union or federation with an independent Poland.

Through the years of the Russian civil war, Lithuanian lands were contested by the nationalists whom the Germans had patronized, the Communists backed by the Red Army, and the independent Poles under Pilsudski. When the Germans evacuated Vilnius at the end of World War I, a Communist government was installed by the Red Army. In April 1919 the Poles took Vilnius, and the nationalists, installed in their new capital of Kaunas, used the Soviet-Polish antagonism to secure Moscow's recognition of their independence. Only with the conclusion of the Russo-Polish War in 1920 and intricate negotiations through the League of Nations were firm borders established between a reduced Lithuania, a Soviet state pushed back eastward, and a bloated Poland that included Vilnius as well as Ukrainian and Belorussian territories. Although it was unable to gain Vilnius until the destruction of Poland in 1939, independent Lithuania seized the German town of Memel (Klaipeda) on the Baltic in 1923 in order to have a port in the Baltic.

The creation of the independent states of Belorussia, Estonia, Latvia, and Lithuania was not the result of broad-based and coherent nationalist movements that realized long-held aspirations to nationhood. Rather, it was initially the artificial result of German politics and the immediate weakness of the central Russian state. Here nationality was the instrument that a Great Power used to destroy the Russian Empire and create ministates it could control, as elsewhere and at other times class would be the basis on which the Soviets would reconstruct a multinational state. At the same time, the principle of national self-determination, promoted both by Lenin and Woodrow Wilson, had gained an enormous influence and legitimacy. As the twentieth century opened, leaders of almost every significant ethnic group not only aspired to statehood but had the backing of powerful leaders of powerful states. The anti-imperial age had dawned.

The Finns

Finland was under Russian control from 1809 until 1917. Finnish speakers were a subordinate people within a region in which they composed the majority. The dominant group within the country was the Swedish-speaking upper class, who made up the nobility, bureaucracy, and much of the middle class. Their relationship to the Finnish peasants was reminiscent of that of the Baltic German nobles to Estonian and Latvian peasants and Polish landlords to Lithuanian and Belorussian peasants. From the moment Russia took Finland from Sweden and incorporated it into the Russian Empire, Finland, which had never been a historic state, achieved the status of an autonomous polity, with its own local Diet, or senate, at the apex of the bureaucracy, guarantees for the Lutheran religion, and the continuance of the Fundamental Laws of the Swedish period. The emperor Alexander I (1801–25) declared himself grand duke of Finland and was formally recognized by the Diet. He pledged to observe the constitution and laws of Finland. For the next eighty-odd years Finland existed as a constitutional anomaly within the empire, a distinct country with its own army, legal system, currency, and taxation, separated from the rest of the empire by tariffs and a frontier.

Thanks to tsarist policy, the Finns for the first time in their history enjoyed political autonomy and began the process of building a nation around an ethnic core. Though distinctions remained between the privileged Swedes and the Finns, the geographic and political unity of the country, the economic ties between Finnish towns and the countryside, the creation of a regional market in Finland, and the relative weakness of social and class conflicts in the nineteenth century created a sense of Finnish nationality that included both Swedish and Finnish speakers. The first generation to advocate Finnish culture and language came from the Swedish-speaking elite. In 1835 Finnish folk poems were compiled into the *Kalevala*, which was celebrated as the Finnish national epic and provided a heroic ingredient for a new Finnish identity. By the end of the century the upward mobility of Finnish speakers and the linguistic adaptation of the elites encouraged the peoples of Finland to share a single national conception. Socially, however, the country remained divided between the Swedish-speaking bureaucracy and bourgeoisie, on one side, and the bulk of the population, which was Finnish-speaking, on the other. Finnish workers gradually grew away from their former bourgeois and intellectual allies, and in the new century the majority of the workers identified with the Social Democratic intellectuals.

As political nationalisms were increasingly perceived by tsarist officials as threats to the unity of the empire, the Russian autocracy, beginning in 1890, attempted to curtail the autonomy of the Grand Duchy of Finland. The Young Finns and the Swedish party resisted the Russian inroads, and after the general strike that swept Russia and Finland in October 1905, Nicholas II was forced to restore Finland's former rights. Most importantly for its future political development, Finland became the first country in Europe to be granted universal suffrage, in which women voted alongside men. In the elections to the Diet in 1907 the Social Democrats won over a third of the vote, achieving the largest representation of any socialist party in Europe. In 1916 the Finnish Social Democrats became the first socialist party in the world to win an absolute majority in the legislature. But unlike the victorious Left in Georgia (or in Latvia in 1917), the Finnish Social Democrats were neither able nor particularly anxious to overwhelm their conservative opponents.

In the first year of revolution the Finnish socialists became the principal advocates of Finland's independence from Russia. In one of its first acts the Provisional Government restored the constitution of the Grand Duchy of Finland and recognized its full "internal independence." The Finnish Social Democrats pushed for a law that ascribed sovereignty to the Finnish Diet. But until the very last days of its existence, the Provisional Government refused to concede full independence to Finland and proved willing to use armed force to enforce its policy in Finland. The only major political party in Russia willing to grant Finland full independence was the Bolsheviks. The delays in establishing an authoritative government in Helsinki aided the process of deepening social division in Finland, which would eventually lead to a bloody civil war.

On December 6, 1917, Finland declared itself an independent state and was recognized by the new Soviet government in Petrograd. The newly formed Finnish Army, under General Karl Mannerheim, began to disarm Russian troops. Fearing the loss of the revolutionary gains of 1917, workers and socialists prepared to defend Helsinki against the Whites and their allies. Aligned with the German army, the Finnish Whites launched a brutal attack on the socialists and the Red Guard to eliminate their hold on the capital and on southern Finland. The Germans took the capital in April, and by early May the whole of Finland was in White or German hands. The upper and middle classes, most of the intellectuals, and the independent peasantry backed the Whites, whereas workers and landless peasants joined the Reds. Middle and poor peasants remained largely passive. In the fighting, 3,500 Reds were killed, 78 percent of them workers. In the subsequent White terror, 200 people a day were killed, and 12,500 Red prisoners died in prison camps. Though all social groups in Finland favored independence, the common national program could not overcome class and regional cleavages. The result was a bloody civil war; the defeat of the Social Democrats, who had led the struggle for democracy and independence; and the coming to power of a conservative, pro-German elite.

The Jews

Jews have lived in parts of what became the Soviet Union since at least the fourth century B.C., first settling along the Black Sea coast and in the Caucasus. In the eighth century A.D. the king of the Khazars, a Finno-Turkish tribe that migrated through southern Russia, adopted Judaism as the official religion of his empire. After the conversion of Russia to Orthodox Christianity in the tenth century, Russian rulers often persecuted Jews, who were considered, in the words of Ivan IV, to "have led our people astray from Christianity, [to] have brought poisonous weeds into our land, and also wrought much wickedness among our people." Both the Orthodox Church in Russia and the Catholic Church in Poland propagated extremely negative images of the Jews that fed into popular stereotypes of these non-Christian people as deceitful and unclean. In the reign of Catherine the Great (1762–96) hundreds of thousands of Jews became Russian subjects with the partitions of Poland. Though herself an enlightened supporter of religious freedom and special privileges for Jews, the empress approved discriminatory legislation that restricted their political and economic rights, imposed higher taxes on them, and limited their habitation to specific areas in the western part of the empire, which became in 1835 the so-called Pale of Settlement. When Jewish merchants began to compete effectively with Russian merchants in Moscow, Catherine acceded to Russian demands that the Jews be expelled from the city.

Russia's Jews lived apart, spoke their own distinct language, Yiddish, and worshipped differently, and the more traditional wore distinctive clothing. The effect of state policy on the Jews was to reinforce differences between them and the Christian majority. Even in the mid-nineteenth century when many educated Jews gravitated toward Russian and European culture, popular and state attitudes placed them in a double bind. Jews could assimilate into Russian life fully only by ceasing to be Jews, but continually met obstacles when they tried to live as Jews equal to Russians. Some Jews sought to reconceive their community less as one of common faith and more in the idiom of modern nationalism. The Haskala, or Jewish Enlightenment, involved secularizing Jewish life and creating a modern nonreligious literature in Hebrew and eventually also in Yiddish. But after 1881 restrictions on and persecution of Jews increased, and the Enlightenment idea of integration into Russian life through education lost much of its appeal. The government imposed quotas on the numbers of Jews admitted to schools of higher learning and barred them from practicing law. In the early 1880s hundreds of pogroms against Jews broke out. Russian and Ukrainian peasants and workers beat up and killed Jews in Kiev, Odessa, Warsaw, Nizhnyi Novgorod, Kishinev, and Ekaterinoslav, often with no interference from the authorities. As racist and anti-Semitic language and rhetoric became more prevalent, supported by the biological and anthropological "science" of the time, superstitions that claimed that Jews used the blood of Christians in their rituals (the "blood libel") or that they plotted to control the world (as claimed in the infamous forgery *Protocols of the Elders of Zion*) spread widely.

Those Russian Jews who were no longer willing to acquiesce to the rising waves of anti-Semitism and persecution either emigrated or turned to opposition politics. Many turned toward the new movement of Zionism, which promoted Jewish settlement in Palestine; others toward socialism, particularly Marxist social democracy, or liberalism; while still others turned inward toward orthodox Judaism. A second wave of pogroms broke out during the Russian Revolution of 1905–07. Radical reactionary movements, like the Black Hundreds, rallied their followers with cries of "Beat the Jews! Save Russia!" During World War I the tsarist government forcibly expelled Jews from western borderlands, though at the same time it permitted Jews to settle outside the Pale. Jews grew steadily more alienated from the Russian *ancien régime* and progressively solidified their enthusiasm for a revolutionary alternative. For many conservatives and reactionaries revolution and the revolutionary movement was a disease that they identified with the Jews, even though the Jews who were most prominent in the dominant revolutionary parties had long abandoned their Jewish religion and identity.

The revolution of 1917 swept away the civil and economic restrictions on the more than 6 million Jews of the Russian Empire. Jewish political parties and newspapers flourished, but scattered and divided as the community was, no single movement or party represented the majority of Russian Jewry. Zionists and Bundists (Jewish socialists) debated each other at the All-Russian Jewish Conference in July 1917, though ultimately they agreed to work for "national self-rule for Jews in Russia." The October insurrection only further divided the Jewish community, with Zionists, Bundists, Mensheviks, and SRs opposing the Bolsheviks. In Ukraine Jewish voters overwhelmingly backed Zionists in the elections to the Constituent Assembly. When Jewish leaders opposed the Ukrainian Rada's move in early 1918 to separate from Russia, their decision created resentment among the Ukrainian nationalists. Jews were caught between antireligious and anticapitalist Bolsheviks on one side and anti-Semitic, anti-Bolshevik nationalists on the other. Tens of thousands of Jews perished at the hands of Ukrainian nationalists under Petliura, the troops of Denikin's Volunteer Army, and the Red cavalry commanded by Budennyi. Thousands of others migrated from the Pale to Petrograd and Moscow.

During the civil war the virulent attacks on Jews, particularly in Ukraine, and the high visibility of Jews among the Bolsheviks convinced many Jews to join the Soviet cause. In 1919–20 Jewish socialist parties split, with many members entering the Communist Party. Stalin's Commissariat of Nationalities formed a Commissariat of Jewish Affairs within it at the beginning of 1918, and the RKP (b) established a Jewish section within its ranks in October. From the other side Zionists and Bundists organized an All-Russian Congress of Jewish Communities in the summer of 1918 and elected a Community Center, but a year later the Commissariat of Jewish Affairs decreed that such organizations be disbanded. Jewish life in the Soviet republics would be determined by the programs and policies of the ruling Communist Party.

Bolshevik theorists were divided on the question of whether Jews constituted a nationality or a religious sect. Stalin's definition of nationality included possession of a specific territory, a criterion that appeared to exclude Jews, but Jewish Communists argued that Russian Jewry constituted a nationality with its own secular culture and Yiddish language, though not a clearly defined territory. The Soviets rejected both Zionism and Judaism, repressed Hebrew and religious studies, and instead promoted a Soviet socialist Jewish nation based on agricultural settlements, Yiddish language and culture, state-sponsored schools, and subsidized cultural institutions. The Communists carried out periodic campaigns against popular anti-Semitism and set up dozens of Jewish soviets and national districts in Ukraine, Belorussia, and Russia. The 1920s witnessed an efflorescence of Jewish theater and literature and the upward social mobility of ordinary Jews, as restrictions on their traditional occupations were lifted. Jews were prominent in the Soviet bureaucracy, in police agencies, and at the very top of the Communist party hierarchy.

In the early 1920s party activists discussed creating a Jewish republic along the Black Sea, stretching from Bessarabia through Crimea to Abkhazia, but local leaders opposed the idea. Eventually, as Jewish autonomous units were gradually dissolved in the former Pale of Settlement, a Jewish Autonomous District was formed in Birobidzhan in the Soviet Far East. This Soviet "Zion," however, never attracted the numbers of settlers that its sponsors hoped, and as official enthusiasm for the rights and culture of Soviet Jews waned in the 1930s, the ever-present anti-Semitism among Soviet peoples seeped back into daily life and bureaucratic practice. That anti-Semitism would burst out with a vicious power in the late 1940s when Stalin himself encouraged a major repression of Soviet Jews.

Islam and the Peoples of the East

By the time of the Russian Revolution there were more than 15 million Muslims in the Russian Empire. The overwhelming majority spoke Turkic languages, including the nomads of Central Asia—the Kyrgyz, Kazakh, and Uzbek tribes—as well as the Tatars of the Volga region and Crimea, some of the peoples of the northern Caucasus, and the Azerbaijanis of Transcaucasia. The major Iranian-speaking people were the Tajiks of Central Asia, who tended to settle in the larger towns of the region, such as Samarkand and Bukhara. Among the Central Asians distinctions between peoples were ill-defined and fluid. Rather than identifying with a nation or a specific ethnic group, the Muslim peoples, particularly in Central Asia, felt loyalty primarily to their tribe or clan, to their dynastic leader, and in a general sense to Islam. The clearest sense of difference was between nomads and settled peoples, often referred to as Sarts. Because of their longer association with Russia and the effects of tsarist economic development, the most prosperous and best educated of the Muslim peoples were the Volga and Crimean Tatars, followed by the Azerbaijanis. In the Volga region the nomadic Bashkirs resented the more settled Tatars and resisted their cultural and economic dominance.

Earlier centuries of Eurasian history can be viewed as a perennial struggle between the nomads from the East and the settled peoples of the West. Across the great Russian plains the contact between Mongols and Muslims on one hand and Slavs and other Christians on the other was often violent and destructive, but over time the domination of the Muslims over the Christians receded until it was reversed in early modern times. When Ivan IV conquered Kazan in 1552, Russia established its hegemony over the non-Russian peoples of the Volga, and Muscovy became a multinational empire. With the decline of the major Mongol and Muslim states, Russia took over where the Golden Horde had once held sway, from the borders of China to the Crimean peninsula. Nowhere was the imperial nature of the Russian state more evident than in those borderlands where Russian rulers and settlers moved into Muslim-populated areas.

Tsarist policy toward Islam and the Muslim peoples was inconsistent. At times the state attacked Muslim religious institutions or abrogated the rights of Muslims, closing mosques, confiscating lands, removing their serfs, and restricting Muslim proselytizing. At other times, as under Catherine II, the government granted privileges to Muslims, freeing them from certain taxes, exempting them from military recruitment, occasionally allowing mosques to be built, and setting up official religious institutions for Muslims. Catherine encouraged the development of a Tatar commercial class that mediated for the Russians along the Volga and into Siberia and Central Asia. Repression of Islam and forced conversion proved to be wasteful and bred resistance and rebellion, while the more tolerant policies reaped a significant loyalty among many Muslims, particularly the elites.

Russian leaders, clergy, and thinkers believed that Russians were the most civilized people of the empire, with the possible exception of the Baltic Germans, and they were convinced that eventually smaller peoples of the realm would assimilate into the Russian nation. Russians felt this sense of cultural superiority most acutely toward Muslims. Allied closely with the Russian state, the Russian Orthodox Church supported its imperial mission, shaped Russian attitudes toward the "heathen" Muslims, and worked to proselytize the Christian faith. To the Orthodox clergy Muslims were misguided and depraved, and the way for them to become full subjects of the Russian tsar was to be brought into his church. As Nicholas I pursued a foreign policy that liberated Greeks from the Ottomans and annexed Georgians and Armenians from Persia, he also revived efforts to Christianize Russia's Muslims.

Through the nineteenth century scholarly interest in the languages of the non-Russians grew, and influential pedagogues advocated the teaching of Tatar and other local languages as a means to spread the Gospel and create loyal subjects. As one educator put it, "The native language speaks directly to the mind and the heart. As soon as Christian concepts and rules have taken root in the hearts of aliens, the love of the Russian people arises by itself." In 1870 the government adopted this idea and set up schools in Tatar and other languages. Though some Tatars opposed the program as an effort at Russification, and many Russians feared this concession to national culture, the effect of the new schools was both to create an educated stratum among non-Russians and a new sense of national distinction. Education opened the way for young Muslims to reconceive the traditional definitions of who they were, to borrow what was useful and progressive from Russian civilization, and to attempt to reform their own community.

Growing initially out of a "new method" (usul-i jadid) of teaching Arabic, an influential movement called Jadidism, dedicated to intellectual and social renewal, emerged among educated Muslims in the last decades of the nineteenth century. The leading figure in the movement was the Crimean Tatar Ismail-bey Gaspirali, publisher of an influential Turkic newspaper, but other popular writers, such as the Caucasian Muslim Mirza Fath Ali Akhundzada, a playwright and publicist who wrote in Azeri, helped spread a sense of Turkic pride and a commitment to modernization. Some Jadids, like Gaspirali, were critical of Russian policies, but in Central Asia Jadids avoided confrontation with the state and instead met resistance from more conservative Muslim religious leaders. Muslim reformers hoped to learn about the modern world from Russia and the West while at the same time they remained wary of Russian threats to their own cultural traditions. Their role was to bring enlightenment, knowledge, and the benefits of the West to the Islamic community. Their faith was in progress rather than religion, and for them Islam was less a sacred practice than a cultural identification and an aspect of self-definition. Not surprisingly, once alternative political movements were eliminated during the Russian civil war, many Jadidists eventually joined the Communists in trying to transform Muslim society.

During the revolution Muslim leaders attempted to forge institutions of Muslim unity, through congresses, conferences, and committees, but in each part of the disintegrating empire local movements pitted reformers against traditionalists and Russian settlers against Muslim activists. In Central Asia ethnic nationalism and class conflict were muted, and Muslims contended with one another over who would lead the community and define their future. Religious conservatives won the July 1917 elections to the Tashkent duma, marginalizing the Jadid reformers. Local Bolsheviks and soviets, like the Tashkent soviet, tended to identify with the local Russians, which only antagonized and alienated the Muslims. After the October 1917 revolution the Tashkent soviet claimed power in the region and explicitly excluded Muslims since the "natives" possessed "no proletarian class organizations." Early in 1918 soviet forces from Tashkent overthrew the reformist Muslim government in Kokand and laid siege to the walled city of Bukhara, driving out the reactionary emir. When faced with a choice between Russian Bolsheviks and ultratraditional Muslims, many of the Jadidist intellectuals sided with the Russians, who at least promised to modernize Muslim society along secular lines.

Soviet policy among Muslims had both domestic and international ambitions. Faced with trying to govern millions of Muslims with very few Muslim Communists and interested in winning over Muslim support and weakening the anti-Bolshevik forces among the Muslims, the Communists granted political and cultural autonomy to various Muslim peoples. But even when the Soviet leadership in Moscow tried to support the aspirations for autonomy of certain Muslim peoples, such as the Bashkirs in 1918–19, they encountered hostility from the local Bolsheviks. After failing to convince Volga Muslims to work within a joint Tatar-Bashkir republic, the Politburo created an autonomous Bashkir Soviet Republic in March 1919 and a separate Tatar Soviet Socialist Republic in January 1920.

Tensions between Muslims and Russians did not dissipate, however, and within the Communist ranks there were serious fractures. In January 1919 Tashkent's Commissar of War mutinied against the soviet government and executed most of its members. The rebellion was quickly suppressed by the Cheka, which brutally cut down thousands in retaliation. Soviet Russia faced not only local Muslim hostility but also nearby British troops allied with the Whites. Moscow sent a high-level commission to Turkestan to replace the Tashkent soviet, and Lenin personally intervened to shift Communist policy in Turkestan in favor of the non-Russians. But though the Central Committee in Moscow was prepared to encourage the recruitment of Muslims into the Communist party and grant a degree of autonomy to Muslims, it balked when Muslim activists began to agitate for a single, unified state of all Turkic peoples. Moscow opposed unification of all Muslims and grew suspicious of nationalist tendencies within Communist ranks.

Deep in Central Asia, in the Ferghana Valley, a popular anti-Soviet movement emerged from a small number of bandits until it became a powerful opposition to the Communists. Known as the Basmachi movement, it fought to eliminate Russian rule in Central Asia. To increase their local support, the local Communists reluctantly acceded to Moscow's demands that Turkestan be declared an autonomous republic. The last Basmachi rebels, under Enver Pasha, were defeated in 1922. As the civil war came to an end and the danger of foreign intervention receded, the Soviets organized Central Asia around an autonomous Turkestan republic and two "people's republics"—Bukhara and Khwarezm—loosely affiliated with Soviet Turkestan.

Figure 4.1. Kyrgyz Red Army cavalrymen bringing Soviet power to Central Asia (SOVFOTO).

Lenin and Stalin were anxious to consolidate Soviet power in the Volga region and Central Asia as the first step toward launching a revolutionary assault on Asia and the Middle East. Their policy was directed against "the most rapacious imperialist government on Earth," as Lenin referred to Great Britain in a telegram to Amir Amanullah of Afghanistan. Early in 1918 Soviet Russia renounced the 1907 Anglo-Russian Convention, which had given tsarist Russia a sphere of influence in northern Persia and Britain a sphere in the south. As Russian troops withdrew, the British moved in, but the Soviets could do little but support a number of local rebels. Direct links were made with the

Persian revolutionary Mirza Kuchuk Khan and the Turkish nationalist forces under Kemal Pasha. After the easy Sovietization of Azerbaijan in April 1920, Russia was once again a player in the northern Middle East. In September the Communists organized a Congress of the Peoples of the East in Baku, and Zinoviev proclaimed a revolutionary jihad against European imperialism. Soviet governments appeared in Enzeli and Gilan in northern Iran.

But the Kremlin reassessed its revolutionary strategy in 1921. When at the beginning of that year the British backed the takeover of Persia by the soldier Reza Shah, the Soviet government signed a treaty with Reza that permitted Russia to intervene in Persia if a third power attacked it. To solidify relations with its unstable neighbor to the south, Soviet Russia abandoned rebels like Kuchuk Khan and acted in Persia in ways not very different from its tsarist predecessor. Similarly in Turkey, the Soviet government supported the westernizing nationalist Mustapha Kemal against the West and signed an agreement with him dividing Armenia, but it later turned a blind eye when Kemal Pasha imprisoned and executed local Communists. State interests took priority over the elusive quest for the international revolution.

Nationalist and Class Struggles

The revolution of 1917 and the subsequent civil war were interpreted by the Marxists as a civil war of class against class, worker against peasant and bourgeois, city against country. Nationalists, in contrast, interpreted the struggle as a national war of Russians against minorities, the center against the peripheries. But ethnic and class conflicts were complexly intertwined. Although in the national peripheries the conflict took on aspects of a national war, the social struggles between workers and industrialists, propertied society and the lower classes, city and countryside were present almost everywhere. Reformist or revolutionary intellectuals among non-Russians, like the Jadidists among the Muslims, were torn between their ethnic compatriots and the modernizing agenda of the Russian-led socialist revolution.

For most non-Russians in Russia and along its periphery a sense of nationhood that overrode and superseded local, religious, tribal, or class identities hardly existed before the revolution. Nationalism was still largely concentrated among the ethnic intelligentsia, the students, and the lower middle classes of the towns, with at best a fleeting following among broader strata. Nationalist leaderships were most successful where they were able to combine social reform with their programs of self-definition, autonomy, or independence. This occurred in Georgia, where the Mensheviks carried both the banner of the nation and the red flag of social revolution. But in Estonia the Bolsheviks lost out when they neglected national aspirations in favor of exclusive focus on social cleavages. Where social, particularly agrarian, reform was delayed or neglected, as in Ukraine under the Rada, ethnic political aspirations alone did not prove strong enough to sustain nationalist intellectuals in power. For ethnic leaders who faced a peasant majority indifferent to their claims to power and were caught up in an uneven struggle with the Bolsheviks, as in

Belorussia, Lithuania, or Latvia, an appeal to the Great Powers of central and western Europe became the last resort. And the intervention of foreigners, particularly by the Germans in the crucial first months after the October Revolution and the Poles at the end of the civil war, radically altered the way the revolution turned out in the borderlands.

Suggestions for Further Reading

For overviews of the nationalities of the Russian Empire and the early Soviet years from very different perspectives, see Richard Pipes, *The Formation of the Soviet Union: Communism and Nationalism, 1917–1923* (Cambridge, Mass., 2nd ed., 1964); Ronald Grigor Suny, *The Revenge of the Past: Nationalism, Revolution, and the Collapse of the Soviet Union* (Stanford, Calif., 1993); Walker Connor, *The National Question in Marxist-Leninist Theory and Strategy* (Princeton, N.J., 1984); and Hélène Carrère d'Encausse, *The Great Challenge: Nationalities and the Bolshevik State, 1917–1930* (New York, 1991).

On the nationalities of Transcaucasia, see Firuz Kazemzadeh, *The Struggle for Transcaucasia (1917–1921)* (New York, 1951); Tadeusz Swietochowski, *Russian Azerbaijan, 1905–1920: The Shaping of National Identity in a Muslim Community* (Cambridge, 1985); Audrey L. Altstadt, *The Azerbaijani Turks: Power and Identity Under Russian Rule* (Stanford, Calif., 1992); Richard G. Hovannisian, *Armenia on the Road to Independence, 1918* (Berkeley, Calif., 1967); and his *The Republic of Armenia,* 4 vols. (Berkeley, Calif., 1971–96); Ronald Grigor Suny, *The Making of the Georgian Nation* (Bloomington, Ind., 2nd ed., 1994); *Looking Toward Ararat: Armenia in Modern History* (Bloomington, Ind., 1993); (ed.), *Transcaucasia, Nationalism and Social Change* (Ann Arbor, Mich., 2nd. ed., 1996).

On Central Asia, see Teresa Rakowska-Harmstone, *Russia and Nationalism in Central Asia: The Case of Tadzhikistan* (Baltimore, 1970); Martha Brill Olcott, *The Kazakhs* (Stanford, Calif., 2nd ed., 1995); Edward A. Allworth (ed.), *Central Asia. A Century of Russian Rule* (New York, 1967) and his *The Modern Uzbeks, from the Fourteenth Century to the Present: A Cultural History* (Stanford, Calif., 1990).

On the Baltic peoples, see Toivo U. Raun, *Estonia and the Estonians* (Stanford, Calif., 1987); Andrejs Plakans, *The Latvians: A Short History* (Stanford, Calif., 1995); Andrievs Ezergailis, *The Latvian Impact on the Bolshevik Revolution* (Boulder, Colo., 1983); Alfred Erich Senn, *The Emergence of Modern Lithuania* (New York, 1959); and Georg von Rauch, *The Baltic States: The Years of Independence, 1917–1940* (London, 1974).

The best book on the Jews in the early Soviet period is Zvi Y. Gitelman, *Jewish Nationality and Soviet Politics: The Jewish Sections of the CPSU, 1917–1930* (Princeton, N.J., 1972). A broader look is taken by Benjamin Pinkus, *The Jews of the Soviet Union: The History of a National Minority* (Cambridge, 1988).

On Ukraine, the following books are indispensable: John Armstrong, *Ukrainian Nationalism* (New York, 1963); John Reshetar, *The Ukrainian Revolution, 1917–1920: A Study in Nationalism* (Princeton, N.J., 1952); Arthur E. Adams, *Bolsheviks in the Ukraine: The Second Campaign, 1918–1919* (New Haven, Conn., 1963); and James E. Mace, *Communism and the Dilemmas of National Liberation: National Communism in Soviet Ukraine, 1918–1933* (Cambridge, Mass., 1983). On Belorussia, see Nicholas P. Vakar, *Belorussia, The Making of a Nation: A Case Study* (Cambridge, Mass., 1956). For Finland, see Anthony F. Upton, *The Finnish Revolution, 1917–1918* (Berkeley, Calif., 1988); and Risto Alapuro, *State and Revolution in Finland* (Berkeley, Calif., 1988).

PART II

RETREAT
AND
REBUILDING

CHAPTER 5
The Evolution of the Dictatorship

Five Easy Steps

In its earliest incarnation soviet government was potentially one of the most democratic in history. It was to be immediately responsible to the Central Executive Committee of Soviets (VTsIK), which was elected by the congresses of soviets, which in turn were to be elected from the democratically elected local and regional soviets. No one party was to dominate; rather, any socialist or democratic party could in theory take power through free elections. But very rapidly democratic forms became the foundation stones of a dictatorial state. The political arena was steadily limited in five successive steps: the exclusion from political activity of the propertied classes, the establishment of a one-party government, the elimination of rival political parties and the monopolization of politics by the Communist Party, the suppression of dissent and factions within the Communist Party, and finally the rise of a single faction dominated by Stalin. The immediate effect of the October Revolution and the drive for a soviet government was to exclude the upper and middle classes of Russia from political participation. Only workers, peasants, and soldiers were permitted to vote for the soviets. The old Duma parties, from the liberal Kadets to the monarchists and nationalists, were completely eliminated from the soviet structure. The Kadets and some other "bourgeois" parties were, however, represented in the Constituent Assembly and in local municipal dumas until these bodies were dispersed by the Bolsheviks in their first months in power. Thus, the first step toward dictatorship—the elimination of the upper classes, the bourgeoisie, and the clergy from political participation—occurred between October 1917 and January 1918. This exclusion was officially incorporated in the constitution of the Russian Soviet Federated Socialist Republic (RSFSR) of July 10, 1918.

One-Party Government

The soviets were made up of leftist parties: Bolsheviks, Mensheviks, Left and Right SRs, anarchists, and other smaller groups. From November 1917 to March

1918, the highest Soviet governmental bodies—the Sovnarkom (Council of People's Commissars), the VTsIK, and the occasionally convened congresses of soviets—were multiparty. Sovnarkom had a Bolshevik majority, but the Left SRs held important ministries from November 1917 to March 1918 and were influential in the Cheka and throughout the state apparatus. When the crisis over Brest-Litovsk ended the coalition of leftist parties in the government, the Communists alone remained in power. Here was the second major step toward dictatorship—the formation of a one-party government by the summer of 1918.

Still more important in the formation of an authoritarian state, however, were the effects of the postrevolutionary economic and social collapse and the outbreak of civil war. The Bolsheviks were an extremely weak party in early 1918. They dominated a few of the largest cities and had a precarious following among urban workers and soldiers. As the Russian economy and social order dissolved and anarchy threatened, and as the prospects of a European revolution coming to Russia's aid receded, Lenin pulled away from his vision of radical democracy. Other themes appeared in his speeches: the need for executive authority (as in one-person management), the need for skill and a high cultural level (in recruiting specialists), the need for discipline and order, even compulsion, and the role of the party as the leader of the masses. A tougher understanding of the dictatorship of the proletariat, one that increasingly emphasized direction from above (though with support from below), came to replace the idea of the commune-state.

The Weakening of the Soviets

Already in 1917, before the October days, the grassroots organizations, such as factory committees and soviets, were losing elements of democratic participation from below and gradually becoming less responsive to the workers and more bureaucratic. Almost immediately after the Bolshevik insurrection, the local soviets, began to act as administrative organs, rather than representative institutions. The trade unions, instead of working to improve workers' conditions of employment, began to operate as instruments to increase production, and in the process they lost their autonomy from the government. Elections of soviets and factory committees were often postponed, and it was frequently difficult to achieve a quorum. Despite demands for new elections by workers, the Bolsheviks tended to resist new elections, which would have registered the growing worker discontent. As hundreds of thousands of workers either migrated to the countryside or were mobilized into the Red Army or turned into party or state officials, the very social base of the Bolshevik regime eroded. The Bolsheviks dominated the soviets through the civil war, often by manipulating elections or dissolving soviets that had opposition majorities. In the first months after the October insurrection the central government did not exclude the Mensheviks and SRs from soviets, but very often local Bolsheviks, soldiers, or Red Guards expelled non–Bolshevik party members from local soviets. Yet the other socialist parties continued to maintain a precarious existence and even to elect deputies to the congresses and be represented in VTsIK.

Already in 1918 an emerging political culture of Bolshevism was being forged. Bolsheviks felt besieged and vulnerable. With enemies all around them, they restricted dissent within their own party, which only fostered a less democratic, more bureaucratic structure within the party. The party, which had moved from a small conspiratorial cluster of professional revolutionaries before the revolution to a quite loose and decentralized mass party in 1917, now increasingly became a large party with power concentrated in the center and at the top. Local committees no longer chose higher committees but acted as subordinate agents of the upper party organs. By placing its loyal cadres in soviets, factory committees, trade unions, the bureaucratized party dominated decision-making in all mass organizations.

Emerging from the civil war, Bolshevik political culture conceived of opposition as the enemy. Not only did the Bolsheviks look upon the bourgeoisie and the Whites as enemies to be crushed, but they also saw other socialists, such as the Mensheviks and SRs, and the anarchists as threats to be repressed. Over time, and certainly by the summer of 1918, the Communists became increasingly intolerant of any opposition to their right to rule. Since all political parties had some quarrel with the Bolsheviks, on the use of terror or undemocratic behavior, the conduct of the war, or peasant policy, the Communists harassed them with expulsion from the soviets, suppression of their newspapers, and arrest. They defined anti-Soviet behavior broadly and labeled the other socialist parties, including the Mensheviks and Right SRs, "petty bourgeois," "counterrevolutionary," and "anti-Soviet." Even though the Mensheviks had abjured armed struggle against the Soviet government and declared itself a legal opposition, Lenin saw them as counterrevolutionary; in his words, "Whoever is not for us is against us." There was no acceptance of the idea that the Bolsheviks, in the normal rough and tumble of politics, might have to give up power to another party that had won popular support.

At times the Communists reconsidered their policy toward the opposition. In late 1918 there was a noticeable thaw in Bolshevik policy toward other parties. Lenin wrote in November, "It would be preposterous to insist solely on tactics of repression and terror toward petty-bourgeois democracy when the course of events is forcing it to turn toward us." A week later the authorities readmitted Mensheviks to the soviets and the Central Executive Committee of Soviets, and in February 1919 they readmitted the Right SRs. But as the civil war raged on through 1919, the Soviet government repeatedly closed Menshevik and SR newspapers, raided their meetings, and arrested their members. The thaw was over by late March 1919 when the Soviet government, endangered by the White offensive, cracked down hard on critics. In the first three months of 1921, it is estimated, five thousand Mensheviks were arrested in Russia, including their entire Central Committee. Martov had left Russia for Germany in September 1920, never to return to his homeland. The party was forced to dissolve itself within Russia and the other Soviet republics. In April 1921 Lenin declared, "The place for the Mensheviks and the SRs, both the open ones and those disguised as 'non-party,' is in prison (or on foreign newspapers, by the side of the White Guards)—we willingly allowed Martov to go abroad."

No law was passed outlawing other parties. In mid-1922 prominent Right SRs were put on trial and found guilty, but under foreign pressure they were given relatively light sentences. Anti-Bolshevik newspapers were eliminated, and hundreds of dissident intellectuals were shipped abroad. Lenin sneered at the opposition:

> We do not believe in absolutes. We laugh at pure democracy. Freedom of the press in the RSFSR . . . is freedom of political organization of the bourgeoisie and its most faithful servants—the Mensheviks and SRs. . . . The bourgeoisie (all over the world) is still many times stronger than us. To give it still another weapon, such as freedom of political organization (freedom of the press, for the press is the center and foundation of political organization) means to make things easier for the enemy, to help the class enemy.

All the power of the state was now to be used to eliminate political alternatives. This was the third step toward the dictatorial state—the elimination of multiparty politics in the local and central soviets; the closing of oppositional newspapers, and widespread repression of dissident opinion outside the Communist Party.

Backwardness and war nourished the authoritarian and hierarchical impulses of the Bolsheviks and starved the more democratic and egalitarian ones. Economic and political collapse had aided the Bolshevik ascent to power; now they inhibited alternatives to the creation of a disciplined state machine. From a decentralized and fluid political structure, Soviet power quickly became a highly centralized and bureaucratic form of political organization. Efforts to combat bureaucratization repeatedly proved to be far weaker than the forces that pushed for control from the center and from above. The building of the new state was a remarkable achievement, especially in the midst of civil war, but its agents and officers responded to command far more willingly than they sought consent.

The economic and social conditions in Russia were certainly not propitious for building a democratic state, but the Bolsheviks repeatedly made political choices and acted in ways that discouraged grassroots efforts at self-government and eliminated tolerance for dissident views. It was not only material deprivation and the imperatives of war that disempowered the class of workers but also the policies that Bolsheviks pursued. Workers did not have economic power of their own and were dependent on the state, which had to win the war at all costs. Two ideals were in conflict. From one side, many workers fought for the democratic ideal of self-management in both the economy and the state, as did millions of peasants in their own way. But, from the other, many party leaders, including Lenin, feared political pluralism and defended instead the "productivist" ideal of a highly efficient and productive economy that could eliminate scarcities, which they thought could be achieved only with discipline, regulation, one-person management, and eventually militarization. Wartime was not very conducive to experiments in new ways of organizing production and administration, and democratic ideals withered, though not without a fight, before more authoritarian methods. Communists became the managers of an economy of scarcity and an authoritarian state that claimed to be the heir of the revolution even as it buried the more egalitarian and participatory aspirations of those who had come out into the streets in 1917.

The Party-State

At first the real organ of state power was the Sovnarkom, the Council of People's Commissars, led by Lenin. While he was alive, Lenin preferred to govern through the Sovnarkom. Here he dealt with all manner of issues, even matters of great detail, which he referred to as "vermicelli." Personally modest, with a sly sense of humor, Lenin used his considerable powers of persuasion to bring his closest comrades around to his point of view. "Simple greed for power," political scientist T. H. Rigby writes, "does not seem to have been in Lenin's character," but he often felt that "erstwhile comrades were leading his cause astray and only his guidance could confirm it on the right path." Early in 1919 Lenin rejected the suggestion that he set up a "personal dictatorship" as "utter nonsense." As long as Lenin was its chair, Sovnarkom benefited from his energy and his enormous prestige. But Lenin made no provision for a successor, and once he was gone Sovnarkom declined rapidly in importance as the highest party committees gained in power.

The Bolshevik government took the occasional congress of soviets seriously and used them for debating policies and mobilizing opinion. But the Sovnarkom subordinated itself neither to the congresses nor to VTsIK, even though they were formally sovereign over the government. After Sverdlov became chairman of VTsIK in early November 1917, he managed this ostensible parliament in the interests of the Bolsheviks. VTsIK legitimized decisions taken elsewhere. Once the Left SRs and other parties were driven out, it lost its function as an arena for the opposition. After March 1919 VTsIK was chaired by Mikhail Kalinin, and in the early years of NEP it acted as a symbolic legislature promulgating the decrees of the New Economic Policy.

The Bolsheviks were anxious to enhance state power during the civil war and end the administrative anarchy that threatened the war effort. In the months following the October Revolution several revolutionary towns— Petrograd, Moscow, and Baku among them—had declared themselves communes, set up their own local sovnarkoms, and even appointed their own commissars of foreign affairs. But this practice was brought to a halt as the central state established its authority. On November 30, 1918, the Council of Workers' and Peasants' Defense was created to replace the Revolutionary Military Council of the Republic. Its members included Lenin, Trotsky, and Stalin, as well as commissars for railways and food supplies. From here the leading figures in the party directed the war effort.

At first, after October 1917, the Bolshevik party was not involved on a regular basis in governmental decisions. Party members worked in the soviets, the army, and the government and had little time for party affairs and meetings. Though the soviets were run by Communists, they often rejected party control over their day-to-day operations. Many party-focused Bolsheviks feared in 1918 that the party would atrophy. There was even talk that the party might be abolished now that there were soviets composed of Communists.

For the first six months after October, Lenin rarely mentioned the guiding role of the party, as he contemplated the establishment of a "commune state," like that of the Paris Commune. In this vision, initiative would come from below; politics would be replaced by administration, and repression would be a popular effort. As Lenin said in February 1918, "The exploiters must be suppressed, but they cannot be suppressed by the police; they must be suppressed by the masses themselves." Lenin based his hopes for socialism on the self-activization and self-actualization of the workers, but already in mid-1918 he had become quite ambivalent in his attitude toward the workers. "Many members of the working class," he wrote in June 1918, "have given way to despair." In December 1919 he noted, "The working class is exhausted and is naturally weak in a country that is in ruins." In place of that weakened working class, he reasoned, the most advanced workers and their leaders had to lead, and that meant the Communist Party. The "vanguard of the proletariat" was substituted for the workers themselves.

Throughout the civil war the Communist Party gained in influence until it became a state within the state. War encouraged quick, clear, effective decisions on major issues, rather than long deliberations and consultations. A habit of command developed among party leaders. Victory in war, some Communists argued convincingly, required coordination and the swift implementation of central state directives, but the soviets were by their nature local organs. The party was better suited to play the role of overall coordination and direction. At the end of 1918, a new party organ was created—the Political Bureau, or Politburo. Soon to be the most powerful political institution in Soviet Russia, the Politburo had five full members—Lenin, Trotsky, Stalin, Kamenev, and Krestinskii—and three candidate members—Zinoviev, Bukharin, and Kalinin. A month later, in January 1919, the Organizational Bureau, or Orgburo, was established. With the government bogged down with myriad minor matters and the country flying apart through the centrifugal forces of war and the rise of local power, the Central Committee and its two bureaus functioned increasingly as the most effective instruments to carry out the instructions of top leaders. The party had means of disciplining its members and had greater control over its local committees than the government did over local soviets, while Sovnarkom acted like a cabinet and carried out policies and made decisions within the general framework set by the party. By 1921 the Politburo was the most powerful institution in Russia, the seat of the oligarchy that ruled the country through the far-flung institutions of the Communist Party.

By the end of the civil war the relations of the party, state, and workers had been transformed in at least three important respects. First, during the years of war the conviction that the Soviet state had to be centralized in order better to defend itself gradually won out over those who favored local power or a more decentralized political structure. Second, Communists increasingly came around to the notion that the party should have primacy over the state. Third, decision-making had gravitated upward, away from workers to autonomous party and state leaders, who did not consult with the rank and file. Centralization, party control, and bureaucratic decision-making all made sense

Figure 5.1 Vladimir Lenin (center) in conversation with Lev Trotsky (left) and Lev Kamenev, Moscow, May 1920 (VA/SOVFOTO).

in the emergency conditions of the civil war. These developments in Bolshevik thinking and practice occurred against the background of the bitter perception that Russia's enfeebled working class was unable to carry out the awesome historical tasks with which the Communists had burdened them.

Everywhere soviets lost power to party committees. In Petrograd, where Lenin's lieutenant Grigorii Zinoviev headed the soviet executive committee, the soviet had dominated over the party committee, whose secretary was a close ally of Zinoviev. But over time the city's party committee tried to strengthen its position against the soviet. A knockdown political squabble over which institution should be paramount divided the local party through 1921. Finally, Moscow stepped in, reprimanded Zinoviev, and established the Petrograd party committee as the supreme power in the old capital. That power would have no check on its activities from below, from the soviets or the workers, but would be ultimately responsible to Moscow and the Central Committee. All over Soviet Russia party committees and soviet executive committees were becoming executives no longer responsible to their ostensible constituents below. When the gap grew too large between the party-state and the people, meetings or commissions might be held, complaints would be heard, and resolutions taken, but no permanent institutions effectively linking society to the state or giving voters control over their representatives were established. The Communist Party ruled over the Soviet people, in their name, determined to transform their society into a vision of the Communists' own imagination.

Opposition within the Party

With the elimination of other effective parties, all politics centered within the Communist Party. For the first five years of Soviet power, party meetings and congresses were like little parliaments where the top leadership, often divided itself, battled with various factions, such as the Left Communists, the Democratic Centralists, and the Workers' Opposition. This brings us to the fourth step in the formation of an authoritarian state—the gradual suppression of internal party politics, which began in earnest in 1921 with the decree against factions and continued through the 1920s.

The idea that the Bolshevik party was a monolithic, highly centralized and disciplined party is a myth that Soviet historians propagated for many years by repressing the real history of the party and that Western observers, without access to the inner workings of the party, reproduced in their writings. In actuality, Bolshevism, from its very birth as a faction in the Russian Social Democratic Workers' Party, was riven by personal and political differences among its leaders. At the time of the February Revolution, the party was still a small collection of radical internationalist socialists loosely united by their respect for Lenin. During the revolutionary year, hundreds of thousands of ordinary workers and soldiers joined the party swelling the membership of the party from about twenty thousand in February to more than two hundred fifty thousand by October. During the civil war the party pulled in peasants and soldiers, until by 1921 it had nearly three-quarters of a million members. The official census of the party in 1921 concluded that 41 percent of members had been workers on the eve of the revolution, 28.2 percent were of peasant origin, and 30.8 percent came from the intelligentsia and white-collar strata. The statistics reveal that the worker component in the party had actually declined in the civil war years as the percentage of the peasants increased and the intelligentsia quotient stayed roughly the same. Many of the new recruits had no or only rudimentary knowledge of Marxism or the past controversies that had divided the Social Democratic movement.

Even at the moment of the seizure of power the party had not been unified. Two of Lenin's closest comrades, Zinoviev and Kamenev, publicly opposed the armed insurrection. In the first month of the new government more than a dozen Communist leaders resigned in protest against Lenin's resistance to broadening Sovnarkom by including members of other parties. And in early 1918 the Left Communist faction formed to oppose the signing of the Brest-Litovsk peace with the Germans.

The Left Communists were led by Bukharin and included important figures like Uritskii, Radek, David Riazanov, N. Osinskii, Emelian Iaroslavskii, and the radical feminist Aleksandra Kollontai. They held a majority in the Moscow Regional Bureau of the party and were powerfully represented in the Petrograd Committee, the Urals organization, and the Central Committee. Once they lost on the war issue, they became the most fervent advocates of a rapid transition to socialism. For the Left this meant immediate nationalization of industry with workers' in control of the factories. Their touchstone was the principle of democratic administration of the economy by the workers. Osinskii's was the loudest voice criticizing one-person management, the hiring of bourgeois specialists, and the coercive measures adopted to increase labor productivity. Many of the former Left Communists, like Bukharin, became enthusiastic advocates of civil war economic policies, and the fullest theoretical treatment of what would later be labeled "War Communism" was contained in Bukharin's influential book *The Economics of the Transition Period*.

As a faction, the Left Communists did not last beyond the summer of 1918, but many of their ideas were taken up by two other factions, the Democratic Centralists and the Workers' Opposition. The Democratic Centralists appeared in 1918 as opponents of Lenin and Trotsky's notion of one-person management. For them the collegial principle was "the strongest weapon against the growth . . . of the bureaucratic deadening of the soviet apparatus." Like the Military Opposition, with which they shared members, the Democratic Centralists were wary about the employment of "experts," who invariably supplanted workers; they were upset with the disempowering of the soviets and urged measures to restore their vitality. But their suggestions to reintroduce more discussion into soviet and party affairs ran up against the suspicion of leading Bolsheviks that they were advocating "parliamentarianism." Arguments for greater intraparty or soviet democracy, were met with retorts urging greater solidarity against the enemy. "The experience of the triumphant dictatorship of the proletariat in Russia," Lenin stated in his polemical pamphlet *The Infantile Disease of "Leftism" in Communism*, "proves that unqualified centralism and the strictest discipline of the proletariat are among the principal conditions for the victory over the bourgeoisie. . . . Whoever in the least weakens the iron discipline of the party of the proletariat (especially during its dictatorship), aids in reality the bourgeoisie against the proletariat."

Even as the power of workers at the bench declined, as decisions were made by specialists and worker-administrators, the Bolsheviks fiercely debated the role of workers in the new socialist system they were building. Early in 1919 the Second Congress of Trade Unions adopted the idea of eventual "statization" of the trade unions, that is, the merging of trade unions and the state industrial administration. A few months later, in March 1919, the Eighth Party Congress adopted a party program that called for the trade unions to take over economic administration. A year later, at the Ninth Party Congress in March and April 1920, party members again debated the role of trade unions and the implementation of one-person management in factories. Trotsky argued for militarization of the trade unions:

> The militarization of labor is unthinkable without the militarization of trade unions, without the introduction of a regime under which every worker feels himself a soldier of labor who cannot dispose of himself freely. If an order is given to transfer him, he must carry it out. If he does not carry it out, he will be a deserter who is punished.

Osinskii, the longtime Bolshevik, whose Democratic Centralist faction feared the bureaucratization of the party, spoke against both militarization and one-person management:

> What is happening now at the Congress is a clash of a number of cultures. . . .
> We have created a military-Soviet culture, a civilian-Soviet culture, and the

> trade union movement has created its own sphere of culture. Each of these
> cultures has its own approach to events and has created its own routine. . . .
> We are against stretching the concept of militarization too far; we are against
> the blind imitation of military models.

The Congress ended by compromising. Trade unions would not be made part
of the state administration but would keep a degree of autonomy. One-person
management would be implemented in factories and shops, but higher up in
the industrial system, there would be collegial boards. Bourgeois specialists
would be employed, while compulsory labor for all would be imposed. Trotsky was allowed to apply his militarization scheme most forcefully in the transportation system, which fell under his new post of commissar of railroads.

With the civil war coming to an end, party members began to raise questions that they had suppressed during the war years, questions about the atrophied soviets, one-person management of factories, and the militarization of
labor. The Democratic Centralists won a significant victory in their assault on
growing bureaucratization in the party and state in September 1920 at the Ninth
Party Conference. The party decided to establish "control commissions" to curtail bureaucratic practices and protect the interests of the rank-and-file members. The final resolution of the conference rejected the practice of appointing
local party secretaries from the center and the heavy-handed repression of di-
vergent views within the party. At about the same time opposition grew to
Trotsky's highhanded methods of running the railroads and his insistence on
militarization of the trade unions. Trotsky's vision was an extreme one of state
socialism with an overall plan for the development of the economy and the
subordination of trade unions to the needs of production. "The worker does
not merely bargain with the Soviet state," he said; "no, he is subordinated to
the Soviet state, under its orders in every direction, for it is *his* state." In November 1920, however, the Central Committee of the party pulled back from
its earlier endorsement of militarization and warned against "bureaucracy, bul-
lying, red-tapeism, and petty tutelage over the trade unions." Controversy
raged over the activities of the new central executive committee of the transport workers (Tsektran), and the party remained deeply divided over the key
issues of the building of a socialist system: the role of workers and trade unions,
the ties between the party and the working class, and the relations between the
workers' state and the vast mass of peasants growing more and more hostile
to the proletarian dictatorship. Lenin joined those who opposed Trotsky's operation of Tsektran and worked out his own position on the role of trade unions.
Zinoviev, Kamenev, Stalin, trade union head Mikhail Tomskii, and others
adopted Lenin's "Platform of the Ten." Instead of immediate "statization" or
militarization of trade unions, Lenin proposed that the unions become "schools
for communism," in which political educators would mobilize the masses of
workers. Unions should not completely merge yet with the Soviet state but
needed to defend the interests of workers for the time being. "Our present state
is such," wrote Lenin, "that the entire organized proletariat must defend itself;
we must use these workers' organizations for the defense of workers from their
state and for the defense by the workers of our state."

The debate climaxed at the Tenth Party Congress in March 1921, when three variant positions were presented: the "Platform of the Ten," the statization position of Trotsky and Bukharin, and the radical democratic platform of the Workers' Opposition. The "Platform of the Ten" attempted to reconcile democratic and dictatorial principles, the "method of persuasion" and the "principles of proletarian compulsion (compulsory mobilization of tens of thousands of trade union members, disciplinary courts, etc.)." But it emphasized the revival of earlier democratic practices.

> The methods of workers' democracy, which were so sharply curtailed in the three years of cruel civil war, should be re-established first of all, and on a wide scale, in the trade union movement. It is necessary first of all to re-establish the system of electing officials for the various trade union organs, instead of appointing them from above. The trade unions should be built on the principle of democratic centralism.

Trotsky argued that trade unions ought to organize workers and draw them into the life of the Soviet state. Rather than worry about workers' welfare, unions had to concern themselves primarily with production. The state had long been using unions to register workers, set output and wage norms, and punish workers for infractions of labor discipline. Now the unions should gradually fuse with the soviet apparatus to run the economic machine more effectively.

The Workers' Opposition, led by Aleksandr Shliapnikov and Aleksandra Kollontai, favored bringing the unions into the management of the entire economic structure through a congress of producers that would be elected by trade unions and organize control over the economy. In this vision workers and their unions would no longer be subordinated to state institutions but would themselves run industry and organize the work process. In Kollontai's words,

> Bureaucracy is a direct negation of mass self-activity. . . . There can be no self-activity without freedom of thought and opinion. . . . We give no freedom to class activity; we are afraid of criticism; we have ceased to rely on the masses: hence, we have bureaucracy with us.

Kollontai castigated the party's policies of relying on bourgeois specialists as a "jump off the rails of scientific Marxist thought." She demanded that "the party must become a workers' party," and that nonworkers must go through a period of manual labor before joining the party. Party officials should be elected rather than appointed, and full democracy should exist within the party. But the party should also exercise control over the soviets, for as the representative of the workers it should push the interests of the workers over any competing interests of the state or other classes.

The debate at the congress was fierce, but in the end the vote was overwhelmingly in favor of Lenin's position: 336 to 50 for Trotsky's resolution and 18 for the Workers' Opposition. Weary of the divisions within the party ranks and fearful of rebellion and signs of discontent in the country, Lenin then set out to crush the Workers' Opposition and unify the party. He pushed through a resolution that required "the rapid dispersal of all groups without exception that have formed themselves on one platform or another" and ordered "all organizations to deal strictly with any factional manifestations by prohibiting them." Though the principles of free discussion and election of officials were reaffirmed, the congress voted officially to ban the organizing of factions within the party. Members of the party guilty of factionalism could be expelled from the party by a two-thirds vote of the Central Committee. Directed against the Workers' Opposition, the resolution was born out of the fear that organized factions within the party would encourage opposition within society.

The wartime habits of command and the imagined (and real) dangers from counterrevolution and the "petty bourgeoisie" (the peasantry) combined to lead the party leaders away from the more democratic, decentralizing, and worker-oriented tendencies that existed within the party and in the country. The conspiratorial practices of the prerevolutionary underground party and the militarized behavior of the leather-jacketed party of the civil war years were too deeply ingrained to be vitiated with rhetoric about internal party democracy. Yet the freewheeling debates that had always been a part of party meetings could not be completely stifled. Factions of various kinds continued to exist, and party leaders repeatedly found it necessary to crack down on them. Political pressure, supplemented by arrests, put an end in 1921 to other dissident Communist factions, such as the Workers' Group and the Workers' Truth, both of which had attacked the growing bureaucratization of the party and its undemocratic behavior. Lenin renewed his attack on factionalism at the Eleventh Party Congress in March and April 1922, and from this point on the disciplinary mechanisms within the party became ever stronger. The solidification of the party apparatus, headed by the Secretariat, would in the future have the power to appoint and transfer party officials and thus disperse potential and actual oppositions. The congress appointed Josef Stalin general secretary of the Communist Party to head the growing apparatus of the party.

As for the trade unions, they too were brought under party control in 1921–22. When the powerful metalworkers union met in May 1921 and voted for the Workers' Opposition, the party's Central Committee simply appointed its own men to lead the union. Lenin, Stalin, and Bukharin appeared at the Fourth All-Russian Congress of Trade Unions to beat down a resolution that emphasized that union leaders should be selected by the organized workers. The congress then demoted chairman Tomskii and other trade union leaders. But six months later, the party leaders gave in to the supporters of autonomy who remained strong within the unions. Tomskii was restored as leader of the central council of trade unions and soon elevated to the Politburo. In the mixed economy of the 1920s trade unions were permitted to defend the interests of workers, and in January 1922 the Politburo resolved that unions were to protect workers against dangers stemming from the capitalist influences of the New Economic Policy. But unions were not to interfere in production and certainly not to run the economy. The Left's dream of worker management or union control of the economy had been deferred indefinitely.

Resistance, Rebellion, and Mutiny

Once the civil war wound down in the fall of 1920, new problems faced the Communists in power. Victorious over the huge space soon be known as the Soviet Union, the Leninists could no longer justify the hardships imposed on the country for nearly three years by claiming that they were necessitated by the war effort. As the Red Army was demobilized, returning soldiers who could find no work in the devastated industries or agriculture turned to banditry. Hundreds of thousands of men roamed the countryside in bands, often stirring the peasants to revolt. In the huge province of Tambov tens of thousands of peasants revolted against Soviet authority, under the leadership of A. S. Antonov. Starvation was widespread, and the peasants hated the grain requisitions and the workers' food detachments. Gathering around a Union of Working Peasants, they called for an end to forced seizures of grain, full political equality of all citizens "except for the house of Romanov," personal economic freedom, denationalization of industry, fixed prices for industrial goods but no firm prices for agricultural produce, freedom to form cooperatives and freedom of teaching in the schools. Their program was a complete rejection of the Communist economic program. The Cheka reported 118 peasant uprisings. Besides the fifty thousand rebels in Tambov province, another sixty thousand guerrillas were active in Western Siberia. Everywhere could be heard the slogans "Down with requisitioning!" "Away with food detachments!" "Down with the Communists and the Jews!"

The rural rebellions compounded the food crisis in the towns, which led to strikes by workers. The price of bread rose. The winter of 1920–21 was exceptionally cold, and famine spread through the Volga basin. Over 22 million head of livestock were lost, and 10,000,000 people lived on the verge of starvation. Workers grew more alienated from the Communist Party, and many gravitated toward the Mensheviks. Particularly worrying to the government were strikes in Petrograd in February 1921. Workers demanded food, boots, and a return to the soviet democracy of 1917. A workers' resolution proclaimed, "After October 25, 1917, we saw workers in all the departments, but now we do not see a single worker in soviet institutions; only white hands sit there and destroy faith in Soviet power." Workers wanted an end to "the growth of a new Soviet bourgeoisie." The city government unleashed the Cheka to arrest Mensheviks and SRs once again and to crack down on the strikers. At the same time they gave in to the economic demands and began distributing food and clothing. The strikes ended in early March.

Yet, even in the face of the growing social crisis, Lenin resisted shifting his economic policies away from the war economy. At the Eighth Congress of Soviets in December 1920, Mensheviks and SRs, who were still represented in the congresses, called for an end to the militarized economy. Peasant delegates as well spoke strongly against the grain seizures. But Lenin argued that the threat of attack from Poland or Wrangel in Turkey still existed, and that reform was premature. He was backed by the Democratic Centrists, who called for more, rather than less, compulsion against the peasantry. The Congress, with its overwhelming Bolshevik majority, passed Lenin's proposals.

The worst and most threatening blow to the Bolshevik regime came from the Baltic sailors who mutinied at the Kronstadt naval base in March 1921. Kronstadt was one of the great tragedies of the years of revolution and civil war. The rebels, who were demanding greater democracy, aroused great sympathy around the world, particularly from anarchists and democratic socialists, but at the same time the beleaguered Soviet state was determined to eradicate this threat at the heart of the revolution. Lenin warned that Kronstadt could be a "step, a ladder, a bridge" for a White victory, and he convinced his comrades that they must use force to crush the rebellion.

The program of the Kronstadt sailors harkened back to the goals of 1917. It favored a decentralized, democratic soviet-based state and called for "all power to the soviets, but not the parties." Borrowing ideas from anarchists and SR-Maximalists, the sailors declared they wanted "not state management and workers' control, but workers' management and state control." The sailors made no threatening move toward Petrograd, twenty miles away across the Finnish Gulf, even though workers in the city were also discontented with Communist rule. Kalinin tried to talk to the sailors but was shouted down. Trotsky arrived in Petrograd and issued an ultimatum demanding unconditional surrender. On March 7 Soviet forces opened an artillery barrage on the fort, but the infantry advancing over the ice under cover of a snowstorm failed to take the base. The sailors now called for "a third revolution," this time directed against "the dictatorship of the Communist Party with its Cheka and its state capitalism, whose hangman's noose encircles the necks of the laboring masses."

Trotsky appeared at the party congress in Moscow and inspired three hundred delegates to come with him to Petrograd to help in the battle for Kronstadt. Fearful that they were losing time and that warmer weather would melt the ice and make Kronstadt impregnable to an infantry invasion, Trotsky ordered another advance. On March 17 a force of fifty thousand men, under the command of Tukhachevskii, took the fortress and ended the rebellion.

A Retreat to State Capitalism

March 1921 marked a major turning point in early Soviet history. At the same moment that popular rebellion shook Soviet power internally, the external position of Soviet Russia stabilized. Poland and Russia signed the Treaty of Riga, and the British agreed to open trade with Soviet Russia. While he toned down his international revolutionary expectations, Lenin pursued internal policies that moved in two directions at once. To contain the simultaneous political and economic crises he decided to tighten up political control by the party, while at the same time loosening the economic hold of the state. The party dictatorship would be retained; factions in the party would be prohibited and opposition parties would be eliminated. But at the same time, on the economic front, the unpopular, unproductive, and draconian policies of the war years would be replaced by a New Economic Policy. In his notes for a speech to the Tenth Party Congress, Lenin wrote: "The lesson of Kronstadt: in politics—the closing of the ranks (+ discipline) within the party, greater struggle against the Mensheviks and Socialist Revolutionaries; in economics—to satisfy as far as possible the middle peasantry."

The Congress opened on March 8, the day that the first attack on Kronstadt failed, and closed on March 16, the day before the successful second attack. In that eventful week the Communists passed the resolution banning factions within the party. Lenin coolly assessed the isolation of Soviet Russia and the precarious position of a proletarian party in a peasant country:

> We know that so long as there is no revolution in other countries, only agreement with the peasantry can save the socialist revolution in Russia. . . . The peasantry is dissatisfied with the form of our relations; it does not want relations of this type and will not continue to live as it has up to now. . . .
> . . . Russia emerged from the war in a state that can most of all be likened to that of a man beaten to within an inch of his life; the beating has gone on for seven years, and it is a mercy Russia can hobble about on crutches. That is the situation we are in!

On March 15 Lenin proposed a new strategy in the period of the transition to socialism, a kind of retreat on the economic front:

> There is no doubt that in a country where the overwhelming majority of the population consists of small agricultural producers, a socialist revolution can be carried out only through the implementation of a whole series of special transitional measures which would be superfluous in highly developed capitalist countries where wage workers in industry and agriculture make up the vast majority. . . . This is not the case in Russia, for here industrial workers are a minority and petty farmers are the vast majority. In such a country, the socialist revolution can triumph only on two conditions. First, if it is given timely support by a socialist revolution in one or several advanced countries. . . . The second condition is agreement between the proletariat, which is exercising its dictatorship, that is, holds state power, and the majority of the peasant population.

Though Lenin could not know it at the time, neither of these conditions ultimately would be met. More immediately, he noted, there was class conflict within Soviet Russia between workers and peasants:

> The interests of these two classes differ; the small farmer does not want the same thing as the worker. . . . The peasantry in general has acquired the status of the middle peasant. . . . It will take generations to remold the small farmer, and recast his mentality and habits. The only way to solve this problem of the small farmer—to improve, so to speak, his mentality—is through the material basis, technical equipment, the extensive use of tractors and other farm machinery and electrification on a mass scale.

The New Economic Policy was a concession to the peasantry, giving them incentives to plant, expand production, and to market their grain. The small peasant, "ruined, impoverished, miserably hungry," must be helped, said Lenin, "or he will send us all to the devils." He argued that the Soviet order was "founded on the collaboration of two classes, the workers and the peasants." This *smychka*, or linking of the town and the countryside, was symbolized in the crossed hammer and sickle on the Soviet flag. The government declared that peasants would pay a set percentage of their production in grain as a "tax-in-kind." Their grain would no longer be forcibly requisitioned. Any surplus above the tax could be sold freely by the peasants. Peasants were individually responsible for paying the tax, and their land, though officially publicly owned, was theirs to work. Land tenure was guaranteed. Lenin saw the NEP as a "retreat to state capitalism," but he also emphasized that Russia was still building socialism, though now through "a reformist approach," rather than a revolutionary one. As Lenin told his comrades, a year later at the Eleventh Party Congress,

> We Communists are but a drop in the ocean, a drop in the ocean of the people. We shall be able to lead the people along the road we have chosen only if we correctly determine it not only from the standpoint of its direction in world history. . . . We must also determine it correctly for our native land, for our country. . . . The peasants will say: "You are splendid fellows; you defended our country. That is why we obeyed you. But if you cannot run the show, get out!" Yes, that is what the peasants will say.

Lenin's model of state capitalism was based on the wartime economy of Germany, the *Planwirtschaft*. He saw this highly planned, regulated, and centralized economy as the transition stage to socialism. Though market mechanisms were permitted to operate, Soviet leaders retained many of the institutions and instruments of planning that had been initiated during the civil war. An overall coordinator of the economy, the Council of Labor and Defense (STO), had been formed in March 1920. Just before NEP was introduced, in February 1921, a state planning agency called Gosplan was formed under STO. Planning and the market were to be combined with the importation of western technology and machines to lay the foundation for the future socialist economy. Enthralled with the power of modern technology, Lenin proclaimed in one of his more bizarre statements, "Communism is Soviet power plus electrification of the whole country." Under STO, the government established a commission to supervise the electrification of Russia, known as Goelro, in November 1920.

Compared to what went on before (the civil war and war communism) and what was to come later (Stalinism, collectivization, and the Great Terror), NEP was a bright spot in the first decades of Soviet history. The state eased up on the people, both economically and in terms of repression and compulsion. Peasants were free to trade their surpluses. Workers could move from job to job. Private trade was legalized. Though most wholesale trade was still carried on by the state, retail trade was on the whole private. Cooperatives grew in number and in strength. Middlemen, the so-called Nepmen, flourished. Foreign trade revived, especially after the March 1921 Anglo-Soviet Trade Agreement. Foreigners were offered concessions to attract foreign capital. Some, like the young Armand Hammer and Averell Harriman, invested in local plants, such as a pencil factory, and in Georgian manganese mines. Despite widespread unemployment, the standard of living for most gradually rose.

NEP had aspects of a market economy but with strong input from the state. Though in future decades, particularly in the last years of the Soviet system, NEP would look to many like a golden age, a model society to be reinstated, Communists argued through the 1920s about how long it would last, what the degree of planning should be in this mixed economy, and if state capitalism was the right road to socialism or would lead to a restoration of a bourgeois society. For most Communists, NEP was transitional and temporary, a retreat that would eventually be halted.

Suggestions for Further Reading

On the evolution of the Soviet state and party, see Oskar Anweiler, *The Soviets: The Russian Workers, Peasants, and Soldiers Councils 1905–1921* (New York, 1974); Carmen Sirianni, *Workers' Control and Socialist Democracy: The Soviet Experience* (London, 1982); John L. H. Keep (trans. and ed.), *The Debate of Soviet Power: Minutes of the All-Russian Central Executive Committee of Soviets, Second Convocation, October 1917–January 1918* (Oxford, 1979); Leonard B. Schapiro, *The Communist Party of the Soviet Union* (London and New York, 1970); *The Origin of the Communist Autocracy: Political Opposition in the Soviet State, First Phase, 1917–1922* (London and Cambridge, Mass., 1955); T. H. Rigby, *Lenin's Government: Sovnarkom, 1917–1922* (Cambridge, 1979); Robert Service, *The Bolshevik Party in Revolution, 1917–1921: A Study in Organisational Change* (London, 1979); Marcel Liebman, *Leninism under Lenin* (London, 1975); Thomas F. Remington, *Building Socialism in Bolshevik Russia: Ideology and Industrial Organization, 1917–1921* (Pittsburgh, 1984); Robert V. Daniels, *The Conscience of the Revolution. Communist Opposition in Soviet Russia* (Cambridge, Mass., 1960); Robert H. McNeal (ed.), *Resolutions and Decisions of the Communist Party of the Soviet Union, Vol. 2, The Early Soviet Period, 1917–1929* (Toronto, 1974); and Mark Ferro, *October 1917: A Social History of the Russian Revolution* (London, 1980).

On state policies toward the population, see Lars T. Lih, *Bread and Authority in Russia, 1914–1921* (Berkeley, Calif., 1990); and Mary McAuley, *Bread and Justice: State and Society in Petrograd, 1917–1922* (Oxford, 1991). On the Kronstadt mutiny, see Israel Getzler, *Kronstadt, 1917–1921: The Fate of a Soviet Democracy* (Cambridge, 1983); and Paul Avrich, *Kronstadt 1921* (Princeton, N.J., 1970).

A classic work on the early Soviet period that covers all aspects of state and party policy is E. H. Carr, *The Bolshevik Revolution, 1917–1923*, 3 vols. (London and New York, 1950–53). Fascinating documents from Soviet archives can be found in Richard Pipes, *The Unknown Lenin: From the Secret Archive* (New Haven, Conn., 1996).

CHAPTER 6
Socialism in One Country

By 1922 interparty politics were a historical memory, and the only arena for political discussion and infighting was within the Communist party. The bar on factions in 1921, the progressive elimination of political opposition through the 1920s, and the steady accumulation of power by a single faction reduced the political arena even further, until a handful of influential figures decided the course for the rest of the party. The closing of the ranks within the party at the end of the civil war was a response to the sense that the rule of the Communist Party was still in serious danger. In a country populated largely by peasants, the New Economic Policy was a tactical retreat to secure peasant support for, or at least acquiescence in, the rule of the Communist Party. And in the multinational environment of the Soviet republics appeals and concessions also had to be made to the non-Russian peoples. Here a serious conflict developed between Lenin and Stalin, one that resulted in Lenin winning the battle and Stalin the war.

The Nationality Question

Long before the revolution the Social Democrats had proclaimed their support for the "right of self-determination of nations," and Lenin had extended that idea to include the right of the oppressed peoples of the Russian Empire to separate and form independent states if they so desired. At the beginning of the twentieth century, Russian Marxists had two somewhat contradictory goals: to win over the non-Russian nationalities and to combat the nationalists' attempts to splinter the unitary state. They believed that "national differences and antagonisms between peoples are vanishing gradually from day to day" and that "the supremacy of the proletariat will cause them to vanish still faster." Bolshevik theorists were adamant in their opposition to federalism and resisted the administrative division of the state along ethnic lines. They preferred "regional autonomy," in which political units would not have ethnic designations.

The Bolsheviks' prerevolutionary thinking on the national question did not survive the revolution intact. The actual nationality policy of the Soviet government was, like its economic policies during NEP, a compromise in the context of underdevelopment. Though many of his comrades consistently favored subordinating nationalism strictly to class considerations, Lenin refused to oppose the independence of Finland, Poland, and, for a time, Ukraine and Georgia. Though he hoped that such separations could be avoided, he was wary of the use of force to keep the empire whole. He was unequivocal in his public commitment to "the full right of separation from Russia of all nations and nationalities, oppressed by tsarism, joined by force or held by force within the borders of the state, i.e., annexed." At the same time, he argued that the goal of the proletarian party was the creation of the largest state possible and the rapprochement and eventual merging of nations. Such a goal was to be reached, not through force, but voluntarily, by the will of the workers.

Immediately after taking power, the Bolsheviks set up the People's Commissariat of Nationalities under Stalin and issued a series of declarations on "the rights of the toiling and exploited peoples," to "all Muslim toilers of Russia and the East," and on the disposition of Turkish Armenia. Most importantly, and with little real ability to effect its will in the peripheries, the Soviet government responded to the centrifugal movement of non-Russians away from the Russian center and accepted by January 1918 the principle of federalism. Even as they launched an attack on Ukraine, the Bolsheviks announced that they recognized the Central Executive Committee of Soviets of Ukraine as "the supreme authority in Ukraine" and accepted "a federal union with Russia and complete unity in matters of internal and external policy." By the end of the month the Third Congress of Soviets resolved: "The Soviet Russian Republic is established on the basis of a free union of free nations, as a federation of Soviet national republics." Both federalism and national-territorial autonomy were written into the first Soviet constitution, adopted in July 1918. Soviet Russia was the first state in history to create a federal system based on ethnonational units.

With the civil war raging, many Communists, particularly those on the peripheries or of non-Russian origin, opposed Lenin's idea of national self-determination, fearing the breakup of the unitary state. As early as December 1917, Stalin argued that the freedom of self-determination should be given only to the laboring classes, not to the bourgeoisie. At the Eighth Party Congress in March 1919, Bukharin supported Stalin's position and tried to separate the national from the colonial question. Only in those nations where the proletariat had not yet defined its interests as separate from the bourgeoisie should the slogan of "self-determination of nations" be employed. Lenin's formula, he claimed, was appropriate only "for Hottentots, Bushmen, Negroes, Indians," whereas Stalin's notion of "self-determination for the laboring classes" corresponded to the period in which the dictatorship of the proletariat was being established. Lenin answered Bukharin sharply. "There are no Bushmen in Russia; as for the Hottentots, I also have not heard that they have pretensions to an autonomous republic, but we have the Bashkirs, the Kyrgyz, a whole series of other peoples, and in relation to them we cannot refuse recognition." All nations, he reasserted, have the right to self-determination, and Bolshevik support for this principle would aid the self-determination of the laboring classes. The stage of a given nation as it moved from "medieval forms to bourgeois democracy and on to proletarian democracy" should be considered, he said, but it was difficult to differentiate the interests of the proletariat and the bourgeoisie, which had been sharply defined only among the Russians. The final resolution of the Congress was a compromise between Lenin's tolerance of nationalism and the more militant opposition to it. Maintaining the principle of national self-determination, the resolution went on to say, "As to the question who is the carrier of the nation's will to separation, the Russian Communist Party stands on the historico-class point-of-view, taking into consideration the level of historical development on which a given nation stands."

The Bolsheviks reached no consensus on nationality policy, and many, like Stalin and his Georgian collaborator Sergo Orjonikidze, were not reconciled to Lenin's softer line on nationalism. For Stalin, unity, centralism, and subordination of the national to the proletarian were the principles on which he based his nationality policy. Far from Moscow, in the everyday battles of the civil war, Communists decided themselves who was the carrier of the nation's will, and after the initial recognition of independence for Finland, Poland, the Baltic republics, and (for a time) Georgia, few other gestures were made toward separatists. The civil war was a new round of gathering the lands that had once belonged to Russia.

As the strategic situation improved for the Bolsheviks and their allies by the summer of 1920, the national-colonial question was put squarely on the agenda. For a moment it seemed that the revolution would be carried beyond the borders of Russia into the Near East and Asia. But despite the enthusiasm of internationalist radicals like the leftist adventurer John Reed, a founder of the American Communist Party and the author of an eyewitness account of the October Revolution, *Ten Days That Shook the World*, the revolutionary wave receded as rapidly as it had arisen, and the Soviet government began to see itself as one state among many, albeit with a different historical role. The Soviet state needed to consolidate internally, many leading Communists thought, before it could effectively inspire revolutionary resistance to international capitalism. In 1921 there were six Soviet republics: the Russian Soviet Federated Socialist Republic (RSFSR), Ukraine, Belorussia, Armenia, Azerbaijan, and Georgia. The relations among them were loose and ill-defined. Though all were ruled by Communist parties, they maintained a considerable amount of independence. Late in 1921 Stalin attempted to establish greater central control over the republics, beginning with the republics of Transcaucasia.

Stalin and Orjonikidze wanted the three republics south of the Caucasus—Armenia, Azerbaijan, and Georgia—to merge into a single Transcaucasian Federation, but the independent-minded leaders of the Georgian Communist Party protested against the merger. Nevertheless, the centralizers managed to win over the delegates to the first congress of Georgian Communists, as well as the leaders of Armenian and Azerbaijan, and in March 1922 a Federal Union of Soviet Socialist Republics of Transcaucasia was formed. An influential group of

Georgian Communist leaders continued to protest the infringements on their sovereignty, but Stalin argued that the economy of all three republics would develop more rapidly if they remained united.

The Georgian conflict soon became entwined in the larger issue of forming a union of all the Soviet republics. In early September 1922 Stalin introduced a plan to bring the five non-Russian republics into the RSFSR as autonomous republics. Communist leaders in Armenia and Azerbaijan were enthusiastic about the plan, but the Georgians opposed this "autonomization" plan. The Orgburo in Moscow approved Stalin's model, and it seemed certain to be accepted by the Politburo. But Stalin failed to win Lenin over to his more centralized idea of union. Lenin was ill, the victim of what would soon be a fatal series of strokes, but from his convalescence outside of Moscow he began a last-ditch effort to scuttle Stalin's plan. Lenin preferred that all six republics enter on an equal basis a new Union of Soviet Socialist Republics. On October 6, 1922, he wrote to Kamenev:

> I declare war to the death on dominant-nation chauvinism. I shall eat it with all my healthy teeth as soon as I get rid of this accursed bad tooth. It must be absolutely insisted that the Union Central Executive Committee should be *presided* over in turn by a Russia, Ukrainian, Georgian, etc. *Absolutely!*

Stalin shrewdly decided not to confront Lenin, though he thought Lenin's view amounted to "national liberalism." The Central Committee approved Lenin's version, and the Soviet Union was formally inaugurated on December 30,1922. But Lenin's last struggle with Stalin continued through the fall of 1922 and into the winter of 1923. Lenin was furious over Stalin's handling of the Georgian "national Communists," as well as a personal affront to his wife, Nadezhda Krupskaia. He began dictating a series of thoughts to his secretaries, which were later labeled Lenin's "testament." In one note, he compared the qualities of Stalin and Trotsky:

> Comrade Stalin, having become Secretary General, has unlimited authority concentrated in his hands, and I am not sure whether he will always be capable of using that authority with sufficient caution. Comrade Trotsky, on the other hand, . . . is distinguished not only by outstanding ability. He is personally perhaps the most capable man in the present Central Committee, but he has displayed excessive self-assurance and shown excessive preoccupation with the purely administrative side of the work.

In a prescient warning to his comrades, Lenin called for Stalin's removal from his high office:

> Stalin is too rude, and this defect, though quite tolerable in our midst and in dealings among us Communists, becomes intolerable in a General Secretary. That is why I suggest that the comrades think of a way to remove Stalin from that post and appoint in his place another man who in all respects differs from Comrade Stalin in his superiority, that is, more loyal, more courteous and more considerate of the comrades, less capricious, etc.

Lenin was appalled at Stalin's "Great Russian chauvinism" and feared the consequences of his attempts to force the nationalities into an artificial unity. He warned that "it is better to oversalt on the side of conciliation and softness toward the national minorities than to undersalt."

From his sickbed Lenin managed to delay the process of centralization but not to stop it. Stalin largely had his way on the national question at the Twelfth Party Congress in April 1923. The Congress reprimanded the Georgian Communists. In his address on nationality policy Stalin agreed that Great Russian chauvinism was the principal danger to national peace in the Soviet republics, but he also emphasized the danger of local nationalisms by the non-Russians, which threaten "to turn some republics into arenas of national squabbles, tearing there the ties of internationalism." And he pointedly ended up by saying, "It is just as forbidden to oversalt in politics as it is forbidden to undersalt."

Soviet nationality policy for the next thirty years was largely the work of Josef Stalin. Though formal commitments were made to autonomy for non-Russians, ultimate authority remained with Moscow. The Soviet state permitted, indeed at times encouraged, the development of national cultures, but strictly within the framework of the socialist system and ideology. "National in form, socialist in content" eventually became the usual formula for describing the permissible expression of ethnic culture. In non-Russian regions and republics a program of national "affirmative action" called "nativization" promoted the use of local people in local organs of government. Though all decisions were strictly subordinated to the "class interests" of the Soviet proletariat as a whole, the party encouraged the use of the local non-Russian languages in schools and official institutions. The six republics received a formal right to secession from the union, but that right was considered a fiction for the next sixty-five years. The new union had a bicameral legislature, elected by the Congress of Soviets, in which one house, the Soviet of the Union, was selected on the basis of population, and the other, the Soviet of Nationalities, represented national groups; but they were largely formal bodies that did not seriously debate issues. The constitution of the new Soviet Union was ratified on January 31, 1924, just days after Lenin died.

The kinds of guarantees for national autonomy that Lenin had hoped for, however, were not realized, though his concessions to the non-Russian peoples brought a level of peace and acquiescence to Bolshevik rule. For both Lenin and Stalin, the key players in the formation of the multinational Soviet Union, nationality policy was a temporary tactical adjustment, not unlike the party's agrarian policy and New Economic Policy, to deal with problems that would be resolved once the international proletarian revolution occurred. Far more than most other party members, Lenin promoted the concept of national self-determination, even to the point of separation from Russia, but it was Stalin's vision of a much more centralized union, with the non-Russian republics reduced to culturally distinct autonomies, that prevailed. As his own power increased, Stalin consistently shifted the emphasis in Lenin's nationality policy until it became an ideology for a new, disguised form of empire in which the center and Russia emerged superordinate and the non-Russian peripheries fell into a state of tutelage.

The General Secretary

Even before Lenin died, Stalin had accumulated enormous power within the party, and though he was not generally recognized outside party circles as one of the most influential leaders, his authority grew steadily. Within the party political manipulation, Machiavellian intrigues, and a willingness to resort to ruthlessness were certainly part of Stalin's repertoire, but he also managed to position himself in the immediately post-Lenin years as a pragmatic and moderate man of the center, a person who supported the compromises and concessions of the New Economic Policy and was unwilling to risk Soviet power in efforts to pursue elusive revolutions abroad.

In his prerevolutionary career Stalin had been a party operative, working within the illegal party committees, rather than as an activist among the workers. Never gifted in the theoretical analysis and synthesis so prized by party intellectuals, he prided himself on being a practical man who got things done. He proved to be a skillful political infighter able to sense when he needed to retreat or keep silent and when he could act with impunity. Most of his biographers have portrayed a man with a personal determination to achieve unchallenged personal power. He was unable to accept frustration of his ambitions or criticism of his errors, and his most dominant feature was a visceral suspiciousness directed even at those close to him. In later years that suspicion would border on behavior that observers considered paranoid. Whatever the influences of his impoverished childhood and fractured family, Stalin was also the product of the particular political culture and internal party practices of Bolshevism. Disputes among party members were fierce and often personal; subordination to higher authorities within the movement was required; and force and repression were available to be used in the service of socialism, which eventually seems to have been defined in Stalin's mind as identical to his own policies and preservation of his personal position. Once he reached his exalted position as chief oligarch, he spoke in the name of the party and the Central Committee without consulting anyone else. And he molded his own version of Leninism as an effective weapon against pretenders.

Stalin was born the son of a poor Georgian shoemaker in the town of Gori on December 21, 1879. His mother was the most important influence in his early years, and it was she who determined that he would have a religious education and become a priest. But when he entered the Orthodox seminary in Tbilisi (Tiflis), the young Iosep Jughashvili turned away from religion to a new faith in revolution and socialism. In the Georgian Marxist circles Jughashvili was known as a hothead, the instigator of a demonstration in Batumi, a Georgian port on the Black Sea, that ended in bloodshed. He soon left Georgia for Baku and rose in the ranks of the Transcaucasian Bolsheviks. Arrested several times, he spent years in Siberian exile. Under instructions from Lenin, he wrote his most important theoretical work, on the nationality question, in 1913.

In the early months of Soviet rule Stalin worked at the very center of power, in Smolny, close to Lenin, constantly in contact with party members and state officials by telegraph. Over time, like other high party leaders, he took on a wide range of assignments, including people's commissar of nationalities

(1917–23), of state control (from 1919), and of worker-peasant inspection (1920–22), membership in the Military-Revolutionary Council of the Republic, the Politburo, and the Orgburo (from their creation in March 1919), political commissar of various fronts in the civil war, and participant in a variety of commissions set up to solve specific problems. In what at the time seemed to many to be a trivial appointment, the Eleventh Party Congress in the spring of 1922 elected Stalin a member of the party Secretariat with the title general secretary.

By the time of Lenin's incapacitation in 1923, Stalin was fast becoming indispensable to many powerful figures. He joined with his political allies, Zinoviev and Kamenev, to prevent the growth of influence of Trotsky. On the eve of Politburo meetings, this troika would meet, at first in Zinoviev's apartment, later in Stalin's Central Committee office, to decide what positions they would take on specific issues and what roles each would play in the meeting. In 1924–25 the group was expanded to seven with the addition of Nikolai Bukharin, Aleksei Rykov, Mikhail Tomskii, and Valerian Kuibyshev.

Stalin's Secretariat was supposedly subordinate to the Orgburo, which in turn was subordinate to the Politburo, but by statute any decision of the Secretariat that was not challenged by the Orgburo became automatically the decision of the Orgburo. Likewise, any decision of the Orgburo unchallenged by a member of the Politburo became the decision of the Politburo. A decision by the Politburo might be challenged by a member of the Central Committee, but unless a plenum of the Central Committee annulled that decision it remained in force. In general, the Politburo was to decide on policy, and the Orgburo was to allocate forces, under the authority and guidance of the Central Committee, but in practice no strict division was maintained between political and organizational questions. Both of these small committees met more frequently and proved more effective in day-to-day decision-making than the larger, more unwieldy Central Committee. Power moved upward to the very institutions in which Stalin played a key role. He was the only person who was a member of all three groups.

With his complete dominance over the Orgburo, Stalin was able to use this institution to make appointments throughout the party and to work out his own policies. He built up his own staff, which soon amounted to a personal chancellery. Despite his suspicious nature and his intellectual limitations (certainly exaggerated by political rivals and opponents), Stalin was able to attract a number of loyal subordinates, whose fortunes would rise with him. Most important were Viacheslav Molotov, with whom he worked from 1917; his comrades from the Caucasus, Anastas Mikoyan and Orjonikidze; and his civil war buddy, Kliment Voroshilov. Among Stalin's assistants within the apparatus of the Central Committee were Georgii Malenkov, secretary of the Politburo; and eventually Aleksandr Poskrebyshev, who rose from clerk in the Central Committee mailroom to become Stalin's principal secretary. Stalin's relationship with all of them was never one of partnership or equality but of superiority.

As Lenin had warned his comrades too late, Stalin was accumulating enormous power almost unnoticed. The growth of bureaucracy within the party and state aided Stalin, who controlled appointments and patronage. Politics had steadily narrowed since 1917, from wide-open brawls between political parties and between state and society to internal factional fights within the Communist Party to the bureaucratic intrigues of a few powerful men at the very top of the party. The road to dictatorship had wound its way through dangerous thickets of revolution and war to end up in the marshy morass of paper pushers and the police.

Lenin's Mantle

In the first years of the NEP, as Lenin suffered a series of strokes that would ultimately incapacitate him, Zinoviev and Trotsky were considered the two party leaders most likely to succeed Lenin. Zinoviev was chairman of the Petrograd soviet and the Communist International, an exciting orator, and one of Lenin's oldest associates. But he was tainted by his failure to support the Bolshevik insurrection in October 1917. Trotsky, for all his intellectual and organizational talents, had even more disadvantages. He was a latecomer to Bolshevism, having joined the party only in the spring of 1917 after years of criticizing Lenin and wandering between the Menshevik faction and his own company of followers. Lenin had immediately accepted Trotsky as a man of extraordinary talent and elevated him to the highest positions in the party and the Soviet state, but other Bolsheviks were wary of Trotsky's ambitions. Briefly serving as the first Soviet people's commissar of foreign affairs, Trotsky displayed exceptional ability as commissar of war, when he organized the 5-million-strong Red Army that preserved Soviet power and defeated its principal enemies in the civil war. But none of the other of Lenin's closest comrades wanted the party to be dominated by Trotsky, who had demonstrated his dictatorial and authoritarian tendencies during the war.

On March 9, 1923, Lenin had a third stroke and lost the power of speech. With his right side paralyzed, he was unable to write and his participation in political affairs ended. When the Twelfth Party Congress opened a month later, Trotsky, whose influence had largely come from Lenin's support, was outnumbered and outmaneuvered. Speakers at the Congress emphasized the theme of party unity, and dissident voices were squeezed out of the debate. In early October Trotsky wrote a letter to the Central Committee attacking what he called "secretarial bureaucratism," that is, the procedure of nomination, rather than election, to key party posts. A week later (on October 15), a group of party members issued the "Platform of the Forty-Six," which also attacked the rising bureaucratism:

> Free discussion within the party has practically vanished; the public opinion of the party is stifled. Nowadays, it is not the party, not its broad masses, who promote and choose members of the provincial committees and of the CC of the RKP. On the contrary, the secretarial hierarchy of the party to an ever greater extent recruits the membership of conferences and congresses, which are being to an ever greater extent the executive assemblies of this hierarchy.

The Central Committee rejected Trotsky's letter and labeled it "a profound political error." The internal party conflicts soon became public when in November 1923, *Pravda* opened its pages to the economic debates then dividing leading members of the party. Trotsky wrote another letter denouncing "the bureaucracy of the machine" as "one of the chief sources of factionalism," and Stalin replied by openly attacking Trotsky in print. Different critical tendencies in the party were lumped together and branded as the Opposition. A significant group in the Young Communist League, the Komsomol, was sympathetic to Trotsky at the time, and students and some party intellectuals were critical of the bureaucratic, antidemocratic practices within the party. But the Opposition remained small and divided. Only the Moscow party organization had a large oppositional fraction, just over a third of the membership.

On January 21, 1924, Lenin died. At that moment Trotsky was in the south recovering from one of his perennial illnesses. Misinformed about the date of Lenin's funeral, he chose not to make the long journey north, and people noted his absence. In the months that followed Lenin's death, party leaders promoted a cult of the dead leader. They renamed the city of Petrograd Leningrad and, against the wishes of his widow, ordered Lenin's body mummified and placed in a marble mausoleum in Red Square, a religious-like relic to be viewed by the faithful. In February the party announced a "Lenin Enrollment" of factory workers into the party, and almost 240,000 new members, almost all of them workers, joined. The party grew by more than 50 percent, and its worker proportion reached over half the membership. In April and May Stalin gave a series of lectures at Sverdlov University that were soon published as *Foundations of Leninism*. Everyone wanted to wrap themselves in the mantle of Lenin. More than any past service, association with Lenin gave a political leader legitimacy and authority in the post-Lenin years. In the new political environment in which loyalty to Lenin was the touchstone of political orthodoxy, Stalin, who had seldom differed openly with Lenin, flourished, while Trotsky, whose prerevolutionary writings had often polemicized against Lenin, withered.

In the spring of 1924, Leon Trotsky told the old Bolshevik Vladimir Smirnov, "Stalin will become the dictator of the USSR." "Stalin?" Smirnov reacted. "But he is a mediocrity, a colorless non-entity." "Mediocrity, yes," Trotsky mused, "non-entity, no. The dialectics of history have already hooked him and will raise him up. He is needed by all of them—by the tired radicals, by the bureaucrats, by the Nepmen, the kulaks, the upstarts, the sneaks, by all the worms that are crawling out of the upturned soil of the manured revolution."

Stalin might have been wounded by the public exposure of Lenin's criticism of him in his so-called testament, but on May 22, 1924, a party meeting decided not to release Lenin's bitter denunciation of Stalin. Despite Lenin's warning, Stalin was kept on as general secretary of the party. That same month the Thirteenth Party Congress condemned the "petty bourgeois deviation" of the Opposition, and debate within the party became nearly impossible. In an article in September, Trotsky tried desperately to prove his loyalty to Lenin as well as his own historic role as leader of the October Revolution, but his opponents reminded readers of Trotsky's earlier opposition to Lenin and Bolshevism. They claimed that he had systematically disregarded the peasantry, an accusation that applied to most Social Democrats, and organized an entire campaign condemning Trotsky's prerevolutionary advocacy of "permanent revolution." The phrase seemed to imply Soviet backing of all revolutionary activity everywhere, whereas in fact it had had a much narrower meaning, that one phase of the revolution in Russia, the bourgeois, would "grow over" inevitably into another, the proletarian. The debate around Trotsky was artificial, like so much political debate, and was directed at destroying and enhancing political reputations. Later Kamenev confessed that "the Trotskyite danger was invented for the purpose of our organized struggle against Trotsky."

Zinoviev, the most adamant opponent of Trotsky in late 1924 and early 1925, tried to convince other leaders to have Trotsky expelled from the party, but Stalin, presenting himself as a moderate and a centrist, opposed expulsion. In January 1925 the Central Committee removed Trotsky from one of his most powerful posts, president of the Revolutionary Military Council, and replaced him with Mikhail Frunze, a hero of the civil war. Trotsky remained a member of the all-powerful Politburo, however, ironically thanks to the votes of Stalin and his associates Orjonikidze, Kalinin, and Voroshilov.

Early Crises of the NEP Economy

Certainly as important as the political conflicts over the rise of bureaucratic practices and the decline in democracy within the party were the deep and developing disputes within the Communist elite over economic policy. The introduction of the New Economic Policy in March 1921 had been a radical turning point in Soviet history, and for many in the party it was only a temporary solution to a difficult economic situation, not the straight road toward the building of socialism. Few thought of the market-oriented NEP as permanent; rather, it was seen as a retreat, a concession to the peasantry, a detour to the ultimate goal. And many feared that it could lead to a restoration of capitalism.

NEP looks better in retrospect than it did at the time. The first year of NEP had been an economic nightmare. Large areas of the country suffered from the ravages of the civil war, and famine was widespread in the Volga and other regions. Hundreds of thousands died from hunger, and the Soviet government, whose requisitioning policies had contributed to the mass hunger, was desperate to feed the starving population. In the summer of 1921 Kalinin authorized the formation of a committee of prominent intellectuals, including Maxim Gorky, to work in the food campaign and appeal to the West for food aid. From the Kremlin Lenin dispatched telegrams ordering that food supply be organized like a military operation. In August the Soviets signed an agreement with Herbert Hoover, the head of the American Relief Administration (ARA), to have American food sent to the famine areas. In the next two years ARA shipments fed over 10 million people, saving lives that would have otherwise been lost. Still, more than 5 million died in the famine. Along with hunger, typhus stalked the land, killing the weakened and the hungry. Millions of orphaned and homeless children, begging and stealing what they could, wandered the streets and roads, their feet bare or wrapped in old newspapers. When a boy of ten or twelve grabbed some bread in a bazaar, he was severely beaten with a cane, "but the boy, on hands and knees, continued hurriedly to bite off piece after piece so as not to lose the bread." He received no sympathy from passers-by. "Adults—women—gathered around and shouted: 'That's what the scoundrel deserves; beat him some more! We get no peace from these lice.' "

Industrial output was only 21 percent of what it had been in 1913. Shortages of fuel led to the closing of those factories not destroyed by the war. Russia was far worse off than it had been before the revolution. Yet there were some hopeful signs. The decline in industry was largely due to the ravages of war, the dispersion of the workers, and disruption of rail traffic. Actual capital stock remained at roughly 95 percent of prewar industry. At the same time agriculture had declined by 1921 to 60 percent of the prewar level. The harvests of 1920 and 1921 were particularly poor, but the coming of NEP began to reverse the decline, both in agriculture and industry.

Fortunately, the 1922 harvest was bountiful. By 1924 agricultural production had reached the prewar level. Disturbing for the party leaders, however, was the drop in the percentage of grain that was marketed by the peasants. Russian peasants in 1921 were, in fact, marketing only 43 percent of the absolute amount they had marketed in 1913, and that figure would rise to only 60 percent of prewar levels by 1924. Clearly, NEP meant that the peasants were eating better to the detriment of the towns and cities. More importantly, the peasants had control of the major economic resource of the country, agriculture.

Russian towns and industry needed agricultural products, not only to feed the population but as raw material for processing industries and to export abroad in order to buy foreign machinery. Though industrial output rose rapidly in the first three years of NEP, as bridges and rail lines were repaired, roofs put on old buildings, and machines repaired, by 1924 industrial production was still only 45 percent of the 1913 level. Industry could not grow without greater inputs from agriculture. Workers could not work if they were hungry; productivity could not be significantly raised without mechanization. The problem of Soviet industry, therefore, was the problem of squeezing more grain out of the peasantry.

Central to the whole imbalance of the NEP economy were the terms of trade between towns and the countryside. In 1920–21, when agriculture was doing badly, prices for farm products were high. Since peasants had little money to spend and industries were selling off their stock, prices for industrial goods remained low. To raise industrial prices the state lowered output in industry. But at the same time the middlemen and merchants known as "Nepmen" held back many industrial goods to force the prices even higher. Within a year this "sales crisis" led to a scarcity of industrial goods and higher industrial prices, while the good harvest of 1922 caused farm prices to fall. By 1923 the Soviet Union was experiencing what Trotsky referred to as the "scissors crisis"; retail and wholesale prices of industrial goods were almost double their prewar levels, while agricultural prices were at half the prewar levels.

Up to 1922–23 all crises in the Soviet economy had been caused by scarcities, but the so-called scissors crisis was due, not to a failure to produce, but

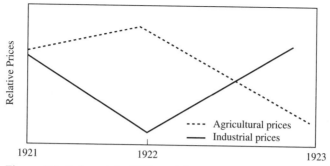

Figure 6.1. Sales crisis, 1922, and Scissors crisis, 1923

to a failure to establish terms and methods of trade to bring about a smooth flow of goods from town to country and vice versa. NEP was a hybrid combination of petty capitalism and state regulation, and suspicious Communist economists were unwilling to allow markets to set prices without interference. A laissez-faire policy in trade could not work when organized trading syndicates controlled industrial prices. When the price "scissors" opened to its widest extent in the fall of 1923, economists called for state-controlled prices. Bukharin, the party's most enthusiastic defender of NEP, advocated the forcible lowering of industrial prices, which, he claimed, would result in increased peasant demand, stimulate sales, and eliminate inefficient producers who were benefiting from artificially high fixed prices. On December 24 the Politburo approved the regulation of wholesale prices of articles of consumption in order to force prices down. Legal maximums were set on the retail prices of necessities like salt, paraffin, and sugar. At the same time the government limited credits to industry. The harvest of 1923 was excellent, and it might have contributed to falling grain prices had not the government resumed foreign trade in grain. By the end of the year, grain prices rose and the "scissors crisis" was over. For the next three years the Soviet Union enjoyed a steadily improving economy, though not one without problems of unemployment in the towns and the constant need to appease the demands of the peasantry.

Socialism in One Country

Within months of Lenin's death at the beginning of 1924, one of his central ideas, that socialism could not be built in Russia without the aid of the international revolution, was revised by Stalin and Bukharin. Once radical socialists had failed in their efforts to hold power in any European country and the prospect of revolutionary allies in the West diminished, the full isolation of the USSR on the capitalist continent convinced key Communists that Lenin's internationalist views had to be adjusted. One prominent Bolshevik, Avel Enukidze, told an American journalist that when the revolution abroad did not break out "it was up to us to uncook the kasha [porridge]." When Trotsky affirmed that "the real rise of a socialist economy in Russia will become possible only after the victory of the proletariat in the most important countries of Europe," Stalin replied that this was "a variant of Menshevism," lacking faith in the possibility of Russia building socialism. Furthermore, he stated, Lenin himself had argued for "socialism in one country" (which was, in fact, not true). Stalin and Bukharin's new position was that socialism could be built in one country, though the "final victory of socialism" required "the aid of the world proletariat in alliance with the main mass of our peasantry." As Bukharin confidently proclaimed, "We will win final victory because revolution in other countries is inevitable." Their innovation in Lenin's thought marked a profoundly important shift in Soviet domestic and foreign policy—away from the militantly internationalist and revolutionary policy that made Soviet socialism dependent on revolution abroad toward a more national commitment to the building of a new socialist society within a single state.

Another important question was whether the Soviet Union would build its economy in isolation from the rest of the world or integrate it with the capitalist economies. Trotsky had earlier argued that Russia was both politically and economically alone in the world and needed to generate its own capital internally. No Western nation would aid a socialist Russia. But beginning in 1925 Trotsky revised his view and argued that in order to industrialize Russia had to develop foreign trade relations, grant concessions to foreign businesspeople, and respond to the world market. He opposed Stalin's attempt to isolate the USSR from Europe and create an autarchic economy. "To reduce the whole question of our development to the internal relation between the proletariat and peasantry in the USSR, and to think that correct political maneuvering ... frees us from world economic dependencies means falling into a dreadful national limitation." Europe needed Soviet grain, and the Soviet Union needed the machinery that Europe had in abundance. By developing foreign trade with the West, the Soviet Union would advance technologically, be able to industrialize more rapidly, and become strong militarily, even before the international socialist revolution. In order to succeed socialism had to achieve a higher productivity of labor than capitalism, but that was impossible in one country alone. "We know the fundamental law of history," wrote Trotsky, "in the end that regime will conquer which ensures human society a higher economic standard."

The real author of economic policy in the mid-1920s was Nikolai Ivanovich Bukharin (1888–1938), the son of teachers, who had joined the Bolsheviks in 1906 and impressed Lenin with his theoretical powers displayed in his first major work, *Imperialism and World Economy*. Lenin later called him the "darling of the party." After the October insurrection, Bukharin was a Left Communist, favoring a revolutionary war with Germany, breaking with Lenin over the Brest-Litovsk Treaty, and favoring what became known as War Communism. Yet in the 1920s he emerged as the major opponent of Trotsky's industrializing strategy and the principal defender of NEP. He reasoned that if peasants were productive they would trade with the towns for industrial goods and industry would then grow as well. As long as industry was using up its prewar capacity, the policy made sense. Profits would be garnered by the state through exchanges with the peasants and then would be plowed back into industry. "The greater the buying powers of the peasantry," reasoned Bukharin, "the faster our industry grows."

From 1923 through 1926 the economic policies of Stalin and Bukharin prevailed in the Soviet Union. They involved the continuation, and even expansion, of the concessions to the peasants, some moderate investment in industry, and reliance on market forces. Bukharin opposed the idea of his former collaborator, Evgenii Preobrazhenskii, that "primitive socialist accumulation" of capital required forcible removals of buying power from the peasantry. Rather he advocated gradual accumulation through commercial circulation between the state and the peasantry. But what recovery industry was making in the mid-1920s was due only in part to careful investment in sensitive parts of the economy and the sale of goods from small-scale industries to the peasants, which stimulated peasants to grow more crops, increase their income, and buy more goods. Much growth was simply the result of the unused capacity of industry, damaged in the civil war, being put back into operation. Deterioration and depreciation of industry continued, and eventually existing capital stock needed to be expanded or industrial output would stagnate. Without significant new investment in industry, Soviet industry would not only not grow but would arrive at an equilibrium point lower than prewar production. Investment had to be raised above the minimum necessary to make up for depreciation.

Trotsky, Preobrazhenskii, and the Left called for more state planning and a redistribution of resources from the peasants to the industrial sector by raising the prices that peasants had to pay for industrial goods. On the political front, the Left claimed that the proletarian state and the party were experiencing "degeneration" and becoming excessively bureaucratic. Trotsky argued that the ban on factions, which he believed had been appropriate in 1921, was no longer applicable. "Without temporary ideological groupings, the ideological life of the party is unthinkable," he complained. Yet the evident splits in the top party leadership could not be smoothed over by compromises. This was a struggle for dominance between strong personalities with very different programs for economic development, internal party organization, and interna-

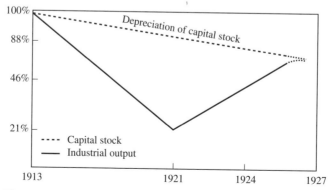

Figure 6.2. Capital stock and investment output in the 1920s. Industrial output reached 21 percent of the 1913 level in 1921, 46 percent in 1924, and 88 percent sometime in 1927.

tional communist policy. The various oppositions were themselves disunited both internally and from one another. Despite the 1921 ban on factions, the Communist Party remained through the decade deeply factionalized and in many ways was several parties within one.

The slow and steady improvement in the Soviet economy in the mid-1920s appeared to vindicate the moderate propeasant policies associated with Bukharin and Stalin. Their support within the party solidified. Though the Opposition made several futile attempts to appeal to the public to support their position, by the mid-1920s politics had long been removed from society at large to the corridors of party headquarters. The idea of "socialism in one country" appealed to the pragmatism and caution that many in the party preferred after the years of civil war. Stalin argued that only the final victory of socialism in the Soviet Union could not be achieved by the USSR alone, because of the threats posed "by the bayonets of capitalist armies." But this revision of Lenin's view that Soviet socialism was contingent on aid from revolutionary allies abroad was unacceptable to Trotsky and the Left Opposition, and disturbed Zinoviev, Kamenev, and many others. At the Fourteenth Party Conference (April 1925), however, the Stalin-Bukharin formulation carried the day: "In general the victory of socialism (*not* in the sense of *final* victory) is unconditionally possible in one country."

In the spring of 1925 the strains within the top party leadership began to tear apart the ruling faction. On April 17, 1925, Bukharin made his most forthright statement of the party's agricultural policy: "We must say to the whole peasantry, to all its strata: enrich yourselves, accumulate, develop your economy." He specifically called for support for the better-off peasants, the kulaks, who had in the past suffered from Soviet discrimination. Zinoviev, with his political base in the Leningrad party organization and after January 1924 in the Komsomol, took a more militantly proworker position and began making speeches against the propeasant policies of Bukharin, which only weeks before he had supported. He rejected Bukharin's view that Soviet state industry was already socialist in character and labeled it instead "state capitalist." He publicly questioned in what direction the USSR was moving, toward socialism or toward a restoration of capitalism. For Zinoviev, NEP was "state capitalism in a proletarian state" and would not lead to socialism in one country. Like the Opposition of 1923 (Trotsky, Preobrazhenskii, Iurii Piatakov), the emerging Leningrad Opposition wanted no further concessions to the peasants and demanded expansion of industry and state planning.

Even nature seemed to support the Stalin-Bukharin line. The harvest of 1925 was excellent, the largest since the revolution. The government was determined to support high prices for agricultural goods. But richer peasants now made it a habit to hold back grain until spring to benefit from even higher prices. The Opposition expressed its alarm at the accumulation of resources in the hands of the kulaks and the Nepmen, but for all their hostility toward Bukharin's propeasant program of NEP, it did not advocate the resumption of coercion against the peasantry, only the raising of taxes and prices of industrial goods.

The Stalin-Bukharin position triumphed at the Fourteenth Party Congress at the end of 1925. With Stalin in control of the apparatus of the party and playing a key role in the selection of delegates, most delegates backed the moderate NEP position. Now in opposition, Kamenev revived the criticism of Stalin that Lenin had vented more than two years earlier: "We are against creating the theory of a 'leader'; we are against making a leader. . . . I have reached the conclusion that comrade Stalin cannot perform the function of uniting the Bolshevik general staff." The argument for internal party democracy by those who had earlier rejected Trotsky's pleas for open discussion in 1923 must have sounded hollow. Zinoviev tried to justify his recent conversion to greater democracy: "The year 1926 is not 1921 and not 1923; today we have different workers, greater activity in the masses, other slogans. . . . In 1926 we must proceed otherwise than in 1923."

Joining the opposition, Lenin's widow, Nadezhda Krupskaia, criticized the concessions given to the richer peasants and deplored the suppression of free discussion within the party:

> For us Marxists truth is what corresponds to reality. Vladimir Ilich used to say: the teaching of Marx is invincible because it is true. And it must be the business of our congress to seek and find the right line. That is its task. One must not lull oneself into the belief that the majority is always right.

Stalin was particularly incensed by Krupskaia's remarks, and he later wrote secretly to Molotov that Krupskaia "has to be beaten, as a splitter, if we want to preserve the unity of the party." Though the story is apochryphal, a popular anecdote claimed that Stalin confronted Krupskaia and told her, "Nadezhda Konstantinovna, be careful or we shall have to find someone else to be Lenin's widow."

In the end only 65 delegates voted with the Opposition, and 559 voted against. Though victorious, Stalin did not use his influence in the Central Committee to force changes in the Politburo but merely to keep his shifting majority in the Politburo in power. Before 1926, no voting member of the Politburo owed his position to Stalin, and the Politburo elected at the Fourteenth Party Congress was still divided. Its continuing members were Stalin, Bukharin, Rykov, Tomskii, Zinoviev, and Trotsky. Kamenev was demoted to candidate status, and close supporters of Stalin—Molotov, Voroshilov, and Kalinin—joined the Politburo. Zinoviev remained a powerful figure, with his base of support in the Leningrad party organization but not for long. After the Congress, Molotov, the popular Mikhail Kalinin, and Kliment Voroshilov traveled to the former capital, met with factory workers, and convinced them to side with the party majority against Zinoviev. A month later Sergei Kirov, a protégé of Stalin's from the Caucasus, replaced Zinoviev as head of the Leningrad organization.

Stalin won every round in his fight with the Oppositionists in 1926, but he seemed to believe that they remained a serious threat to his majority. In mid-June he wrote to Molotov:

> If Trotsky tells Bukharin that he soon hopes to have a majority in the party, that means he hopes to intimidate and blackmail Bukharin. How little he

knows and how much he underestimates Bukharin! But I think pretty soon the party will punch the mugs of Trotsky and Grisha [Zinoviev] along with Kamenev and turn them into isolated splitters, like Shliapnikov [of the Workers' Opposition of 1921].

Zinoviev remained a few months longer as head of the Communist International, and he attempted to involve the Comintern in the internal politics of the Russian Communist Party. When Zinoviev and Kamenev joined Trotsky in July 1926 in the United Opposition and issued a joint "Declaration of the Thirteen" against the propeasant line of the majority, Zinoviev was dropped from the Politburo and as head of the Comintern. Ian Rudzutak, and Orjonikidze, both close to Stalin, joined the Politburo, and in October Trotsky and Kamenev were dropped.

Stalin's rise was not only the product of his skillful manipulation of internal party politics and his success at positioning himself as the champion of a successful economic policy. The party itself had changed since the revolutionary years, and Stalin's moderation and pragmatism meshed well with the aspirations of ordinary party and state officials. By 1927 the party had over a million full and candidate members, of whom more than half could claim working-class origin. Many of those workers had graduated from the factories into the burgeoning party apparatus and state bureaucracy where they held prestigious and powerful positions. Workers were particularly highly represented in the higher ranks of the Communist Party, and their rapid upward mobility bound them to the leaders and system that had improved their lives and status. The RKP (b) of the late 1920s was a far cry from the small groups of revolutionary intellectuals steeped in Marxism and radicalized workers ready to overthrow the bourgeoisie that had made up the RSDRP in 1917. Only at the very top of the party were "Old Bolsheviks" still in command. After the years of revolutionary sacrifice and the destructive effects of civil war and famine, the workers, peasants, soldiers, officials, and members of other political parties who had joined the Communist ranks supported those leaders who seemed able to provide the greater degree of orderly progress and moderate material rewards. Yet revolutionary fervor had not been completely diluted, and in the coming years of crisis moderates would turn overnight into radicals.

The Final Crisis of NEP

The years 1925–26 can be seen as the apogee of NEP. The harvests were good; and the supply of and demand for grain was in equilibrium. The peasantry was prosperous and as content as it had ever been since the revolution. There was no current crisis, political or economic, and the leadership was confident that its policies were working well. Bukharin explained the logic behind the concept of "socialism in one country":

> If we knew in advance that we were not equal to the task, then why the devil did we have to make the October Revolution? . . . Then there was no

reason for us to go to the barricades in October, then the Mensheviks would have been right when they said that in so backward a country as Russia it was pointless to plan a socialist revolution, then Trotsky would have been right in affirming that without state aid from a victorious western European proletariat we shall necessarily come into collision with the peasants, who will necessarily overthrow us.

But behind the rosy rhetoric there were storm clouds gathering. By 1926, the restoration of the pre–World War I economy had been completed. There would be little more real economic growth without significant new investment. The problem for the Soviet economy would soon be a dearth of industrial goods, and without goods to buy the peasants, as rational sellers in a market economy, would simply hold on to their grain. Gradually, each of the major leaders began to reevaluate the current situation, and steadily they began to abandon their confidence in the market and the private economy and move toward reliance on the state. The Left Opposition continued to favor giving priority to heavy industry. Even Bukharin shifted toward the "left," that is, toward greater emphasis on developing industry. Though he remained a passionate advocate of the NEP system, Bukharin began to call for greater investment in consumers-goods industries. "It is absolutely clear that our socialist industry ought to grow not only at the expense of what is produced by the working class inside the state industry itself, but also that we have to pump resources from the nonindustrial reservoir into industry, including some means to be taken from the peasant economy." Bukharin realized that the peasant demand that he had encouraged had become a curse. With no more unused industrial capacity to absorb, industrial capacity had to be increased by major investments. The capital would have to come from the peasants paying higher prices for factory goods. Still, he opposed prices that were so high that the rich peasants would be unable to save and invest in their agriculture.

All through 1926 the United Opposition attempted to organize rank-and-file members of the party. Denouncing these activities as factional, Stalin offered the Opposition a compromise: if they agreed to renounce factional activities and unconditionally accept decisions of the party, they would be free to express their views within the limits of the party line. Six leaders of the Opposition—Zinoviev, Kamenev, Piatakov, Sokolnikov, Trotsky, and Evdokimov—agreed. But when the Politburo decided that Stalin could refute the views of the Opposition at the forthcoming party conference, Trotsky exploded in anger and called Stalin "the gravedigger of the revolution." Stalin condemned the Opposition as "a social democratic deviation in our party." At the Fifteenth Party Conference in the fall, Bukharin told the Opposition to "come before the party with head bowed and say: Forgive us for we have sinned against the spirit and against the letter and against the very essence of Leninism. . . . Say it, say it honestly: Trotsky was wrong. . . . Why do you not have the common courage to come and say that it is a mistake?" Some of the dissident party members humiliated themselves and asked for forgiveness, but those that failed to repent were censured and demoted. The conference then went on to emphasize the need to mobilize internal resources for industrialization and to seek foreign sources for investment. Even as economic policy gravitated to the left, the Stalin majority crushed the political Left.

Stalin and Bukharin were firmly in the saddle when a series of foreign policy crises in China and Europe shook their confidence and revived the fortunes of the Opposition. The Opposition made a last attempt to unseat the Stalin-Bukharin majority. In May a vigorous debate took place in the Comintern at which Trotsky spoke against the leadership. At a Moscow factory, some people shouted, "Down with Stalin's dictatorship! Down with the Politburo!" On May 26 Trotsky, Zinoviev, and others sent the Politburo a declaration signed by eighty-four members of the Opposition that argued that the mistakes of the Stalin leadership had weakened the Soviet Union and made war against the USSR more likely. Trotsky let it be known that his loyalty was to the "socialist fatherland" but that he never would support Stalin. At the end of July 1927 the Central Committee met to deal with the Opposition once more. The majority demanded that the Opposition revoke its idea that there was a degeneration in the party and that the leadership must be changed. When the Opposition refused, the majority voted to reprimand Trotsky and Zinoviev. Krupskaia, who had supported the Opposition a year earlier, now condemned them for not seeing the "construction going on in the country" and for being divorced from "real life" and the masses. The struggle with the United Opposition entered its final phase, but now with the use of the police. After the Opposition issued its official platform in September, many of its leaders were arrested, and Trotsky and Zinoviev were expelled from the Central Committee.

In this moment of international and domestic political problems for the Stalin-Bukharin leadership, the economy contributed to the mood of crisis. The 1927 harvest was several million tons below that of 1926. Grain prices offered by the state were relatively low, and industrial consumer goods were in short supply. Peasants simply withheld grain from the market and chose to sell other products, like meat and dairy products that fetched higher prices. To make matters worse, industrial production fell in 1927, and the unfavorable balance of foreign trade led to a curtailment of imports. The supply of industrial goods shrank significantly, and the value and buying power of the ruble deteriorated. This time the government refused to raise grain prices as they had in 1925, when peasants held back grain. Instead, officials decided to push ahead for industrialization and introduced compulsory seizures of grain.

At the Fifteenth Party Congress in December 1927, the majority adopted agricultural and industrial policies that seemed designed by the Left. The resolutions called for a Five-Year Plan of economic development, for a "socialist offensive," and for the liquidation of capitalist elements in the countryside and in the towns. Even moderates like Bukharin and Rykov were prepared to speed up the tempo of industrialization and put pressure on the kulaks, though they believed that the free market had to be maintained. Stalin cautioned against those who called for harsh measures against the kulaks and condemned the use of administrative pressure or police measures. Still appearing to be a moderate, he told the Congress, "The kulak must be dealt with by economic methods and on the basis of socialist legality."

NEP was in its final crisis. By the last months of 1927 grain and food procurements were falling below demand. Cotton growers in Central Asia were
short of food. In the early weeks of the new year, Stalin reacted by ordering
military-type operations against peasants. Cadres were mobilized and sent to
various "fronts." Even Politburo members left Moscow for Ukraine, the Volga,
and the North Caucasus. Stalin himself went to Siberia and pushed through
emergency measures using Article 107 of the Penal Code (three years for speculation) against so-called grain hoarders. On February 13, 1928, Stalin blamed
the kulaks for the crisis and reinterpreted the line of the Fifteenth Party Congress in his own way: collectivization of agriculture was to be directed against
"not only the kulaks but individual peasant agriculture [in general] as the de-
liverer of grain to the state." By moving to this militant position, Stalin was
challenging Bukharin and other pro-NEP moderates in the Politburo.

The crisis over grain collection strained Stalin's alliance with Bukharin. Almost overnight Stalin changed (in the words of T. H. Rigby) from being "the
soul of caution and moderation" to "intransigence itself." By December 1927
he achieved a majority of loyal supporters in the Politburo, and by 1930 he removed the so-called Right, those unwilling to follow him unreservedly into
collectivization. With the fall of Bukharin, Rykov, and Tomskii, Stalin established an unchallenged oligarchy with himself as chief oligarch. The trend toward a more authoritarian and dictatorial regime within the USSR was paral-
leled by developments throughout Europe, as democracy and liberalism
appeared to be in retreat and anti-Soviet forces in the ascendency.

Retreat and Retrenchment

Weakened by war and revolution, Europe recovered slowly. It would never
again dominate the globe without challenge as it had in the prewar period.
World War I was estimated to have cost $600 billion at a time when the na-
tional income of the United States was approximately $50 billion. Sixty-five
million men had been mobilized, 9 million had been killed, 5 million were missing, 15 million had been seriously wounded, and 7 million were permanently
disabled. Europe's economic growth had been set back by eight years, while
its rivals—the United States, Canada, and Japan—had leaped ahead during the
war. In 1920 the United States produced 22 percent and Japan 76 percent more
manufactured goods than they had in 1913, while European industrial output
had fallen by 23 percent.

In the decade after World War I the popular enthusiasm for Wilsonianism
propelled European states toward parliamentary democracy. Authoritarian
systems were transformed into constitutional democracies, and most of the
newly formed states in east-central Europe adopted liberal, western-style constitutions. The franchise was extended to women in most countries. But within
a decade one after another of the smaller states succumbed to dictators and a
new authoritarianism. In 1920 Admiral Nicholas Horthy became the dictatorial "regent" of a nonexistent monarchy in Hungary. Two years later Benito

Mussolini marched on Rome and set up a fascist regime in Italy that lasted until 1943. In 1926 coups overthrew parliamentary governments in Portugal, Lithuania, Poland, and briefly Greece, and in 1928–29 Albania and Yugoslavia succumbed to royal dictatorships. The next decade proved even worse. In 1933 Adolf Hitler came to power in Germany, and Austria, Latvia, Estonia, Greece, Bulgaria, and Rumania all became dictatorships by 1938. A year later the rebel forces under General Francisco Franco took power in Spain. By the outbreak of World War II in 1939, only Britain and France, Belgium and the Netherlands, the Scandinavian countries, Switzerland, Luxemburg, and Czechoslovakia retained democratic political systems.

Given the isolation and weakness of the Soviet Union, Soviet foreign policy makers, following the lead of Lenin, generally practiced a policy of peaceful coexistence with the imperialist world. Normal relations were established with foreign governments, even as Communist parties worked to subvert those same governments. Despite conservative opponents, such as Winston Churchill and Lord Curzon, British Prime Minister Lloyd-George opened trade negotiations with a Soviet representative in June 1920. At times the antics of revolutionary Bolsheviks, such as Kamenev, who passed out money to left-wing newspapers, threatened the talks, but in March 1921 an Anglo-Soviet treaty granted the RSFSR de facto recognition and opened the doors to commercial exchange. The Soviet Union was not party to the European order set up by the Versailles Treaty of 1919, and like Germany, Bulgaria, Hungary, and other "revisionist" countries that had lost out in the Versailles settlement, they hoped to "revise" the terms of that treaty. In the 1920s the Soviet Union desperately tried to develop an alliance with Germany, the other major anti-Versailles power, to prevent a British-led coalition on the European continent directed against the USSR. Though Soviet policy became more cautious toward the major capitalist powers in Europe, it continued to work to undermine British power in the colonial world.

The turn toward more moderate policies within Soviet Russia, beginning in 1921, was reflected in both Soviet foreign policy and in the debates in the Comintern. There Lenin tended to be among the most cautious of the Communists when it came to assessing the potential for revolution abroad. Some of Lenin's closest comrades, including Bukharin, Zinoviev, and Radek, called for an offensive revolutionary strategy in Europe. When German Communists in Berlin launched an insurrection in March 1921 and were quickly suppressed, Lenin's more pragmatic approach began to prevail. Comintern policy and Soviet foreign policy adjusted to the reality of Communist weakness in the West, the postwar stabilization of the capitalist economy, and the international isolation of the battered Soviet state. Lenin denounced attempts at armed uprisings at the Third Comintern Congress in June and called for a longer period of preparation. The new slogan of the Comintern was "first and foremost, to the masses, with all means." Communists could not win state power by coups and conspiracies; they had to win over the mass of workers first. "Whoever does not understand that we must conquer the majority of the working class in Europe, where nearly all proletarians are organized, is lost to the Communist movement," Lenin told the delegates. Trotsky echoed this view: "Now for the first time we see and feel that we are not so immediately near to the goal, to the conquest of power, to the world revolution. . . . In 1919 we said to ourselves: 'It is a question of months.' Now we say, 'It is a question of years.' " By the end of the year the Communist International adopted a new strategy, "the United Workers' Front," that required Communist parties everywhere to work with other socialist parties and trade unions for common aims. This was a radical reversal of the strategy that had brought the Comintern into being.

To ease its international isolation the Soviet leadership agreed in the fall of 1921 to pay back the huge loans that the tsarist government had contracted before 1914. But the Soviets wanted recognition and economic assistance in exchange for settling the largest debt incurred by any country in the world up to that time. In April 1922 delegates from the USSR met in Genoa with representatives of the major European powers to discuss the reintegration of Russia into the European system. The Soviet negotiators hoped to attract European aid to rebuild the Russian economy, but at the same time they were very suspicious of Western interference in the Soviet economy. From Moscow Lenin kept in close touch with the Soviet delegation and held them back from making certain concessions to the West. Lenin opposed paying back any debts except prewar state loans or restoring property in Russia to foreign capitalists. An agreement with Britain or France proved impossible, but the German and Soviet delegates met secretly and on April 16 signed the Treaty of Rappallo. By this agreement the Soviet government, exploiting the divisions among the European powers, formed an economic, political, and quasi-military alliance with Germany. Soviet grain was traded for German machines. The German military, forbidden by the victorious powers to train pilots on their own territory, secretly carried on its training on Soviet soil. Like a good ally, the Soviet Union protested the occupation of the Ruhr by the French in 1923, but this did not prevent Comintern enthusiasts for revolution from continuing to work for a Communist insurrection within Germany.

Just as the Soviet state had adopted a policy of peaceful coexistence with the "bourgeois" world in 1921, so the Comintern had adjusted its revolutionary policy toward the capitalist states. The Soviet Union could no longer depend on revolutions abroad and was falling further behind the growing economies of the European states. Abandoning their earlier militance, Communists tried to recruit more broadly among workers and socialists. Many Communists, however, were appalled at the new moderation of the Comintern. Briefly, in late 1923, as an economic crisis gripped Germany, the Soviet Communist leadership gave in once more to its hopes for revolution and backed a desperate plan of the German Communists for a revolutionary seizure of power. At the last minute the German comrades tried to call off the planned uprising, but Communists in Hamburg launched their own insurrection on October 23. Government troops crushed the Communists while workers watched passively. This third major defeat for the German Communists only served to accelerate the Comintern's move toward moderation and caution, and though there would be a few more relapses (in Bulgaria and Estonia in 1924), revolutionary adventures were abandoned, and the politics of peaceful coexistence dominated over the politics of revolution. At the same time the Comintern directed all Communist parties to Bolshevize themselves, that is, to eliminate deviant political tendencies and align themselves with the policies of the Russian Communist party. Under pressure from Moscow foreign Communist parties steadily became conformist followers of the Soviet Communist party. Each time the RKP (b) eliminated organized factions within its ranks, Comintern parties around the world followed in lock step.

The Soviet Union Isolated

By the mid-1920s the Soviet Union was recognized by all the major powers except the United States. Yet it remained isolated and fearful of Western hostility. Just before a British election in 1924, a conservative newspaper published a letter purported to be from Zinoviev, head of the Comintern, calling on British Communists to form cells within the British army as a first step to creating a Red Army. The "Zinoviev Letter," which was a forgery, was given banner headline in the British press—"Civil War Plot by Socialists," "Moscow Order to Our Reds," "Great Plot Disclosed Yesterday"—and contributed to the failure of the Labour party at the polls. Relations between London and Moscow chilled to the freezing point. At the same time Germany, the Soviet Union's one friend in Europe, drew closer to Britain and France, signing the Dawes Plan on payment of war reparations and the Locarno treaties, and joining the League of Nations. The Soviets feared that Germany would join an anti-Soviet coalition with Britain and France. Commissar of Foreign Affairs Chicherin proposed a military alliance with Germany but was unable to convince either the Germans or the French that they ought to join the USSR in an anti-British "continental bloc." By 1924–25 the Germans saw a greater advantage to closer ties with the Western powers than expanding their relationship with the Soviet Union.

More than others in the foreign policy establishment Stalin perceived ominous signs of danger from the West. "The conflict of interests among the victor countries is growing and becoming more intense," Stalin told his comrades. "Collision among them is becoming inevitable, and, in anticipation of a new war, they are arming with great energy." For Stalin capitalist stabilization was inherently unstable, war remained inevitable, and intervention against the Soviet Union was becoming ever more likely. In this period the delay of the international revolution necessitated the construction of "socialism in one country" and a less aggressively revolutionary policy by the Comintern abroad. Yet in no sense, Stalin believed, did the present calm among capitalists portend a long peace.

From late 1925 through 1927 the Soviet Union worked hard to create a secure environment along its borders through a series of bilateral treaties. In December 1925 the USSR signed a treaty of friendship and mutual nonaggression with Turkey, followed by similar treaties with Germany (April 1926), Afghanistan (August), Lithuania (September), Latvia (July 1927), Estonia (August), and Persia (October). Poland, however, refused to sign such a treaty. The treaties were the Soviet Union's "reply to Locarno" and were directed at preventing any hostile political or economic blocs against the USSR. The normalization of relations with its neighbors meant the subordination of the revolutionary goals of the Comintern to the official state-to-state relations of the USSR.

Figure 6.3. "Long live the Third Communist International." Poster by Sergei Ivanov, 1920 (Courtesy of Hoover Institution Archives, Poster Collection, RU/SU807).

Continuing Revolution in Asia

By 1921 Soviet power extended from Ukraine and Belorussia in the West to Vladivostok and Mongolia in the East. In November of that year the Mongolian People's Republic, which had been established by the Red Army in alliance with local Communists, signed a treaty with its protector, Soviet Russia. Though the period of militance and enthusiasm for the spread of the revolution was ending, the Soviets continued to support revolutionaries around the world. Their aid and advice to nationalists in the Middle and Far East irritated the British, who were concerned about any threat to their empire in India and political dominance in Persia. In May 1923 the British foreign secretary, Lord Curzon, sent an ultimatum to Moscow protesting the financial support by the USSR of anti-British revolutionary movements and threatening a break in relations. Though offended by Curzon's tone, Moscow responded in a conciliatory manner, agreeing to curb revolutionary activity in Persia, Afghanistan, and India.

The Communist International focused much of its attention in the 1920s on the revolutionary potential of China. Though the Chinese state was divided and weak, the country was so underdeveloped and so overwhelmingly peasant in population that the Comintern decided that China was ready only for a nationalist revolution, rather than a socialist one, and that the nationalist party, the Guomindang, was the only serious national revolutionary force in China. Comintern and Soviet agents worked to organize radical Chinese students into

Leninist party cells and, at the same time, to convince the Chinese authorities to recognize the Soviet government. Communists were ordered to work within the Guomindang and turn it toward the goal of proletarian revolution. This "bloc within" strategy was not popular with Chinese Communists, some of whom, like the young Mao Zedong, tried unsuccessfully to convince their leaders to break with the nationalists.

The Soviet Union was the only major power that supported Chinese opposition to European dominance. For this reason the leading Chinese nationalist, Dr. Sun Yatsen, hailed the Russian Revolution and convinced his followers to approve the treaty of mutual recognition of May 1924. The Soviets, for their part, renounced any extraterritorial privileges enjoyed by the tsarist government in China, even to the point of recognizing Chinese sovereignty over Mongolia. China and the USSR agreed to manage jointly the Chinese Eastern Railroad. From 1925 to 1927 Soviet Russia, the Comintern, and the Chinese nationalists were allies against the warlords and imperialists in China. Soviet agents in China helped reorganize the Guomindang and train its military. Sun Yatsen sent his chief of staff, Chiang Kai-shek, to Moscow to learn strategy. But when Sun Yatsen died in March 1925, tensions developed between those in the Guomindang who favored the Communists and those who feared them. Chiang Kai-shek carried out a coup within the party in March 1926, arrested several Communist leaders, and established his own power. The Comintern, largely under the influence of Stalin, reluctantly supported Chiang Kai-Shek as Sun Yatsen's successor. Though Trotsky expressed some doubts about the alliance with the Guomindang, Stalin argued that Chiang would be "used until the end, squeezed dry like a lemon, and then flung away." The Soviets backed the nationalists' military campaign in northern China in 1926 with advisors, munitions, and even aircraft, and gloried in their victories.

After the spectacularly successful northern campaign, Chiang Kai-shek decided to move against the Left Guomindang and their Communist allies, who wanted to accelerate the revolution in China. In April 1927, the Guomindang leadership arrested Communists and brutally suppressed a workers' rebellion in Shanghai, killing more than thirty thousand people in the subsequent anti-Communist repressions. The Soviet advisors left China for the USSR, while the nationalists seized the Chinese Eastern Railroad and broke off diplomatic relations with the Soviet Union. This catastrophe for Soviet policy in China reflected badly on Stalin and those who had favored the alliance with the nationalists. But so secure was Stalin's grip on the party that the efforts by Trotsky and the Left to stir up opposition to the ruling faction, both in the party and in the Comintern, had almost no palpable effect.

The War Scare of 1927

A cascade of events in 1926–27 stirred the deepest sources of Soviet paranoia about the West. Even though the Soviet Union was allowing Germans to train secretly on Soviet soil, the Germans were unwilling to help the Soviets build a modern weapons industry in the USSR. Suspicious of Western intentions, Soviet foreign policy spokespersons escalated the rhetoric of fear in the summer of 1926, adding to the usual references to capitalist encirclement and the danger of war more specific threats of military attack. The British Conservative government broke off relations with the USSR in May 1927, setting off a "war scare" among the Soviet leaders. The press whipped up emotions, and a panicked sense of impending war swept the Soviet elite. Inside the USSR the secret police (GPU) reported nationalist rumblings in Georgia and Ukraine. When the Soviet ambassador to Poland was assassinated in June, the Soviet government responded by executing twenty Russian nobles it had detained as hostages. The head of the GPU, the Soviet secret police, said: "We must show the monarchists we still exist." At this moment of perceived domestic and foreign crisis, Stalin urged a tougher policy toward his opponents at home and threats from abroad. Rejecting the views of his foreign minister, Chicherin, who played down the seriousness of the crisis, Stalin pushed for a more hostile position toward the capitalist world. A month later *Pravda* announced the arrests of engineers, many of them German, in the coal industry in Shakhty, in Ukraine. Both in foreign and domestic policy the Soviet Union was entering a new period of militancy and revolutionary enthusiasm.

Stalin and the Comintern

For all their militant rhetoric, the sacrifice of thousands of revolutionaries, and the material and spiritual backing of the Soviet Union, the international Communist movement never managed to take power in any country outside the former Russian empire in the interwar years, with the single exception of Mongolia. The most important reason for this was the relative weakness of the Soviet Union in comparison with the capitalist countries and the rapid and successful economic recovery of the European states after the war. While Social Democrats became major political actors in interwar Europe, forming governments in Germany, Austria, France, Spain, and other countries, Communists remained largely on the margins of legal politics. In many countries—Hungary, Italy after 1922, Poland, Germany after 1933—Communist parties were outlawed. The uneven strength of the Russian Communist Party and the other parties led to the gradual control of the Comintern by the largest party. After 1924, Communist parties were Bolshevized, or turned into smaller models of the Russian party. By the end of the 1920s all opposition groups that sided with Trotsky, Zinoviev, or Bukharin were purged from Communist parties, and they were effectively Stalinized. In 1926 Zinoviev was removed from his post as chairman of the Comintern, and the International denounced his Opposition as "essentially a right-wing danger to the party, frequently concealed behind left phrases." The Comintern went on to endorse Stalin's policy of "socialism in one country." Through persuasion, pressure, and purges, Communist parties around the world were largely reduced by the 1930s to international instruments of the ruling Soviet Politburo. Communists were required to demonstrate full ideological conformity to the official line of the Comintern, no matter which way it zigged or zagged. That line always involved an unquestioning devotion to the Soviet Union, defined as the first socialist state in the world. In time defense of the USSR was considered by Communists a more important priority than the domestic interests of workers in their home country. Here was a new form of "proletarian internationalism," one that demanded allegiance to a foreign state. Because the interests of the Soviet Union did not always conform to the interests of one's own country, Communists were caught in the unenviable dilemma of having to choose between their own workers and the USSR. For a true Communist in the Stalinist sense there could be no conflict. The first duty was to defend and protect the socialist homeland.

Balance and Power

From 1917 to 1928 the USSR moved from being a revolutionary power to become a more normal state in the constellation of international politics. Highly suspicious of the capitalist states, Soviet Russia had bold global ambitions, at first not so much for itself as a state as for itself as the first representative of a new stage of history, the foundational stone in a future multinational socialist world order. Its revolution was without limits. Because of the threat such a vision presented to the rest of the world, the enemies of Soviet socialism imagined the Soviet Union to be an expansionist state dedicated to world domination, like the imperialist ones that Europe already knew. Both sides felt threatened by the other: Soviet Russia by the interventionist capitalist powers; capitalist Europe by the virus of Bolshevism. Political scientist Stephen M. Walt has argued that revolutions increase the likelihood of war because they alter the balance of power, make it difficult for states to measure the threat from the other side, exaggerate the hostility of their opponents, and weaken the state that has experienced revolution, opening a window of opportunity for other states. Revolutionary regimes convince themselves that their revolutions can easily be spread, while counterrevolutionary powers believe that they can easily reverse the gains of the revolution. The first decade of Soviet foreign and Comintern policy demonstrated that revolutions produce instability, a threat of war, and interventions, but also that, in Walt's words, "revolutions are harder to reverse or to export than either side expects."

Once the Bolsheviks had won the civil war and the Allies had retreated from Russia, both Europe and the Soviet Union each realized that they could not achieve their maximal goal, the destruction of the other, and would have to learn to live with their enemy. After 1921 a self-proclaimed socialist state coexisted with states about which it believed sooner or later it would have to fight a war. The Western powers, on the other hand, had to reassess the Soviet government, which it had initially seen as nothing more than a deceitful agent of the Germans and later as a dangerous subversion of civilization. Though the initial suspicions never completely dissipated, as both sides learned more about each other, leaders became convinced that the conflicts between camps could be managed without war. The Soviet Union remained a relatively weak state, without dependable allies, and because much of the rest of the world failed to respond to its revolutionary inspiration, it turned inward to build its own economy, culture, and society. This more nationally oriented, less internationalist and revolutionary outlook was well represented by Stalin, the Soviet leader who exemplified a program of strengthening the state and its economy internally and subordinating its sympathizers abroad to the preservation of the "first socialist state."

Stalin's Path to Power

The political achievement of Stalin still astounds historians. The son of a shoemaker from Georgia, consistently underestimated by those around him, Stalin rose from an obscure associate of more radiant revolutionaries to become the undisputed ruler of the largest country in the world and arguably, by the time of his death, the man with the greatest power over the greatest number of people in history. His rise to power, like that of Napoleon before him, was made possible by a revolution that reshaped the rules of the political game. Older ruling elites were replaced by a new one of professional revolutionaries, and within the first few years of Bolshevik rule politics narrowed from interparty to intraparty politics. Soviets and lower party bodies played no significant role by the end of the civil war, leaving the party's Central Committee and its Politburo as the key political arenas. The ban on factions in 1921, prompted by the Bolsheviks' desire to centralize power, and the practice of command from the top that became the rule during the years of war all favored anyone who could control the majority of the nine-member Politburo. By 1923 Stalin was the man of the majority, a key coconspirator in preventing Trotsky from dominating the central party organs.

A second advantage for Stalin was his control of the party secretariat, which allowed him to build up personal support at lower party levels and have his men elected to party congresses and the Central Committee. He turned an internal party organization based on political orthodoxy and loyalty into a system of patrons and clients, in which personal as well as political fidelity to Stalin and his majority became the principal source for advancement. By late 1927 Stalin had a firm majority within the Politburo.

While some historians see Stalin as the supreme Machiavellian, who carefully planned his every move and foresaw his eventual path to the top, others argue that his victory was only in part due to his lust for power and personal security, that it was also the result of good fortune and seizing opportunities as they arose. Though his innermost thoughts remain elusive, even after the initial opening of Soviet archives, Stalin probably did not choose his policies only because of future personal political advantages they might provide, which would have been unknowable, but rather because they would help to achieve the kind of socialist society he sought to build. For Stalin, as for many politicians, personal power and political goals were complexly intertwined, and he probably saw little contradiction between what was good for him personally and what was good for the country. From 1923 to 1927 he identified with the successful NEP policies crafted by Bukharin, but as the crisis over grain procurements and industrialization deepened, he made a dramatic break with the

propeasant policy and moved to the opposite extreme. He did not adopt this
new policy simply to eliminate rivals and enhance his personal position, but
once he shifted his position old allies became new enemies. With little hesitation he prepared to destroy them.

Stalin's personality, both his apparent moderation and his ruthlessness,
aided him in his climb to the top. He positioned himself as the most loyal follower of Lenin, even though he had broken with Lenin over very serious issues, such as the nationality question, at the end of his mentor's life. Politically
shrewd, Stalin appealed in the 1920s to those tired of revolutionary excesses
and fearful of Trotsky's notion of exporting the revolution. The general secretary was able to base his power on the party apparatus and the state bureaucracy, which in the general exhaustion of the postrevolutionary years became
the most potent actors in what was left of politics. Trotsky and many of his followers believed that the Soviet bureaucracy had replaced the working class as
the effective ruling stratum in Soviet society, but social historians have shown
how former workers filled the niches of that bureaucracy. While having former workers sitting behind desks is not the same as workers in factories choos-
ing representatives to act in their interests, in a sociological sense the new ruling elite of Stalin's Soviet Union was made up largely of the children of the
working class. Those former workers, now bureaucrats, became the loyal cadres
of the Stalinist majority in the party.

Finally, Stalin won the power game because of the weaknesses of his opponents: Trotsky's lack of genuine sympathy within the old Bolshevik elite and
the newly recruited party members, Zinoviev's egotism and indecision, and
Bukharin's inability to compete with Stalin in the rough-and-tumble of postrevolutionary politics. In the political world of the Communist party, a world that
shared characteristics with the internal infighting of large business corporations, the political machines of large cities, and the Mafia, Stalin was in his element.

Suggestions for Further Reading

For overviews of the 1920s, see E. H. Carr, *A History of Soviet Russia: The Interregnum*
(New York, 1954), *Socialism in One Country*, 3 vols. (New York, 1958–64), and *Foundations of a Planned Economy*, 3 vols. (vol. I with R. W. Davies) (New York, 1969–78). On
the struggle for power within the Soviet Union, see Moshe Lewin, *Lenin's Last Struggle*
(New York, 1968); Isaac Deutscher, *The Prophet Unarmed: Trotsky, 1921–1929* (London
and New York, 1959); Stephen F. Cohen, *Bukharin and the Bolshevik Revolution: A Political Biography, 1888–1938* (New York, 1973): Robert C. Tucker, *Stalin as Revolutionary,
1879–1929* (New York, 1973). A classic study of the economic discussions within the
party is Alexander Erlich, *The Soviet Industrialization Debate, 1924–1928* (Cambridge,
Mass., 1960).

On Soviet foreign policy in the first decade, see Richard Debo, *Revolution and Survival: The Foreign Policy of Soviet Russia, 1917–1918* (Toronto and Buffalo, N.Y., 1979);
Louis Fischer, *The Soviets in World Affairs: A History of the Relations between the Soviet
Union and the Rest of the World, 1917–1929)* (Princeton, N.J., 1951); Jon Jacobson, *When
the Soviet Union Entered World Politics* (Berkeley, Calif., 1994); Stephen White, *Britain and*

the Bolshevik Revolution: A Study in the Politics of Diplomacy, 1920–1924 (London, 1979); Gabriel Gorodetsky, *The Precarious Truce: Anglo-Soviet Relations, 1924–1927* (Cambridge, 1977); George Kennan, *Russia and the West under Lenin and Stalin* (Boston, 1961); and Adam Ulam, *Expansion and Coexistence* (New York, 1968); and Stephen M. Walt, *Revolution and War* (Ithaca, N.Y., 1996).

On the Comintern and international communism, see Jane Degras (ed.), *The Communist International, 1919–1943: Documents*, 3 vols. (London and New York, 1956–65); Albert S. Lindemann, *The "Red Years": European Socialism versus Bolshevism, 1919–1921* (Berkeley, Calif., 1974); Allen S. Whiting, *Soviet Policies in China, 1917–1924* (New York, 1953); Conrad Brandt, *Stalin's Failure in China, 1924–1927* (New York, 1958); and the collections of documents in Helmut Gruber (ed.), *International Communism in the Era of Lenin: A Documentary History* (Ithaca, N.Y., 1967), and John Riddell (ed.), *The Communist International in Lenin's Time*, 5 vols. (New York, 1987–93).

CHAPTER 7
NEP Society

Cultures and Classes

The Soviet Union in the NEP years (1921–28) was a postrevolutionary society full of contradictions. Politically it was a workers' state, while its economy was officially state capitalist. Workers and artisans made up a tiny fraction of the whole population, which was mostly peasant. Besides the "toiling masses," other groups, strata, and social classes coexisted. At the top of society was the Old Bolshevik party leadership, the men and women who had made the long journey from underground, prison, and exile to political power. Under them were the newer party members, former workers and Red Army soldiers who, together with some "bourgeois specialists," top bureaucrats, managers, and loyal intellectuals, made up the ruling groups. In towns visitors came across the new petty bourgeoisie, the Nepmen, small merchants, traders, peddlers, and hustlers, who moved goods from place to place, hand to hand. Those most favored, the workers and party members, lived a more privileged life than the so-called former people—nobles, clergy, and prerevolutionary intellectuals and professionals—who had no real place in the new society. Whole groups of people, such as veterans of the White armies or children of former capitalists, whom the regime considered exploiters or counterrevolutionaries, were deprived of the right to vote and found it difficult to make a living.

Side by side the old and the new coexisted in an uneasy tension. NEP society was an amalgam of cultures ranging from the traditional peasant culture, omnipresent but now pushed back to the edge of towns by working-class culture, to the new youth culture with its enchantment with new cultural forms (or at least the fox trot). Embattled bourgeois culture coexisted with intelligentsia traditions from the tsarist period and the militant political culture of Bolshevism. Old Russian habits were confronted by radical challenges to patriarchalism, passivity, localism, and xenophobia. Claims by party intellectuals to a superior internationalist point of view contested with more the traditional ethnic cultures of Russians and non-Russians alike. NEP was an enforced compromise between the radical vision of the Bolsheviks and the backwardness of Russian and non-Russian society.

The Communists were convinced that NEP society was a class society, much like that of the capitalist world, but the party, through its control of the state, would guide society toward socialism and eliminate any chance of a bourgeois restoration. For all Communists class was an objective reality, something tangible that marked people's behavior and mentality. It might be hidden but it could not be eradicated without revolutionary transformations and social development. To be a "proletarian" or a "poor peasant" gave an individual special status and privilege, while being a clergyman or former noble or bourgeois only created unwanted difficulties. Poor peasants could vote but kulaks could not; sons and daughters of proletarians found the doors of schools and universities open to them, while children of clergymen or merchants were often barred from entry. Though individuals might move from class to class through education and social advancement, many Bolsheviks believed that the stigmata of class origins remained indelibly with people. In some ways such party ideologues thought of class as racists think of race, as an essential characteristic that determines consciousness, loyalty, identity, and activity. Others believed that since class behavior and attitudes were produced socially they could be radically altered with social change and honest labor.

Though Marxists believed in the reality of class and class conflict, in the 1920s they had great difficulty describing and analyzing the fluid and gelatinous social formations of the NEP years. Classes that had been more fixed and bounded, whose members were conscious of who they were and were not, were no longer so clearly marked in the years after the civil war. If classes had been shaped by the progress of capitalism in the late tsarist period, they had been disassembled and distorted during the civil war and early NEP period. The middle class of property owners, or "bourgeoisie" in Marxist terms, had been battered; having lost their economic base, many had emigrated to the West. A sizable part of the working class, or proletariat, had evaporated into the countryside. NEP society was stratified, divided, and highly mobile, but the kind of hard class divisions that had polarized prerevolutionary Russia did not congeal in the 1920s.

The attitude of the Communist Party toward class friends and enemies betrays both a crude ideological simplification of a complex and fluid social reality and a great insecurity before the population. Communist officials spent much time determining what a person's class origin and political orientation was. Seven or more years working in a factory or service in the Red Army during the civil war qualified one for admission to the proletariat. Since advantages and disadvantages came with one's class affiliation, many people tried to improve their social pedigree by claiming to be from the working class or poor peasantry. Communist watchdogs then had to work diligently to unmask the "hidden class enemies" in their midst. Though the so-called bourgeois specialists were needed by the state to restore the economy, they were barely tolerated and often punished. "No matter what you feed a wolf," a provincial deputy to the central soviet told his comrades, "he still looks to the forest."

The early Soviet conceptualization of class, as a relatively fixed category with a clear essence that manifests itself in consciousness and behavior, was too rigid and schematic to capture the complexity of a dynamic society. Though many scholars reject entirely the concept of class, it is useful to employ a more fluid, historically contingent, and less economically determined idea of class. Class can be understood to be not only determined by one's relationship to the economic order but also by culture, experience, education, and one's relationship to others in society. Classes can be made and unmade through time. They vary in degree of cohesion and self-awareness, or consciousness. Their members might have a high or low sense of belonging to a social class, of identity with other members of a class. Whatever social position an individual or group finds itself in, whether as workers in a factory or managers in an office, their sense of belonging to a class is highly subjective. Consciousness of belonging to a class, like one's sense of being part of a nation, is an act of imagination and perception, deeply influenced by education, experience, and the dominant forms of social thinking in a society. By officially promoting and energetically propagating a sense of class, by rewarding and punishing according to class criteria, the Communists in the 1920s both infused a sense of class throughout the Soviet population and gave class a somewhat artificial firmness and stability.

Workers under State Capitalism

Historically the Russian working class had always grown when peasants came into towns from the countryside, either because of seasonal work patterns or because they sought a higher standard of living. Old workers, those who had been in the factories for a generation or two, were hostile to the new unskilled migrants from the villages. And their trade union leaders resented the influx of cheaper, more easily exploited labor. Lenin, on the other hand, applauded the migration, seeing it as a healthy social process that dragged backward peasants into modern life, weakened the traditional patriarchal family, and contributed to the equality of women.

As industry shrank during the civil war, so many people left the towns for the countryside in search of food that there were not enough factory workers left to run the working plants. To find hands for factories the Sovnarkom decreed on September 3, 1918, that people without fixed employment must take the work offered them. Three months later the government ordered conscription of labor. Employers were not permitted, by decrees in 1918 and the Labor Code of 1922, to hire workers directly. Hiring was permitted only through labor exchanges, which were set up in late January 1918. But because the unemployed were required to work at the jobs offered them, many were reluctant to register with the exchanges. Less than half the trade-unionized workers registered with the exchanges, and it is estimated that about one-fifth of hiring took place outside the exchanges.

As early as 1921–22, with cities recovering from the war and the countryside still reeling from the famine, former townspeople and starving peasants streamed into the cities. The peasants in the towns competed with local work-ers for jobs and put a strain on social services and housing. The number of workers bottomed out in 1922 at about 1.6 million, only 64 percent of what it had been in 1913. Then the number of workers grew steadily. By the middle of the 1920s the Soviet Union's population had reached 147 million, of whom 5.6 million were counted as workers. Slightly less than half, about 2.3 million, worked in heavy industry, most of them in the Russian Republic (1.7 million). Overpopulation in the countryside, along with the demobilization of the Red Army, constantly fed the cities, and according to the 1926 census the popula-tion of the cities had reached their prewar level. But industry could not keep up with the new migrants, and at the end of 1926 over a million workers were unemployed.

Tired of the sacrifices that they had been forced to make during the civil war, workers wanted higher wages and more say in the running of their lives. But once again they ran up against the demands of the state for cheaper goods to sell to the peasants (i.e., lower wages for workers) and greater discipline un-der a single, powerful manager in the factories. Civil war had given way to a kind of capitalism, and workers who had fought hard for a better life that they identified with socialism or Soviet Power found themselves in an intense con-flict with their new, socialist bosses. Instead of finding security in their jobs, they were threatened by unemployment. In the first years of NEP (1921–23) a series of strikes disrupted industry, and the government reluctantly had to give in and allow wages to rise. After 1924 wages rose steadily, and with prices rel-atively stable, the workers' standard of living improved up to the end of the decade.

Already in 1918 women made up almost half (43 percent) of the workforce in Soviet Russia. They had entered into the working class in record numbers during World War I (from 1913 to 1918 the number of women workers grew by 60 percent, compared to 7.8 percent for men). During the civil war women held their own in the working class, remaining somewhere just under half of the industrial workforce, even as absolute numbers of both women and men workers were dropping because of migration to the countryside. In 1921 women made up the majority of workers in the textile, tobacco, and garment indus-tries, though in heavy industries they represented only about 28 to 30 percent of the workforce.

With NEP skilled male workers were encouraged to reenter the working class to take up their old jobs, and women were displaced to some degree. By 1923 women and adolescents made up over half the unemployed. Employers preferred male workers and discriminated against women. In 1921 the Red Army was reduced from 4.1 million to 1.6 million, and many demobilized Red Army soldiers went to towns to find work. There they were hired first, if they accepted work in their trade, but women from the armed forces were not given such preferential treatment, because, it was argued, they had joined the war effort voluntarily and had not been conscripted. Women generally had lower skill levels than male workers and were considered less fit for the heavy man-ual labor that made up much of the work of the time. Labor laws prohibited women from working in certain jobs, and employers were unhappy that women required long maternity leaves or time off to take care of sick children. Overall, traditional ideas about what kind of work was appropriate for women, as well as the fact that women workers were generally less skilled than urban male workers, combined with other forms of gender prejudice and discrimination to add extra burdens on women workers.

The NEP was dedicated to restoring and expanding industry in order to produce the consumer goods necessary to satisfy the vast majority of the Soviet population, the peasantry. At the same time the Communists had a long-term goal of founding an industrial economy based on advanced heavy industry that would rival the most developed countries of the West. To satisfy the peasants, NEP favored light industry, which consisted of artisan and handicraft production, at least until the mid-1920s, by supporting those branches of peasant domestic industry that met immediate consumer demand. Textiles, rubber, matches, tobacco, and printing flourished in the first years of NEP, though a number of other light industries—food, leather, sewing, and paper—suffered. In the first five years of NEP (1921–25) wages rose faster in consumer industries than in heavy industries as trade and markets grew. Labor productivity was higher in light industries, and influential party leaders, such as Nikolai Bukharin, argued for more support for labor-intensive light industry. Trotsky and the Left in the party called for greater subsidies to heavy industry, and indeed the need for basic producer goods, such as iron and steel, encouraged investment in heavy industry. Most workers (84.5 percent in March 1923) continued to work in the larger-scale state-owned industries. The emphasis on heavy industry, which grew stronger in the second half of the decade, favored that portion of industry that employed primarily men. As early as the middle of 1925 officials were forced to report, "The displacing of female labor in almost all branches of production is a fact that has been firmly established and raises no doubts whatsoever."

The pressures on workers in an economy designed to favor the peasantry created tensions between workers and the Communist party. Fearful of the growing chasm between the leadership and its ostensible constituents, Communists initiated meetings, conferences, and consultations with workers in factories to hear grievances, scold insensitive trade union officials, and head off labor unrest. In 1924 the party initiated the "Lenin Enrollment" to recruit more workers into its ranks. Efforts were accelerated to promote able workers into responsible positions of management or administration and foster their higher education, so as to create leaders from the working class. Thus, those workers who might have become the spokespersons of the workers were instead coopted by the party; they quickly moved up the social ladder and became the next generation of bosses and officials.

The working class was rather rustic in the 1920s, and many workers preserved traditional forms of organization, carryovers from peasant life, through the years of NEP. A group of anywhere from five to fifty workers joined together voluntarily, usually with people from their home village or district to form what was called an *artel* to sell their labor. They chose an "elder" to run the affairs of the *artel*, and older members of the *artel* passed on their skills to younger members, though not to outsiders. *Arteli* were particularly popular among construction workers, miners, lumberers, and seasonal industrial workers, who pooled their labor, tools, and even their horses to sell at the best price. Wages were divided equally, or by the elder on the basis of some accepted principle (in some cases, by the length of each member's beard!). Though the *arteli* were collectivist and egalitarian, many Communists considered them throwbacks to peasant life, premodern, and paternalistic. The *arteli* were made up of people from the same region or village, and the party was unhappy about this localist rather than class loyalty. In December 1924 labor *arteli* were recognized in Soviet law as having the right to make contracts, hire workers, and operate with limited working capital. But members of labor *arteli*, or the even more collective "labor communes," were excluded from trade unions. Though Communists tolerated the *arteli*, the more production-oriented, like Aleksei Gastev, continued to believe that collective labor and egalitarianism were inefficient and therefore inappropriate in the modern Soviet economy. Some more skilled or harder-working workers resented the principle of equality on which the *artel* was based; often younger workers were frustrated by the rigid reverence for seniority, and the unions too fought against the *arteli*. Over time the state limited the powers of the elders and tried to replace them with appointed leaders. In 1926 the miners' union, for example, banned *arteli* in its industry.

Briefly, at the very end of the 1920s, during the push for the First Five-Year Plan, a renewed enthusiasm for egalitarianism and collectivity gave the *arteli* a second wind. The party and unions came out in favor of "collective wages" and "collective bonuses," instead of individual wages and bonuses. By 1929 new production units called shock brigades, complete with elected leaders, emerged. Many *arteli* turned themselves into brigades. But very quickly this short-lived experiment faded. By 1931 the productivist ethic overwhelmed the collectivist and egalitarian. Some workers protested and resisted, for they preferred to work in the traditional collective forms. Eventually the *arteli* would disappear, some survived under the rubric of the *brigady* (brigade) but without the elected elders. Ironically, just at the moment when the Communists were forcing peasants to collectivize, they pushed workers to individualize. At the same time the party thwarted the workers' own impulses for egalitarian organization and tried to institute greater control over workers in the interest of productivity.

The New Economic Policy ended the militarization and forced mobilization of labor of the civil war years, allowed a free market in labor, and introduced wage differentials. The egalitarianism of the civil war years, which was mostly an equal sharing of poverty, gradually gave way to greater differentiation among workers. Wages were negotiated between enterprises and the unions, which became more independent of the state, though the party still played a controlling role. Unions attempted to protect the interests of the workers, while remaining careful not to interfere in the running of industries. Workers were even allowed to use the traditional weapon of capitalist working classes, the strike. Freer to move around, bargain for their labor, and express their discontents than they had been during the civil war, Soviet workers under NEP found that their lives were still insecure and that the state's interest in productivity overrode consideration of workers' own needs.

During the NEP years the Communist Party expanded its role steadily from politics into economics until it intervened and interfered in all aspects of production and consumption. State agencies as well as unions and local party committees all gave orders, issued recommendations, often at cross purposes with one another. Though the "command economy" of the earlier civil war period and the later Stalinist period was not in place under NEP, the party and state constantly overruled industrial directors, and party committees drew up lists of acceptable candidates for workers to "elect" to factory committees. But on rare occasions when the party-state attempted to push workers too far or too fast there was a backlash. When enthusiasts for Taylorism attempted to introduce greater intensification of labor in textile mills in 1925, a series of strikes involving about 100,000 workers, most of them female, broke out. The party bosses were forced to back down, ease the new regulations, increase wages, and allow greater democracy on the shopfloor.

Protests and strikes, however, were the exception. Generally Soviet workers in the 1920s were marked by what might be called "low classness." Though a class of workers existed as a demographic fact, it was not an organized, conscious, mobilizable force that acted in its interests to oppose either the state or the ruling elites. Its most successful members were continuously siphoned off to become crew leaders, managers, or state and party operatives. Workers did not develop their own leaders and were not permitted to organize a political party of their own. The Communist Party occupied the public space that under the more liberal versions of capitalism allowed workers' parties, unions, newspapers, and clubs to flourish. Party leaders proclaimed themselves to be the best representatives of the working class and were unwilling to surrender their exclusive role to outsiders or even to the workers themselves.

Certainly the revival of industry under NEP, the reurbanization of part of the population, and the positive image of labor in the official ideology contributed to a reconsolidation of the working class after the ravages of the civil war. But at the same time other factors worked against the formation of a cohesive working class. The decomposition and dispersal of the pre-1917 working class, the influx of peasants into the towns, high unemployment, the absence of an antagonistic bourgeoisie of any significance, the limits on workers' protest, the difficulty of forming class institutions independent of the party and its union officials, and the appropriation by a self-styled workers' state of the role of representative and spokesperson for the working class—all made the formation of a class-conscious working class in the 1920s a near impossibility. Still, on occasion, though rarely, groups of workers went on strike or protested labor conditions, and at such times their voices rang with the old rhetoric of class hostility.

Peasant Russia

Peasants had won enormous gains by the mid-1920s. During the revolution and civil war peasants had chosen to revive their own preferred form of landholding and governance, the peasant commune, with its periodic redistribution of the land. Their egalitarian division of the land created millions of small farmers and had the effect of driving Russia into an even more backward state. There were fewer large farms producing primarily for the market, and when not compelled to give up their produce by the state, the smallholding peasants increased their own consumption.

The village commune remained largely autonomous of the official state and party authorities, and was much more independent than it had been before the revolution. A kind of dual power existed in the villages, with the peasant-run village communes vying with the soviet institutions in the district towns, which were controlled by urban, literate men. A leading Bolshevik wrote, "In 1925, an almost total swallowing-up of the rural soviets by the commune gatherings was to be observed."

The unity of the hammer and the sickle preoccupied Lenin in the early years of NEP. At times, like many other Bolsheviks, he considered the peasants the most potent force in the USSR for restoring capitalism and periodically encouraged the polarization of the poor, "proletarian" peasants and the richer kulaks. But in his last years, desperate to maintain the alliance of the peasants and the workers, on which he believed Soviet power was based, he talked of taking a more gradualist approach toward converting the peasants to Bolshevik ideals, emphasizing education and the slow nurturing of culture. And he remembered the injunction of one of the cofounders of the Marxist tradition, Friedrich Engels, that compulsion should not be used against the peasantry. As he reconsidered the nature of rural Russia, Lenin envisioned the countryside as containing a number of interrelated and contradictory social structures, among them patriarchalism, capitalism, and socialism. Peasants might naturally gravitate toward capitalism, but the state and the traditional peasant commune could work against such a development. Opposed to the compulsion of some of his comrades to "propagate purely and strictly communist ideas in the countryside," he instead advocated coaxing peasants into cooperative agriculture. As he neared the end of his active political life, he wrote, "Given social ownership of the means of production, given the class victory of the proletariat over the bourgeoisie, the system of civilized cooperators is the system of socialism." Even without understanding the specifics of what Lenin may have meant, Communists tried in a variety of ways to encourage peasants to leave their communes and join cooperatives or collective farms. But they were met with sullen resistance and achieved little success. At times the party turned its "face toward the countryside," as in a notable campaign in the mid-1920s, but the bulk of the peasantry turned its back on the party.

In the 1920s there were approximately 20 million peasant households in Russia, organized into roughly three to four hundred thousand communes. For peasants the household was the center of peasant society, the work unit and the social unit, the source of help, discipline, and learning. The Soviet Land Code of 1922 also recognized the legal status of the peasant household and the head of the household as its "elected" representative. The peasants treated the land as the property of the household, subject to the rules and distributions of the commune. In Soviet law, however, the land was technically the property of the state. Both government and commune agreed that the land could not be

Figure 7.1. *Haymaking.* Painting by Kasimir Malevich, 1928 (Scala/Art Resource, NY).

sold or bought and that the actual holders should be those who worked the land.

The equality created by the peasants' revolutionary land settlement was lost somewhat during the NEP years. By the mid-1920s commentators spoke regularly about three levels of peasants. The poor peasants were seen by the Communists as true "rural proletarians." They were either paid agricultural laborers, peasants without land, or those with so little land that they were forced to work for others to supplement their income. Perhaps as many as one-third of Russian peasants were poor, without livestock or even a horse, unable to support their families from their farms. Middle peasants made up the majority of the peasantry, or about 60 percent. They were able to eke out a bare subsistence on their farms and usually had some livestock. At the top of peasant society were the kulaks, the richer peasants who possessed livestock, perhaps even some farm machinery, and were able to hire labor. While they were the best-off peasants materially, they had certain disadvantages. In Soviet Marxist theory they were class enemies of the working class and the poor peasants. From 1918 until 1936 they were denied the right to vote and burdened with special taxes. Poor peasants, on the other hand, received various privileges, and like urban workers were freed from most taxes. The 90 percent or more of the peasantry labeled poor or middle produced three-quarters of the marketable grain, while the kulaks made up about 3 to 5 percent of the peasantry and produced fully one-quarter of all the marketable grain.

As Russian agriculture recovered from the ravages of civil war in the first half of the 1920s, many observers noticed two contradictory tendencies among the peasants: greater differences between richer and poorer peasants on the one hand and a striking class cohesiveness among all peasants on the other. These paradoxical outcomes were the result of the larger, richer households dividing over time into smaller households and the poorer families combining their limited resources with other poor households to become larger households. When the periodic redistributions of land took place in the communes, the poorer households, now with more mouths to feed, received more land and tended to become richer, while the once-richer households, now with fewer mouths to feed, received less land and tended to become poorer. Instead of absolute polarization, there was a kind of cyclical mobility in the Russian village.

Though there were fractures and disagreements within villages, peasants preferred their own to outsiders. The peasants looked upon the kulaks, not as a class enemy, the way the Communists saw them, but rather as leaders of the village. But this class cohesion, rather than class warfare, in the countryside meant that the Communists in the towns faced a relatively united and conservative social force in the villages, one that was unwilling to change their farming practices, resistant to certain effects of the capitalist market economy, and even more obstinate in the face of any city-imposed program of industrialization. Though they were largely uninterested in joining collective farms, in their own lives the members of a peasant household pooled all their income and shared everything except clothing and shoes. As one village correspondent wrote, "As long as there is only one family pocket, then there is a family, but as soon as things get hidden in separate pockets, then you know that tomorrow there will be a partition."

People from the towns thought of the peasants as "dark people" who were unenlightened and backward. Outsiders saw them as living in superstition and fear of the unknown. In 1926, 55 percent of the rural population could not read, and 40 percent of children (7 to 11 years old) had no schooling. There was only one schoolteacher for every seven hundred rural dwellers, only one doctor for every seventeen thousand. Russian peasants were religious but not very in-

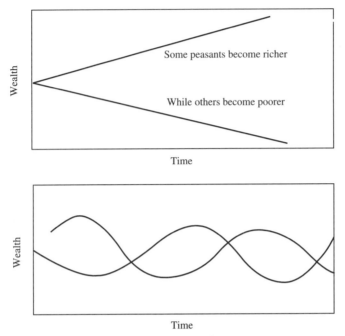

Figures 7.2 and 7.3. Peasant polarization or cyclical mobility? Absolute polarization model (Figure 7.2; top) and cyclical mobility model (Figure 7.3; bottom). Poorer peasants, usually in smaller families, join others to form larger family groups and become, over time, richer; larger, wealthier families break up and, over time, become poorer. Cohesion of the peasantry, rather than polarization, results.

volved in the church. They identified themselves as orthodox, but they adapted Russian Orthodoxy to their needs, preserving pagan rites and festivals and incorporating magic and belief in witches, demons, and unclean spirits. While they believed in God and Christ, and venerated icons and observed the cults of the saints, peasants had little respect for the villages priests, who often came from the peasantry and were known for their drunkenness and their greed. Parish clergymen were poor and dependent on the charity of the villagers, and they were alarmed at the growing indifference to religion, particularly among peasants who had been to the city. Though peasants had long had an ambivalent attitude toward the church, most were not happy with the harsh treatment of local parish priests by Soviet officials. In the early 1920s villagers began to elect their own priests to reduce the power of the church hierarchy locally. Many peasants looked upon Communists simply as people who did not believe in God. When the government required that education, most of which had been in church hands, be taken over by the state, the clergymen resisted and were occasionally joined by whole villages. The state tried to replace religious holidays with official secular holidays, but tradition proved more powerful than the innovations of outsiders.

Whatever suspicions the Bolsheviks may have had about peasants, they realized that without their support the workers' revolution would have suffocated in the cities and the old regime might have been restored. It was the peasantry that destroyed the whole structure of power in the countryside, dividing up the landlords' estates and replacing the old district assemblies and the local administrations of tsarist times with ad hoc peasant committees that eventually evolved into soviets. By defeating the Whites, who had threatened to take back the land from the peasants, Soviet power had won some degree of prestige and legitimacy in the eyes of the villagers. By their very location in the traditional Russian capital of Moscow, the Bolsheviks enjoyed the trappings of rightful authority. Their propaganda and dedicated agents, the discipline of party members, and the confidence that history was on the side of the cities and the workers worked to win over some elements in the countryside. If peasants were not enthusiastic about the Communists in power in the 1920s, neither were they openly hostile.

Younger peasants or those who had been in the army responded more enthusiastically than their elders to the Communists' efforts to bring education, technology, and modern medicine to the villages. Most peasants relied on the traditional healers in the villages, who mumbled secret prayers or used combinations of herbs to cure the ill, while others looked toward the Soviet doctor, most likely a paramedic, and the village clinic. The struggle between the old and the new sometimes turned violent, particularly when the patriarchal hold of men over women was challenged by the Communists, but in general the NEP years were an uneasy standoff between the modernizing trends from the cities and the stolid resistance of peasant society.

Even at the end of the first decade of Soviet power, the Communist Party had made few inroads into the countryside. There were only 333,300 Communists in rural areas, organized into about 23,000 party cells. Over half the chairpersons of the rural soviets were former Red Army soldiers, many originally from the peasantry but now identified in their own minds and the peasants' as party members. In 1929 only 15 percent of party members could be considered peasant, even when generously defined by their social status at birth rather than by current occupation. Forty-two percent were factory workers, and another 43 percent were officials and other white-collar professionals. On the eve of collectivization and the demise of NEP, the Soviet countryside was extremely undergoverned, and the presence of state authority was only intermittently experienced by the peasants.

The Nepmen

Though NEP was Lenin's own creation, the semicapitalist system was never fully accepted by the more militant Communists. The very word *nepovskii* (of or belonging to NEP) had a negative ring to it. To many NEP looked like the slippery slope back toward capitalism, and its only justification was that it was a necessary evil that would eventually be abolished. The most visible effect of

NEP was the reemergence of private trade and manufacturing, which was legalized in 1921, even as most wholesale trade was still carried on by the state. Cooperatives grew in number and in strength. Middlemen, the so-called Nepmen, flourished, and peddlers multiplied. As if by magic, goods that had been hoarded and hidden away during the civil war suddenly appeared, not only necessities but English cloth, Havana cigars, and fine French wines. Foreign trade also revived, especially after the signing of the March 1921 Anglo-Soviet Trade Agreement, and foreigners were offered concessions to attract foreign capital. In October 1921 a state bank (Gosbank) was established to supply credit to industry and agriculture. The currency was stabilized, based in part on gold. Somewhat disillusioned, one Bolshevik remarked, "We Young Communists had all grown up in the belief that money had been abolished once and for all."

Lenin put the best face on the need for free domestic trade. Since the weak state could not supply consumers with all they needed, "We must not be afraid to admit that there still is a great deal that can and must be learned from the capitalist." And Bukharin, the most enthusiastic defender of the NEP compromise, wrote that formerly "we believed it was possible to destroy market relations immediately with a single stroke. As it turned out, we will reach socialism only through market relations." He favored competition between the state sector and the private to see which could better satisfy consumer demand. But most Communists barely tolerated the Nepmen and expected them to be eliminated eventually. Stalin castigated the "merchant and usurer [who] have wedged themselves between the state, on the one hand, and the peasantry, on the other." As early as 1924 the government cracked down on the petty merchants, closing shops and restaurants. But a year later the party softened its hard line on free trade and promoted the private sector. Taxes on the Nepmen were eased, and they were allowed to reap higher profits.

At the height of the NEP free market, in the mid-1920s, Nepmen controlled three-quarters of all trading operations in the Russian Federation and over 90 percent in Transcaucasia and Central Asia. Millions of people were producing goods in small workshops and factories. Rather than coming from the prerevolutionary bourgeoisie, the new entrepreneurs were either state employees who had access to goods or former shop clerks or small producers who saw an opportunity to get rich. Former black marketeers now turned to legal businesses. Doctors, dentists, architects, publishers, entertainers, and restauranteurs all plied their trade in relative freedom but under the suspicious glance of the party, which feared that the peasants might prefer the Nepmen to the working class. In central Moscow the Sukharevka market bustled with trade to the dismay of the more ascetic Communists. To its shoppers it was a veritable feast for the eyes, as a visitor reported:

> Everywhere you look is an agitated, noisy human crowd, buying and selling. The various types of trade are grouped together. Here currencies are bought and sold, there the food products; further along, textiles, tobacco, cafes and restaurants, booksellers, dishes, finished dresses, all sorts of old junk, and so on. . . . Urchins scurry all about with kvass [a beer-like drink

made from bread]—huge bottles of red, yellow, or green liquid in which
float a few slices of lemon. One million rubles a glass [this at a time of runaway inflation]. Everyone drinks this poison from the same glass. . . .

The tide turned again in 1927 when state regulation on private trade increased. With the swing in 1928–29 toward collectivization of agriculture and
a planned economy, the state cracked down hard on the private traders. The
government raised taxes, confiscated the goods of the Nepmen, and closed their
shops. The merchants were driven from state housing and their children expelled from schools of higher learning. By 1930 even private medical and den-
tal clinics and barbershops were forbidden. Private trade was condemned as
"speculation," a crime that by 1932 could result in five to ten years in a labor
camp and loss of property.

The Red Army

Millions of people, mostly peasants, had gone into the Red Army during the
civil war. Their hardening in battle was also a kind of political education. At
one point half the Communist Party served in the army, and over two hundred thousand party members died in the fighting. When the war ended, some
5 million Red Army men and women were demobilized and had to be absorbed
into civilian society. Some found work in the state and party apparatus, about
562,000 remained in the small central standing army, and another million and
a half participated in regional militias, but millions returned to their villages,
where they became an important link between Soviet power and the peasantry.
Here they found work as local police officers, soviet officials, village corre-
spondents, or reintegrated into local life as library workers, administrators, and
activist peasants.

At the war's end the old socialist suspicions of standing armies resurfaced.
Some Communists, like Nikolai Podvoiskii, wanted to resurrect the idea of a
people's militia, but the army commanders, most importantly Commissar of
War Frunze, defended the need for a regular army by raising the specter of a
possible attack on the Soviet republics from the capitalist West. The army was
preserved but not without significant reforms. In 1923–24 the government
worked with top officers to increase discipline and morale among the ranks,
reduce the power of political commissars and "military specialists" in the army,
and improve the living standards of officers. The army once again became a
respectable career for many upwardly mobile young men.

The army was more than just the military force defending the country
against its enemies. It was a school for socialism in the countryside. The largest
state institution, the army of peasants in uniform that had brought the Bolsheviks to power and defended the "workers' state" in the civil war became in
the 1920s one of the state's principal links to the rest of the population. The
Red Army was a huge welfare agency for its soldiers and their families. Not
only did it provide health benefits and housing credits, it also carried out a
vast educational effort to turn hundreds of thousands of soldiers into literate,

cultured citizens. The army, thus, worked to create a large group of loyal supporters with a sense of patriotic duty and dedication to the new socialist order. In this way it was also a school for nationalism, at least for the particular Soviet variant of nonethnic supranational patriotism.

The army was one of the institutions of the Soviet state that reached furthest into the countryside. Disturbed by its lack of authority in the villages, where many local soviets were run by peasants who disregarded the policies of the central state, the government put forth former soldiers in the local elections in 1926 and won half the seats in the district executive committees, one-third in the rural soviets, and more than one-half of the chairmanships of those soviets. These new officials had all gone through a common experience and education in the military, and their mentality as well as their careers were tied to the further development of the Soviet system. The army, as the long arm of the state, would be powerfully flexed at the end of the 1920s when tens of thousands of soldiers were mobilized to drive the peasants into the collective farms.

The New Soviet Man and Woman

Part of the appeal of Marxism came from its utopianism, its vision that under communism a new society without violence and class conflict would be built and within it a new human being would be created. The most extravagant statement of that hope was expressed by Trotsky in an elegant passage at the end of his *Literature and Revolution* (1924), where he described life under the highest stage of communism:

> Man will become immeasurably stronger, wiser and subtler; his body will become more harmonized, his movements more rhythmic, his voice more musical. The forms of life will be dynamically dramatic. The average human type will rise to the heights of an Aristotle, a Goethe, or a Marx. And above this ridge new peaks will rise.

The achievement of a more just, egalitarian, nonexploitative society was based on the prior achievement of material abundance. The abolition of competition and greed, the elevation of cooperation, was contingent on the end of shortages. Yet the first self-proclaimed socialist government came to power in one of the most backward parts of Europe, in a country beset by hunger, disease, and poverty. The material base for the vision did not exist, but that did not stop the most radical elements in the party and intelligentsia from pursuing their dreams of democracy and egalitarianism.

The tension between the utopia of freedom and justice and the reality of backwardness and poverty was most evident in the policies and practices of the Soviet party-state that affected women, private life, and the family. Here a small group of activist Communists attempted to institute a radical transformation of the subordinate position of women. Marxists began with a belief in the historical mutability of human nature and the family. Not completely consistently, Marxists believed that the family was both a natural and a social relationship. Marx had written that the first division of labor was in the family, between men and women. Women's maternal function, the reproduction of the species, created the conditions for women's oppression, and only the communal organization of domestic chores would liberate women from their burdens within the home. In his famous work *The Origin of the Family, Private Property, and the State* (1884), Engels concluded that the nuclear family with its male dominance was not natural and necessary, that communal marriages had preceded nuclear families, and that monogamy was based "on the subjugation of one sex by the other." Capitalism had transformed the family, bringing women into the world of wage labor. Though its effects on family life were destructive, the economic fruits of capitalism, nevertheless, made possible the liberation of women. Under socialism housework would be turned into social work.

The most influential Marxist writer on gender questions was the German worker-socialist August Bebel, who in 1879 published *Women and Socialism*. He proposed that sexuality was a natural impulse, like hunger or thirst, and should not be treated as moral or immoral. "What I eat and drink, how I sleep and dress is my private affair, and my private affair also is my intercourse with a person of the opposite sex." Under capitalism sexuality had been distorted, and marriage had become a "forced relationship." Socialism would change that and permit a "free union of love." Among Russian socialists the "women's question" was usually subordinated to other issues, as in Nadezhda Krupskaia's essay "The Woman Worker," where she argued that female liberation depended on the liberation of all workers from the oppression of capitalism and autocracy. In general Marxists were more concerned about production than reproduction. Production was public, but reproduction was private, in the home, a female issue that was neglected in favor of issues considered more important.

A singular exception to the neglect of gender issues among Russian Marxists was the work of Aleksandra Kollontai (1872–1952), who had been inspired by the oppression of women to join the Social Democratic movement. Kollontai abandoned her husband and small son to become a full-time revolutionary and organize women workers. Constantly coming up against the indifference or even hostility of male socialists, Kollontai grafted the sexually libertarian ideas of the Russian radical intelligentsia onto the sparse references to sexuality found in Western Marxist literature. All the male writers on this topic, from Marx and Engels to Bebel and Karl Kautsky, were firm monogamists. They wanted marriages based on love rather than compulsion, but they remained committed, at least publicly, to marriage. Kollontai proposed a new "proletarian morality" in place of "bourgeois marriage." By this she meant that sexual union based on love could exist outside marriage, though she was careful to warn against promiscuity. Socialism alone could bring full freedom to women, for it could make them economically independent, politically equal, and give them state and social support for raising children. Kollontai was not a political feminist who saw women's issues separate from the socialist movement in general. Women, like men, were in her view divided by class, and she was hostile to middle-class feminists who ignored social questions like the dependency of working-class women.

The Russian Revolution opened opportunities for a new agenda for women. After February the Provisional Government granted women the vote for the first time, and after October the Soviet government steadily dismantled the whole edifice of tsarist family law. Under the old regime marriage and divorce had been left to the churches. A wife was obligated to obey her husband, to live with him, take his name, and assume his social status. Up to 1914 a women could not take a job or enroll for further education without her husband's consent. The husband was obligated to support his wife according to his status and abilities. A father had almost unlimited power over his children for life, and parental consent was required before a child could marry. Divorce was almost impossible according to the teachings of the Orthodox Church. Only in cases of impotence, prolonged absence, or adultery witnessed by two or more people would the Church allow divorce. A woman had only a few rights. She could control her dowry, special purchases, and gifts and hold property separately from her husband. But an illegitimate child had no legal rights and up to 1902 could not be adopted or recognized without explicit imperial consent.

The early record of the Soviet state in the area of female liberation was mixed. The intentions and legislative record were the most progressive of any major country, but their actual effects on the position and power of women were meager. Lenin became the first head of state to address a woman's congress, at which delegates cheered the suggestion that the derogatory Russian word for a woman, *baba*, be outlawed. Already, in December 1917, the state had mandated the principle of equal pay for equal work and granted paid maternity leaves for women workers. Marriage was secularized, and common-law marriages were legally recognized. The language of submission and dominance in the marriage ceremony was eliminated, and spouses were free to choose either the name of the wife or the husband or a combination of the two. Soon "Red weddings" replaced church weddings for dedicated Communists. Complete sexual equality in marriage was declared the law of the land. The first Soviet constitution, in July 1918, declared men and women equal, and the soviets adopted a new code of family laws. Divorce was simplified to the point that mutual consent meant immediate divorce. If only one party wanted divorce, a brief court hearing was held. No grounds for divorce had to be stated, no evidence presented, and no witnesses heard. The courts then decided matters of property and children. Alimony was granted to either party if he or she was needy. No distinctions were made between children born in or out of wedlock. The whole concept of "illegitimate children" was eliminated. This most radical family law in Europe was extended in 1920 when abortion was legalized—fifty-three years before *Roe v. Wade* in the United States—and the costs of abortion were borne by the state.

Yet women did not reach positions of power in either the state or the party. Women Bolsheviks organized the Women's Section of the party (Zhenotdel) in 1919 with the Franco-Russian socialist Inessa Armand as its first director. The party saw Zhenotdel as the representative of the party among women, but Kollontai and others saw it as the representative of women's interests within the party and state. Well over seventy thousand women fought for the Reds in the civil war, though few held high rank. The political commissar Zemliachka, however, cut her hair short, wore boots, pants, and leather coat and proved to be as tough in meting out punishment as the men with whom she worked. Kollontai became the first female people's commissar (of public welfare) and later the first female ambassador in history (to Norway). Still, women were less likely to be admitted to the Communist Party than men. Since the party recruited the more skilled and literate workers and women fell heavily in the less-skilled category, admission to the party simply reproduced the inequities within society. Only seven women, among them Kollontai and Krupskaia, sat on the Central Committee in the years before World War II. In the 1930s women held only one-sixth of the administrative posts in the party, mostly at the lower levels. In 1932 just over 16 percent of party members were female. Female delegates to party congresses until 1939 never reached 10 percent of the total.

Even more telling was the failure to implement the Marxist social program so essential to the emancipation of women. Lenin polemicized against housework as "petty and containing nothing that can in any way further the development of women." He called for the creation of daycare centers, communal kitchens, and other institutions to free women from compulsory labor in the home. Bukharin spoke of the family as "the most conservative stronghold of all the squalors of the old regime," and Kollontai declared, "The family ceases to be necessary." Society was to take over the bringing up of children. During the civil war labor shortages drew millions of women into the workforce, but the social services needed to provide for home and children were woefully inadequate.

The social disruptions of the world war, revolution, civil war, and postwar famines that had left 16 million people in the Soviet world dead hit women and children hardest. Besides homelessness and unemployment, poverty and economic dislocation led to the growth of prostitution. The immensity of these problems undermined the position of those who advocated the weakening of the family. Many poorer working-class and peasant women were unhappy with the easy divorce rules and the loose marriage practices of the early 1920s, and peasants in particular spoke out against marriages unsanctioned by church or ceremony. A few party leaders, such as Mikhail Kalinin, pulled back from the radicalism of the early years and argued that law should not move too far ahead of the mass of the people.

In 1926 a new Family Law Code was issued. Personal relations were freed as much as possible from legal interference. The new law code made divorce even easier. Either party could simply declare a divorce and notify the other by postcard. As a result, divorce doubled in 1927. The law recognized extramarital sex as legitimate and in no way punishable, and extended alimony to wives of common-law marriages. Particularly controversial was the extension of all legal rights to de facto unregistered marriages. One activist woman complained, "Some men have twenty wives; they live with one for a week, another for two, and leave each one with a child!" The divorce rate in Russia was fast becoming the highest in Europe, three times above that of Germany and twenty-six times higher than in England and Wales. In Moscow one out of every two marriages ended in divorce.

With all the rights they had received in law, women were not doing well in the years of the NEP. Divorced and single women were often left with children. Men often failed to pay child support. Unemployment remained high for women, and women's pay was only about 65 percent of that of men in the mid-1920s. Officials repeatedly delayed the building of childcare centers or social-ized dining halls and gave little attention or support to the development of contraception. In Muslim areas Communist activists used women as a "surro-gate proletariat" to pry apart the patriarchal society, which the party sought to dismantle. In the steppes of Central Asia and the mountains of Caucasia women wore the veil or the *chadra*, a full covering from head to toe, were kept from public activity, and denied education. The party enrolled activist women to lead the way in unveiling Muslim women and to explain elementary ideas of cleanliness, contraception, and childcare. The campaign opened new op-portunities for women of the East, and the first female brigade leaders and trac-tor drivers were celebrated in stories and films. But more traditional Central Asian and Caucasian men turned on the Bolshevized women. Azerbaijani men attacked a Zhenotdel meeting in Baku with wild dogs and boiling water. In Central Asia a twenty-year-old woman who had dared wear a bathing suit was sliced to pieces by her father and brothers. By the early 1930s the Communists pulled back from this frontal attack on Muslim practices and took a more grad-ualist approach through education and persuasion.

The attempts to liberate women were heroic. Largely carried out by women themselves, they often found little support from male party members. Sadly, the utopian plans for rapid emancipation withered before a harsh reality. The society and state were too poor to realize fully their ambitious plans, and re-sistance from patriarchal peasants who clung to traditional family patterns overwhelmed the urban radicals. With tens of thousands of orphans roaming the streets and roads, the idea of weakening the family unit further or collec-tivizing childrearing on a mass scale seemed perverse. Ordinary women and the peasants in general pushed for limiting divorce, fighting male promiscu-ity, and enforcing the laws on alimony. In the next decade many of their de-mands would be reflected in the family policies of the Stalinist regime.

Religious Wars

Atheism had long been part of the Russian revolutionary movement, as it had been for international Marxism. From the time of Marx, Social Democrats op-posed religion as the "opiate of the people," a form of deception and false con-sciousness, from which people had to be liberated. Marxism was defiantly a sec-ular humanism dedicated to the full realization of human potential on Earth. Atheism and antireligious feeling were compounded by anticlericalism, oppo-sition to the official church and its priests, which grew in intensity during the revolution and civil war. At the time of the revolution the Russian Orthodox church had almost 55,000 churches, 57,000 priests and deacons, 1,500 monas-teries with almost ninety-five thousand monks, nuns, and novices. With the ab-dication of the last tsar, the church convened an all-Russian council, the Sobor, to restore the patriarchate that had been abolished two hundred years earlier by Peter the Great. The newly elected patriarch, Metropolitan Tikhon of

Moscow, proved to be an implacable enemy of the Soviet state, and in January 1918 he anathematized the Bolsheviks, calling them "outcasts of the human race." The Soviets replied by disestablishing the church, that is, ending its privileged connection to the state, and eliminating religious instruction from schools.

Church and state were henceforth to be separate, and the Soviet Constitution of 1918 declared that there would be freedom of both religious and antireligious propaganda. A year later the party program warned that insulting religious believers would only lead to greater religious fanaticism. Many Communists, however, were anticlerical zealots, and while the fierce battles of the civil war raged, some turned their anger against priests and monks. Most priests favored the Whites over the Reds, and a few even fought against the Bolsheviks. Trotsky spoke of religion as "the principal moral arm of the bourgeoisie," and antagonizing or harming priests, called "priest-eating," remained popular with many party members. Church lands were seized, monasteries ransacked, and members of the clergy murdered. It was estimated that by 1923 twenty-eight bishops and more than a thousand priests had been killed.

Soviet policy toward the church vacillated between harsh opposition and halfhearted efforts at conciliation. In June 1921 the state declared that no religious instruction was permitted to groups of people over eighteen years of age. In March 1922 the government, desperately in need of money to aid the economic recovery and alleviate famine, demanded that gold, silver, and other precious objects be handed over by the church. The patriarch ordered resistance, and a virtual war broke out between the party and the church. When the Politburo decided to delay confiscations, Lenin urged using firing squads against the religious rebels. Priests and laypersons were tried for counterrevolution, and some were executed. The patriarch himself was put under house arrest. A number of priests opposed the hard line taken by the church hierarchy toward the state, broke with Tikhon, and formed the "Living Church," which supported the October Revolution and began to reap the benefits of state backing. Trotsky called the new church "an ecclesiastical NEP." The state turned churches over to the insurgents, who soon controlled almost two-thirds of the parishes in Russia. But fearful of the effects on the peasants of the hostility between the church and the government, the Communists soon backed down. When the patriarch confessed to "hostility to the Soviet authorities and anti-Soviet acts," he was released from arrest and fully reinstated. The state in turn lessened its support for the Living Church, which soon withered. Tikhon died in 1925, and Metropolitan Sergei of Moscow attempted a reconciliation with the Soviets. In 1927 he proclaimed:

> We wish to be Orthodox and at the same time to claim the Soviet Union as our civil motherland, the joys and successes of which are our joys and successes, the misfortunes of which are our misfortunes.... Remaining Orthodox, we remember our duty to be citizens of the Union "not from fear, but from conscience," as the Apostle has taught us (Romans 13:5).

Sergei's accommodation with the state was widely rejected by the faithful. Ninety percent of the churches refused to disseminate his proclamation, and the government was forced to publish it in *Izvestiia*. A new schism loomed when dissident priests formed an oppositional group of believers known as the Tikhonites. The Soviets now supported the official Orthodox Church against the more conservative dissidents.

But the Communists never gave up their efforts to rid the "new Soviet man and woman" of religion. Museums of atheism were opened, and Red weddings and christenings were organized to substitute for religious rituals. In 1925 the Bolshevik Emelian Iaroslavskii, who had been publishing an atheist newspaper, *The Godless*, for three years founded the League of the Godless. The Godless opposed aggressive action against believers or harsh treatment of priests. Instead they advocated education, agitation, propaganda, and even mockery. With the launching of the First Five-Year Plan at the end of the 1920s, the party once again became more aggressive in its anticlerical efforts. Peasant resistance to collectivization appeared to be supported by parish priests, and the party launched antireligious campaigns to break the back of the opposition. Antireligious instruction was introduced into schools, and thousands of churches were closed. By the end of 1930, it is estimated, four-fifths of all village churches were no longer operating.

Building Legitimate Authority

The paradox of the October Revolution was that the Bolsheviks possessed the physical power to overthrow the Provisional Government and disband the Constituent Assembly but did not yet have either a popular mandate to rule all of Russia (let alone the non-Russian peripheries) or an unassailable legitimizing myth to sanction their claim to govern. Even as they successfully built a new state during the years of civil war, the Bolsheviks were (as Lenin usually admitted) a minority party that needed to justify its hold on power. But unlike many other political parties, the Bolsheviks required more than passive acquiescence in the new order; they wanted active support that could be mobilized toward heroic goals. One of the central problems of the Communists in the first two decades of their rule was how to move from exercising power through force toward persuading people to accept their right to rule. The Bolsheviks had to supplement their coercive power with discursive power.

Whatever benefits military victory, the practice of state terror, or the repression of opposition might bring a regime in the short term, authority-building, as political scientist George Breslauer has noted, "is necessary to protect and expand one's base of political support." "Authority is legitimized power," and Soviet leaders had to legitimize their power and policies by demonstrating their competence or indispensability as rulers. In their own search for legal authority in the 1920s, the Bolsheviks could rely neither on tradition (associated with the *ancien régime*) nor religious faith, and they chose not to exploit Russian nationalism either. They had to create their own hegemonic culture that would bind the people to the new order.

In the post-October scramble to hold on to the reins of government, Lenin and the Bolsheviks had justified their actions by reference to a variety of historic claims: that they represented the vanguard of the proletariat organized in the soviets, that they were the only party able to bring peace and order to the country and willing to give the land to the peasants, and that the transition to socialism was at hand and the weakest link in the capitalist chain had been broken. Russia's second revolution would receive its ultimate sanction in the rising of the European working class, and all talk of the prematurity of the Bolshevik seizure of power would cease. But that did not happen.

The civil war provided a new justification for holding power: the fight against enemies domestic and foreign was directed toward the preservation of the victories of 1917 and the prevention of a restoration. Both of these goals had considerable popular support, especially among workers and peasants. As unpopular as the Communists were in many parts of the country, they were accepted as the lesser evil, and acquiescence to, if not positive acceptance of, Lenin's government spread through different social strata and groups: workers, many peasants, intellectuals, and certain nationalities, like the Jews, who were particular victims of White anti-Semitism.

With NEP and Stalin's notion of "socialism in one country," the Soviet leadership substituted pragmatism and domestic development for the flights of revolutionary imagination and international aid to the suffering masses abroad. The symbols of the revolution were reemployed to justify the new order as it existed as well as what it would become in time. The iconoclasm of early Bolshevik political culture changed into a quasi-religious faith in the icons of Soviet power. The most powerful official image was that of Lenin, the nearly deified leader of the revolution, untimely ripped from life by an early death. Though Lenin himself was a modest man who shunned publicity, his comrades began to create a cult around his name and deeds soon after they came to power. The first manifestation came in September 1918 after a would-be assassin wounded Lenin. Zinoviev praised Lenin as "the chosen one of millions . . . , the leader by the grace of God . . . , the authentic figure of a leader such as is born once in five hundred years in the life of mankind." Such idolatry was uncharacteristic of the Social Democratic movement, which had mourned its martyrs but had not usually spent much energy on living individuals. Indeed, Marxist historical theory tended to play down the importance of heroes in history and to emphasize instead great and impersonal economic, social, and political forces. Lenin survived the assassination attempt, which helped his political popularity and inspired expressions of extreme affection. Trotsky proclaimed, "When you think that Lenin may die, all our lives seem useless and you stop wanting to live."

Lenin discouraged the growing cult, but on his fiftieth birthday, April 22, 1920, the press celebrated the occasion with poems and eulogies. The revolutionary poet Vladimir Maiakovskii wrote:

> I know it is not the hero who precipitates the flow of revolution. The story of heroes is the nonsense of the intelligentsia! But who can restrain himself and not sing of the glory of Ilich? . . . Kindling the lands with fire everywhere where people are imprisoned, like a bomb the name explodes: Lenin! Lenin! Lenin!

Ordinary people had quite different views of the leaders of the republic. In a village near Moscow in 1922, a peasant told a visitor: "Lenin is a Russian man; he respects the peasants and does not allow them to be robbed, driven into village communes; whereas that other ruler—Trotsky—is a Jew; he does not know their work and life and does not value them and does not care to know them." As they sacralized Lenin party leaders took serious note of popular attitudes. They were distressed a few years later to discover that Lenin had a Jewish grandparent and suppressed that information, against the advice of Lenin's sister, for fear of arousing the anti-Semitic prejudices of the peasants. About the same time a Moscow cab driver told an American journalist about two giant portraits of Marx and Lenin: Comrade Marx was "the chief Bolshevik of the world, the little one with the beard was Lenin, the Bolshevik tsar of Russia." Pointing with his whip toward the Kremlin, he added, "The two of them live over there."

The Lenin cult began in earnest after Lenin's major stroke in March 1923 and then accelerated after his death on January 21, 1924. Not only was Petrograd renamed Leningrad and a "Lenin Enrollment" organized to bring workers into the party, but Lenin institutes and museums were built all over the country. A Lenin corner could be found in many workers' clubs and public halls in imitation of the corner in religious homes where icons were hung. Demobilized soldiers carried back to their villages special booklets, called *pamiatki*, filled with Lenin's pictures and words. Just as people made the pilgrimage to Lenin's mausoleum in Red Square to show their socialist piety, so party leaders claimed authority by reference to their faithfulness to the dead leader and his ideas. A new political formulation, Leninism (later Marxism-Leninism), was created as the emerging canon of sacred Leninist ideas.

The official character of the Lenin cult contrasted with earlier Bolshevik and revolutionary rituals. During the revolution and civil war, a carnival spirit had prevailed in which public festivals and mass demonstrations celebrated the new freedom and hope associated with the revolution. But by the 1920s many of these mass celebrations had been tamed by the authorities, regularized and ritualized, losing their spontaneity and emotional appeal. Official holidays, like May Day and the anniversary of the revolution (November 7), remained important for mobilizing public support for the regime, but they were no longer generated from below by ordinary people and activists but from above by state organizations and institutions. This trend toward state-initiated festivities grew stronger through the 1920s and developed into the highly orchestrated mass celebrations of the Stalinist period. Though they were no longer genuine, spontaneous expressions of enthusiasm, they became rituals that attempted to maintain the new status quo. Though Soviet culture was hardly dominant in all parts of Soviet society—certainly not among the peasants—it found its adherents among many young people, much of the urban population, and those who had moved up into the new elites thanks to the Soviet system.

The Soviet Union was for many of its supporters at home and abroad a dream world, a vision of the future in the present. The building of a new society with a new culture was a utopian effort attempted under the most difficult social and material conditions. The most fantastic plans were made, most of them never realized. "Utopias," wrote the philosopher Aleksandr Bogdanov, "are an expression of aspirations that cannot be realized, of efforts that are not equal to the resistance they encounter." But at the same time more mundane but equally impressive achievements were made. By the end of the 1920s the Soviet people enjoyed greater security, better health care, higher literacy, better nutrition, greater social mobility, and more social equality than most of them had ever experienced. Not surprisingly, looking forward from the civil war years and back from the Stalinist decades, NEP retains a brighter glow than many other periods of Soviet history. For the Bolsheviks it was a retreat, a detour, but for millions of Soviet citizens it was a time of relative peace and steady improvement in their lives.

Suggestions for Further Reading

For overviews of NEP society, see Sheila Fitzpatrick, Alexander Rabinowitch, and Richard Stites (eds.), *Russia in the Era of NEP* (Bloomington, Ind., 1991); Sheila Fitzpatrick, *The Russian Revolution* (New York, 2nd ed., 1994); Roger Pethybridge, *One Step Backward, Two Steps Forward: Soviet Society and Politics in the NEP* (New York, 1990); as well as Lewis H. Siegelbaum, *Soviet State and Society between Revolutions, 1918–1929* (New York, 1992). A classic work that covers the entire interwar period is Moshe Lewin, *The Making of the Soviet System: Essays in the Social History of Interwar Russia* (New York, 1985). A volume of additional essays by Lewin is *Russia/USSR/Russia: The Drive and Drift of a Superstate* (New York, 1995).

On the utopian plans for transforming society and relations between men and women and in the family, see Richard Stites, *Revolutionary Dreams: Utopian Vision and Experimental Life in the Russian Revolution* (New York, 1989), and his *The Women's Liberation Movement in Russia: Feminism, Nihilism, and Bolshevism, 1860–1930* (Princeton, N.J., 1978); Wendy Z. Goldman, *Women, the State, and Revolution: Soviet Family Policy and Social Life, 1917–1936* (New York, 1993); Barbara Clements, *Bolshevik Feminist: The Life of Aleksandra Kollontai* (Bloomington, Ind., 1979); Beatrice Farnsworth, *Alexandra Kollontai: Socialism, Feminism, and the Bolshevik Revolution* (Stanford, Calif., 1980); Vladimir Shlapentokh, *Love, Marriage, and Friendship in the Soviet Union: Ideals and Practices* (New York, 1984); and Dorothy Atkinson, Alexander Dallin, and Gail Warshofsky Lapidus (eds.), *Women in Russia* (Stanford, Calif., 1977). On the problem of orphaned children, see Alan M. Ball, *And Now My Soul Is Hardened: Abandoned Children in Soviet Russia, 1918–1930* (Berkeley, Calif., 1994).

On workers, see Lewis H. Siegelbaum and Ronald Grigor Suny (eds.), *Making Workers Soviet: Power, Class, and Identity* (Ithaca, N.Y., 1994); William Chase, *Workers, Society and the Soviet State: Labor and Life in Moscow, 1918–1929* (Urbana, Ill., and Chicago, 1987); Chris Ward, *Russia's Cotton Workers and the New Economic Policy: Shop Floor Culture and State Policy, 1921–1929* (New York, 1990).

On the peasantry, see Dorothy Atkinson, *The End of the Russian Land Commune, 1905–1930* (Stanford, Calif., 1983); Sula Benet, *The Village of Viriatino* (Garden City, N.Y., 1970); D. J. Male, *Russian Peasant Organization before Collectivization: A Study of Commune and Gathering, 1925–1930* (Cambridge, 1971); and Teodor Shanin, *The Awkward Class: Political Sociology of Peasantry in a Developing Society, Russia 1910–1925* (Oxford, 1972). For an account by a respected Soviet historian, see V. P. Danilov, *Rural Russia Under the New Regime* (London and Bloomington, Ind., 1988). The journalistic accounts by Maurice Hindus are extremely informative: *The Russian Peasant and the Revolution* (New York, 1920), *Broken Earth* (New York, 1926), and *Humanity Uprooted* (New York, 1929).

On the Lenin cult, see Nina Tumarkin, *Lenin Lives! The Lenin Cult in Russia* (Cambridge, Mass., 1983). On the atheist campaigns, see David E. Powell, *Anti-Religious Propaganda in the Soviet Union* (Cambridge, 1975). On businessmen in NEP Russia, see Alan M. Ball, *Russia's Last Capitalists: The Nepmen, 1921–1929* (Berkeley, Calif., 1988). On the army, the major work is Mark Von Hagen, *Soldiers in the Proletarian Dictatorship: The Red Army and the Soviet Socialist State, 1917–1930* (Ithaca, N.Y., 1990). Douglas R. Weiner, *Models of Nature: Ecology, Conservation, and Cultural Revolution in Soviet Russia* (Bloomington, Ind., 1988) is a pioneering work on environmentalism. The efforts at delivering health care to the new republic are dealt with in Susan Gross Solomon and John F. Hutchinson (eds.), *Health and Society in Revolutionary Russia* (Bloomington, Ind., 1990).

CHAPTER 8
Culture Wars

Intelligentsia and Revolution

When the Bolsheviks took power in October 1917, the vast majority of the old intelligentsia, everyone from renowned artists to local schoolteachers, opposed the new regime. Officials and clerks from the former government either refused to come into work or sat on their hands. Early in November, the new Soviet authorities sent out a call to intellectuals urging them to attend a meeting to show their support for Soviet power. The only noteworthy intellectual to show up at the meeting was the Futurist poet Vladimir Maiakovskii. Especially bitter for the regime was the open hostility of Maxim Gorky, Russia's most famous living writer and a personal friend of Lenin's. Almost unanimously the old writers and artists, and the university professors and other professionals, considered any collaboration with the Bolshevik "usurpers" to be a betrayal of intelligentsia traditions. Yet Lenin remained hopeful that eventually the "intelligentsia will have to arrive at the position of helping the workers precisely on a Soviet platform."

The prerevolutionary Russian intelligentsia did not survive the revolution and civil war intact but divided into four major communities: those who stayed in Russia and supported the Bolsheviks, those "internal émigrés" who stayed but had little sympathy for the Bolsheviks, those who temporarily emigrated (or were deported) only to return when the Soviet system stabilized, and those who left and never returned from exile. In the early years the Soviet government allowed intellectuals who opposed the regime to emigrate. Besides thousands of political émigrés, the permanent cultural émigrés included the philosopher Nikolai Berdiaev, pianist Vladimir Horowitz, painter Marc Chagall, composer Igor Stravinsky, and some of the most talented poets and writers that prerevolutionary Russia had produced, including short-story master Ivan Bunin, who, along with another émigré, Vladimir Nabokov, would later win the Nobel Prize for Literature. The Bolsheviks, who feared that the struggle between the few Marxist intellectuals and the rest of the intelligentsia was an uneven fight, expelled 160 liberal intellectuals from the country in 1922. This "group of ideologists of the 'new' bourgeoisie," it was claimed, was responsible for "the growing influence of a revitalized bourgeois ideology in the young Soviet Republic."

Temporary émigrés included short-story writer Aleksandr Kuprin, poet Maria Tsvetaeva, journalist and novelist Ilia Ehrenburg, novelist Count Aleksei Tolstoi, literary critic Prince Dmitrii Mirskii, composer Sergei Prokofiev, and Maxim Gorky. Once the USSR was established and signs of social and economic progress were evident, a significant number of intellectuals sought reconciliation with the regime that had driven them from their homeland. Among those who remained in Soviet Russia in an uneasy armistice with the party-state were the prose writers Konstantin Fedin and Mikhail Zoshchenko and the poets Valerii Briusov and Nikolai Gumilev (who was shot by the Cheka in 1921), and his wife Anna Akhmatova. More enthusiastic in their support of the revolution were filmmaker Sergei Esenin and the poets Maiakovskii, Demian Bednyi, and Aleksandr Blok.

For a century before the revolution Russia's intelligentsia had its own clear sense of itself as a voice of culture and progress; it was ready to sacrifice itself for the good of the people. But its writers and philosophers were split between those who gauged their activities by a criterion of social utility and those who claimed that their value stemmed from the individual's inner life. The utilitarian view of art, held by the realist critics of the 1840s to the 1860s and by Gorky in the immediate prerevolutionary period, asserted that art should be produced that would serve the liberation of the people. Art was needed by the revolutionary cause. But at the end of the nineteenth century and the beginning of the twentieth, many artists reacted against this utilitarian view and insisted on the primary value of artistic form over content, of subjectivity and experimentation. This new attitude was worn like a badge of honor by the Russian Symbolists, whose main aim was self-development of the individual in whatever direction that individual desired. Life was identified with art, instead of the other way around. For the Symbolists, and followers of other avant-garde schools such as Acmeism, Futurism, and Formalism, individual, personal experience was the ultimate value, no matter how strange that experience might seem to the ordinary citizen.

Among the most individualist of prerevolutionary artists to remain in Russia was the young poet Aleksandr Blok (1880–1921), an aristocratic eccentric already well known by 1905 for his Symbolist lyrics. Blok vacillated between reveling in his splendid poetic isolation and a desire to connect with the society in which he lived. Briefly in 1905 he flirted with politics, but then he decided to build a bridge to society through the theater, linking up with the famous avant-garde director Vyacheslav Meyerhold. Blok wrote, "More than any other art, the theater gives the lie to the blasphemous abstraction of the formula 'art for art's sake.' For the theater is the very flesh of art—that lofty sphere wherein 'the word is made flesh.' "

When other prominent intellectuals recoiled at the Bolshevik victory, Blok declared to a friend:

> A revolution, like a violent whirlwind or snowstorm, always brings new and unexpected things and cruelly disappoints many people. Its whirlpools

devour the good and save the worthless, but that is in the nature of revolutions and changes neither the total direction of the current nor the terrible deafening tumult which accompanies it. The roaring noise is an expression of its sublimity.

With an almost erotic approach to revolution, Blok submitted to the whirlwind around him. This was the same man who five years earlier had written, "The sinking of the Titanic yesterday has given me unspeakable joy—there is still an ocean!" In the first winter of Soviet power Blok wrote two of his greatest poems, "The Twelve" and "The Scythians." In these the revolution was pictured as an elemental, irresistible movement destroying the old civilization of Europe. At the head of the Red Army Blok puts the figure of Jesus Christ. With Blok a leading artist in the revolutionary camp, poetry and theater became the emblematic forms of literature in the civil war years. Sadly, Blok himself did not survive the revolution by very much, dying in 1921.

Most Bolsheviks were not particularly enthusiastic about the avant-garde poets and artists who supported the revolution in the early years, but they were very pleased with the decision of the realist writer Gorky to collaborate with the Soviet government in late 1918. Describing himself as a "heretic everywhere," Gorky had taken upon himself the role of the conscience of the revolution and in late 1917 and early 1918 published critical articles in his own newspaper attacking Bolshevik repression. In July 1918 the government, with Lenin's personal approval, closed it down. Gorky sought to use his influence to protect the intelligentsia during the "time of troubles" of the civil war and to appeal to the Americans for food relief during the famine of 1921. He was angered and frustrated by Soviet censorship and acted as a one-man loyal opposition. On Lenin's urging, a sick Gorky left for Europe in 1921. He remained abroad until he made several triumphal trips to the USSR in 1928 and 1929 in an attempt to bridge the growing distance between the Soviet Union and the Russian emigration. Only in 1933, after being courted by the Stalinists, did he return to Russia for good.

The state agency that dealt most directly with the intelligentsia was the People's Commissariat of Enlightenment, or Narkompros, headed for its first twelve years by Anatolii Lunacharskii (1875–1933), a cultured man of broad tastes. Lunacharskii had nearly impeccable revolutionary credentials. He had adhered to the Bolshevik faction almost from its inception, though he was a member of a dissident group between 1905 and 1917, when he and his brother-in-law, Aleksandr Bogdanov (1873–1928), developed the heretical view that Marxist materialism was a kind of metaphysics, since the real world is knowable only through one's perceptions. Along with Gorky, Lunacharskii held that Marxism was a new scientific, godless religion. This somewhat unorthodox Bolshevik, who wept openly when he heard of art treasures being damaged by revolutionary fighting, was a major player in formulating Soviet policy toward culture and the intelligentsia. His first official declaration was to end the tutelary relationship between the government and institutions of culture and to proclaim that "the people themselves, consciously or unconsciously, must evolve their own culture."

Desperate for support from the intelligentsia, Lunacharskii promoted the fortunes of a group of radical intellectuals who advocated the development of a proletarian culture. Influenced by Bogdanov, who held that art was the product not only of social environment but of a particular class, they called themselves Proletkult and were soon a semiofficial arm of Narkompros. For them art was "a most powerful weapon for the organization of collective forces, and in a class society, of class forces." The proletariat had to have its own class art "to organize its own forces in social labor, struggle, and construction." Even art from the past might be useful, but instead of the bourgeois principle of individualism, proletarian class culture would adopt collectivism as its touchstone. The more militant members of Proletkult denounced all bourgeois culture as "old rubbish" and called for workers' universities, a workers' encyclopedia, and a proletarian theater with an entirely new repertoire.

As its critics often noted, Proletkult leaders were not themselves proletarians, but Proletkult responded by claiming that real proletarian culture did not have to emanate from actual proletarians but from people with a "proletarian orientation." Both Lenin and Trotsky spoke out against Proletkult's attempts to dominate the cultural scene. Lenin called them "escapees from the bourgeois intelligentsia, who often looked on the newly created workers' and peasants' educational institutions as the most convenient field for their own personal fantasies in the sphere of philosophy or culture." Proletkult offended Lenin, who was a cultural conservative who preferred the Russian classics and traditional representational painting to modernist avant-garde experiments. In 1920 he pushed for Proletkult to be subordinated more directly to the Commissariat of Enlightenment. Gradually the organization lost its autonomy. But the greatest blow against its efforts came with the introduction of the New Economic Policy, when state subsidies ceased and the proletarian culturalists were forced to adapt to market conditions.

Soviet writers and artists in the 1920s, even those committed to the socialist project, were very contentious and continually formed small groups to promote their own view of the new culture. As Proletkult attempted to mobilize people in the creation of a workers' art, a small group of writers split off in 1919 to found a magazine called *Smithy* and celebrate machines, factories, and labor in their poetry. A year later, in October 1920, writers with a prolabor orientation formed the All-Russian Association of Proletarian Writers (VAPP). Writers divided into those more concerned with professional literary matters, like some of those connected with *Smithy*, and others dedicated to the organization of literature among the masses, like those affiliated with the journal *October*. The *October* group soon controlled VAPP and petitioned the party to recognize it as the exclusive voice of the Communist Party in literary affairs.

The party, however, declined to sanction one literary faction over another. In the early years of Soviet power the government gave artists a degree of autonomy while policing the boundaries of what was permissible. Censorship against political enemies was practiced by the Bolshevik government from its first days, but only occasionally was it extended to literature and the arts. Rather than state persecution, writers during the civil war suffered from lack of paper, the breakdown of printing presses, and the collapse of the book market.

In conditions of desperate shortages the Soviet government promoted the free distribution of printed matter and thus determined what might appear. Private publishing barely survived during the civil war and revived only with the advent of NEP.

For the Bolsheviks art was a means to securing support for their new order as well as transforming the backward peoples of the Soviet land into conscious proletarians. Besides the printed word, those means included mass spectacles, public readings and lectures, the visual arts, theater performances, and films. Almost immediately after the revolution, interest in theater exploded. Thousands of people formed dramatic groups; three thousand theaters performed in the Russian Republic alone, and the Red Army and Fleet operated over a thousand theaters. Artistic enthusiasts organized street festivals and mass spectacles to displace religious festivals and processions. Great artists participated, such as Marc Chagall, who painted murals in his native Vitebsk, and Natan Altman and K. S. Petrov-Vodkin, who redecorated the Palace Square in Petrograd. Thousands of participants reenacted the storming of the Winter Palace on its third anniversary. In these public presentations the chaos and confusion of revolution and civil war were given clear meaning. History was retold in the Bolshevik interpretation. Not only did audiences discover what October was about, but the makers of October found out what they had done. Bolshevism was now imagined as the end result of a long and inevitable social evolution, and this imagined march through time toward a brilliant future gave the Soviet state a precarious legitimacy that it worked constantly to prop up.

Wild experiments in theatrical form competed with the more traditional theaters of Konstantin Stanislavskii and Aleksandr Tairov. The poet Maiakovskii's play *Mystery Bouffe*, a fantastic allegory of the struggle of good and evil, was designed by the Suprematist artist Kazimir Malevich and staged by the avant-garde director Meyerhold on the first anniversary of the revolution. The play so confused its audiences that it lasted only one performance. But the revolutionary temper of the times encouraged experiment, and even a sober revolutionary like Bukharin was moved to chastise the producers of Chekhov's *The Cherry Orchard* for not staging *The Cherry Factory* instead.

Fellow-Travelers and Proletarian Writers

NEP turned out to be one of the most experimental and creative periods in Russian and Soviet literature, though it was rivaled by the explosion of literary modernism in the West that produced James Joyce, Marcel Proust, Thomas Mann, T. S. Eliot, and William Butler Yeats. The New Economic Policy created a new relationship between the state and the intelligentsia as it eased up on artists and writers by the authorities. This "soft line on culture," in the words of historian Sheila Fitzpatrick, "rested on the premise that the Soviet state needed the services of bourgeois specialists and would have to pay for them." From the expulsion of intellectuals from Soviet Russia in 1922 until the turn toward ideological militancy in 1928, the Soviet government was extraordi-

Figure 8.1. *Death of the Commissar.* Painting by Kuzma Petrov-Vodkin, 1928 (Scala/Art Resource, NY).

narily accommodating and tolerant toward the intelligentsia. The party stood aside from literary squabbles, except to encourage a variety of views and prevent a monopoly of any one group. As Zinoviev put it, both sides understood the need to work together and "we will no longer remember the past." He even invited scholars to return from abroad to celebrate Soviet power. While censorship continued and works deemed to be counterrevolutionary were proscribed, the party broadened its tolerance for non-Communist literature. For six years the living conditions and salaries of academics improved, job security became a reality for professors, and intellectuals managed their own institutions with relatively little interference from the state or party. In the universities the system of favoring the admission of workers was replaced in 1926 by an open competition with entrance examinations that, in effect, favored the children of the intelligentsia.

    The chasm separating the Soviet authorities and the intelligentsia remained deep, however. Many intellectuals who had chosen to stay in the Soviet republic were, in Trotsky's words, "not artists of the proletarian revolution but its artistic fellow-travelers." Typical of the attitude of many intellectuals was a group of twelve exceptionally talented young writers known as the Serapion Brothers, who proclaimed the inviolability of independent artistic creation. They included Fedin and Vsevolod Ivanov, the satirist Zoshchenko, and the Formalist critic, Viktor Shklovskii. They rejected the experimentalism of radi-

cals like Maiakovskii and used traditional forms to express their ambivalent
attitude toward the revolution. In a sense, they were the literary NEP—half
bourgeois, half accepting of the revolution as the condition under which they
had to work. Fedin, for example, in his 1924 novel *Cities and Years* dealt with
the adaptation of a middle-class youth to the revolution. Or, in the words of
the writer Boris Pilniak:

> In so far as I want to follow . . . Russia's historic destinies, I am with the
> Communists—that is, in so far as the Communists are with Russia, I am
> with them. . . . I acknowledge that the destinies of the RKP are far less in-
> teresting to me than the destinies of Russia.

The national patriotic strain expressed by the fellow-travelers within the
Soviet Union was also deeply felt by certain émigré intellectuals. In July 1921
a group of Russian expatriates in Prague published a volume called *The Changing of Signposts*, which argued for reconciliation with the Soviet regime. Russia
was now ruled by the Communists and this harsh fact had to be accepted. In
any case, they argued, Russia is greater than Bolshevism and irresistible forces
were compelling the Reds toward a more conservative policy. These artists and
intellectuals were "national Bolsheviks," neo-Slavophiles, who were prepared
to accept the Russian Revolution as the national destiny of their beloved homeland. The Changing Signposts movement found an enthusiastic response
within the Soviet republic, and Lenin himself believed that these reconciled patriots "express the mood of thousands and tens of thousands of bourgeois of
all sorts and Soviet officials who participate in our New Economic Policy."
In the tolerant atmosphere of the early and mid-1920s the leading voice for
literature was the journal *Red Virgin Soil*, edited by the Marxist critic Aleksandr
Voronskii. Often in trouble with the party leadership because of his association with the Trotskyist opposition, Voronskii was most eloquent in his support of the fellow-travelers. He believed that art was one of the means by which
people obtain knowledge of the external world. Like science, art must provide
knowledge, "cognition of life" and an understanding of reality. But whereas
science analyzes, art synthesizes; whereas science is abstract, art is concrete.
Science is aimed at people's minds and apprehends life by means of concepts,
while art is directed at their sensuous nature and illuminates life through images. By means of intuition, rather than reason alone, artists uncover the real
world, seeing beyond appearances to the underlying reality. For Voronskii
beauty, rather than utility, was the key to art's purpose. "Art," he wrote, "has
always sought and must seek to recover, restore, and reveal the world, which
is beautiful in itself, to represent it in the purest and most direct impressions."
Voronskii took aesthetics seriously, equating it with a kind of objectivity and
truth. For him, great literature, no matter what its class origin or nature, was
a revelation of the world and had a value for the proletariat.
Voronskii's views, which were shared by Trotsky and Lunacharskii, were
consonant with the soft line on culture. In a series of literary essays Trotsky
criticized the proletarian writers who treated literature as propaganda and defended the fellow-travelers who believed in the unique and irreducible quali-

ties of literature. In May 1924 a party conference on literature resolved that "no single movement, school or group can or should act in the name of the party." Early the next year the party rejected VAPP's call for "a seizure of power by the proletariat in the field of art." The decisive voice in the debate was that of Bukharin, then at the height of his power. He believed that in the long, gradual transition to socialism tolerance for a broad range of cultural activities was necessary. "It seems to me," he wrote, "the best way to destroy proletarian literature is to reject the principle of free and anarchic competition." On July 1, 1925, the Central Committee echoed Bukharin's approach and resolved that "as the class war in general has not ended, neither has it ended on the literary front." Though at some time in the future the proletariat would conquer positions in the field of belles-lettres, "the hegemony of proletarian literature does not yet exist, and the party should help these writers earn for themselves the historic right to that hegemony." But fellow-travelers must be tolerated. "Communist conceit" must be combated, and "Marxist criticism should have as its slogan 'to learn.' "

The literary radicals, like Maiakovskii and the Futurists gathered around the journal *Left*, were appalled by the fellow-travelers' dominance of the literary scene in the early NEP years. The militant literary critical journal *On Duty* declared that "all ideological doubts are absolutely *inadmissible*." Young Communists in the Komsomol (Communist Youth League), Red Army veterans, and literary politicians, such as Leopold Averbakh, the editor of the Komsomol journal *Young Guard*, all polemicized against the fellow-travelers. But a wide public appreciated the more classical styles of writing of the moderates, and influential party leaders, weary of the formalistic and often inaccessible work of the avant-garde, cultivated them.

Bolshevik-minded proletarian writers produced their own literature, soon to become part of the official canon of Soviet reading, primarily in the form of novels about the civil war and the construction of socialism. Dmitrii Furmanov, who had been a political commissar at the front during the civil war, wrote a semiautobiographical account of his experiences with the raw-boned partisan leader Chapaev that later was turned into a popular film. Written in the realist style with romantic heroes that would in the 1930s be enshrined in the Socialist Realism school, *Chapaev* (1923) was a model work that contrasted what is with what ought to be. Chapaev, the rough-hewed partisan chief, who is all impulse, spontaneity, and courage, meets up with Klychkov (Furmanov in real life), the disciplined, sober, intellectual party man, who ultimately brings the necessary political consciousness to the partisans. Aleksandr Fadeev's *The Rout* (1925), Fedor Gladkov's *Cement* (1926), and Mikhail Sholokhov's novel about the Don Cossacks, *Quiet Flows the Don* (1928), also borrowed the realist style and psychological characterization of classic writers like Tolstoy to promote the values of the Bolshevik revolution and the party. Whereas earlier in the decade the stylistic inventions of the avant-garde had been associated with the revolution, increasingly realism was adopted as the proper literary expression of the proletarian writers. At least in form and style, if not content and political commitment, the Communist writers approached the traditionalists among the fellow-travelers.

Two poets were emblematic of Russian literature in the 1920s: Sergei Esenin (1895–1925) and Vladimir Maiakovskii (1893–1930). Esenin was the golden-haired youth of Soviet poetry, an immensely popular platform artist who inspired a cult following with his melodic poems about lost village life. Born in Riazan and continually invoking his peasant roots, he fell in love with and married the American modern dancer Isadora Duncan. But when he traveled with her to the United States, he was repelled by modern urban life. In one poem he proclaimed, "My mother, homeland, I am a Bolshevik!" His life as well as his poems celebrated rebellion, both personal and social, and he found unbearable the deceptions and constraints imposed by officialdom. "I am not your tame canary!" he exclaimed, "I am a poet!" Alcoholic and depressed, he hanged himself in the Angleterre hotel in Leningrad at age 30, leaving behind a poem written in his own blood: "Dying is nothing new in this life / But then, living is nothing new either." A rash of suicides of young people followed. Maiakovskii, who hated Esenin for his popularity, his poetry, and his pessimism, wrote a bitter reply: "Maybe / if there'd been ink / in that room in the "Angleterre," / You wouldn't have had to / cut open your veins . . . Dying/ in this life / is not hard. / Making life / is much harder."

Maiakovskii's was a thundering, self-confident voice, and he posed as the champion of the October Revolution as he toured factories reading his opaque Futurist poems to workers. Along with the painter Malevich and others, he called for the death of the old art: "It's time / for bullets / to pepper museums." His iconoclasm and youthful bravado antagonized more conventional writers and even the cultural commissars. Lunacharskii considered him an adolescent whose boyhood had continued too long. Maiakovskii wrote frankly propagandistic poems, like *150,000,000* (1919) and *Vladimir Ilich Lenin* (1924), but ironically Lenin himself despised much of Maiakovskii's work and called it "nonsense, stupidity, double-dyed stupidity, and pretentiousness!" Maiakovskii's efforts to link the Futurists with the Soviet state failed repeatedly. Discomforted by the retreats of NEP, the poet wrote "About Scum" (1921):

> The storms of revolutionary depths are stilled.
> The Soviet brew is overgrown with slime.
> And from behind the back of R.S.F.S.R.
> Peers out
> The snout
> Of the philistine.

His brash criticisms of Communist pretensions found more sympathy with Lenin, who told a meeting of metalworkers that he did not know if it was good poetry, "but I guarantee you it's absolutely right from a political point of view." Maiakovskii also experimented with the theater, first in *Mystery Bouffe* (1918), which mystified audiences, then in *The Bedbug* (1928), his greatest success, and finally in *The Bathhouse* (1930), which flopped badly. In these works he caricatured Soviet bureaucrats, whose revenge after his death would be to remove his plays from the Soviet repertoire for decades. Maiakovskii's bohemian lifestyle, his challenges to those in authority, and his alienation from many

Figure 8.2. Vladimir Tatlin's monument to the Third International, 1919–20 (Bildarchiv Preussischer Kulturbesitz).

other writers led him into social and political isolation. Depressed by the constant attacks on his work by critics and his inability to convince his greatest love, the married Lily Brik, to marry him, Mayakovskii shot himself in the heart on April 14, 1930. He ended his suicide note by addressing his "comrades of the Proletarian Literary Organization:" "Don't think me a coward. Really, it couldn't be helped." Briefly after his death, Maiakovskii faded into a shadowy disgrace, but he soon was elevated to the highest ranks of officially sanctioned Soviet literature. Once Stalin uttered his judgment—"Indifference to his memory and his works is a crime"—Maiakovskii officially became "the poet of the revolution."

Film and Popular Culture

The power of poetry in the 1920s came from its public performances. Public art, like theater and film, were the most appropriate media for expressing the revolution to a multinational country in which the great majority of the people outside of towns were illiterate. Lenin was particularly enthusiastic about the development of a Soviet film industry. He is reported to have said, "Of all the arts, for us the cinema is the most important." Its purpose would be education, propaganda, selling the values of socialism to the masses. As film critic Dwight MacDonald put it, "Propaganda, instead of being the fatal weakness of the Soviet cinema, is, philosophically and historically considered, its greatest source of strength." The Soviet film industry was not to be based, as was the capitalist cinema, on making money by appealing to the immediate interests and appetites of ordinary people. Rather, Lunacharskii declared:

> The moving picture will be used to the fullest extent for amusement and education. The story of humanity will be told in pictures, and heroic deeds recorded. There will, however, be no glorification of bloodshed and violence; no appeal to race or religious bigotry and hatred: the cinema will be used to teach citizenship and love of humanity.

Early Soviet filmmakers were inspired by the first hit movie in Soviet Russia, the American film *Intolerance*, written and directed by D. W. Griffith. Like Griffith, they had their own epic moral vision and wanted to affect their audiences more than simply please them. Experimenting with new techniques to stimulate reactions from the audience, Soviet directors developed a complex editing form called montage, in which frames of film were rhythmically arranged to convey specific effects. Unexpectedly, the fledgling film industry in Russia produced an extraordinary group of young directors, including Sergei Eisenshtein, Vsevolod Pudovkin, Lev Kuleshov, Aleksandr Dovzhenko, and Dzhiga Vertov. Film production extended to most of the Soviet republics. Revolutionary messages were combined with folkloric evocations of an exotic past. In Azerbaijan an early film, *Legend of the Maiden Tower* (1924), was filled with images of a colorful and cruel Orient ruled by an evil khan, played by an Armenian actor. Though Soviet films were not as popular with Soviet audiences as American thrillers, Tarzan movies, or German horror films, they won international critical acclaim with such works as Eisenshtein's *Strike* (1924), *Battleship Potemkin* (1925), and *October*, or *Ten Days That Shook the World* (1927), Pudovkin's *Mother* (1926) and *End of Saint Petersburg* (1927), and Dovzhenko's *Arsenal* (1929) and *Earth* (1930). In the evolving Soviet film style a wholesomeness and humanism infused the heroes and heroines, and through struggle and sacrifice the carriers of socialist values ultimately overcame enemies of the revolution. Optimism and hope infused the films, anticipating what would become the officially sanctioned style a decade later.

Just as the interests of party authorities conflicted with the artists who produced the high culture of the early Soviet years, so the party's ambition to create a new Soviet man and woman ran into problems when it met the counterattractions of popular culture. The public wanted to be entertained much more than it wanted to be educated, and many of the more politically correct novels and plays of socialist writers were far less attractive to readers than detective thrillers or imaginative science fiction. Politically savvy but commercially astute writers and filmmakers tried to combine what was popular with socialist themes. One of the most successive novelists was a young Armenian woman, Marietta Shaginian, who in 1923 turned out a popular adventure novel with revolutionary values, *Mess-Mend*, written under the pseudonym Jim Dollar. This story of an evil capitalist plot to subvert the Soviets that is foiled by heroic American workers became a popular Soviet movie three years later. But beyond the popular art manufactured by professionals, a huge realm of popular cultural expression existed in the cafes and bars, on the streets, in music halls, and around kitchen tables. Here people shared rude jokes and irreverent poems and sang gypsy romances or the sad ballads of prisoners. A popular joke of the time tells of an old man on a trolley car, upset by the conditions of his life, sighing, "Oi." His wife quickly hushes him with a warning, "Fool, don't talk counterrevolution in public." A guitar or balalaika, a few glasses of vodka, followed by bits of potato, bread, or pickle, was enough to carry a gathering of friends through an evening. The songs might include "Little Buns," the sad tale of a poor peddler of hot buns whose father drinks too much and sister walks the street. The song was too dark and pessimistic for the authorities, and eventually it was banned from public performance, but around the table at night it could still be heard.

Soviet School Days

At the turn of the century Russian educators, like their counterparts in the West, were engaged in a search for new and more relevant forms of educating young people. Convinced that proper education was essential for developing citizenship in the modern world, many reformers sought to link the schoolroom with the real workaday world, while others optimistically argued that schools and scientific knowledge could play a transformative social role. Many leading figures, particularly among university professors, adopted liberal attitudes favoring autonomy for intellectual institutions, the spread of knowledge throughout the population, and guarantees for the free development of the individual. Briefly, during the eight months of the Provisional Government, censorship had been largely eliminated, and academics enjoyed an unusual degree of power and influence within the state. They used this fleeting opportunity to enact a liberal program that abolished quotas on Jewish admission to institutions of higher education, empowered faculty and students within universities, and expanded the autonomy of higher education from state control. A few reforms in elementary and secondary education aimed at local community control of schools. But when the Bolsheviks came to power, scholars and scientists feared a reassertion of state control to the detriment of learning.

Somewhere buried in his writings Marx had noted, "On the one hand, a change of social circumstances is required to establish a proper system of education. On the other hand, a proper system of education is required to bring about a change of social circumstances." Soviet educators believed that they were halfway out of this dialectical dilemma: the revolution had changed social circumstances, and now it was up them to create the educational system that would produce a new understanding and psychology among Soviet citizens. As one of the leading figures in Soviet education, Nadezhda Krupskaia, wrote, "Socialism will be possible only when the psychology of people is radically changed. To change it is the task standing before us." Immediately after the Bolsheviks came to power, the government handed all educational institutions to Lunacharskii and Narkompros, and the People's Commissar of Enlightenment immediately opened the schools to all and abolished fees and entrance requirements. Though the resources were unavailable for quality mass education, and the teaching personnel was resistant to the Bolshevik reforms, Narkompros worked out a plan to create a United Labor School, a single coeducational school system combining vocational and academic education without regard to the class origins of the pupils. Its goal was compulsory universal education available at no cost to all children.

The early Bolshevik reforms met resistance from teachers who resented the new curriculum with its emphasis on labor, and parents who opposed efforts to take religion out of the schools and introduce new pedagogies. Yet another major obstacle was the lack of material resources. Schools were unable to take on the utopian goal of reshaping mentalities when Narkompros could supply only one pencil for every sixty pupils, one quill pen for every twenty-five, a fountain pen for every ten, and a notebook for every two. Given the multinationality of Soviet Russia, the government planned to have education available in dozens of non-Russian languages, but it found that textbooks and materials in those languages simply did not exist. The grandiosity of Narkompros's vision met up with a harsh reality, and Lenin and other more pragmatic leaders demanded that more practical measures be taken. By 1921 Narkompros compromised its notion of a single school for all and gave in to pressure to set up special vocational and technical schools for workers to produce the skilled hands that the economy desperately needed.

During the civil war the hostility of the intelligentsia toward the regime was most clear among university professors. Some served the Whites as government ministers, and others worked secretly against the Bolsheviks, but the majority bided their time, hoping for a more liberal government. The Bolsheviks were divided between those who tweaked and provoked the academic intelligentsia and those who tried to win them over to the new order. The Bolshevik historian Mikhail Pokrovskii, now in a position of power in the Narkompros, threatened his former colleagues with arrest, while his superior Lunacharskii, was far more tactful. But all in the government hoped to squeeze "bourgeois" social science out over time and replace it with Marxism. Lenin suggested to Pokrovskii that the old professors might be forced to teach about colonialism and, thus, despite their liberalism they would be obliged to inform their students about the dark side of capitalism.

At first the Soviet government allowed universities to remain autonomous, though they ordered that they be open to all. Since poorer people were less prepared for higher learning, special departments for workers were opened for adults needing preparatory training for university. The resistance of professors to Narkompros's programs for "democratizing" education convinced the government to end university autonomy in 1921 and to appoint Communist rectors to direct institutions of higher learning. In order to promote the ideological agenda of the party, the state created a parallel system of Communist schools, universities, and an academy in which Marxist teachers trained prerevolutionary students.

With the coming of NEP central state spending for schools declined, and a greater burden was placed on local governments. The number of public schools and teachers fell precipitously from 1920 to 1924; enrollments shrank in the lower grades, and the school population did not reach its pre-NEP level until the very end of the decade. In 1925 pupils on average spent less than two and a half years in school. A year later it was reported that over 20 percent of elementary school pupils in rural areas of the Russian Republic did not finish the year. The state spent its money on professional and technical training in institutions of higher learning and on political education, rather than on mass education as it had earlier promised. Parents ended up paying for much of early education, thus reintroducing privatization of education. This meant that better-off families received education while the poorest had difficulty staying in school. Schools continued to be badly supplied, and many closed in winter for lack of heat. Whereas earlier schools had been governed by councils that represented pupils, teachers, and parents, after 1923 power fell to local educational departments and appointed school directors.

The educational zealots at Narkompros continued through the 1920s to advocate educational reform. Teaching was to be organized around the "complex method," in which the themes of labor, nature, and society replaced traditional subjects. Instead of grading and testing, evaluation was to be based on the pupil's participation in group discussions and collectively written assignments. But teachers, poorly paid and sometimes not paid at all, subverted the reformers and adapted traditional methods to new circumstances. Though religion and classical languages disappeared, science, mathematics, Russian language, and social studies continued. Radicals wanted more workers and peasants in the schools, but they remained poorly represented. Peasants particularly suffered. The lower the grade, the higher the percentage of peasants enrolled; the higher the grade, the lower the percentage of peasants. In the highest grades the largest percentage of pupils came from the families of white-collar workers, officials, and managers.

The schools during NEP had been burdened with the enormous social tasks of democratizing the school population, inculcating socialist values, eradicating illiteracy, and introducing learning into the countryside and the non-Russian areas—all without adequate material resources or personnel. They were attacked for not being proletarian enough, for fostering bourgeois values, for being elite, and for not developing skills needed in an industrializing economy. At the end of the decade the government adopted a radical proletarianizing program that ended many of the programs of the NEP period and brought class warfare into the classroom.

Cultural Revolution

The Central Committee resolution of 1925 that had expressed tolerance for fellow-travelers in literature did not remove the bitterness in literary politics. Personal squabbles were tied up with broader conflicts over style, content, and the politics of a socialist literature. As the intraparty struggle between the Stalinists and the opposition intensified in 1926–27, the literary Left made a bid to take over the newly formed Federation of Soviet Writers. VAPP's leader, Averbakh, openly accused Voronskii and the moderates of Trotskyism, only to have accusations of Zinovievist sympathies hurled back at the Left. As Stalin turned against Bukharin and the Right within the party, the party also abandoned its soft line in culture.

Beginning in 1928 and for the next three years, the party promoted a policy that emphasized class war against the party's enemies, the end of favors to the bourgeois specialists and the promotion of the interests of proletarians. This period in culture and literature, which corresponded roughly with the First Five-Year Plan (1928–1932) and the militant "Third Period" (1928–1935) in Comintern policy, came to be known as the "Cultural Revolution." The shift toward the new policy was abrupt and sudden. As late as December 1927, at the Fifteenth Party Congress, Stalin spoke about strengthening "the bond of the working class with the toiling Soviet intelligentsia of town and country." But in March 1928 he launched a campaign "against bourgeois elements that are supported by the remnants and survivals of the influence, traditions, and customs of the old society." From that moment until June 1931, the state and party sanctioned a broad attack on "specialists," which before and after this episode would be labeled "specialist-eating."

For Lenin the term "cultural revolution" had meant the mass education and cultivation of civilized behavior and values that he considered a prerequisite for the building of a society run by the people. But in the late 1920s and early 1930s cultural revolution took on a new and more militant meaning. The Left in literature and art had long pressured the party leaders to crack down on fellow-travelers and "bourgeois" elements in the intelligentsia. Other militants had urged less tolerance of economic specialists and greater support for simple workers. Now the party mobilized young people against bureaucrats and backed the militants in the intelligentsia to take over and radicalize their disciplines. The mood of the civil war was revived, the floodgates were opened for reviving utopian schemes of social engineering, and instead of coexisting with fellow-travelers and specialists, a wave of Communist intolerance swept through the country.

In the rhetoric of the late 1920s a "class war" had been declared on the remnants of the old society. But a principal target of much of the campaign was the so-called Right in the Communist Party, led by Bukharin, Rykov, and Tom-skii, who were the most determined critics of Stalin's rush into collectivization and rapid industrialization at the expense of the peasants. Lunacharskii and his closest associates at Narkompros fell victim to charges of cultural rightism, and the Commissar, who had been appointed by Lenin and had held his post for twelve years, resigned in the spring of 1929. The Stalinist leadership heated up the accusations against the bourgeois specialists and their sympathizers. They believed that some intellectuals had entertained hopes that they might gain access to positions of political power, that Soviet power might become the first real technocracy. Though such pretensions hardly presented a serious threat to the Communist hierarchy, the Stalinists hit back hard, particularly at engineers, of whom as many as seven thousand may have been arrested. Zealots from the Komsomol led attacks on bureaucrats, and the authorities ex-pelled the sons and daughters of social groups considered privileged in the past (nobles, priests, merchants, and kulaks) from universities and secondary schools.

The campaign against bureaucrats and specialists was complemented on the positive side by a massive campaign for literacy, the admission of workers into educational institutions and the party, and the promotion of workers into technical and managerial positions. Schooling was expanded in the country-side, and in 1930 primary school education was made compulsory. Educational levels for Communist Party officials had been abysmally low. In 1927 only 8.7 percent of all Communists had higher or full secondary education, and those in white-collar positions had completed on average only four or five years of schooling. Over one hundred thousand Communists entered higher educa-tional institutions during the years of the First Five-Year Plan. At the same time about two hundred thousand working-class students flooded the higher edu-cational institutions, a significant jump from the forty thousand workers or children of workers who had been in Soviet universities in 1928. Hundreds of thousands of workers were propelled into the ranks of engineers, displacing the older generation of technicians and specialists, and by 1933 half of the in-dustrial plant directors were from the working class. A new proletarian intel-ligentsia was formed that eventually would become the ruling elite of the So-viet Union.

Russian science had a long and distinguished tradition of pure theoretical science, especially in mathematics (Nikolai Lobachevskii) and chemistry (Dmitrii Mendeleev, the author of the periodic chart of the elements), and Russ-ian scientists had managed to stay above or outside politics in the first decade after the revolution, with some exceptions. But that became less possible with the Cultural Revolution. The cathedral of Soviet science was the Academy of Sciences, founded at the beginning of the eighteenth century by Peter the Great and becoming in the years before the revolution, not merely a scientific soci-ety, but the leading force in the scientific life of the country. The academy held its own from 1917 to 1927, fending off state interference in its activities and maintaining itself as the most powerful unreformed institution surviving from tsarist times. Through shrewd maneuvering the academy's permanent secre-tary, the aristocrat Sergei Oldenburg, kept the Academy independent of the state, despite the growing desire on the part of Marxist scholars to penetrate it and take it over.

The Communist Party had long held that Marxism was not simply another philosophy but was in fact science, the most powerful tool for apprehending society and nature. But in the 1920s one school of Marxists, the "mechanists," believed that science was Marxist whether the scientists knew it or not. A rival school, led by Abram Deborin, held that science had class aspects and that Marxists must combat "bourgeois" philosophy to assure the victory of dialectical materialism. During NEP, however, the evolving dogma of Marxism-Leninism existed side by side with other philosophical and scientific schools, and skeptics and doubters, like the prominent earth scientist Vladimir Vernadskii, were free, within limits, to express their doubts about the official ideology. Vernadskii and other scientists tried to block Marxist philosophers from being elected to the Academy of Sciences, which until 1928 could boast that no academician was a party member.

In April 1928 the Politburo informed the Academy of Sciences that it had to undergo radical reforms. It was ordered to increase the number of members and create certain new chairs in socioeconomic and technological sciences and philosophy. A disciple of Deborin announced that "The Academy of Sciences stands as if before an examination. It is expected to demonstrate that it is in step with Soviet society." In the fall, after much contention with the academicians, the party pushed through its candidates. Along with a majority of traditional scientists, the academy reluctantly elected a number of Marxists who qualified as scholars, including Bukharin, Deborin, and Pokrovskii. More pressure was applied to the Academy in a second round of elections in 1929, and in subsequent elections the party established its dominance over the academy. Tolerance of diversity radically diminished, and Deborin, who had emerged as the dominant Marxist philosopher, attacked those who questioned the authority and scientific soundness of dialectical materialism. Of his rival Vernadskii he wrote, "The whole world view of V. I. Vernadskii is deeply hostile to materialism and to our contemporary life, our construction of socialism." If Vernadskii had not been such a respected scientist, a trophy proudly displayed by those in power, despite his liberal, anti-Marxist views, he would have ended up badly. But the Soviet state valued the contributions of certain nonconformists, such as the behavioral psychologist Ivan Pavlov, and protected them against the attacks of self-proclaimed orthodox Marxists. But other, less prominent scientists and intellectuals fell victim to the cultural revolutionaries.

A major purge hit the academy in 1929. Several distinguished historians, including Sergei Platonov and Evgenii Tarle, were arrested, and Oldenburg was forced to resign. The following year the academy was reorganized. The government increased its control and directed the scientific community to orient its work toward socialist construction. With the introduction of graduate students, the academy became dominated by Communists. In April 1931 Bukharin called for "planning of science," which largely translated into state support for scientific research. A huge organizational apparatus of scientific research institutes, where scholars would work without the burdens of teaching, was created, and branches of the academy were set up in the various union republics. The scientific intelligentsia now was dependent on the state, an ally of the party in the industrialization campaign, and had to appear, at least publicly, sympathetic to Marxism. Stalinism created the world's largest state-subsidized intelligentsia, and though never completely subordinate to the party and usually able to maintain a degree of autonomy in their research, Soviet scientists were nevertheless the privileged partners of the state, materially dependent on the authorities and dedicating their intellect to the modernizing project of Stalinist socialism.

At the same time the literary proletarians, now led by the newly renamed RAPP (Russian Association of Proletarian Writers), ascended to power in the cultural sphere. Party leaders praised RAPP and allowed it to become the official mouthpiece for the party in literature. The theorists of RAPP took a position between those who argued that art is a class instrument and those who saw art as a means of understanding life. Concerned about eliminating illiteracy, reeducating the masses, and carrying out a successful cultural revolution in the Soviet Union, Averbakh proclaimed, "We look upon art not only as a means for cognition, but also as a means for changing social reality." Proletarian writers were to cultivate a Marxist worldview, revealing the real social relationships hidden below appearances. Their slogan was to be "Tear off the masks!" and their aim to deal with "the living man" underneath the illusions and idealizations. Writers and critics suffered from the enforcement of the new, militant orthodoxy. The young literary critic Mikhail Bakhtin, for example, was forced to leave Leningrad as an "alien class element" because he was the son of a nobleman. Already the author of a brilliant book on Dostoevsky, Bakhtin spent the rest of his career teaching Russian literature in Mordovia, a remote republic in the north of Russia to which political prisoners were sent. Miraculously he survived the years of Stalinism to be rediscovered by young literary scholars in Moscow in the 1950s, and before his death the power of his literary and theoretical work made him famous in the West.

In December 1928 the Central Committee of the Communist Party called for the publication of more socially useful books. Rather than tolerating many different kinds of literary production, the party now sought to mobilize the intelligentsia in the service of the First Five-Year Plan. Writers were to be sent out as journalists to write up reports on outstanding workers and farmers. To redeem herself and imbibe the full experience of the Stalin industrial revolution, the adventure novelist Marietta Shaginian spent four years as a construction worker. Party leaders wanted writers to be even more the servants of the current policies of the state than RAPP had envisioned. Rather than making the proletarian writer an objective observer and unprejudiced judge, writers were to attack the social ills of alcohol, sabotage in industry, and illiteracy. By the spring of 1931 RAPP was criticized for failing to grasp the necessity of "party attitude" in literature. Politburo member Lazar Kaganovich told the writers that they should be dealing with themes of collectivization and industrialization. Referring to the building of Magnitogorsk, the steel center of the Urals, he said, "What we need is a Magnitostroi of literature." The proletarian writers, who had been waiting impatiently for party support, now were found wanting by their patrons. As writers they looked upon literature as a lens through which to reveal life, but the Stalinist leaders wanted a literature that was primarily geared toward educating people in the spirit of the new state-directed "revolution from above." In April 1932 the party dissolved RAPP and the other proletarian writers' associations.

By 1932 the culture wars were over. The party had disciplined scientists and established Marxism-Leninism as a dogma not to be questioned publicly. It had disbanded the various literary camps and emerged as the single arbiter of literary style and content. All writers and artists were organized into unions under state control, and those intellectuals who wanted to continue working became, in Stalin's words, "engineers of the soul."

Suggestions for Further Reading

The writing on Soviet culture in the NEP years is rich and varied. Two of the finest works are by Katerina Clark: *The Soviet Novel: History as Ritual* (Chicago, 1981), and *Petersburg, Crucible of Cultural Revolution* (Cambridge, Mass., 1995). Much of the discussion of the cultural politics of the period has been defined by three seminal works by Sheila Fitzparick: *The Commissariat of Enlightenment: Soviet Organization of Education and the Arts under Lunacharsky* (Cambridge, 1970); (ed.), *Cultural Revolution in Russia, 1928–1931* (Bloomington, Ind., 1978); and *The Cultural Front: Power and Culture in Revolutionary Russia* (Ithaca, N.Y., 1992).

On early Soviet cultural visions, see Abbott Gleason, Peter Kenez, and Richard Stites (eds.), *Bolshevik Culture: Experiment and Order in the Russian Revolution* (Bloomington, Ind., 1985); Lynn Mally, *Culture of the Future: The Proletkult Movement in Revolutionary Russia* (Berkeley, Calif., 1990); William G. Rosenberg (ed.), *Bolshevik Visions: First Phase of the Cultural Revolution in Soviet Russia* (Ann Arbor, Mich., 1984); and James von Geldern, *Bolshevik Festivals: 1917–1920* (Berkeley, Calif., 1993). On literature and literary politics in the early Soviet years, see Maxim Gorky, *Untimely Thoughts: Essays on Revolution, Culture, and the Bolsheviks, 1917–1918* (New Haven, Conn., new ed., 1995); Edward J. Brown, *Mayakovsky, A Poet in the Revolution* (Princeton, N.J., 1973); Robert A. Maguire, *Red Virgin Soil: Soviet Literature in the 1920s* (Princeton, N.J., 1968); and Helen Muchnic, *From Gorky to Pasternak: Six Writers in Soviet Russia* (New York, 1961).

On science, outstanding works are Kendall E. Bailes, *Science and Russian Culture in an Age of Revolutions: V. I. Vernadsky and His Scientific School, 1863–1945* (Bloomington, 1990); and the many works by Loren Graham, particularly *The Soviet Academy of Sciences and the Communist Party, 1927–1932* (Princeton, N.J., 1967). On education, see Sheila Fitzpatrick, *Education and Social Mobility in the Soviet Union, 1921–1934* (Cambridge, 1979); and Larry E. Holmes, *The Kremlin and the Schoolhouse: Reforming Education in Soviet Russia, 1917–1931* (Bloomington, Ind., 1991). On film, see Denise Youngblood, *Soviet Cinema in the Silent Era, 1917–1935* (Ann Arbor, Mich., 1985); and Richard Taylor, *The Politics of Soviet Cinema, 1917–1929* (Cambridge, 1979). A unique book is Peter Kenez, *The Birth of the Propaganda State: Soviet Methods of Mass Mobilization, 1917–1929* (Cambridge, 1985).

PART III

STALINISM

CHAPTER 9
The Stalin Revolution

Revolution from Above

The 1930s were both a heroic and tragic period in Soviet history, a time of compressed industrial revolution, the victory of the party over peasant resistance to collectivization, and the creation of a new society. The price paid for the social and economic changes was high indeed: millions of lives lost or broken in the dekulakization, the resulting famine, and the purges. Collectivization, which was supposed to pay for the industrialization by providing marketable surpluses of grain and other agricultural products, in fact led to a permanently depressed agriculture and created a sullen and passive peasantry. Workers as well lived at near subsistence levels and fared little better than their rural cousins during Stalin's five-year plans. The Soviet state expanded enormously, swallowing up much that been left to the market and to society in the 1920s. The political apparatus took over the economy, dominated all aspects of culture, and eliminated any social movements it did not initiate or could not control. But it was not the Communist Party that emerged at the end of the decade as the ruling class of the Soviet Union. The party itself fell victim to the dictator who set the police on those he decided were disloyal or threatening to his monopoly of power. The revolution that had begun twenty years earlier in a popular uprising for liberation petrified into a leviathan state headed by a leader with totalitarian ambitions.

For many decades after the forced collectivization, many historians, both in the West and in the Soviet Union, claimed that "Stalin's revolution" in the countryside, with all its attendant brutalities, had been unavoidable, given the need to industrialize and the unwillingness of the peasants to part with their grain at low prices. The argument went, that if the USSR was to industrialize rapidly, it had to exploit the peasants; yet if the peasants were taxed too heavily or the terms of trade turned against them, they would simply withdraw from the market and withhold their grain. In 1927–28 that was precisely what happened; relatively low prices for agricultural goods and shortages of industrial goods led to peasant hoarding of grain. Therefore, in order to feed the towns and acquire cheap grain to sell abroad to finance industrialization, Stalin decided that confiscation was necessary. He convinced his supporters that force was required to break the back of the peasantry in order to secure the capital needed for the building of industry.

Eventually historians in the West challenged the idea that Stalinism, or at least collectivization, was necessary for the building of an industrial society in the Soviet Union. Instead they argued that a slower rate of growth had still been possible under conditions of NEP and that the decision to use coercion against the peasants was extremely costly for Soviet development and ended in catastrophe. A growing consensus among scholars held that Stalinism destroyed the budding civil society of the NEP and suppressed the market at a time when the state could not provide the material goods that its people required. Repression of the peasants resulted in the creation of a coercive state apparatus that a few years later was employed by the dictator against the party itself. Rather than being inevitable or necessary, the Stalin revolution in agriculture could have been avoided, and more moderate, less violent alternatives would probably have led to slow, steady growth in the agricultural sector, which would have aided industrialization more in the long run.

War on the Peasants and the Final Opposition

The process of collectivization went through several initial stages, each one embodying a more radical policy toward the peasantry. First, the party ordered the forced requisitioning of grain in late 1928 and 1929 as a temporary, emergency measure. Then, with the political victory of the Stalinists over the Bukharinists, a campaign for "dekulakization" drove the richer and more productive peasants from the land in 1929–30. Still later, as kulaks were being deported, exiled, or shot, the regime plunged the country into a frenzied campaign to achieve rapid and complete collectivization by the application of maximum force.

In December 1927, within weeks after the Fifteenth Party Congress had decided in favor of voluntary collectivization, Stalin pushed for a more confrontational approach with the peasantry. Applying the so-called Ural-Siberian method, agents of the central government descended on the provinces and coerced peasants to give up their grain. The state treated the peasants like criminals, even though peasants were acting like rational producers for a market, holding on to their grain, not as an act of sabotage as they were accused, but because grain prices were too low and there were few cheap goods for which to exchange their produce. The return to coercive measures against the peasants stunned the moderates in the Politburo and Central Committee, led by Bukharin, and brought the five-year alliance of Stalin and Bukharin to an end. For much of 1928 neither Stalin nor the Bukharinists, whom Stalin now labeled the "Right," could have their way completely. Party policy drifted between force and pressure on the one hand and concessions on the other.

Rather than have independent peasant producers deliver grain to the state, the Stalinists were determined to have collective farms as the point of grain production and collection. Though Stalin blamed the kulaks for the crisis, he aimed collectivization not only against the rich peasants but against individual peasant agriculture in general. Local party officials began closing markets to control the trading in grain. Stalin's associates Kuibyshev and Kaganovich stated frankly that the new agricultural policy was aimed at subordinating market forces to the will of the state. Trade in agricultural goods would no longer be determined by the market as the Stalinists moved step by step toward a state-directed economy.

But the moderates still had significant support in the leadership. In June the central party officials came out against closing markets and fixing prices. They decided that the grain crisis would be met, at least in part, by buying grain from abroad. The party moderates, including Bukharin, Rykov, and Tomskii, interpreted the grain crisis of 1927–28 as the result of a mistaken policy that had upset the equilibrium of the market. They continued to believe that the problem could be solved within the basic structure of NEP. Stalin, however, no longer had confidence in the market and concluded, as had the exiled Left Opposition, that the "bourgeois" elements within NEP, namely, the Nepmen and the kulaks, would in time overwhelm the party. His mistrust of the peasantry deepened through 1928 as the grain crisis dragged on. For Stalin, peasants were unreliable allies and potential restorers of capitalism. Collectivization was at one and the same time a way of solving the immediate problem of the grain crisis and the deeper problem of peasant control over the Soviet Union's principal economic resource. The "war on the peasants," thus, was as much, if not more, a political strategy than it was an economic policy.

While the government claimed that the kulaks were the enemy in the countryside and attempted to ally itself with the middle and poorer peasants, almost all peasants resisted the forced requisitioning of grain in every way they could. They argued with the authorities, protested the seizures, and wrote to their sons in the army to inform them how they were being treated by the state. Most ominously for the country as a whole, they simply sowed less grain. The government tried desperately to entice peasants to form collective farms and promised them tax breaks, credits, and tractors. But the program was implemented in such haste that there simply were not enough funds or farm machinery available for the new collective farmers. The industrial sector of the economy was simply too weak to supply the agricultural sector, and peasants had little incentive to give up their grain or voluntarily join the collective farms. By the end of 1928 the government was forced to introduce food rationing.

State force and repression steadily tore apart the framework of the New Economic Policy, which involved relatively free markets and peasant discretion over their grain. Stalin attacked party members who held the very opinions he had held a few years earlier. In April 1928 he said, "He who believes that our alliance with the peasantry . . . means an alliance with the kulaks, has nothing in common with the spirit of Leninism." Stalin did not fear class warfare in the villages as did Bukharin, and he claimed that the closer the country moved toward socialism, the more intense would be the class struggle. "As we march forward," he claimed in his peculiar logic, "resistance from these capitalist elements will steadily increase, and the class struggle will grow more and more bitter, while the Soviet regime, with steadily mounting strength, pursues a policy aimed at encircling the hostile forces." For Bukharin this kind of inverted Marxism was "ignorant nonsense" and portended disaster. Rather than coercion and forced collectivization, Bukharin advocated preservation of individual farms, encouragement of productivity, and heavier taxation of the rich peasants.

Though the struggle within the Politburo was kept from public view, both sides made cryptic and meaningful allusions in the press to the different approaches in the countryside. By mid-1928 Bukharin and Stalin were no longer on speaking terms and were in fierce competition for control of the Politburo. Of the nine full members Bukharin could count on Rykov and Tomskii, with the candidate member Nikolai Uglanov a close ally and Grigorii Petrovskii siding with them as well. Stalin relied on Molotov, with the candidate members Mikoyan, Kaganovich, and Kirov firmly in his camp. Both sides tried to woo the uncommitted Kalinin, Kuibyshev, Rudzutak, Voroshilov, and the candidate Andreev. Stalin maneuvered cleverly, offering concessions and then taking a harder line. At the July 1928 Central Committee session the propeasant members called for concessions to the middle peasants. Stalin dismissed them as "peasant philosophers looking backward instead of forward." In the end the resolution was a compromise between the moderates and the militants. The waverers in the Politburo moved closer to Stalin, but the Central Committee was still divided. Bukharin foolishly complained to the disgraced Kamenev about Stalin's intrigues. Stalin, he warned, "has made concessions now, so that [later] he can cut our throats." Stalin soon learned of this conversation and interpreted it as a conspiratorial alliance of the Left and Right against him.

Through the summer and fall the Stalinists tried to make the emergency measures used to collect grain a permanent feature of Soviet policy toward the peasants. In September Bukharin published a bold article in *Pravda* entitled "Notes of an Economist." His target in the article was ostensibly Trotsky and his followers, but in fact his polemic was directed against those around Stalin who were destroying the link with the peasantry and promoting planning to the detriment of the market. He called for an equilibrium between agriculture and industry, a balance that allowed the development of agriculture for industry and vice versa. He concluded his article with the same complaint expressed by all previous oppositions within the party, that bureaucratization and centralization had gone too far and had to be combated. Resurrecting an idea that had seemed moribund since the civil war, he wrote, "We must ask ourselves, should we not take a few steps in the direction of the Leninist commune-state?"

Stalin's reply to Bukharin's attacks was to undermine his bastions of support in the trade unions and the Moscow party organization. In November Uglanov was removed as Moscow party chief, and a month later the loyal Stalinist Kaganovich was placed next to Tomskii in the trade union hierarchy. The general secretary carefully crafted a myth of a "rightist danger" in the party that was calling for a slower rate of economic growth, underestimating international dangers, and willing to compromise with the kulaks. When the Central Committee met in November, the mood of anxiety and struggle created by the grain crises, the perceived danger of war, and the growing sense that sabo-teurs were threatening the Soviet economy worked to Stalin's advantage. Party leaders were more inclined to sanction confrontational policies with the peas-ants to guarantee high industrial growth rates.

In February 1929 Bukharin, Rykov, and Tomskii presented their position to the Politburo, accusing Stalin's followers of "military-feudal" exploitation of the peasantry and destroying democracy in the party. They proposed slowing the tempo of industrialization and maintaining the free market. But the ma-jority refused to change its line and began public attacks on the Right. Bukharin was removed as editor of *Pravda* and head of the Comintern; Tomskii was dis-missed as head of the trade unions; and both were dropped from the Politburo. Rykov lost his post as chairman of the Sovnarkom of the RSFSR. The defeat of the last opposition was complete, and Stalin's "general line" was now the only permissible position for Communists.

The vicious factional struggle within the leadership in 1928–29 and the de-feat of the Bukharinists opened the way for the creation of a new kind of po-litical regime in the Soviet Union—Stalinism. Though to many historians this system appeared to be the culmination of what Marxism or Leninism intended, Stalinism was much more the product of the particular context of economic and social backwardness in which the Communists found themselves. The vic-tory of Stalin and his followers within the party apparatus, and their impro-vised responses to a series of crises that they themselves had caused, laid the foundation for a political system that the Stalinists themselves did not envi-sion. Backwardness and ruthlessness combined with the personal ambitions of Stalin to forge an autocratic regime that single-mindedly would try to drive a continent into the industrial age. Stalin had turned 180 degrees from 1926 to 1929, from a moderate and a centrist to an extreme radical, outdoing the Left in his own party. The very radicalism of his program was a response to a grain-collection crisis and a stagnating industrial economy that had been created by his former moderate policies. But rather than shifting his policies in a gradual, modulated way, he broke completely with the Bukharinist approach and the concept of NEP and launched the country into a chaotic experiment in non-market economics based on coercive state practices.

Collectivization and Dekulakization

The agricultural crisis continued through 1928 and 1929. Though the harvest of 1928 was higher than 1927, it was still 5 million tons lower than the record 1926 harvest. Grain collections were below those of 1926 and 1927, as peasants had no material incentives to part with their grain. The demand for agricul-tural products soared as the party pursued a program of greater investment in industry, and rationing was introduced in 1928–29, first on bread, then sugar and tea, and in autumn 1929 on meat. Food and grain prices rose on the mar-ket, but the state kept state prices lower. The shortages might have been re-lieved by imports of grain—and, indeed, Russia, usually an exporter of grain, did buy grain abroad in June 1928—but in the spring of 1929 the Politburo rejected Rykov's call for imports and decided to intensify its efforts to squeeze grain from its own peasants. Stalin insisted on the application of the Ural-Siberian method more broadly, pressuring village assemblies to sell all their surpluses to the state and impose quotas for delivery of grain on the kulaks. Instead of allowing peasants to trade at free-market prices, the peasants were to be given contracts for acquiring industrial goods in exchange for grain. Stalin spoke of the need to bring the poor and middle peasants over to the side of the state against the kulak. The question once again for the Communist leaders was "who will defeat whom." But this primitive understanding of the village failed to recognize that large numbers of middle peasants, along with their poorer neighbors, were more likely to resist the state grain collections than to fight against the richer peasants. The degree of peasant solidarity only increased when the village was threatened from outside. Once launched, the attack on the peasantry would have to be carried to its bloody end, and the alliance between worker and peasant, city and countryside, which Lenin had believed essential for maintaining Soviet power in Russia, would be destroyed.

As a plaintive article by Krupskaia stated early in 1929, Stalin's methods of dealing with the peasants were contrary both to the Marxist tradition, as expressed by Engels—"Our task in relation to the small peasants will consist first and foremost in converting their private production and private ownership into collective production and ownership—not, however, by forcible means, but by example and by offering social aid for this purpose"—and to Lenin's own views—"The transition to collective cultivation must be carried out by the proletarian state power with the utmost caution and gradualness, by force of example, without the slightest constraint on the middle peasantry." Step by unanticipated step Stalin destroyed the relationship with the peasants built up by the Soviet regime and in its ruins founded a new social and political system that fundamentally altered the meaning of the revolution. In the words of historian and political scientist Robert V. Daniels, "Regardless of its labels, the Stalinist regime no longer represented the same movement that took power in 1917."

In the summer and fall of 1929 the Stalinists applied the Ural-Siberian method of grain collection, which had been conceived at first as a temporary measure to meet the crisis, to the whole country. With grain prices artificially low and inadequate goods available for exchange, peasants continued to resist giving up their grain. Under the command of Anastas Mikoyan, a close associate of Stalin since the civil war, one hundred thousand party members were sent to the countryside to assist in grain collection. Threats and force worked to pry grain from the reluctant peasants and pressure them to join the collective farms. Because the state could more easily extract the grain from those peasants who had been pushed onto collective farms, the collectivized peasantry, which made up just over 5 percent of the peasantry, accounted for 14 percent of the marketable grain. From July to October 1929, twice as much grain was collected each month as had been in 1928.

With the Right broken within the party, Stalin's policies had no serious opponents. The timetables for collectivization were speeded up. At the end of 1929 the party decided that all Soviet agriculture should be collectivized, with the exception of Central Asia, Transcaucasia, and some northern regions. Dekulakization went into full swing. All leniency toward the kulaks ended. They were not to be admitted into the kolkhozy. Their "means of production," that is, their tools and horses, were to be confiscated. They were to be resettled on distant and poor-quality land or, in the case of "malicious kulaks," exiled to Siberia, Kazakhstan, or the far north. In November Stalin wrote an article entitled "The Year of the Great Breakthrough" in which he claimed that the middle peasantry was enthusiastically joining the new collective farms. Molotov called for acceleration of the pace of collectivization and warned about kulaks entering the kolkhozy: "Treat the kulak as a most cunning and still undefeated enemy." Stalin was even more forceful in his denunciation of the kulaks.

> We have gone over from a policy of *limiting* the exploiting tendencies of the kulak to a policy of *eliminating* the kulak as a class.... Dekulakization is now an essential element in forming and developing the kolkhozy. Therefore, to keep on discussing dekulakization is ridiculous and not serious. When the head is cut off, you do not weep about the hair.

In early 1930 the government called for rapid and complete collectivization, a final push that was to lead to the overall socialization of the countryside. Month by month more and more villages were declared collective farms. Red Army units and secret police troops were sent, along with a quarter of a million workers and party members from the cities to organize the new order

Figure 9.1. Running tractors on the new collective farms, early 1930s (Brown Brothers).

in the countryside. These urban volunteers, backed by the state, provided the necessary number of people to establish the power of the state in the country-side. They took over local administrations and dismissed local officials who stood in their way. A frenzy of activity, spurred on by the slogan "Time does not wait," resulted in massive arrests and deportations. At the beginning of 1930 kulaks were divided into three groups: counterrevolutionary activists, who were to be imprisoned, sent to camps, or shot; the "arch-exploiters," the richest kulaks, who were to be exiled to remote parts of Russia or Kazakhstan; and the loyal kulaks, who were allowed to resettle on new lands outside the collective farms. Since the term "kulak" had never been very precisely defined, the judicial *troiki* (three-person courts) that dealt with the kulaks often pun-ished middle and poor peasants who resisted collectivization as "ideological kulaks."

Many peasants fought hard against the onslaught from the cities and the state, most ferociously in January and February 1930. Women particularly protested the "socialization" of cows, pigs, and poultry. They were joined by men offended by the antireligious campaign, the persecution of so-called ku-laks, and the joining of different villages in a single collective farm. The injus-tice and brutality of the campaign that reduced once prosperous peasants to outlaws in their own country was reflected in the plaintive words of peasants from the Urals: "You turned us into worse than serfs; earlier we did not get clothes and industrial goods, and now they have taken away our last few pounds of flour and meat." More than sixteen hundred cases of armed resis-tance broke out in the first three months of 1930. In the North Caucasus rebel peasants shouted, "For Soviet Power without Communists and *kolkhozy*!" "Down with the *kolkhoz*!" "Long live Lenin and Soviet Power!" and "We are for Soviet Power but without collectivization!" All over the country peasants slaughtered their livestock rather than surrender it to the collectives. Soviet of-ficials were threatened by violence and the total collapse of their power in some areas. At the end of February prominent party leaders close to Stalin returned to Moscow from the provinces, shaken by the peasant resistance and bringing with them reports of the chaos in the countryside. With the state facing a ver-itable civil war on the horizon, Stalin decided to act.

On March 2 Stalin called a halt to the headlong rush into collectivization. In an article, "Dizziness from Success," he announced that "the basic turn of the village to socialism may be considered already secured." But the easy suc-cesses have caused some comrades to become drunk with success and to have gone too far. Collectivization requires voluntary choice by the peasants, he said disingenuously, and force was inappropriate. He blamed local party officials, even though the central party leaders had both initiated and insisted on the rapid tempo of collectivization. Like the father figure he was becoming, he ad-monished the party cadres, telling them that "it is wrong to run ahead, for run-ning ahead means to lose the masses and isolate oneself."

By this cynical maneuver Stalin may have saved his power. Peasants re-sponded with joy, carrying the article on placards, showing it to local officials, and demanding changes in policy. Some thought of it as the Soviet equivalent of the Emancipation Decree of 1861 that had freed the landlord serfs. For weeks local officials did not dare show themselves in many villages. Stalin became an instant hero to many peasants, who blamed the local officials for collectivization. Party and soviet personnel were under attack from above and below, and a few prominent leaders were removed from office for "leftist excesses." But the central party leaders, who were responsible for the acceleration of collectivization in the first months of 1930, refused to blame themselves or the Central Committee publicly. Rather, they blamed regional party leaders, who in turn blamed their subordinates. One bold and foolish party member, a certain Mamaev, asked in *Pravda*, "Whose head got dizzy?" and sarcastically noted that "it appears 'the tsar is good and the local *chinovniki* [officials] are useless.' " Mamaev dared to suggest that conditions were not ready for collectivization, that mechanization was inadequate for large-scale farming, and that the middle peasantry was not actually in favor of the kolkhoz. Mamaev was pilloried as "an agent of the kulaks within the party," and his was one of the last articles critical of Stalin to appear in print within the USSR for almost a quarter century. When the party leaders gathered in Moscow in June 1930 for their Sixteenth Congress, no voice was raised against major party positions.

Just before "Dizziness from Success" appeared, 15 million households had been collectivized. This included 79 percent of households in the North Caucasus, 64 percent in Ukraine, and 57 percent in the central Volga region. But after Stalin's retreat, peasants spontaneously decollectivized. Within a few months the total number of households considered collectivized fell from 59.3 percent to 23 percent. Nine million families left the *kolkhozy*, and the move away from the collectives continued until the fall of 1930. Most who left were middle peasants; most who stayed were poor. But the war on the peasants had had enormous effects. Though it would now take several more years for collectivization to be completed, the old Russian village as it had been was gone forever. A new structure of Soviet power based on village soviets replaced the former communes and village gatherings, which were officially abolished on July 30, 1930. The collective farm became the point of contact between the state and the peasant.

Despite all the disruptions, dislocations, violence, and shifts in policy, the harvest of 1930 was a good one. Some 77 million tons of grain was brought in, a total equal to the record harvest of 1926. But animal products were severely reduced, down 22 percent, largely because of peasant slaughter of livestock. This fall in animal products was greater than the increase in crops, and overall agricultural production was lower in 1930 than it had been a year before. By law collective farms were required to deliver no more than one-third of their harvest to the state, but in the lawless atmosphere of the period state officials pressured the farmers to give up much more of their surpluses. Of the 77 million tons produced, 54 million tons were left with the peasants after the collections and 23 million were delivered to the state. Grain went to feed the towns and cities and to be sold abroad to buy machinery for industrialization. The record harvest and record grain collections worked in late 1930 to convince many people far from the farms of the correctness of the collectivization campaign. Though collectivized peasants made up only 25 percent of the peasantry at that point, they provided 40 percent of the state deliveries.

Figure 9.2. Peasants listening to the decision of the Communist Party to give preferential treatment to those who join the collective farms, 1930 (VA/SOV-FOTO)

The Soviet government requisitioned grain to sell abroad, just as the tsarist government had done, in order to build industry. The bumper crop of 1930 made it possible to expand grain exports from 100,000 metric tons in 1929 to nearly 3 million metric tons in 1930—a twenty-three fold increase. But world wheat prices had been steadily falling since the mid-1920s, and the Soviets were unable to reap large returns for their grain. Their exports took in only ten times the 1929 level of foreign exchange, and even when exports rose to over 5 million metric tons in 1931, their value on the world market failed to rise significantly. Soviet grain only helped to drive world grain prices down further. As the government dumped grain on a world market that did not need it, there was rationing in Soviet cities, and peasants in Ukraine and elsewhere starved.

Millions of people were uprooted during collectivization. By the end of 1930, the authorities had "expropriated" about 1.5 million peasants. Hundreds of thousands of others, said to have voluntarily "self-dekulakized," fled the villages. Two hundred fifty thousand families who had lost their lands were resettled locally on marginal land. The police imprisoned or executed at least 63,000 heads of households by the end of 1930. Police chief Genrikh Iagoda reported to Stalin at the beginning of 1932 that since 1929, they had deported 540,000 kulaks to the Urals, 375,000 to Siberia, more than 190,000 to Kazkhstan, and over 130,000 to the far northern regions. Battered and beaten, with the odds against them and the costs of resisting collectivization rising, peasants reluctantly joined the collectives over the next few years rather than risk losing everything.

Famine in Ukraine

Ukraine was the breadbasket of the USSR. There collectivization was carried out more rapidly, and probably more violently, than in the Russian Republic. By mid-1932, only 59.3 percent of RSFSR peasants were in *kolkhozy*, while 70 percent of Ukraine's peasants had been collectivized. Although Ukraine produced only 27 percent of the total Soviet grain harvest, it supplied 38 percent of all grain deliveries. Still, the government in Moscow was suspicious that Ukraine was not giving up enough of its grain and rejected complaints by local Communist Party officials that the state was collecting too much grain. In 1930 the state took one-third of the Ukrainian harvest, and the next year it demanded 42 percent of the Ukrainian harvest, though it was unable to collect that much. In 1932 Stalin called for a figure that would have equaled just over half the Ukrainian harvest. To the pleas of the Ukrainian Communists Molotov responded that "there will be no concessions or vacillations in the problem of fulfillment of the task set by the party and the Soviet government."

The full force of the law and the police was brought down on the Ukrainian peasants to collect the grain. Local party and soviet officials suspected of aiding or protecting peasants were arrested. Brigades of grain collectors went from house to house to search for grain and took everything they found, leaving people with nothing to eat. Lev Kopelev, then a young political activist and later a dissident writer, remembered how he and his comrades took the last food of starving people:

> With the others, I emptied out the old folks' storage chests, stopping my ears to the children's crying and women's wails. For I was convinced that I was accomplishing the great and necessary transformation of the countryside; that in the days to come the people who lived there would be better off for it; that their distress and suffering were a result of their own ignorance or the machinations of the class enemy; that those who sent me—and I myself—knew better than the peasants how they should live, what they should sow, and when they should plough. In the terrible spring of 1933, I saw people dying from hunger. I saw women and children with distended bellies, turning blue, still breathing but with vacant, lifeless eyes.

Despite all the brutalities, the collectors failed to meet the targets set by the government. Moscow called for a more resolute struggle against the kulaks and charged the Ukrainian Communists with a "lack of class vigilance." Stalin sent Pavl Postyshev as special plenipotentiary to enforce Moscow's policy. In answer to requests from local army commanders, such as Iona Iakir, who feared rebellion by Ukrainian soldiers, Postyshev brought some grain with him. Stalin turned a deaf ear to stories of famine, and the press printed nothing about starvation. Some Western journalists found out about the famine; a few, like Malcolm Muggeridge, wrote about the disaster in Ukraine, but others, most notably *New York Times* correspondent Walter Duranty, deliberately avoided any mention of the famine, fearing that his tenure in the Soviet Union would be cut short if he were too critical of Stalin's policies.

The height of the famine was reached in early 1933. Corpses lined the roads, whole families disappeared, and instances of cannibalism were reported. In January the government replaced forced requisitioning with a simple grain tax, and a month later grain trading was allowed in some provinces. By mid-March grain collections had ended in Ukraine, and by May the famine had dissipated. But not before an estimated 5 million people died. Many Ukrainians, particularly outside the USSR, as well as some historians, have argued that the famine of 1932–33 was the result of a deliberate policy of genocide aimed at eradicating Ukrainian nationalism. Indeed, just as the famine subsided, the central party launched an attack on Ukrainian "national Communists." Mykola Skrypnyk was dismissed as commissar of education, and a number of intellectuals, including the prominent historian Matvii Yavorsky, were arrested. The Ukrainian writer Mykola Khvylovy shot himself in May, and two months later Skrypnyk did the same. By November the regime had arrested or exiled two thousand people considered to be nationalists.

The events in the countryside and the capitals (in 1933 Kiev replaced Kharkiv as the capital of Ukraine) were connected but not in the way that those who see a deliberate genocide imagine. The famine was a particularly vicious episode in the general collectivization campaign, a badly conceived and miscalculated policy, but it was not directed specifically against ethnic Ukrainians. Along with Ukrainian villages, German, Jewish, and Russian villages in Ukraine suffered. Famine occurred outside Ukraine as well, in the North Caucasus and the Volga region, and the per-capita population loss in Kazakhstan, where the government forcibly settled nomadic tribes, exceeded that in Ukraine. Still, famine, unlike food shortages, is not the result of natural disaster but of government failure. Moscow's procurement policies led to the famine, and Stalin was determined to break the back of the independent Ukrainian peasantry, the local Ukrainian Communists, and the nationalist intelligentsia. His regime both initiated the famine through its excessive extractions of grain and allowed it to continue by ignoring the evident consequences of the state's actions.

The Countryside after the Storm

The aims of collectivization were contradictory. At one and the same time the regime wanted to break the resistance of the independent peasantry and expropriate its grain at the lowest possible price, as well as eliminate traditional agriculture, increase productivity, and modernize the countryside. The result of the war on the peasants, however, was to depress agricultural production and consumption and create a sullen, recalcitrant peasantry, the bulk of which was hostile to the regime that had taken their land, horses, and grain. Most peasants were worse off after the collectivization than before and looked nostalgically back to the NEP as a period of prosperity and forward to an imagined time when war or revolution would bring down the Soviet system and disband the collective farms. A smaller group of peasants accommodated themselves successfully to the new agricultural system. Some rose to become chairpersons of the *kolkhozy*, while others, particularly young men, trained as mechanics or tractor drivers and worked at the machine-tractor stations that controlled the large farm equipment.

Though collectivization was supposed to end the social polarization in the countryside and create a more egalitarian rural society, in fact the village became more stratified than ever. At the top of the collective farm was the white-collar elite, largely appointed by district party and state officials to act as chairpersons, *kolkhoz* board members, brigade leaders, and other administrators. Below them was a blue-collar elite of machine operators, drivers, and blacksmiths, who like those at the top were freed from field labor. At the bottom were the field workers, who received less pay than the elites and saw themselves, not as masters of the collectives, but as serfs after a second enserfment.

Stalin's government tried to improve its relations with the peasants in the years after collectivization but failed miserably. As early as May 1933 Stalin and Molotov signed a secret instruction to party and police officials that stated that "as a result of our successes in the countryside. . . , we no longer need the mass repressions which, as is well known, have injured not only kulaks but also independent peasants and part of the *kolkhoz* population." Mass deportations of peasants ceased, and the power of arrest was restricted to the police. The government involved peasants in the discussions on the new Kolkhoz Charter, convening a congress of outstanding collective farmers early in 1935. The charter granted peasants private plots of about an acre to cultivate their own vegetables and fruits. The peasants could keep cows but were not permitted to possess their own horses, which would remain exclusively the property of the collective farms right up to the collapse of the *kolkhoz* system in the 1990s. In 1935 the state granted amnesty for collective farmers and chairpersons arrested for economic crimes. The authorities made concessions toward former kulaks and for a few years in the middle of the decade eased pressure on priests. Freedom of religion was proclaimed in the 1936 constitution, and civil rights were restored to priests and the other categories of disenfranchised people. Priests and their children, however, remained the one group not permitted to join collective farms.

The state and its allies in the world of culture and mass media made a concerted effort to convince the peasants that the new agricultural system was in their best interest. In official propaganda, films, novels, and songs, they depicted the Soviet countryside as a kind of arcadian paradise with happy peasants energetically working for the common good. In reality the great majority of the peasants had a completely different experience. All the rhetoric of socialism was belied by the day-to-day exploitation by party and state bosses, the privileges that the elites accrued, and the gap between the idea that the farmers had voluntarily joined the collective and elected their leaders and the fact that they had been coerced into the collectives and had to obey appointed officials. The constitution of 1936 proclaimed, "He who does not work, does not eat." A peasant woman from Voronezh suggested that the clause should be rephrased, "He who works should eat."

For all its revolutionary implications, the collective farm system preserved many aspects of traditional peasant agriculture. Though the village commune was gone, the *kolkhoz* essentially cultivated the same lands as had the commune, and the peasant household remained the basic unit of agricultural production. Households joined together in a brigade to work. Traditional patriarchy took on a Soviet form. While there was still a pretense that the collective farm was run democratically, in fact the chairpersons of the *kolkhozy* carried themselves as "little tsars" and referred to themselves as *"khoziainin"* (bosses), the same term used for Stalin by his closest subordinates. Peasants saw collectivization as a restoration of serfdom. Required to do forced labor on roads and to work the collective farm fields against their will, and restricted in their movements, collective farmers had many of the characteristics of serfs. But the absence of a hereditary class of nobles and their subordination, instead, to state officials suggests that they were more analogous to the state peasants of tsarist times than to landlord serfs. Like serfs under tsarism, many collective farmers used whatever opportunities were at hand to escape the bondage of the countryside. But unlike tsarist officials, Soviet authorities did not capture and return runaways. Though the government sometimes worried about uncontrolled emigration from the countryside and refused to grant peasants an official right to move around freely, the need for labor in the burgeoning industries made the leadership tolerant of peasant movement. When at the end of 1932 the law gave workers and urban dwellers internal passports, which they were required to carry with them when they moved from place to place or sought new residence, it did not give them to peasants, effectively attaching them to their villages.

Peasants got their revenge against the bosses during the Great Purges, when local trials gave ordinary farmers the chance to denounce these officials as "enemies of the people." But life grew tougher for peasants in the last prewar years as well. In 1937 Stalin secretly ordered the deportation and execution of tens of thousands of "former kulaks and criminals." The government renewed its persecution of priests. Two years later the state imposed a minimum number of labor days on collective farmers, tightened the penalties for infractions of labor discipline, and cut back the size of their private plots.

Soviet peasants never recovered from the blows of collectivization. Their material and moral life suffered. Birthrates and fertility fell. Divorces increased. Many of the traditional craftspeople, often branded as kulaks, left the villages or gave up their craft work. Villages were contentious, factionalized societies, in which meager resources were bitterly fought over. Rival families contended for positions of power and influence. Corruption, drunkenness, and violence were part of the fabric of Soviet rural life. Despite the state's attempt to restrict migration, the battering of rural society led millions to leave the village and migrate to towns and construction sites, laying the foundation of the expanded Soviet working class. In this way many peasants entered Soviet life in a way that their elders had not experienced in the 1920s. And Soviet life entered the villages as well in the 1930s. Along with the expansion of state control over the countryside came the costly building of Soviet-style infrastructure, including schools, clinics, and other governmental services. The local educational system was expanded, and seven years of primary and secondary education were made compulsory. Most peasants utilized the schools as a means to leave the village. Medical facilities increased in the countryside, though they remained woefully inadequate, and peasants continued to turn to traditional healers rather than trained doctors. Elementary rules of hygiene had to be taught to many peasants, and posters of the time attempted to expose villagers to the idea that germs cause disease and that washing with soap prevents the spread of sickness.

The results of collectivization were mixed and contradictory. Many economists believe that there was no economic payoff for industrialization from collectivization. The most productive farmers had been driven out of farming, and there had been so much destruction caused by resistance to collectivization that the agricultural sector became a net importer of material products in the early 1930s. While the state was taking grain and foodstuffs from the peasants at prices far below market level, it had to turn around and use resources to invest in agriculture. Total per-capita peasant consumption of food declined in 1930. With half the horses and most other livestock slaughtered by the peasants, meat consumption fell. The killing of livestock meant a loss in tractive power as well as an absence of manure as fertilizer. The perverse benefit of killing the animals was that less fodder was needed for livestock and could be sent to the state. In fact, it is estimated that the entire gain in grain procurements came from the savings on animal feed. Collectivization did not improve production of grain very much at all. It only made it easier for the state to take what was available without negotiating with the peasantry.

The colossal effort to uproot the rural population and push them into collective farms coincided with forced and rapid industrialization and the creation of a huge state-controlled economy that systematically sacrificed agriculture to the demands of industry. As the state steadily took over more and more of the economy, it became more directive of the whole of society, and as a consequence enlarged the coercive apparatus of the state. The disorganization of agriculture, the chronic wastefulness, and the devastation visited upon the peasants created a permanent economic crisis in the country that threatened disorder and rebellion. Millions of people were on the move, their lives disrupted, their very existence threatened, trying to find a place for themselves in a new world that was out of their control. The regime that had carefully restored the economy after the civil war and assiduously tried to build support in the population during the NEP years had in a series of blows destroyed its ties with the rural masses. Stalin's party elevated coercion in place of persuasion and set loose a monstrous machine to enforce its rules. That machine would soon devour the very operatives that had set it in motion.

Suggestions for Further Reading

Reading on collectivization should begin with one of the earliest and most influential studies, Moshe Lewin, *Russian Peasants and Soviet Power: A Study of Collectivization* (Evanston, Ill., 1968), and continue with R. W. Davies, *The Industrialisation of Soviet Rus-*

sia, I: The Socialist Offensive—The Collectivisation of Soviet Agriculture, 1929–1930 (Cambridge, Mass., 1980) and *The Industrialisation of Soviet Russia, II: The Soviet Collective Farm, 1929–1930* (Cambridge, Mass., 1980). The major study of the postcollectivization settlement is Sheila Fitzpatrick, *Stalin's Peasants: Resistance and Survival in the Russian Village After Collectivization* (New York and Oxford, 1994). A more specialized monograph, on worker participation in collectivization, is Lynne Viola, *The Best Sons of the Fatherland: Workers in the Vanguard of Soviet Collectivization* (New York and Oxford, 1987). See also, her *Peasant Rebels under Stalin: Collectivization and the Culture of Peasant Resistance* (New York and Oxford, 1996).

In a category of its own is the work of economic historian Alec Nove, *An Economic History of the USSR* (London, 1969), who asked the famous question "Was Stalin Really Necessary?" in an article in *Encounter* (April 1962). Nove had an important debate about collectivization and its effects with James Millar. See, James A. Millar, "Mass Collectivization and the Contribution of Soviet Agriculture to the First Five-Year Plan: A Review Article," *Slavic Review*, 33, no. 4 (December 1974): 750–66; and "Was Stalin Really Necessary? A Debate on Collectivization," *Problems of Communism*, 15 (July–August 1976): 49–62.

Eyewitness accounts include Maurice Hindus, *Red Bread: Collectivization in a Russian Village* (1931; reprinted, Bloomington, Ind., 1988); and Lev Kopelev, *The Education of a True Believer*, trans. Gary Kern (New York, 1980). On the Ukrainian famine, see Robert Conquest, *The Harvest of Sorrow: Soviet Collectivization and the Terror-Famine* (New York, 1986).

On the power struggle in the party between Stalin and Bukharin, see Catherine Merridale, *Moscow Politics and the Rise of Stalin: The Communist Party in the Capital, 1925–1932* (New York, 1990); Michal Reiman, *The Birth of Stalinism: The USSR on the Eve of the "Second Revolution,"* trans. George Saunders (Bloomington, Ind., 1987); Roy Medvedev, *Let History Judge: The Origins and Consequences of Stalinism* (New York, 1989); and the fascinating memoirs of Anna Larina, *This I Cannot Forget: The Memoirs of Nikolai Bukharin's Widow* (New York, 1993).

There are a number of important biographies of Stalin: Isaac Deutscher, *Stalin: A Political Biography*, 2nd ed. (New York, 1967); Robert H. McNeal, *Stalin: Man and Ruler* (New York, 1988); Leon Trotsky, *Stalin: An Appraisal of the Man and His Influence*, trans. Charles Malmuth (New York, 1967); Robert C. Tucker, *Stalin in Power: The Revolution from Above, 1928–1941* (New York, 1990); Adam Ulam, *Stalin: The Man and His Era* (New York, 1973); and Dmitri Volkogonov, *Stalin: Triumph and Tragedy*, trans. Harold Shukman (New York, 1988).

CHAPTER 10
Stalin's Industrial Revolution

Industrialization Stalin-Style

For Stalin and the Stalinists socialism meant collectivization, industrialization, urbanization, and a welfare system for working people, all without capitalism or the market, and carried out and managed by a state directed by the Communist Party. "We are advancing full steam ahead along the path of industrialization—to socialism," Stalin told his followers, "leaving behind the age-old 'Russian' backwardness. We are becoming a country of metal, an automobilized country, a tractorized country." The whole endeavor was carried out by the most authoritarian means, which were dubbed democratic. For Stalinists democracy came to mean the formal support by the peasants, workers, and intelligentsia of the dictatorship of the party, registered in one-candidate elections, enthusiastic public demonstrations, and their energetic participation in the building of socialism. While the Stalinists' vision of socialism coincided with certain aspects of earlier ideas of Marxism—collectivized agriculture, industrial society, and a centrally planned noncapitalist economy—it broke radically with other, more democratic aspects: the empowerment of ordinary people, democratic control over the economy and state, and egalitarianism. Marxism had proposed that the socialist revolution would lead to the state being absorbed into society; under Stalinism the opposite occurred, as society was taken over by the state. Alternative ideas of socialism, however, were considered counterrevolutionary and anti-Soviet. Any dispute with the ends or the means decided by Stalin and sanctioned, in the view of the party, by history and doctrine could end with the dissident voices being silenced by prison or execution.

The first ten years of the Soviet regime had simply restored the industry that had been destroyed by war, revolution, and civil war. By the end of the 1920s the level of industrial production in the USSR had reached roughly that of 1913. But the Soviet population had grown, technology had not developed any further than the prewar years, and the Soviet Union's relative backwardness vis-à-vis the major capitalist industrial countries was even greater than it had been just before the revolution. In many ways the USSR was more back-ward than tsarist Russia. Not only had war and revolution set back economic development, but the loss of Poland and the Baltic states had cost the Soviet Union much of its engineering and metallurgical industry. All factions within the party were convinced by 1927 that more of the limited resources of the country had to be shifted to industry, that only greater investment would fos-ter further growth, and that there should be greater reliance on state planning and less on the market. Year by year more capital was turned from agriculture toward industrialization, and that effort led rapidly to the breakdown of the NEP system.

As the leadership considered its industrial strategies, it adopted a number of priorities to which it remained constant. Industrialization, it was agreed, had to be based on the most advanced technology, emphasize heavy industry and capital goods production, and develop a wide range of industries to make the country relatively self-sufficient. Only industrialization could end the country's backwardness and military weakness, and the party confidently, even arro-gantly, saw itself as possessing the tools and ideology to propel the USSR into the industrial future. As Kaganovich immodestly proclaimed in 1930, "We are convinced that 1940 will see only one great world power—the USSR!"

Soviet leaders asserted that planning and the massive mobilization of re-sources and people gave the Soviet Union a distinct advantage over chaotic, anarchic capitalism. In August 1928 Gosplan, the principal planning agency of the country, drafted a five-year plan for economic development, but only in the spring of 1929 did the Politburo approve a more ambitious plan. Though it was hardly a blueprint for development, this Five-Year Plan became the sym-bol of the Soviet system of rational planning. In fact the plan was a set of tar-gets that the Politburo kept raising, until they had chosen an optimal version that projected fantastic goals, including a 110 percent increase in worker pro-ductivity and a 65 percent rise in real wages. The Stalinists set impossibly high targets for industrial production, not so much as real guides or measures of success, but as distant goals to stimulate the maximum effort. Economists knew what the party leaders wanted, and they agreed to ridiculously high rates of growth. The Stalinist economist Stanislav Strumilin said that his planners pre-ferred to "stand for higher tempos than sit [in prison] for lower ones." By the fall of 1929 the new slogan was "Fulfill the Five-Year Plan in four years." Since targets changed all the time, real planning was impossible, but the plan re-mained a sacred myth which all had to revere.

Stalinist industrialization had its own unique characteristics, its own lan-guage, slogans, strategies, and costs. It was carried out as a massive military campaign, along "fronts," scaling heights, conquering the steppe, vanquishing backwardness, all while being encircled by capitalism. All obstacles, natural and technical, were to be overcome. In his November 1929 article "The Year of the Great Breakthrough," Stalin spoke of human will as the essential force for achieving the economic plan. Paraphrasing Marx, who had said a century ear-lier that "the task of philosophers was not to interpret the world but to change it," Strumilin asserted that "our task is not to study the economy but to change it." "Our laws," Kaganovich claimed, "are governed by revolutionary expediency at each given moment." Perhaps the most pungent words came from Stalin a few years later, when he proclaimed that "there are no fortresses Bolsheviks cannot capture!" In the same speech, in February 1931, Stalin explicitly linked the need to industrialize rapidly with the dangers that the USSR faced from the great capitalist and imperialist powers:

> It is sometimes asked whether it is not possible to slow down the tempo somewhat, to put a check on the movement. No, comrades, it is not possible! The tempo must not be reduced. . . . To slacken the tempo would mean falling behind. And those who fall behind get beaten. But we do not want to be beaten. One feature of the history of old Russia was the continual beatings she suffered because of her backwardness. She was beaten by the Turkish beys. She was beaten by the Swedish feudal lords. She was beaten by the Polish and Lithuanian gentry. She was beaten by the British and French capitalists. She was beaten by the Japanese barons. All beat her—because of her backwardness, because of her military backwardness, cultural backwardness, agricultural backwardness. . . . Such is the law of the exploiters— to beat the backward and the weak. It is the law of capitalism. . . . That is why we must no longer lag behind.

Rapid economic development was linked to national security, and any hesitation or footdragging could easily be construed as "wrecking" the plan or treason.

Class War on the Specialists

A vicious campaign by the superindustrializers came down hard on "specialists"—engineers, technicians, and economists—who argued for more rational, less impulsive economic development. The initial attack came in the famous Shakhty trial of 1928, the first important show trial since the trial of the Socialist Revolutionaries in 1922. Late in 1927 the police arrested a group of engineers in the town of Shakhty in the North Caucasus and accused them of conspiring with the former owners of coal mines, now living abroad. On March 10, 1928, *Pravda* announced that sabotage was being used as a new form of class struggle by the bourgeoisie. A month later, Stalin mentioned the Shakhty case as evidence that class struggle was intensifying as the country moved closer to socialism. Bukharin, Rykov, and Tomskii opposed Stalin's view, but Stalin turned up the heat, arguing that international capital was trying

> to weaken our economic power by means of invisible economic intervention, not always obvious but fairly serious, organizing sabotage, planning all kinds of "crises" in one branch of industry or another, and thus facilitating the possibility of future military intervention. . . . We have internal enemies. We have external enemies. We cannot forget this for a moment.

In May 1928 the trial began. Fifty-three engineers were accused of sabotage. The only evidence produced as to their guilt was their own confessions and statements of workers who had worked for the engineers. Ultimately, five men were sentenced to death, forty-four sent to prison, and four acquitted.

Besides finding scapegoats for the chronic waste, breakage, and chaos in industry, the trial was also meant to nip in the bud any notions among technicians or "bourgeois specialists" that they were powerful enough in their own right to bargain with the party leadership. The Stalinists were aware that many specialists had personal and political links with Bukharin and the Right. In November 1929 Kaganovich accused the specialists of "wrecking," and a month later G. M. Krzhizhanovskii declared, "Who is not with us is against us." By 1930 the slogan "Destroy the wreckers" expressed the official view of anyone standing in the way of higher tempos for industrial production or trying to challenge the party's authority by appealing to technical expertise. At the Sixteenth Party Congress in June 1930, Stalin spoke of "people who chatter about the necessity of *reducing* the rate of development of industry" as "enemies of socialism, agents of our class enemies."

Later that year former employees of Gosplan and the Supreme Council of the People's Economy (VSNKh), along with some engineers, were put on trial as the alleged members of an "Industrial Party" that had plotted to aid the French to attack the Soviet Union. Eight prominent intellectuals in the field of economics and planning were tried, and two thousand people were directly implicated in the alleged conspiracy. The Stalinists purged the doubters among the planners in Gosplan, as well as officials in the major economic ministries, the People's Commissariats of Labor and Finance, and VSNKh. Up to this point Gosplan, and economics in general, had been intellectually dominated by non-Communists, particularly by former Mensheviks, and they provided the example of what happened to those who considered ever faster tempos unattainable.

That same month, forty-eight officials from the People's Commissariat of Trade were indicted for sabotage in the food trade. All were shot three days later. About this incident *Pravda* editorialized "A Blow for a Blow": the Soviet proletariat had hitherto shown "too much forbearance to its accursed enemies." The wave of terror directed against the "bourgeois specialists" hit some thirty thousand senior engineers, about two to three thousand of whom were accused of being "wreckers." One estimate holds that the police had arrested seven thousand engineers by the spring of 1931. Though it was the breakneck Soviet industrialization that created inefficiencies, waste, breakage, and bottlenecks, these trials and arrests placed the blame for failures squarely on the engineers rather than the Stalinist leadership and its policies. As experts trained before the revolution were removed, new Soviet-trained graduates and foreign specialists took their place.

Scapegoating, however, could not solve the problems caused by the pell-mell industrialization of 1928–30. Stalin moved the loyal Stalinist Valerian Kuibyshev, who had headed VSNKh since 1926 and directed the early industrialization drive, to Gosplan and chose his old comrade from Georgia, Sergo Orjonikidze, as industrial tsar. The two Georgians had known each other since the 1910s. Stalin had brought his fiery friend up from the Caucasus in 1926 to head the party's watchdog committee, the Central Control Commission, and then put him in charge of the Workers' and Peasants' Inspectorate (Rabkrin), the state watchdog, which along with the Politburo became the major formulator of economic policies. Once he took over VSNKh and became a full member of the Politburo, Orjonikidze was Stalin's right-hand man in the industrial economy. When VSNKh was abolished in 1932 and new industrial commissariats were created, Orjonikidze became the first people's commissar of heavy industry.

Orjonikidze, soon adopted a more conciliatory line toward specialists than his predecessor had. Within half a year, the attacks on the specialists and technicians ceased. Though Stalin and Molotov, in particular, remained suspicious of people from the old privileged classes, the conciliatory line toward the intelligentsia and technicians won support at the June 1931 plenum of the Central Committee. Stalin continued to speak about turning Bolsheviks into industrial specialists and repeatedly told his audiences that potential saboteurs had to be rooted out: "There are and will be wreckers as long as we have classes and as long as we are encircled by capitalism." Nevertheless, the Central Committee responded to the growing mood among party leaders concerned with industry by declaring that the technical intelligentsia should no longer be terrorized.

For the beleaguered technicians and engineers the militance of the Cultural Revolution came to an end in the summer of 1931. Technical education now was open to all who passed difficult entrance examinations, rather than only those with the right class background (as in the years 1928–31). Instead of class warfare the party promoted cooperation and civil peace among social classes. Instead of extremely high industrial tempos, industrial leaders now emphasized quality work and education. These concessions toward the intelligentsia and skilled workers marked the beginning of a gradual moderation of economic and social policies that would reach its apogee in 1934–36.

Extension and Centralization

Stalin's command economy was hierarchical, with those above issuing orders and expecting obedience from those below. The top officials in Moscow made all major and many minor decisions concerning industrialization throughout the vast country. Industry was one huge state enterprise with corporate headquarters in the Kremlin. One of Stalin's innovations in Marxist theory was to declare that the state would become stronger before it would disappear altogether: "The higher development of state power in order to prepare conditions for the withering away of state power—this is the Marxist formula."

The Stalinist industrial economy was based on the constant expansion of labor and capital stock. Coercion operated at every level. Huge numbers of people were herded onto building sites and into new factories. Compulsion and command were the means to get people to work, for the material rewards were few at the beginning. Not surprisingly, orders and threats from above were met by resistance and inertia below. The grandest of plans often drained away in the summer mud or winter frosts across the great expanses of the country. Untrained labor and poor materials were simply not up to the tasks of a modern industrial economy. An exemplary plant, the Stalingrad tractor factory, was completed in June 1930 and was supposed to produce about five hundred tractors a month. In fact, only eight tractors rolled off the lines in June, none at all in July, ten in August, and twenty-five in September. Sadly, after about seventy hours of operation, the tractors began to fall apart.

All over the country the government organized huge building projects—the Turkestan-Siberian Railroad (Turksib), the Dneprstroi dam, and the steel center, Magnitogorsk. Perhaps the most impressive building project was the attempt to create a steel-producing city to rival Gary, Indiana, in the barren steppe at the southern end of the Ural Mountains. The "magnetic mountains" that gave rise to the steel mills and city of Magnitogorsk were the site of one of the most lauded achievements of Stalinist industrialization. Here high-quality iron ore was easily accessible, as well as limestone and firebrick clay, which could provide the raw materials for making steel. Missing, however, was coking coal, which had to be brought two thousand kilometers from the Kuznetsk Basin of western Siberia. Though Ukrainian economists argued in favor of building new steel plants in Ukraine where all the needed ingredients could be found, the party decided to go ahead with the Magnitogorsk project, probably to locate one major metallurgical center far from the Soviet Union's vulnerable western frontier. By late spring 1930 American engineers arrived in the empty steppe to design a steel mill and a city, only to find themselves involved in endless conflicts with their Soviet counterparts. The Soviets demanded building the plant at the fastest possible pace, while the Americans worried about technical feasibility. On February 1, 1931, the first pig iron was produced at Magnitogorsk to wild celebration. A few hours later an accident caused the blast furnace to be shut down.

Soviet propaganda proclaimed the triumphs of industrialization in the USSR and left out any mention of accidents, faulty construction, or bottlenecks. When problems were discussed, it was inevitably the result of sabotage or wrecking by bourgeois specialists or foreigners. Soviet engineers at Magnitogorsk soon replaced the Americans, and as problems with production accumulated, Soviet directors were replaced one after another. Inefficiencies were rampant. Bureaucratic centralization, supply shortages, pilfering, shoddy work, and the inability to calculate values for inputs and outputs without markets contributed to the chaos of a supposedly planned economy. The problems and successes of Magnitogorsk were repeated throughout the Soviet Union. Everywhere red tape gummed up the works. In January 1930 Orjonikidze complained, "If we don't put a stop to the paper flow it will drown us. We defeated Denikin and Iudenich, Wrangel and every other counterrevolutionary scum, but paper of all things will smother us."

The rush to modernity, with its celebration of smokestack industry and mammoth hydroelectric dams, meant that attention was paid almost exclusively to output and productivity and almost no notice was taken of the impact of rapid industrialization on the natural environment. This insensitivity to the limits of nature was characteristic of capitalist industrialization as well, but in the Soviet Union general ecological ignorance was compounded by the

Figure 10.1. Building the Ferghana Canal in Uzbekistan, 1939 (Bildarchiv Preussischer Kulturbesitz).

bravado of the Communists, who looked upon nature simply as an obstacle to be overcome on the road to progress. Bolsheviks could control nature rationally through planning, the party argued, while anarchic capitalism would only ruthlessly despoil the natural world. The Soviet Union was so large and so rich that pollution, it was thought, was not a major problem. The USSR possessed 10 percent of the world's rivers (155,000 rivers in Siberia alone), was watered by 10 percent of the globe's precipitation, and contained vast inland seas (the Caspian and Aral) and lakes, including the deepest in the world, Lake Baikal. In the early years the Soviet authorities set aside protected natural areas, provided for the supply of clean water to consumers, and regulated the use of forests. But with the industrialization drive of the 1930s, a major assault was launched on the environment. Stalin projected thirteen dams along the Volga, which would create huge reservoirs behind them. But the reservoirs and irrigation led to a decreased flow of water into the Aral and Caspian Seas, and the levels of the two seas fell over time. As millions moved to cities, little public notice was taken of the environmental effects of urbanization. In a society in which automobiles would not be a mass phenomenon until the 1960s, the effects of air pollution were delayed, but an ecological disaster on a gargantuan scale lay in the future.

Still, industrial output grew. Because of the inflated claims of Soviet sources, it is difficult to say for certain what the actual levels of growth were, but both Soviet and Western economists consider Soviet industrial growth in the 1930s to have been extraordinary. American economist Holland Hunter estimates that Soviet industry expanded by at least 50 percent in five years and 80 percent in six years. The annual rate of industrial growth ranged between 15 and 22 percent during the First Five-Year Plan. From 1928 to 1940 industrial output grew on average by 17 percent per year, agriculture by half a percent, and overall income (gross national product) by 15 percent. A rate of income growth of 15 percent per year over twelve years is unparalleled in history. Tsarist Russia in its period of greatest growth sustained a growth rate of 3 percent over twelve years, and the United States attained a growth rate of 4.5 percent over its twelve years of most rapid growth. Only West Germany and Japan after World War II came close to the Soviet rate of growth. Japan grew at an average yearly rate of 10 percent between 1945 and 1967, reaching peaks of 15 percent for periods as long as four years, but like Germany its growth was aided by the rebuilding of prewar industrial capacity, massive inflows of foreign capital, and very low spending for national defense. As inefficient, ecologically unsound, and costly in human and material terms as Soviet industrialization was, it transformed a basically agrarian society into an industrial one in record time. What the industrialists of England and America had done over half a century or more, the Soviet Communist Party tried to achieve in a decade.

Stalin's Working Class

From a relatively small social class in the 1920s the Soviet working class expanded into a huge, amorphous social conglomerate in the 1930s. In 1928 there were 11.6 million hired workers in Russia; by 1937 that number had grown to 27 million. Eighty percent of people in industry by 1940 had entered the workforce in the 1930s. This was a new working class that came largely from the displaced peasantry (half of the industrial workforce by 1933 was made up of peasant recruits) and simply swamped the old one. Only in the late 1930s did new workers come in significant numbers from urban families. Tens of thousands of former kulaks arrived in boxcars at Magnitogorsk, where they lived (and often died) in tents before they moved into drab barracks. There and at other building sites they were joined by recruited peasants and workers, some foreign enthusiasts ready to "build socialism," and thousands of others who simply drifted in looking for work. As outcasts, kulaks tried to blend into the most favored class in Soviet society, often concealing their origins. The working class, in turn, lost some of its prestige as it was diluted by new dekulakized peasants.

The working class at the end of the 1920s was polarized between the older generation of skilled workers and newer, younger, less skilled peasant workers. In 1929 half the workers in the Soviet Union had entered the workforce before the revolution and might be considered "hereditary proletarians." Thirty-five to forty percent had been born peasants, and twenty-five percent still had some ties to the land. Party leaders considered the miners, metalworkers, and textile workers, two thirds of whom had fought with the Red Army in the civil war, to be the workers most loyal to Soviet power, and their reliable social support. When the crisis over grain collections occurred in 1928–29, over seventy thousand workers volunteered to go to the "grain front." More than three-fourths of these mobilized workers were party members or Komsomols. The skilled workers displayed a pride in their work and enjoyed a craft solidarity based on the older, pre-Soviet work culture. They resented upstart workers, as well as foremen and bosses, and resisted the speed-up policies of the party-labor specialists, such as Gastev, who tried to introduce Taylorist work patterns on the plant floor. The older workers looked down on the newer workers as uncultured, politically ignorant outsiders who did not appreciate the traditions of the working class. Foremen and administrators, as well as the older workers, harassed and discriminated against new workers.

Party leaders had ambivalent views of the workers. They noted periodically that parts of the working class, particularly "newcomers from non-proletarian classes" on the one hand and "labor aristocrats" on the other, were often unreliable politically. These "marginal strata" of workers were thought to be potential "conduits for bourgeois influences on the proletariat." Many party leaders were suspicious that a "labor aristocracy," with close ties to the trade unions, was a source of "opportunism," which in this case meant that they were too comfortable with the status quo and not eager to take on the sacrifices of rapid industrialization. Every once in a while party leaders tried to head off the growing social differentiation among workers with more egalitarian policies, as in the years 1927–29 when wage differentials were narrowed. As trade union autonomy was eliminated at the end of the 1920s, the skilled labor elite was battered from above and below. With tens of thousands of new workers who did not share the traditional deference to the older workers moving into the factories, the older workers lost their traditional status on the factory floor. At the same time Stalin used the Komsomol to promote a third group of workers, a young, skilled group who had been teenagers during the revolution and civil war. Some were sent to the countryside during the collectivization campaigns; others went to school to become engineers.

In September 1929 the government moved to increase the power of managers over workers by reviving the system of one-person management that had been tried early in the decade and ending the dual decision-making of so-called Red managers, who were often political appointees, and chief engineers. This was part of the campaign against "bourgeois specialists" that characterized the years 1928–31, as well as one more attempt to impose greater labor discipline on the workers. In the same years the trade unions lost their autonomy and power, and only factory committees were left as organs through which workers could pressure managers. Managers also received the right to fire workers without clearing their decisions with factory committees, and at about the same time the bosses gained full control over wage rates. In theory, then, managerial power increased, as managers were less accountable to technical experts.

As the one person held responsible for everything in the factory, the manager was soon being referred to as a "feudal lord." But managers' actual authority remained quite limited for some time. Party and union organizations continued to interfere in management decisions, and even during the attacks on the specialists during the years of the Cultural Revolution, the managers had little choice but to rely on the expertise of engineers and technicians. Even the workers were supposed to be able to exercise workers' control through their representative institutions.

As the distance between workers and bosses grew, the distance between village and city was shrinking. Some 23 million peasants moved to towns and cities between 1926 and 1939, 2 million to Moscow alone. Many young peasants, especially those who had tasted the city doing seasonal work or had left the village for the army, had long desired to leave the village, but the chronic unemployment of NEP had discouraged such a dangerous move for many. For some young men and women city life meant freedom from patriarchal authority and a family of their own. For those who had been forced off the farm as kulaks and forbidden by law to join the collective farms the city also meant freedom from the stigma of their past. For still others there was no future in the countryside. One migrant wrote in 1933:

> Here on the collective farm I am living the life of a badly fed animal. I have been robbed of my grain and all my reserves. My cattle have been taken. . . . Life is impossible. I go into town, get a job as a workman, and there will be fed.

Ordinary Soviet workers entered the age of industrialization poor and vulnerable, and their status grew worse in the 1930s. Living standards dropped, and their power to negotiate with management was curtailed. Yet workers found ways to protect their interests, despite the state's backing of the managers. The industrial expansion of 1930–31 ended unemployment and created a desperate need for workers. In the summer of 1930 the Soviet Union officially proclaimed itself the first country to experience full urban employment in peacetime, and early in October the government canceled unemployment benefits. Labor shortages allowed workers to gain some degree of leverage with managers, carve out some autonomy at the workplace, determine their own pace of work, and attempt to better their pay and working conditions. Their unions were no longer able to speak for the workers, but now became the providers of welfare benefits. As part of the state apparatus, they were given the specific functions of doling out social insurance funds, dealing with compensation for injuries, and working out the arrangements for vacations at state resorts.

A constant problem for the government was low labor productivity. In 1926–27 the average Soviet worker produced only one-half as much as a British worker and a quarter as much as an American worker. In part this might be explained by the recent arrival of workers into industry or their lack of skills or labor discipline, but it was largely the result of a yawning technological gap between Russia and the West. In the fall of 1927, the government launched a campaign to increase labor productivity that proved remarkably successful. Productivity began to increase after 1928 as the amount of fixed capital (machinery and plants) advanced as rapidly as the number of workers. In the first years of industrialization, 1927–29, over 60 percent of the increase in industrial output was due to greater productivity. One method of increasing productivity was "uninterrupted work," which involved machines being operated day and night by three or more shifts of workers. Workers were given one day of rest after five days of work, but the machines were never allowed to idle.

Marxists had long complained that workers under capitalism were "wage slaves" faced with the harsh choice of working for capital on the bosses' terms or facing unemployment and starvation. In the Stalinist system workers resisted being tied down to the industrial system by constantly changing jobs. The state tried to regulate workers' movements by introducing the internal passport at the end of 1932 and issuing ration cards on different occasions. To live in any major city required a permit stamped into one's passport. Since housing was provided by companies or local administrations, most workers could be said to be living in company towns with little option for opposing the will of their employers. Despite increasingly harsh disciplinary measures imposed from above, workers continued to move, riding the rails and living out of their cheap suitcases. In 1930 the average industrial worker changed jobs every eight months and took off four and a half days without permission. Coal miners changed jobs on average every four months and were absent from work almost fourteen days a year. The passport system only slightly affected the high rates of worker migration, and enterprising forgers were always ready to make up a passport for a paying customer. As late as 1937, it is estimated, some 30 percent of all workers changed their job each quarter of the year.

Workers held off the growing power of managers and foremen in the first years of industrialization by maintaining their traditional *arteli,* which gave them some control over work and wages. Like other egalitarian production collectives and communes in the first, more radical phase of the industrialization drive between 1929 and 1931, the *arteli* gave the workers considerable clout in negotiating with managers, who were forced in many cases to give up making unilateral decisions on rates of production. Managers wanted workers to form nontraditional "brigades," which did not involve relatives and friends from the same village or region, but workers subverted the change by electing the *artel* elder as brigade chief. When managers encouraged workers to compete with one another to maximize output in what was euphemistically called "socialist competition," the worker collectives and communes proved to be very productive. In conditions of shortages and fluctuating wages, collectives and communes were, in the words of historian Lewis Siegelbaum, "fortresses erected by workers to defend themselves" against the blows of forced industrialization and collectivization, "even while those policies elicited much support among them."

Abruptly on June 23,1931, Stalin clamped down on proworker radicalism. In a groundbreaking speech, he denounced equality in wages and proclaimed that henceforth skilled workers would receive more than unskilled workers in order to curb labor migration. In 1932 better rations and bonuses were introduced for the most productive workers, or "shock workers," who were usually of working-class, rather than peasant, origin. The party agreed to give factory directors more freedom from party officials in the factory, and the powers of the police in the economy were limited. Stalin's attack on the practice of equal wages and promotion of differentiation in wages encouraged a new stratification of the working class and the breakup of the egalitarian workplace culture favored by many workers. Confused by the party's policy shift, one worker complained, "In the village you are driving peasants into collective farms, whereas here you divide us up into individuals." "We don't want to work individually," another said boldly; "many died in Solovki [labor camps] because they wanted to work individually in the village."

In Marxist terms an essentially "bourgeois" system of remuneration was introduced: "from each according to his or her ability, to each according to his or her work." Stalin was convinced that only a system of unequal material rewards could improve productivity, and a few years later he expressed his contempt for "infantile egalitarian exercises":

> There cannot be any doubt that the confusion in the minds of individual party members concerning Marxian socialism and their infatuation with the egalitarian tendencies of agricultural communes are like two peas to the petty bourgeois views of our 'Leftist' blockheads, who at one time idealized the agricultural communes to such an extent that they even tried to implant the commune in the factories, where skilled and unskilled worker, each working at his trade, had to put his wages into the common fund which was then shared out equally.

In the spring of 1934 a new wage system known as the progressive piecework system was introduced. Wages were tied to the number of pieces produced, with higher-producing workers receiving higher remuneration per piece as well. Skilled workers steadily improved their standard of living.

Yet at the same time managers gained power when the state backed the factory directors by issuing a series of disciplinary laws against workers. In January 1931 prison sentences were introduced for labor-discipline violations on the railroads, and a month later compulsory labor books were required for all industrial and transport workers. In March punitive measures against negligence were announced. Late in the year employers were permitted to transfer workers from one job to another without their consent, thus abolishing Article 37 of the 1922 Labor Code, and in November managers were empowered to dismiss workers, take away their ration cards, and evict them from company housing for a single day's absence. The next month the state granted managers responsibility for issuing ration books, without which it was difficult to survive. Workers were incensed by these decrees and in some places physically assaulted officials. Managers tried to appease their employees by suggesting that they should obey the letter of the law for a few weeks and then everyone could relax. Managers, who desperately needed their workers on the job, ended up covering for absentees, rather than turning them over to the police. Still both the government and managers remained nervous about worker mobility, and neither was ultimately able to control it.

For the Soviet worker the rewards for hard work were in part material—increased monetary sums and a better standard of living—and in part spiritual—participation in the great enterprise of creating a better way of life called socialism. When Ilya Ehrenburg, a novelist and then the Paris-based correspondent for the government newspaper *Izvestiia*, returned to the USSR and traveled about the country in the summer and fall of 1932, he noted the complex attitudes of the workers he observed:

> The word "enthusiasm," like so many others, has been devalued by inflation, yet there is no other word to fit the days of the First Five-Year Plan; it was enthusiasm pure and simple that inspired the young people to daily and unspectacular feats. Many workers felt a real affection for their factories. . . . Life was hard; everyone talked about rations, about distribution centers. In Tomsk the bread was like clay. It reminded me of the year 1920. . . . This vast canvas was painted in two colors: rose and black; hope lived side by side with despair; enthusiasm with dark ignorance—some were given wings, others were destroyed by the experience.

The Soviet worker of the 1930s was a very different person from his counterpart of 1917. He (and increasingly she) was more likely to have been born a peasant and to have moved to the city as a young adult. She or he never knew the labor struggles of capitalist society, never enjoyed protection by a trade union, and was constantly being reminded that the Soviet state was a workers' state. The novelty and anxiety of urban life and factory work were compounded by political fears generated by the official media, in stories of how saboteurs and wreckers were secretly operating in the factories, how foreign fascists and Trotskyite spies were attempting to undermine the great Soviet experiment, and how the sole socialist country in the world was encircled by capitalist states intent on war. Hard work and discipline were essential to constructing socialism and defending the first proletarian state. A program of "socialist emulation" recognized and rewarded outstanding workers, whose pictures were hung on "honor boards," and awarded red banners to exceptionally productive brigades.

Because peasants now worked in a factory or on a building site did not mean that they understood the culture and discipline of industrial work. They were resistant to the new way of life, worked slowly, broke their tools, and got drunk. Alcohol played the same role in Soviet industrialization as it had one hundred years earlier in the early stages of the English industrial revolution. Life was harsh and unforgiving. Real wages fell by 50 percent in the years of the First Five-Year Plan, and only began to rise in 1936. Housing was woefully inadequate, and many families shared a single room with other families. The comic prospects of communal living inspired Valentin Kataev to write his play *Squaring the Circle*, but for the real denizens of the shared apartments such communal living was far less funny. The state invested most heavily in plant and machinery, not in social overhead like housing or consumer goods. Still, per-capita consumption rose from 1928 to 1937, and many Soviet people would later remember the mid-to-late thirties as a time of relative plenty, a golden age before the years of war and renewed famine.

Tempo was everything for the planners, and the speed with which new plants were built precluded efforts to make them safer or more humane than pre-Soviet factories. Accidents were common. The American worker John Scott, whose idealism brought him to Magnitogorsk, tells of the hardships and dangers faced by ordinary workers:

> Standing on the top of the huge [gas-]pipe at its highest point, nearly one hundred feet up in the air, and looking along its tortuous track over the bare steppe, one got the impression that some obscure designer had gone mad, and we pawns were blindly executing the senseless pattern of his pen.
>
> This pipe line was absolutely unprotected from the wind. During the winter the workers nicknamed it "Sakhalin," after the Soviet Union's icy Pacific island. The north wind would race across the endless barren steppe and sway our columns back and forth like reeds. Once two columns and a section of pipe fell and a rigger and a welder were killed. But the line was finished nonetheless, and went into operation in due course of time.

The working class, which was growing rapidly, remained a class in flux, without its own autonomous organizations or independent representatives. Workers certainly knew that they were a subordinate social group, inferior to the managers, engineers, and foremen, but favored over the peasantry. They made up a social conglomerate with an extremely low sense of class solidarity or consciousness or ability to affect their own future. The most mobile of social groups, workers migrated, not only from place to place seeking better conditions and higher pay, but also upward by joining the Communist Party and becoming managers and administrators. Still, workers in the factories were distinguished from the peasantry, who did not receive passports or ration cards, and from the rulers who rose from them but grew increasingly distant.

The New Class of Bosses

The new elite class of managers and administrators that emerged in the 1930s was a distinctively Soviet phenomenon. If American presidents were often born in log cabins, Soviet managers and politicians after 1930 came from the huts of peasants and tenements of workers. Before the great leap into industrialization, most administrators in Soviet industry were from the middle classes, and only about one out of six came from the working class. In the 1930s the government pushed some half million worker Communists and another half million non-Communist workers into managerial and technical positions. In Stalin's Soviet Union workers could rise as individuals through hard work, education, and appropriate political behavior into the ranks of the rulers. These people pushed up from the working class into the elite would become the governing class of the Soviet Union for the next half century.

Historian Moshe Lewin has graphically described the creation of Soviet bosses as "a process in which not leaders but *rulers* were made." The party promoted a new style of harshness, rudeness, and even cruelty. The boss could use fines, fire workers, and threaten them with arrest. He had the police to enforce his decrees. The legacy of the revolution, which had encouraged more familiar relations between managers and workers, was discarded, and a new, authoritarian elite stood above workers. One industrial boss declared, "The ground must shake when the factory director enters the plant." An engineer later commented:

> For us bosses, these new instructions were not so bad, that is from our personal interest. We thought that as older and experienced people we deserved this respect. but for the workers this was very disagreeable, and you could feel this. From talks with foremen, with whom we had close relations, we learned that the workers were very dissatisfied.

At the same time managers found their position between the party-state authorities and the workers very precarious. Their tenure in office was insecure and dependent on the arbitrary will of their superiors and their own good luck and skill to make things work in chaotic conditions. To survive they too had to learn to manipulate the system and skirt the limits of legality. Managers were given benefits and privileges if they were successful: cars and chauffeurs, special well-stocked stores in which to shop, better housing, vacations at discrete resorts, and monetary bonuses. Engineers and technicians also gained access to special dinning rooms and better apartments. In Lewin's words, "The *chinovnik* [bureaucrat] was 'swallowing' the masses, the state was swallowing those same *chinovniki*, and the proletariat was quite irrelevant to the question."

As a "ruling class without tenure," the managers grew increasingly dependent on being in favor with those even higher up. Their success required absolute and unquestioning obedience, enforcement of the decisions from the top with determination, even ruthlessness, and a willingness to acquiesce and participate in what can only be considered criminal activity (denunciations of the innocent, approval of lawlessness, and collaboration with a regime based on deception). Their dilemma was that they had to satisfy the demands of those above them while trying to increase production and get the workers to work harder. Managers and directors and party and state officials were under a constant threat of demotion, expulsion from the party, arrest, and even death.

The Second Five-Year Plan and Stakhanovism

As the First Five-Year Plan came to an end and the second began, the material hardships of workers eased up. The years 1934–36 were known as "the three good years." The famine had ended, more consumer goods were produced, agricultural products were easier to obtain, and by December 1934 rationing, first in bread and later in other products, came to an end. Higher-paid workers were able to live quite comfortably. New factories built in the early 1930s now came on line and newly trained worker-engineers and managers took over important positions in the industrial economy. During the years of the Second Five-Year Plan (1932–37), labor turnover slowed down, as did absenteeism, but the problem of labor productivity persisted. Managers and technicians often argued that there were fixed technical limits on productivity, but the government called for higher levels, above the technical limits defended by managers. In May 1935 Stalin changed the slogan "Technology decides everything" to

"Cadres decide everything." Like other vague pronouncements of the leader, this new slogan was interpreted differently by different people. Technicians thought it meant that they would be treated better by authorities. Factory directors thought it meant they ought to treat workers better.

The decline of worker power and the increase of manager and technician power accelerated during the Second Five-Year Plan. Directors were given discretionary power over certain funds. An attempt was made to introduce "technical norm determination"; that is, specialists were to determine the normal levels of worker productivity mathematically. This effort failed, and more customary forms of norm determination survived. But it was extremely difficult to know how much a worker could produce when so many workers had just arrived from the farm and the state kept pushing workers to break out of their work routines and produce extraordinary outputs. Setting a standard pace for work was very difficult when record-breakers disrupted the normal pattern of work. Soviet industrializers rewarded the so-called shock workers, who overfulfilled the normal levels of production, but these efforts only undermined any normalizing or routinizing of work rates. Ordinary workers often resented the shock workers and would set upon them and beat them up.

Late in August 1935 a miner in the Donbass, in Ukraine, Aleksei Stakhanov, accepted the challenge of local party leaders to attempt to set a new record in hewing coal. With all the necessary helpers and supplies at the ready, Stakhanov took up his pneumatic pick and cut 102 tons of coal in five hours and forty-five minutes. The local press picked up the story, and when Commissar of Heavy Industry Orjonikidze read about it, he demanded that Stakhanov's feat be featured in the all-Union press. A new campaign began to increase productivity, using Stakhanov as the principal example but engineers and directors were to "head up and organize" the movement. Stakhanov was a kind of super shock worker, but unlike other shock workers, the Stakhanovites were also to introduce new production techniques and innovate patterns of work.

The Stakhanovite movement was a state-initiated form of pressure on both workers and managers to make them work harder, faster, and more efficiently. Foremen, engineers, and plant directors often resisted the record-setting methods of the Stakhanovites, which upset the normal ways of working. But a kind of recordmania swept the country. Everywhere teams of workers reorganized their work to set new records. These highly skilled workers, usually with privileged positions on the shop floor, such as brigade leaders and instructors, worked as a collective, but their records were touted as if they were the achievements of individuals. Stakhanovism became an explicit criticism of old ways of working and of those workers and bosses who did not improve productivity. Orjonikidze warned, "Whoever wavers, we will straighten them out," He was echoed in a more sinister voice by Leningrad party boss Andrei Zhdanov: "All saboteurs, routinizers, and bureaucrats will be swept away by the victorious march of the Stakhanovites."

The Stakhanovite movement in its first flush lasted just over a year. In early 1936 the government raised the output norms in various industries and decreased the remuneration for piecework. Stakhanovites had made havoc of the old norms and the targets of the Five-Year Plan. Managers found it impossible to support both labor heroics like Stakhanovism and keep order and productivity in the enterprises. Those managers who did not keep up with the spirit and efforts of Stakhanovism often fell victim to the Great Purges, which dealt another disruptive blow against industry. In the years before the war, 1937 to 1940, productivity fell off, just as the country turned decisively toward military preparation. In December 1938 new punishments were imposed on late or absent workers. In June 1940 the six-day workweek, introduced in 1929, was extended to seven days. In October 1940 the state decreed that it could transfer workers and engineers from one enterprise to another. The government imposed a harsh military discipline on Soviet workers as the country moved into the years of World War II.

Making the Socialist City

"Soviet urbanization, in tempo and scale," wrote historian Isaac Deutscher, "is without parallel in history." In the first fifty years of Soviet power the urban population of the USSR rose from 15 percent of the total population to 60 percent. That same growth took one hundred years in the United States. The first great leap into cities came with the Stalin revolution. In 1926, 26 million, or less than a fifth of the population, lived in towns and cities; by 1939, 56 million, almost a third of the total population, did. These 30 million new city dwellers came largely from the peasantry in a massive influx of people that led to what Moshe Lewin calls "the ruralization" of the cities. Instead of a small stream of people from the provinces flowing into cities and being acculturated by the dominant urban population, the flood of rural migrants into towns overwhelmed the weakly developed urban culture, not to mention the fragile institutions and available services.

Old cities and towns, especially industrial ones, exploded in size, and hundreds of new towns were built. Between 1926 and 1939 Moscow, Leningrad, and Kharkiv doubled in population, and the city of Gorky (Nizhnyi Novgorod) tripled. New cities, such as Magnitogorsk, grew where no town had existed before. These cities were envisioned as planned socialist municipalities with broad thoroughfares and rationalized apartment dwellings. "Superblocks" of apartments, all looking alike to discourage inequalities and envy, were to be built according to the radical ideas of urban planning and architecture set down by the authorities during the Cultural Revolution. Everyday life was to be socialized, with communal kitchens and services. Form was to follow function in the dominant aesthetic. But even before the foundations could be laid, the realities of shortages and chaotic settlement distorted the plans. Moreover, the radical visions of the Cultural Revolution were diluted by the arrival of a new aesthetic, Socialist Realism, which dictated more traditional designs, heroic statuary, and monumental and neoclassical architectural forms.

By the mid-1930s egalitarianism in design was replaced by a variety of residences and neighborhoods of different quality and comfort, which were more appropriate to the hierarchies of the Stalinist order. Special buildings were reserved for high officials, foreigners, and others favored by those in power. In Magnitogorsk a separate village called Amerikanka was constructed in a birch grove for American specialists. A few years later, after most of the Americans had left, its name was changed to Berezhka (Little Birchtree), and its inhabitants included Soviet officials who lived a life apart from ordinary workers. The elite had cars and drivers to bring them to work, while workers had to use the crowded public transportation system, which could not keep up with the burgeoning demand. Moscow underwent a radical reconstruction as much of the old center of the city was torn up (or torn down) and replaced by new hotels and government buildings and huge squares and parks to be used for demonstrations and public recreation. Stalin ordered the massive Cathedral of Christ the Savior to be demolished and a skyscraper called the Palace of Soviets to be built in its place. The cathedral was destroyed, but the palace was never built. For the next half century, a large public swimming pool operated on the site, until with the fall of the Soviet Union the new Russian government rebuilt the cathedral. One of the most ambitious and successful projects of the Stalin Revolution was the building of the Moscow metro, a subway that whisked commuters to and from work in comfort and speed. Each station on the limited line was built like a small palace with sculptures, mosaics, and paintings in marble settings. The drabness and drudgery of everyday life in a backward, industrializing country could for a moment be forgotten in this concrete vision of the socialist future. Here was the physical representation of what the Soviet system could achieve. The steel and stone buildings, the subway, and the grand parks of culture were a promise to the people of the coming rewards for the sacrifices and pain that they had endured during the "Great Stalinist Breakthrough."

The transformations of the 1930s, which have been called a revolution from above, left a mixed legacy for the Soviet people. Peasants opposed the collective farm system, and it was decades before they became reconciled to it. In contrast, workers and most other Soviet people considered industrialization, for all the dislocations and deprivations it imposed on working people, as one of the great successes of Soviet power, which would pay off big in years to come. Sadly, the future was to be continually delayed, and the great edifice of Stalinist industrialization would ultimately be exposed as built on shoddy scaffolding. Though the gains made in the 1930s certainly helped the USSR stave off the Nazi onslaught in World War II and provided steady improvement in the standard of living for the Soviet population for the next fifty years, the form in which industrialization took place had built-in liabilities that would eventually catch up with the system. Stalinist industrialization promoted gigantic constructions over more rational ones and emphasized central planning and orders from above rather than local decision-making or initiative from below. Managers pushed for productivity and neglected safety and working conditions. Technology was more important than human requirements, whether in housing, consumer goods, or the small things that made life more pleasant. Output rather than ecology was first in the industrializers' minds. Achieving power, overcoming backwardness, and protecting the country against its many enemies had become the primary goals of the socialist system.

The end result was an industry built too quickly to be safe and efficient, concentrated too heavily on heavy industry, and unable to supply the range of consumer goods that capitalist societies take for granted. The colossal costs of inefficient and wasteful smokestack industries would eventually be paid by nature and people, whose health would deteriorate. Improvements were slow but steady, except for the years of war, yet the promise of a better life only raised expectations of a glorious future that never came. The dismal reality was one of hard physical labor and meager material rewards for most of the Soviet people for most of their lives.

Suggestions for Further Reading

The literature on Stalinist industrialization is rich and includes works already mentioned by Moshe Lewin, Shelia Fitzpatrick, and the collection of essays on workers edited by Lewis H. Siegelbaum and Ronald Grigor Suny. More specialized studies of workers include Vladimir Andrle, *Workers in Stalin's Russia: Industrialization and Social Change in a Planned Economy* (New York, 1988); Donald Filtzer, *Soviet Workers and Stalinist Industrialization: The Formation of Modern Soviet Production Relations, 1928–1941* (London, 1986); Hiroaki Kuromiya, *Stalin's Industrial Revolution: Politics and Workers, 1928–1932* (New York, 1988); David L. Hoffman, *Peasant Metropolis: Social Identities in Moscow, 1929–1941* (Ithaca, N.Y., and London, 1994); Lewis H. Siegelbaum, *Stakhanovism and the Politics of Productivity in the USSR, 1935–1941* (New York, 1988); and the extraordinary memoir, John Scott, *Behind the Urals: An American Worker in Russia's City of Steel* (Cambridge, Mass., 1942; reprinted, Bloomington, Ind., 1989).

For studies of Soviet industrialization, see William G. Rosenberg and Lewis H. Siegelbaum (eds.), *Social Dimensions of Soviet Industrialization* (Bloomington, Ind., 1993); Anne D. Rassweiler, *The Generation of Power: The History of Dneprostroi* (New York, 1988); Joseph S. Berliner, *Soviet Industry from Stalin to Gorbachev: Essays on Management and Innovation* (Ithaca, 1988); two works by Eugene Zaleski, *Planning for Economic Growth in the Soviet Union, 1918–1932* (Chapel Hill, N.C., 1962) and *Stalinist Planning for Economic Growth, 1933–1952* (Chapel Hill, N.C., 1980); and the groundbreaking work by Stephen Kotkin, *Magnetic Mountain: Stalinism as a Civilization* (Berkeley and Los Angeles, 1995). Also see the important article and discussion by Holland Hunter, "The Overambitious First Soviet Five-Year Plan," with comments by Robert Campbell, Stephen F. Cohen, and Moshe Lewin, *Slavic Review* 32, (June 1973): 237–91.

The best study of the technical intelligentsia remains Kendall E. Bailes, *Technology and Society under Lenin and Stalin: Origins of the Soviet Technical Intelligentsia, 1917–1941* (Princeton, N.J., 1978). See also Michael Gelb (ed.), *An American Engineer in Stalin's Russia: The Memoirs of Zara Witkin, 1932–1934* (Berkeley, Calif., 1991).

CHAPTER 11
Building Stalinism

Stalin came to power in the absence of a broad consensus within the party and within society as a whole on the legitimacy and necessity of his personal rule. Indeed the ruling party did not yet enjoy a firm ideological or cultural hegemony among the population, and repression and even mass terror had been periodically used, during the civil war and the collectivization of agriculture, to enforce the power of the state and remove potential sources of opposition. Yet at the same time the regime confidently proclaimed that it possessed a popular and historically sanctioned mandate and worked assiduously to create real support for itself, through education and propaganda, leadership cults, election campaigns, broad national discussions (for example, on the constitution), public celebrations (such as the Pushkin centennial of 1937), show trials, and political rituals. Most importantly, the regime made real concessions to the populace and satisfied the ambitions and aspirations of many (certainly not all) for social mobility and an improved living standard. Peasants who became workers and workers who became managers and party bosses were moving up the social ladder, and they repaid the party-state for their new status with loyalty. At the same time, however, many of their envied social "betters" of the past were experiencing an enforced downward mobility that ended in the infamous prison system known as the GULag—or against a dank wall in a prison basement.

Stalinism was at one and the same time revolutionary and conservative. It differed from many traditionally authoritarian dictatorships that simply sought to preserve the status quo. Stalin was unwilling to accept backward Russia as it was, but while radically transforming it, he also wanted to solidify and stabilize his regime by restoring certain traditional values like patriotism and patriarchy. His political legitimacy was to be based on more than victorious revolution and naked force. The ideological props of the Stalin dictatorship were a seriously revised Marxism and a pro-Russian nationalism and statism. Because, according to the Stalinists, the country was surrounded by hostile capitalist states that would eventually launch a war against the only socialist state, the USSR had to remake itself into a great industrial and military power. These alleged foreign threats were matched by imagined internal dangers. When Stalin declared the Soviet Union to be socialist in 1936, he tempered praise of this positive achievement of reaching a higher stage of history than the rest of the world with constant reminders that the enemies of socialism existed both within and outside the country. Repeated references to deceptive and concealed enemies that "vigilant" Communists had to "unmask" were used to justify Stalin's enormous reliance on the "steel gauntlets of Ezhov," the sadistic chief of the secret police.

Like any ruling class, the Communist Party needed to work constantly at justifying its right to rule. In the Stalinist formulation the revolution from above of the 1930s, though initiated by the state, was supported from below by millions of peasants and workers, but in fact it destroyed the basis of the regime's relationship with the great majority of the population and created a new crisis of legitimacy and authority. The regime painted a picture of progress and harmony, even as peasants resisted collectivization and workers struggled against the enormous difficulties of early industrialization. The forced images of energy, joy, and purpose did not easily mesh with the harsh daily experiences of most people. This disjuncture created unease among those in the party-state apparatus, who were attempting to govern a vast country and transform it according to a vision that only a minority within a minority shared.

Politics and the Party

In November 1930, at a moment of crisis in industry, Stalin moved decisively to establish a more complete monopoly over decision-making at the highest levels. Not only did he replace the disorganized Kuibyshev, the chief economic authority, with Orjonikidze, but he dismissed Prime Minister Rykov, who had been associated with Bukharin, and replaced him with Molotov. Stalin feared any schism between party and state and sought to end discussion in the Sovnarkom, which delayed the carrying out of his policies. "With this combination we will have full unity of the soviet and party summits that will undoubtedly double our strength," he wrote to Molotov. Yet filling top jobs with Stalinists and centralizing the bureaucracy did not in fact contribute to more effective government. Concentration of power at the top often had the opposite effect, fostering local centers of power and low-level disorganization. The trend toward authoritarianism created "Little Stalins" throughout the country, and in the national republics ethnopolitical machines threatened the reach of the central government.

Likewise, Stalin-faction rule failed to eliminate disagreements within the party. Instead new oppositions and potential oppositions were produced and reproduced, though they could no longer be expressed openly. In his own statements Stalin refused to accept any blame for the economic chaos or the famine and dealt with the failures of collectivization and industrialization by increasing repression. In a letter replying to the Cossack writer Mikhail Sholokhov's protests against the systematic brutality of the grain collection, Stalin took a hard line:

> One must take into account . . . the other side. And that other side amounts to the fact that the respected grain-growers of your region (and not only your region) have gone on a sit-down strike (sabotage!) and shown no concern about leaving the workers, the Red Army, without grain. The fact that the sabotage was peaceful and outwardly bloodless in no way alters the realities—that the respected grain-growers have in essence carried out a "peaceful" war with Soviet power. A war by starvation, dear Comrade Sholokhov.

The oligarchy that carried out the Stalin revolution was a very narrow political elite, but it had not effectively closed the party to debate and consideration of alternatives. Each time a shift in party line occurred, and another group or faction was defeated, a purge (*chistka*) was carried out. Originally the word *chistka* meant a thorough rechecking of the party membership to determine qualifications and orthodoxy. The first such purge had taken place in 1921, when 156,900 members (out of 585,000) were expelled. Other purges in the 1920s were directed against various oppositions, but there had always been an unwritten rule within the party, based on Lenin's warning, that the Bolsheviks should not repeat the mistake of the French revolutionaries, the Jacobins, and exterminate each other. With very few exceptions this rule was kept until 1936, though the death penalty was carried out against nonparty opponents and victims of the regime.

The growing gap between the public statements and images put forth by the state, on the one hand, and the real destruction in the countryside and the phony, "Potemkin village" factories that failed to produce, or the other, convinced some prominent party members to speak up against the covering up of the failures. In the fall of 1930, S. I. Syrtsov, chairman of the Sovnarkom of the RSFSR, and Beso Lominadze, the party chief in Transcaucasia, criticized the party line on collectivization. Shocked by the costs of collectivization and the extremely high investment in industry, they began privately to circulate memoranda and lobby for moderation. Lominadze unwisely told a friend that there must be a clean sweep of the party leadership. "What about the General Secretary?" asked his friend. "If there is a spring cleaning, every piece of furniture has to be removed, including the biggest one." Stalin swiftly removed both Syrtsov and Lominadze from their posts and expelled them from the Central Committee. He transferred Lominadze to Magnitogorsk, where he was to prove his loyalty. But in January 1935, when he was summoned to Moscow to meet with Stalin, Lominadze took his own life.

The swift retribution against Syrtsov and Lominadze (demotion in these cases) did not deter a number of other critical groups from emerging. Within the Central Committee and the Politburo more moderate elements opposed the rapid tempos in industry and proposed a more conciliatory attitude toward society, particularly the peasantry. Martemian Riutin's appeal of 1932 is symptomatic of the views of those opposed to Stalin's emerging dictatorship, who

Figure 11.1. "Religion is poison. Safeguard the children." Anti-religious poster by N. B. Terpsikhorov, 1930 (Courtesy of Hoover Institution Archives, Poster Collection, RU/SU650). The child reaches toward the school, while her grandmother drags her to church.

saw it as the negation of Leninism and the collective leadership of the Central Committee and the principal cause of the growing disillusionment of the people with socialism. Those around Riutin, who formed a union of Marxist-Leninists, believed that the only way to save Bolshevism was to remove Stalin and his clique by force. If Riutin was right that "the faith of the masses in socialism has been broken, [and] its readiness to defend selflessly the proletarian revolution from all enemies weakens each year," then the regime had either to move immediately toward conciliation and the rebuilding of confidence or turn to even more radical and repressive measures. Once discovered, Riutin and seventeen associates were expelled from the party for "having attempted to set up a bourgeois, kulak organization to reestablish capitalism and, in particular, the kulak system in the USSR by means of underground activity under the fraudulent banner of 'Marxism-Leninism.' " Stalin, it was reported, called for Riutin to be put to death, but Kirov and other moderates opposed using the death penalty against a party member.

Riutin's circle was an unusual instance of coherence and organization among those who opposed Stalin. Much more evident was a broad, inchoate discontent with Stalin's rule that permeated political and intellectual circles. Several highly placed and loyal Stalinists harbored serious doubts about Stalin's agricultural policies. Others, like Mykola Skrypnyk, a cofounder of the Ukrainian Communist Party who had sided with Stalin in the 1920s and early 1930s, criticized the growing centrism in the party and state and the evident pro-Russianness of Stalin's nationality policies. Perhaps most ominously, tensions arose between the Red Army commander Mikhail Tukhachevskii, who called in 1930 for expansion of the armed forces, particularly aviation and tank armies, and Stalin and Voroshilov, who opposed what they called "Red militarism." During the famine in Ukraine high military officers such as Iona Iakir angered Stalin by reporting their concern with peasant resistance, which, they felt, could spread to the troops, and demanding that more grain be kept in the region.

Stalin was able to turn quickly against even his closest comrades if they crossed him. In 1933 he severely criticized Orjonikidze for objecting to remarks by prosecutor Andrei Vyshinskii that attacked those working in the industrial and agricultural ministries: "The behavior of Sergo (and Iakovlev) . . . is impossible to call anything else but anti-party, because it has as its objective goal the defense of reactionary elements of the party against the Central Committee." Stalin repeatedly called for harsher measures against real and potential enemies of the party's general line, and Molotov, his closest collaborator in the 1930s and throughout World War II, usually backed him up.

Stalin received regular reports from the police official Genrikh Iagoda and insisted that Molotov circulate them among the members of the Central Committee and the Central Control Commission, as well as among "the more active of our economic specialists." He told Molotov that he was convinced that conspiratorial elements were linked with the Rightists within the party. Though the mass killing of the Great Terror did not come until the late 1930s, Stalin all along was prepared to execute those he considered his enemies. Already in 1930 he wrote to Molotov, "It is absolutely essential to shoot [the economists] Kondratiev, Groman and a pair of the other bastards. . . . It is absolutely essential to shoot the whole group of wreckers in meat production and to publish this information in the press." Stalin trusted very few people and those not for very long. One exception was his prime minister, Molotov, one of the few people whom he addressed with the familiar pronoun *ty*. As the Yugoslav Communist Milovan Djilas remembers,

Molotov, though impotent without Stalin's leadership, was indispensable to Stalin in many ways. Though both were unscrupulous in their methods, it seems to me that Stalin selected these methods carefully and fitted them to circumstances, while Molotov regarded them in advance as being incidental and unimportant. I maintain that he not only incited Stalin into doing many things, but that he also sustained him and dispelled his doubts.

Police officials spread the concocted stories of anti-Soviet conspiracies throughout the top bureaucracy and created an atmosphere of suspicion that justified the use of precisely the kinds of harsh measures that Stalin advocated. Kirov, the young party chief in Leningrad, agreed with Stalin. "Now everyone can see," he said in October 1932, "that we were right, that the further we go along the road of constructing socialism, the more evident is the counter-revolutionary character of every oppositional tendency." In November 1932 Stalin demanded that resistance from "individual detachments" of collective farmers be dealt "a shattering blow." At about the same time he arrested critics of his agricultural policy, including the former commissar of agriculture, A. P. Smirnov. A few weeks later the Politburo called for a purge of party members because many organizers of kulak sabotage had come from within the party. "Such an enemy with a party card in his pocket," the resolution stated, is more dangerous than the open counter-revolutionary, and must be punished with every severity of revolutionary law." Early in January 1933 Stalin told the Central Committee that the famine and economic chaos in the country was the fault of saboteurs, "the last remnants of moribund classes," some of whom had "even managed to worm their way into the party." "All the enemy can say is that nothing would be lost if Stalin were removed." He called for greater repression: "The abolition of classes is not achieved by the extinction of the class struggle, but by its intensification.... We must bear in mind that the growth of the power of the Soviet state will intensify the resistance of the last remnants of the dying classes." Stalin skillfully fostered an atmosphere of fear and mistrust. That fear and the constant calls for "vigilance" against enemies were in large part artificially generated by deliberate political rhetoric and the activities of the political police, but fear fermented in an environment of social disruption and uncertainty and the real weaknesses and insecurities of the Soviet state. Surrounded by imagined enemies and real hostilities throughout Soviet society, the beleaguered Communists drew together around the leader who projected a powerful image of Bolshevik toughness.

Retreat

The brash leap from a market economy into a state-organized economy led to chaos and repeated crises in the early 1930s. The harvests of 1931 through 1934 were abysmally low, only recovering in 1935 to pre-1928 levels. Excessively high procurements of grain and the peasants' killing off of livestock led to food shortages in the towns and hunger, even famine, in much of the countryside. Living standards collapsed faster than they had anytime before in history. The winter of 1932–33 was a time of severe economic dislocation both in industry as well as agriculture, and anxiety about the future was heightened by the news that Adolph Hitler had come to power in Germany. The Communist Party gradually shifted toward more moderate economic and social policies. By the middle of 1932 the government had lowered production targets for the Second Five-Year Plan and given consumer goods higher priority. It announced that the harvest of 1933 had been unusually abundant, though this was not true, and Stalin was seen as largely responsible for compelling the collection of the crop. Arrests and deportations declined. The number of people executed by the state fell from 20,201 in 1930 and 10,651 in 1931, during the height of collectivization, to 2,728 in 1932 and 1,118 in 1936. Criminal convictions, which had numbered between 142,000 and 240,000 in 1930–33 dropped to their lowest point, 79,000, in 1934 before beginning a steady rise in the mid and late 1930s. In an extraordinary gesture in May 1933, Stalin and Molotov released half of those in labor camps who had been confined because they had resisted collectivization.

The apparent successes in agriculture and the enthusiasm for industrialization contributed to Stalin's popularity, at least among the urban population. Yet in his public rhetoric of these years Stalin maintained his severity and toughness, qualities that had long been part of Bolshevik culture. He seemed not only a competent commander to many but an indispensable leader in a time of political stress and economic crisis. A high party official wrote about this period (1932): "Loyalty to Stalin was based principally on the conviction that there was no one to take his place, that any change of leadership would be extremely dangerous, and that the country must continue in its present course, since to stop now or attempt a retreat would mean the loss of everything." Stalin was dealt a personal blow when his second wife, Nadezhda Allilueva, killed herself in November 1932. Molotov reported that the only time he ever saw Stalin cry was at Allilueva's funeral. Rumors that Stalin suggested he might resign were embellished by reports of his associates rallying around him—a scene reminiscent of an episode from the life of Ivan the Terrible, later to feature in a major motion picture by Eisenshtein.

At times Stalin could be pressured to be more flexible and accommodating. Neither a consistent moderate nor radical, Stalin himself had shifted from center-right during his alliance with Bukharin in the mid-1920s to the left during the Cultural Revolution and Great Breakthrough of 1928–31, and then back to a more moderate position around 1931–32. Whether or not this policy shift in 1931 was imposed on Stalin or corresponded to a genuine reevaluation of his position, during the next half decade the Soviet leadership steadily began to reverse many the more radical social and economic policies of the end of the 1920s and the early 1930s and pull back from egalitarianism and collectivism toward a promotion of hierarchy, cultural traditionalism, and social conservatism. This move toward accommodating the Soviet system to native Russian traditions has come to be known as the "Great Retreat," a term coined by the émigré sociologist Nicholas Timasheff. Socially, sexually, and artistically conservative, the Great Retreat preceded and overlapped with the most politically repressive period in all of Soviet history, the years of the Great Purges

(1936–38). Soviet policies in many areas shifted around 1932 to more moderate positions. Concessions were made to the collective-farm peasants and codified in the Kolkhoz Statute of 1935. In the industrial economy the Great Retreat meant the end of egalitarianism for the working class and greater power for technicians and managers. State policies aimed at integrating different social groups and classes into a single Soviet people rather than accentuating conflict between classes. The state now favored the educated and ambitious, softened its line toward the intelligentsia, and rewarded materially those who worked hard and proved their loyalty. The tensions and fears of the First Five-Year Plan period rapidly dissipated, at least for a few years. In every field, from the arts, where experimentation and abstraction were forbidden in favor of Socialist Realism, to state policies toward woman and the family, where prohibitions were placed on abortion and restrictions on easy divorce, a palpably conservative tone dampened the once militant attitudes of the Communists.

The Great Retreat of the mid and late 1930s was in part a response to the failures and difficulties of Stalin's revolution from above, in part a renewed effort to reconstruct links between the state and ordinary people, and in part a massive attempt to mobilize a diverse and divided population around the great tasks of "socialist construction" and national defense. Revolutionary appeals were supplemented with more traditional patriotic ones. Egalitarian aspirations and methods were replaced by rewards and privileges based on performance and loyalty. The Stalinist settlement involved the creation of a highly hierarchical system of access to information and influence that elevated a small number of party and state officials, intellectuals, and managers. The end of rationing in 1934–35 forced everyone below the privileged upper levels of society to forage in government stores and peasant markets for what they could afford. Social inequalities grew in an economy of permanent shortages where money talked less effectively than one's position and personal connections.

When the delegates to the Seventeenth Party Congress gathered in Moscow in late January 1934, they dubbed their meeting "the Congress of the Victors." Stalin declared that "the party today is united as it has never been before." Yet he tempered his message by mentioning that "at times unhealthy moods penetrate into the party from outside. . . . There still exist in town and country certain intermediate strata of the population who constitute a medium that breeds such moods." Though Stalin was enormously popular and powerful in 1934, fractures still existed within the party, even among Stalin's closest associates, though the public was largely unaware of them. An open disagreement at the Congress between Orjonikidze and Molotov over industrial targets was a rare public sign of a deeper split between those moderates who wanted to consolidate the gains of the First Five-Year Plan and the radicals, who wanted to continue to plunge ahead. Molotov spoke in favor of raising the rate of industrial growth to nearly 19 percent, five or six percentage points above the targets set by the party a year earlier. Orjonikidze, who worked closely with those most involved in industrial production, objected and proposed a rate of 16.5 percent. His proposal carried the day, to the evident relief of engineers and plant managers.

Some dissident party members tried to collect like-minded delegates to oppose Stalin. They approached the popular Sergei Kirov, who had opposed using the death penalty against Riutin, and proposed that he run for general secretary. But Kirov was a loyal Stalinist who wanted nothing more than to remain head of the Leningrad party, and he rejected their offer: "You are talking rubbish! What kind of General Secretary would I make?" Though he often emphasized the need for "revolutionary legality," which was understood to be a lessening of repressive measures, Kirov was in all his public and political appearances completely loyal to Stalin, who in turn favored his younger protégé. For the majority of party members Stalin still represented the militant turn toward socialism—collectivization, rapid industrialization, and the destruction of organized political opposition—and there was no significant challenge to his authority.

Though a few Communists feared Stalin's inclination toward personal autocracy, the oligarchic bureaucratic system seemed more secure than ever. The dominant faction had rendered all oppositions impotent, and a new emphasis on "revolutionary legality" seemed to promise a more orderly, procedural, less disruptive mode of governance. The government eliminated expedient judicial procedures, such as the three-person courts set up during the recent famine, and gave the Procuracy, which was somewhat like the American attorney general's office, the authority to oversee arrests by the secret police. At the same time the police were reorganized. In July 1934 the OGPU, the secret police that succeeded the Cheka, and the regular civil police, the militia, were merged into the People's Commissariat of Internal Affairs (NKVD), now headed by Genrikh Iagoda, a reliable ally of Stalin's. Five months later NKVD took control of all prisons in the various union republics of the USSR and established the infamous Main Administration of Labor Camps (GULag). The huge police and security apparatus was centralized and brought closer to Stalin's personal control, but there were still legal and traditional restraints on the unleashing of the police against party members. The event that sharply changed the atmosphere in the Soviet Union from the prevailing moderation to a frenzy of mass terror occurred suddenly and unexpectedly on December 1, 1934.

As Sergei Kirov was entering an office in the Smolny Institute in Leningrad, he was shot from behind by an assassin. From Moscow Stalin sped by train to Leningrad and took over the investigation. The killer, Leonid Nikolaev, was a disgruntled former party member with a history of mental illness. Many historians in the West believe that he was an agent, wittingly or unwittingly, of the secret police and perhaps Stalin himself. Whether Stalin was involved in the killing of Kirov (which is doubtful) or not, he used the occasion of the murder to turn up the heat on the remnants of the opposition. He appointed Nikolai Ezhov and Aleksandr Kosarev, head of the Komsomol, to "look for the killer among the Zinovievites." When Kosarev and police chief Iagoda balked at Ezhov's tactics, Stalin called in Iagoda and told him that if he did not cooperate "we will smash your mug." Two weeks later the police arrested Kamenev and Zinoviev and announced that Kirov's murder was the work of a mysterious "Leningrad Center" that included members of the Zinoviev opposition. The Central Committee circulated a secret letter to all party committees linking the assassination with oppositionists. In mid-January 1935 Zinoviev and Kamenev were tried and sentenced to prison terms.

Fear spread widely. The American ambassador, William Bullitt, reported back to Washington: "It is difficult to exaggerate the fear which now exists among the leading members of the Communist Party in Moscow. Relations with foreigners are restricted to an irreducible minimum." The Central Committee called on all party members not "to rest on their laurels and turn gullible. It is not complacency that we need, but vigilance, genuine Bolshevik vigilance." A rising hysteria could be felt within the party as Communists searched for enemies. Deviance of any kind could lead to expulsion from the party or arrest. A general investigation of party members in 1935 led to 177,000 Communists being expelled from the party and 15,000 arrested. This campaign, as well as an "exchange of party documents" in 1936, was directed by Ezhov, who was prepared to flout legal means and regular procedures to ferret out political enemies. Some party officials and even secret police agents tried to stay within the boundaries of Soviet law, clearing arrests with the local procurators and honestly seeking evidence of treachery. But Ezhov and others escalated the rhetoric about hidden enemies and arbitrarily linked various kinds of offenders to the Trotskyists and Zinovievists, who by this time presented no palpable threat to the Stalinist clique.

The police investigated thousands of cases of alleged counterrevolutionary activity. Even Vyshinskii, later the vicious prosecutor during the Great Purge trials of 1937–38, complained to Stalin that the police were arresting people for "everyday babbling, grumbling, dissatisfaction with the poor work of individual persons or organizations . . . and also for singing popular ditties and songs with anti-Soviet content." A general attack on organizations of "Old Bolsheviks," party members who had joined the movement before or during the revolution, led to the closing of their clubs, the Society of Old Bolsheviks and the Society of Former Political Prisoners. One of the most venerable old Communists, Abel Enukidze, who had worked in the Transcaucasian party organization from its inception and knew Stalin when he first joined the Social Democrats, was expelled from the party after he was accused by Ezhov of protecting enemies of Stalin. Enukidze was forced to criticize his own memoirs of the early days of the revolutionary movement, which did not adequately elevate the role of the young Stalin. The unscrupulous head of the Transcaucasian party organization, Lavrentii Beria, constructed a new account of that history, which was reprinted in thousands of copies around the world. History was pressed into service of the growing cult of Stalin, as libraries were ordered to remove works by oppositionists.

The Great Purges

The period from 1928 until December 1934 might be seen as the prehistory of Stalinism, the period when the political structures and social conditions were formed that created the possibility for a regime of extreme centralization of power, overwhelming dominance of a weakened society, and particular ferocity. A bureaucratic regime had pacified the country, though it remained extremely wary of any form of dissent. In many ways the bureaucracy was creating its own "normal" way of governing the vast country, but Stalin did not want to be simply the chief bureaucrat. Suspicious of potential opposition to his rule and unwilling to tolerate the slightest restraint on his absolute power, Stalin turned on his own administrative elite.

Repression intensified in 1936. Even as the new "Stalin constitution," lauded as the most democratic in the world, was being ratified, secret communiqués within the party linked the defeated oppositionists with foreign spies, White Guards, and kulaks. All Communists were required to unmask the hidden enemies. The principal targets were former oppositionists and anyone who had known them. When Tomskii, the long-time head of Soviet trade unions and former ally of Bukharin, was accused, in August 1936, of belonging to an anti-Soviet conspiracy, he shot himself. A few days later Zinoviev and Kamenev were tried again in a widely reported show trial where they were accused of forming a counterrevolutionary, terrorist "Moscow Center" that was responsible for the murder of Kirov. The court claimed that Zinoviev and Kamenev had joined with Trotsky, who was in exile abroad, to form a bloc against the Soviet leadership with the aim of assassinating Stalin. Though there had been some contact between Trotsky's son, Leon Sedov, in France and oppositionists in the Soviet Union, the idea of a conspiratorial bloc that presented any palpable threat to Stalin was pure fantasy. Yet the defendants, after being tortured in secret and promised their lives if they admitted guilt, confessed to their invented crimes in open court. Vyshinskii, who prosecuted the case, ended his final speech with "I demand that dogs gone mad should be shot—every one of them!" Though Zinoviev and Kamenev begged Stalin to spare their lives, he ordered that these two close comrades of Lenin and leaders of the opposition to Stalin in the late 1920s be executed.

Stalin was still not content with the efforts of his police, and in September he wrote a letter critical of Iagoda, who "has definitely proved himself to be incapable of unmasking the Trotskyist-Zinovievist bloc." For not being ruthless enough against the oppositionists, Iagoda was replaced by the much more vicious Ezhov, who began his reign as chief policeman by purging the police itself, ridding it of moderate elements that hesitated to use extralegal methods. The number of arrests rose monthly, and Ezhov personally participated in the brutal interrogations of many prisoners. Where there was no crime or conspiracy, Ezhov and his henchmen found one by torture. Stalin encouraged this practice and personally signed thousands of death warrants. When the confession of an imprisoned Trotskyist was not satisfactory, Stalin wrote to Ezhov: "One might think that prison for Beloborodov is a podium for reading speeches, statements that refer to the activities of all sorts of people but not to himself. Isn't it time to squeeze this gentleman and make him tell about his dirty deeds? Where is he, in prison or in a hotel?"

The height of the terror was reached in 1937, a date that still connotes fear and repression. Iurii Piatakov, an "Old Bolshevik" close to Orjonikidze and a leading figure in the industrialization drive, had been hounded throughout 1936 with a series of false accusations. He tried to defend himself, wrote to Stalin directly, and told Ezhov that he was prepared personally to carry out the execution of Zinoviev, Kamenev, and even his own wife to prove his loyalty—all in vain. In January Piatakov and other prominent leaders—Radek,

Grigorii Sokolnikov, and Leonid Serebriakov—were tried and executed. This and other attacks on leading figures in the industrialization effort grieved Commissar Orjonikidze, who was already concerned about the arrest of his brother. Almost any accident at a factory led to accusations of sabotage and the arrests of technicians and managers. The police had lists of suspicious people, many former members of various oppositions, and arrests were imminent. On February 18, 1937, after a bitter argument with Stalin over the telephone, Orjonikidze, one of Stalin's oldest comrades, shot himself. The press suppressed the news and announced that he had died of a sudden heart attack. But what Orjonikidze did not have heart for was participating any longer in the inner-party intrigues revolving around fabricated conspiracies that were destroying old comrades.

Within a week the Central Committee met to discuss the case of Bukharin. Ezhov began with a long indictment, accusing Bukharin, Rykov, and other Rightists of collaborating with Trotskyist-Zinovievist terrorists. When Bukharin rose to defend himself, he was in his fourth day of a hunger strike to protest the false accusations made against him. As he denied the fantastic charges of treason leveled against him, the Central Committee members interrupted his reply repeatedly. Bukharin pleaded that he was speaking the truth, that he could not bring himself to confess falsely to such monstrous crimes. Disingenuously, Stalin asked why would all Bukharin's accusers have lied about his role in the anti-Soviet conspiracy, and he ended the session by saying he was surprised by nothing, for "Trotsky and his pupils Zinoviev and Kamenev had at one time worked with Lenin and now these people have made an agreement with Hitler." The Bukharin case lingered on until March 1938, when he was tried along with his comrade Aleksei Rykov and the former police chief Iagoda. All were executed. This grandest of the show trials, with its fabricated plots and forced confessions, warned the Soviet people that their country was the target of vicious forces conspiring internally and from abroad. The staging was convincing enough that the American ambassador, Joseph E. Davies, believed that the charges had been proven beyond a reasonable doubt. He wrote home to his daughter:

> For the last week I have been attending daily sessions of the Bukharin treason trial. . . . It is terrific. . . . [The proceedings] disclose the outlines of a plot which came very near to being successful in bringing about the overthrow of this government. . . . The extraordinary testimony of Krestinsky, Bukharin, and the rest would appear to indicate that the Kremlin's fears were well justified. . . . But the government acted with great vigor and speed. The Red Army generals were shot and the whole party organization was purged and thoroughly cleansed. . . . I must stop now as the trial reconvenes at 11 a.m. and I'll have to run.

Before he died, Bukharin was able to dictate a final testament to his wife, Anna Larina, who committed it to memory:

> I am leaving life. I bow my head, but not before the proletarian scythe, which is properly merciless but also chaste. I am helpless, instead, before an infernal machine that seems to use medieval methods, yet possesses gigantic power, fabricates organized slander, acts boldly and confidently. . . .

> Since the age of eighteen, I have been in the party, and always the goal of
> my life has been the struggle for the interests of the working class, for the
> victory of socialism. These days the newspaper with the hallowed name
> *Pravda* [Truth] prints the most contemptible lie that I, Nikolai Bukharin,
> wanted to destroy the achievement of October and restore capitalism. This
> is an unheard-of obscenity.... In what may be the final days of my life, I
> am certain that sooner or later the filter of history will inevitably wash the
> filth from my head. I was never a traitor: I would have unhesitatingly traded
> my own life for Lenin's. I loved Kirov and never undertook anything against
> Stalin. ... Know, comrades, that the banner you bear in a triumphant march
> toward communism contains a drop of my blood, too!

Most devastating for the security of the USSR was the purge of the army
that began in May of 1937. Marshall Tukhachevskii, the hero of the civil war,
was arrested, tortured until he confessed (the confession had telltale bloodstains
on it), secretly tried, and shot. General Iakir was tortured but insisted on his in-
nocence. When it was reported to Stalin that Iakir had exclaimed "Long live the
party! Long live Stalin!" at the moment of his execution, Stalin cursed furiously.
General Gamarnik did not wait for the ax to fall on him and shot himself. The
purge fell heaviest on civil war veterans; as many as thirty-seven thousand officers were purged, about one-half the officer corps; only ten thousand would be
reinstated by 1940. Often their wives, children, and other relatives were also arrested. Tukhachevskii's wife and two brothers were executed; his three sisters
were sent to camps, and his mother died in exile; when his young daughter came
of age, she too was arrested. The cause of the military purge lay in Stalin's suspicions that the army was disloyal, that a plot by Soviet generals was being
hatched against the party leadership. The president of Czechoslovakia, Eduard
Benes, passed on such information in good faith to Soviet intelligence after receiving it from Russian émigrés and German diplomats. This material was in fact
forged, probably by a Russian anti-Soviet organization in Paris headed by a White
general. As a result, Stalin killed more Soviet generals than would be killed in
World War II. Fifteen out of the 16 army commanders, 60 of the 67 corps commanders, and 136 of the 199 divisional commanders were executed.

The Great Purges began as a bloody retribution against the defeated political opposition to Stalin. They spread through the ranks of political bosses,
economic officials, and the army brass. When the top party leaders called for
vigilance and unmasking of enemies, cascades of denunciations swept millions
of people into the frenzied search for saboteurs and spies. On July 3, 1937, the
Politburo ordered Ezhov to round up and try "anti-Soviet elements" and deal
with them ruthlessly. Ezhov set quotas for the numbers in each district to be
arrested, exiled, and shot. He projected a total of 177,500 people exiled and
72,950 executed. The numbers actually tried by the revived three-person courts
and shot exceeded the planned totals. The number of accusations and arrests
overwhelmed the police, and they quickly and crudely processed people
through the investigations, forcing confessions by torturing them, and sent
them to labor camps or prisons or on to execution.

The number of labor camps and slave laborers increased dramatically in
the 1930s. During collectivization and dekulakization the number of inmates
rose rapidly, from thousands to hundreds of thousands, and with the purges

to over a million. The infamous camps dotted the Soviet landscape, particularly in the far north of European Russia, in the Volga and Ural regions, and in far eastern Siberia. The names Solovki, Kolyma, Vorkuta, and Magadan became chilling metaphors for subhuman confinement in a frozen wasteland and life-destroying work in gold and coal mines. The earlier Soviet interest in rehabilitation of prisoners had given way to a productivist mentality; the aim was to sweat out whatever labor one could from the prisoners and make the camp economically self-sufficient. Evgeniia Ginzburg, the wife of a highly placed Communist official in Tatarstan, spent seventeen years in such camps, and in her memoirs she remembered one of the worst:

> Elgen was covered in thick mist as we drove along its main street toward the low wooden building which housed the state farm officials' administration. It was the time of the midday break, and long lines of workers surrounded by guards trudged past us on their way to the camp.... "I thought Elgen was only for women, but don't some of these look like men to you?" ... They were indeed sexless, these workers in padded breeches and footwear made of cloth, with caps pulled down low over their eyes, and rags covering the lower part of their brick-red, frostbitten faces.... "Elgen is the Yakut word for 'dead,' " said one of our company.

Though these camps were not designed, like the Nazi death camps of World War II, to exterminate their inmates, the treatment was so bad that the number of deaths in the camps jumped from 20,595 in 1936 to 90,546 in 1938. Political prisoners were separated from common criminals, and even as they tried to preserve their intelligentsia traditions and solidarity, they often stirred up the resentment of the more sadistic guards and fell victim to the violence of the criminals.

Though tens of thousands of ordinary citizens fell into the terror machine and ended up in the camps, the Great Purges devastated particularly the political leadership, the army, and the intelligentsia. By 1939, 60 percent of those who had been party members in 1933 had been driven out of the party. Of the 139 members and candidates of the Central Committee elected at the Congress of Victors in 1934, 98 (i.e., 78 percent) were arrested and shot, mostly in 1937–38. Of the 1,966 delegates to the Seventeenth Party Congress, 1,108 were arrested as counterrevolutionaries. In many ways the purges eliminated the power of much of the Old Bolshevik elite. Only 6 of the 10 Politburo members of 1934 survived until 1939: Stalin, Molotov, Andreev, Kalinin, Kaganovich, and Voroshilov. They were later joined by Mikoyan, Zhdanov, and Khrushchev. Gone were the assassinated Kirov, the suicide Orjonikidze, the purged and shot S. V. Kosior, and Kuibyshev, dead of a heart attack. Whereas in 1934 about 81 percent of the party elite had joined the party before 1921, by 1939 that percentage had fallen to 19 percent.

It is particularly instructive to consider the fate of those who had served in Lenin's first government. Lenin himself died in 1924, and a few others also died naturally: Nogin (Trade and Industry) in 1924, Skvortsov-Stepanov (Finance) in 1928, and Lunacharskii (Enlightenment) in 1933. The rest—Miliutin (Agriculture); Krylenko, Dybenko, and Antonov-Ovseenko (Military); Lomov-Oppokov (Justice)—perished in the purges. Shliapnikov (Labor), Glebov-Avilov (Post and Telegraph), and Teodorovich (Food) were arrested and died in camps. Trotsky, Soviet Russia's first commissar of foreign affairs and the founder of the Red Army, was murdered in 1940 in Mexico when a Soviet agent plunged an ice ax into the back of his head. The lone survivor of Lenin's first government was the people's commissar of nationalities, Joseph Stalin. As Trotsky had put it in the late 1930s, a river of blood separated Lenin and Stalin.

The most accurate estimates of the number of victims of the purges come from the official KGB numbers revealed for the first time in the early 1990s. By the end of the 1930s, 3,593,000 people were under the jurisdiction of the NKVD, 1,360,000 of whom were in labor camps. In just the years 1937–38, according to official figures from the archives, the authorities executed 681,692. When you add the estimated 4 to 5 million people who perished in the famine of 1932–33 to the figures of prisoners, exiles, and executed, the total number of lives destroyed in the 1930s runs from 10 to 11 million. Over a longer span of time, from 1930 to 1953, 3,778,234 people were sentenced for counterrevolutionary activity or crimes against the state; of those, 786,000 were shot to death. At the time of Stalin's death there were 2,526,000 prisoners in the Soviet Union and another 3,815,000 in special settlements or exile, many of them non-Russians deported from their homelands during and after World War II.

The Great Purges were like a self-injected virus tearing the body politic apart. By early 1938 several high-ranking party members complained that the number of arrests and expulsions of Communists was excessive and must be brought to a halt. Malenkov and Vyshinskii, both of whom had been involved in the purge process, now called for caution. Vyshinskii condemned the conditions in labor camps and the widespread use of torture. Stalin reined in Ezhov by replacing him with the Georgian Lavrentii Beria. In March 1939 Ezhov himself was arrested; he was shot a year later. Almost immediately after Beria's ascension to head of the NKVD, the number of arrests fell precipitously, conditions improved in camps and prisons, and torture was employed less frequently. In the next few years the government quietly released many prisoners, including thousands of officers who were reinstated in the military. Beria carried out his own purge in the ranks of the police to get rid of Ezhov's men. At the Eighteenth Party Congress in March 1939 surviving party leaders let the country know that the hunt for internal enemies was largely finished and that attention now had to be turned to external enemies.

The Great Purges removed all limits on the unbounded despotism of Stalin. They simultaneously eliminated all possible resistance and created a new and more loyal elite with which the tyrant could rule. Yet why the purges occurred and took on the mammoth dimensions they did remains a difficult question to answer. Some analysts, like political scientist Zbigniew Brzezinski, propose that purging was a permanent and necessary component of totalitarianism in lieu of elections. The novelist Alexander Solzhenitsyn sees the purges as simply the most extreme manifestation of the amorality of the Marxist vision, an inherent and inevitable part of the Soviet system. Others have explained the purges as a more extreme form of political infighting and have attempted to reduce the role of Stalin himself. "The existence of high-level personal rivalries, disputes over development or modernization plans, powerful and conflicting centrifugal and centripetal forces, and local conflicts," writes historian J. Arch Getty, "made large-scale political violence possible and even likely." Several writers have focused on the effects of the purges rather than its causes, implying that intentions may be read into the results, and have shown how a new "leading stratum" of Soviet-educated "specialists" replaced the Old Bolsheviks and "bourgeois specialists." "Stalin—and, for that matter, the majority of Soviet citizens—saw the cadres of the mid-1930s less in their old role as revolutionaries than in the current role as bosses," writes Sheila Fitzpatrick. "There is even some evidence that Stalin saw them as Soviet boyars (feudal lords) and himself as a latter-day Ivan the Terrible, who had to destroy the boyars to build a modern nation state and a new service nobility."

Recently uncovered evidence seems to support a quite banal and traditional explanation for the Great Purges. The opening of the Soviet archives, even though still incomplete, reveals conclusively Stalin's initiation and personal direction of the purges and supports the view that the dictator's ambition and morbid suspiciousness was the catalyst for thousands of smaller settlings of scores. Whether Stalin was actually paranoid in a clinical sense (he probably was not) is largely irrelevant. He and his most faithful lieutenants, like Molotov and Kaganovich, shared a mentality that divided the world into enemies and friends and justified the harshest of measures against all opponents. They judged the slightest deviation from solid support of Stalin as a sign of possible defection that needed to be prevented. Forty years after the purges, Molotov, then an old man living out his last days, continued to justify the repression: "In the main it was the guilty, those who needed to be repressed to one degree or another, who were punished." He still expressed venomously his contempt for one of his victims, the head of the police, Iagoda, "a filthy nobody who wormed his way into the party and was only caught in 1937." He sneered at this "skunk" who pleaded for his life: "Let me live, for I have rendered a good service to the court!" "We had to work with reptiles like that," Molotov went on,

> but there were no others. No one! Now you understand why so many mistakes were made. They deceived us, and innocent people were sometimes incriminated. Obviously one or two out of ten were wrongly sentenced, but the rest got their just desserts. It was extremely hard then to get at the truth! But any delay was out of the question. War preparations were under way. That was the way it was.

In the context of deep and recurring social tensions, with the threat of war looming, the state gave the green light to resentment of the privileged, the intelligentsia, other ethnicities, outsiders, and nonconformists. The requirement to find enemies, to blame and punish, worked together with self-protection and self-promotion (and plain sadism) to expand the purges into a political holocaust. An official had to appear willing to find enemies, even among the innocent, or faced possible incrimination himself.

At the end of the Great Purges, the Soviet Union, seriously weakened economically, intellectually, and militarily, resembled a ruined landscape, but at the same time it was dominated by a towering state apparatus made up of new loyal apparatchiki, disciplined by the police, and presided over by a single will.

By the outbreak of World War II the central government, the military, the republics and local governments, the economic infrastructure had all been brutally disciplined. The vastness of the bloodletting crushed for a time the local political cliques, known as "family circles," and the local political machines, particularly in the union republics, but by 1938 the mass arrests and executions brought in their wake not only concentration of power at the top and center but even greater disorder and insecurity. The foundations had been laid for what the West would call a "totalitarian state," but it was in actuality a disorganized, inefficient, and unresponsive leviathan. Rather than orders from the top being obeyed without contradiction, fear and lethargy, conformity and unwillingness to take responsibility eliminated most initiative or originality. Safe in the Kremlin or his well-guarded summer homes, Stalin ruled without challenge for the rest of his unnatural life.

Suggestions for Further Reading

The literature on the Great Purges is broad-ranging and controversial. For a review of events and a traditional explanation, see Robert Conquest, *The Great Terror: A Reassessment* (New York, 1990); David J. Dallin and Boris I. Nicolaevsky, *Forced Labor in Soviet Russia* (New Haven, Conn., 1947); Boris Levytsky, *The Stalinist Terror in the Thirties: Documentation from the Soviet Press* (Stanford, Calif., 1974); and Robert C. Tucker and Stephen F. Cohen (eds.), *The Great Purge Trial* (New York, 1965). A systemic reading is given in Zbigniew K. Brzezinski, *The Permanent Purge* (Cambridge, Mass., 1956). The revisionist accounts include J. Arch Getty, *Origins of the Great Purges: The Soviet Communist Party Reconsidered, 1933–1938* (Cambridge, 1985); the collection edited by Getty and Roberta T. Manning, *Stalinist Terror: New Perspectives* (New York, 1993); Robert W. Thurston, *Life and Terror in Stalin's Russia, 1934–1941* (New Haven, Conn., and London, 1996); and Gabor Tamas Rittersporn, *Stalinist Simplifications and Soviet Complications: Social Tensions and Political Conflicts in the USSR, 1933–1953* (Chur, Switzerland, 1991). A Soviet discussion of the show trials and their star performer can be found in Arkady Vaksberg, *Stalin's Prosecutor: The Life of Andrei Vyshinsky* (New York, 1990). On the Red Army in the 1930s, see John Erickson, *The Soviet High Command, 1918–1941* (New York, 1962). For a post-Soviet discussion, see Oleg V. Khlevniuk, *In Stalin's Shadow: The Career of Sergo Ordzhonikidze* (Armonk, N.Y., 1995).

Memoirs of the period include Joseph E. Davies, *Mission to Moscow* (New York, 1941); Alexander Barmine, *One Who Survived* (New York, 1945); Arvo Tuominen, *The Bells of the Kremlin: An Experience in Communism* (New York, 1983); and the stunning accounts of the experience of Eugenia Semyonovna Ginzburg, *Journey into the Whirlwind* (New York, 1967) and *Within the Whirlwind* (New York, 1981). A collection of memories of the Stalin years can be found in Adam Hochschild, *The Unquiet Ghost: Russians Remember Stalin* (New York, 1994). And a book in a class of its own is the collection of interviews over many years with Stalin's right-hand man, *Molotov Remembers: Inside Kremlin Politics, Conversations with Felix Chuev* (Chicago, 1993).

The classic statement of the "Great Retreat" thesis is Nicholas S. Timasheff, *The Great Retreat: The Growth and Decline of Communism in Russia* (New York, 1946). On the clash of views on Stalin, see Giuseppe Boffa, *The Stalin Phenomenon*, trans. Nicholas Fersen (Ithaca, N.Y., 1992).

CHAPTER 12
Culture and Society in the Socialist Motherland

"Art has always been free of life," wrote the iconoclastic Soviet literary theorist Viktor Shklovskii, "and its colors never reflected the colors of the flag waving over the city." The attempt beginning in the 1930s to dictate to artists and writers the form as well as the content of what they could create came up against another of Shklovskii's warnings about the relationship of art to politics: "You cannot control the unknown." In a real sense artists in the very nature of their activity "speak back to power," and writers are, as the dissident novelist Aleksandr Solzhenitsyn said, "a second government." As Stalinism extended the state's power over all aspects of public and social life, the Soviet leadership no longer was willing to tolerate the autonomy of art and culture that it had allowed in the 1920s. Artists were to be mobilized as "engineers of the soul," in Stalin's words, to become one more tool in the construction of socialism. Instead of revealing the contradictory realities of life, art was to educate in a particular direction; instead of subverting conventions and assumptions, literature was to support the Soviet status quo and indoctrinate the population in the ever narrowing ideology of the victorious Stalinists. Yet even as orthodoxy and conformity became the mark of loyalty, intellectuals and politicians struggled to define the content of what was "socialist" and acceptable.

Socialist Realism

In the years of the Cultural Revolution (1928–31), the leftist "proletarian" writers, musicians, and artists briefly realized their long-held ambitions to become the arbitrators of the Soviet cultural world. The regime initiated a cultural class war against "fellow-travelers" and "bourgeois intellectuals," which derided traditionalism and classicism of all kinds yet was highly ambivalent about experimentation and new forms. "The proletarianists," writes cultural historian Richard Stites, "assaulted science fiction, detective stories, fairy tales, folk music, jazz, urban song, and escape movies as the effusion of decadent intellectuals produced for the unhealthy appetites of degenerate businessmen and allowed to flourish in dark and noisome corners of the NEP." In music, for example, the Russian Association of Proletarian Musicians (RAPM) condemned the modernism of Western contemporary music as well as "light music" such as jazz, gypsy songs, music hall, and even the fox-trot. The radicals called for the banning of the saxophone (which would actually be banned at the end of the 1940s!) and rejected the operas of Tchaikovsky—*Evgenii Onegin* and *The Queen of Spades*—as well as *The Nose* (based on Gogol's short story), the first opera by the budding Soviet composer Dmitrii Shostakovich. RAPM proposed that musicians create mass marching songs, like Aleksandr Davidenko's "They Wanted to Beat, to Beat Us," which was played incessantly on the radio.

Proletarian writers used their pens to expose corruption and vice, to portray complacency or disillusionment among Communists, and to attack bureaucracy. Still committed to a literature that reflected the world as it was as well as the internal psychological conflicts of individuals, the newly empowered Russian Association of Proletarian Writers (RAPP) was nevertheless dogmatic and doctrinaire. RAPP opposed the "varnishing of reality" and called "for the removal of any and all masks." But in the First Five-Year Plan the party decided that all artists were to be mobilized to assist in the project of socialist construction. Official policy called for the creation of "positive socialist heroes" that could be emulated by simple people.

In April 1932 the party dissolved RAPP, RAPM, and the other proletarian artistic associations and organized all whom it regarded officially as artists, whether they were Marxists or fellow-travelers, into single unions, one for each branch of the arts. In the summer of 1932 Maxim Gorky, who had made his peace with the Soviet state and returned permanently to Moscow a year later, chaired a committee to form the new writers' union, which would become the model for the other creative unions. In October Stalin himself met with leading writers in Gorky's Moscow apartment and listened inscrutably to the debate on how Soviet art should be conceived. When he finally intervened, his conclusion was decisive: "If the artist is going to depict our life correctly, he cannot fail to observe and point out what is leading it toward socialism. So this will be socialist art. It will be socialist realism."

The new Union of Soviet Writers, chaired by Gorky, began operations in 1934 as an umbrella organization that was at one and the same time the principal police agency in literature and the major dispenser of rewards for loyal writers. In August Andrei Zhdanov, a rising young favorite of Stalin's, opened the First Congress of Soviet Writers and proclaimed that Soviet literature was "saturated with enthusiasm and heroism. . . . It is fundamentally optimistic, because it is the literature of the rising class of the proletariat, the only progressive and advanced class." He went on to define the official literary doctrine of Socialist Realism, now the only permissible style in which to write. Life was to be depicted

> in its revolutionary development. In doing so, truthfulness and historical concreteness of artistic depiction must be combined with the task of ideological remolding and re-education of the toiling people in the spirit of socialism. . . . Our literature . . . must not shun romanticism, but it must be a romanticism of a new type, revolutionary romanticism.

Socialist Realism demanded that an author depict reality in a realistic way but that the depiction anticipate the socialist future. Thus, the doctrine contained elements of both literary realism and romanticism while it eschewed experimentation with form. The party rejected the complex and experimental avant-garde styles of the first three decades of the century, for they were not easily apprehended by ordinary people. Karl Radek spoke at the congress against those exemplars of "bourgeois formalism" Marcel Proust and James Joyce. Joyce's methods, he said, were able only to describe insignificant people and emotions and "would prove utterly bankrupt the moment the author were to approach the great events of the class struggle." Art was now a mode of pedagogy, the source of models for inspiration and imitation, and the producer of revolutionary myths by which the past, present, and future might be understood. Collectivism was emphasized over disruptive and egotistic individualism. Writers and artists were to promote self-abnegation in the interest of the collective cause and to eliminate personal erotic or hedonistic experience. As an example of the new form, the authorities circulated to all congress delegates a book edited by Gorky that purported to show how convicts working on the White Sea canal were regenerated through labor.

Although the formulation of an official artistic creed set limits on creative expression, those limits were broader than the ones laid down by the militants of the proletarianist movement. The turn away from the Cultural Revolution loosened the strictures on social and cultural life, at least for a few years. Stalin himself proclaimed in 1935, "Life has become better, life has become more joyful." For three or four years, roughly 1932 to 1936, there was a brief effervescence of a pluralistic popular culture and just plain fun. For those years jazz again flourished in the USSR, with bands touring the country and people dancing the tango. Though the regime reined in the more excessive expressions of fun and joy in 1936, it sanctioned a new amalgam of official socialist culture and popular tastes that was neither as rigid and purposeful as revolutionary militants wanted nor as free and spontaneous as the popular culture of the NEP period had been. The new Soviet culture, writes historian Richard Stites, "promoted optimism over self-pity, exuberance over introspection, comradely devotion over sex, directed satire over open-ended comedy, and systematic formula over experiment." The hybrid culture actually "gave the public part of what it wanted: 'realism,' adventure, and moral guidance," a simple, readable prose, and an accessible, representational art. Stalinist art contained both the socialist message as defined by the regime and traditional forms that appealed to the public. In the theater, for example, critics attacked the challenging and disturbing productions of the avant-garde stage director Vsevolod Meyerhold and praised the realist work of Konstantin Stanislavskii of the Moscow Art Theater, which became the officially approved style for theater. Directors and authors employed stereotypes and folkloric genres to reach the broader public. Comedies became prevalent on the stage, as official values met popular tastes.

The larger-than-life heroes of such works as Nikolai Ostrovsky's novel *How the Steel Was Tempered* (1932–34) or the film *Chapaev* (1934) were models for young Soviet people to emulate. They lived in a world of daring adventures, dangers, and triumphs with the guiding presence of dedicated party members

to show the proper path. More tortured was the hero of one of the most popular novels of the time that began to appear in 1928, *Silent Don* (or *Quiet Flows
the Don*), by the Cossack writer Mikhail Sholokhov. But here too Soviet power
is victorious and resistance is futile. During the collectivization campaign
Sholokhov interrupted the writing of his multivolume masterpiece to accept a
party assignment to write the quintessential novel of the agrarian revolution.
In 1931 the first part of his *Virgin Soil Upturned* appeared, but critics generally
agreed that it did not match his earlier and later epic treatment of the civil war
in the Cossack lands. History was also mobilized for the Soviet cause. The novelist Aleksei Tolstoi published a mammoth work on *Peter the Great* (1929–40)
that depicted the modernizing tsar as a powerful leader who launched an earlier revolution from above. All these works combined realism of portrayal with
the romanticism of an anticipated future.

One of the most severe attacks on modernist art came in January 1936, after Stalin and Molotov attended a performance at the Bolshoi Theater of
Shostakovich's second (and, as it turned out, last) opera, *Lady Macbeth of
Mtsensk* (or *Katerina Izmailova*). Two days later a brutal editorial in *Pravda* denounced the opera as primitive, vulgar, and crudely naturalistic. "The music
shouts, quacks, explodes, pants and sighs, so as to convey the love scenes in
the most naturalistic manner." Echoing some of the earlier attacks on modernism of the Cultural Revolution, the editorial said the opera was too influenced by Western musical experiments. Shostakovich was accused of the "most
negative traits of 'Meyerholdism,' multiplied to the nth degree." Within days
works by Shostakovich were removed from the repertoire, and Stalin's earlier
call for "Soviet classics" reverberated throughout the artistic world. Composers
were to return melodically to the great Russian composers of the nineteenth
century (Tchaikovsky, Borodin, Mussorgsky, and Rimsky-Korsakov); no experimentation or twelve-tone scales, but back to Beethoven and the European
Romantics. Music was to be life-affirming, positive, inspirational, just as Gorky
had proclaimed literature should be.

Shostakovich recovered from the blows he received in 1936 to become a
prominent author of film scores and turn more intensively to symphonic works,
but he lived with the ever present fear that he might again tread over the boundary of the permissible. The warnings about opera had a palpable effect within
and beyond the musical world. Soviet music was tamed; it became more
melodic, folkloric, often heroic, and popular. Light music was revived, particularly in films, on the radio, and in music halls, and jazz thrived in the years
up to the war. When the great composer Sergei Prokofiev decided to return to
the Soviet Union in 1933, he quickly discovered that he had to adjust to the
new, more popular style of composition. His less accessible works of the 1920s
found little favor with Soviet audiences and critics, while his opera *The Love
for Three Oranges* (1927) was quite popular, as was *Lieutenant Kije* (1934), the
ballet *Romeo and Juliet* (1935–36), and the musical tale *Peter and the Wolf* (1936).
He understood, as he put it, that "music in our country has become the heritage of vast masses of people. Their artistic taste and demands are growing
with amazing speed. And this is something the Soviet composer must take into
account in each new work."

Stalinist cultural policy reintegrated the classical Russian literary canon of the nineteenth century into the school curriculum, from the great poet Aleksandr Pushkin to Nikolai Gogol, Ivan Turgenev, Lev Tolstoy, and Anton Chekhov. The pessimistic, conservative Fedor Dostoevsky, who did not fit well into the new narrative of a progressive Russian intelligentsia as the precursor of the Bolsheviks, was given a less prominent place. The classics were sacred, no longer to be questioned. The Soviet regime simply appropriated them as the proper heritage of the new socialist society by rechristening many traditional authors as "revolutionary democrats." In 1937, with the Great Purges raging, the whole country was host to an enormous commemoration of the one-hundredth anniversary of Pushkin's death in a duel. Translated into dozens of Soviet languages, Pushkin's works represented the best in Russian culture, which now was officially to become the cultural legacy of all Soviet peoples. Through the dead poet and the other greats of the nineteenth century, the Soviet cultural establishment imposed Russian cultural dominance over the "lesser" artists of the non-Russians.

At the same time, however, the national republics also canonized certain writers and artists and relegated others to oblivion. Those now accepted by the regime and introduced into the school curricula were not always the most revolutionary or progressive, particularly since many opponents of tsarism had ended up in the anti-Bolshevik camp. In Georgia, for example, writers associated with the Menshevik Party, which had dominated Georgian politics for a quarter century before the Soviet invasion, were anathema, while more conservative nationalist writers, such as the poets Ilia Chavchavadze and Akaki Tsereteli, were honored—once their more offensive writings had been censored. In Armenia the godfather of Armenian music was the priest and ethnomusicologist Gomidas, who had been largely apolitical and died in a mental asylum in France, and the most important poets were Hovannes Tumanian and Avetis Isahakian, both of whom had made their peace with the Soviet regime; but the group of writers from the diaspora, particularly those associated with the nationalist party, the Dashnaktsutiun, which had ruled independent Armenia, were written out of Armenian literature as taught in the schools of Stalinism.

Among those promoted by officialdom were the "enlightened" non-Russian writers and artists who had been associated with Russian "revolutionary democrats." If a Caucasian or Central Asian writer had met Pushkin or corresponded with the radical intellectual Chernyshevskii or expressed sympathy for Russia, he or she was likely to be admitted to the ranks of those favored by the regime. This process of admitting non-Russian writers into the canon continued into the 1940s and 1950s as Kazakhs, like Abai Kunanbaev, Kyrgyz folk poets, like Togolok Moldo, Azerbaijani playwrights, like Mirza Fatali Akhundov, and early Armenian novelists, like Khachatur Abovian, were adopted as unwitting forerunners of Bolshevism.

Stalinist art was traditional and conservative in many ways. The new official canon of acceptable literary and artistic works was, in the words of literary historian Katerina Clark, "the official repository of state myths." As a popular, didactic form of art, Socialist Realism rejected artists who ventured toward experimentation in form and condemned them as "formalists," a devastating accusation always available in the arsenal of critics and politicians who wanted to warn against Western influences. Art during Stalin's time, and Soviet art for years after Stalin's death, was also extremely puritanical and sexually repressive. The denunciation of modernist art as "decadent," "coarse," and "depraved" suggests the association of avant-gardism with deviant sexuality. On October 17, 1935, a law was passed that punished pornography in art or literature with a five-year prison sentence.

At the same time Stalinist art was deliberately provincializing and nationalist. Stalinism attempted to establish a unified Soviet people, multiethnic to be sure, but one with its own lingua franca, selected traditions and myths, and literary school. Folklore was elevated to a concert art form with the dance ensemble of Igor Moiseev, the balalaika orchestra of Nikolai Osipov, and the chorus founded by Mitrofan Piatnitskii. The use of balalaikas instead of saxophones was part of state policy. Stalinist culture established what was acceptable or possible, but within that permissible range art could provide emotional and aesthetic pleasure, bring people to tears or laughter, and make them feel good about the lives they lived. What it could not do is what many avant-garde artists saw as their primary mission: subvert unquestioned assumptions and render the familiar unfamiliar, question common sense and undermine the commonplace, make uncomfortable the complacent and destabilize the normal.

Going to the Movies with Stalin

The 1930s saw the emergence of the first mass media and communications in the Soviet Union. Radios became more widespread, and though most of the programming was music (96 percent in 1928 but declining through the next decade), dramas, news, and children's programs linked Moscow with the provinces and the state to invisible listeners. Film as well became a mass art form in the 1930s. From 1933 to 1940, 308 Soviet films were distributed, and tickets sales tripled betweem 1928 and the war, reaching 9 million in 1940. The number of cinemas grew from just over 7,000 to more than 29,000, with 17,000 of them in the countryside. Though Soviet people were reading more in more languages year by year, film remained the art form that reached into the most distant corners of the Soviet Union and had the greatest impact. Film and other media, like the national newspapers, such as *Pravda* ("Truth," the party paper) and *Izvestiia* ("News," the government paper), connected diverse and scattered peoples into a single "national" community.

Soviet film art had a worldwide reputation at the beginning of the decade for being revolutionary both in form and content, but with the Cultural Revolution and the later turn toward Socialist Realism, Soviet film was forced to become a more popular and conventional medium, one that could supply movies for the millions. The experiments of the 1920s with montage, filming outdoors, and using nonprofessional actors quickly gave way to more conventional narrative forms of storytelling and studio productions with professional actors. The state bureaucracy more directly dominated filmmaking starting in 1930 and enforced strict rules governing both form and content.

The film community quickly adjusted to the new order, and Soviet films of the thirties ranged from masterpieces of Socialist Realism to light comedies that delighted audiences. One of the first successful sound films in the USSR was Nikolai Ekk's *Road to Life* (1931), a story of homeless boys who come under the tutelage of a wise but firm educator. This Soviet precursor to the American film *Boys Town* (1939) was based on the pedagogical work of Anton Makarenko, who despite critical attacks on his work and on the film eventually became the most authoritative writer on education in the Soviet Union. A more conventional film, and one that in effect launched the Stalin school of filmmaking, was F. M. Ermler and S. Yutkevich's *Counterplan* (1932), the quintessential film on industrialization. Scored by Shostakovich, the film, like many other films (and novels) of the period, was about coming of age or gaining of consciousness, in this case by a pair of workers, aided by a party secretary.

The major success of the early Stalinist cinema was the film about the civil war hero *Chapaev* (1934) by the brothers Sergei and Giorgii Vasilev. A great box-office hit, the film is realistic in style but romantic in theme. A simple partisan leader of great integrity and courage, Chapaev learns to use his talents and control his impulses thanks to a wise, cool-headed political commissar. The simplicity and humanism of the film give it an emotional power. At the end of the film Chapaev is killed, but as historian Peter Kenez notes, "A socialist realist film . . . is by definition optimistic. It ends in a major key as Chapaev's death is avenged by the victory of the Red forces. The hero might die, but the cause is invincible." With *Chapaev* the Soviets had essentially made a successful Hollywood film, and the remarks by the leading experimentalists of the 1920s are not without irony. Eisenstein announced that *"Chapaev* is the answer to the very deep solving of party problems in art." Dovzhenko predicted that *"Chapaev* is tied up with the future of the cinema." But forty years after the film, and fifty after the memoir by D. A. Furmanov on which it was based, the heroic Chapaev was forgotten, and the simple peasant became the butt of a whole series of irreverent jokes.

The most inventive of the early Soviet filmmakers, Sergei Eisenshtein, found it difficult in the 1930s to receive approval for his own work, and his production of *Bezhin Meadow* (1935) fell afoul of the censors and was never completed. The story of the film was loosely based on the actual murder of a peasant boy, Pavlik Morozov, by his relatives for denouncing his father as a kulak to the authorities. Party propagandists had transformed Pavlik posthumously into a hero for young people, and such a subject might have seemed safe for filmic treatment. But critics considered Eisenshtein's approach to the drama of collectivization too personal and denounced him for "formalism" and not showing "passionate hatred for the class enemy" and "genuine love for those who build the *kolkhozy*." The great director was forced to capitulate to his critics and renounce the film. Abjectly (but not without irony), he wrote that he had been mistaken to think that his talent gave him the right to be original, "to give my own special, as if it were independent, views of the world, instead of carefully studying the statements of the party and expressing them. I thought I had the right, but it turned out that I did not."

Though the stories within the films might be about resistance or revolution, the films of the 1930s worked to create support for the status quo, never to question it. Instead of the revolutionary documentaries of Dziga Vertov, which had stunned cinemaphiles in the West in the 1920s, musicals, comedies, and dramas based on plays and novels became the staple of the Soviet film industry in the 1930s. Sixty-one films were made about the revolution and the civil war. Many were operatic in style, with Lenin and Stalin at center stage, grand in gesture but petty in conception. The most popular films were the musical comedies directed by Grigorii Aleksandrov—*Joyful Guys* (1934), *Circus* (1936), *Volga, Volga* (1938), and *Radiant Road* (1940)—which starred his wife, Liubov Orlova, and were scored by the popular composer Isak Dunaevskii. Historical epics, like V. Petrov's *Peter I* (1937–38) and Pudovkin's *Minin and Pozharskii* (1939) and *Suvorov* (1941), glorified the Russian past as the USSR geared itself for war. The most extraordinary patriotic film, *Alexander Nevsky* (1938), marked Eisenshtein's return to the forefront of Soviet cinema. Scored by Prokofiev, the film told the story of the epic struggle between the medieval Russians and the Teutonic knights. In the climatic battle on the ice earthy, hearty Russians, led by Prince Alexander, defeat the arrogant Germans, and the film ends with a warning against all who would dare to invade the Russian land. Russian nationalism was blended smoothly into Soviet patriotism, and at the same time the multinational unity of the Soviet motherland (*rodina*) was underlined in films from the national republics. Films like *Karo* (Armenia, 1937), *Shchors* (Ukraine, 1939), *Bogdan Khmelnitskii* (Ukraine, 1941), *Georgi Saakadze* (Georgia, 1942), and *Arshin-Mal-Alan* (Azerbaijan, 1943) were examples of "official nationalism," the permitted expression of ethnic pride that was never allowed to extend to chauvinistic hostility to other nationalities, Russophobia, or political separatism.

Disciplining the Intelligentsia

The Soviet intelligentsia as a single social and cultural category came into being in the 1930s. Distinctions between "bourgeois intellectuals" and "Red specialists" disappeared, as a common elite with its own functions and privileges was created. Though outbursts of state-initiated attacks on elites would still occur, as in the Great Purges, Stalinism sanctioned the existence of an elite with privileges that it had properly earned through hard work and achievement. The Soviet intelligentsia, which included those in political power, was conceived in the official view as a classless social group that coexisted with (and was clearly above) the two great nonantagonistic classes of Soviet society, the working class and the collectivized peasantry. The former emphasis in official rhetoric and practice on class struggle and conflict that had marked the years of the Cultural Revolution was gradually replaced by a more conciliatory, homogenizing view of all members of society as part of a unified Soviet enterprise. New men and women of humble origins could rise to power, influence, and material comfort in the Stalinist social order without embarrassment about their new status.

The intelligentsia in the Soviet Union had always been a reluctant partner of the state. Though most of them had been hostile to the Bolshevik Revolution, intellectuals enjoyed a degree of freedom during the NEP years. But already under Lenin there was a call from the party to interpret the word in Marxist terms, to establish the primacy of Marxism in theory and science. Lively debates ensued in the 1920s, until Stalin called a halt to the discussions and decreed the orthodox position in each field. With the Stalin revolution in intellectual life politicians began to intervene in all fields of learning in the name of Marxism-Leninism. Politics and practical results were the criteria by which science and scholarship, as well as art, could be judged. Stalin claimed that theory was to guide practice but that practice would decide the truth of theory. The problem was that Marxism, however construed, did not have simple answers or clear principles that could be applied to all fields of knowledge. In each branch of science, therefore, leading scientists and politicians fought over what was properly and practically Marxist-Leninist. Vicious infighting divided those in genetics, biology, and other scientific disciplines. The ultimate arbiter was Stalin or his satraps.

The costs of resistance or opposition were enormous, and the Great Terror took its toll on writers, artists, and scientists. In the late 1930s party-appointed hacks who had been placed in charge of the artists' unions attacked their colleagues as Trotskyites or "wreckers," thus casually condemning many to prison or death. It was quite arbitrary who might fall victim and who might be spared. Among those who perished were the short-story writer Isaak Babel, the author of *Red Cavalry*; the Georgian poets Paolo Iashvili and Tsitian Tabidze; the Armenian poet Eghishe Charents and his countryman writer Aksel Bakunts; the leader of the proletarianist writers' organization RAPP, Leopold Averbakh; and thousands of others. The writer Boris Pilniak, who had told a friend that "there isn't a single thinking adult in this country who hasn't thought he might be shot," was arrested in 1937 and shot sometime later. The experimental stage director Vsevolod Meyerhold, who had fallen out of favor for his avant-garde stagings, tried to redeem himself by a new production of his greatest success, Lermontov's *Masquerade*. But the authorities closed his theater in 1938. After exclaiming, "In hunting down formalism, you have eliminated art!" he was arrested. In February 1940 he was shot. A few days later his wife was brutally murdered in her apartment.

The poet Osip Mandelshtam had written a poem against Stalin in 1933 and was briefly arrested. Four years later he wrote an ode to Stalin, but it failed to save his life. Mandelstam died for having written these earlier words:

> We live, deaf to the land beneath us,
> Ten steps away no one hears our speeches,
> But where there's so much as half a conversation
> The Kremlin's mountaineer will get his mention.
> His fingers are fat as grubs
> And the words, final as lead weights, fall from his lips,
> His cockroach whiskers leer
> And his boot tops gleam.
> Around him a rabble of thin-necked leaders—
> fawning half-men for him to play with.
> They whinny, purr or whine

As he prates and points a finger,
One by one forging his laws, to be flung
Like horsehoes at the head, the eye or the groin.
And every killing is a treat
For the broad-chested Ossete.

The rewards of conformity and service to the Soviet cause brought the vast majority of intellectuals and educated people into line with the aims of the leadership. While thousands perished in the prison camps of the GULag, once the bloodletting slowed down in 1938–39, those who had survived became part of the privileged elite of a great country, and though their tenure was never completely secure, they were among the principal beneficiaries of the Stalinist system.

Women and the Family

Nowhere is the sense of a great retreat (or great reversal) clearer in the Soviet experience than in the shift in policies toward women and the family. The revolution had aimed at the full emancipation of women, that is, their liberation from the drudgery of housework and their full equality with men in society. Lenin had declared:

Petty housework crushes, strangles, stultifies and degrades [the woman], chains her to the kitchen and to the nursery, and wastes her labor on barbarously unproductive, petty, nerve-racking, stultifying and crushing drudgery.

Though many advances were made in women's rights in the 1920s, the general poverty of the country, the high unemployment among women, and the millions of homeless children precluded the full implementation of a policy of socializing housework and childraising. As divorce and abortion became easier to obtain and the number of failed marriages increased, critics of the radical program of the Bolsheviks, which had been put into law in the 1918 and 1926 family codes, became more numerous. Peasant men and women tended to be resistant to the emancipatory aims of the feminist Communists, and they made it clear that they wanted limits on divorce, enforcement of alimony responsibility, and an end to the flagrant male promiscuity. The signal that a major change in policy was about to occur came when Zhenotdel, the woman's department of the party, was closed down in 1930. Separate women's sections attached to party committees lasted for four more years until the party leaders abolished them as well.

The Stalinist regime desperately needed labor for its industrial revolution, and its policy toward women was aimed at bringing them into the workforce. Women's labor was no longer primarily seen as liberating but as a duty to socialist society. Women would henceforth carry the infamous double burden of work inside and outside the home. During the drive to industrialize, from 1929 to 1941, more than 10 million women entered the wage-labor force, and the percentage of women at work rose from 24 percent to 39 percent of the total number of waged workers. Women particularly dominated light industry, where they eventually made up two-thirds of the workforce, but Soviet women were also increasingly found in occupations formerly closed to them, such as construction, lumbering, electronics, and machine-building. Though prejudices remained that heavy lifting or skilled labor was not appropriate for women, over time women gained many jobs designated earlier as men's work.

From a program of socializing household work and loosening the ties of the family, Soviet family policy after 1931 put new emphasis on maintaining and strengthening the traditional family unit. In order to recruit women with children into the labor force, the state embarked on a more vigorous effort to build daycare centers and nurseries. Whereas the number of nursery places per thousand women had declined in the 1920s, it doubled from late 1928 to 1930, as did places in preschools. And childcare facilities continued to expand during the Second Five-Year Plan, though they remained woefully inadequate and of poor quality. The state insisted that the family be made more clearly responsible for the child and liable to fines for its children's criminal activity. The regime adopted a harder, more conservative attitude toward juvenile crime, which was increasingly seen as stemming, not from material hardship, but from family breakdown. Often working women would be blamed for their children's deviance. In the same year (1935) that Stalin, in an act of public filial piety, visited his aged mother in Tbilisi, a harsh law ruled that children over twelve years old would be tried by the courts as adults.

New rules were passed in 1935 discouraging divorce, and the following year a new family law code encouraged women to have as many children as possible. The law prohibited all abortions, except those in which the mother's life was threatened, and guaranteed pregnant women job security and lighter work. The state increased monthly nursing allowances and other subsidies and extended maternity leaves up to sixteen weeks for all female workers. Since contraception was hardly available and abortion banned, women were compelled to carry all pregnancies to term. Stalin's pronatalism stemmed, not from the original Bolshevik program of female liberation, but from his own agenda of industrialization and defense:

> We need men. Abortion which destroys life is not acceptable in our country. The Soviet woman has the same rights as the man, but that does not free her from a great and honorable duty which nature has given her: She is a mother, she gives life. And this is certainly not a private affair but one of great social importance.

The burden imposed on women was heaviest on working-class and peasant women. Women of the working class were encouraged to become socially productive by entering the workforce, just as they had been in the 1920s. Peasant women were supposed to increase output and strive to become model producers, like the famous tractor driver Praskovia Angelina. Yet at the same time, more-privileged women, like the wives of factory managers or engineers, were

not necessarily to enter the workforce but rather to be helpmates for their husbands. The Soviet elite were the primary recipients of the Stalinist version of
cultured life, which emphasized domesticity and propriety. Being cultured took
on a new meaning in the 1930s. It meant the acquisition of a kind of middle-
class lifestyle and materialist values. People whose parents had been peasants
and workers now strove to send their children to the more prestigious schools
and institutes, to teach them the violin or piano, and even, in the best bourgeois tradition, to do "social work." Wives of Soviet executives and professionals had their own journal, *The Socially Active Woman*, which suggested ways
to bring culture to their husbands' work place. The state encouraged industrialists' wives to hang curtains in workers' quarters, demonstrate hygienic practices, and organize drama and study groups. In a subtle way class distinctions
not only remained but were reinforced, and women remained divided along
social lines. With no permissible forms of female organization or expression
outside the most circumscribed and prescribed official channels, women had
no means to act collectively or develop a politicized gender consciousness.

Mind, Body, and Soul

One of the long-lasting achievements of the Stalin revolution was the expansion of mass popular education and the achievement of mass literacy. In 1930
the government decreed that all children ages eight to eleven were to be enrolled in schools by the end of summer. The number of pupils increased from
14 million in 1929 to over 20 million in 1931, with the bulk of the increase (90
percent) occurring in rural schools. Education was the means by which the
Communists could realize their goals of overcoming religion and superstition
and the resistance of traditional practices and patriarchal authorities. Schools
were made coeducational after the revolution, and special effort had to be made
to teach women to read. Fourteen million of the 17 million illiterate adults in
Russia in 1917 were women. By 1939, 83.4 percent of all women in Russia could
read.

In the late summer of 1931 the Central Committee repudiated progressive
educational experiments and the idea, promoted during the Cultural Revolution, of the eventual "withering away of the school." The eighth, ninth, and
tenth grades, which had been eliminated at the end of the 1920s, were reinstated in August 1932. What became the Soviet orthodoxy on education was
laid out in the work of Anton Makarenko (1888–1939), particularly in his au-
tobiographical text *Pedagogical Poem* (1933–35). Incensed by the experimental-
ism of the Cultural Revolution, which had opposed punishment of pupils and
promoted individual creative impulses of children, Makarenko stressed instead
developing a "strong, enthusiastic, if necessary a stern collective" to which individuals would have a sense of duty.

The party increased the powers of teachers, instituted new hierarchies and
stability in schools, and emphasized once again traditional subjects and pedagogy. Authorities gave students more instructional hours in mathematics and
science and reemphasized grammar. On February 12, 1933, it was decided that

Narkompros had to approve school textbooks and that each subject was to have a mandatory textbook. A few months later, on May 16, 1933, the state reintroduced traditional school structures, abandoning the experimental educational practices of the 1920s. At about the same time, the authorities criticized the teaching of geography as too schematic and restored the history faculties in Moscow and Leningrad universities (which had been abolished in favor of social studies). In September 1935 they standardized class schedules, examination procedures, and promotions, restored the traditional grading systems (1–5, with 5 the highest grade), and reintroduced school uniforms. School directors became the virtual bosses of their schools, and the basic means of instruction was through lectures by teachers. Teaching had great prestige in the 1930s, and instructors received relatively high salaries and the highest level of rations along with managers, engineers, and factory workers. Though teachers' material conditions remained at a low level and conditions of work were poor, the number of men entering teaching rose sharply. The recruitment programs that had favored workers in 1928–31 had increased the percentage of students from the working class in technical schools to 65 percent by 1933–34, but in the following years that percentage steadily declined until it reached 44 percent at the end of the decade. More and more Soviet schools began to look like tsarist *gimnaziia* (classical high schools), and in 1943 coeducation was abolished and males and females attended separate schools. Corporal punishment, however, was not reintroduced.

Schools in the non-Russian regions were the battlegrounds on which the struggle against backward aspects of ethnic cultures could be combated and the new Stalinist culture of "national in form, socialist in content" could be propagated. Non-Russians particularly distrusted women teachers. In some cases, as in the Tatar autonomous republic, local people saw the teachers, who were largely Russian, as foreign agents of the Soviet state and resisted their teaching. Parents took matters in their own hands and killed hundreds of teachers during the first years of the First Five-Year Plan. Nevertheless, instruction was carried out in seventy different languages, and the government worked hard to recruit non-Russian teachers. In Armenia, Belorussia, Georgia, and Ukraine, more than 70 percent of the teachers were natives, though in the Muslim republics of Azerbaijan and Central Asia, 40 percent or more were Russians.

Education and ideology were the areas where the Great Retreat from radicalism toward tradition was most evident. In 1931 Stalin himself intervened in the debates among historians in a pointed letter to the journal *Proletarian Revolution* admonishing a historian for being critical of Lenin and demanding a new level of conformity among historians. History-writing was too important a weapon in the arsenal of culture and ideology to be left outside party control. But the most ferocious attack came a little later when party leaders, including Stalin himself, came out against the strict class interpretation of Russian history by the Old Bolshevik historian Mikhail Pokrovskii (1868–1932), which then dominated Soviet historiography.

As head of the Society of Marxist Historians, Pokrovskii spent much of his career in battle against the prerevolutionary "statist school" of historians, which emphasized the role of tsarist absolutism in shaping the Russian past. Instead he proposed using the methodology of class analysis to show that the tsarist state had in fact been the representative of the landed aristocracy and the capitalist bourgeoisie. During the years of the Cultural Revolution, Pokrovskii's Marxist historians attempted to sweep the last "bourgeois" historians from the field, rejecting any idea of patriotism or nationalism, and in so doing antagonizing not only some of the most distinguished scholars of the old school but also several within the Marxist establishment.

The attacks on Pokrovskii (without mentioning his name) began in the years before his death in 1932, and they grew into a major campaign by 1936. The principal problem with his work was that it left little room for national pride in the achievements of prerevolutionary Russia. Soviet leaders and pedagogues were looking for reliable textbooks that would tell the story of a great country and its leaders. Stalin himself became personally involved in the rewriting of history. In March 1934 the Politburo discussed the inadequacies of history instruction in the schools, and commissions were created to write new standardized textbooks for different grades by June 1935. The general secretary read the drafts of the textbooks and pronounced them failures. Incensed by the characterization of Minin and Pozharskii, the seventeenth-century leaders of the uprising to oust foreign rulers from Muscovy, as counterrevolutionary, he wrote in the margins of one Pokrovskii-inspired textbook, "What do you mean, the Poles and Swedes were revolutionaries? Ha, ha! Idiocy!" He edited *The History of the Civil War in the USSR* in early 1935. And he personally inserted the first open criticisms of Pokrovskii in an official Central Committee report in January 1936, in which "the well-known errors of Pokrovskii" were characterized as "anti-Marxist, anti-Leninist, essentially liquidationist, [and] anti-scientific." He approved the team-produced text that became the standard history of the USSR for the next twenty years, the *Short Course in the History of the Soviet Union*. At a dinner at Voroshilov's on November 7, 1937, Stalin expressed his own views of history, which were reflected in the official high school textbook about to be published:

> The Russian tsars did a great deal that was bad. They plundered and enslaved the people. They waged wars and seized territories in the interest of the landowners. But they did do one good thing—they put together a vast state reaching as far as Kamchatka. We have inherited this state. And we Bolsheviks were the first to establish and consolidate this state as a unified, indivisible state, not in the interests of the landowners and capitalists but for the benefit of the working people.

He warned ominously that the unity of the Soviet state was indivisible:

> Anyone who attempts to destroy this unity of the socialist state, anyone who strives to remove a particular part or nationality from it, is an enemy, a damnable enemy of the state and the peoples of the USSR. And we will annihilate any such enemy—even if he is an Old Bolshevik—we will annihilate all his kind, all his family.

Stalin's dinner-table remarks coincided with the arrests and executions of most of the top Communist leaders of the national republics and regions who were condemned as "bourgeois nationalists" who, it was claimed, had separatist ambitions for the non-Russian peoples.

Each field of learning was disciplined to one degree or another in the 1930s. Authorities and orthodoxies were established in every branch of knowledge. The behaviorist school of Ivan Pavlov (1849–1936) was the officially approved methodology in psychology and physiology. Nikolai Marr (1864–1934), with his grandiose theories linking language to the economic base, was the authority in linguistics, and the infamous Timofei Lysenko (1898–1976), who proposed an erroneous theory of environmental influence on heredity, in genetics. Some sciences suffered more than others. Genetics was devastated, as the most prominent scientists, such as Nikolai Vavilov, who opposed Lysenko, ended up in the camps or were shot. Mathematics, on the other hand, remained a vital field of great achievement. Physics as well managed to produce seven Soviet physicists who later shared four Nobel Prizes for work done in the Stalin period. After intensive philosophical discussion in the 1920s, Soviet philosophers recognized in 1929 that relativity and quantum theory were "triumphs of dialectical materialist philosophy" only to find these theories condemned in 1936. The internationally renowned physicist Boris Hessen died in the purges. Others, however, fared better. Igor Tamm, then doing work that would later bring him and two colleagues the first Soviet Nobel Prize in physics, was denounced but not imprisoned. Lev Landau, another Nobel laureate, was imprisoned briefly in the 1930s. Petr Kapitsa, who had returned to Russia from England for a visit and was not allowed to go back, defended Landau but was not touched by the police. Several of these men were colleagues and friends of the leading Western physicists, including Niels Bohr, and would later play key roles in the development of Soviet nuclear weapons. Historian of Soviet science David Joravsky characterizes the period from the 1930s to the early 1950s as one in which "brilliant scientific achievement coexisted with scandalous political assault on higher learning."

Most people in the USSR were not touched directly by the quarrels, tensions, and persecutions that affected the intellectual and political elites. Their lives were lived in a rhythm of work and leisure, with more time at the former than the latter in the 1930s. Yet the authorities also set aside time and places for people's rest and recreation. Parks of culture were built throughout the country, the most important near the center of Moscow, and houses of culture were set up in urban districts and collective farm centers. Because so many holidays and celebrations, feasts and festivals had traditionally been associated with religion, the Soviets tried either to substitute their own rituals for the religious ones or to reinvent their meanings. Once the militant antireligious campaigns of the early 1930s came to an end, the government made some conciliatory gestures toward religious traditions. In 1935 the *elka* (New Year's Tree), which had been banned in 1928, was once again permitted. The Christmas holiday had been displaced to the turn of the year but the trappings included colored lights, the exchange of presents, festive feasting, and *Ded moroz* (Father Frost), who looked quite like Santa Claus. At Easter that year it was possible to buy the ingredients for the traditional cake and cheese (*kulich* and *paskha*) in state stores. Almost every month of the year was punctuated by notable days or holidays, substituting for the dozens of religious holidays. February 23 was Red Army Day, March 8 International Women's Day, and May Day was followed in the same month by Press Day and Borderguard Day. The most important holiday of the year, at least in the official Soviet calendar, was the anniversary of the October Revolution, celebrated on November 7 with a mammoth parade through Red Square. As thousands of soldiers in uniform, glowing young gymnasts, and representatives of the hundreds of Soviet peoples in national costumes marched past Lenin's mausoleum, on top of which stood the Soviet leaders with Stalin in the center, a perfect microcosm of the harmonious, unified, trouble-free Soviet Union was presented to an enthralled public. The sea of red flags and giant posters represented a radiant new world, at least for the moment.

Indestructible Union

The Soviet Union was the first state in history to be formed of political units based on nationality. In name it was a federation of sovereign states that had "voluntarily" combined to form a union of national republics. In fact the republics lost their real political sovereignty to the center in the first few years as members of the union, and all parts of the Soviet Union were governed by branches of a single all-union Communist party. Yet the constituent nationalities were given territorial identity, educational and cultural institutions in their own languages, and members of the non-Russian peoples were promoted into positions of power. National Communist leaders retained much local autonomy, at least until the mid-1930s, and could lobby for the interests of their republics before the central leaders.

Though Stalin considered Lenin too liberal in nationality policy and preferred a more centralized state, he carried out the policy of developing national regions and republics, ethnic cultures, and the use of local languages quite vigorously until the early 1930s. The radical, experimental policies of the 1920s and early 1930s favored the "rooting" of native peoples in their republics and national districts and promoted equality among peoples. Even quite small ethnic groups were given their own republics or autonomous districts. This elaborate territorialization of ethnicity, which in the 1920s often extended down to villages, actually promoted cultures and languages that had languished in the tsarist period.

Ironically a state that saw itself as internationalist and based its claim to power on its identification with a social class worked to harden the differences between nationalities and create the conditions for greater national consciousness. In general non-Russian Communist elites in the union republics and autonomies supported the nationalizing policy of the Soviet government, but occasionally the center's program went further than the population desired. Russians living in Ukraine or Belorussia were resistant to promotion of the Ukrainian or Belorussian language, but there were also instances when Belorussians, a people without strongly defined national consciousness, or

Ukrainians, many of whom were Russian-speakers, opposed being forced to become more ethnic. Of the number of potential identities that people might adopt—national, religious, regional, class, gender, or all-Soviet—the state actively promoted the national one for non-Russians.

Over the first decade of Soviet rule the percentage of non-Russian party members and officials increased in the non-Russian areas at the expense of Russians. In 1922, 72 percent of all Communists were Russians, with only fifteen thousand from the traditionally Muslim peoples. Five years later Russians made up only 65 percent of the whole party, while almost half the members of the party in national republics and regions (46.6 percent) were non-Russian natives. In Kazakhstan the Kazakh membership in the party rose from 8 percent in 1924 to 53 percent in 1933. In Ukraine the percent of Ukrainians in the party jumped from 24 percent in 1922 to 59 percent ten years later. The one nationality that did not develop ethnic national institutions and could not promote its national traditions forcefully in the 1920s was the Russians.

Soviet nationality policy was closely tied to foreign policy. The USSR was to be a model for a future world political order in which the rights of all nations would be respected. The party believed that fair treatment of non-Russians would be a magnet to attract Ukrainians, Armenians, and other peoples with diaspora populations beyond the Soviet Union to support their compatriots within the Union. In the case of Ukrainians and Belorussians, who lived on territory that had been part of the Russian Empire but now found themselves in Poland, or Rumanians in Bessarabia, which had been annexed by Rumania, Soviet policy sought to attract them back into the Union. In 1924 the USSR created a Moldavian Autonomous Soviet Socialist Republic as a prelude to the eventual joining of Bessarabia to the Soviet Union. That same year Moscow transferred a large territory with 2 million inhabitants from the Russian Federation to Belorussia, both to consolidate the Belorussian nation in its own republic and to serve as an example of the political generosity of Soviet nationality policy. Likewise, the government made a series of border adjustments between the Russian Republic and Ukraine, expanding Ukraine but ultimately leaving millions of Ukrainians in the RSFSR.

The years of the Cultural Revolution represented a continuation, and even an acceleration, of the nationality policies of the 1920s. The state enthusiastically promoted education in the non-Russian languages to bring the less developed peoples up to the level of the more developed. Whereas in 1925–26 only 30 percent of non-Russian school-age children were enrolled, in contrast to 62.5 percent of Russian children, by 1929, 70 percent of the non-Russian school-age children were in school. Ukraine had been at the forefront of the development of national culture in the 1920s. By 1927, 94 percent of Ukrainian pupils, as well as 66 percent of the Russian pupils in Ukraine, were taught in Ukrainian. The extension of Ukrainian language and culture to Russians in the republic was anathema to many Communist leaders, who saw it as a dangerous nationalist tendency. But the high levels of Ukrainian instruction continued into the 1930s, and in 1935–36, 83 percent of all school children in the republic were being taught in Ukrainian.

Soviet scholars created more than forty written languages for small Soviet peoples who had never had an alphabet and written language of their own, sixteen in 1932–33 alone. Some of these peoples had under a thousand members. To make the written word more accessible to ordinary people, and to cut the modern language off from its Islamic roots, a movement began to Latinize the languages of the Turkic and Persian peoples who used Arabic script. From 1925 to 1938 eighteen Turkic languages received a Latin alphabet, and the movement spread to non-Islamic peoples. All but a few alphabets (among them the ancient Armenian and Georgian scripts) were replaced by Latin. There was even talk in the early 1930s of changing the Cyrillic alphabet used by Russian to Latin.

In 1930–31 the state officially elevated the so-called small peoples of the north, the reindeer herders and hunters of northeastern Siberia, from tribes to "nations" and gave them designated territories of their own. To complete the process of nation-making Stalin-style, the government granted the Jews, who did not quite fit Stalin's definition of a nation because they did not inhabit a fixed territory, a "homeland" of their own in Birobijan, near the Chinese border. Few Soviet Jews, however, migrated out to this Soviet Zion, and in the 1920s and early 1930s many Jews availed themselves of the officially sanctioned revival of Yiddish schooling and culture. The state and Jewish Communist activists discouraged the use of Hebrew, a language identified with the religion of Judaism and political Zionism. As they moved out of the shtetl into towns and cities, many Jews lost their religious traditions and assimilated into the general Soviet Russian culture.

The radical phase of nationality policy came to an end in December 1932. In the ferocity of the campaign to collectivize the peasantry, the resistance of non-Russians in Ukraine, the North Caucasus, Kazakhstan, and Transcaucasia was notably greater than in the central Russian provinces. Massive rebellions broke out in western Ukraine and in the Ferghana Valley in Uzbekistan. Agents of Stalin traveled to the national areas and reported back that resistance to the agrarian revolution was linked with local nationalism. Tens of thousands of people were deported from their home villages, and tens of thousands of others were sent to prisons or labor camps. Precipitously the government called a halt to the Ukrainization policies outside Ukraine and accused its most enthusiastic supporters of counterrevolutionary activity.

The slap at Ukrainization signaled a major shift in nationality policy. The government now abolished the dozens of nationality districts and soviets that had been formed to represent non-Russian minorities at the local level (and outside designated autonomous regions) in the Russian, Ukrainian, and other republics. Though nativization would continue, the nationality that was to be promoted would be the titular nationality of the union republic, the autonomous national republic, or national region. Nationality was steadily territorialized, and the predominantly Russian areas in the RSFSR were cleansed of nationality institutions, newspapers, and schools. In the Cossack regions of Kuban in the North Caucasus, where a vigorous effort at Ukrainization had been carried out, the government closed Ukrainian schools after 1932 and ordered all pupils to be taught in Russian. Within the RSFSR there would be no officially recognized Ukrainian or Belorussian minorities, and over time more and more Ukrainians and Belorussians in the Russian Republic began identifying themselves as Russians.

Nationality policy had an enormous effect on national identity. When the nativization policy was encouraged, citizens identified with their non-Russian nations, but when the state's policy became less enthusiastic about non-Russian national consciousness, the tendency toward assimilation with the Russian population became stronger. Whereas earlier Soviet policymakers had recognized, and even emphasized, differences between (and within) peoples, the policy after 1932 was to unify and homogenize smaller nationalities. In 1934 a single Chechen-Ingush Autonomous Region was created to bring two related peoples into a single political unit with a single literary language, and the autonomous Russian city of Groznyi was included in the new national region. While earlier some ethnographers and officials had encouraged Mingrelian pretensions to distinguish themselves from the dominant population of the Georgian Republic, for example, now such activities were considered risky, and could potentially lead to charges of nationalism. Whereas some 188 ethnic groups had been included in the 1926 census, that number was reduced to 107 in the 1937 census. With the adoption of the 1936 constitution two autonomous republics within the RSFSR—Kazakhstan and Kyrgyzstan—were raised to full union republic status and five autonomous regions became autonomous republics. The Transcaucasian Federation was broken up into its constituent republics, and Armenia, Azerbaijan, and Georgia became full union republics within the USSR.

Though the rhetoric of internationalism and revolution remained part of the Soviet language, a more patriotic, pro-Russian, even nationalist tone entered Soviet culture. The government promoted Russian language instruction throughout the Union. In national regions Russian, which was now spoken of openly as a language of a higher culture, was to be the first foreign language. Non-Russians in the RSFSR lost some of their former privileges. No longer would special places be reserved for minorities in Russian universities. Minority children were no longer compelled to study in their own language, but they (or their parents) could chose to study in Russian. This new "freedom" led to a fall in the number of non-Russians studying in their native languages in the Russian republic. The official opposition to assimilation of non-Russians, which had marked the 1920s, now gave way to a new enthusiasm for free, spontaneous assimilation. The right to choose one's nationality was proclaimed widely. As a result the Russian Republic became more Russian in ethnic composition. For nationalists this new permissiveness spelled disaster, but in fact some non-Russians saw it as opportunity to escape the ghetto of nationality and enter the more cosmopolitan world of greater social mobility.

Soviet patriotism had a Russian flavor to it. The word *rodina* (motherland), which had not appeared in the press for more than a decade, was resurrected, first in a decree on high treason that spoke of "betrayal of the motherland" (June 9, 1934). In July an editorial in *Izvestiia* argued that every citizen ought to love his or her fatherland (*otechestvo*), meaning the Soviet Union. The second half of the decade saw a veritable carnival of Russian nationalist films, the centennial of Pushkin's death, and relentless emphasis on Russian culture, not only in the Russian Republic but in all the national republics and regions of the USSR. The historian Evgenii Tarle, who had earlier been persecuted for his non-Marxist approach and arrested in 1929, was now commissioned to write a history of General Kutuzov and the war of 1812. At the end of 1937 all non-

Russian schools in Russian regions of the RSFSR were closed. In March 1938 Russian became a compulsory language in all Soviet schools, though in the national republics the local languages continued to be taught as well. Moscow called a halt to the program of Latinizing alphabets and began replacing them with Cyrillic.

As Russian culture was elevated to the first among a family of cultures, the other Soviet republics were encouraged to replicate, on a smaller scale, the official celebration of their historic experiences and national cultures. But non-Russian republics were to emphasize the fraternal ties with Russia and the progressive achievement of annexation to the Russian Empire. Before the late 1930s scholars and journalists treated Russian expansionism as imperialist and colonialist. They even criticized the great nineteenth-century Russian masters Lermontov and Pushkin for their "reactionary" colonialist tendencies. But by the last years of the decade a new formulation described annexation of non-Russians by the tsarist empire as "the lesser evil," and at the Pushkin centennial his poetry and prose was lauded for promoting "friendship of the peoples."

National culture was a growth industry in the 1930s but within the strict limits established by Soviet policy. Even peoples who had not had a national or independent state experience in the past now acquired all the trappings of a long national tradition. The Uzbeks adopted the fifteenth-century Chagatay poet Mir Ali Shir Nawaiy as their national poet, and the Persian-speaking Tajiks appropriated the Persian writer Firdousi. The government promoted cultural exchanges between nationalities, sending troops of Georgian dancers to Ukraine and Uzbek ensembles to Belorussia. Thousands of works were translated into Russian and the other Soviet languages, all in an effort to promote "friendship of the peoples." Relative peace was maintained between nationalities, though ethnically based clashes, and even rebellions, occurred at times. The state came down hard on the slightest manifestation of nationalism, even as it promoted what it called patriotism. The distinction between the two often depended on the official political line at the moment. National cultures were pieced together into a multicolored Soviet quilt sewn tightly by the Communist Party. Anyone who attempted to tear the quilt or claim that one part was more beautiful than another would suffer the wrath of the state.

Non-Russians as well as Russians suffered and benefited from the social transformations of the decade. The fruits of Lenin's "rooting" program did not disappear, and pro-Russian tendencies coexisted uneasily with nationalizing processes in the non-Russian republics. The campaigns for literacy continued, and the literacy rate for people 9 to 49 years of age rose from 56.6 percent in 1926 to 87 percent in 1939. For non-Russian republics the result was truly spectacular, notably in Tajikistan, where literacy for that age group rose from just under 4 percent in the mid-1920s to nearly 83 percent at the end of the 1930s. Newspapers continued to be published in the non-Russian languages and were often more easily available than Russian equivalents. In the Belorussian republic at the end of the 1930s, three-quarters of the newspapers and over four-fifths of the books were published in Belorussian.

The largely peasant peoples of the non-Russian republics developed their own national intelligentsia and national proletariat. They moved into cities in record numbers, turning their towns and capitals into their own national urban centers. Those educated cadres who sought to rise in the party and state learned Russian, for that language was essential for upward social and political mobility. Russian was clearly the language of Sovietization, and its mastery was necessary for unencumbered access to the corridors of power. Not surprisingly, ambitious parents sent their children to Russian language schools, and after intermarriage between Russians and non-Russians offspring were given (or chose) Russian as their official passport nationality. The advantages of adopting Russian ways, pulled many people into the Russian nationality, while others were pushed by officialdom to adopt a Russian identity. It is estimated that between 1926 and 1939 some 10 million non-Russians adopted Russian nationality.

The irony of Soviet nationality policy was already evident by the 1930s. A state that believed it was moving beyond nationalism and nationality was in fact creating new nations and consolidating others as a result of its nationality policies. At the same time relations between the center and the non-Russian republics and autonomies were unequal, hierarchical, and imperial. The number of all-union commissariats increased as the center took over one prerogative of the republics after another. In 1929 agriculture became an all-union commissariat, followed in 1934 by internal affairs. In 1936 federal councils at the center were formed for higher education and art, justice, and public health. By 1943 only public education below higher education, local industry, local transportation, local public utilities, and social security were in the hands of republic-level or autonomous-unit level commissariats. Once national Communist leaders had been brutally tamed in the Great Purges, all meaningful decision-making shifted to Moscow, and the Soviet Union, founded by anti-imperialist ideologues, took on the practices of an empire.

For Stalin and the Soviet leaders nationality was an objective reality, and when the Soviet internal passport was introduced in 1932, it fixed a nationality for each adult Soviet citizen. Ethnicity was usually inherited from one's parents and, therefore, had a biological even more than linguistic or cultural origin. In the case of mixed marriages, however, a person could choose the nationality of one parent or the other, though it was usually that of the father. Yet in the successive Soviet censuses (1926, 1937, and 1939) respondents were asked to give their own subjective sense of to what nationality they belonged. Thus, nationality remained a somewhat fluid category. In the Soviet federation, in which administrative units were national in character, membership in the titular nationality in a republic or national region often gave an individual privileged access to resources. Minorities without their own administrative units had little protection from the state after the abolition of national soviets. Their fate was to be blended eventually into the dominant nationality of the territory they lived in. In much of the Soviet Union that meant Russification, but in national republics it could mean that a Kurd or Talysh in Azerbaijan would become Azerbaijani or an Armenian in Georgia would become Georgian.

The Soviet leaders never adopted a completely Russifying or forcibly assimilationist policy. The center never attempted to homogenize the multinational country and create a single nation-state. There was a Soviet people but no Soviet nation. No one was permitted to choose "Soviet" as their passport nationality, as would later be permitted in Tito's Yugoslavia. Instead of urging a single Soviet nation, the USSR became the crucible for dozens of smaller nations below the all-union level. By the late 1930s an "empire of republics," many of them little empires in their own right, had been created in the USSR, and the state promoted a new Soviet patriotism, with a heavy Russian cultural overlay, as the binding cement to hold the union together.

Suggestions for Further Reading

Besides the works mentioned at the end of Chapter 8, readers interested in Stalinist culture should look at Richard Stites, *Russian Popular Culture: Entertainment and Society Since 1900* (Cambridge, 1992); James von Geldern and Richard Stites (eds.), *Mass Culture in Soviet Russia: Tales, Poems, Songs, Movies, Plays, and Folklore, 1917–1953* (Bloomington, Ind., 1995); Regine Robin (ed.), *Soviet Literature of the Thirties: A Reappraisal* (Montpelier, Vt., 1986); Frank J. Miller, *Folklore for Stalin: Russian Folklore and Pseudofolklore of the Stalin Era* (Armonk, N.Y., 1990); and Hans Gunther (ed.), *The Culture of the Stalin Period* (New York, 1990). On Soviet cultural practices and their effects, see Christel Lane, *Rites of Rulers* (Cambridge, 1981); James Riordan, *Sport and Soviet Society* (Cambridge, 1977); Robert Edelman, *Serious Fun: A History of Spectator Sports in the USSR* (New York, 1993); William C. Fletcher, *A Study in Survival: The Church in Russia, 1917–1943* (London, 1965); and Walter Kolarz, *Religion in the Soviet Union* (London, 1961).

On film and music, see Peter Kenez, *Cinema and Soviet Society, 1917–1953* (Cambridge, 1992); Jay Leyda, *Kino: A History of the Russian and Soviet Film* (London, 1960); S. Frederick Starr, *Red and Hot: The Fate of Jazz in the Soviet Union* (New York, 1983); Boris Schwarz, *Music and Musical Life in Soviet Russia, 1917–1981*, enlarged ed. (Bloomington, Ind., 1983); Elizabeth Wilson, *Shostakovich, A Life Remembered* (Princeton, 1994); and Sheila Fitzpatrick, "The *Lady Macbeth* Affair: Shostakovich and the Soviet Puritans," in her *The Cultural Front* (Ithaca, N.Y., 1992), pp. 183–215. One might with caution also look at Solomon Volkov, *Testimony: The Memoirs of Dmitri Shostakovich* (New York, 1979).

The memoirs and novels of the period are extremely informative and moving. See, for example, Nadezhda Mandelshtam, *Hope against Hope* (New York, 1970) and *Hope Abandoned* (New York, 1974); Elena Bonner, *Mothers and Daughters* (New York, 1992); Raissa Orlova, *Memoirs* (New York, 1983); Anatoli Rybakov, *Children of the Arbat* (Boston, 1988); Arthur Koestler, *Darkness at Noon* (New York, 1970); and Vassily Aksyonov, *Generations of Winter* (New York, 1994) and *The Winter's Hero* (New York, 1996).

On women, a key text is Gail Warshofsky Lapidus, *Women in Soviet Society: Equality, Development, and Social Change* (Berkeley, Calif., 1978).

On Soviet nationalities policies, two works are indispensable: Yuri Slezkine, *Arctic Mirrors: Russia and the Small Peoples of the North* (Ithaca, N.Y., 1994); and Terry D. Martin, "An Affirmative Action Empire: Ethnicity and the Soviet State, 1923–1938" (Ph.D. diss., University of Chicago, 1996).

On Soviet science, see Loren R. Graham, *Science and Philosophy in the Soviet Union* (New York, 1972); and David Joravsky, *The Lysenko Affair* (Chicago, 1970) and *Soviet Marxism and Natural Science, 1917–1932* (New York, 1992).

CHAPTER 13
Collective Security and the Coming of World War II

The Fascist Menace

In the years between World War I and World War II, Soviet and Comintern leaders confronted a seemingly senseless doctrine emerging in Italy and Germany and spreading to Austria, Spain, and other European countries. This new political phenomenon brought together nationalist, racist, anti-Communist, and anticapitalist ideas into a single mass movement. From its origins in Mussolini's Italy to its apogee in Nazi Germany, fascism preached a message of heroism and violence, celebrated the state and nation, and promoted shamelessly imperialist foreign policies. As the antithesis of liberalism, this radical conservative movement saw itself as the resolution of the crisis of bourgeois society and the most potent answer to the threat of Marxism. Fascism rejected pacifism and embraced war. "War alone," Mussolini wrote, "brings up to its highest tension all human energy and puts the stamp of nobility upon the peoples who have the courage to meet it." Fascists did not believe in majority rule or democratic representation but in the "fruitful inequality of mankind." As Mussolini put it, "Fascism is the purest kind of democracy, so long as people are counted qualitatively and not quantitatively." The state was seen as "the custodian and transmitter of the spirit of the people." And, "for fascism, the growth of empire, that is to say the expansion of the nation, is an essential manifestation of vitality, and its opposite a sign of decadence. Peoples that are rising, or rising again after a period of decadence, are always imperialist; any renunciation is a sign of decay and death."

The German dictator Adolf Hitler openly proclaimed his hostility to all forms of egalitarianism, communism, and the USSR. In his 1923 autobiography, *Mein Kampf* (My Struggle) he had outlined a program of conquest and colonization and spoke of winning *Lebensraum* (living space) for the German people in the East, either through diplomacy or war. Germans were to be settled in Poland and Russia and exploit the local population in order to ensure the dominance of the German race for a thousand years. He told his associates, "What India was for England, the territories of Russia will be for us. If only I could make the German people understand what this space means for our future! Colonies are a precarious possession, but this ground is safely ours."

Hitler's racist outlook convinced him that the Soviet Union was weak and that war in the East could easily rid the world of the virus of Bolshevism. Earlier he had written of Bolshevik Russia as a Jewish empire that had to be destroyed: "The colossal empire in the East is ripe for dissolution. And the end of Jewish domination in Russia will also be the end of Russia as a state." Since Stalin's regime, in Hitler's view, was politically and racially rotten, strong pressure from Germany would cause it to collapse from within. "Bolshevism," Hitler said, "is Christianity's illegitimate child. Both are inventions of the Jew." "The Slavs are a mass of born slaves who feel the need of a master," he told his followers during the war.

Fascism was a reaction to the initial successes of the Bolsheviks and their allies in Europe in the years 1917–21. But Communists both in the Soviet Union and outside consistently underestimated the potential threat of fascism. In the 1920s the Comintern saw fascism as a radical mass movement that was essentially like other forms of bourgeois rule and often equated it with social democracy, which they claimed was "fascism wearing a socialist mask." Only after Hitler's coming to power in Germany in 1933 did the Comintern intensify its condemnation of fascism as "the open, terrorist dictatorship of the most reactionary, most chauvinist and most imperialist elements of finance capital." Still, the leading Communists remained complacent for a few more years, expecting that the current crisis of capitalism would soon provide them with the mass backing they needed to overcome both fascism and capitalism.

The 1930s seemed to be a moment of both danger and opportunity for Communists. The capitalist world had plunged into the Great Depression, the greatest economic collapse that the international economy had ever suffered. Between 1929 and 1939 total production in the world dropped by one-half, and total world trade dropped by two-thirds. In the major industrial powers 30 million people were out of work, 6 million in Germany alone. Governments reacted by attempting to isolate their economies from the world economy by imposing tariffs on foreign imports. The Great Depression shook capitalism and liberalism to its foundations, and the capitalist countries adopted various forms of state capitalist policies, using government to intervene in and regulate the economy. Political systems as different as Franklin Delano Roosevelt's New Deal and Adolph Hitler's Nazi state adopted programs of public works, which in the case of Germany became increasingly oriented toward the military. By gearing up early for war, Hitler was far more successful in reducing unemployment and bringing the depression to an end in his country than was Roosevelt. The United States had 8 million unemployed at the end of the 1930s and only managed to end the depression when the war created a new customer for industrial production, namely the military. Whether in liberal democratic, fascist, or socialist countries, the effect of the depression all over the developed world was to increase the power of the state in the economy and to make alternatives to liberal capitalism appear more attractive to many.

Even before the depression began, the Comintern predicted a general capitalist crisis that would develop a "trend toward state capitalism" and turned sharply toward a more militantly anticapitalist policy. The Sixth Congress of the Communist International, which met in the summer of 1928, resolved that the world had entered a "Third Period" since the world war. The first period, of crisis and revolution, had ended in 1923, and the second period of "gradual and partial stabilization" was now being superseded by a third period of "intense development of the contradictions in the world economy." This period would be one of new revolutionary opportunities. The enemy on the Right was fascism but equally dangerous was social democracy, which would henceforth be referred to as "social fascism." Communists were instructed not to build coalitions with other working-class parties or trade unions but to tighten up their own ranks, suppress any critical thinking within the party, and expel those who were considered Rightists.

As a result of this new Comintern line, Communist parties turned inward, cut themselves off from the broad ranks of workers, and became even more sectarian and dependent on the Soviet Union for support. Within the next few years Communist parties became Stalinist the world over, as the defeat of Bukharin within the USSR was mirrored in the expulsion of moderates in other Communist parties. The victorious Stalin faction in the Soviet Union crudely disciplined foreign Communist leaders, demanding full acceptance of the new line. A prominent Italian Communist later reported that Stalin had demanded of the Italians "either complete capitulation or we could leave" and sadly concluded that "if we don't give in, Moscow won't hesitate to fix up a left leadership with some kid out of the Lenin School." For many old militants expulsion from the party meant a life without meaning, political impotence just at the moment when the struggle for socialism was intensifying.

The international atmosphere was generally hostile to the USSR in the early years of the Great Depression, and this was felt in the area of foreign trade. Desperate for machinery and industrial goods from the more developed countries, the Soviet Union increased its imports by more than a quarter from 1929 to 1932. By 1931 the USSR was the largest single buyer of British and American machinery, and in 1932 it was buying 50 percent of world machine imports. To pay for these imports, the Soviets unloaded tons of grain and other raw materials on the weak world market. The Western press charged that the USSR was dumping cheap goods to undermine further the capitalist economy. The United States retaliated by restricting Soviet imports in July 1930; the French placed sanctions on the USSR in October, and Great Britain cut off trade with the Soviet Union altogether at the end of 1932. The Soviets responded by buying from the Germans.

Soviet security had been based since 1922 on an entente with Germany, a fellow "revisionist" state opposed to the Versailles settlement. Both powers were hostile to Poland, but the German government, never pleased by Soviet support of the German Communist Party, gravitated steadily toward the West in the second half of the 1920s. At the same time Soviet support for Comintern militants and anticolonial struggles in India and Southeast Asia created tensions both with Britain and France. From India and Afghanistan the British aided the anti-Soviet Basmachi rebels in Central Asia, and the French suppressed the nationalists and Communists in their Indochinese colonies. In the early 1930s, except for its troubled relationship with Germany, the Soviet Union was isolated and without foreign friends. A debonair Old Bolshevik, Maxim

Litvinov, who replaced Chicherin as Commissar of Foreign Affairs in July 1930, favored abandoning the existing alliance with Germany and shifting to an alliance with Britain and France. To many observers Litvinov seemed an odd choice for Stalin to make for the top position in foreign affairs. The son of a Jewish bank clerk and a Bolshevik since 1903, married to an Englishwoman who was also Jewish, Litvinov was sophisticated, cosmopolitan, and stubborn, and a savvy political infighter within the bureaucracy. Stalin, who was personally anti-Semitic, had hardly ever traveled outside Russia and was suspicious of intellectuals. Stalin was isolationist in his foreign policy, while Litvinov was an internationalist, ready to conclude agreements with potential allies. But both men shared a pragmatic approach to foreign affairs, and neither man was particularly interested in fostering revolution abroad.

Often Stalin delayed making decisions in foreign policy and allowed matters to drift, and Litvinov was given an unusual degree of independence. He developed a nonrevolutionary foreign policy that sought more stable relations with established states, even fascist Italy. As he told the British ambassador in 1931, "The Soviets wanted no revolution in Germany or elsewhere today; world revolution was undoubtedly 'on their books' but for the moment they were entirely concentrated on the Five-Year Plan and wished to show concrete results in their own country as the best form of propaganda." Litvinov was prepared to turn away from the Rapallo strategy favoring Germany and toward improved relations with Britain and France. The Western powers embraced him as a man who seemed less confrontational and more cooperative than his predecessors. Litvinov's positions in the early 1930s were clearly at odds with the more militant, anti-Western revolutionary strategy of the Communist International.

The world became much more dangerous for the USSR in the early 1930s, with the Japanese on the march in Asia and the Nazis coming to power in Germany. In 1931 Japan invaded Manchuria, an indisputable part of China, and the members of the League of Nations failed to react to the aggression. To strengthen the Soviet Union's international position, the Foreign Commissariat concluded a series of nonaggression treaties and trade agreements, in 1931 with Turkey and Afghanistan and the following year with Finland, Latvia, Estonia, Poland, and France. Only Rumania and Japan refused to sign such treaties, Rumania because the USSR refused to recognize her claim to Bessarabia, and Japan because of complications arising from its invasion of Manchuria. Soviet officials also tried to show that the USSR was committed to international peace. Litvinov became an articulate speaker favoring disarmament, and the USSR backed the peace movement. Soviet authorities forced reluctant Comintern leaders to support the call for a world antiwar congress. When the congress met in Amsterdam in August 1932, it adopted a pro-Soviet, anti-French manifesto and condemned Japanese aggression. Many in the West saw the peace movement as an artificial front for Soviet foreign policy interests.

The Popular Front and Collective Security

The intransigent policy of the Comintern in its Third Period (1928–35) was disastrous for the Communist movement internationally and further isolated the

Soviet Union. If Italian fascism was in many ways the reactionary response to the failure of socialists to gain power in Italy in the early 1920s, Nazism was the beneficiary of the Great Depression and the divisions within the political Left. In the context of economic collapse, unemployment, and fear of Communism, Hitler used his extraordinary oratorical talents to inspire millions with his fantasy of a powerful and purified German nation. Backed by important figures in big business, the army, and the political elite, Hitler was named chancellor of Germany on January 30, 1933. Within a few months he brought the liberal Weimar Republic to an end, destroyed the Communist and Social Democratic parties, dissolved the socialist trade unions, and established a one-party dictatorship.

Four months after Hitler came to power, German Communists argued that "the worse, the better"; the crisis in capitalism would lead to a brief fascist triumph, " 'the last stage of imperialism," after which

> the revolutionary tide in Germany will grow.... The establishment of an open fascist dictatorship, which is destroying all democratic illusions among the masses and freeing them from the influence of Social Democracy, will speed up Germany's progress towards the proletarian revolution.

Throughout 1933 and 1934, both communists and socialists rejected attempts by the others' International to come to an agreement, and only a few leaders attempted to forge links between the two movements. Meanwhile, the USSR renewed its treaty of alliance with Germany (May 1933), declaring that it could live in peace and friendship with Germany, despite its fascist government, just as it had done since 1922 with Italy. Stalin still conceived of Britain and France as a greater threat than the weaker central European fascist states.

The menace from the new Nazi state grew month by month. Hitler withdrew from the League of Nations in October 1933, signaling his independence in foreign policy. The Nazis won election victories in the Free City of Danzig (May 1933) and a plebiscite in the Saar Basin (January 1935), which brought the latter territory into the German state. Rightists clashed with leftists in Austria and France. Hitler violated the Versailles Treaty in March 1935 by decreeing compulsory military service in Germany. Although his relations with Mussolini were strained at first, Hitler backed the Italian invasion of Ethiopia in October, and a Berlin–Rome axis was soon consolidated. Fascism was clearly spreading through Europe and beyond and needed to be contained.

In 1933–34 Soviet foreign policy shifted toward greater accommodation with the West. In November 1933 Litvinov traveled to Washington, where he reached an agreement with the new Roosevelt administration on recognition of the Soviet Union. A month later the Politburo passed a resolution in favor of the policy of collective security, the idea, embodied in the concept of the League of Nations, that nations would act in concert against an aggressor. In January 1934 Litvinov's stature was enhanced by membership in the Central Committee, and nine months later the USSR joined the League of Nations. On May 2, 1935, the Soviet Union signed a pact of peace and friendship with France, followed two weeks later by a treaty with Czechoslovakia. The USSR was now allied with countries that it had denounced only a short time before, one of which it viewed as a major imperialist power. Though it was committed to come to the aid of its allies in case of "an unprovoked attack on the part of a European state," fulfilling that obligation would be difficult, for the Soviet Union had no common border with Czechoslovakia or, more significantly, with the potential aggressor, Germany. An agreement with Poland or Rumania was essential to make these treaties effective, but neither of those states would join the USSR in a military pact. Moreover, the treaty with France contained no military arrangements, and the suspicions of the French army delayed serious discussions about military matters with the Soviets. Still, from 1934 until 1939, the Soviet Union drew closer to the powers that supported the Versailles settlement, like its old adversaries Britain and France, and moved away from Germany and Italy, the "revisionists" that wanted to overthrow the Versailles arrangements.

Soviet foreign policy moved more quickly toward cooperation with the major Western capitalist powers than did Comintern policy. The costs of passivity or disunity in the face of fascism became clearer to the Left after Hitler came to power, and pressure mounted to unite the socialist and Communist movements. As early as May 1934, *Pravda* editorialized that united action with socialist leaders was permissible, and the Communists in France signed an agreement with the Socialists on an electoral alliance in July. But not until 1935 did the Seventh (and last) Congress of the Communist International adopt formally the strategy of "popular front" with democratic and socialist parties.

The new Comintern policy was identified with the Bulgarian Communist leader, Georgi Dimitrov, who had been arrested and tried in Germany for his alleged role in the burning of the Reichstag building. Dimitrov had brilliantly defended himself, and after his acquittal he emerged as an international hero of the Left. After he arrived in Moscow, late in February 1934, he began speaking out in favor of the unity of all antifascist forces. Typically, Stalin did not make a firm decision on this question, but early in April he agreed that Dimitrov would become secretary-general of the Comintern. Only after individual parties had moved toward alliances with socialist and "petty bourgeois" parties, as in France, did the Comintern executive committee embrace the idea of a popular front of progressive, antifascist parties. At the Seventh Congress Dimitrov spoke at length on strategy, warning that "the bourgeoisie would rather drown the labor movement in a sea of blood than allow the proletariat to establish socialism by peaceful means." But, he went on, distinctions had to be made between fascism, which was reactionary, antidemocratic, and imperialist, and the rest of the bourgeoisie and petty bourgeoisie that honored democratic freedoms. Broad fronts had to be formed with reformist socialist parties and bourgeois parties against fascism and imperialism in defense of democracy. Dimitrov shored up his position with an obligatory quote from Lenin: "Just as one cannot have a victorious socialism without realizing full democracy, so the proletariat cannot prepare itself for victory over the bourgeoisie without waging a comprehensive, consistent, and revolutionary struggle for democracy."

With the Popular Front the boundaries of the Left were expanded to include "bourgeois democratic" forces. The Comintern now directed Communists to fight fascist imperialism, not bourgeois capitalism and democracy, and to carry out that struggle in tandem with middle-class allies, not just workers and socialists. That Popular Front strategy was in large part generated from outside the Soviet Union, by foreign Communists, who pressured the divided Comintern leadership to shift its tactics. Once the leadership, and most importantly Stalin, decided in favor of the new strategy, the recalcitrant hard-liners were forced to toe the new line. The final disciplining of the Comintern occurred around this time. Soviet police officers were added to the Executive Committee, and Dimitrov had to take his orders from Ezhov. A few years later the defeated militants, who had opposed the turn toward the Popular Front, paid a heavy price for their loyalty to the old line. They perished in the Great Purges, while the moderates, led by Dimitrov, survived and remained important players in Communist politics.

Communism versus Fascism

The second half of the 1930s was a kind of golden age for Communists, Socialists, and their fellow-travelers on the Left. In 1934 the Swedish Social Democrats had won a clear majority in parliamentary elections and through the decade began to bring Sweden out of the depression through public works, financed out of increased death duties. The Swedish "middle road" was based on nonmilitary deficit spending, establishing greater social equality through law and taxes, and guaranteeing working people social protection and benefits. In 1936 Popular Front coalitions triumphed in national elections in both France and Spain. In France millions of workers went on strike, stimulating a furious few weeks of prolabor legislation. Maurice Thorez, the leader of the French Communist Party, spoke on radio about reconciling the tricolor flag of the republic with "the red flag of our hopes." Everywhere the language of the Popular Front was less that of "the proletariat" and much more of "the people" and "the nation."

The Comintern gained a new prestige as part of an international antifascist movement, and for many intellectuals and workers in the West Soviet-style communism seemed a preferable political alternative to either fascism or the decrepit, crisis-ridden liberalism and capitalism of the depression years. When right-wing Spanish generals revolted against the democratically elected republic and plunged Spain into civil war (1936–39), the crusade against the fascists in Spain became closely identified with the Communists and the Soviet Union. Sympathetic journalists and travelers hailed the Soviet Union as "a new civilization," and playwright George Bernard Shaw contrasted the Soviet "land of hope" with "our Western countries of despair." In 1936 Stalin declared that socialism had been built in the Soviet Union, and in December of that year he issued what was proclaimed to be the "most democratic constitution in the world."

But fascism was unrelenting in its growing power and influence in the second half of the 1930s, and the Soviet Union's attempts to put teeth in the idea of collective security against fascism ran up against the suspicions of Western governments about Stalin's intentions. Britain and France desperately wanted to avoid war, and their repeated passivity toward and concessions to Italy and Germany developed into a policy of appeasement. When Italy invaded Ethiopia in October 1935, the USSR protested and imposed economic sanctions on Italy, but the other great powers continued to trade with the Italians, thus undermining the effectiveness of collective security. The emperor of Ethiopia, Haile Selassie, spoke in Geneva to the League of Nations, whose covenant called for sanctions against an aggressor, but his pleas, as well as Litvinov's, went unheeded. When Germany reoccupied the Rhineland, another clear violation of the Versailles Treaty, the French did not move against the Germans. Even France's Popular Front government did not come to the aid of beleaguered Spain during its civil war, though Germany and Italy sent arms and soldiers to aid the insurgent General Franco.

The Soviet Union secretly sent advisors and arms to Spain. Some forty thousand volunteers from around the world came to Spain, joining the International Brigades, to fight fascism. But the Soviet Union was wary of frightening the British and French governments and instructed Communists to shore up the "bourgeois republic," not to carry out a socialist revolution. The Communists in Spain, who gained by their association with the USSR and their role as fighters in the defense of Madrid, alienated the more revolutionary elements, who were fighting to create a socialist society. The anarchist and Trotskyist Left, which hoped to turn the civil war into a revolution, clashed with the Communists, who together with the government of the republic crushed a popular leftist rebellion in Barcelona in May 1937. The splits on the Left and the consequent dampening of the ardor of the revolutionaries, as well as the aid from international fascism and the lack of support from the democracies, led to the defeat of the Spanish Republic and the triumph of Franco's brand of Spanish fascism early in 1939. As the war wound down Stalin recalled his agents and advisors in Spain, but instead of being honored for loyal service, most of those involved in the Spanish Civil War were executed when they returned home.

The USSR was caught between a hostile Germany and Japan and a West that was unwilling to link itself firmly to the Soviet idea of collective security. Many foreign policy experts in the United States and other Western countries took Marxist-Leninist ideology, with its rhetoric of eventual Communist victory over capitalism, much more seriously, as a short-term goal of Soviet policy, than did the more pragmatic associates of Stalin. The American ambassador to Moscow, William C. Bullitt, for example, after becoming disillusioned with Stalin, cabled the State Department that the Soviet Union was a "nation ruled by fanatics who are ready to sacrifice themselves and everyone else for their religion of communism." And later he told them, "Neither Stalin nor any other leader of the Communist party has deviated in the slightest from the determination to spread communism to the ends of the earth." On the other hand, other experts, like the young diplomats George F. Kennan, Loy Henderson, and Charles Bohlen (who would become major policymakers during the Cold War), proposed that state interests and defense were the paramount concerns of Soviet policy.

Judging from Soviet behavior in the 1930s, Stalin's own reasoning was probably based far more on the power politics of states vying for advantage in a chaotic world than on dreams of revolutionary expansion. In a circular way ideology was subordinated to state interests, but interests were understood in terms of ideology. Stalin wanted to defend and preserve the USSR, and enhance its prestige, power, and influence, but as the "first socialist state" with a special role to play in history. He suspected that the capitalist West, which saw its interests threatened by Marxist socialism, might attempt to come to an agreement with Hitler against the Soviet Union. His principal aim was to avoid war and to prevent a European bloc directed against the USSR. To that end the Soviet leaders kept up their own contacts with Germany throughout the 1930s, through their trade representative in Berlin. It was little comfort, then, to receive the report of the Soviet ambassador in Berlin that "Hitler has three 'obsessions': hostility toward the USSR (toward communism), the Jewish Question, and the Anschluss [annexation of Austria to Germany]." Germany signed an agreement with Italy in October 1936 and with Japan in November, effectively forming an anti-Comintern, anti-Soviet alliance.

With the West unwilling to stand up against fascism, Litvinov's policy of collective security was vulnerable to attack within the Soviet leadership. Some historians believe that Molotov and Zhdanov favored a more isolationist policy in which the USSR would strike out on its own or perhaps come to an agreement with Germany. As the purges fell hard on the Commissariat of Foreign Affairs, Soviet watchers speculated that Litvinov would soon perish. His wife prudently left for the Urals to teach English. His closest associates were imprisoned or shot, among them high Commissariat officials and a number of ambassadors. But the ax did not fall on Litvinov, and collective security continued to be Soviet policy for another two years. Litvinov told a French journalist at the end of 1937 that the Soviet Union was becoming isolationist because "at the moment no one wants anything to do with us. We will carry on waiting . . . and then we will see." When the correspondent asked if a rapprochement with Germany were possible, Litvinov grimly replied, "Perfectly possible."

Germany annexed Austria in March 1938. The Soviet media did not denounce the Anschluss but directed its anger at the appeasers. As Germany turned its attention to Czechoslovakia and called for the secession of the German-inhabited Sudetenland, the Soviets made it clear that they were ready to defend Czechoslovakia if the French also agreed to come to its aid. The Red Army prepared to march, mobilizing secretly some ninety divisions. The Czechoslovaks also prepared to fight. The French, however, only partially mobilized, and the government sought a diplomatic way out. Poland and Rumania refused to allow troops to cross their territory to reach Czechoslovakia, but Rumania agreed to shut its eyes to Soviet aircraft flying over its territory. Hitler was prepared to go to war despite the possibility of Soviet aid to its Czechoslovak ally. On September 29, 1938, the French premier, Edouard Daladier, and the British prime minister, Neville Chamberlain, met with Mussolini and Hitler in Munich and agreed to cede Czech territory to Germany, without consulting with or securing the agreement of the Soviets or the Americans. Chamberlain proclaimed to his anxious nation that he had brought them "peace for our time," but in fact by capitulating to Hitler the British and French governments had weakened Czechoslovakia and isolated the USSR from France. The war in Europe was delayed another year, but in that year Nazi Germany prepared much more effectively for the coming battles than did its future enemies.

Munich marked the collapse of Litvinov's policy of collective security. The Soviet Union was alone, faced by a rearmed Germany, now the strongest power in Europe, and Japan, with which it had several armed clashes on the Manchurian border. On its western border were the hostile states of Finland, Estonia, Latvia, Lithuania, Poland, Hungary, and Rumania. Shortly after the Munich Conference, Litvinov told the French ambassador:

> I merely note that the Western powers deliberately kept the USSR out of negotiations. My poor friend, what have you done? As for us, I do not see any other outcome than a fourth partition of Poland.

Munich probably convinced Stalin that the West was plotting to unleash Hitler against the Soviet Union. Though this was not in fact the aim of the Western powers, an alliance with the USSR did not promise great benefits. They were aware that the Red Army had been devastated by the purges, and if Hitler were to march they preferred war in the east rather than the west. Suspicious of Stalin, Western leaders were not interested in strengthening the Soviets. Both Britain and France, in fact, secretly supported a group of Ukrainian exiles in Germany who hoped to create an independent Ukraine at the expense of the Soviet Union. As Chamberlain wrote to his sister early in 1939,

> I must confess to the most profound distrust of Russia. I have no belief whatever in her ability to maintain an effective offensive, even if she wanted to. And I distrust her motives, which seem to me to have little connection with our ideas of liberty. . . . Moreover, she is both hated and suspected by many of the smaller states, notably by Poland, Romania, and Finland.

Soviet policy was confused and hesitant after Munich. At the Eighteenth Party Congress in March 1939, Stalin laid out Soviet thinking on the current crisis:

> A new imperialist war is already in its second year. . . . The war is being waged by aggressor states (Germany, Italy, Japan), who in every way infringe the interests of the non-aggressive states, primarily England, France, and the USA, while the latter draw back and retreat, making concession after concession to the aggressors. . . .

The West is trying to push Germany against the USSR, he went on, "promising them easy spoils and saying again and again: just start a war with the Bolsheviks and henceforth everything will work out well." When a few days later the Nazis occupied the Czech capital, Prague, and proclaimed Slovakia an independent state, the USSR protested and offered Europe a joint effort to stop

Nazi aggression. The offer was refused, but this time Britain and France pledged to lend support to Poland if attacked. A similar guarantee was given shortly thereafter to Rumania and Greece. The Soviets might have been pleased at these pledges, but they were unsure if the West would really act in case of German aggression. Litvinov proposed that France, Britain, and the USSR guarantee military defense of all the East European states that bordered on the USSR. The Western powers hesitated, and discussions dragged on for months. Stalin later told Winston Churchill that

> we had formed the impression that the British and French governments were not resolved to go to war if Poland were attacked, but that they hoped the diplomatic line-up of Britain, France, and Russia would deter Hitler. We were sure it would not.

War was on the horizon, and it increasingly looked as if it would begin over Poland. On March 23, the Germans seized the Baltic port of Memel from Lithuania. The Baltic region, which had been Russian from the eighteenth century until World War I, was seen as a possible area of expansion by both Germany and Poland. The USSR had its own interest in the area, and Litvinov issued a statement that "the Soviet government . . . continues to attach immense importance to the preservation of the complete independence of . . . the Baltic republics."

On May 3, 1939, Litvinov was replaced as foreign commissar by Molotov. The change seemed to portend that the policy of collective security might be abandoned and that some agreement with Germany might be possible. By August the Soviets were negotiating both with the British and, secretly, with the Germans. Stalin invited Hitler's foreign minister, Joachim von Ribbentrop, to Moscow. At six in the evening on August 23, Ribbentrop and the German ambassador to Moscow were ushered into the Kremlin where they met Stalin and Molotov. Stalin explained that although they had "poured buckets of filth" over each other for years, the quarrel could now end. He proposed that eastern Europe be divided into spheres of influence. After a recess during which Hitler's agreement was secured, the talks resumed. Before midnight the foreign ministers had signed both a Soviet-German pact and a secret protocol on the division of eastern Europe. A late dinner followed, at which Stalin described Hitler as a man whom he "had always greatly admired." "I know how much the German nation loves its Fuhrer," Stalin went on. "I should like to drink his health."

The Nazi-Soviet Pact pledged ten years of peaceful cooperation between the USSR and Germany, nonaggression toward the other party, and no aid to a third party that attacked the other signator. From reliance on collective security the Soviet Union had basically taken a position of neutrality in the coming European conflict, increasing both its isolation and its freedom of maneuver. The secret protocol, which the Soviets would not publicly admit existed until well into the Gorbachev period, established the border between the Soviet and German spheres of influence. Finland, Estonia, and Latvia, as well as Bessarabia, were to be in the Soviet sphere; Lithuania, including Vilno, would be in the German. And Poland would be divided into German and Soviet spheres of influence. Germany declared "its complete political distinterested-ness" in southeastern Europe. A week after the agreement was signed, Molo-tov tried to justify the turnabout in Soviet policy in terms of state interests and by laying blame on the Western powers:

> People ask with an air of innocence how the Soviet Union could consent to improve political relations with a state of a fascist type. "Is it possible?" they ask. But they forget that this is not a question of our attitude toward the internal regime of another country but of the foreign relations between the two states. They forget that we hold the position of not interfering in the internal affairs of other countries and, correspondingly, of not tolerat-ing interference in our own internal affairs. . . .
> . . . The Soviet Union signed the Non-aggression Pact with Germany [because] the negotiations with France and England had run into insuper-able differences and ended in failure through the fault of the ruling classes of England and France.

The Nazi-Soviet Pact stunned the world, not least the millions of Com-munists and Soviet sympathizers around the world. Even Politburo members had been kept in the dark. When they brought some ducks they had shot to Stalin's country home the next day, he informed them of the treaty. "I know what Hitler's up to," he told them. "He thinks he's outsmarted me, but actu-ally it's I who have tricked him." As Khrushchev remembered, "Stalin told Voroshilov, Beria, myself, and some other members of the Politburo that be-cause of this treaty the war would pass us by for a while longer. We would be able to stay neutral and save our strength. Then we would see what happened." By signing the treaty Stalin gained time and space, though the Soviets failed to make good use of the delay. The West had given him little choice by its de-lays and suspicions. Given that the USSR was not really prepared for war with Germany, he managed to prevent a common front of capitalist powers, demo-cratic and fascist, against the USSR, something he feared but that probably was not in the making anyway. And the Japanese-German Axis was severely dam-aged. As a result of the pact, the Soviet Union recovered some lost lands for Ukraine and Belorussia and was able to annex the Baltic countries and some territories from Finland. But the price for the breathing spell was high indeed. Stalin probably did not expect Britain and France to declare war on Germany when Hitler invaded Poland but to act as they had in the past and acquiesce in the Nazi expansion. By allying with Germany, Stalin allowed Hitler's armies to knock the Western powers out of the war and off the continent and gave the Nazis the opportunity by 1941 to launch a devastating one-front war against the Soviet Union.

War in Europe

On September 1, 1939, Germany invaded Poland with a ferocious air and land attack known as the *Blitzkrieg* (lightning war) and began World War II. Two days later Britain and France declared war on Germany. Stalin hesitated at first to move into the part of Poland reserved for the USSR in the secret protocol, but the Germans pressured him to occupy the territory reserved for the Soviets. After revising his sphere of influence to include only areas taken from Russia by the Poles in the Treaty of Riga (1921) and largely inhabited by Ukrainians and Belorussians, Stalin issued marching orders to the Red Army on September 16. A new and brutal phase of Soviet foreign policy began. From a largely defensive policy Soviet strategy now turned to military expansion, first in Poland, then in the Baltic republics and Finland, and still later in Rumania.

To legitimize the attack on Poland, the Soviets depicted it as the liberation and unification of historically Ukrainian and Belorussian lands. The Red Army units were made up largely of Ukrainians and commanded by a Ukrainian, Semen Timoshenko. The political commissars told the soldiers that they were entering eastern Poland not as conquerors but as liberators, and leaflets were dropped to tell the local peasants that the Red Army was coming to rid them of their oppressive Polish rulers. Though there was some resistance from Polish troops, the Red Army suffered less than two thousand casualties. Local peasants were sympathetic to the Red Army, and the Soviets created peasant militias and workers' guards, along with local revolutionary councils, and held a series of rigged elections. On October 24 the People's Assembly of Western Ukraine requested to become part of the USSR. Once the region was made part of the Soviet Union, land was socialized and industry nationalized, though only about 13 percent of the peasants were collectivized by the time the Nazis invaded a year and a half later. As the region was Sovietized, it was also made more Ukrainian and Belorussian. The Soviets arrested thousands of Polish officials, landlords, and officers and sent them to prison camps. There they soon became an inconvenient presence, and Beria's NKVD eventually executed more than ten thousand of them.

With Poland partitioned and Germany allowing the USSR a free hand in much of eastern Europe, Stalin turned his attention northward. Finland, Estonia, Latvia, and Lithuania were governed by right-wing dictators and had been pro-German and anti-Soviet in their foreign policy. In the fall of 1939 Stalin demanded that Estonia sign a military alliance with the USSR and join the Soviets in a war with Finland. Though Estonia, whose people were linguistically and culturally close to the Finns, refused to agree to fight Finland, it conceded bases to the Soviets. Lithuania was forced to allow nearly thirty thousand Red Army troops to be stationed on Lithuanian territory, and Latvia as well was required to house Soviet soldiers. In October Stalin turned up the pressure on the Finns. In a meeting in the Kremlin with Finnish representatives, he demanded that the Gulf of Finland be closed to all enemies of the Soviet Union, that Hango become a Soviet base, and that the Finnish-Soviet border be moved westward to protect Leningrad. Parts of eastern Karelia would be given to Finland in compensation. The Finns agreed to only minor concessions but refused to give up any of their territory. On November 30 the Soviets claimed that they had been attacked by the Finns and launched an offensive in which they bombed Helsinki. The war was started so cynically and seemed such an uneven struggle that the Soviet Union's aggression was condemned by much of the world. Even the Finnish Communist Party refused to aid the USSR and fought for Finland. Stalin used his own loyal Finnish Communists to set up a puppet Finnish government on Soviet territory.

The Russo-Finnish War exposed the military weakness of the Soviet Union to the whole world. The Finns had set up a belt of defenses, the Mannerheim Line, across the isthmus leading to Viipuri (Vyborg) and Helsinki. The Finnish defenses and their highly mobile ski troops stopped the poorly prepared Red Army. By the end of December the first Soviet offensive had collapsed. Winston Churchill praised the courageous Finns: "Finland alone—in danger of death, superb, sublime Finland—has shown what free men can do." Stalin was furious. He berated his subordinates:

> Why aren't we advancing? Ineffective military operations may hurt our policies. The whole world is watching us. The authority of the Red Army is the guarantee of the USSR's security. If we get bogged down for a long time in the face of such a weak adversary, we will encourage the anti-Soviet forces of the imperialist circles.

The Red Army then changed its tactics, bringing in new divisions and making Timoshenko the new front commander. The second offensive began in February 1940 and soon overwhelmed the Finns. On March 12 they signed a harsh peace with the USSR. The Soviet Union took over Hango, Viipuri, and Finnish Karelia but allowed Finland to remain independent. Official Soviet statistics estimate that the Finns had lost 60,000 men killed to their 48,745, but Finnish and Western sources estimate that the Soviets lost somewhere between 230,000 and 270,000 killed and another 200,000 to 300,000 wounded, while the Finns lost 25,000 killed and 43,500 wounded. For Finland the losses were dear indeed, and 420,000 Finns lost their homes and had to move into what was left of independent Finland.

For the Soviets the war was a rude awakening. Clearly the Workers' and Peasants' Red Army (RKKA) was not yet battle-ready. It had expanded enormously in the 1930s, from 542,000 men on active duty and 842,000 in territorial reserve units in 1930 to 1,300,000 in 1936, when two-thirds of the reserve forces were converted to active duty units. Conscription was raised to 600,000 men a year, as the Red Army became a predominantly standing army in 1936. But the doubling of the size of the army was not met with a simultaneous doubling of the officer corps. Moreover, the Russian and Soviet armies did not have professional noncommissioned officers, like sergeants, to train the troops. As a result, the Red Army was extremely poorly trained. Problems only became worse in the years 1937–41. The army tripled in size in those years until it reached nearly 5 million men, while the shortage of officers grew even more acute when more than 22,000 officers were arrested and many of them killed during the Great Purges. About 11,500 were released from prison camps and reinstated by May 1940, but as late as the summer of 1941 three-quarters of Soviet officers had been in their jobs less than a year. A mere 7 percent of them had higher education, and only a little over a third had finished intermediate military schooling.

In early May Stalin removed his pal Voroshilov as commissar of defense, "promoting" him to deputy chairman of the Defense Council, and replaced him with Timoshenko, who was raised to the rank of marshall of the Soviet Union. The new commissar began a vigorous program of military reforms, re-instituting iron discipline among the troops, placing more emphasis on rank and hierarchy, and introducing new field regulations and training manuals. He reduced the powers of the political commissars, who had been equal to commanders, instituted unity of command, and introduced new mechanized corps and more advanced tanks, artillery, and aircraft. But it was too little too late. The army sent into the field in 1941 remained unwieldy, inadequately trained and led, and poorly equipped.

Soviet propaganda backfired on the army. The public and the military had been told repeatedly that the Red Army was invincible. No other assessment was permissible, and officers who had doubts about the battle-worthiness of the army kept silent. The purges had sown great suspicion of officers among the ranks, and morale was low. Discipline declined, accidents and suicides increased. When Soviet soldiers crossed the border into eastern Poland, they were shocked to see how much better people lived on the other side. They greedily bought up what consumer goods they could find—alarm clocks and ladies' shoes were popular—to the dismay of their commanders. Much of the idealism of the antifascism struggle had been dissipated by the partnership with the Nazis, and the territorial aggrandizements in the Baltics and Finland were difficult to rationalize.

During the twenty-two months of the Nazi-Soviet Pact foreign Communist parties lost what support and sympathy they had enjoyed during the Popular Front period. At first Communists defended the pact but declared their continued opposition to and willingness to fight Hitler. Unable to change overnight from antifascists to supporters of an alliance with the Nazi state, Communists in France voted for war credits and supported their government's war effort against Germany, calling for the defense of "the national independence and freedom" of Poland. In Britain Communists backed the war as "antifascist." But by mid-September agents from the Soviet Union were forcing foreign Communists to bow to the Soviet line, renounce their pledge to fight Hitler, and condemn the war as imperialist. When the Red Army invaded Poland, the British Communist newspaper, *Daily Worker*, proclaimed, "The Red Army is bringing bread to the starving peasants." In France, the Communists changed their line to "revolutionary defeatism." Party leader Thorez, who had been the first Communist parliamentary deputy to join the French Army, now deserted his unit and escaped to Moscow. The rigid loyalty to the Soviet Union of the Communist core did not extend to much of the rank and file and their sympathizers, who drifted away. The French government arrested over thirty-four hundred Communists, outlawed the party, and dissolved over 600 trade unions. By the end of September 1939, only two Communist parties, the British and the Swedish, were legal in Europe.

The USSR had completed a circular evolution from being an enemy of the Versailles settlement through the period emphasizing collective security, in which it defended the European status quo, to its rapprochement with Germany and a policy of ruthlessly rearranging the map of the continent. The Soviet Union and the Comintern branded the Western powers aggressors for attempting to restore the old Poland and for continuing an imperialist war to defend their empires. Stalin asserted that "it was not Germany that attacked France and England, but France and England that attacked Germany." On December 14, 1939, a majority in the League of Nations voted to expel the Soviet Union. Stalin probably hoped that the war would end soon, without further German gains. After the partition of Poland and the war against Finland, there was little real fighting in Europe. The "phony war," in which France and Britain stood ready to fight the Germans but no real battles occurred, lasted until the spring of 1940. Then the Germans invaded Denmark and Norway on April 9 and turned toward Belgium, Luxembourg, and the Netherlands on May 10. They drove into France, around the hardened Maginot Line, and in little over a month had defeated the French (June 15) and driven the British off the continent at Dunkirk. The precipitous fall of France left the Soviet Union alone in Europe to face Germany.

Dropping all pretense about respecting the sovereignty of the Baltic republics, Stalin now moved to solidify his position in that region. Step by step he took over the republics. In Lithuania he began by accusing the government of breaking its treaty with the Soviet Union and joining in a Baltic entente with Estonia and Latvia that was aimed at the USSR. On June 15 Soviet troops entered Lithuania, and its ruler fled to Germany. A "People's Government" was formed, and a month later the newly elected Lithuanian Seim voted to join the USSR. Similar "revolutions" occurred in Estonia and Latvia. On August 3, the Supreme Soviet officially accepted the Lithuanian, Latvian, and Estonian Soviet Socialist Republics into the USSR. Here the integration of foreign states into the Soviet Union was accompanied by massive brutality and repression. In the first year alone the Soviets executed some two thousand Estonians and exiled about nineteen thousand. In mid-June 1941 the police rounded up thousands in all three republics, targeting officials of the independent government, landowners, industrialists, clergy, and intellectuals. Sovietization in the Baltic decimated the political, economic, and intellectual elites among the Baltic peoples and left a legacy of hostility toward the Soviet Union and communism that festered for the rest of the century.

Tensions tore at the Soviet-German alliance. Even though Finland had been placed in the Soviet sphere of influence, German troops entered the country. Particularly annoying to Hitler was the Soviet occupation of Bessarabia and northern Bukovina, which the Soviets took from Rumania and incorporated into the Soviet republic of Moldavia. Hitler intervened in Balkan affairs and transferred part of Transylvania from Rumania to Hungary (the "Vienna Award," August 1940). After the fascist Iron Guard took over Rumania in September and King Carol fled to the West, German troops arrived, expanding the German sphere of influence further into the Balkans. Hitler wanted the Soviets to give up the Balkans and turn their interest to Central Asia and India. Molotov flew to Berlin in November 1940 to work out the differences with the Germans over Finland and the Balkans. As he and Von Ribbentrop were negotiating, a British air raid began, and the foreign ministers were evacuated to an underground shelter. As they continued their talks about dividing up the world, Molotov asked, 'What will England say?" Von Ribbentrop snorted, "England is finished. She is no more use as a power." To which Molotov replied, "If that is so, why are we in this shelter, and whose bombs are falling?" The Soviets refused to budge from their position on the Balkans. After Molotov reported to the Politburo, its members became convinced, as Khrushchev later remembered, that war was "inevitable and probably imminent."

Indeed, Hitler had long been contemplating an attack on the USSR for both strategic and ideological reasons. At first his plan was to carry out a "crusade against Bolshevism" once Germany had destroyed the resistance of Great Britain. But after the Royal Air Force met and outmatched the Luftwaffe in the skies over Britain in 1940, Hitler realized that invasion of the island kingdom was impossible in the absence of German air superiority. With the British holding out hope that the Soviets would soon enter the war against Germany, Hitler concluded that the USSR had to be crushed as a condition for British capitulation. Since the Soviets were rearming, Germany had to deal with them sooner rather than later. At the end of July 1940 Hitler decided to attack the USSR in the spring of 1941, and he set about securing allies for the coming campaign. Germany concluded the Tripartite Pact with Italy and Japan, and soon after Slovakia, Hungary, Rumania, and Bulgaria joined as well. Pressure was applied to Turkey, but cool calculations of who was likely to win the war ultimately prevailed over pro-Nazi sympathies among Turkish leaders, and though friendly to the Germans, Turkey remained neutral for most of the war. Finland, wounded by its defeat in the Russo-Finnish War, was already cooperating with the German military. On December 5, 1940, Hitler approved "Operation Barbarrossa," the plan to invade the Soviet Union.

Before Hitler was able to attack the USSR, however, he turned toward the Balkans where his ally Mussolini had faltered in his attempt to conquer Greece. In March 1941 a coup d'etat overthrew the pro-German regent of Yugoslavia, Prince Paul, and installed the young king, Peter II. The new Yugoslav government signed a treaty of friendship and nonaggression with the Soviet Union on April 5. Hitler was furious, and the very next day Germany declared war on Yugoslavia and Greece and sent its bombers over Belgrade. By the end of April Hitler's armies had conquered Greece, eliminated Yugoslavia as a united state, and moved troops into Bulgaria. The war in the Balkans delayed his move into the USSR by a few weeks, though the late thaw and the heavy mud made a May invasion very unlikely in any case. Now a new date was set for Barbarossa: June 22, 1941.

Suggestions for Further Reading

We are fortunate to have the excellent studies of Soviet foreign policy before and during the period of collective security in Jonathan Haslam, *Soviet Foreign Policy, 1930–33: The Impact of the Depression* (London and New York, 1983), *The Soviet Union and the Search for Collective Security, 1933–1939* (London and New York, 1984), and *The Soviet Union and the Threat from the East, 1933–41: Moscow, Tokyo and the Prelude to the Pacific War* (London, 1992). See also Jiri Hochman, *The Soviet Union and the Failure of Collective Security, 1934–1938* (Ithaca, N.Y., 1984); and the older classic, Max Beloff, *The Foreign Policy of Soviet Russia*, 2 vols. (Oxford, 1947–49).

On various aspects of Soviet foreign policy, see Gustav Hilger and Alfred G. Meyer, *The Incompatible Allies: A Memoir-History of German-Soviet Relations, 1918–1941* (New York, 1953); Gerald Freund, *Unholy Alliance: Russian-German Relations from the Treaty of Brest-Litovsk to the Treaty of Berlin* (New York, 1957); Gerhard L. Weinberg, *Germany and the Soviet Union, 1939–41* (London, 1954); Anthony Read and David Fisher, *The Deadly Embrace: Hitler, Stalin, and the Nazi-Soviet Pact, 1939–1941* (New York, 1988); Hugh D. Phillips, *Between the Revolution and the West: A Political Biography of Maxim M. Litvinov* (Boulder, Colo., 1992); and Jan T. Gross, *Revolution from Abroad: The Soviet Conquest of Poland's Western Ukraine and Western Belorussia* (Princeton, N.J., 1988); and for a broad and interpretative comparative biography of the two principal leaders of Europe in the 1930s, see Allan Bullock, *Hitler and Stalin, Parallel Lives* (New York, 1992).

On the Comintern, see the superb history by Paolo Spriano, *Stalin and the European Communists* (London, 1985), as well as Franz Borkenau, *World Communism: A History of the Communist International* (1938; reprinted, Ann Arbor, Mich., 1962); E. H. Carr, *Twilight of the Comintern, 1930–1935* (New York, 1982); Fernando Claudin, *The Communist Movement: From Comintern to Cominform*, 2 vols. (New York 1975); the excellent volume of documents edited by Helmut Gruber, *Soviet Russia Masters the Comintern: International Communism in the Era of Stalin's Ascendancy* (New York, 1974); and the fascinating memoir of Arvo Tuominen, *The Bells of the Kremlin: An Experience in Communism* (Hanover, N.H., and London, 1982).

CHAPTER 14
The Great Fatherland War

In the twentieth century the peoples of the Soviet Union experienced six phases of general catastrophe and destruction: World War I, the civil war and famine, collectivization and famine, the Great Purges, World War II, and the period of decline and collapse in the 1990s. In between they lived through four periods of restoration and recovery: the New Economic Policy, which raised the economy to pre–World War I levels; the industrialization, urbanization, and spread of popular education and upward mobility of the mid-1930s; the recovery after World War II; and the years of the post-Stalin reforms. The pain and costs of the periods of destruction were borne by the Soviet people, who had little other choice, as were the costs of the periods of recovery and restoration. In the vicissitudes of seventy-four years of Soviet power, undoubtedly the most catastrophic experience occurred in the years 1941 to 1945.

Invasion

On June 21, 1941, Marshall Timoshenko called Stalin to tell him that several German deserters had crossed into Soviet territory and reported that a German attack was planned for that night. Stalin ordered him to come with Generals Georgii Zhukov and Nikolai Vatutin to the Kremlin. When they arrived, the full Politburo was gathered. Stalin asked them, "Well, what now?" There was silence, until Timoshenko spoke up: "We must immediately order all troops in the frontier districts on to full battle alert." Stalin disagreed: "It would be premature to issue that order now. It might still be possible to settle the situation by peaceful means. We should issue a brief order saying that we might attack if provoked by German action. The border units must not allow themselves to be provoked into anything that might cause difficulties." The military leaders had no choice but to agree, and as they prepared to leave, Stalin added, "I think Hitler is trying to provoke us. He surely has not decided to make war." At three o'clock in the morning, the meeting of the Politburo broke up. Half an hour later, at 3:30 A.M., on June 22, 1941, the German army invaded the Soviet

Union, beginning the most massive military confrontation between two states in history. By that time Stalin had returned to his villa at Kuntsevo on the outskirts of Moscow. He was awoken by a telephone call from Zhukov, who informed him of the attack. Stalin was silent. "Did you understand what I said, Comrade Stalin?" Zhukov asked. Again, silence. Only when Zhukov asked again, did the stunned Stalin answer that he understood and ordered Zhukov, Timoshenko, and the Politburo members to return to the Kremlin.

Stalin had refused to believe that Germany would attack the USSR without first knocking England out of the war. He later told the British newspaper publisher Lord Beaverbrook, "I knew war would come, but I thought I might gain another six months or so." He had ignored Churchill's warnings in April 1941 of an imminent attack; rejected the reports from the German Communist spy Richard Sorge, who had infiltrated the German Embassy in Tokyo and sent Moscow information on the exact date of attack; and had not taken seriously a Soviet report a few weeks earlier that 4 million German soldiers had been massed on the Soviet borders. Most astonishing of all he brushed aside as "disinformation" the treasonous revelation of the German ambassador to the Soviet Union, who told his Soviet counterpart in May that Hitler had decided to launch a war against the USSR on June 22. Stalin reasoned that the German military wanted to instigate a war with the Soviet Union but that Hitler could be trusted to prevent it for the time being.

Despite all the warnings, Stalin refused to issue a command for combat readiness until two and a half hours before the actual invasion began. Only at 7:15 A.M., nearly four hours after the invasion had begun, did the government order "open active offensive operations against the enemy" to begin. Two hours later Timoshenko issued Directive No. 3, ordering all three Soviet fronts to launch offensives against the Germans. But ordering offensive action at a moment when entrenchment or retreat was called for only worsened the situation. By that time Soviet forces had no capability to take the offensive. The Germans had pushed far into the Soviet Union, smashing the land defenses and obliterating much of the air force while it was still on the ground.

Stalin was so shaken by the invasion that he went into a depression. Molotov received the German ambassador, who read him Hitler's proclamation. "Surely we have not deserved this," Molotov replied. Later the foreign minister, not Stalin, announced to the Soviet people that war had begun. Distraught and confused as he left the People's Commissariat of Defense a week later, he burst out: "Lenin left us a great inheritance, and we, his heirs, have fucked it all up!" Stalin may have thought that his comrades were about to overthrow him or that a revolutionary uprising might sweep away the Soviet regime itself. When Stalin did not emerge from his country home, the Politburo members went to see him. As Mikoyan remembers,

> We found him in an armchair in the small dining room. He looked up and said, "What have you come for?" He had the strangest look on his face, and the question itself was pretty strange, too. After all, he should have called us in.

On our behalf, Molotov said power had to be concentrated in order to ensure rapid decision-making and somehow get the country back on its feet, and Stalin should head the new authority. Stalin looked surprised but made no objection and said, "Fine."

On June 30 the State Defense Committee was created with Stalin as its chairman. Finally, on July 3, Stalin made a radio address to the nation. "Comrades! Citizens! Brothers and sisters!" he began. This war with fascist Germany, he said, is not simply a war between two armies but "a great war of the whole Soviet people against the German-fascist forces. The goal of this all-people's patriotic war against the fascist oppressors is not only to liquidate the danger handing over our country but to help all the peoples of Europe groaning under the yoke of German fascism." The USSR is not alone, he went on, but allied to Europe and America in a struggle for "independence and democratic freedom." And he concluded, "Forward to our victory!" A few months later when Khrushchev came from Kiev to see Stalin, he noted a changed man:

> He had pulled himself together, straightened up, and was acting like a real soldier. He had also begun to think of himself as a great military strategist, which made it harder than ever to argue with him. He exhibited all the strong-willed determination of a heroic leader.

Outside the Kremlin ordinary people were stunned by the news of the German invasion. Largely convinced by Soviet propaganda that the USSR was invulnerable, many considered the attack to be the act of a madman and were convinced that the war would be over in a week. Some believed that German workers would rise up to support the USSR. Soviet workers voted in their factories to increase the workday by two hours, and thousands of volunteers signed up for military duty. Others rushed to the banks to withdraw their savings or to food stores to stock up. Some made excuses to avoid service. The sudden vulnerability of the government emboldened critics to raise their voices. People questioned why a treaty had been signed with the Nazis. Others were open about their hostility to the Communists. A drunk doorman at a brakes factory told his boss, "You're a Communist, but just wait, soon the time will come when it will be the end for all you Communists." Signs of open anti-Semitism appeared in Moscow; "Good, the war's begun—they'll kill the Jews," some workers at the Stalin Automobile Plant were overheard to say. The popular mood in this hour of national danger included much pessimism, fear, griping, and complaining but also patriotic determination to drive back the enemy.

The German invasion was the largest land invasion ever launched in history. Joined by Rumanian, Hungarian, and Finnish troops, the German army met Soviet forces unprepared for war. "At the outbreak of the war," Khrushchev would reveal after Stalin's death, "we did not even have sufficient numbers of rifles to arm the mobilized manpower." The twenty-two-month respite gained by the Nazi-Soviet Pact had allowed some increase in military production and preparedness but not nearly enough to withstand such a massive German force. Though the Soviet frontier had been moved hundreds of miles to the west after the partition of Poland, the Soviets had managed to dismantle the old fortifications on the 1939 border but not to complete building defenses along the new border.

In many ways the Nazi-Soviet Pact had lulled Stalin and the General Staff into a false sense of security. Soviet strategy was based on the assumption that there would be no war in 1941 and that the Soviet Union still had time to prepare for the likely conflict, that a surprise attack by Germany was impossible and any offensive from the West would be preceded by an ultimatum, a declaration of war, or small-scale military operations. The Soviets believed they would have time to take up defensive positions, quickly repel the enemy, and move the war to foreign territory. The Red Army did not develop operational or tactical army groups to repel a surprise attack. A slogan of the time confidently proclaimed: "The Red Army will win any future war with little expenditure of blood and will carry the fight into the enemy's own territory." Such a miscalculation led Stalin to overrule his advisors, who cautiously suggested

Figure 14.1. Europe and the Soviet Union during World War II.

placing supply dumps beyond the Volga; instead, Stalin ordered that they be concentrated in border regions, where the Germans found them in the first weeks of the war.

The Soviet Union had become an industrial power thanks to the colossal efforts of the forced industrialization of the 1930s, but it still lagged far behind the other Great Powers. The USSR's gross domestic product (GDP) per capita in 1940 was 87 percent as much as Japan's, 69 percent of Italy's, 61 percent of France's, but only 45 percent of Germany's, 36 percent of Great Britain's, and 29 percent of the United States' GDP. In many ways the Soviet economy of the 1930s had been a war economy. Much of the Soviet industrialization effort had been stimulated by and directed toward the requirements of military defense. The defense budget had grown from 12 percent of the total state budget in the early 1930s to 43 percent by 1941. But after the Great Purges industrial growth slowed down. Pig iron, steel, and rolled metal production fell after 1938, and automobile and tractor outputs declined by more than a quarter. Though there were some improvements on the eve of the war, they were uneven.

Even more telling was the inferior quality of Soviet armaments. More than three-quarters of all airplanes and half of the tanks in the border districts were obsolete. The dismal showing of Soviet aircraft in the Spanish Civil War, where they had been outgunned by German planes, had demonstrated Soviet vulnerability in the air. Several noted airplane designers were arrested in the purges, and the most up-to-date new planes, like the YAK-1 and MiG-3 fighters, were hardly in mass production by 1941. New tanks were designed and built on the eve of the war, as well as a rocket mortar, later nicknamed "Katiusha" after a popular song, that was mass-produced starting in June 1941. But there were serious deficiencies in the production of artillery. Against the advice of the commissar of armaments, Stalin ordered production to be shifted from a smaller- to a larger-millimeter cannon despite the time lag in availability that would occur. The commissar warned Zhdanov, "You are permitting the disarmament of the army before the war." As a result of this decision, mortar production was disrupted, and the innocent commissar was arrested.

Like the German military command, the Soviet leadership had rethought the nature of modern warfare in the 1930s, moving away from the static concepts of wars of position, like the trench warfare of World War I, to warfare employing the movement of mechanized formations. A motorized mass army would be deployed in depth, with frontline troops in the field of operations and mechanized reserves behind ready to deal with any enemy breakthroughs and to reinforce the attacking forces. In the USSR Marshall Tukhachevskii had argued for dealing a swift, decisive blow against the enemy by launching in-depth operations to take advantage of the new technologies. But he was opposed by Voroshilov, the people's commissar of defense, who believed that rapid victory was impossible and that the Soviet Union had to prepare for a long war of attrition. In this view defensive operations were the way to achieve victory. For them the infantry and artillery units were more crucial than reliance on armor. Once Tukhachevskii fell victim to the purges, the defensive strategy prevailed.

Though the Soviets had been among the first to develop mechanized military units, as early as 1932, after the execution of Tukhachevskii and the disasters of the Spanish Civil War, the Soviet high command decided that large tank formations were unnecessary and abolished the mechanized corps. They had to be reconstituted just before the war. During the Great Purges the government also disbanded the schools and bases for partisans that had been set up in the late 1920s and early 1930s in Ukraine, arrested their leaders, and accused them of organizing guerrilla warfare against the Soviet people. For all its ruthless efficiency in crushing domestic resistance, Stalin's dictatorship, with its inherent suspicion of deviance or initiative and its arbitrary and callous treatment of its own loyalists, proved to be completely unprepared for its greatest trial.

From Blitzkrieg to War of Attrition

Hitler's calculation that Germany could defeat the Soviet Union quickly was shared by many in Britain and the United States. The powerful German offensives in Western Europe, the so-called *Blitzkrieg*, had eliminated all of Hitler's opponents on the continent except the USSR. What was less appreciated at the time was that Germany was fighting the war in the West without the total mobilization of its economy, and even after the Battle of Britain the Nazis had not shifted to a fully mobilized wartime economy. Their successes were dependent on short, massive attacks. If the Germans became bogged down in a long war of attrition against the combined economic and military might of the USSR, Great Britain, and the United States, they were bound to lose, given their far more limited resources. Thus, the war in Russia became the killing ground on which the racist and imperialist hopes of the Nazis foundered.

The fascist forces that invaded the Soviet Union on June 22 numbered 190 divisions: 3.6 million men, 50,000 pieces of artillery, 5,000 aircraft, and 3,648 tanks. The Soviet Union had 2,900,000 troops and 15,000 tanks (more tanks than the rest of the world combined) and soon would be producing the finest tanks in the world. They also had more aircraft than the Germans had on the eastern front (9,000 to 2,510), but the Soviet planes were inferior to the German. The German surprise attack was so swift and effective that some 5,000 Soviet airplanes were destroyed on the ground. The German plan was to launch a three-pronged attack. Army Group North was to march north of the impenetrable Pripet Marshes in western Belorussia, through the Baltic states toward Leningrad; Army Group Center would move eastward toward Moscow, 650 miles from the border; and Army Group South would push through Ukraine to the Dnieper River and Crimea and then on toward Rostov and the Caucasus, ultimately capturing the oil center at Baku.

The lightning war worked well at first. The advance through the first two Baltic states was swift. In Lithuania nationalists overthrew the Soviet government in Kaunas and declared the republic independent. Tens of thousands of people turned on the pro-Soviet forces, and when the Germans entered the town just a few hours after the war had begun, it was already securely in the hands of local nationalists. On July 1 the Germans took the Latvian capital, Riga, and moved into southern Estonia. A fierce battle raged around Tartu, the Estonian university town, where nationalist partisans fought Soviet troops. The Soviets staunchly defended the Estonian capital, Tallinn, home to much of their Baltic fleet. But at the end of August the city was abandoned and the fleet attempted to flee to Leningrad. Dozens of ships and about ten thousand lives were lost in what has been called "the Russian Dunkirk." Further south the Germans captured Minsk, the capital of Belorussia, and Bialystok on July 9, after destroying two Soviet armies completely and decimating a third. The Germans captured hundreds of thousands of prisoners and thousands of tanks. Smolensk fell on July 16, and several hundred thousand more prisoners fell into German hands. At the end of July the Germans paused for a month to resupply. Though they had advanced rapidly, the Germans nevertheless had been held up by resistance in Ukraine and around Smolensk. The German Ostheer (Eastern Army) was surprised to find that the Soviet soldiers fought fiercely, even when surrounded.

Hitler's war in the East was to be a war of extermination, plunder, and enslavement, driven by Nazi ideology and intended to be extraordinarily brutal. The Soviet Union represented the mortal enemy of Nazi racism, an obstacle to German expansion, and an opportunity for colonial exploitation. This was, in Hitler's words, a "war between two ideologies."

> A Communist is not and can never be considered a fellow soldier. This war will be a battle of annihilation. . . . It will be very different from the war in

Figure 14.2. A German officer deals with five suspected partisans in occupied Kishinev, Moldavia, July 1941 (Bildarchiv Preussischer Kulturbesitz).

the West. In the East harshness will guarantee us a mild future. Military
leaders must overcome their [humanitarian] reservations.

Goering urged the commanders in the East to intensify exploitation of the local population: "I do not care if you say that your people [the Russians] are
dying of hunger. So they may, as long as not a single German dies of hunger."
German policy was to kill all Communist leaders outright without trial, as well
as partisans, the guerrillas fighting behind enemy lines, and not to prosecute
German soldiers for crimes against the civilian population. As a result of such
an openly vicious policy, some 57 percent of Soviet prisoners of war died before the end of the war (about 3 million people), while only 3.5 percent of British
and American prisoners in Germany perished. Even Soviet treatment of German prisoners, harsh as it was, was not as devastating as the German treatment of the Soviets; of the 3.1 million German prisoners of war in the USSR,
35 to 37 percent died and over a longer period of time.

Ordinary soldiers absorbed the attitudes of the Nazi and Soviet leaders.
Both sides believed that defeat would lead to annihilation of their way of life.
Whereas German soldiers in the West did not make last-ditch efforts or fight
to the last man against the Allies, they fought much more fiercely in the East.
There the Germans lost more men in one month of fighting than in the entire
war in the West. Between November 1942 and October 1943 the Ostheer suffered 1.5 million casualties and was reduced to just over 2 million men by December. By the end of March 1945 the total casualties of the Ostheer were over
6 million, a number that represented four-fifths of all German losses on all
fronts since June 1941. Historian Omer Bartov argues that the major reason for
the greater effort in the East, and the greatest motivation for German soldiers
on the Eastern Front, was Nazi ideology. Nazi propaganda presented Hitler as
an instrument of God, the protector of German culture and blood. Russians
and other Slavs were pictured as *Untermenschen*, a species of subhumans, and
soldiers were seldom punished in Russia for raping or brutalizing the population as they were on the Western Front. Letters from rank-and-file soldiers
reflected the inverted reality of the Nazi vision. One soldier wrote home that
Russians were "a people which needs long and good schooling in order to become human." Another wrote that Russians were "no longer human beings,
but wild hordes and beasts, who have been bred by Bolshevism during the last
twenty years."

Both Hitler and Stalin made major miscalculations early in the war. In anticipation of the German invasion, the Soviet General Staff in September 1940
had argued that the Nazi attack would be concentrated in the center toward
Moscow and in the north toward Leningrad, but Stalin overruled his commanders and ordered deployment in the south, believing that the Germans
would make a major effort to capture Ukraine. Hitler's generals in fact urged
the Fuhrer to concentrate the main blow against Moscow, but Hitler favored
the three-pronged attack and decided in the summer of 1941 to divert even
more of his troops into Ukraine to take Crimea and Kiev. The drive to Moscow
would be continued only after Ukraine had been conquered. In late August the
Ostheer began the southern campaign, with General Heinz Guderian making

Figure 14.3. "Tractor in the field, so that there can be tanks in battle!" Poster by Viktor Ivanov and Olga Burova, 1942 (Courtesy of Hoover Institution Archives, Poster Collection, RU/SU2159).

a major breakthrough. His Panzer army surrounded five Soviet armies on the southwestern front. Stalin's generals urged withdrawal, but Stalin refused to give up the Ukrainian capital, Kiev. On September 18, Kiev fell and the Germans captured over half a million prisoners and annihilated the Soviet southwest front.

Meanwhile Leningrad was besieged by Finns from the north and Germans from the south. The Finns regained much of the territory they had lost in the Russo-Finnish War and came within twenty miles of Leningrad. The deep hatred of the Finns for the Russians, who had beaten them just over a year earlier, was evident in the vicious fighting. A Finnish officer taunted a wounded Komsomol in Russian: "And you stupid kids think you are going to save Russia. What's the idea of this suicide, I ask you? Soviet Russia is kaput." The boy raised himself, and with blood flowing from his mouth, he shouted, "Hitlerite baboons! I spit on you. Go ahead. Shoot." The officer kicked him, then shot him. The Finns and Russians stayed in position roughly on the 1939 border for the next three years. The German Army Group North advanced toward Leningrad and on September 8 cut it off almost entirely from the outside world. Only a tiny window was left open where the Germans had failed to cross the Neva River and link up with the Finns. For the next three years Leningrad endured the longest siege of any city since biblical times (900 days).

Of the nearly 3 million people trapped in Leningrad, the second largest city in the Soviet Union, almost half would be dead by the end of the war. During the ferocity of the siege, the city's inhabitants displayed a gritty determination not to succumb to the enemy. Over two hundred thousand people volunteered for military duty in the first week. The tragic poet Anna Akhmatova stayed in the city, along with the composer Dmitrii Shostokovich, who wrote much of his Seventh Symphony there, later dedicated to Leningrad, until ordered by the government to leave the city. The city authorities made special arrangements for the rapid evacuation of children and the treasures of the Hermitage Museum. But Stalin, who unrealistically expected forces from Leningrad to stop the German advance, grew angry at local party chief Zhdanov and the chief local commander, Voroshilov, whom he called "specialists in retreat." In September he sent General Zhukov to organize the defense of the city, just as Hitler decided not to take Leningrad by storm but to starve it into submission.

The city was pounded from the air and from long-range artillery. Fires broke out, gutting historic buildings and Soviet-built apartments. Slowly starvation gripped the city. The food supply dwindled until whole families perished, with no one left to take their corpses to the cemetery. "Today it is so simple to die, a woman noted in her diary. "You just begin to lose interest, then you lie on the bed and you never again get up." Another woman spent an evening looking for a cat, not to pet, but to eat. There were instances of cannibalism. Malnutrition led to disease, disinterest in sex, and a fall in the birth rate. There was no electricity, little water, and not enough fuel to keep people warm through the bitterly cold winters. But the cold froze the river and Lake Ladoga and allowed the Soviets to build an ice road, a "road of life," across the lake over which supplies could reach the city. Leningrad held out until it was liberated in January 1944. As the workers of the Kirov Works had predicted almost three years earlier, "Soon death will be more afraid of us than we of death."

Many military analysts believe that Hitler's decision to divide his forces in the summer of 1941 was the most fateful error that he made. Even though the campaign in Ukraine and the capture of Kiev proved to be a great military triumph, the southern campaign interrupted the drive toward Moscow for 78 days, sent tens of thousands of men 300 miles south and then back north again, exhausting the men of the southern flank and straining supplies. Muscovites were able to use those months to stiffen the defenses of the capital. In September Hitler decided to consolidate his troops in the center and concentrate on the capture of Moscow in what was called "Operation Typhoon." The Battle of Moscow went through three phases: the first German offensive from September 30 through October, the second offensive from November 17 to December 5, and the Russian counteroffensive, which began on December 5 and continued into the spring of 1942. Three million soldiers fought in this battle, 40 percent of all Soviet ground forces and 38 percent of all German infantry on the eastern front. With characteristic ferocity and speed the Germans broke through the Russian front, carried out another huge encirclement at Viazma and Briansk, and again captured over half a million men. Almost eight Soviet armies, commanded by Timoshenko, were wiped out. When Orel was taken on October 8, General Jodl reported to Hitler, "We have finally and without any exaggeration won the war!" But Soviet resistance had slowed down the German advance and gained time for the Russians to prepare Moscow's defense.

Still, the Soviet capital was in mortal danger of capture, and the government was prepared to evacuate to Kuibyshev. The university was evacuated, and plans were made to move defense industries eastward, but workers and other Muscovites were upset by the idea of abandoning the city. When People's Commissar of Armaments Dmitrii Ustinov arrived at a defense plant to convince the workers of the need to evacuate, the plant director told him:

> The situation is pretty bad—actually it is awful. . . . The workers are saying "We will not surrender Moscow!" and that they do not want to leave. They say we have to do everything necessary to defend the capital city, not abandon it. It is better, they say, for us to die here in battle than to go someplace else.

Only with difficulty did Ustinov manage to convince the workers that they had to leave. But on October 16 panic spread through the city and government officials fled for the east. Crowds of people, numbering tens of thousands, gathered in the streets and beat up the police. Workers at a dairy discovered the director with some dairy products; they seized them and his car and stuffed him upside down in a barrel of sour cream. A plane was on the runway for Stalin, but after paying a visit to his wife Allilueva's grave in Novodevichii Monastery, he decided to remain in the Kremlin. Zhukov, whom Stalin had recalled from Leningrad to take charge of the capital's defense, mined the bridges and rail junctions, and one hundred thousand Muscovite women dug trenches.

Stalin spoke to the people on the eve of the anniversary of the October Revolution (November 6), calling on them to remember the great commanders of the Russian past, invoking Russian nationalism to stir the defenders of the city, and blending the heroic military traditions of the Russian Empire with the cause of Lenin and the Soviet Union.

> Comrades, Red Army and Red Navy men, officers and political workers, men and women partisans! The whole world is looking upon you as the power capable of destroying the German robber hordes! The enslaved peoples of Europe are looking upon you as their liberators. . . . Be worthy of this great mission! The war you are waging is a war of liberation, a just war. May you be inspired in this war by the heroic figures of our great ancestors, Aleksandr Nevskii, Dmitrii Donskoi, Minin and Pozharskii, Aleksandr Suvorov, Mikhail Kutuzov. May you be blessed by great Lenin's victorious banner. Death to the German invaders! Long live our glorious country, its freedom and independence! Under the banner of Lenin—onward to victory!

Stalin's presence in the city and his speech helped to strengthen resistance to the German offensive. Fierce battles raged at the edges of the city. Stalin ordered a counterattack on November 13. When Zhukov protested, Stalin called Bulganin, the political commissar at the front, and ominously told him, "You and Zhukov there have been giving yourselves airs. But we will find a way to deal with you." The Germans countered, and the Soviets, largely without reserves, retreated, fighting with their backs to the Moscow-Volga Canal. Temperatures fell to minus twenty degrees Fahrenheit. "Are you certain we can hold Moscow?" Stalin asked Zhukov. "I ask you this with pain in my heart. Speak the truth, like a Communist." Zhukov replied that they would hold Moscow without doubt, but they needed two more armies and 200 more tanks. On December 5 seven hundred thousand Soviet troops, many of them brought in from the east, launched their counteroffensive along a 560-mile front. The Germans fell back several hundred miles, losing half a million men and thousands of guns and tanks. General Guderian urged Hitler to allow German troops to withdraw, but Hitler proved as stubborn and determined as Stalin. The German retreat halted and the front stabilized.

The Battle of Moscow, many military analysts believe, was the military turning point of the war on the Eastern Front. Along with the Battle of Britain, it stopped the further expansion of Nazi power. The winter was one of the harshest in a century, and some analysts have maintained that the ultimate German defeat and Soviet victory were actually won by "General Winter." But the weather, of course, was the same for men and machines on both sides of the front, and the Soviets simply were better prepared and clothed and therefore endured the subzero temperatures better than their enemies. Germany, though the master of Europe in the winter of 1941, had became bogged down in a long war deep in Russia. The Nazis failed to win a quick victory on the Russian steppes, and the *Blitzkrieg* was proving to be a far riskier tactic in the East where vast spaces, poor roads, mud, and the cold took a heavy toll on the machines of war. As it moved further into Russia, the German army steadily became demodernized. Its supply lines grew ever longer, until they stretched

1,000 miles, to feed a German front that extended 1,500 miles. The 142 German divisions in the East suffered 750,000 casualties, about a quarter of their forces, in the first six months of the Soviet war. From June 1941 until March 1942, 15,000 German officers were killed, compared to only 1,233 killed from 1939 to 1941. The war in the East was bleeding the German Army and weakening it, but it was still not clear whether the Soviets or the Germans would be the first to collapse.

Soviet losses in the first six months of the war were also staggering. The Germans captured 3,355.000 Soviet prisoners of war, one of whom was Stalin's older son, Iakov (who, like millions of others, died or was killed in a Nazi concentration camp). Soviet dead may have numbered 4 million by the end of 1941. The Germans occupied most of the European part of the Soviet Union. This area included both important grain-producing regions and the heartland of Soviet industry, as well as the access to the Baltic and Black seas. Though the Soviets had built new industrial centers in the Urals and Siberia in the 1930s, they had, nevertheless, concentrated most armaments facilities in Ukraine and European Russia, the very areas seized by the Nazis. Over 70 percent of iron ore, pig iron, and rolled steel came from this region, as well as 90 percent of the aircraft and nearly three-quarters of tank production, 38 percent of Soviet grain, 84 percent of its sugar, and 38 percent of the cattle and 60 percent of the pigs

Figure 14.4. "Grief (The dead won't let us forget)." Soviet survivors search for their war dead on the Kerch Peninsula, January 1942. Photograph by Dmitrii Baltermants (SOVFOTO).

of prewar USSR. By November 1941 the Germans occupied territory where 40 percent of the prewar Soviet population had lived.

By delaying the German army, however briefly, the Soviets managed to evacuate thousands of industrial enterprises from the west to the east. Under committees directed by Kaganovich and Mikoyan, a colossal effort was undertaken in the summer and fall of 1941, and again in June–September 1942, to coordinate the movement of industry and people. As early as the second day of the war women and children were evacuated from Minsk. Tens of thousands of people, a million from Belorussia, fled to the east, clogging the roads and straining the railroads. Four hundred thousand people were evacuated from Leningrad and 1.4 million from Moscow in the fall of 1941. Vulnerable populations, like Soviet Jews, were sometimes given priority for evacuation. Altogether 16.5 million people were evacuated through official channels and another 6.5 to 10 million fled from the front. This extraordinary flow of people, however, still left four-fifths of the people in the western Soviet Union in areas occupied by the Germans.

The Soviets evacuated some 2,592 plants, along with 30 to 40 percent of the workers and staff, to the Volga region, the Urals, Siberia, Kazakhstan, and Central Asia. By 1942 the eastern parts of the Soviet Union accounted for nearly all pig iron production, over 80 percent of crude and rolled steel output, and nearly 80 percent of coal production. Though a huge proportion of prewar industry was lost to the Germans, the massive shift of the center of industry from Ukraine and the west to the Urals and Siberia was a key factor in the ultimate Soviet victory over Nazism. But this heroic effort barely prevented the total collapse of defense production and could not make up for the evaporation of the civilian economy. Just after the invasion the government ordered the conversion of civilian plants to wartime production. As historian Mark Harrison reports, "A children's bicycle factory started making flame-throwers, at a die-stamping plant teaspoons and paperclips gave way to entrenching tools and parts for anti-tank grenades, and a typewriter works began to manufacture automatic rifles and ammunition." Finally, besides the evacuation and conversion of industries, Soviet military procurement was aided by more than $10 billion worth of Lend-Lease aid from the United States.

The Soviet economy was highly centralized, in fact, too highly centralized. Though in some ways it had long been on a wartime footing and could be easily mobilized, decisions that might have been taken locally were delayed until the center sanctioned them. In the chaos of war the state tried to tighten its control over basic industries, while it allowed greater autonomy for local people to use their own resources and ingenuity in less vital industries. The Germans delayed shifting to a full wartime economy until the winter of 1941–42, when the losses suffered on the eastern front forced them to undertake total economic mobilization for war. But time was on the side of the Soviets. Germany would by 1944 produce 22,000 light and medium tanks and over 5,000 superheavy tanks a year; it would increase its aircraft production from 12,000 in 1941 to 40,000 in 1944. But the Soviets would already be producing 30,000 tanks in 1943 and 2,000–3,000 aircraft per month in 1944–45. Added to these totals would be the 36,000 tanks produced between late 1941 and the end of

1943 by Great Britain and the 88,000 tanks and the hundreds of thousands of fighters and bombers built by the United States that the Nazis would have to face on various fronts. Twentieth-century warfare was war fought in factories as well as on the battlefields, and in this regard the Soviet economy proved to be mightier than the German.

Agriculture suffered even more than industry. Whereas the industrial workforce dropped by 12.5 percent, from 31.2 million to 27.3 million during the war (1940–45), agricultural labor fell by a third, from 36 million to 24.7 million. Over 12 million men left the farm for the front. In the two years 1941–43 the number of collective farmers fell from 35 to 15 million. Women, young people, pensioners, and the infirm were mobilized to work in agriculture until by the beginning of 1944 there were four times as many able-bodied adult women working the farms as able-bodied adult men. With fewer draught animals, less than half the number of the early war years, the burden on farmwomen was horrendous. Their workday lengthened by 50 percent, and humans had to pull plows as if they were animals. Agricultural output declined precipitously until people were consuming dangerously low amounts of calories—780 for dependents, 1,100 for employees, and between 3,000 and 4,400 for workers in heavy industry and mining.

The war had an enormous effect on the place of women in Soviet society. The number of women exceeded that of men by 7 million just before the war and by some 20 million a decade and a half after the war. Deaths were far greater among men during the war, and among the generation of women who would have been in their twenties during the war less than 60 percent were married. Women not only dominated agricultural labor but made up the majority of industrial workers (52 percent) by 1942. Three-quarters of workers in Leningrad during the siege were women. Eight hundred thousand women were mobilized into the Soviet armed forces during World War II, with half of them serving in frontline units. Dressed in male uniforms with American-made men's boots, women soldiers endured the taunts of their male compatriots and the withering waste of war to emerge with over one hundred thousand decorations and 91 Hero of the Soviet Union medals, the highest award for valor.

The Supreme Commander and the Road to Stalingrad

By the outbreak of World War II Stalin was in all but name an autocrat with powers greater than any tsar had enjoyed. He had brutally disciplined the central government, the military, the republics and local governments, and the economic infrastructure. After decimating the high command of the armed forces, his control over his military was greater than Hitler's over his, at least at the beginning of the war. He intervened and interfered in both minute and major decisions, reading through the piles of reports on his desk and even letters from ordinary soldiers. He was often abrupt and threatening, yet he was more willing to rely on his generals than was Hitler, who became progressively more involved with operational command and more contemptuous of the military leaders.

Stalin stood at the center of all strategic, logistical, and political decisions. He was chairman of the State Defense Committee, which included the highest party officials (Molotov, Beria, Malenkov, Voroshilov, Kaganovich, and later Voznesenskii and Mikoyan); the chairman of Stavka, the supreme military headquarters; general secretary of the party and chairman of the Politburo; chairman of the Council of Ministers and people's commissar of defense. Real business often took place in late-night meetings at Stalin's apartment or dacha, and the exigencies of total war reinforced and accelerated the centralization of power.

The way war was waged on the Soviet side reflected Stalin's personality and views, just as the war on the Nazi side reflected Hitler's. Hundreds of thousands of people died because of Stalin's stubbornness about pulling troops back from the early encirclements by the Germans. His suspiciousness was evident in his infamous Order No. 270 of August 1941, which declared all Soviet prisoners of war traitors and turncoats and persecuted their families and denied them benefits. Often when a prisoner escaped from the Germans and made it to the Soviet lines, he was arrested and shot. Discipline in the army was a constant problem, and Stalin once again strengthened the authority of the officers. In July 1942 braid and epaulettes were brought back, to the dismay of many soldiers. Harsher penalties were instituted for disobedience. In October 1942 the political commissars, whose powers had been reduced in 1940 but increased after the invasion, were abolished, and single command by the officer was restored.

After the Battle of Moscow the Soviet-German war settled down to a long, bloody, brutal war of attrition, punctuated by bursts of dynamic campaigns, but the balance of forces had dramatically changed. After the Japanese attack on Pearl Harbor and Hitler's gratuitous declaration of war on the United States, the European war had become a global war, and the world's most powerful economy was now on the same side as Britain and the Soviet Union. Germany was overextended and much weaker than it had been in June 1941. The Red Army, despite all its losses and sacrifices, had dealt withering body blows to the Ostheer, and the Germans had to reassess their capabilities as they planned their second campaign eastward, "Operation Blue." In 1942 the Germans were more concerned with securing the oil and other raw materials they needed to continue the war than they were with the anti-Bolshevik crusade. Without consulting his generals, Hitler decided to drive toward the Caucasus where the oil-producing and refining centers of Groznyi, Maikop, and Baku were located. But he also decided, against the advice of his army chief of staff, to divide his forces between those moving toward the Caucasus and those advancing toward the Volga with the goal of taking the symbolic city of Stalingrad.

On January 5, 1942, Stalin summoned his commanders to hear his plan for a massive offensive against all three German army groups. Zhukov argued for a concentrated attack on Army Group Center, but Malenkov and Beria agreed with Stalin, who then issued the directives for an all-out offensive along a thousand-mile front. Supplies were so low that each soldier was given only one or two rounds of ammunition each day. The offensive continued for seventy days, until the end of March, but few gains were achieved. Both armies bogged down.

The Soviets needed time to recover, rebuild, and expand their industrial production before they could knock out the Germans.

Impatiently, Stalin pushed for another offensive in May 1942. He approved Timoshenko's plan to move against Army Group South and retake Kharkov in Ukraine. Thinking that Hitler would attempt once more to attack in the center, Stalin refused to believe intelligence reports that the Germans were actually planning an offensive in the south toward the Caucasus. Stalin forced his generals to concentrate troops near Orel to prevent another German thrust toward Moscow. The Red Army around Kharkov found itself encircled, and Stalin's delay in ordering their retreat resulted in 237,000 soldiers taken prisoner. Further losses near Leningrad and Voronezh and in the south at Kerch, Sevastopol, and Rostov brought any thoughts of a Soviet offensive in 1942 to an end. For the Soviets the summer of 1942 was known as the "Black Summer" of the war. For the Germans the road was now open for their own move toward the south, to Stalingrad on the Volga and the Caucasus.

On June 28 Operation Blue began with a drive toward Voronezh and the Don River. Soviet resistance was weak, and the Germans slogged through rain to cross the Don and take Voronezh (July 6). For the first and only time in the war Stalin ordered a retreat, and the remnants of the Soviet armies in the south pulled back across the Don opening up broad stretches of the steppe to the Germans. The retreat soon turned into a rout, and Soviet commanders were unable to gain control. On July 28, Stalin issued Order No. 227, "Not One Step Back!" Since the Germans had formed special barrier detachments behind their frontline troops with orders to shoot them if they retreated, the Soviets were to "take a lesson from our enemies on this score." "Every position, every meter of Soviet territory must be defended down to the last drop of blood."

After capturing Rostov-on-Don, Hitler ordered the splitting of his forces to move on to the Caucasus and Stalingrad. The Germans took Maikop on August 9, scaled Mount Elbrus, the highest peak in Europe, and entered the Terek Valley. But they never crossed the mountains into Transcaucasia or reached the Caspian Sea, as German attention turned toward the Stalingrad operation. On August 21 the Germans, under General Friedrich Paulus, began their drive toward Stalingrad. Both Hitler and Stalin understood the symbolism of capturing or keeping the city that bore the Soviet leader's name. Neither dictator would permit his forces to withdraw. Stalin appointed General Vasilii Chuikov commander of the city's defense. The Germans managed to split Chuikov's forces, push them to within a thousand yards of the Volga, and even reach the banks of the river themselves in places. By November 8 the Germans held nine-tenths of the city, but in the ruined buildings of the city, with their backs to the Volga, the defenders held on, house by house, factory by factory. A Sergeant Pavlov held a four-story house with sixty men for fifty-eight days. On November 19 the Soviet forces launched their counter attack, a huge pincer movement against the Rumanians in the north, where Soviet tanks managed to break through, and the Germans in the south. After five days the Red Army closed its envelopment of the Axis forces, trapping 250,000 Germans. The Luftwaffe tried to supply food and fuel by air, but bad weather and Soviet artillery prevented effective resupply. The Soviets kept moving westward, not back into

Stalingrad, pushing the exhausted Germans back and widening the gap between the German lines. No rescue came to the Germans as the Soviets gained mastery in the air. Grouping seven armies around the city, the Soviets launched a final assault on January 10, 1943. Paulus signaled Hitler that further resistance was impossible, but Hitler refused to let him pull his troops out and instead promoted him to field marshall, for no German field marshall had ever surrendered. The next day, January 31, Marshall Paulus surrendered. Two thousand German officers and 90,000 soldiers were taken prisoner, 150,000 Germans were dead, and another 50,000 would die in the next few weeks in camps. Of the survivors of the battle of Stalingrad, only about 6,000 Germans ever returned home.

War and Diplomacy at Home and Abroad

Until early 1943 most observers could not tell which side, Nazi Germany or Soviet Russia, would emerge victorious in the European war. The Germans were laying siege to Leningrad and had reached the environs of Moscow, the slopes of the Caucasus, and the banks of the Volga. Only after the colossal battle at Stalingrad, which lasted six months (from August 1942 to February 2, 1943), did it become clear that the German forces, which had been superior up to this point to the Soviets, were now more evenly matched by their stubborn opponents. A mammoth struggle still lay ahead, even though by the summer of 1943 military analysts could see that Soviet superiority had been established. After Stalingrad both the Germans and Soviets were exhausted, and a general lull marked the Eastern Front from March to July 1943. The USSR desperately needed Western aid in the form of war materiel and a second front that would speed Germany's collapse. Stalin feared that Western delays would bleed the country white.

Relations with the Western Allies became strained in the spring of 1943. On April 13, 1943, German radio announced the discovery of mass graves of thousands of Polish officers in the Katyn forest. They claimed that the Poles had been executed by the Soviet secret police after the last partition of Poland. The Polish government-in-exile, then in London, called for an international investigation. Stalin bristled at what he considered an anti-Soviet insult, a "monstrous invention by the German-fascist scoundrels," and on April 26 the USSR severed relations with the London Poles. On May 9 the Soviets formed their own Polish Army to advance with the Poles in the liberation of Poland. The Soviets kept silent about the Katyn massacres for the next fifty years, and only in the Gorbachev years was it finally admitted that the executions had indeed been ordered by Stalin and carried out by Beria and the NKVD. Official figures revealed that 4,443 Polish officers had been executed at Katyn and another 16,000 at other sites.

Anxious to preserve the Grand Alliance, Stalin made a series of conciliatory gestures toward the Western powers. On May 1 he denounced any thought of a separate Soviet peace with the Germans and adopted the Casablanca formula of Roosevelt and Churchill that favored "unconditional surrender" of the enemy. Many Westerners, including Vice President Henry Wallace, who feared that Bolshevik Russia might "again embrace the Trotskyist idea of fomenting world-wide revolution" after the war, were stunned, and pleased by the surprise announcement on May 23 that the Executive Committee of the Communist International had decided to dissolve the Comintern. As he buried the Third International, which Lenin had founded, Stalin emphasized that the end of the Comintern would "facilitate the organization of the common onslaught of all freedom-loving nations against the common enemy." Once again Stalin reversed Lenin. Whereas Lenin had created the Third International as an instrument to overthrow capitalist states and foster the international socialist revolution, Stalin dissolved the Comintern to pave the way for collaboration with the capitalist world. The dissolution actually gave Communist movements in different countries a bit more room to maneuver and adapt to local needs, but only within strict limits. If any party deviated too far from Moscow's preferences, it could be called into line. The Stalinization of Communist parties around the globe was so complete by 1943 and national Communist parties so loyal to Stalin that the formal apparatus of the Comintern had become superfluous.

As if to underline the new moderation of Soviet policy, Stalin soon after received the head of the Russian Orthodox church, Metropolitan Sergius, with whom he held a long and friendly talk. He agreed to restore the Holy Synod, to allow churches to open, and to give the church a spiritual but not a social or political role in public life. The church was not permitted to run Sunday schools or carry on charitable activity. Other innovations followed: the segregation of boys and girls in schools and the return of stricter ranks, epaulets, and formalities in the army. People's commissariats were renamed ministries, and on January 1, 1944, after a competition in which the leading composers participated, a new patriotic Soviet anthem replaced the "Internationale." Instead of "Arise, ye workers, from starvation," Soviet patriots now sang, "Indestructible union of free republics, forged together through the centuries by Great Rus."

Stalin's move to a more conservative, less revolutionary posture was not popular with many Communists and workers, who considered the dissolution of the Comintern an unnecessary concession to the Allies. Peasants and religious people were pleased by the state's rapprochement with the church, but others, who had little interest in religion, were unenthusiastic. At the great Uralmash plant in the Urals, a rumor spread that singing the "Internationale" would be forbidden, and several workers asked cynically, "So what the hell will we sing now, 'God Save the Tsar'?" Soldiers were appalled by the more formal address and the fancy braid introduced into the Red Army (soon renamed the Soviet Army). In a metal factory some workers complained, "Since the army is wearing the tsarist uniform, Soviet power is changing the class character of its policies. It has turned back. Soon we will choose a tsar. This is the result of Allied pressure. They are dragging us back to the old order." On the other hand, peasants hoped that the war would bring about the abolition of the collective farms, and intellectuals looked forward to the war's end, which, they believed, would usher in a new era of greater freedom. Workers looked forward to the reintroduction of the eight-hour workday, the end of wartime taxes, and the easing of the draconian labor laws of the late 1930s. Everyone wanted an easier life, the end to the unending, unbearable sacrifices.

Ordinary Soviet citizens made superhuman efforts both at the front and in the rear to win the war. Though they never stopped complaining about shortages, inefficiencies, and the hardships they suffered, they worked until exhaustion to produce the shells and weapons needed at the front. Most people seemed to have had a clear idea of the chasm that lay between the official idealized formulations of Soviet life and the harsh reality in which they lived day by day. Soviet people expected the state to provide for their needs and were outraged when the official bread ration was reduced in November 1943, fearful of the effect even fewer calories would have on their children. "After living twenty-five years in the Soviet Union," one director of a food distribution center complained, "they cannot even feed us our fill of bread, and one cannot even talk about the rest." The social ideology of the Soviet system had been long internalized in many ordinary Soviet citizens, and popular attitudes were often not that far from those of the official ideology. People desired security and welfare and a bright future; both state officials and the people distrusted foreigners, even their Allies, and had little love for the West and its capitalism; and much of the regime's rhetoric of class warfare fit in well with people's resentment of elites and the privileged. Popular discontent was less about socialism or the Soviet regime than about the failure of the regime to live up to its own promises of plenty or its ideology of egalitarianism and popular empowerment.

Tens of thousands of ordinary citizens who found themselves behind enemy lines heeded Stalin's call, just weeks after the outbreak of war, to form partisan units to create "intolerable conditions in the occupied areas" for the Germans. Cut off from the regular Red Army and Soviet institutions, the partisans formed their own Soviet-type societies, electing their leaders and carrying out raids on their own initiative. Party control was quite weak at first, though as the Soviet Army moved westward, Communists asserted their control over the partisans. Many of the self-styled "people's avengers" resented the interference from Soviet authorities, and some remained lone wolves, resisting all imposed authority. Pro-Soviet partisans not only fought against the Germans but against anti-Soviet, anti-Semitic, and nationalist partisans. Whatever their military contribution to the final victory over fascism, the Soviet partisans managed to maintain some Soviet presence in the occupied territories— a reminder to both friend and foe that the Nazis could be effectively challenged.

Though the overwhelming majority of the Soviet population fought against the Nazi invaders, a significant minority collaborated with the enemy. Wartime defection in the USSR, which included over a million soldiers, was the largest of any country fighting in World War II. When the Germans moved into Ukraine in 1941, they were often greeted with bread and salt, the traditional greeting for a guest, by peasants who hoped for relief from the Soviet regime that had collectivized their farms and allowed them to die in the famine ten years earlier. Tens of thousands of Ukrainians joined the nationalist, anti-Soviet partisan movement. Late in 1942 a captured Soviet general, Andrei Vlasov, organized a volunteer army to fight alongside the Germans against the Red Army. Hitler was highly suspicious of a free Russian movement and allowed its organization solely for propaganda purposes. Joining the Russian Liberation Army commanded by Vlasov was for many Russians more a way to save their lives than to support the Nazi war aims, and as the Soviet forces advanced, Vlasovite soldiers often deserted, surrendered, or joined the Soviet partisans. At the war's end thousands of Soviet citizens who had collaborated with the German occupiers or been compromised by association with them followed the retreating German army and lived in refugee camps in Germany, eventually to be resettled in the United States. The Americans captured Vlasov and eleven other high-ranking officers and turned them over to the Soviets, who executed them in 1946.

The Red Army, confident and energized after Stalingrad, moved westward to take Kursk on February 8 and Kharkov in Ukraine on February 15, pushing the Germans toward the Dneiper. Exhausted by their losses on the Eastern Front but desperate for a victory, the Germans took advantage of the last weeks before the spring thaw and threw the Soviets back. With just over 3 million German troops in the Soviet Union facing 6.6 million Soviet soldiers, Hitler decided to attack the bulge around Kursk. On July 5, 1943, the Germans launched their last great offensive on the Eastern front, named "Citadel," and the largest tank battle in history began. When Marshall Zhukov launched his counterattack, the German attack turned into a stubborn defense. Just at that time the Americans and British landed on Sicily and began their drive to liberate Italy. Hitler withdrew troops from the Eastern Front to rescue his Italian ally. By early August the Soviet Army had liberated Orel and Belgorod, and Stalin proclaimed proudly that the "German legend" that the Soviets were unable to fight a summer campaign had been obliterated. While the battles of Moscow and Stalingrad were both moments that changed the balance of forces in favor of the Soviets, Kursk was the point at which the Soviet victory was assured. Stalingrad had stopped the German advance eastward, but it had ended with the two armies bogged down in central Russia. After Kursk the Soviet Army moved steadily westward, liberating Kharkov again on August 23, cleaning out the Donbass in early September, retaking Smolensk on September 25, and marching into Kiev on November 6. The outcome was no longer in doubt, only the time when the war would end.

Endgame

After the siege of Leningrad was broken in January 1944, Soviet troops far to the south moved through Ukraine destroying the Germans' southern army. In May the Soviet armies cleared the Crimean peninsula of Germans, and in June offensives in the Baltic area pushed the Finns out of Vyborg, which had been theirs up to 1940. By July Finnish politicians were looking for a way out of the war, and in September they accepted the harsh conditions for peace set down by the Soviet Union. By summer the main obstacle to Soviet victory lay in Belorussia, where the Germans still held a huge territory, called the "Belorussian

Balcony," that barred the Soviet advance toward Warsaw. Since the roads and railroads of the region were better developed than in Russia proper, the Germans were mobile and able to pin down large numbers of Soviet troops. Belorussia was one of the principal centers of partisan activity, with nearly 374,000 partisans organized in units by the summer of 1944. Just before the major thrust into Belorussia by the Soviet Army, the partisans were ordered to soften up the enemy by demolishing railroads, highways, and bridges. In one night ten thousand explosions tore up railroad tracks west of Minsk. On June 22, 1944, the third anniversary of Hitler's invasion of the USSR, the Soviet Army launched a massive offensive along the Baltic, Belorussian, and Ukrainian fronts. The Germans had lost the dynamism and confidence of the early phase of the war. Zhukov noted in his memoirs that "the German command had become sluggish and devoid of ingenuity, particularly in critical situations. Their decisions betrayed an absence of correct assessments of the capacities of both their own troops and those of the enemy." The Germans were late in withdrawing troops under heavy attack and lost men in Soviet encirclements, as the Soviets had in the first months of the war. In the first week of the summer offensive the Germans lost over 130,000 men, half of them prisoners, 900 tanks, and thousands of other vehicles. On July 3 the Soviets liberated Minsk, a completely devastated city, and moved on through the countryside of ruined, burnt-out villages, sparsely populated by the barely surviving peasants. By the middle of the month the Soviets had destroyed Army Group Center—a stupendous victory that annihilated more than twenty-five German divisions, 350,000 men, more than had been destroyed or captured at Stalingrad. In Moscow a victory parade was held; fifty-seven thousand German prisoners of war marched through the streets of the capital to the damning silence of the Russian crowds.

Soviet troops next advanced toward Lvov in annexed western Ukraine, crossed deep into prewar Poland, and drove on toward Warsaw. Moscow announced the formation of a Polish Committee of National Liberation, which, Stalin hoped, would be the core of a new, pro-Soviet Polish government to rival the hostile Polish government-in-exile in London. In late July Soviet troops reached the suburbs of Warsaw but were unable to cross the Vistula River. Suddenly, on August 1, just five hours after the Soviet soldiers had dug in across the river, the Polish underground within Warsaw ordered an uprising against the Germans. Stalin was angry that the Poles had started an uprising, clearly aimed at strengthening the hand of the London Poles, without coordination with the Soviet army command. He was not interested in helping the Warsaw insurgents, and later many writers would claim that he deliberately allowed the rising to be crushed by the Germans. In fact, the Soviet Army was not able to aid the Poles. It was overextended, and when the Germans counterattacked, they drove Soviet forces back 65 miles. The Soviets haphazardly parachuted supplies to the insurgents but many of them were lost, and they were extremely reluctant to let their allies fly into the area. An attempt was made to take the city in September but to no avail. The First Belorussian Front, then in Poland, suffered 123,000 killed in a few weeks. Within Warsaw the Germans were ruthless, massacring more than 40,000 Poles and razing the city. All together between 200,000 and 250,000 noncombatants and 15,000 insurgents were killed. Warsaw surrendered to the Germans on October 2, and it was not until January 17, 1945, that the Soviet army was able to liberate the Polish capital.

Similarly, toward the end of August Slovak partisans, Communists, and regular army troops launched their own uprising against the pro-German regime of the Slovak puppet state. The Soviet Army tried desperately to cross the Carpathian Mountains to reach the rebel Slovaks, but they lost ninety thousand men and did not reach the rebels before the Germans took their revenge on the Slovaks. The uprising was completely suppressed by the end of October.

Soviet troops crossed the border with Rumania in early August, and on August 26 Rumania switched sides and declared war on Germany. The Soviets imposed harsh terms on Rumania, forcing them once again to cede Bessarabia and northern Bukovina, and dictated their form of government. The Soviets meant to be well paid for the Rumanian participation on the Nazi side and the more than 46,000 soldiers it had lost in driving the Germans from Rumania. As the Soviet troops moved into East-Central Europe and on into eastern Germany, many engaged in acts of rage and savagery against the local population. Though they seemed to have been restrained in Bulgaria, Soviet soldiers were vicious in Hungary and Germany particularly. Brutalized by war and the atrocities carried out in Russia by the Germans, Soviet soldiers now descended into barbarity, reproducing the horrors their own people had suffered. Red Army soldiers took their revenge for what the Germans had done to their countrymen even as they liberated concentration camps and bore witness to the worst excesses of Nazism. Though a few looters or rapists were punished, most often officers looked the other way, and rape, looting, and arbitrary killing became routine in the Soviet occupation zones.

Early in 1945 Stalin took over the strategic planning and coordination of the final push against the Germans. He gave Zhukov command of the First Belorussian Front with the honor of taking Berlin and on January 12, 1945, ordered the heaviest offensive of the war, sending 3.8 million men against the main German forces. By February 3 the Soviet Army had reached the Oder River, but while the Yalta Conference was in session Stalin had the offensive slow down. Only on April 16, 1945, did the Soviets launch their last great offensive of the war and begin the battle for Berlin. Two and a half million soldiers moved toward the German capital. Some three hundred thousand Soviet soldiers and two hundred thousand German soldiers were killed before the Soviets entered Berlin on April 21. Four days later the first Soviet soldiers joined up with the American First Army on the Elbe River.

The "Great Fatherland War" between Nazi Germany and the Soviet Union lasted 1,418 days, almost four years, from June 22, 1941, to May 9, 1945. The Soviets destroyed or disabled 506 German divisions and 100 more of their allies. Of the 13.6 million Germans killed, wounded, missing, or made prisoner during World War II, 10 million of them met their fate on the Eastern Front. The Soviets lost between 7 and 8 million soldiers, compared to 405,000 for the United States and 375,000 for Great Britain, and about 19 million civilians. Twenty million of the 26 to 27 million killed on the Soviet side were men. Es-

Figure 14.5. Victorious Soviet soldier raises the flag over the Reichstag Building in Berlin, May 1945 (RIA-NOVOSTI/SOVFOTO).

timates for losses in the besieged city of Leningrad range from 650,000 to 1 million dead. The overwhelming number of victims in the Soviet-German war were ethnic Russians, but along with Communists, Gypsies, the handicapped, and homosexuals, the Nazis singled out Jews for slaughter.

Of the more than 5.2 million Jews in the USSR on the eve of the war, 2.2 million were killed by the Germans, in killing fields like Babi Yar outside of Kiev or in gas chambers in concentration camps. In Minsk where seventy-five thousand Jews remained in the city, the Nazis first forced them to wear yellow tags, then resettled them into a ghetto surrounded by barbed wire. Thousands were shot in periodic mass executions; others died of torture or mistreatment. Late in 1941 German Jews were shipped to the Minsk ghetto. Finally, on October 21, 1943, the ghetto was surrounded by the Gestapo, and the last Jews, reduced to just two thousand, were loaded onto trucks and sent off to die. The soldiers blew up the apartments and eliminated the Minsk ghetto. This pattern was repeated in Riga, Vilnius, and dozens of other cities and towns. In Ukraine and Lithuania local people sometimes aided the Nazis on carrying out atrocities against the Jews; in Latvia Baltic Germans collaborated with the invaders. A German corporal wrote in his diary:

> Women who had just given birth, children, and old men were forced to kneel and barely alive, like skeletons, were dragged out and shot indiscriminately. People died while suffering cruelties worse than any mankind had known. Houses were ravaged. Corpses lay in houses for six days. Both men and women were unclothed. It was a horrible sight. In spite of this, I stealthily made my way into the houses. I looked for people whom, with a shot, I could put out of misery. Not one soldier went into the ghetto on his own. The doors and windows creak.

The economic effects of the war were colossal. The Soviet Union suffered $128 billion in damage; 1,700 towns and 70,000 villages were destroyed; 25 million people were made homeless; 31,000 industrial enterprises were destroyed, along with 65,000 kilometers of railroad track; 17 million cattle, 27 million sheep and goats, and 20 million pigs were slaughtered. By 1944 the Soviet Union was producing approximately 22 to 31 percent less than it had in 1940. Thirty percent of capital stock had been lost. Agricultural output was only 60 percent of the 1940 level, and people were eating only two-thirds of what they had consumed before the war. Vast areas of the country faced starvation. American Lend-Lease helped sustain many Soviet citizens in the last years of the war, and the United Nations Relief and Rehabilitation Administration (UNRRA) aid continued for almost a year after the war. Agricultural output would not reach the prewar level until 1948. Consumption, which had been 74 percent of gross national income in 1940, fell to 66 percent of a lower national income in 1945. Along with a corresponding fall in investment, these "savings" paid for the war effort.

Industry had collapsed completely in Ukraine, Belorussia, and western Russia, where more than 80 percent of enterprises had been destroyed or dismantled. Hundreds of thousands of people were transported eastward to the Urals and western Siberia, where new plants were built. The industrial workforce there grew 65 percent in the first three years of the war. Steel production was down to only 35 percent of the 1940 output, oil to 40 percent, and timber to 50 percent. During the war the percentage of national income used for the war effort rose from 11 percent in 1940 to 44 percent in 1943. About 30 percent of capital stock in the USSR was lost. The Soviet Union would not reach pre-war levels of industrial production until 1948.

The victory over Germany was seen by Stalin as the ultimate vindication of his policies in the 1930s. Though it cannot be denied that rapid Soviet industrialization made possible the mammoth effort against Nazi arms, historians have attempted to evaluate just what aspects of the Stalin revolution were necessary for victory and what policies and practices were not. Stalinist industrialization stressed heavy industry and those aspects of the economy geared toward defense, which a more balanced, more gradualist form of industrialization would not have. Soviet economic growth might have been smoother, more efficient, less painful if it had not been so ambitious, but it would not have been as focused on those branches of industry that most directly contributed to the war effort.

Stalinism pushed people hard, forced them to accept unbearable sacrifices, and terrorized them into silence and conformity. A successful war effort requires more than adequate materiel; it also requires commitment to the cause, and the high costs of the Stalinist collectivization and industrialization, the Great Purges, and the initial failures at the front battered the morale of the Soviet people. Ultimately the regime was able to inspire the people to fight for it, and it was aided by the evident viciousness of the Nazi invaders. Stalinism was a mass of inefficiencies that became institutionalized, and they only increased the burdens on ordinary citizens. Sometimes the most apparently rational and efficient decisions turned out to have unexpected costs. Soviet planners of the 1930s had continued the pattern of concentrating industry in the old centers of industry along the western border, in an area vulnerable to an invading force. Though there was considerable investment during the First Five-Year Plan in other regions, as in Magnitogorsk in the Urals, the high costs of developing industry in new regions led to investing in existing industrial centers. The unfounded confidence—one might say arrogance—of the regime that there would be no fighting on Soviet soil led to the almost immediate loss of much of the metallurgical industry and military engineering, which were located in the Soviet west. When the Nazis broke through Soviet defenses in 1941, the USSR lost one-third of its vital capital stock. Yet it revived and survived. "No society in modern times," writes economist James R. Millar, "has absorbed a blow of the severity of Operation Barbarossa and survived as a political, economic, and social entity."

The Soviet Union emerged from the war physically ravaged but at the same time the principal victor over fascism and an ally of the most powerful states on the globe. British historian John Erickson has written, "Whatever the scale of measurement, the decisive role in defeating the 'Fascist Bloc' was played by the Soviet Union." Throughout most of the war the Soviet Army confronted 70 to 75 percent of the German forces, while the rest of the Allies dealt with the other quarter to a third. Even at the time of the Normandy invasion, the western armies met only 27 of the 81 German divisions on the western front, while the Soviets faced 181 German divisions and a third as many satellite divisions in the East. World War II left the USSR as the single strongest military power on the European continent. Globally, only the United States stood as an effective military rival. The war ended Russia's East European isolation and turned the Soviet Union into a world power. Russia's historic goals—expansion to the West, creation of a buffer zone of friendly states on its western border, dominance in the Balkans and the Turkish Straits—seemed to be in the realm of the immediately possible. Internally the Soviet system had survived the war without major disruption. Though millions of Communists and state officials had been killed, the party and state rapidly rebuilt themselves. Stalin had no rivals for power and ruled absolutely.

The "Great Fatherland War" proved to be an enormous psychological support for Stalin's regime. The struggle against fascism brought Russians and the non-Russian peoples into a closer relationship with the Soviet system, which now became more difficult to separate from their allegiances to their traditional homelands. National integration of the people, the state, and the party was accomplished in a more complete way than in the prewar years. The victory over Nazism, which was at one and the same time convincingly identified with the superiority of the Soviet system, its organic link with the motherland, and the personal genius of Stalin provided the Communists with the kind of legitimacy and popular authority that had eluded them in the prewar period. Russia and the Soviet Union melded into a single image. Patriotism and accommodation of established religious and national traditions, along with the toning down of revolutionary radicalism, contributed to a powerful ideological amalgam that outlasted Stalin himself. The war became the central moment of Soviet history for generations to come, eclipsing the revolution of 1917 and the "revolution from above" of the early 1930s.

Suggestions for Further Reading

Among the most authoritative works on the war are John Erickson, *The Road to Stalingrad* (New York, 1975) and *The Road to Berlin* (Boulder, Colo., 1983). The controversy over Soviet historian Aleksandr Nekrich's heretical account of the German invasion is contained in Vladimir Petrov, *"June 22, 1941": Soviet Historians and the German Invasion* (Columbia, SC, 1968). See also the extraordinary account by eyewitness and journalist-historian Alexander Werth, *Russia at War* (New York, 1964); as well as Albert Seaton, *The Russo-German War 1941–1945* (London, 1971); Harrison E. Salisbury, *The 900 Days: The Siege of Leningrad* (New York, 1969); Georgii Zhukov, *The Memoirs of Marshall Zhukov* (London, 1971); Catherine Andreyev, *Vlasov and the Russian Liberation Movement: Soviet Reality and Émigré Theories* (Cambridge, 1987); and Seweryn Bialer (ed.), *Stalin and His Generals: Soviet Military Memoirs of World War II* (New York, 1969). A fascinating account of the effect of the war in the East on the Ostheer can be found in Omer Bartov, *Hitler's Army: Soldiers, Nazis, and War in the Third Reich* (New York, 1991).

On the German occupation and the Soviet home front, see Alexander Dallin, *German Rule in Russia, 1941–1945: A Study in Occupation Policies* (1957); John Armstrong, *Soviet Partisans in World War II* (Madison, Wis., 1964) and *Ukrainian Nationalism*, 2nd ed. (London, 1963); Mark Harrison, *Soviet Planning in Peace and War, 1938–1945* (Cambridge, 1985); William Moskoff, *The Bread of Affliction: The Food Supply in the USSR during World War II* (New York, 1990); Richard Stites (ed.), *Culture and Entertainment in Wartime Rus-*

sia (Bloomington, Ind., 1995); John Barber and Mark Harrison, *The Soviet Home Front, 1941–1945: A Social and Economic History of the USSR in World War II* (London, 1991); Ilya Ehrenburg, *The War: 1941–1945* (Cleveland, Ohio, 1964); Susan J. Linz (ed.), *The Impact of World War II on the Soviet Union* (Totowa, N.J., 1985); and Richard Joseph Brody, "Political Work on the Soviet Home Front: Political Culture and Party Ideology During World War II" (Ph.D. diss., University of Michigan, 1993). On the diplomacy of the war years, see Ivan Maisky, *Memoirs of a Soviet Diplomat: The War, 1939–1943* (New York, 1968); Milovan Djilas, *Conversations with Stalin* (New York, 1962); Gabriel Kolko, *The Politics of War* (New York, 1968); and Vojtech Mastny, *Russia's Road to the Cold War: Diplomacy, Warfare, and the Politics of Communism, 1941–1945* (New York, 1979).

CHAPTER 15
The Big Chill: The Cold War Begins

By 1945 Europe was emerging from the most intense period of social disloca-tion since the Thirty Years' War of the seventeenth century. The decade and a half from 1930 to 1945 had been one of economic depression, military de-struction, mass murder, and the collapse of social and political order. Alto-gether it is estimated that more than 60 million people died in World War II. The great bulk of them were from the Soviet Union, upwards of 26 million. Perhaps as many as 15 million Chinese died, 6.5 million Germans, 6 million Jews, 4 million Poles, over 2 million Japanese, and almost 2 million Yugoslavs. France lost 600,000, Britain about 400,000, mostly soldiers, and the United States about 405,000.

The war had created a new bipolar world, with the USSR the strongest sin-gle military power on the European continent. Many of its historic goals had been or seemed about to be realized. The interwar cordon sanitaire against Bol-shevism was gone, and Russia had ended its isolation in Eastern Europe. Now the Soviets could build their own buffer zone of friendly, dependent states along their western border. Dominant in the Balkans and ready to flex its mus-cles in the Middle East against Turkey and Iran, the Soviet Union was threat-ened only by the United States with its newly acquired atomic weapons. De-spite its evident weakness and need to rebuild itself, the Soviet Union with its large armed forces was the only power that stood in the way of American global hegemony.

The international Left, particularly the Communists, were given a new lease on life by the Soviet victory, the prestige gained by the antifascist resistance, and the apparent acceptance of the USSR into the councils of the Great Pow-ers. The capitalist economy was in shambles in Europe and Asia, and no one could predict how long Europe's recovery would take. The war had been pre-ceded by the Great Depression, and many thought that the war's end would bring back the economic troubles of the 1930s. Some in the West anticipated that social revolution and the breakup of the world capitalist system were on the horizon. Conservative and rightist parties had been discredited for their collaboration with fascism. Yet within a few years the recovery of Europe would be underway; the Soviet Union would be isolated behind the "Iron Curtain"; the Left in Europe would be divided, and the Communists once again under attack; and the United States would be the major economic player in most of Europe and Asia and the keystone of an Atlantic alliance directed against the USSR.

Historians Look at the Cold War

Debate about the Cold War has raged since the mid-1940s. Why did the Grand Alliance of the United States, the Soviet Union, Great Britain, France, and China, with its enormous promise for a peaceful and united world, break down into rival nuclear blocs staring each other down over a divided Europe? Were the long years of the arms race necessary or avoidable? Was the USSR largely to blame for the frustrating and futile conflicts of the late 1940s and 1950s, or should blame to be shared by both East and West? Two great schools of thought have been shaped in this debate: the "orthodox" and the "revisionist."

The orthodox (sometimes referred to as the liberal) view sees the Cold War as largely caused by Soviet expansionism. The United States was forced by the international danger posed by the USSR to shoulder an unwanted burden and become the reluctant leader of the Free World. Given the global ambitions and aggressive behavior of the Soviet Union, the United States had no policy alternative but containment of the USSR. Only the formation of NATO, the generosity of the Marshall Plan, and the determination of American military might prevented further territorial gains by the Soviet Union. In historian Arthur Schlesinger's words, the Cold War was "the brave and essential response of free men to communist aggression." For orthodox historians of the Cold War, the two sides were hardly equivalent. On one side was Soviet aggression, on the other the American defensive response.

The revisionist historians have elaborated the view that the Cold War was the product of mutual suspicion on both sides and that neither side can be singled out for blame. They argue that the USSR, rather than being aggressive and expansionist after World War II, was actually cautious and conservative. Because the country had endured four years of war and Nazi occupation, it was weak and wanted nothing more than aid from and cooperation with the West. Most revisionists see Stalin as coldly rational and cautious rather than paranoid, expansionist, or revolutionary. A few historians, who might be called "hard revisionists," turn the orthodox view upside down and contend that the blame for the Cold War lay with the United States, an expansionist capitalist economy that required the breaking down of trade barriers everywhere in the world. Whereas the "soft revisionists" see the Cold War as a failure of American statesmanship, the hard revisionists go further and argue that the need for capitalism to expand required the creation of an "open world." When the Soviet Union refused to concur in American ambitions and to restrict access to its own economy and Eastern Europe, American leaders saw the USSR as a hostile force.

In the 1990s, as the archives of the formerly Communist states were opened to historians, researchers found evidence of much more confusion and hesitation in Stalin's foreign policies and behavior than many had anticipated. Rather than possessing a blueprint for world conquest or expansion across Europe or the fomenting of foreign revolutions, Stalin's behavior was marked by a cold realism and pragmatism, the subordination of ideology to state interests, which was enforced by brutal and cynical methods. Stalin based his policies on an appreciation of the weakness of the USSR, a fear that the West would try to take advantage of that weakness, and a desire to ensure the continuance of the Grand Alliance and material aid from the West. But at the same time Stalin wanted recognition of a Soviet sphere of influence in Eastern Europe. This did not necessarily mean the Sovietization of the countries along the USSR's western border, but it did mean that no potentially hostile government would be permitted in that region. As reflected in his actions and directives to Communist leaders abroad, Stalin was conservative and cautious, not particularly interested in promoting revolution in the early postwar years and at times positively counterrevolutionary. He was prepared to allow the West a free hand in Western Europe, Greece, and Japan if he were permitted the same in Eastern Europe. Stalin's dilemma, however, was that the United States would not agree to maintaining the Grand Alliance and giving aid to the Soviet Union if Stalin insisted on his foothold in Eastern Europe.

The United States, on the other hand, feared the spread of Soviet and Communist influence, was anxious about the rising forces on the Left, including the Social Democrats, and wanted to reintegrate as much of Europe as possible into a revived capitalist world economy. This included dislodging the Soviet Union from Eastern Europe, a task for which the United States had neither the power nor the will. American actions created new suspicions in Stalin's minds, encouraged him to tighten his grip on the governments and societies in his zone of occupation, and eventually, as the Grand Alliance disintegrated, convinced him to install obedient Communist regimes.

Soviet policy during the Cold War can usefully be divided into two phases. The first phase, 1945–47, was a time of flux and missed opportunities, when Stalin was much more flexible and moderate in his dealings with Eastern Europe. The second phase, 1947–53, was marked by a steady elimination of opposition within the countries of Eastern Europe, the coming to power of Communist parties, and, after 1948, even the destruction of "national communist" alternatives and the full coordination of policy in the region through the use of Soviet police agents.

Diplomacy and the War Effort

The Grand Alliance began to take shape shortly after the Nazi invasion of the Soviet Union. Prime Minister of Great Britain Winston Churchill told an associate, "If Hitler invaded Hell, I would make at least a favorable reference to the Devil in the House of Commons." In the summer of 1941 President Roosevelt's trusted aide, Harry Hopkins, traveled to Russia and reported to the President and to Churchill that, contrary to the prevailing opinion at the time, the USSR would be able to hold out against the Germans. But a bitter debate

Figure 15.1. The USSR and Europe at the end of World War II.

raged in the United States, which was not yet at war, about sending Lend-Lease aid to the Soviet Union. The then-senator from Missouri, Harry S. Truman, calculated, "If we see that Germany is winning the war, we ought to help Russia, and if Russia is winning we ought to help Germany and that way let them kill as many as possible." Eventually aid was sent, and it proved very important in the early days of the war, both materially and psychologically.

The Big Three were allies of convenience, bound together by their determination to defeat the Axis powers. They signed no treaty of alliance and never managed to develop the degree of trust and mutual long-term interest that sustainable alliances require. Even during wartime the alliance suffered many strains. Stalin's principal request of the West was that they open a second front in Europe and draw German troops from the Eastern Front, but in this he was to be bitterly disappointed. Churchill preferred a pinprick strategy against Germany, which involved an invasion of North Africa, knocking Italy out of the war, and the Mediterranean before launching the invasion of France. But later when Churchill suggested an invasion of the Balkans, the Americans pushed harder for the second front in the West. Still, the West did not launch its cross-channel invasion into France until June 1944, by which time the Soviets were already advancing into East-Central Europe.

With the Soviet victory at Kursk in the summer of 1943, it was clear that the time had come for the Allied leaders to concentrate on the political problems that would shape the postwar world. The Soviet ambassador to London told the British foreign minister, Anthony Eden, at the very end of August that "there were two possible ways of trying to organize Europe after the war." Either the USSR and the West "could agree each to have a sphere of interest" or they could "admit the right of the other to an interest in all parts of Europe." The Soviets prefered the latter solution, but the British favored a spheres-of-influence policy, and Great Britain signaled the Soviets in the early fall of 1943 that they recognized Russia's interest in moving its borders westward and its historic interests in Eastern Europe. On principle the United States was opposed to spheres of influence, though it vigorously defended the historic American sphere in the Western Hemisphere. The United States refused even to accept the Soviet Union's 1941 borders, which included parts of prewar Poland and the formerly independent states of Estonia, Latvia, and Lithuania. In November 1943 Churchill, Stalin, and Roosevelt met for the first time together in Teheran. Roosevelt was still unwilling to sanction Soviet borders, but he privately agreed with Stalin that the Soviet-Polish frontier should run along the "Curzon Line," which roughly approximated the border between ethnically Polish and non-Polish territories. All three agreed that Germany should be dismembered after the war, and the West promised once again to launch an invasion of France. Stalin agreed to join the war against Japan once Germany had been defeated.

As Soviet forces moved relentlessly westward and it became evident that they would be the principal power in East-Central Europe after the retreat of the Germans, the nature of the relationship between the small countries on the USSR's borders and Moscow had to be worked out. In December 1943 Edvard Beneš, head of the Czechoslovak government-in-exile, came to Moscow and negotiated a treaty of alliance with the Soviets. He agreed to check all important international questions with the Kremlin before taking action. Stalin saw this treaty as a model for Soviet relations with their other Western neighbors— independent, friendly governments, who posed no security threat to the USSR.

World War II had begun over Poland, and the Cold War as well would center on that strategically important country. Much of Poland had been part of the Russian Empire from the late eighteenth century until the revolution of 1917, and tsarist rule had left a powerful legacy of anti-Russian feeling in Polish nationalism. At the end of the 1930s Stalin wiped out many of the leaders of the Polish Communist Party and forced the party to dissolve itself just before the Soviets invaded eastern Poland and took back the ethnically Belorussian and Ukrainian lands they had lost in 1920. Relations between the Polish government-in-exile in London and the Soviet Union collapsed in 1943, and Stalin soon formed his own Polish Army, resurrected the Polish Communist Party and established a committee that would form the embryo of a pro-Soviet Polish government to rival London. He offered to negotiate the frontier issue with the London Poles if they accepted several pro-Soviet Poles into the exile government. The London Poles refused, hoping that the Americans would support restoration of Poland in its prewar frontiers. The Czech foreign minister, Jan Masaryk, mused at the time that he "had never seen a group of politicians who could by their every act commit suicide with such professional thoroughness." Churchill warned the Polish prime minister, Stanislaw Mikolajczyk, that "Great Britain and the United States would not go to war to defend the eastern frontiers of Poland." Stalin tried to reassure the London Poles that he was not interested in imposing a Communist government on them. "Communism," he told Mikolajczyk, "does not fit the Poles. They are too individualistic, too nationalistic. . . . Poland will be a capitalist state." But when the London government again refused to accept the Curzon Line, Stalin installed a pro-Soviet government, the Lublin Committee, in Warsaw.

The Soviets also advanced in the summer and fall of 1944 into the Balkans, where they quickly established friendly pro-Soviet coalition governments. Fearing that Britain would be excluded from influence in the Balkans, Churchill flew to Moscow in October to bargain with Stalin. In his memoirs Churchill remembered how the famous "percentages agreement" was made:

> The moment was apt for business so I said, "Let us settle about our affairs in the Balkans. Your armies are in Rumania and Bulgaria. We have interests, missions, and agents there. Don't let us get at cross-purposes in small ways. So far as Britain and Russia are concerned, how would it do for you to have 90% predominance in Rumania, for us to have 90% of the say in Greece and go 50-50 about Yugoslavia?" While this was being translated I wrote out on a half-sheet of paper: Rumania—Russia 90%; the others 10%; Greece—Great Britain 90% (in accord with USA); Russia 10%; Yugoslavia— 50-50%; Hungary—50-50%; Bulgaria—Russia 75%; the others 25%.
>
> I pushed this across to Stalin, who had by then heard the translation. There was a slight pause. Then he took his blue pencil and made a large tick upon it, and passed it back to us. It was all settled in no more time than it takes to set down. . . .

After this there was a long silence. The penciled paper lay in the centre of the table. At length I said, "Might it not be thought rather cynical if it seemed we had disposed of these issues, so fateful to millions of people, in such an offhand manner? Let us burn the paper." "No, you keep it," said Stalin.

The "percentages agreement," made so callously by two world leaders as if they were real estate brokers, was in fact an explicit acknowledgment of Soviet hegemony in much of the Balkans, with Britain dominating in Greece. The United States did not participate and would later protest the arrangement, but the Soviets abided by the agreement faithfully. When the British occupied Greece in December 1944 and used military force to quell any pretensions of the Left to power in Greece, the Soviets sat silently by as their supporters were shot down or imprisoned.

Yalta and Its Aftermath

Roosevelt and Churchill flew to Yalta in the Crimea in early February 1945 to meet with Stalin and deal with the most vexing questions of the postwar settlement. Germany, it was agreed, would emerge from the war far weaker than it had been. Officially the communiqué from the conference spoke of the "complete disarmament, demilitarization, and dismemberment of Germany," but in fact Britain and the United States were already convinced that a strong Germany was needed to balance Soviet power. Stalin asked for $10 billion in reparations from Germany, but Britain balked, and in the end only a vague agreement as to reparations in kind was made. On Poland, the conference agreed that that Stalin's Lublin government would form the core of a new Polish government to which would be added émigré Poles, but free elections were to determine the final shape of postwar Poland. The eastern frontier would generally follow the Curzon Line, and Poland would be compensated by significant former German territories in the west.

Stalin also obtained significant agreements from Britain and the United States concerning the war and the peace in Asia. The status quo would be maintained in Mongolia, where the Soviets dominated a Communist government. The USSR would be given long-term leases on the port of Dairen and a naval base at Port Arthur in China, reversing losses suffered in the Russo-Japanese War of 1904–05. The Chinese eastern and southern Manchurian railroads would be jointly operated by the Soviets and Chinese. Southern Sakhalin Island would be returned to the USSR by the Japanese, and the Soviet Union would annex the Kurile Islands. China would have to agree to these arrangements, and the Soviet Union committed its army to join the war against Japan, taking on the land forces in Manchuria, within three months of the ending of the war in Europe.

Yalta marked the peak of the Grand Alliance. As Harry Hopkins wrote, "We really believed in our hearts that this was the dawn of the new day we had all been praying for and talking about for so many years." Even the fierce old anti-Bolshevik Churchill now could say without embarrassment that "Stalin's life [was] most precious to the hopes and hearts of all of us." The Soviets had gained much at the conference, but they had given up much as well. Secretary of State Edward Stettinius said, "The record of the Conference shows clearly that the Soviet Union made greater concessions at Yalta to the United States and Great Britain than were made to the Soviets." But within a month disagreements, particularly over Poland, soured the Yalta mood. The Soviets arrested leading Polish politicians and Resistance leaders and dragged their feet on reconstituting the Lublin government. In the midst of these quarrels, on April 12, President Roosevelt died suddenly of a brain hemorrhage and was succeeded by Harry S. Truman, who was much more suspicious of Soviet intentions. Stalin, upset at Roosevelt's death and the uncertainties it promised, sent Molotov to the United States to speak to the new president and attend the founding meeting of the United Nations. Truman berated Molotov for Soviet actions. The foreign minister protested, "I have never been talked to like that in my life." "Carry out your agreements," Truman replied, "and you won't get talked to like that."

Truman's policies did not in essence differ from those of Roosevelt's, though the brusque style of "give-'em-hell" Harry convinced Stalin and Molotov that the new president was hostile to Soviet interests. More willing than Roosevelt to apply pressure on the Soviets to make concessions in East-Central Europe, Truman abruptly cut off Lend-Lease aid to the Soviet Union on May 8, the very day that the war in Europe ended. Ships were turned around at sea. Yet the door was left open for negotiations, and after a mission to Moscow by Hopkins, Stalin agreed to a broader Polish government, which received Western approval in June. At this point Stalin was willing to allow Poland to be independent but not outside the Soviet sphere of influence.

At the Potsdam Conference in July–August 1945, Truman tried to push Stalin to make changes in the Rumanian and Bulgarian governments and allow free elections. Stalin was annoyed and told his colleagues that "he had been hurt by the American demand. . . . He was not meddling in Greek affairs and it was unjust of them [to meddle in Rumania and Bulgaria]." A few days later, after receiving news that American scientists had successfully exploded the first atomic bomb in Alamagordo, New Mexico, Truman casually mentioned to Stalin that the United States had just developed a new weapon of unusual force. Stalin seemed disinterested, but in fact he had been informed by spies that the Americans were experimenting with an atomic bomb. The conference ended indecisively, with few agreements, and Stalin left disappointed that he had not been able to convince his allies to fix a definite amount for reparations from Germany.

Within a few days of the end of the Potsdam Conference, the United States dropped an atomic bomb on the Japanese city of Hiroshima, killing about 145,000 people through the blast and radiation effects. Stalin had underestimated the importance of this new weapon, and only after Hiroshima did he agree to accelerate the Soviet atomic bomb program. Two days later, on August 8, the Soviet Union carried out its promise to fight the Japanese and informed the Japanese that they would be in a state of war the next day. Stalin had announced as early as April 5, 1945, that the USSR would not renew its neutrality pact with Japan, and in the months after the European war ended half a million troops had been moved from the Western fronts to eastern Siberia. When the Japanese tried through back channels to feel out the Soviets about brokering a peace, the Soviets were cool and evasive. Stalin did not want Japan to surrender before the Soviet Union had entered the war in Asia. After a second U.S. bomb was dropped on Nagasaki on August 9, killing another 70,000 people, Japan decided to surrender. Stalin tried to convince Truman to allow the Red Army to land on Japan's northernmost island, Hokkaido, but the President refused. Some of his advisors pushed him to go ahead anyway, but Stalin backed down "to avoid the creation of conflicts and misunderstanding with respect to the allies." With the physical presence in northern China of 1.5 million Soviet soldiers, facing the defeated Japanese army, the Nationalist Chinese government signed a Treaty of Friendship and Alliance with the USSR, agreeing to the concessions in China granted to Stalin at Yalta.

Atomic Diplomacy

Stalin was dismayed that after all the Soviet sacrifices in the war to defeat Germany the American bomb had radically transformed the balance of world power. At a single stroke the huge Soviet conventional army was rendered far less powerful. "No doubt "Washington and London are hoping we won't be able to develop the bomb ourselves for sometime," Stalin told his subordinates. And meanwhile, using America's monopoly, . . . they want to force us to accept their plans on questions affecting Europe and the world. Well, that's not going to happen." After Hiroshima he called in the physicist Igor Kurchatov, who before the war had been doing research on atomic weapons, and told him, "Provide us with atomic weapons in the shortest possible time. You know that Hiroshima has shaken the whole world. The balance has been destroyed. Provide the bomb—it will remove a great danger from us." The bomb project was given the highest priority and was placed under the direct supervision of the chief of the secret police, Lavrentii Beria. Aided by information received from Klaus Fuchs and other Soviet spies in the West, Soviet scientists saved about a year or two in their rush to build a bomb.

Ironically, the powerful new weapon in the hands of the United States, which had altered the global balance of power, did not convince Stalin to be more conciliatory to the West. Instead, it resulted in greater intransigence on both sides. The Soviets believed that they had to demonstrate how tough they were, that they could not be pushed around, and so they repeatedly turned up the heat on the West. Atomic weapons were largely symbolic, and in the years of the Cold War they would never be used. Yet they were powerful signs of great power, and at times American officials considered brandishing the bomb to gain points in international diplomacy. When the Allied foreign ministers gathered in London in September 1945 to thrash out the outstanding differences between their countries, the new secretary of state, James Byrnes, joked with Molotov, "If you don't cut out all this stalling and let us get down to work,

I'm going to pull an atomic bomb out of my hip pocket and let you have it." Later Byrnes complained that the Russians were "stubborn, obstinate, and they don't scare," and he told an aide, "Well, pardner, I think we pushed these babies about as far as they will go and I think that we better start thinking about a compromise." Later in December Byrnes met privately with Stalin and made a proposal on his own, a Big Power guarantee against German resurgence in exchange for a reduction of Soviet influence over East-Central Europe. Stalin was cautious but interested. When Byrnes returned to Washington, however, Truman castigated him for negotiating with Stalin without keeping the White House informed. Truman told his secretary of state, "Unless Russia is faced with an iron fist and strong language another war was in the making. . . . I do not think we should play compromise any longer. I am tired of babying the Soviets." Though Byrnes's ill-fated attempt to deal with Stalin had landed him in hot water, it showed that negotiation with the Soviets was possible. But the mood in Washington was shifting rapidly toward a much more intransigently anti-Soviet stance, while in Moscow Stalin was ever more reluctant to give up his positions in the Balkans and Poland for vague promises of aid and reparations.

A New World Order

The balance of power in the world in 1945 was quite unbalanced. The United States emerged from World War II as the strongest economic power on the globe. Though it had been preeminent among the Great Powers since the early part of the century, thanks to the two world wars her rivals—Great Britain, France, Japan, Germany, and the USSR—had fallen even further behind. In 1945 the United States held 75 percent of the world's gold reserves. Its gross national product (GNP) had grown by 63 percent during the war, and its standard of living had risen by 11 percent. When compared to the much smaller Soviet economy, then still emerging from the rubble of the war, the gap between the two leading world powers was enormous. Formerly a reluctant Great Power with strong isolationist tendencies, the United States reconceived its interests to include the Mediterranean, the Middle East, Southeast Asia, and the Pacific, taking over where the now-defunct British and Japanese empires had retreated. American political leaders began developing a consensus on the need for American international leadership in the postwar world. From Truman down American leaders believed that peace and prosperity had to march together, that a stable peace required a stable international economy, and that poverty and dissatisfaction would lead to war, revolution, and communism. Leading economists and politicians feared a revival of the depression and believed that prosperity depended on healthy world trade. But states that controlled their country's foreign trade, like the Soviet Union, privileged trading systems, like the British Sterling bloc, and colonial empires stood in the way of global free trade. Truman expressed the new confidence of the American leadership in 1945 when he stated that "America should take the lead in running the world in the way the world ought to be run."

The "Communist menace" was a psychological reality for the West at the end of the war, but it was based on both a misreading of Soviet intentions and an overestimation of the USSR's military and economic capabilities. The Soviets had steadily demobilized their vast wartime army, from over 11 million in 1945 to 2,874,000 in 1948. In Europe, outside the USSR, the Soviets had about 800,000 troops, roughly equivalent to Western occupation forces. Though the Soviets reported these demobilizations, the Western press played down their significance and failed to note that only one-third of their 175 divisions were full strength; another third was partial strength; and the final third were essentially paper units. The higher Western estimates of Soviet strength allowed speculation that the Soviet units were able and willing to consider an invasion of Western Europe. But in fact the Soviet Army was in poor shape after the war. As late as 1950 half of their military transport was horsedrawn. Morale was low, desertion rates high. The army in Europe was used primarily for occupation, repressing anti-Soviet activity, and dismantling factories for reparations. And the rear was not secure. Anti-Communist rebels were active in western Ukraine and the Baltic republics, not to mention Poland. Most bridges, rail lines, and roads had been destroyed in the western parts of the USSR and were slowly being repaired, often by German prisoners of war. The Soviet army was incapable of launching an effective invasion of Western Europe in the postwar years. Yet even though the Central Intelligence Agency and many in government knew the true dimensions of Soviet capabilities, politicians and journalists believed in a Soviet threat and saw their every action as proof of aggressive intentions. Convinced of Soviet superiority in conventional weapons and forces, American politicians proposed strategic air power using atomic weapons.

The Left in Europe

The Nazi invasion of the Soviet Union gave Communist parties in Europe and Asia a new lease on life. Ideologically the moribund popular front was broadened into a "national front" against fascism, and the war became a "national patriotic war." Stalinist Communists, whose loyalty to the Soviet Union was nearly unshakable, took leading roles in the resistance movements against fascist occupation. These were supposed to be liberationist movements to restore democracy, not to promote socialist revolution. But very often underground Communist parties in occupied Europe did not restrain their radical impulses. Though Dimitrov sent a secret message from Moscow to the Yugoslav Communist leader, Tito, saying "Keep in mind that in the present stage the issue is liberation from fascist oppression and not socialist revolution," it hardly deterred the Yugoslav partisans from combining liberation with revolution. Many of the newly recruited Communists did not treat directives from the Comintern as holy writ; interpretation was varied and nuanced and differed from party to party and within parties between leadership, middle-level cadres, and the rank and file. The very goal of creating a broad national front required a loosening of control from the top and a responsiveness to specific national contexts.

The success of the national front policy was already apparent by 1944–45. The prestige of the Soviet Army, the major force in the defeat of Nazism, was high; the conservative and status quo parties of Europe were discredited; a yearning for unification of the workers' movement was palpable; and many of the antifascist fighters in Europe and Asia regarded socialism, not restored capitalism, as the preferred alternative to defeated fascism. When the war ended, Communist parties officially went only as far as calling for social reforms and did not place socialism on the agenda. Given that American power was intact in Western Europe, liberation movements were forced to recognize that only a democratic, not an anticapitalist, transformation was possible at the time.

The moderate tactics of Communists on the ground conformed to the overall strategy of Stalin not to antagonize the Western powers and to secure their agreement to Soviet hegemony in Eastern Europe. At first this cautious and measured policy garnered concrete results. The French Communist Party grew to nearly a million members in 1945, while the Italian Communist Party reached 1,770,000. In Eastern Europe Communists fared unevenly but emerged as a far more potent force than they had been between the wars. In Czechoslovakia the Communists polled 38 percent of the vote in April 1946, becoming the largest party in the country, but in another relatively free election in Hungary, in November 1945, Communists received a mere 17 percent vote. In Poland oppressive methods created a contrived majority in January 1947 for the "anti-fascist bloc." In Rumania and Bulgaria Communist-dominated fronts were installed as governments through Soviet pressure. In Yugoslavia and Albania Communist-led partisans swept to power without Soviet assistance, while in Greece a broad-based, Communist-led guerrilla movement was challenged by the military intervention of the British. In Asia Communist-led national liberation movements emerged as the most powerful political forces in China, Vietnam, and North Korea.

Communist parties in the early Cold War years were an odd hybrid. They remained in the hands of hardened, Stalinized leaders and factions were not permitted, but at the same time the parties had become mass organizations, having recruited thousands of new members during and immediately after the war. In the context of Soviet economic weakness, the atomic monopoly of the United States, and the desire of local Communists to win support among the peasants and workers, the Soviet policy of "national roads" to an ultimate socialist future was eminently practical. Even the most Stalinist of Communists were enthusiastic about their national reform programs. Klement Gottwald, the Czech leader, told the Yugoslav Communist Milovan Djilas, "The Soviet Union is still undeveloped. We are developed, we have strong democratic traditions, and socialism here is going to be different." As each party took its own path, the Yugoslavs pushed for a more aggressively anticapitalist, anti-Western policy and urged the Soviet leaders to adopt a more coordinated strategy. With the Comintern dissolved, East European Communists consulted bilaterally with one another without directly involving the Soviets. Though all were unquestioningly loyal to the Soviet Union and Stalin, the years of war had loosened ties between Moscow and the underground parties in occupied Europe and Asia. For some time Stalin did not pronounce on many questions and tolerated an unusual degree of autonomy, as long as Soviet interests did not seem threatened. But the independence and diversity of the foreign Communists soon went too far for the Soviet dictator. When the American Communist leader Earl Browder called for transformation of the American Communist Party into a "political association," the limit was reached. Communist parties were to remain Leninist in organization, and the French Communist Jacques Duclos, who was evidently speaking for Stalin, blasted Browder's idea. This response signaled that the euphoric period of national Communism would soon end, and in 1947–48 the Soviets began systematically to discipline Europe's Communists.

The Soviets in Eastern Europe

With the old ruling classes either having been killed off or dispersed and Soviet officers and officials the most powerful actors in the region, the real question was not *whether* the Soviet Union would dominate East-Central Europe— that was a foregone conclusion given military realities and Soviet notions of security—but rather *how* Stalin would dominate his borderlands. Would it be through "friendly governments," as in Finland, or through allied but autonomous Communist-led states, as in Czechoslovakia and Bulgaria, or through fully Stalinized, Soviet-controlled police regimes as were finally established in the years 1949 to 1953?

In the initial postwar period, from 1945–47, the Soviet government agreed to the formation of coalition governments of democratic, socialist, and Communist parties. As early as September 1944 a pro-Soviet Communist-dominated coalition, called the Fatherland Front, came to power in Bulgaria. In March 1945 coalition governments, with Communists and socialists as members, were formed in Czechoslovakia and Rumania. On June 28, 1945, the Polish government based on the Lublin Committee was reconstituted. Now led by a socialist, it included the peasant party leader Mikolajczyk as deputy prime minister. In Hungary national elections resulted in a Peasant Party majority, but the Communists and Social Democrats, each receiving 17 percent of the vote, were included in a coalition government.

East-Central Europe was ripe for social change. Though the region was basically agricultural, it experienced near famine in 1944–45. As the most backward part of Europe, it still maintained semifeudal structures in some places. One of the first tasks of the new Soviet-backed governments was land reform. In Hungary, for example, where less than 1 percent of the population owned 48 percent of the land, the Soviet Army ordered the "abolition of feudalism," and, against the resistance of the Catholic church, which alone held 17 percent of the land, it confiscated and distributed over 3 million hectares to 663,000 peasants, many of whom had been landless. In September 1944, 1 million hectares of large Polish estates were redistributed to peasants. Later 5.5 million Poles were resettled on former German lands in the west from which Germans were expelled. Rumania distributed over 1 million hectares to individual landholders. Through the land reform the left-leaning governments and the Soviet occupiers gained some sympathy and support from a generally hostile population.

Rather than spontaneous change arising from below, Communists preferred governmental initiative. In many places workers and students favored
radical reforms, but the Communists in government worked with other parties to quash the revolutionary workers' councils and liberation committees
that had arisen at the end of the war. They agreed to outlawing strikes and
promoting social order rather than revolution. They pushed for nationalization
of industry, particularly foreign and German-owned companies. In late 1945
and early 1946 Czechoslovakia and Poland nationalized most of their industry, to the protests of the United States.

Eastern Europe quickly became the major bone of contention between the
United States and the Soviet Union. Truman opposed the Soviets building a
sphere of influence there and was concerned about the economic isolation of
the region as well as the violations of democratic norms. The Americans had
very little direct economic interest in Eastern Europe; their holdings amounted
to just over a half a billion dollars, only 4 percent of U.S. investments abroad.
Nevertheless, the American minister to Hungary feared that that country would
soon "become an economic colony of [the] USSR from which western trade will
be excluded and in which western investments will be totally lost." For most
American officials, however, the damage to these investments and to trade was
less worrisome than the threat to its goal of unrestricted world trade and the
elimination of economic and political spheres of influence. The Soviets, on the
other hand, were primarily concerned with state security. Stalin was comfortable with a sphere-of-influence policy in which the Soviets would have the
dominant political say, but he was willing to have the West trade and invest
in Eastern Europe. For the first few postwar years no economic Iron Curtain
cut Eastern Europe off from the West. The Soviet Union, too poor, underdeveloped, and devastated by the war to supply East-Central Europe's economic
needs, wanted trade, loans, and investment from the West to develop the area
but stopped short of allowing its neighbors to be integrated into a Western economic bloc.

From 1943 on, the Soviet government made it clear that it hoped to be
granted a large American loan, perhaps $1 billion, at low interest to aid the
USSR in its postwar reconstruction. As the war wound down, Molotov made
a formal request for a postwar loan. Roosevelt delayed deciding on the loan,
and no mention was made of such a credit at the Yalta Conference. When Soviet-American relations cooled after Roosevelt's death, the probability of a loan
like the one granted to Great Britain in early 1946 faded fast. In March 1946
the State Department announced that the Russian loan request had been "lost"
since August of the previous year. The United States told the Soviets that it
would be willing to discuss a loan of a billion dollars but that such a discussion would require examination of Soviet relations with Eastern Europe and
the promise of the USSR to join the International Monetary Fund and the World
Bank and adopt their rules in international commerce. The Soviets found such
terms impossible. They argued that complete free trade as advocated by the
United States would result in a reproduction of the prewar economic division
of Europe into an advanced, industrialized Western Europe and a backward,
agrarian Eastern Europe. Protectionism, they contended, was necessary to de-

velop industry in Eastern Europe, which Stalin wanted to develop in cooperation with the Soviet Union. The USSR concluded bilateral trade treaties with its neighbors and began setting up joint-stock companies that combined the interests of East European and Soviet firms. These agreements heavily favored the Soviet economy. The Soviet sphere of influence in East-Central Europe was to be both political and economic.

Perceptions and Misperceptions

Three important statements in early 1946 shaped the coming Cold War decisively: Stalin's so-called pre-election speech, George F. Kennan's "Long Telegram," and Winston Churchill's "Iron Curtain speech" in Fulton, Missouri. On February 9, 1946, Stalin spoke to a packed house at the Bolshoi Theater in central Moscow. Stalin characterized the recent war as originating in the conflicts between monopoly-capitalist states over raw materials and markets, which had led to the formation of two hostile capitalist camps. Both world wars had been imperialist wars bred by a great crisis in capitalism, but the Second World War differed from the First in that the fascist powers were antidemocratic, terroristic, and expansionist. World War II, therefore, had the character of an antifascist war of liberation with the task of reestablishing democratic freedoms. Freedom-loving countries, like the USSR, the United Kingdom, and the United States formed an antifascist coalition to destroy the armed might of the Axis Powers. Though the speech was a fairly conventional statement of the Soviet interpretation of the causes of war, it was read by many in the West as an aggressive statement of Soviet hostility to the West. Supreme Court Justice William O. Douglas called the speech the "declaration of World War III."

A few weeks later George F. Kennan, the U.S. chargé d'affaires in the Moscow embassy, sent his famous "Long Telegram" to the State Department. This memo, with its clear and forceful presentation of Soviet ideological premises, was extraordinarily influential on the subsequent American thinking on policy toward the USSR. Kennan began by noting that the Soviets were concerned about "capitalist encirclement," which he saw as "not based on any objective analysis of [the] situation beyond Russia's borders" but arising "mainly from basic inner-Russian necessities which existed before [the] recent war and exist today."

> At bottom of [the] Kremlin's neurotic view of world affairs is [the] traditional and instinctive Russian sense of insecurity. . . . Basically this is only the steady advance of uneasy Russian nationalism, a centuries old movement in which conceptions of offense and defense are inextricably confused.

For Kennan Soviet thinking could be explained as a kind of "self-hypnosis," with no belief in objective truth. The Soviets were "impervious to the logic of reason" and "highly sensitive to the logic of force." Soviet policy was aimed at increasing its own power and weakening that of the capitalist powers.

> We have here a political force committed fanatically to the belief that with [the] US there can be no permanent modus vivendi, that it is desirable and necessary that the internal harmony of our society be disrupted, our traditional way of life be destroyed, the international authority of our state be broken, if Soviet power is to be secure.

In contrast to the United States and its values, Kennan concluded, "world communism is like [a] malignant parasite which feeds only on diseased tissue."

On March 5, 1946, former British prime minister Winston Churchill addressed students and faculty at the small Westminister College in Fulton, Missouri. He had been invited by President Truman, who sat on the stage. Though at the time no country then occupied by Soviet troops had a purely Communist government and in many there would be years of relatively free elections ahead, Churchill intoned dramatically that Eastern Europe had been lost to the West:

> From Stettin in the Baltic to Trieste in the Adriatic, an iron curtain has descended across the continent. Behind that line lie all the capitals of the ancient states of central and eastern Europe. Warsaw, Berlin, Prague, Vienna, Budapest, Belgrade, Bucharest, and Sofia, all these famous cities and the populations around them lie in the Soviet sphere and all are subject in one form or another, not only to Soviet influence but to a very high and increasing measure of control from Moscow. Athens alone, with its immortal glories, is free to decide its future at an election under British American, and French observation.

Besides the disagreements over Eastern Europe in 1946, the West was also nervous about Soviet intentions in the northern Middle East. Soviet troops were occupying northern Iran in line with a Soviet–Iranian treaty, but at the same time Azerbaijani radicals were being encouraged to create their own autonomous state in the region. The USSR also made territorial claims on Turkey, first on the behalf of Armenia and later of Georgia, and demanded a base in the Dardanelles. Stalin's muscle-flexing in Iran and Turkey only drove the governments of those countries into the Western camp and confirmed the West's demonic vision of the Soviet Union as a state with an insatiable appetite for expansion. In March 1946 the Soviet Union agreed, under Western pressure, to withdraw troops from Iran and ceased pushing the claims to Kars and Ardahan in eastern Anatolia. But the image of the Soviets as expansionist was by this time indelibly etched into the minds of Western policymakers. In a long memorandum to the president in September, a key advisor wrote, "The language of military power is the only language which disciples of power politics understand." More ominously, he went on, "In order to maintain our strength at a level which will be effective in restraining the Soviet Union, the United States must be prepared to wage atomic and biological warfare." When Truman read the memo, he told his advisor that it was too hot to be circulated and locked it away in his office safe.

Soviet views on the United States were in many ways ideological mirror images that reflected back the same distorted images of Soviet aggression and expansionism that were becoming fixed in American minds. The Soviet ambassador to the United States sent his own "long telegram" to Moscow, in which he accused American "monopolistic capital" of "striving for world supremacy." Truman was seen as "a politically unstable person but with certain conservative tendencies." The ambassador's greatest fear was that hundreds of U.S. bases were to be built around the globe, demonstrating the "offensive nature of [American military's] strategic concepts" and the "plans for world dominance by the United States."

The Division of Europe

On March 12, 1947, President Truman spoke before Congress for a brief eighteen minutes about international affairs and dramatically changed the direction of American foreign policy for decades to come. He talked of "the gravity of the situation which confronts the world today" and of the need for the United States to aid Greece as a "democratic" and "free" state. Turkey, which was not spoken of as democratic, nevertheless needed to have its "integrity" defended.

> We shall not realize our objectives . . . unless we are willing to help free peoples to maintain their free institutions and their national integrity against aggressive movements that seek to impose upon them totalitarian regimes. . . .
>
> I believe that it must be the policy of the United States to support free peoples who are resisting attempted subjugation by armed minorities or by outside pressure.

Truman's speech marked the end of American retreat and isolation and the acceptance of what it considered its global responsibility. The president accentuated the anti-Communist tone in his speech in order to assure passage of his aid program to Greece and Turkey through Congress, which it did by lopsided majorities. A Gallup poll showed that three-quarters of Americans favored Truman's new policy. The Soviet response to Truman's speech was cautious. Molotov told his ambassador in Washington that "the President is trying to intimidate us, to turn us at a stroke into obedient little boys. But we don't give a damn." Yet within a few months Soviet policy toward the West, and East-Central Europe, began to harden, in part in response to a bold new initiative on the economic front by the United States.

On June 5, 1947, Secretary of State Marshall announced at Harvard University that the United States was willing to offer grants to European states if they worked out plans for economic integration. American policymakers were concerned that European poverty made Western Europe both a poor trading partner for the United States and a potential target for the Left. Desperate to trade its postwar surpluses, the United States through the Marshall Plan could establish stable, viable trading partners in democratic states. The offer seemed to be open to the USSR as well as other East European states, though there was divided opinion among American leaders about the wisdom of including the Soviets. A very influential group around George Kennan was convinced that the West must form its own bloc, which would include Western-occupied zones in Germany. Three weeks later the foreign ministers of the Great Powers met in Paris to discuss a joint proposal for American aid. Molotov wanted the aid to be given without preconditions, but the Western ministers agreed with the American advisors that a coordinated plan for the entire European economy should be drawn up. The Soviet Union was unwilling to integrate their state economy into an international capitalist system, and Molotov claimed that the American conditions would allow foreign interference into the internal affairs of states.

Molotov left the conference without an agreement, convinced that the Marshall Plan would subordinate the Soviet Union and Eastern Europe to Western capitalism, but Foreign Trade Minister Mikoyan tried to convince Stalin of the advantages of joining the Plan. As he remembered in his memoirs,

> His only reaction was: "We shall be dependent on the West." In vain I argued that we were independent enough politically, and that with the aid from the USA we would be able to restore the economy of the European part of the country, which was in ruins, much faster and on a new technological level. Which would have made us more independent! But Stalin, a clever man able to understand economic issues when one explained them to him, could be also stubborn as a donkey, to the extent of being a fool.

Once Stalin had made up his mind, the Soviets forced their East European allies, including the Czechoslovaks, who were particularly anxious to receive Marshall Plan aid, to reject the American offer. Stalin warned Jan Masaryk, "If you take part in the conference you will prove by that act that you allow yourselves to be used as a tool against the Soviet Union." By August the East European states were coordinating their own mutual trade ties as a separate trade bloc. The "Molotov Plan" was adopted, and Europe split into two antagonistic economic blocs. From that point on, an even closer political and economic integration of Eastern Europe with the USSR became inevitable.

In late September 1947 leading Communists met at Szklarska-Poreba in Poland to work out a common strategy in the Cold War world. Stalin's principal representative was Andrei Zhdanov, who mapped out the division of the world into two major camps: the anti-imperialist and democratic camp versus the antidemocratic and imperialist. He stressed, as Stalin had, that war between the two was not inevitable. But his major aim was to stiffen the back of European Communists for a more militant struggle ahead. He attacked the French and Italian Communist parties for their mild and conciliatory policies and praised the Yugoslavs as the most militant and revolutionary party. The meeting ended with the formation of a Communist Information Bureau, or Cominform, which included the parties of the East-Central European states (with the exception of Greece) plus the French and Italian parties. The Cominform conference marked as clearly as any event the turn of the Communist movement toward a more militant strategy.

Despite Stalin's overwhelming authority, the Soviet Union did not have a single, consistent foreign policy in the Cold War years. Stalin had no blueprint for Eastern Europe and up to 1947 played with various possible arrangements for the countries in the region. But in the last years of the decade he tightened his grip on the neighboring regimes, and the options narrowed rapidly. Calculating that Truman was a weak leader and that anti-American sentiments were growing in Europe, the Soviets overreacted in 1947, underestimated the power of the American economy, and adopted a new defensive policy that consolidated the division of Europe.

Poland

Stalin was determined to have a Poland that presented no threat or hostility toward the Soviet Union. He attempted to use the resurrected Polish Communist Party as a wedge into Polish politics. Under Soviet patronage and in an atmosphere of enthusiasm for social renewal, the party grew rapidly, from a few hundred members in 1943 to eight thousand in 1944 to a million in 1948. The Communists toned down their rhetoric, appealed to Polish nationalism, and spoke of a "Polish road" to socialism. Even so the Polish Communists were too independent and radical for Stalin, who hoped to enlist the more conservative Polish parties in the common cause of reconstructing Poland and creating a friendly state on the Soviet Union's most vulnerable border.

The Soviet Union became the guarantor of the new borders of Poland. In moving of its frontiers to the west, Poland lost agricultural lands in the east but gained a highly-developed German industrial and transportation complex in the west. Stalin forced the new government to accept the new frontiers in the east and north. On January 3, 1946, Poland nationalized all industries employing over fifty workers. A virtual civil war raged in the country between 1945 and 1948, with nationalist Poles and Communists ambushing and killing each other by the thousands. The Communists gained support from the reforms they carried out but were not above using force and violence against their political enemies. After consulting with Stalin, the Communists and Socialists, formed a government bloc of five parties to contest the January 1947 elections against the Polish Peasant Party. The Democratic Bloc won 9 million votes to the Peasant Party's 1 million, but the elections were marked by pressure on voters and the stuffing of ballot boxes. The West protested, and Peasant Party members resigned from the government. But in February the new Communist-led parliament elected a Communist president of Poland, and within months a new constitution and economic laws transformed Poland into a partially socialized economy. With their political range severely circumscribed, the Peasant Party carried on as an opposition party until the fall of 1947. In October, fearing that he would soon be arrested, its leader Mikolajczyk, fled to the West.

The Communists dominated Poland from the summer of 1947. Stalin turned from restraining the Polish Communists to promoting those who wanted to move toward socialism rapidly. Poland was defined as a "people's democracy," a transitional political form on the road from capitalist to social-ist democracy, and government policy was closely coordinated with Moscow. The Socialist Party merged with the Communists in December 1948, and the former socialist Joseph Cyrankewicz served as prime minister from 1948 to 1972. By the early 1950s Poland was completely subordinated to the Soviet Union, a state dominated by a submissive Communist elite who listened at-tentively to the orders of Soviet police agents.

Czechoslovakia

In contrast to Polish–Soviet relations, Czechoslovak–Soviet relations were quite cordial. Czechs and Slovaks shared a latent pro-Russian feeling of Slavic soli-darity with the Russians, and they were aware that the USSR had been pre-pared to fight for Czechoslovakia at the time of the Munich agreement. As the war came to an end, President Beneš spoke of Czechoslovakia as a bridge link-ing East and West in Europe. In March 1945 he agreed secretly to allow the So-viet Union to mine uranium ore and ship it to the USSR, not understanding the new importance that uranium had in the world balance of power. As in Poland, the Communists in Czechoslovakia were in a moderate phase; they emphasized the idea of national roads to socialism and reacted to Stalin's pri-vate musings that in certain instances it was possible to achieve socialism with-out the dictatorship of the proletariat. In June the new coalition government expelled most of the Germans and Hungarians in the country, accusing them of collaboration, and Beneš made an extraordinary concession to Stalin: he agreed to cede Ruthenia, the easternmost part of his country, which was in-habited by people close to the Ukrainians, to the USSR. In exchange the Czechs were permitted to keep Teschen, which the Poles had annexed after Munich. In late October the president ordered the nationalization of most industry. By December both the Americans and the Soviets had withdrawn their troops from Czechoslovakia, and Beneš's policy of bridging East and West seemed to be paying off.

The major beneficiary of the popular reforms and the good will toward the Soviet Union was the Communist Party, which by spring of 1946 could claim over 1 million members. In the elections of May 1946, the Communists won 38 percent of the votes, the largest of any party, and their leader, Klement Gottwald, became prime minister of a coalition government. The government intended to deal with both with the Soviet Union and the West, but the Amer-icans soon began to treat Czechoslovakia as if it were already a Soviet satel-lite. When Stalin forbade Czechoslovakia to participate in the Marshall Plan, the policy of bridging East and West collapsed. A political crisis exploded in Prague when in February 1948 the National Socialists, suspicious that the Com-munists were preparing a coup d'etat, tried to bring down the government and force new elections by resigning. Mass meetings were held in the Old Town Square, where crowds cheered Gottwald, who accused the departing ministers of having formed a "reactionary bloc" to obstruct further reforms. Given the popularity of the Communists and the growing dependence of Czechoslovakia on Soviet aid and good will, Beneš had little choice but to agree to appoint a new coalition government that was more firmly in Communist hands. These events, which were soon characterized as "the Czech coup," in fact were legal and constitutional. But within a few weeks, the non-Communist foreign minister, Jan Masaryk, was mysteriously killed, either by murder or suicide. In May a new constitution was adopted and elections overwhelmingly supported the new government. On June 7 Beneš resigned and Gottwald succeeded him as president. From 1948 until 1989 Czechoslovakia was dominated by the Communist Party.

Yugoslavia

The most leftist of the Communist parties in Eastern Europe was the Yugoslav party led by Josef Broz, known as Tito, an ardent Stalinist and the battle-hardened leader of the antifascist partisans. The Communists came out of the mountains determined to abolish the prewar monarchy, which Stalin did not want them to do, and carry out militant policies toward the political opposition and the church. They came to power on their own, with little Soviet help, and their policies were more radical than their Soviet mentors. But the Yugoslav Communists believed themselves to be loyal to Stalin. A leading party member said, "I would have taken poison if Stalin had offered it." Yet after years as partisans waging their own antifascist struggle Tito and his comrades had gained in self-assurance and independence and became the spokesmen for "national roads to socialism." Tito publicly announced in May 1945 that "our goal is that everyone be the master in his own house."

The Soviets proved to be difficult comrades for the Yugoslav Communists. The Yugoslavs expected more economic aid from the USSR than they received and were appalled by the unfair terms of trade agreements and joint-stock companies established by the Soviets. Though he spoke highly of Tito, Stalin maintained his own agents among the Yugoslav party members. Stalin was prepared to have Yugoslavia "swallow" Albania, where local Communist partisans under Enver Hoxha had come to power with Yugoslav assistance, but when Tito pressed for unification with Albania and Albanian leaders resisted, Stalin's suspicions increased. He feared that Yugoslavia was becoming a regional Communist center and might dominate the proposed federation of Balkan states. The Yugoslav Communists were the principal supporters of the Greek Communist Party in its civil war against British-backed monarchists. Early in 1948 Stalin told Tito that the revolution in Greece should be "folded up." Underlying the estrangement between Moscow and Belgrade was Yugoslav reluctance to subordinate their country to the USSR.

On March 27 Stalin and Molotov sent a letter to the Yugoslav leaders claiming that their Central Committee was not Marxist-Leninist. Tito quickly rallied his party, convened the Yugoslav Central Committee, which had not met since 1940, and arrested pro-Soviet party members, the so-called Cominformists. The Cominform met in June and condemned Yugoslavia. Stalin believed that he could wiggle his little finger and Tito would fall, but his effort to pressure Yugoslavia failed. While the other Communist parties turned against Tito, Soviet troops sent specialists and munitions to his allies in Eastern Europe in preparation for an invasion. The attack never came, but Yugoslavia was driven from the Soviet bloc. By 1949 Stalin had leading "Titoists" in the parties under his control in Eastern Europe arrested and executed. National Communism was buried for several decades. Meanwhile, Tito developed his own non-Soviet brand of socialism. The Communist Party maintained its monopoly on political power, but workers' councils were given increased power in factories and plants. Yugoslavia drew somewhat closer to the West and received weapons from both Britain and the United States, though it played a leading role in the emerging movement of "nonaligned" countries.

The Finnish Exception

By 1944 Finland was a defeated former ally of Nazi Germany. Forced to give up territory and pay reparations of $300 million to the USSR, the country's very independence seemed threatened. Soviet forces set up a base in Porkkala, thirty minutes driving time from Helsinki, but Soviet troops did not occupy Finland. After free elections in March 1945, a coalition government was formed, based on a program of cooperation with the USSR and the maintenance of a democratic, capitalist system. Communists eventually joined the government, but here as elsewhere in Eastern Europe, the Soviet Union supported a non-Communist as head of government.

In 1947, when the Soviet leadership took a harder line toward its neighbors, Moscow instructed the Finnish Communists to stiffen up their policy. Workers marched in protest against the ending of food rationing, and rumors ran rampant that the Communists were about to seize power by force. The Socialists pushed the Communists out of government. As the crisis heated up, Stalin proposed a mutual assistance pact like that concluded with Rumania and Hungary, but Finland held out for a quite different relationship with the Soviet Union: it remained an independent parliamentary democracy with a capitalist system, but its foreign policy was carefully coordinated with the interests and desires of its mammoth neighbor to the east. It agreed not to participate in the Marshall Plan, rather than antagonize the USSR, but at the same time it was able to receive aid from the West. This position of formal independence and sovereignty with full autonomy in domestic policy but nonantagonistic foreign policy became known as "Finlandization." At a dinner party late in 1947 Stalin remarked that it had been a mistake not to occupy Finland. "We were too concerned about the Americans, and they wouldn't have lifted a finger." "Ah, Finland!" Molotov added, "That is a peanut." For Stalin, at least in this case, independence along with foreign policy coordination was an acceptable solution to the national security insecurities of the Soviet Union.

At the beginning of 1947 Communists held a monopoly of power only in Yugoslavia and Albania, where they had come to power without direct Soviet help but as the leaders of national partisan movements. Hungary, Rumania, Bulgaria, Czechoslovakia, and Poland all had coalition governments. Soviet control was formalized through bilateral treaties signed with the Communist governments of Eastern Europe, the first with Rumania on February 4, 1948. Two weeks later a similar treaty was signed with Hungary and a month later with Bulgaria. Stalin's earlier tolerance of diversity in Eastern Europe turned quickly into backing the takeover of governments by the Communist parties. By mid-1948 all of the countries of Eastern Europe, with the exception of Finland and Greece, had Communist governments.

The German Question

For the Soviet Union prevention of a third war launched from Germany through Poland was paramount in their strategic thinking. As Soviet leaders contemplated the future in Europe, they might have considered five possible solutions, at least in theory, to the problem of how to deal with their defeated enemy, Germany. The first hypothetical solution was a four-power agreement on a harsh, Carthaginian peace, with annexation of German territory, demilitarization, and a limit placed on future German industrial growth. Though Stalin and France's Charles de Gaulle liked the idea and Roosevelt had supported it, Churchill opposed it and convinced the president that it would leave the USSR too powerful on the continent. A second possible solution was a four-power agreement on a neutralized, united Germany, the same solution that would be applied to Austria in 1955. The USSR favored such an arrangement, but many in the West feared a united neutral Germany because the strength of the Left in eastern Germany might have led to a pro-Soviet Germany. The third solution would be Soviet domination of all of Germany, but the West was determined to prevent this. And the fourth solution was Western domination of all of Germany, and the Soviet Union was opposed to that. Thus, the only solution left was what eventually occurred: the partition of Germany.

After the Yalta Conference Stalin committed himself to securing a united Germany, but he could not secure agreement from the West. Fundamental reforms were delayed, awaiting the outcome of discussions with the West, but by early 1946 the occupation authorities had expropriated and nationalized nearly all large industries in the Soviet zone. They carried out land reform that, though economically a disaster because there was not enough land for those who wanted it and yields fell rapidly, was politically a success. The old social order in the countryside was destroyed, and the former ruling class of Prussia, the aristocratic Junkers, was eliminated. But as quickly as the German Communists revived economic institutions, the Soviets dismantled them and removed them to the USSR as prizes of war. Stalin's first priority was Soviet recovery and only later was he concerned with efforts to aid an allied Germany. Moreover, the Soviets believed that the more radical tendencies among local social groups had to be curbed. Even as the Communists weakened the capitalists and the landlords, they limited the independent power of workers in factory councils, who believed that socialism meant that workers ought to control the means of production. When the Communist Party lost momentum and support in the fall of 1945, the Soviets, along with the trade unions, pressured the increasingly popular Social Democrats to join the Communists in a united party, the Socialist Unity Party (SED), which formed in April 1946.

Soviet and SED policy was geared toward creating a "people's democracy" that could prevent a return to fascism. But the greater social changes in eastern Germany, as well as the merger of the Left into a single party, made the Soviet zone distinctly different from the western zones. The United States was upset that the Soviet Union had failed to implement the all-German economic policies that had been agreed to at Potsdam. In July 1946 Secretary Byrnes authorized the merger of the British and American zones and created "Bizonia," and within a month France moved closer to joining its zone to that of the British and Americans. German partition was becoming a reality.

By the beginning of 1948 Stalin realized that there would be separate East and West German states. He told delegations from Bulgaria and Yugoslavia that "the West will make West Germany their own, and we shall turn Eastern Germany into our own state." However, he wanted the city of Berlin, which was also occupied by the four powers, to be entirely in the new East Germany. On March 6 the Western powers announced that a separate West German government would be formed. The Soviets protested the plan, which they considered a violation of the Potsdam agreements by walking out of the Allied Control Council in Germany. On April 1 the Soviet authorities restricted Western military traffic into Berlin, and the Americans responded with a "little airlift," bringing in supplies by plane. Two months later, on June 1, the United States and Britain agreed to introduce a separate currency, the Deutschemark, in their zones of occupation, replacing the all-German Reichsmark. The Soviets replied by introducing their own currency in their zone and attempted to include all of Berlin. The West retaliated by extending its currency into its Berlin zones. On June 24 the Soviet authorities shut off all surface access from the West through their zone to Berlin. The Berlin Blockade had begun.

The West responded with a massive airlift of supplies for West Berlin, landing planes at the rate of one a minute. For almost a year the airlift "to preserve freedom" continued, and Berlin was transformed from the capital of a defeated fascist power into a symbol of courageous resistance to totalitarianism, in the words of President John F. Kennedy in 1961 "a showcase of liberty, a symbol, an isle of freedom in a communist sea." As anti-Communist rhetoric shaped (and simplified) people's perceptions of complex diplomatic questions, the Soviet Union was steadily reimagined as the heir of Nazism, a "Red Fascist" state engaged in an enterprise of world conquest similar to Hitler's. The only appropriate response to such an aggressor was resistance, not concessions that would appear to be appeasement. One American officer spoke of his adversaries as "Communist rats who walked like bears," and once the Soviets were depicted as vicious enemies who only understood power, recourse to negotiation became increasingly constrained. During the crisis the United States sent B-29 bombers to Britain to signal that it was prepared to defend Western Europe with nuclear weapons if necessary.

Stalin increased pressure on the West in Berlin to show strength, but he carefully limited the degree of pressure and never interfered with the airlift. He did not want the Soviet Union to be humiliated, nor did he want to precipitate a war, and he apparently was convinced that the United States would not use nuclear weapons to resolve the crisis. Finally, in January 1949, after months of tension, the Soviets hinted that they were prepared to shift their position on Berlin and suggested that the whole question of German unity be reopened. Though some American policymakers, such as George Kennan, were interested in ending the division of Germany and Europe, U.S. officials decided that it was more important to link Allied-controlled Germany to the West than to unify the whole country. On May 5 the four occupying powers signed an agreement that brought the yearlong crisis to an end. But no agreement was reached on unification. Secretary of State Dean Acheson noted joyfully that the Soviets "are back on the defensive. . . . They are visibly concerned and afraid of the fact that they have lost Germany."

Stalin lost his gamble in Berlin. Two separate Germanys were created, and the West moved rapidly toward rearmament and the formation of a military alliance directed against the USSR. In 1949 the Federal Republic of Germany and the German Democratic Republic were created, and in April the North Atlantic Treaty Organization (NATO) was formed. The lesson learned in the West from the Berlin crisis was that force, especially air power, was the most reliable weapon against Communism. The lesson Stalin learned was that intransigence and aggressive bluffing, within limits, were tools he could use in an increasingly dangerous world. International politics took on aspects of a global morality play, one in which both sides would soon have the option of using atomic weapons.

Suggestions for Further Reading

Cold War historiography is divided into the competing orthodox and revisionist schools. For the orthodox view, see Herbert Feis, *Churchill, Roosevelt, Stalin: The War They Waged and the Peace They Sought* (Princeton, N.J., 1957); Arthur Schlesinger, Jr., "Origins of the Cold War," *Foreign Affairs*, 47 (October 1967): 22–51; and Winston Churchill, *The Grand Alliance* (Boston, 1950) and *Triumph and Tragedy* (Boston, 1953). For the revisionist view, see Gar Alperovitz, *Atomic Diplomacy* (New York, 1965); Thomas J. Paterson, *Soviet-American Confrontation: Postwar Reconstruction and the Origins of the Cold War* (Baltimore, 1973); Lloyd C. Gardner, *Architects of Illusion: Men and Ideas in American Foreign Policy, 1941–1949*, rev. ed. (Chicago, 1970); Diane Shaver Clemens, *Yalta* (New York, 1970); Gabriel Kolko and Joyce Kolko, *The Limits of Power: The World and United States Foreign Policy, 1945–1954* (New York, 1972); and Barton J. Bernstein, "American Foreign Policy and the Origins of the Cold War," in his (ed.), *Politics and Policies of the Truman Administration* (New York, 1970), pp. 15–77.

Important works have built on this controversy and tried to move beyond it. See, for example, John Lewis Gaddis, *The United States and the Origins of the Cold War, 1941–1947* (New York, 1972) and *Russia, the Soviet Union, and the United States: An Interpretive History* (New York, 1978); Melvyn P. Leffler, *A Preponderance of Power: National Security, the Truman Administration, and the Cold War* (Stanford, Calif., 1992); and Fraser J. Harbutt, *The Iron Curtain: Churchill, America, and the Origins of the Cold War* (New York, 1986). On Stalin's foreign policy, see Marshall Shulman, *Stalin's Foreign Policy Reappraised* (Cambridge, Mass., 1963); Adam Ulam, *The Rivals: America and Russia Since World War*

II (New York, 1971); William Taubman, *Stalin's American Policy* (New York, 1982); Norman M. Naimark, *The Russians in Germany: A History of the Soviet Zone of Occupation, 1945–1949* (Cambridge, Mass., 1995); David Holloway, *Stalin and the Bomb: The Soviet Union and Atomic Energy, 1939–1956* (New Haven, Conn., 1994); Vladislav M. Zubok and Constantine V. Pleshakov, *Inside the Kremlin's Cold War* (Cambridge, Mass., 1995); and Matthew Evangelista, "Stalin's Postwar Army Reappraised," *International Security*, 7, no. 3 (Winter 1982–83): 110–38. For important Cold War documents, see Kenneth M. Jensen (ed.), *Origins of the Cold War: The Novikov, Kennan, and Roberts "Long Telegrams" of 1946* (Washington, D.C., 1991).

CHAPTER 16
Late Stalinism at Home and Abroad

From under the Rubble

World War II represented not only a mammoth military effort by the Soviet people but also a colossal social upheaval. The European part of the Soviet Union was a landscape of ruin and devastation by war's end, far more vulnerable than many in the West suspected. Social, state, and party institutions had broken down and needed to be rebuilt, and Stalin soon made it clear that he intended to restore, not only the economy, but the autocratic political structure that he had built in the 1930s. The population had diminished by more than 26 million from its prewar number of 190 million. Huge movements of population had occurred. In 1939–40 populations were exchanged between the German and Soviet-held parts of Poland; Baltic Germans and Germans living in the Soviet zone were transferred to German-held territory, and Ukrainians and Belorussians and Russians were transferred to the USSR. Over four hundred thousand Finns and Karelians were expelled to Finnish territory. Some 880,000 people, most from the annexed regions of Ukraine, Belorussia, and the Baltic states, were deported to special settlements and labor camps in 1940–41; of those only about half were released before the end of the war. During the war Stalin moved whole peoples from their homelands within the USSR to Central Asian exile. In the fall of 1941 the government removed 400,000 Volga Germans to Central Asia and Siberia, ostensibly out of fear that they might collaborate with the invading Germans. In 1943–44 Stalin ordered the deportation of Crimean Tatars, Chechens, Ingushi, Karachai, Balkars, Kalmyks, Meskhetian Turks, and others, about a million people in all, from their homelands to Kazakhstan and Central Asia. Rounded up by Beria's NKVD, accused of collaboration with the enemy, and sent into exile in boxcars and Studebaker trucks (part of Lend-Lease), hundreds of thousands of North Caucasians and others perished on the way.

During the war the Germans occupied territory in which 85 million Soviet citizens had lived before the war. Some 12 to 15 million were evacuated or fled during the war. Of the 5 million Soviet soldiers and officers captured by the

Germans, only 1 million emerged from German POW camps at the end of the war. Altogether 5.5 million Soviet citizens were repatriated to the Soviet Union in the first seven postwar years. The Western Allies had agreed at Yalta to repatriate all Soviet citizens in the West, but as relations with the USSR cooled (after September 1946) those reluctant to return were no longer forced to repatriate. About half a million Soviets remained in the West, while many of those who returned went from Nazi concentration camps to Soviet labor camps.

At the war's end, Jews and Poles who had lived in prewar Poland were given the option of moving to the newly constituted Poland that had been pushed westward. About 2 million Poles moved to Poland (about half the total of Soviet Poles), along with a large number of Jews, many of whom then moved on to the West or to Palestine. Ukrainians, Russians, Belorussians, and Lithuanians (but not Jews) who had lived in Poland were allowed to move to the USSR, and more than half a million migrated. The new arrivals were not allowed to settle in border regions but were sent further into Ukraine and Russia, while the borderlands were settled by Russian migrants from Siberia and Kazakhstan. Russians and others were also sent to the Baltic states, where new industries were established. One hundred eighty thousand non-Estonians arrived in Estonia between 1945 and 1949, and in Latvia the Russian population rose from 12 percent in 1935 to 27 percent in 1959. Germans in the Konigsberg region on the Baltic, which had been East Prussia but now became the Russian district of Kaliningrad, were replaced by Russians and other Slavs, who, *Izvestiia* announced, "are again settling on this ancestral Slavic soil."

The areas gained by the Soviet Union were rapidly Sovietized, which at this time meant not only the establishment of Soviet institutions—collective farms, party committees, nationalized industry, and statified trade unions—but also demographic and cultural Russification. In the spring of 1949 the state launched a massive campaign to collectivize agriculture in the newly acquired regions. This led to a fall in the rural population and a rise in the urban. In Estonia, for example, the rural share fell from 53 percent in early 1950 to 46 percent in 1954, with 50,000 peasants moving to towns and cities. Because of all the uprooting and movement, as well as the gender imbalance in which women far outnumbered men, intermarriage and linguistic Russification accelerated during and just after the war.

Some 8.5 million soldiers were demobilized and returned to civilian life in the three years after the war. At first, soldiers were simply handed their papers and allowed to go where they wanted, but this put enormous strain on the civilian economy. Later they were ordered to be demobilized at the place where they had been inducted, apparently to ensure that millions of peasant soldiers returned to their collective farms. But given the desperate need for industrial workers, hundreds of thousands of people moved where they liked anyway, and about half the demobilized soldiers found their way into towns and industry. The war proved to be a motor for upward mobility for many peasants who became workers.

The employed labor force grew altogether by 12 million people between 1945 and 1950. Along with ordinary Soviet workers there was a huge convict labor force, estimated to be about 3 or 4 million in various categories. Statistics published from archives opened in the last years of the Soviet Union reveal that the total number of prisoners in labor camps and colonies rose from 1,460,676 in 1945 to 2,468,524 in 1953. To those figures should be added the 300,000 convicts in prisons and the more than 2 million "special settlers" sent from their homelands into exile in Central Asia and Siberia. German POWs were repatriated only in 1955, ten years after the war had ended. Of the estimated 1.9 to 3.7 million German POWs held by the Soviets during the war, only about 20,000 ever returned to Germany. It was these people, along with Soviet prisoners, who built the Volga-Don Canal and the Lenin Hills building at Moscow State University.

Despite the use of POWS and convicts, labor shortages remained chronic in the USSR after the war. During the war women made up much of the industrial labor force. Twenty million men had been conscripted into the Red Army during the war, leaving farm labor and much factory work to women, old people, and children. Four times as many women were working behind the lines as men. Though the female proportion of the industrial workforce dropped in the postwar years as men returned to work, the actual number of women in the industrial labor force continued to rise.

Once again, as in the tsarist empire and the period of the first five-year plans, the Soviet peasantry paid for the recovery of the economy. The peasants numbered 64.3 million in 1944, some 15.4 million less than in 1936. They had diminished by 18 percent in four years of war, while the number of those who were able-bodied had fallen by 38 percent. Whereas in 1936 peasants had made up 60 percent of the whole working population of the Soviet Union, by 1945 they constituted only 45 percent. For the first time in Russia's history, peasants no longer constituted the majority of the laboring population. War and the weakening of party control in the countryside had encouraged the breakdown of established collective farm rules and regulations. In some places collectives even sold land to speculators or in exchange for services. Peasants simply took over and farmed land that belonged to the collective, but in September 1946 the government decreed that such land had to be returned to the collectives. Grain prices had not been raised since the early 1930s, and procurement prices were kept low during and after the war. Deliveries to the state were compulsory, and payments were even lower than before the war. Only cotton, citrus, and tea received higher prices (this favored Uzbekistan and Transcaucasia). Not surprisingly, local government, police, and party officials participated in the illegal distribution of agricultural products to favored customers. Taxes on collective farm income were raised five-fold during the war and again in August 1948. A year later the income of peasant farmers dropped to half of what it had been in 1928. Peasants managed to survive, however poorly, by working their individual plots and selling their surpluses in the collective farm markets. The harshness of rural life drove millions from the countryside each year. From 1950 to 1954, 9 million people left the farms. In the two decades from 1939 to 1959 the rural share of the total population fell from 61 to 56 percent.

A new economic and ecological fact was making itself felt on world leaders: the United States with its enormous food production controlled a vast international resource on which much of the world would be dependent in the

future. Many American officials realized, as others had after World War I, that
food was power. The Soviets and the Americans competed in Europe for influence and support through their rival food-delivery programs. Except for
Sweden and Switzerland, most of Europe was hungry in 1946–47. Food riots
broke out in France in April and May 1947. Rumania, quite dependent on Soviet grain shipments, was starving in 1947 when the USSR failed to deliver
enough grain. The Soviet Union suffered from a disastrous drought in 1946.
Agricultural output fell significantly from 1945 to 1946, and plan targets could
not be met. In 1947 people were dying of starvation in Kursk and in Ukraine.
Three hundred eighty-nine thousand people were suffering from malnutrition
and dystrophy in Moldavia in the winter of 1946–47. For political reasons, however, Stalin continued to export thousands of tons of grain to France, Finland,
Czechoslovakia, and Rumania. When the United States ended its contribution
to UNRRA, which was feeding hundreds of thousands in Ukraine and Belorussia, Soviet officials complained of the "American food blackmail," and the
government was forced to continue wartime rationing and even raise the price
of bread to cut down consumption.

Particularly hard hit was Ukraine, then governed by Nikita Khrushchev.
The combination of German destruction and an exceptionally dry year in 1946
created famine conditions. Stalin ordered Ukraine to meet its quotas to the state
first and only then to satisfy its own grain needs. The central authorities set a
target of 7.2 million tons of grain, which as Khrushchev later reported in his
memoirs, "had been calculated not on the basis of how much we really could
produce, but on the basis of how much the State thought it could beat out of
us." Experts estimated that only one- or two-fifths of the prewar output could
be expected in 1946. Khrushchev was soon receiving letters and reports about
starvation and even cannibalism. Nevertheless, as an obedient party boss he
sent the grain out of Ukraine. Even this did not save him from demotion. Stalin
sent his ruthless enforcer, Kaganovich, to Ukraine in 1947. Only in 1949 did
Ukrainian agriculture recover from the war and drought. Khrushchev, who
survived Stalin's wrath, was rewarded by being called back to work in Moscow
to balance rival factions in the leadership.

A second problem in Ukraine was the resistance of Ukrainian nationalists
to the imposition of Soviet rule, primarily in the western parts of Ukraine,
which had been annexed in 1939. In the spring of 1945 the Organization of
Ukrainian Nationalists (OUN) and its military wing, the Ukrainian Insurgent
Army (UIA), had 90,000 men under arms. From 1944 until they were defeated
at the end of the 1940s, the OUN-UIA killed 25,000 Soviet soldiers and police,
as well as 30 district party secretaries, 32 chairmen and vice-chairmen of district soviet executive committees, and about 30,000 Soviet citizens. The government retaliated brutally, deporting 66,000 families (over 200,000 people)
from Western Ukraine in the years 1944–51.

With both the agricultural and industrial economies devastated by the war,
and the prospect of aid from abroad growing dimmer each year, the Soviet
government was thrown back on its own resources to rebuild the country. Defense industries were rapidly converted to domestic production, but the result
in the short run was a further fall in output. Defense production fell by two-

thirds through 1945, but civilian production rose only one-fifth, and industrial output continued to fall in 1946. The Soviet press admitted the strains imposed on the people by drought and food shortage. Besides malnutrition, food shortages also affected labor productivity and slowed down economic recovery. Only by the end of 1947 was the economic output of 1940 reached. Rationing was then abolished, and a currency reform was initiated in December. Ten old rubles were now equivalent to one new ruble. The inflated money of the war years was replaced by a firmer currency, which at the same time dealt a severe blow to the flourishing black market and wiped out people's savings.

The Fourth Five-Year Plan (1946–50) looked much like the plans of the 1930s, with heavy investment in capital goods industries. Included were large allocations for atomic energy, radar, rocketry, and jet propulsion. Although overall defense spending went down once the war ended, it continued to absorb an inordinately large share of the country's wealth. New investment was made in industry, but repairing old plants and rail lines damaged during the war and bringing them on line proved easier than starting from scratch. Recovery was gradual but impressive. The showpiece of prewar industrialization in Ukraine, the Dnepropetrovsk hydroelectric station, was operating by 1947. The prewar level of steel production was reached in 1948. But in order to foster recovery and a rapid buildup of the military-industrial complex, the government restricted the production of consumer goods. Soviet industry produced fewer pairs of shoes each year than the number of citizens. Again, promises of a better future were used to offset current discontent and discomfort. Each year from 1948 to 1954 the government lowered prices on many essential goods such as bread, which by the mid-1950s cost half of what it cost in 1947. Decades later many older people would remember the late Stalin period as a golden age of peace, low prices, and strict, predictable order.

Party leaders experimented in the late Stalinist period with a flurry of schemes to improve the situation in agriculture, but none of them resulted in any significant improvement. Khrushchev, who had gained a reputation as an expert in agrarian matters, proposed the merger of collective farms into larger farms and the construction of agricultural towns with apartment houses and the amenities of urban life. Stalin himself attacked the notion, and Khrushchev wrote an abject letter pleading with Stalin to help him correct his "crude error:"

> You completely correctly showed me the errors I made on March 4 when I published the article "On Building and Improving the Amenities of Collective Farms." . . . I am prepared to appear in the press and thoroughly criticize my article. . . . I beg you, Comrade Stalin, help me to correct the crude error I have made and at the same time, as far as is possible, to lessen the damage that I have done to the party by my incorrect act.

In July 1950, however, farms were merged into larger collectives, diminishing the number from 252,000 to 123,000 by year's end. Stalin proposed his own grandiose schemes for the "transformation of nature," which involved massive planting of trees in the southern steppes and the building of networks of irrigation canals. But the trees died and the canals contributed little. Like many other large-scale projects, this one ended in colossal waste and expense.

The ruling Communist Party had changed during the war; it now included a new generation of war veterans. The party grew from 3,872,000 in 1941 to 5,760,000 in 1945. Two-thirds of all postwar party members had joined during the war. Over 40 percent of its members had served in the armed services. Many had been killed, and another 8.4 million new members, almost 80 percent of whom had served in the military, had been recruited into the party during the war. The war was a new common experience, not unlike the revolution and civil war for an earlier generation, that bound the party members together. Men or women with distinguished military service received rapid advancement and privileges, while others who had some black mark on their record suffered. Over 40 percent of new party members came from white-collar employees; just under a third were from the working class and a quarter from the peasantry. In 1947 nearly half of the party (48.3 percent) were white-collar; a third (33.7 percent) of worker origin; and 18 percent of peasant origin. Female representation had risen slightly to 18.3 percent. Though the war increased the number of Communists working in rural areas, the penetration of the party into the countryside remained superficial. Rural party leaders were usually poorly educated; few had better than a primary school education.

The war encouraged greater centralization and discipline in the party, but the physical hardships of the time made implementation of central control difficult until the end of the fighting. Then the leadership worked to discipline and centralize the party, even more than in the prewar years, approaching the image of a monolith, which had been the ideal of many Bolsheviks. In 1947 more than a quarter of district party secretaries were removed in a sweeping purge. The party increased its role in the economy, downplaying its role as political guide. While ordinary party members were completely subordinate to and dependent on the top leadership, they were a relatively privileged elite with considerable power over the rest of the population. But life as a party leader remained insecure. Stalin ruled in the name of the party and spoke as the voice of the Central Committee, although he did not bother to call very many sessions of the Central Committee or a single party congress between 1939 and 1952. Party life atrophied in the late Stalin years, and much of the daily decision-making and executive power fell to the state apparatus.

When foreign observers looked at Stalin's Soviet Union in the late 1940s, the immediate comparison that came to mind was with Nazi Germany. An image of "Red Fascism" melded the experiences of the two recently hostile states into a single political formulation. Political scientists borrowed the term "totalitarianism" to conceptualize these one-party ideological regimes that used terror and complete monopoly of the means of communication to control totally a subordinate society. They contrasted totalitarian regimes, with their mass manipulation, suppression of voluntary associations, violence, and expansionism, with liberal democratic, pluralistic societies. In their view the extreme Right and extreme Left were more similar than different, and many concluded that such systems effectively suppressed all internal dissension and would never change unless overthrown from outside. Totalitarianism was a powerful analytical model for describing the late Stalinist Soviet Union, but it failed to adequately account for the differences between Nazi Germany and Stalinist USSR: the contrast between a racist, inegalitarian ideology (Nazism) and an egalitarian, internationalist doctrine (Marxism); the difference between a state capitalist system with private ownership of property (in Nazi Germany) and a completely state-dominated economy with almost no production for the market (in Stalin's USSR); and an advanced industrial economy geared essentially to war and territorial expansion (Nazi Germany) and a program for modernizing a backward, peasant society and transforming it into an industrial, urban one (Stalinist Soviet Union). Moreover, the total control of totalitarianism was never that total, never matched the image of an all-powerful state that atomized its population, turning people into "little screws" (Stalin's words) to do the bidding of the state. And finally, the Soviet regime, at least, did change over time, in the four decades after Stalin's death. What was totalitarian about Stalinism was not the actual achievements of the system but the intentions of the ruler. Stalin and his clique had ambitions to create a society in which the party and people were one, in which interests of all were harmonized and all dissent destroyed. But they never achieved that goal; they never had the power and instruments to control the people completely, yet never realized that that particular distopia was unreachable.

Reconstructing Hearts and Minds

There was widespread yearning for a more peaceful and freer life after the war. Many peasants believed that the collective farms would be dismantled; artists and intellectuals thought that the sacrifices for the war effort would be rewarded with greater creative freedom. Briefly in the first months after the war ended, new literary works appeared that seemed to bear out the promise of a more tolerant and liberal cultural life. At a poetry reading in Moscow young Muscovites wildly applauded the unorthodox poets Boris Pasternak and Anna Akhmatova. Sergei Eisenstein's new film *Ivan the Terrible: Part I* won a Stalin prize in January 1946. But the respite ended quickly.

Even before the war ended, observant people might have noticed signs that there would be no real liberalization in social and cultural policy. When the satirical writer Mikhail Zoshchenko published the story *Before Sunrise* and began it with "I am unhappy and I don't know why," party critics pounced on him for his individualism and avoidance of larger social themes. About the same time the much-lauded writer Konstantin Fedin issued a second volume of his *Gorky among Us*, only to find that in official eyes he had created an example of "apolitical art" and minimized the role of the party. Party officials called writers to task. Stalin had spoken of them as "engineers of the soul," and in the postwar years they were to serve an even more narrowly strict definition of art and conform to an ever more restrictive repertoire of themes.

On August 14, 1946, the Central Committee attacked Zoshchenko and Akhmatova, who were soon expelled from the Writers' Union. This was the first major salvo in what would be known as the *Zhdanovshchina*, a cultural war against innovation, modernism, liberalism, and Western sympathies. Zhdanov, Stalin's lieutenant in Leningrad, made two major speeches in which he defined the role of literature in Soviet society. The writer was to work to educate and unite the people in Bolshevik idealism. Zhdanov reflected Stalin's own hostility toward things Western and condemned "servility before contemporary bourgeois culture." He combined anti-Westernism with a reassertion of Soviet patriotism, with its Russian nationalist undertones, and depicted Russian culture as unique and distinct from anything the West had produced.

One of the most popular novels of the day was Aleksandr Fadeev's *Young Guard*, the story of a band of young partisan fighters fighting the Germans behind enemy lines. Universally praised by critics and dramatized for the stage, it seemed an unimpeachable work. Fadeev himself had been elevated to head the Writers' Union, and *Young Guard* had won the Stalin Prize, First Class, in 1946. Suddenly, in November 1947, the leading literary journals turned on Fadeev for his ambivalent treatment of party leaders in the novel. Even though the story was based on real incidents, it was impermissible to show party leaders as "incapable, inexperienced, and even foolish." Fadeev set to work immediately and four years later produced a new version of the novel, which was approved by party censors.

On January 13, 1948, Zhdanov chaired a meeting in the Central Committee building to discuss the question of "formalism in music." He attacked Shostakovich, Prokofiev, and other composers for "distorting our reality, for not reflecting our glorious victories, and for eating out of the hands of our enemies." Zhdanov said that the new music by contemporary composers was "infiltrated and overloaded to such a degree by naturalistic sounds that one is reminded—forgive the inelegant expression—of a piercing road drill or a musical gas-chamber." On February 12 a special degree singled out the opera *The Great Friendship*, by a minor Georgian composer, which had upset Stalin with its alleged anti-Russian implications. The effect of the state's intervention was to throw a pall over all musicians. Shostakovich's works were not played, and he once again took to writing movie scores for popular films. Only a year later was Shostakovich given a reprieve by a direct intervention from Stalin. A friend remembered:

> The telephone rang, and Dmitri Dmitriyevich picked up the receiver. A second later he said helplessly: "Stalin is about to come on the line." . . .
>
> Stalin was evidently inquiring after Shostakovich's health. Dmitri Dmitriyevich answered disconsolately: "Thank you, everything is fine. I am only suffering somewhat from stomach-ache."
>
> Stalin asked if he needed a doctor or any medicine.
>
> "No, thank you, I don't need anything. I have everything I need."
>
> Then there was a long pause while Stalin spoke. It transpired that he was asking Shostakovich to travel to the USA for the Congress of Peace and Culture.
>
> ". . . Of course I will go, if it is really necessary, but I am in a fairly difficult position. Over there, almost all my symphonies are played, whereas over here they are forbidden. How am I to behave in this situation?" . . .

> Stalin reassured Shostakovich that this was a mistake, which would be corrected; none of Dmitrii Dmitriyevich's works had been forbidden; they could be freely performed.

Though back in favor and at the mercy of the whims of the dictator, Shostakovich courageously continued to write his own modernist music, skirting the boundaries of what was permissible. He wrote a cycle of Jewish songs at the height of the anti-Semitic campaigns of the late 1940s and helped friends and colleagues who had fallen afoul of the regime.

A small number of highly placed intellectuals enjoyed a degree of autonomy and privilege that few others in Stalinist society could claim. But with those exalted privileges came the danger of a long fall. On October 3, 1945, the eminent physicist Petr Kapitsa wrote a strongly worded letter to Stalin criticizing Beria's running of the A-bomb project and the policeman's lack of respect for science. Kapitsa asked to be allowed to resign from the project. Beria made an elaborate gesture of reconciliation with Kapitsa while at the same time asking Stalin privately for permission to arrest the scientist. Stalin told Beria not to touch Kapitsa, but soon the future Nobel Prize winner fell into disfavor; he was removed from the project and lost the directorship of his institute.

Those physicists who did not complain and learned to work under the severe constraints of the Stalinist system, like Igor Kurchatov, received everything they needed for their work and a style of life unimaginable to the average Soviet citizen. Stalin told Kurchatov in 1945, "If a child doesn't cry, the mother doesn't know what he needs. Ask for whatever you like. You won't be refused." Early the next year Stalin promised improved living standards for scientists: "Our state has suffered very much, yet it is surely possible to ensure that several thousand people can live very well, and several thousand better than very well with their own dachas [summer houses], so that they can relax, and with their own cars." Pay raises were ordered for scientists in March, and the budget for science in 1946 tripled that of 1945.

Yet the continued suspicion and excessive supervision of scientists and engineers had a baleful effect on Soviet technological development. Several branches of science, most tragically biology, were subjected to ideological interventions backed by state power. A philosopher was attacked for his overly sympathetic history of Western European philosophy. The agronomist Trofim Lysenko conspired with Stalin to purge the Academy of Agricultural Sciences, where in July 1948 genetics was attacked as bourgeois falsification. Stalin himself denounced the canonical Soviet linguist Nikolai Marr, who had died in 1934, in his own polemic, *Marxism and Questions of Linguistics*, in June 1950, and all of Soviet linguistics had to discard overnight the theory that had dominated their field for nearly twenty years. In psychology Freudianism was rejected, and in 1949 the behaviorism of Ivan Pavlov, the venerated Russian psychologist who had been vehemently anti-Bolshevik, was officially approved as the Soviet approach to human psychology. Speaking at the 100th anniversary of Pavlov's birth, a noted academician said that the great scientist had driven "the soul out forever from its last refuge—our minds." The entire psychological profession in the USSR was forced to turn toward reflexology. Human beings were to be understood as creatures whose character and conduct were controlled at every step by the conditioning process. Rather than allowing for the autonomous development of the personality, every psychic act was considered a conditioned reflex. In such an environmentally determined world, the correct social environment could create good human beings.

Soviet scholars and scientists were potentially prepared to do brilliant scientific work, but the restraints placed on their work by the state distorted the development of scholarship. The economist Eugene Varga published a prescient work of forecasting in 1949 in which he argued that the West would emerge from the war with few difficulties, that capitalism would prosper, and that revolution was unlikely in the West. He went on to conclude that the United States would help Western Europe restore itself on a capitalist basis and that the relations between imperial states and their colonies would be reformed. He boldly suggested that wars among capitalist nations were not inevitable, thus questioning Leninist dogma. Varga was subjected to criticism for underestimating the postwar crisis of capitalism. Though he resisted changing his views for several years, he capitulated to his critics in March 1949. Had the Soviet leadership taken Varga's predictions more seriously, they might have avoided certain foreign policy errors that helped to precipitate the Cold War.

Stalinism was suspicious of any scientific findings that compromised the absolute character of scientific laws. Quantum theorists in the West, who argued that electrons choose their path, were condemned, as was the Danish physicist Neils Bohr, who claimed that the law of the preservation of energy was not an absolute law of nature but a statistical probability that only holds good on the average. Soviet physics, however, because of its importance to the atomic bomb project, was not publicly attacked, though plans for a purge were well underway in 1949. Kurchatov warned his superiors that if relativity theory and quantum mechanics were rejected as idealist, the bomb itself would have to be rejected. Stalin told Beria, "Leave them in peace. We can always shoot them later."

Zhdanovshchina was a severe disciplining of the intelligentsia, particularly against any deviation from the Soviet patriotic line. It instituted a period of xenophobic anti-Westernism, a turning inward that isolated Soviet learning from intellectual currents in the rest of the world. This cultural Cold War of the late 1940s and early 1950s also involved renewed attacks on the nationalism of the non-Russian peoples and an exaggeration of the achievement of Russians. Stalin had signaled as early as May 1945, in a victory speech, that the Russians were the "most outstanding nation of all nations within the Soviet Union." Non-Russian artists were attacked for nationalist sentiments about their own peoples. Poets, such as the author of the poem "Love Ukraine," were depicted as bourgeois nationalists. In April 1948 Stalin ordered a purge of Mingrelians, a west-Georgian ethnic group, in the Georgian party apparatus. The purge was probably a signal to Beria, himself a Mingrelian, to be careful of gaining too much power. At about the same time a vicious campaign was directed against Soviet Jews.

The whole tenor of Lenin's nationality policy had been against all nationalist chauvinism and anti-Semitism. Soviet Jews had enjoyed state support for

Yiddish culture during the 1920s, though religion and Zionism were discouraged and even persecuted. In the 1930s Soviet Jewish cultural life declined as support for Yiddish education dissipated, and enrollments in Yiddish schools dropped 50 percent between 1932 and 1940, until only one-fifth of Soviet Jews were being educated in Yiddish. In 1938 the government shut down the last Moscow Yiddish daily. Assimilation advanced rapidly, particularly among urban Jews, but there was no persecution of Jews as a nationality. The fierce threat of Nazism convinced many Jews around the world that the Soviet Union deserved their support. At the end of the 1930s, just before the Nazi-Soviet Pact was signed, the state organized massive demonstrations throughout the Soviet Union to protest Nazi policies toward the Jews. But once the pact was signed, all such antifascist sentiments or protests were forbidden.

On the eve of the Nazi invasion in 1941 there were 5,250,000 Jews in the USSR, many of them new citizens who lived in newly annexed western Ukraine and western Belorussia. When the Germans crossed the frontier, hundreds of thousands of Jews were evacuated from the occupied areas eastward. Of those left behind over 2 million perished. Others became partisans and fought the Germans, as well as nationalist, anti-Soviet Ukrainian and Belorussian partisans. Jews were active in the war effort, with more than 100 Jewish generals serving in the Soviet Army. Yet rumors slandered them as shirkers and draft dodgers. Leading Jewish activists and intellectuals established the Jewish Anti-Fascist Committee to aid the war effort. But for reasons that still remain obscure, two of the leading lights of the Jewish community, the leader of the Jewish Bund (and former Menshevik) Henryk Erlich and Viktor Alter, were arrested and were killed in prison. (Erlich probably committed suicide.)

In the immediate postwar years there was relative harmony between the Soviet regime and its Jewish citizens. Two leading writers, Ilya Ehrenburg and Vasilli Grossman, collected material on the Nazi crimes against the Jews for a planned *Black Book*, but the project was halted by the authorities. Popular anti-Semitism was rampant in the Soviet Union, particularly in the western republics, and official attitudes toward Jews began to change in the postwar years. On October 12, 1946, the newly appointed minister of state security, V. S. Abakumov, submitted a report to the top party and state leaders "on the nationalist manifestations of some workers of the Jewish Anti-Fascist Committee," and a month later the committee was dissolved. On January 13, 1948, a prominent Yiddish actor and former official of the Jewish Anti-Fascist Committee, Solomon Mikhoels, was mysteriously killed in Minsk. Though he was buried in a magnificent funeral in Moscow, the killing had been organized by the secret police and marked the beginning of a vicious anti-Semitic campaign. The Soviet Union, whose Middle Eastern policy at the time supported the creation of the state of Israel in Palestine, was the second country in the world, after the United States, to recognize the new state in 1948. But Stalin was disturbed by the massive outpouring of enthusiasm that greeted the arrival of Golda Meir, the first Israeli ambassador to Moscow, and the friendliness that high-ranking persons, such as Molotov's wife, Polina Zhemchuzhina, showed to Meir. Stalin had Zhemchuzhina arrested in 1949, and though he remained a high official, Molotov fell into disfavor.

Zhdanovshchina was in full swing, and part of its anti-Western thrust was contained in attacks on "cosmopolitanism." Not limited to anti-Semitism, the anticosmopolitan campaign extolled the glories of Russia and a kind of rooted nationalism. Russians, it was claimed, had achieved the first heavier-than-air flight; they had also discovered insulin and vitamins, synthetic rubber, the electric light bulb, and baseball. Over time more specifically anti-Semitic references crept into the rhetoric of anti-Westernism. The party-state attacked Jewish drama critics, writers, scientists, and historians, closed Yiddish newspapers and journals, with the single exception of one in the Jewish autonomous region, and shut down the last Jewish schools, in Vilnius and Kovno, in 1949, as well as all Jewish professional theaters. Even the libraries and theaters of Birobidzhan were destroyed, and the regional party secretary was arrested. Dozens of Jewish intellectuals were imprisoned, and in July 1952, after a trial, twenty-four were executed for advocating the creation of a Jewish republic in Crimea. The anti-Semitic campaign spread to Eastern Europe, and that fall the Czechoslovak party leader Rudolf Slansky was tried and executed as an "apprentice of Zionism."

The final and most infamous of Stalin's anti-Semitic purges was the so-called Doctors' Plot. In October 1952 Stalin was shown a letter that claimed that Zhdanov's death four years earlier had been medical murder. In early November several of the most prominent doctors in the Soviet Union, who had treated the highest government officials, including Stalin, were arrested. On January 13, 1953, *Pravda* announced the arrest of "a group of saboteur-doctors." Six of the nine accused were Jews, and they were reported to be "connected with the international Jewish bourgeois nationalist organization 'Joint,' established by American intelligence for the alleged purpose of providing material aid to Jews in other countries." The doctors were tortured to obtain confessions, and evidence was prepared for a show trial. A letter, edited by Stalin, calling for the deportation of all Jews eastward was circulated in Moscow among prominent Jewish intellectuals. Under threat of arrest or worse, many signed, though a few, like novelist and journalist Ilia Ehrenburg, refused to sign. Hysteria spread through the country, and Jews expected to be deported. On February 12, after a bomb exploded at its Tel Aviv legation, the Soviet Union broke diplomatic relations with Israel. The Doctors' Plot, many historians believe, would have had wider consequences, possibly including a major purge of the party leadership, had not Stalin suffered a brain hemorrhage six weeks after the arrests.

The late 1940s and first years of the 1950s were the height of the Stalin cult. His image was featured daily in newspapers, emblazoned on giant red banners, and suspended from a balloon above Red Square. The celebration of his seventieth birthday in December 1947 was the occasion for poems and songs, tapestries, rugs, and pottery all lauding the "Leader." The Stalin cult gave a focus and a powerful fatherly image to the loyalty expected of all Soviet people toward the Soviet Union. The love for Stalin was widespread and genuine, and a dangerous merging of the man, the system, and the state was forged that would damage the cause of Soviet-style socialism at home and abroad when his successors attempted to distance Stalin from Soviet socialism.

Instead of freedom Stalin offered what literary critic Vera Dunham calls the "Big Deal." The state made a tacit alliance with the Soviet middle class, that subelite below the top officials and cultural figures but above the "world of plain clerks and factory workers, of farm laborers and sales girls." This class of factory managers, engineers, administrators, organizers, party officials, and military personnel were the new post-Purge, postwar conservative establishment. They wanted security and privileges, a modicum of respect and power, prestige, more leisure time, and material rewards. In turn, this Soviet bourgeoisie repaid the state with political loyalty, silence, obedience, conformity, patriotism, reliable hard work, and a degree of professionalism. They also, when they found the opportunity, lined their pockets and ripped off a considerable share of the scarce goods in Soviet society. Both the government and the middle class wanted social stability, preservation of the status quo, and steady material progress. For them ideology was irrelevant; what was important was upward social mobility and contentment. Dunham concludes that by encouraging this "enbourgeoisement of the entire system," Stalin "put an end to much of the revolution."

The postwar conservatism was a continuation and intensification of trends that began to appear in Soviet life in the mid-1930s and were most evident in the state's policy toward women and the family. On July 9, 1944, a new law on the family was issued that gave women enhanced state support but at the same time underlined the pronatalist goals of the regime. Women were given money upon the birth of each child after the first plus a monthly payment for each child until its fifth birthday. Single women received larger child-support grants, which continued until the child was twelve. Pregnant and nursing mothers received extra food rations and were protected from certain kinds of hard labor. Pregnant women were given paid maternity leave, and no woman was required to work overtime after her fourth month of pregnancy. Mothers of five or six children received the "medal of motherhood," while those with eight or nine were given the "motherhood glory" award and those with ten or more became "heroine mothers." At the same time divorce was made more difficult, unregistered marriages were no longer recognized, and women were not permitted to bring paternity suits against fathers, and thus had to bear full responsibility for extramarital sex. Adding to the initial setbacks of the 1930s, this legislation completely buried the radical reforms of the 1920s. Motherhood became the official ideal for Soviet women, though they were also expected to become exemplary workers. The Soviet discourse on women continued to see women as essentially different from men. Even though women had been able to do "masculine" work in a time of national emergency, at the end of the war men returned to these jobs and women were given lighter, usually less-skilled work. The cultural patterns of the village persisted in factories as well as on collective farms. Yet the chronic labor shortage, along with vestiges of the Marxist commitment to female liberation, made it impossible to push women back into the domestic sphere altogether.

Stalinizing Eastern Europe

Before 1948 the so-called people's democracies were distinguished from the socialist Soviet Union and were thought to be following national paths toward socialism. But once Stalin drove Tito out of the Communist camp, Soviet authorities began intervening more forcefully in the affairs of the states of East-Central Europe, centralizing the economies, collectivizing agriculture, pushing industrialization at the fastest possible rate, while giving absolute priority to heavy industry, and eliminating differences between regimes. Now only the Soviet model of social organization was permissible. When the Polish Communist leader Wladyslaw Gomulka resisted the introduction of collectivization into the Polish countryside, the Cominform denounced him for refusing to support the struggle against the kulaks and for "ignoring the experience of the USSR." He was placed under house arrest in 1948 and expelled from the Central Committee in 1951. The facade of coalition was maintained in the people's democracies, but there was little pretense about which party held real power. A Soviet marshall, who was an ethnic Pole, was named minister of war in Poland and a member of the Politburo. Each Soviet bloc state adopted a new constitution closely modeled on the Stalin constitution of 1936, first in Bulgaria in 1947 and finally in Poland in 1952.

At the end of 1948 the Bulgarian Communist and former head of the Comintern Georgi Dimitrov redefined the concept "people's democracy" and stated that, although it was not as advanced a social formation as Soviet socialism, it was a form of the dictatorship of the proletariat that would destroy the remnants of capitalism. The clear implication of this formulation was that although the Communist states of Eastern Europe had to conform to the Soviet system they remained inferior and subordinate to the USSR. This was a classic example of an unequal, imperial relationship between ostensibly sovereign states.

While some local Communists approved of the shift toward a more strictly Soviet-type regime and pressured the Kremlin to tighten party control over their countries, much of the initiative for the Stalinization of Eastern Europe came from Stalin himself. As Khrushchev revealed in his memoirs,

> Stalin took an active personal interest in the affairs of [Poland and Hungary], as well as of Czechoslovakia, Bulgaria, and Rumania. The rest of us in the leadership were careful not to poke our noses into Eastern Europe unless Stalin himself pushed our noses in that direction. He jealously guarded foreign policy in general and our policy toward other socialist countries in particular as his own special province. Stalin had never gone out of his way to take other people's advice into account, but this was especially true after the war. The rest of us were just errand boys, and Stalin would snarl threateningly at anyone who overstepped the mark.

In the years 1949–52 police terror was launched against non-Communists and Communists alike. All in all over 1 million Communists were expelled from East European parties in those years, and Soviet police organized show trials of prominent Communists, several of whom were executed. Both the victims and instruments of the Soviet secret police, the demoralized and discredited Communists of the Soviet bloc ruled as unpopular agents of a foreign power. Their regimes were artificially imposed and failed to gain a popular social base, even as they radically transformed their societies. The postwar industrial revolution in most of Eastern Europe, except for Czechoslovakia, was

carried out by the Communist parties. Economic growth rates were astound-
ingly high in the early 1950s: 14 percent in Rumania, 11 percent per year in Albania (1951–55) and Poland (1950–55), 10 percent in East Germany, 9.5 percent
in Czechoslovakia, and 8.5 percent in Hungary (1950–54). Yet workers, in whose
name these revolutionary changes were made, were themselves rendered politically impotent and materially impoverished. When Stalin died, his legacy
in East-Central Europe was not only the beginnings of the creation of a modern urban industrial society, but the seeds of political discontent and revolution. The first outburst came in June 1953, a few months after Stalin's death,
when German workers marched in protest against the government's intensification of work norms and were shot down by Soviet tanks.

Cold War and Hot War

Though the USSR had lost the initiative in Europe and remained far weaker
than the United States both economically and militarily, in many ways the balance of power improved for the USSR in 1949. On August 29, 1949, the Soviets exploded their first atomic bomb, thus ending the American nuclear monopoly. In October the Chinese Communists, who had defeated the Nationalists
and driven them off the mainland to the island of Taiwan, founded the Chinese People's Republic. The Chinese Communists wanted the Soviets to help
them attack Taiwan, but Stalin restrained them for fear that an invasion could
trigger war with the United States. Stalin remained highly suspicious of the
Chinese Communists, who had relied less on the tiny working class in China
and more on the peasantry as the principal revolutionary force. He referred to
Mao Zedong as a "margarine Marxist," gave them almost no help in their victory over the Nationalists, and when after victory Mao came to Moscow seeking aid, Stalin forced him to cool his heels for many months. Ultimately Stalin
tied the Chinese into unequal economic relations that were offensive to the Chinese. Nevertheless, the frustrated Mao went home in February 1950 with a
treaty of military alliance that included assurances of nuclear assistance.

The Communist victory in China stimulated greater fear of Communist expansionism in the West, particularly in the United States where hysteria over
Communist "infiltration" and "subversion" spawned the investigations of
Richard Nixon and Joseph McCarthy, the perjury trial of former diplomat Al-
ger Hiss, and the arrests and eventual execution of the alleged atomic spies
Julius and Ethel Rosenberg. When the United States learned about the Soviet
atomic bomb, Truman ended the debate among scientists and officials about
development of a thermonuclear weapon and authorized the H-bomb program.
The key policymakers in the United States saw Soviet leaders as inspired by a
"new fanatic faith, antithetical to our own" and committed to imposing their
"absolute authority over the rest of the world." In a top-secret memorandum
a key administration official argued that American policy should aim to reduce
Soviet power, and even change the nature of the Soviet system, roll back Soviet influence in Eastern Europe, and revive nationalism among the subject
peoples of the USSR. But, he feared, because the Soviet Union would possess

the capability for a surprise nuclear attack in four or five years, the United States had to increase military spending. The American nuclear arsenal grew steadily, from 298 bombs in 1950 to 1,161 in 1953.

In official statements the Soviet Union noted that the balance of forces was shifting in its favor. Each world war had improved the position of socialism. "If the imperialists start a third world war," Georgi Malenkov stated on November 6, 1950, "it will mean the end, not of individual capitalist states, but of all the capitalist world." Though Malenkov then concluded that the world was becoming safer thanks to the existence of the socialist camp, another rising star in the ideological firmament, Mikhail Suslov, argued that the world was becoming more dangerous because the capitalists were increasingly more aggressive. Stalin appeared to favor Suslov's view, and Khrushchev later remembered that the aging dictator now believed that "the capitalist countries would attack the Soviet Union." His foreign policy became more aggressive in Asia. The Kremlin directed the Japanese Communist Party to be more militant in its opposition to the American occupation, and supported leftist rebellions in Malaya and Indochina. In Europe the Soviets built up their forces in Germany and developed and supplied armies for the Eastern European Communist states, which by 1953 numbered over 1 million men. Stalin decided to expand the Soviet Navy and armed forces. The number of Soviet troops doubled, from a low of 2,874,000 in 1948 to 5,700,000 in 1955.

Yet the Soviet Union, which was being surrounded by American military bases, had no way to carry war to the United States. Fearful of atomic attack by the United States, Stalin prodded his engineers and designers to develop an intercontinental turbojet bomber and rocket-powered missiles. In October 1952, the United States exploded the first hydrogen bomb, equal to the explosive power of 10 megatons of TNT. The USSR followed in August 1953 with a much smaller hydrogen bomb of 200–400 kilotons, and exploded its first superbomb, 1.6 megatons, only in November 1955. While the Soviet atomic bomb had been a copy of the American bomb, its new bomb was an original design. By this time the nuclear arms race was ten years on.

The first military clash between the Communists and the Western powers occurred on the Korean peninsula in the early 1950s. At the end of World War II Communists, backed by the Soviet Union, came to power in the northern half of Korea, while pro-Western forces gained control in the south. In 1948 the Democratic People's Republic of Korea, with its capital at Pyongyang, was established north of the 38th parallel, and the Republic of Korea, with its capital at Seoul, to the south. Foreign troops were withdrawn from both countries, and the government of each made it clear that it hoped to unify all of Korea under its regime. The North was militarily superior, and when Secretary of State Acheson announced publicly in January 1950 that the American defense perimeter in East Asia was limited to Japan, Okinawa, and the Philippines, the Communist leader of North Korea, Kim Il-Sung, tried to convince the Soviets and Chinese that the Americans would not fight to defend South Korea. Stalin was hesitant about launching a war in Korea, but in the spring of 1950 both he and Mao accepted Kim's argument that the South was ripe for revolution. On June 25 the North Koreans invaded the South. Three days later they took Seoul. As they moved rapidly toward victory, it became clear that they had made two fundamental miscalculations: the people of the South did not rebel and support the invasion, and on June 27 the United Nations, where the Soviet delegate had walked out and therefore could not use his veto, voted to intervene in the war.

The fighting between the North Koreans and the United Nations troops flowed up and down the peninsula. In September the United Nations forces under General Douglas MacArthur landed at Inchon, behind the North Korean lines, and transformed the war. The UN armies recaptured Seoul on September 26 and moved northward across the 38th parallel into North Korea. The war was now being fought not to restore the status quo ante bellum but to liberate all of Korea. Kim Il-Sung requested Soviet and Chinese troops. Mao agreed, but Stalin refused to send soldiers or even air cover for the Chinese. On October 19 the Chinese crossed the Yalu River into Korea, driving MacArthur's forces back to the 38th parallel. In a new offensive at the end of the year they moved south and took Seoul.

At this moment of crisis at the end of 1950 and beginning of 1951, when it appeared that the Americans might lose the Korean War, the Soviet Union turned on the heat in Europe and Asia, first denouncing the United States and Britain for their proposed rearming of Germany and then ordering its satellites in Eastern Europe to expand their military production. The Communist Viet Minh launched an offensive against the French rulers of Indochina. The United States, reflecting the preferred solution offered by General MacArthur, hinted that it might resort to nuclear weapons and expand the war into China. But in April 1951 Truman fired MacArthur for insubordination and soon initiated conversations to bring an end to the war. American forces resisted the Chinese onslaught, and the war wound down into a long, dreary stalemate as armistice talks began in July.

The first real nuclear crisis of the Cold War had passed, and hot war settled again into cold war. Stalin, now old and infirm, continued to stress that conflict between socialism and capitalism was inevitable as long as the imperialist states existed. In his last major piece of writing, *Economic Problems of Socialism in the USSR*, in October 1952, Stalin concluded that "the struggle of the capitalist countries for markets and their desire to crush their competitors" had proven stronger in the past than "the contradictions between the capitalist camp and the socialist camp." This meant that war could occur again, with a revived Germany and Japan in the lead. Stalin was far more antagonistic and less conciliatory toward the West in 1952 than he had been in 1945. He was no longer looking for a reduction in tensions with the West but instead was building up the Soviet Union and the Soviet bloc for anticipated clashes with the imperialists.

The Cold War was the result of illusions and misunderstandings as well as the conflicting interests of two superpowers. The United States was primarily interested in reshaping the postwar world to create a favorable economic climate that, in turn, would promote prosperity and peace. Security, in the view of American policymakers, depended on free trade, free markets, and, if possible, democratic polities. The Soviet Union, on the other hand, saw its own se-

curity in its dominance of Eastern Europe and was willing to forego the benefits of the Grand Alliance in order to hold on to its sphere of influence along its
western border. The question of how Stalin would dominate East-Central Europe was settled by the end of the 1940s; it would not be through influencing
friendly but essentially independent and sovereign governments (the Finnish
model) or allied but autonomous Communist states (like Czechoslovakia or Bulgaria before 1949) but through the creation of fully Stalinized and Soviet-
controlled police regimes (like those established in the years 1949–53). Stalin
had no blueprint for Sovietizing his neighbors at the end of World War II, but
he was determined to prevent the establishment of hostile governments along
his borders that would permit, for the third time in thirty years, an invasion of
Russia from the West. His policies evolved toward greater control over Eastern
Europe as the value and durability of his relationship with the Allies declined.
At first his policies were cautious and rather conservative, even counterrevolutionary. His behavior was based on his awareness of the weakness of the USSR,
his desire for the continuance of the Grand Alliance, and his hope that the West
would help rebuild the Soviet economy. But his two goals—maintenance of the
Grand Alliance and creation of a sphere of influence in Eastern Europe—proved
incompatible once the United States under Truman decided it would not sanction Soviet hegemony in the region. After the Truman Doctrine and the Marshall Plan were launched in 1947, Stalin rapidly clamped down on the coalition
governments in Eastern Europe and established one-party Communist states.

The Cold War was an uneven series of battles between a much more powerful United States and a weaker Soviet Union. The heavy costs of victory in
World War II, the burdensome costs of recovery without aid from the more
developed states, and the great strength of the United States placed severe limits on Soviet power. After half a decade of the Cold War, the USSR would find
itself once again a pariah state with much of the world arrayed against it. Long
before the Cold War ended, the Soviet Union had already lost it.

High Politics in the Kremlin Court

Stalin's personal attitudes determined the harsh policies of the postwar period
and the continuation of wartime norms and obligations. Not until he died did
his associates carry out rapid changes in policy: loosening of control of the
peasantry, relaxing labor discipline, dismantling the system of convict labor,
and ending overt Russification policies, and searching for ways to lessen tensions with the Western powers. He was slowing down physically and men-
tally in the late 1940s and early 1950s, taking long vacations in the south, usually from late August until late November. He may have suffered several slight
strokes in late 1945 and again in 1947. Yet he maintained his absolute control
over his subordinates through fear, and none of his underlings ever seriously
challenged him. Khrushchev later wrote:

> All of us around Stalin were temporary people. As long as he trusted us to
> a certain degree, we were allowed to go on living and working. But the mo-

Figure 16.1. *The Dawn of Our Fatherland.* A portrait of the aging Joseph Stalin by Fedor Shupin, 1949 (Erich Lessing, Art Resource, NY).

ment he stopped trusting you, Stalin would start to scrutinize you until the cup of his distrust overflowed.

One day Khrushchev overheard Stalin mutter, "I'm finished. I trust no one, not even myself." Everyone around Stalin was insecure. "In those days," Khrushchev remembered,

anything could have happened to any one of us. Everything depended on what Stalin happened to be thinking when he glanced in our direction. Sometimes he would glare at you and say, "Why don't you look me in the eye today? Why are you averting your eyes from mine? . . . Bulganin once described very well the experience we all had to live with in those days. We were leaving Stalin's after dinner one night and he said, "You come to Stalin's table as a friend, but you never know if you'll go home by yourself or if you'll be given a ride—to prison!

The post–World War II leadership was made up of the closest associates of Stalin who had survived the Great Purges. First in line was Molotov, who served as foreign minister until 1949, when Stalin no longer trusted him. Beria, the head of the police apparatus and the Soviet atomic bomb program, was on the ascent in the late war years and became a full member of the Politburo in March 1946. As deputy chairman of the Council of Ministers, he remained in charge of security. Beria was closely allied to Malenkov, who suffered a brief political eclipse in 1946 and was sent to Central Asia. Only after Beria convinced Stalin of Malenkov's value and loyalty was he returned to Moscow early in 1947. Stalin grew suspicious of Beria's growing power and at one point noticed that Beria had surrounded him with Georgians, including a much-decorated shish-kebab chef. Stalin replaced them all with Russians. After a second round of anti-Mingrelian purges in 1951, Beria lost his foothold in the Georgian party. Though seriously threatened, Beria managed to deflect Stalin's wrath and stayed close to the aging dictator.

Zhdanov was the chief rival in Kremlin circles of the Beria-Malenkov group. His principal allies were Nikolai Voznesenskii, a brilliant economist who headed Gosplan and became a full Politburo member in 1947, and A. A. Kuznetsov, the Central Committee secretary in charge of party supervision of the security police. Other important leaders included Lazar Kaganovich, Nikita Khrushchev, Anastas Mikoyan, and Kliment Voroshilov. Zhdanov died suddenly and unexpectedly on August 31, 1948, and the Beria-Malenkov group moved to purge the party of those most closely associated with the former leader of the Leningrad party organization. Both Voznesenskii and Kuznetsov were arrested and executed. A young engineer, Aleksei Kosygin, then a Leningrad apparatchik and almost two decades later prime minister of the USSR, was demoted along with hundreds of other officials. The principal beneficiaries of the "Leningrad affair" were Malenkov and Beria who now had few rivals at the top of the political pyramid. Stalin recalled Khrushchev to Moscow in 1949, after 12 years of service in Ukraine, to act as a counterweight to the growing power of Beria and Malenkov.

In October 1952 the Nineteenth Party Congress was held, the first in thirteen years, and Stalin designated Malenkov to give the all-important general report to the Congress and Khrushchev to report on the new party statutes. These two men then emerged as the most important leaders of the party after Stalin. A new Five-Year-Plan was announced at the Congress, and it emphasized centralized control, investment in heavy industry, and little autonomy for peasants. After the Congress Stalin enlarged the party Presidium to twenty-five members and formed a smaller presidium bureau of nine members: Stalin, Malenkov, Beria, Khrushchev, Voroshilov, Kaganovich, Saburov, Pervukhin, and Bulganin. Ominously missing were Molotov and Mikoyan. On October 16 Stalin spoke briefly to the newly elected Central Committee. As the writer Konstantin Simonov reports, Stalin told them that

> he was old, and that the time was approaching when others would have to continue doing what he had done, that the situation in the world was complex and a difficult struggle with the capitalist camp lay ahead and that the most dangerous thing in this struggle was to flinch, to take fright, to retreat, to capitulate. That was the main thing that he wished not only to say, but to instill into those present and that in its turn was connected with the theme of his own age and possible departure from this life.

He then turned menacingly toward Molotov and Mikoyan and attacked them for their cowardice and softness. He labeled them "Rykovtsy," as if they were right-wing imitations of Aleksei Rykov, who had been executed in 1938. Pale and limp, the latest two victims of Stalin's wrath insisted that "they had never been cowards or capitulationists, were not afraid of new clashes with the camp of capitalism, and would not capitulate before it." Though they were not arrested, Molotov and Mikoyan were no longer invited to the late-night meetings presided over by Stalin. Their colleagues feared that they were already condemned men.

On March 1, at about 5 or 6 A.M., a dinner party ended at Stalin's dacha in Kuntsevo outside Moscow. Stalin was cheerful and drunk. At about 10:30 the next evening his guards checked on Stalin, who had not emerged all day from his room. They found him lying on the floor, conscious but unable to speak. Evidently he had suffered a stroke. They lifted him onto a couch and called Malenkov, who arrived together with Beria at about 3 A.M. Beria berated the guards, told them that nothing was wrong, and left with Malenkov. Later that evening, doctors diagnosed a cerebral hemorrhage, gave Stalin oxygen, and applied leeches. Fear had led to delay. Stalin lingered for several more days, dying slowly and evidently in great pain. On the night of March 4 the Central Committee Presidium met and began the transfer of power to a single small presidium. At 9:50 P.M. on March 5, 1953, Stalin died.

Suggestions for Further Reading

Scholars have not yet turned in great numbers to study the postwar Soviet Union, but among the most important works so far are: Werner G. Hahn, *Postwar Soviet Politics: The Fall of Zhdanov and the Defeat of Moderation, 1946–53* (Ithaca, N.Y., 1982); Sheila Fitzpatrick, "Postwar Soviet Society: The 'Return to Normalcy,' 1945–1953," in Susan Linz (ed.), *The Impact of World War II on the Soviet Union*, pp. 129–56, and "War and Society in Soviet Context: Soviet Labor before, during, and after World War II," *International Labor and Working-Class History* 35 (Spring 1989): 37–52; Barbara A. Anderson and Brian D. Silver, "Demographic Consequences of World War II on the Non-Russian Nationalities of the USSR," in Linz, *The Impact*, pp. 207–42; Robert Conquest, *Power and Policy in the USSR: The Struggle for Stalin's Succession, 1945–1960* (London, 1961); Barrington Moore, Jr., *Soviet Politics—the Dilemma of Power: The Role of Ideas in Social Change* (Cambridge, Mass., 1950) and *Terror and Progress—USSR: Some Sources of Change and Stability in the Soviet Dictatorship* (Cambridge, Mass., 1954); Timothy Dunmore, *The Stalinist Command Economy: The Soviet State Apparatus and Economic Policy, 1945–1953* (London, 1980); William O. McCagg, *Stalin Embattled, 1943–1948* (Detroit, 1978); Amy Knight, *Beria: Stalin's First Lieutenant* (Princeton, N.J., 1993); and the extraordinarily sensitive work on Soviet mentalities by Vera Dunham, *In Stalin's Time: Middleclass Values in Soviet Fiction* (Cambridge, 1976).

Late Stalinism was the classical moment of the totalitarian model. For works on totalitarianism, see Hannah Arendt, *The Origins of Totalitarianism* (New York, 1951); Carl J. Friedrich and Zbigniew K. Brzezinski, *Totalitarian Dictatorship and Autocracy* (Cambridge, Mass., 2nd ed., 1965); and Abbott Gleason, *Totalitarianism: The Hidden History of the Cold War.* (New York, 1995).

For the scholarly debates on Stalinism, see Stephen F. Cohen, *Rethinking the Soviet Experience: Politics and History Since 1917* (New York, 1985); Sheila Fitzpatrick, "New Perspectives on Stalinism," *The Russian Review* 45, no. 4 (October 1986): 357–73; and the discussions that followed: 375–413; 46, no. 4 (October 1987): 375–431; and Ronald Grigor Suny, "Gorbachev and Soviet History," *Tikkun* 2, no. 4 (September–October 1987): 32–35, 91–96; and Nick Lampert and Gabor T. Rittersporn (eds.), *Stalinism—Its Nature and Aftermath: Essays in Honor of Moshe Lewin* (Armonk, N.Y., 1992).

PART IV

REFORM
AND
STAGNATION

CHAPTER 17
From Autocracy to Oligarchy

The Several Deaths of Stalin

The death of Stalin left a huge void in Soviet society, for the regime, and even the revolution, had been identified with him for more than twenty years. The man whom Kaganovich had called "the driver of the locomotive of history" was revered by the overwhelming majority of Soviet citizens, who knew little of the enormity of his crimes against them. The poet Evgenii Evtushenko remembered:

> On March 5, 1953, an event took place which shattered Russia—Stalin died. I found it almost impossible to imagine him dead, so much had he been an indispensable part of life. A sort of general paralysis came over the country. Trained to believe that they were all in Stalin's care, people were lost and bewildered without him. All Russia wept. And so did I. We wept sincerely, tears of grief—and perhaps tears of fear for the future.

Tens of thousands of people swarmed to the center of Moscow to view Stalin's body, and in the chaos many were crushed to death. Abroad there was relief and hope among those who believed that Stalin was responsible for the Soviet hard in line domestic and foreign policy. But among Communists and fellow travelers, there was genuine grief and confusion. The leftist German poet and playwright Bertoldt Brecht wrote:

> The oppressed of five continents must have felt their heart stop beating when they heard that Stalin was dead. . . . I praise him for many reasons. Above all because under his leadership the murderers were beaten. The murderers, my own country.

Stalin's successors were a mixed lot; many of them were sycophants and survivors of the brutal struggle to stay in Stalin's favor, but others had reserves of ability that they were able to display only after Stalin's death. The problematic future would depend on which of Stalin's lieutenants would emerge as the dominant personalities. The succession crisis began in Stalin's dacha, even as the Bureau of the Presidium of the party gathered to watch the old man's death agony. Stalin had not designated a successor, and the top leaders were wary of any one of them emerging as an all-powerful leader. Hours before Stalin died, the bureau members decided to eliminate the large Presidium that Stalin had named and turn the bureau into a smaller ten-man Presidium. But ultimate power lay with a triumvirate that emerged almost immediately after Stalin's passing, with Malenkov as head of government, Beria in charge of the police, and Khrushchev the leading figure in the party secretariat. Molotov, Bulganin, and Kaganovich became first deputy prime ministers along with Beria, and Voroshilov took the largely formal position of president of the Soviet Union. On the government side, the total number of ministries was reduced from fifty-one to twenty-five. Molotov was named foreign minister and Bulganin minister of war. On the party side, Khrushchev was released from his duties as secretary of the Moscow city committee, so he could concentrate on Central Committee Secretariat matters.

At first the leadership was quite united, though the old suspicions among them remained. "Collectivity" or "collegiality" was the watchword of the elite, though Malenkov, who served briefly as head of both state and party, and Beria, in charge of the secret police, quickly emerged as the most important figures in the days following Stalin's death. Malenkov ran the meetings of the party Presidium, and whenever Beria made a proposal, Malenkov agreed to it, stifling discussion with a call for an immediate vote. Only after Khrushchev began to convince him privately that Beria was dangerous did Malenkov begin to loosen his control over the agenda and allow for more discussion. Within a few weeks power was diffused somewhat when Malenkov "requested" to be relieved of his position in the Secretariat, which was thereafter headed by Khrushchev. Malenkov may have calculated that since the government had grown powerful under Stalin, while the party had atrophied, it was to his advantage to head the state apparatus rather than the party. This judgment turned out to be a political error.

A palpable shift in policy occurred in the first weeks of the new regime. The worst excesses of Stalinist terror ended. Though it was not well known at the time, many of the early reforms were initiated by Beria, who carried them further than his comrades expected. Beria halted grandiose and wasteful construction projects, like the Volga-Baltic Canal. When the question of the fate of millions of prisoners was discussed, he suggested that they be released from prison and exile but kept in special regions designated by his Ministry of Internal Affairs (MVD). Of the 2,526,000 prisoners in labor camps, Beria claimed that only 221,000 were "especially dangerous state criminals." Khrushchev angrily disagreed and argued that the entire system of arrests and punishment had to be examined. On March 24 the first amnesty was declared. Shortly afterwards the Kremlin doctors arrested in the Doctors' Plot were rehabilitated.

Beria attempted to build a political base in the elites of the non-Russian republics. In April the so-called Mingrelian affair, which had led to the dismissal of Beria's clients in Georgia, was denounced, and Beria reasserted his control over Georgia. He publicly committed himself to promoting the status of non-

Russian nationalities and suggested that leaders be chosen only from the indigenous nationalities. The Presidium agreed that the post of first secretary in every republic should be held by a local person, not a Russian sent from Moscow. As a rule, however, second secretaries continued to be Russians in almost all republics.

Following the turn toward the "New Course" in domestic policy, the Soviet government adopted a more tolerant and relaxed attitude toward the Soviet bloc countries. But the Kremlin leadership was divided about its policy toward East Germany, a state they had been reluctant to create at the end of the 1940s. The leaders of the German Democratic Republic (GDR) had pushed for a rapid building of socialism, and the policy had led to discontent and apathy among the people. Beria favored a united, neutral Germany, but Khrushchev opposed any moves toward reunification of Germany on a "bourgeois basis" as a reversal of the victory over Nazism. Molotov held out for preserving the GDR as a socialist state but agreed that the "forced construction of socialism" had to be curtailed. Khrushchev sided with Molotov and remained committed for the rest of his political career to preserving a socialist Germany. With Beria taking an active lead in formulating policy toward the GDR, the Soviet leaders agreed that the occupation should end, that the economic flow from the GDR to the USSR would be reversed, and that a slower pace of economic development, along with an easing of the political atmosphere, had to be initiated in East Germany. But when these measures were implemented, the German leaders antagonized workers by raising work norms. Protests broke out in the streets of Berlin, and on June 17 the world watched as Soviet tanks brutally crushed the demonstrations by workers in a "workers' state." Though Beria's policy was hardly to blame for the Germans' failures, the police chief was now vulnerable to charges from his colleagues that he had weakened the socialist hold on East Germany.

After the June 1953 uprising by German workers, Soviet leaders backed the Stalinists in Berlin and argued that the uprising had been part of an American plot to "roll back" socialism in Eastern Europe. But soon Soviet leaders called for economic reforms and political relaxation throughout the Soviet bloc. They substituted economic concessions for terror, retreated from the forced pace of development of late Stalinism, and promoted collective leadership. The alliance was strengthened at the end of 1954 when the Soviets decided to form the Warsaw Pact, the East European answer to NATO. Molotov argued that the GDR should not be included in the pact, for "nobody would fight for the Germans," but Khrushchev pushed for inclusion of "our friend."

Though most of the early liberalizing reforms both inside and outside the USSR were supported by the majority of the top leaders, Khrushchev became increasingly suspicious about Beria's prominence and his control of the secret police. Along with his close friend Malenkov, Beria had increased the role and power of the government apparatus over the party. The discussion of foreign policy moved from the Secretariat to the Council of Ministers. When Beria claimed that there was a serious problem in the Ukrainian leadership, Khrushchev saw this as directed against him, since he was largely responsible for Ukraine. He began to agitate the other members of the leadership, in secret, and managed to convince Molotov, Malenkov, and Bulganin, one by one, of the necessity of arresting Beria. He did not inform Voroshilov and Mikoyan, whom he thought might still be well-disposed toward Beria, of the conspiracy. The plotters garnered support among the top brass in the military—eleven marshalls and generals, headed by Marshall Zhukov—who harbored resentment against the police. On June 26, 1953, Malenkov opened a fateful meeting of the party and government presidia. He immediately gave the floor to Khrushchev, who accused Beria of "relying on nationalist antagonism to undermine Soviet unity." "As a result of my observations of Beria's activities," he went on, "I have formed the impression that he is no Communist. He is a careerist who has wormed his way into the party for self-seeking reasons. His arrogance is intolerable. No honest Communist would ever behave the way he does in the party." Beria was stunned and asked, "What is going on, Nikita? What's this you are mumbling about?" Mikoyan tried to defend Beria, but after others spoke against Beria, Malenkov in panic pressed a secret button, and Zhukov and the generals entered and arrested Beria. Underestimating Khrushchev, Beria had not suspected the danger he was in, and he hoped to alert his bodyguards in an anteroom. The generals held Beria until dark, when they spirited him out of the Kremlin, still guarded by his loyal MVD troops.

The new leadership had no better claim to power than Beria. To legitimize their coup, they worked out a resolution on the "criminal, anti-party, and anti-state activities" of Beria and took it to a Central Committee plenum early in July. The new Presidium presented a united front. Khrushchev and Molotov spoke of the danger to the party that Beria presented, and after almost a week the Central Committee agreed to expel him from the party and try him as a criminal. Beria was kept for months in an underground bunker until he was secretly tried and executed on December 24, 1953. The American ambassador to Moscow wrote wryly to the secretary of state, "There is of course elementary justice in the fate of Beria and [secret police] associates, but it would have been more fitting if retribution had been meted out by his victims rather than his accomplices."

The fall of Beria weakened Malenkov and boosted Khrushchev, but it also had much wider significance. With the help of the army, party leaders had reasserted their primacy over the police and eliminated the danger of any party leader using the police to rule over the party. The Soviet government would never again turn into an autocracy; it had become a bureaucratic oligarchy. In the absence of terror the new elite had to demonstrate its right to rule, its competence, even indispensability, and build up its authority. The party leaders soon worked out a broad economic and political strategy that, with different emphases, would be followed for the next four decades. They agreed not to return to terror, to work instead to increase consumer satisfaction and provide greater material incentives for the working people. Power would be decentralized to a greater extent, and a wider range of people would be included in politics and administration. Leadership would be collective rather than centered on one person. Social and economic security and equality would be promoted, while privileges would remain for the elites. Though much of the excessive repression of Stalinism would be eliminated, the state-centered command economy and the monopolistic rule of the Communist Party would remain intact. No one in the leadership pushed for complete social equality, full democratization of the political system, or the creation of a market economy. They identified socialism with the one-party monopoly over politics and the economy and the absence of capitalism that marked the Soviet system.

In many ways Stalin had brought his country to a standstill. The Soviet Union was isolated and domestically impoverished, with a stagnating economy and a weary population. The Stalinist budget of 1952 was geared to a kind of war economy, emphasizing military spending and heavy industry, with little investment in agriculture, housing, or consumer services. All of Stalin's successors agreed after his death that the poverty of consumers had to be relieved, but they differed on the program to achieve prosperity. At first they continued many of the policies associated with Beria, and now with Malenkov, who was an effective administrator, a details man who was called a "manager by telephone." Malenkov's New Course favored cuts in the military and heavy industry budgets and increased spending on consumer goods. Khrushchev, however, proposed that money be spent both on increasing grain output and strengthening the military. Malenkov's proposals represented a more radical break with the past, whereas Khrushchev's were an attempt to bring together traditional values and the needs of the present. Both Malenkov and Khrushchev fancied themselves experts on agriculture, and success or failure in that field would boost or break any potential leader. Soviet peasants had been forced to pay for industrialization in the 1930s and economic recovery in the 1940s. They were demoralized and apathetic and looked for any opportunity to flee the villages. Malenkov and the Council of Ministers worked out a new approach to agriculture in August 1953, which improved the material life of the peasants by cutting their taxes 50 percent.

In September 1953 Khrushchev became first secretary of the Communist Party, and in his first major speech on agriculture he supported the Malenkov plan. Only in early 1954 did Khrushchev make his first original contribution to the development of agriculture. The party adopted his plan to develop millions of acres of new, "virgin" land in the Volga region, Urals, Siberia, and Kazakhstan. With his characteristic gusto Khrushchev spoke about the need for more agricultural production in order to build communism: "There will be no communism without an abundance of products. There will be no communism if our country has as much metal and cement as you like but meat and grain are in short supply." Here was a new voice with the timbre of the common people:

> And what is that very same communist society without sausage? [laughter] Really, comrades, in a communist society you will not tell people to go and eat a potato without butter. The communist society presupposes the creation of such conditions for our nation whereby people will be assured according to their need. Surely a man living in a communist society will not ask for turnips in the grocery store, but will demand better foodstuffs. But better foodstuffs cannot be created without an abundance of grain.

The "Virgin Lands" program was very successful in its first years. By 1955 grain production was 6 percent above the 1949–53 average in spite of bad conditions. At the same time that new lands were cultivated, the bureaucratic control of thousands of officials over agriculture was reduced. Local authorities in the collective farms and machine-tractor stations were given more power to make decisions locally. As grain yields rose, Khrushchev's stature as an agricultural expert increased, and his position in the leadership grew stronger. At the end of the summer 1953, while on vacation in the Crimea, he met informally with other party leaders, among them Mikoyan and Bulganin, to solicit their support against Malenkov. Khrushchev managed to isolate Malenkov and forced his retirement as prime minister on February 8, 1955. Though Malenkov remained in the party Presidium and as a deputy to Bulganin, his new appointment, as minister of electric power, was a clear signal that he had lost influence. Nikolai Bulganin, a debonair, affable ally of Khrushchev's became head of government.

Khrushchev solidified his power base in the party by elevating allies to the party Presidium and naming Marshall Zhukov minister of defense. He replaced many regional officials with people who had worked with him in Ukraine and Moscow. By the time the Twentieth Party Congress met in February 1956, 44 percent of the members and candidates of the Central Committee elected in 1952 were gone. In the future all successive party leaders would consolidate their power over time by similar personnel policies. Khrushchev reasserted the authority of the Central Committee and the Secretariat over the major government ministries, defense and internal affairs, as well as the new Committee for State Security (KGB). Khrushchev undermined the power of the old Stalinist guard. Most ominous for those who had been closest to Stalin, such as Malenkov and Molotov, was Khrushchev's appointment of a special commission in December 1955 to look into the massive political repression of the 1930s.

When the Twentieth Party Congress opened in February 1956, few anticipated that they were at a historic turning point; when it was over, the international Communist movement and Soviet society had begun a stunning break with their Stalinist past. At first the Congress reaffirmed old themes—the priority of heavy industry, capitalist encirclement of the Soviet Union, progress and peace at home—but Khrushchev had a bombshell waiting for the conclusion of the meeting. On February 25 the delegates listened in stunned silence as Khrushchev delivered what would be known as his "Secret Speech." For hours he told in shocking detail of the repressions of the Stalin era, of forced, false confessions, torture, and judicial murder. He spoke about the unpreparedness of the Soviet Union at the time of the Nazi invasion and condemned "the cult of personality" and "violations of socialist legality," euphemisms for Stalin's dictatorship and terror. Khrushchev hinted broadly that Stalin was responsible for the murder of Kirov, and he rehabilitated several repressed figures but stopped short of rehabilitating prominent oppositionists, such as Trotsky, Bukharin, Zinoviev, and Kamenev, or making any reference to still influential members of the Presidium who were implicated in Stalin's crimes, such as Molotov, Voroshilov, and Kaganovich. The speech was a masterstroke. By denouncing the Great Terror Khrushchev seriously wounded his political rivals at the top of the party and offered those party members who followed his anti-Stalinist program greater security and advancement. Since Khrushchev had been relatively junior at the time of the purges, he emerged unscathed by

Figure 17.1. Nikita Khrushchev and Richard Nixon toast each other after their famous "Kitchen Debate," July 24, 1959 (UPI/CORBI-BETTMAN).

the revelations, but an apocryphal story tells of a note being passed up to Khrushchev asking why he had not protested against the terror at the time. Khrushchev looked out into the audience and asked who had sent up the note. No hand was raised. "That answers your question," Khrushchev commented coolly. After the Twentieth Party Congress Khrushchev was the most powerful political figure in the Soviet Union, though he served at the pleasure and with the confidence of the other members of the Presidium. He was neither a dictator with unchecked power nor a president able to overrule his cabinet.

The Man

In a portrait of his former boss, Fedor Burlatskii writes that Khrushchev "understood his role in our country's history . . . as being to give peace and well-being to the Soviet people," to normalize their lives. But Khrushchev had no clear vision of what needed to be done or what the final system would look like. He tried innovating without any sense of direction, and though his reforms were numerous, they were unconnected and often ephemeral. When he and Bulganin visited England in 1956, Winston Churchill told him: "Mr. Khrushchev, you are undertaking big reforms. And that is good! I would only like to advise you not to be too hasty. It is not easy to negotiate an abyss in two jumps. You might fall in." Burlatsky adds to this story, "Nor can the abyss be negotiated when you do not know which side you are planning to jump to."

Nikita Sergevich Khrushchev was born on April 3 (15 n.s.), 1894, in the Donets region of Ukraine, the son of a Russian coal miner and his wife. As a young man he worked as a shepherd, a factory worker, and a miner before joining the Red Guards during the revolution. In 1918 he became a member of the Russian Communist Party. Four years later he entered the Workers' Faculty (Rabfak) at Iuzovka Industrial Institute in eastern Ukraine. Though he very briefly sympathized with the Trotskyist opposition, he soon aligned himself with the party majority. In 1928 Kaganovich, then party boss of Ukraine (1925–28), called Khrushchev to Kharkov to work on personnel decisions. At the end of the 1920s he studied engineering in Moscow at the Industrial Academy, where he befriended Nadezhda Allilueva, Stalin's young wife, and was soon promoted to party secretary of the academy, where he led the fight against Bukharin's supporters. In 1934, at the age of 40, he became a member of the Central Committee. Four years later he returned to Ukraine as first secretary of the Ukrainian Communist Party, replacing the Ukrainian leader who soon fell victim to Stalin's purges. In Ukraine Khrushchev proved his Stalinist credentials when he carried out a sustained attack on what was left of the Ukrainianization policies of the former leadership and liquidated an alleged "Trotskyist underground" within the republic. For services well rendered he was promoted to full membership in the Politburo in 1939. "I was 100 percent faithful to Stalin as our leader and our guide," he later recalled. "I believed that everything Stalin said in the name of the party was inspired by genius."

During World War II Khrushchev was a political commissar and served in Ukraine and at Stalingrad. He returned to Kiev in the last years of the war and once again headed the party there. Khrushchev remained a dedicated and tough Stalinist while occasionally revealing a softer, populist sympathy for the plight of his constituents. He organized the struggle against armed Ukrainian nationalists in western Ukraine and at the same time attempted to convince Stalin that Ukraine faced another famine and desperately needed aid. Stalin's answer was to send Kaganovich, who from March to December 1947 ran Ukraine ruthlessly, hunting down nationalists and enforcing the outrageously high grain collection quotas. Khrushchev tried on occasion to "rehabilitate" arrested Ukrainian intellectuals or ease the repression but was limited by the independent power of the police, which took orders from Moscow. Khrushchev's experience in Ukraine, his distance from Stalin's "court," and his close knowledge of the human suffering in the republic he ruled probably influenced his later attacks on Stalin and Stalinism.

After briefly being in disgrace, Khrushchev was brought back to Moscow at the end of 1949 and served as party secretary of Moscow. Within the close circle around Stalin, this round-faced bumpkin, who often played the clown at the late-night dinners in Stalin's dacha, seemed relatively harmless, loyal and able but not particularly cunning. In fact, Khrushchev was a man of great ability and deep contradictions. He was supremely self-confident, courageous, and committed to what he believed was the "building of Communism." But he was often willful, impulsive, and susceptible to flattery. According to Burlatsky, he

> had difficult picking the right people. He was always more inclined to rely on flatterers than on true supporters of his reforms. . . . He was little impressed by strong, self-sufficient personalities and people with an independent character. Khrushchev had too much self-confidence to seek support in others.

Sadly for his reforms and his tenure in power, his behavior was marked by rashness and hastiness, and he often interfered in matters beyond his competence. Ultimately his reforms were conservative rather than radical, preserving as much of the old system as possible, and he had more faith than clear vision of the future shape of Soviet society.

The Soviets Enter the Nuclear Age

For nearly five decades the world lived under the threat of nuclear holocaust. Atomic weapons were only used twice, by the United States in its final effort to defeat imperial Japan, but from their invention in 1945 on these ominous weapons played a key role in preventing direct military confrontation between the two superpowers, the United States and the Soviet Union. All-out global war was prevented by the recognition on both sides that the costs of an atomic exchange would be too costly to bear, and for most of the Cold War Soviet and American strategists argued that in a nuclear war there would be no winners.

Soviet foreign policy after 1945 was consistently based, not on great strength in comparison with the United States, but rather on relative weakness vis-à-vis the capitalist world. From the immediate postwar period, when the United States had a nuclear monopoly, through the early Khrushchev years, when the Soviets were finally able to develop a delivery system (the Intercontinental Ballistic Missile, or ICBM) to compete effectively with the Americans, to its last years, the Soviet Union was usually at a considerable disadvantage economically, technologically, and militarily. Only for brief moments and in certain aspects, such as conventional arms, was the USSR superior to the combined military might of the NATO alliance. By the time of Stalin's death, anti-communism had unified the strongest nations of the West into NATO, the

United States dominated the United Nations, forcing the Soviets to use innumerable vetoes, and Americans were leading a multinational force against North Korean and Chinese Communist armies on the Korean peninsula. From this relative weakness derived the extreme Soviet sensitivity to the possibility of foreign attack, which has been characterized as "Russian paranoia."

Given the relative weakness of the Soviet Union, its policies in the post-Stalin years, despite occasional flights of revolutionary rhetoric and aid to Third World liberation movements, were usually conservative rather than revolutionary, defensive rather than expansionist, and the USSR usually reacted to Western initiatives rather than making its own overtures. Almost every major development of new weapons technology, almost every advance in the arms race, and almost every deployment of a new weapons system was first made by the United States and only sometime later by the Soviet Union. Many in the Soviet foreign policy establishment (but far from all) were genuinely interested in building political and particularly economic ties with the Great Powers of the West. They wanted to end their country's political and economic isolation, but not until Gorbachev were Soviet leaders willing to consummate such cooperative relations at the price of losing their hegemony over the countries of East-Central Europe. As much as the Soviet Union may have wanted a lessening of tensions with the West, this goal was always secondary to its primary understanding of its interests, to maintain at all costs a security zone of subordinate states along its western border. For most Soviets security meant holding on to territory. The USSR was faced by a profound "security dilemma." The policies and programs it adopted to increase its security were perceived as threats by the United States, and the rest of the world, which responded to them by building up its military might, thereby making the Soviet Union more vulnerable.

From their vantage point in the Kremlin, the successors to Stalin felt quite vulnerable to American power. Not only had the United States surrounded the USSR with military bases, but in 1954 it deployed tactical nuclear weapons in Europe for the first time. Only three years later did the Soviets introduce similar weapons into their part of Europe. In 1954 the United States had 1,630 nuclear bombs, and a year later it possessed 2,280. Though no Soviet figures on the numbers of bombs have yet been published, the Central Intelligence Agency estimated that the Soviet Union possessed between 50 and 200 bombs in mid-1953. While the Soviet Union was ahead of the United States in rocket development in the 1950s, the United States was ahead in long-range bombers. The first intercontinental bomber, the B-52, appeared in 1955. That plane could deliver a nuclear bomb to the Soviet Union, and the Soviets had no way to respond. While Soviet military theorists speculated in their secret journals about the wisdom of a surprise attack on American bases, the U.S. Department of Defense estimated that after an American atomic offensive 60 million people would die in the USSR.

With new forms of weaponry in their arsenal, Soviet military and political leaders began to reassess their military doctrine, tentatively questioning Lenin's notion that imperialism inevitably generated war and reviving the discussion that Stalin had abruptly brought to a close in 1952. Khrushchev told the Twentieth Party Congress in 1956 that war was no longer "fatalistically inevitable" and that the "camp of socialism," along with the labor movement in capitalist countries, were forces for peace that could "prevent the imperialists from unleashing war." Nevertheless, the USSR had to be prepared to fight a war if the imperialists chose to start one. Soviet foreign policy was aimed, it was claimed, at preventing war, or at least to reducing its risk, and this peace policy required military might. Khrushchev endorsed the strategy of mutual assured destruction, the idea already adopted by the United States that defense required being able to retaliate after being hit by a first nuclear strike from the other side. Such a second-strike capability, which would inflict unacceptable damage, it was thought, would cause the other side to refrain from launching a first strike. The struggle with imperialism would continue but could be carried on without war. Later, in January 1960, a confident Khrushchev told the Supreme Soviet that the USSR would survive a nuclear war because of its vast territory and less-concentrated population, whereas capitalism would be destroyed.

Throughout the 1950s the Soviet military increased its nuclear arsenals while reducing the size of its armed forces. Khrushchev cut back Stalin's naval buildup program, placing greater reliance on war by nuclear rocket and, in December 1959, creating the Strategic Rocket Forces as a separate service. Khrushchev's plan for further cuts in manpower met resistance from the Soviet High Command, which believed that mass armies were still required in nuclear war. The United States also reduced its military spending in the early 1950s and began to rely heavily on air power and nuclear weapons instead of the more expensive conventional forces. In 1955 the Strategic Air Command war plan was designed, as one military officer put it, to reduce the Soviet Union to "a smoking, radiating ruin at the end of two hours."

Peaceful Coexistence and Its Setbacks

The Kremlin was pleased to see President Truman, whom they considered the architect of the Cold War, replaced by former General Dwight D. Eisenhower, a man much beloved in the Soviet Union. Yet the early 1950s also saw the rise of the Republican Party's right wing, as represented in the administration by Eisenhower's vice president, Richard Nixon, and in the Congress by Wisconsin Senator Joseph McCarthy. Instead of the "containment" of communism, the rightists spoke of its roll-back and the "liberation" of Eastern Europe. They were encouraged by Secretary of State John Foster Dulles, who called Soviet peace initiatives "Trojan doves" and talked of "massive retaliation." This "brinksmanship" policy, a willingness to go to the very brink of war, was less enthusiastically embraced by the president, who was genuinely interested in improving relations with the Soviet Union. Just over a month after Stalin's death, President Eisenhower made an important speech (on April 16, 1953) in which he stated that the United States would "welcome every honest act of peace" and called upon the Soviet leaders to help "turn the tide of history" by taking risks for peace. Noting that "an era ended with the death of Joseph Stalin," he outlined a number of concrete moves—an armistice in Korea, a treaty on the fate of occupied Austria, and arms reductions—that would create a new and more cooperative atmosphere between the superpowers. Speaking of the arms race, he said, "This is not a way of life at all, in any true sense. Under the cloud of threatening war, it is humanity hanging from a cross of iron." Though Eisenhower's opening to the Soviets was followed two days later by a Cold War blast from his hard-line secretary of state, the Kremlin decided to respond positively to Eisenhower's invitation. A few months later the two sides in the Korean conflict signed a truce, and at the end of the year Eisenhower introduced his program "Atoms for Peace." Though both sides were highly suspicious of the other, tentative steps were taken away from confrontation and toward negotiation. The USSR dropped its claims to territory in Turkey and relinquished its rights to naval bases in Port Arthur, China. Diplomatic ties were reestablished with Israel and in 1954 the Soviet Union pressed for an international conference to settle the conflict in Indochina.

The thaw in foreign policy accelerated in 1955. The USSR returned the military base at Porkkala to Finland and established diplomatic relations with West Germany. In May a reluctant Molotov went to Vienna to sign the Austrian State Treaty by which Austria became a united neutral country. Soviet occupation troops were removed, and the four-power division of Vienna and the country ended. Khrushchev and Bulganin became a familiar pair of travelers as they visited India, Burma, and Afghanistan, and they frequently met with journalists at diplomatic cocktail parties in Moscow. The new leadership was far more accessible than any Soviet leaders had been since the early 1930s. In July 1955 they attended the first "summit conference" in Geneva, where they met with Eisenhower, Anthony Eden of Great Britain, and Edgar Faure of France. Largely a ceremonial affair, the conference nevertheless demonstrated that all sides understood the dangers, indeed the impossibility, of nuclear war. Khrushchev spoke of "peaceful coexistence" and "détente," and Eisenhower of a "new spirit of conciliation and cooperation." The only significant agreement, however, was on a program of cultural exchanges. Eisenhower proposed a program of "open skies," to permit aerial inspection in line with an agreed-upon disarmament program, but Khrushchev retorted that this was a form of espionage. Eisenhower later remarked, "We knew the Soviets wouldn't accept it. We were sure of that, but we took a look and thought it was a good move." The next year the United States opened Soviet skies unilaterally by secretly sending high-altitude U-2 aircraft over the USSR. John Foster Dulles had a far more cynical view of the negotiations with the Soviets: "We did not actually desire to enter into either negotiation, but felt compelled to do so in order to get our allies to consent to the rearmament of Germany. World opinion demanded that the United Sates participate in these negotiations with the Communists."

As Khrushchev emerged as the most powerful voice in both domestic and foreign affairs, his opening to the West left him vulnerable before the more conservative forces in the leadership. Peaceful coexistence appeared to have little payoff to Molotov, who spoke of this policy privately as appeasement. Khrushchev was especially anxious to improve relations with Yugoslavia, but hard-liners in the Presidium, most importantly Molotov and Suslov, argued that Yugoslavia was no longer a socialist country. Khrushchev prevailed and had Yugoslavia officially qualified as socialist, even though accepting Yugoslavia meant that different roads to socialism were possible once again. This was a decisive blow against Molotov and the hard-liners. Khrushchev explicitly repudiated Stalin's methods of dealing with his neighbors and began to speak of a "commonwealth of socialist states" with relations of equality and fraternal cooperation. In April 1956 the Cominform, long an anachronism, was formally disbanded.

Khrushchev in Crisis

After the "Secret Speech" Khrushchev set out immediately to consolidate his political position. The new Central Committee elected at the end of the Congress had more than one-third new members, almost half of whom had either worked in Ukraine, at the Stalingrad front, or in Moscow under Khrushchev's administration. The same Presidium was kept, but five new candidate members were elected, all of whom owed their election to Khrushchev. Soon after the Congress, Molotov was dropped as foreign minister, and Kaganovich was demoted as well. The power struggle between the more Stalinist Old Guard, some of whom were fearful of changing the basic contours of the system, and those closer to Khrushchev, pushing for reform, accelerated in the next year.

The effects of Khrushchev's speech had a ripple effect both inside the Soviet Union and in the Soviet bloc, and his policies soon began to undermine his political position. Though the actual text of the speech was not circulated in the Soviet Union, it was well known in the West, and rumors about the speech ran through the Soviet elite. Official public attitudes toward Stalin changed noticeably, and in Tbilisi, the capital of Soviet Georgia, students, angry at Khrushchev's denunciations of a native son, organized demonstrations to prevent the removal of a monument to Stalin. The Soviet government sent in tanks, which fired into the crowds on the main street of Tbilisi, killing dozens and wounding hundreds.

The opening of the anti-Stalin campaign had immediate and stunning consequences in the Soviet bloc, particularly in Poland and Hungary. Poland had not been as terrorized or as completely Sovietized as other East European states. Suddenly in June 1956, Polish workers in Poznan, upset by declining wages and the insensitivity of authorities to their grievances, demonstrated. Officials condemned the protesters as provocateurs and traitors and suppressed the demonstrations. Khrushchev attacked the workers as "anti-Soviet" elements. Privately he expressed fears that the West hoped to use such events to overthrow the socialist governments of Eastern Europe. He told the Yugoslav ambassador, "We must give them a rap on the knuckles. . . . The policy of peaceful coexistence will not suffer, however, for imperialism accepted that policy only if socialism was strong. Imperialism would not coexist with a weak socialism." The Soviet leaders offered a large grant of consumer goods to placate the workers; if that failed, they were prepared to use force. The Polish Communists were divided between those who called for broadening workers' democracy and the Stalinists, who wanted a return to the old order. The crisis came to a head in October when Gomulka, who had been arrested under Stalin, was elected to the Politburo. Khrushchev, Kaganovich, Mikoyan, and Molotov flew to Warsaw uninvited, and while Soviet troops stood ready to move out from their bases in Poland, they carried out "serious, difficult, and bitter" negotiations with the Polish leaders. Finally, the Soviets agreed to allow the Poles latitude in domestic affairs, as long as they did not threaten the unity of the Soviet bloc. Gomulka became first secretary of the Polish Workers' Party, and Soviet Marshall Rokossovskii was relieved of his positions in the Polish government. By presenting a united face to the Soviets, the Polish Communists managed to gain control of their internal affairs and prevent a Soviet invasion. The Hungarians were not so fortunate.

Hungary's postwar experience was similar in some ways to that of Poland. In both countries the Communists had little popularity and met strong resistance from the Catholic Church. But unlike Poland, Hungary had experienced the most rapid collectivization, and by 1953 hunger was widespread. A recalcitrant Stalinist, Matyas Rakosi, headed both party and government until the introduction of the New Course, when Soviet leaders reprimanded the unpopular Rakosi for economic excesses that "had driven the country to the verge of catastrophe" and relieved him of his post as prime minister. A moderate, reform-minded Communist, Imre Nagy, became head of government and began to emphasize light industry, reduce taxes on the peasants, and even allow them to leave the collective farms. The rivalry between the two men, who had very different visions of socialism, led to an intense power struggle. In March 1955 Nagy fell from power, and Rakosi announced recollectivization of agriculture and new investments in heavy industry. Rakosi had Nagy expelled from the party and announced that he and four hundred intellectuals were to be executed. At this point the Soviet leaders intervened and forced Rakosi to resign.

This initial phase of the Hungarian crisis simmered until the fall. Once the Polish crisis resulted in Gomulka's victory, Hungarian grievances exploded in mass demonstrations. On October 23 university students, who had been actively discussing politics in circles named after the Hungarian poet Sandor Petofi, marched to the monument to the poet in the city center. There they read poems and sang nationalist songs in support of the Polish struggle and greater freedom in Hungary. Toward evening the crowds in the streets grew more militant. Shots were fired, and the printing plant of the party newspaper was wrecked. About two hundred thousand people joined the demonstrations that first day. The next day Imre Nagy was returned as prime minister, but he was unable to stop the fighting in the streets. Army units joined the insurgents, and a workers' council was formed. Soviet troops entered the fray, but the rebels increased their determination to fight for independence. On the third day Janos Kadar, who himself had suffered from Stalinist repression, became first secretary of the Hungarian Workers' Party. Workers' councils appeared throughout the country to take over factories and organize resistance. The government attempted to meet the demands of the crowds by forming a coalition government with non-Communists on October 27. Two days later the Soviets withdrew their troops to the outskirts of Budapest. The Nagy government made additional concessions to the crowds, abolishing the one-party system and freeing the virulently anticommunist Cardinal Jozsef Mindszenty from house arrest. But Nagy was unable to control the insurgents.

After vacillating about what action to take, the Soviet Presidium decided that intervention was necessary. Khrushchev reasoned that the Soviet Union had no choice: "If we let things take their course the West would say we are either stupid or weak, and that's one and the same thing. We cannot possibly permit it, either as Communists and internationalists or as the Soviet state. We would have capitalists on the frontiers of the Soviet Union." He and his comrades consulted with and secured the agreement of the Polish, Rumanian, Czechoslovak, and Bulgarian leaders, and even flew through a thunderstorm to Tito's retreat on Brioni Island for his approval. On October 31 new Soviet troops entered Hungary. Nagy declared Hungary a neutral state, withdrawing it from the Warsaw Pact. The party chief, Kadar, defected to the Soviets. On November 4 Soviet troops attacked Budapest, overwhelming its defenders. Nagy and his closest associates fled to the Yugoslav Embassy. Later he was lured out of the embassy on promise of free passage, arrested, and secretly tried; in June 1958 he and several other leaders of the Hungarian Revolution were shot. Thousands of Hungarians fled to the West, as the worst crisis in the Soviet bloc was ended by Soviet tanks. The images of Hungarian freedom fighters crushed by the Soviet Army marked the minds of the Western public more indelibly than all the initiatives of Khrushchev for peaceful coexistence.

With disorder in the Soviet bloc, Khrushchev's rivals in the Kremlin had powerful political ammunition against him. By December 1956 the Central Committee took steps against some of Khrushchev's policies by reorganizing the industrial planning system and placing greater power in the State Economic Commission. Khrushchev sat silently while these changes were being discussed in the Central Committee. By February 1957 the first secretary seemed to revive his reform impulses, perhaps buoyed up by the successful harvest of late 1956 and vindicated by the apparent short-term success of the Virgin Lands program. He challenged the powerful, conservative forces in the bureaucracy who favored heavy industry and centralization of decision-making and who were less enthusiastic about greater investment in agriculture. Pushing for decentralization of economic decision-making, Khrushchev abolished a number of industrial ministries and created about a hundred regional economic councils (*sovnarkhozy*). Having allied himself with middle-level party officials, who made up over half of the Central Committee, Khrushchev was prepared to give greater authority to the non-Russian republics and local authorities and hoped to isolate the central ministers.

The opposition to Khrushchev was not united by adherence to a set of principles or a consensus on policy. Rather, Molotov, Malenkov, and Kaganovich came together out of fear of Khrushchev. They recruited Bulganin and Voroshilov into their conspiracy and took action on June 17, 1957. Just after returning from a trip to Finland, Khrushchev was called at his home by Prime Minister Bulganin, who demanded an immediate meeting of the party Presidium. Arriving at the Kremlin, Khrushchev found key members already assembled. They demanded a meeting of the full Presidium (three members were out of town), and all, except Mikoyan, began criticizing Khrushchev—for the lack of unity in the party and the state, his "cult of personality," his conduct of foreign policy, the imposition of his will on the majority, his control of the police, and his campaign to catch up with and overtake America. Khrushchev fought back, even accusing Malenkov of strangling the former Politburo member Voznesenskii, a victim of the Leningrad affair. The majority of the Presidium members present opposed him, but it was clear that they had not prepared their move well and had no political program except to get rid of Khrushchev. A second meeting was held the next day, with candidate members, including Marshall Zhukov, attending. He supported Khrushchev, and made arrangements for Central Committee members from all over the country to fly to Moscow for the showdown. A majority of the Presidium called for Khrushchev's dismissal as first secretary.

Khrushchev insisted that the matter be taken to the Central Committee, and the Presidium majority, confident it would win, foolishly agreed. The Central Committee met for a week, and came out overwhelmingly on the side of Khrushchev. Speakers implicated Malenkov, Molotov, and Kaganovich in the Stalinist purges and condemned the so-called anti-party group. Khrushchev added fuel to the fire: "I think that if two evil geniuses, Beria and Malenkov, had not been around Stalin, then much would have been different. It was possible to speak with Stalin. When Beria was far from Stalin, I decided many questions with Stalin." Khrushchev's opponents were swept from the Presidium, except for Voroshilov and Bulganin, who appealed to Khrushchev. Though no one was imprisoned or killed, his opponents were driven from politics. Molotov was appointed ambassador to Outer Mongolia. Malenkov became director of a cement plant.

By 1957 Khrushchev had proven to be the most talented and shrewd politician among Stalin's heirs. In 1953 he isolated and eliminated Beria, in 1954 he outmaneuvered Malenkov, in 1956 he discredited Stalin and those closest to him, and in 1957 he beat the Molotov-Malenkov-Kaganovich plot against him— all this despite the fact that his destalinization policies had led to serious threats to Soviet rule in Eastern Europe. To further ensure his position, Khrushchev rid himself of a powerful potential threat, the popular, strong-willed Marshall Zhukov. While the minister of defense was visiting Yugoslavia in October 1957, Khrushchev had him replaced and later removed him from the party Presidium as well. Zhukov, shaken by his treatment at the hands of the political leadership he had served, retired in disgrace to write his memoirs.

Khrushchev's power was further consolidated in March 1958 when he replaced Bulganin as prime minister. Now he headed both party and state, backed by a loyal Central Committee and a subordinate police and army. Though he was certainly the most powerful politician in the Soviet Union from 1957 until October 1964, he was still not an all-powerful dictator like Stalin. Rather, he was the chief oligarch, with his power limited by his colleagues in the party Presidium and ultimately sanctioned by the Central Committee. Though the Presidium usually made the decisions, which the Central Committee simply rubber-stamped, it frequently consulted and negotiated with powerful members of the Central Committee. Debate and conflict continued in the top party bodies, and consensus had to be reached. But often, to the dismay of his comrades, Khrushchev made decisions without adequate consultation. He dominated through his personal authority, though occasionally he was forced to retreat from his preferred positions. The events of June 1957 indicated once again that in the post-Stalin Soviet Union the ultimate sanction for power in the USSR was the Central Committee. In order to keep his position, Khrushchev had to appeal to the Central Committee and be confirmed by it—a clear shift from earlier days when Stalin stood above both the party and the Central Committee.

Suggestions for Further Reading

The Khrushchev period has largely drawn the attention of political scientists, but a few historians and memoirists have contributed significantly. Among the best works are Roy Medvedev, *Khrushchev* (Oxford, 1982); Bertram D. Wolfe, *Khrushchev and Stalin's Ghost: Text, Background and Meaning of Khrushchev's Secret Report to the Twentieth Congress* (New York, 1957); Sidney Ploss, *Conflict and Decision-Making in Soviet Russia: A Case Study of Agricultural Policy, 1953–1963* (Princeton, N.J., 1965); Abraham Brumberg, *Russia under Khrushchev: An Anthology from Problems of Communism* (New York, 1962); Howard R. Swearer, *The Politics of Succession in the USSR: Materials on Khrushchev's Rise to Leadership* (Boston, 1964); Stephen F. Cohen, Alexander Rabinowitch, and Robert Sharlet (eds.), *The Soviet Union since Stalin* (Bloomington, Ind., 1980); and the indispensable George Breslauer, *Khrushchev and Brezhnev as Leaders: Building Authority in Soviet Politics* (Boston, 1982).

The indispensable source for the period are Khrushchev's three volumes of memoirs: *Khrushchev Remembers* (Boston, 1970), *Khrushchev Remembers: The Last Testament* (Boston, 1974), and *Khrushchev Remembers: The Glasnost Tapes* (Boston, 1990). These should be supplemented with the memoirs of others such as Fyodor Burlatsky, *Khrushchev and the First Russian Spring: The Era of Khrushchev through the Eyes of His Adviser* (New York, 1988); Vittorio Vidali, *Diary of the Twentieth Congress of the Communist Party of the Soviet Union* (New York and London, 1984); Veljko Micunovic, *Moscow Diary* (Garden City, N.Y., 1980); and Sergei Khrushchev, *Khrushchev on Khrushchev: An Inside Account of the Man and his Era* (Boston, 1990).

On culture in the post-Stalin years, see Deming Brown, *Soviet Russian Literature since Stalin* (New York, 1978); Priscilla Johnson, *Khrushchev and the Arts: The Politics of Soviet Culture* (Cambridge, Mass., 1965); George Gibian, *Interval of Freedom: Soviet Literature during the Thaw, 1954–1957* (Minneapolis, Minn., 1960); and Hugh McLean and Walter N. Vickery (eds.), *The Year of Protest, 1956: An Anthology of Soviet Literary Materials* (New York, 1961).

On foreign policy, see Zbigniew K. Brzezinski, *The Soviet Bloc: Unity and Conflict*, rev. ed. (New York, 1961); and Paul Zinner (ed.), *National Communism and Popular Revolt in Eastern Europe* (New York, 1986) and *The Anti-Stalin Campaign and International Communism: A Selection of Documents* (New York, 1956).

CHAPTER 18
Khrushchev and the Politics of Reform

The Thaw and Destalinization

By introducing what he called "socialist legality," Khrushchev eased the pressure on intellectuals, party and government officials, and ordinary people. Tens of thousands of victims of Stalinism were rehabilitated, and survivors drifted back into Soviet society, as visible witnesses to an irrepressible past. Yet at the same time the complete subordination of law and the courts to the goals and interests of the Communist Party gave little protection to anyone who opposed the party openly. Though the penalties had been reduced—people were no longer shot for political crimes—those who persisted in their opposition were arrested, sent to labor camps, and subjected to physical and psychological pain. The boundaries of discussion, personal autonomy, and possible criticism of the regime had been expanded, but severe limits were maintained on public expression of political dissent.

The post-Stalin leadership was very insecure before the Soviet people. Their first message to the population warned people not to panic because of Stalin's death. Borrowing the word from the title of Ilya Ehrenburg's 1953 novel, they favored a cultural "thaw," but as Khrushchev reports in his memoirs, "We were scared—really scared. We were afraid that the thaw might unleash a flood, which we wouldn't be able to control and which could drown us.... We wanted to guide the progress of the thaw so that it would stimulate only those creative forces which would contribute to the strengthening of socialism." Intellectuals were given more freedom, though restrictions on their works were maintained, and party leaders, especially Khrushchev, felt they had an absolute right to intervene in cultural affairs and dictate style and content to artists and writers. As he put it succinctly,

> The press and radio, literature, art, music, the cinema and theater are a sharp ideological weapon of our Party. And the Party sees to it that that weapon should be kept ready for action at all times and strike telling blows at our enemies.

In the stultifying atmosphere of late Stalinism the world of culture had atrophied. Writers had been compelled to write literature "without conflict" to reflect a Soviet society supposedly free of conflict. The film industry produced only eight feature films in 1951. In the first year after Stalin's death several prominent Soviet writers raised new themes in their work. They spoke of sincerity, bureaucratic corruption, and the tensions between generations. Late in 1954 the Second Congress of Soviet Writers rejected the "theory of no conflict" and made it clear that a somewhat more tolerant period for culture had begun. The puritanism and what might be called "Soviet humanism" of Stalinist literature continued to set the tone for depicting interpersonal relations in art and literature. Kindness and feeling toward other humans, cooperation with family members and fellow workers, honesty and integrity were emphasized, whereas ambition, competitiveness, egotism, and "uncultured behavior" were condemned. The party and the official artistic establishment remained in place as the final arbiters of what was acceptable in terms of content and style. There was to be no return to the NEP years of contending schools and party passivity.

Khrushchev's criticism of the "cult of personality" encouraged intellectuals to criticize the excesses of Stalinist cultural practices. Some critics boldly suggested that administrative controls over art be lifted, others that the artists themselves be the judge of artistic works. Konstantin Simonov wrote that party intervention had not improved but distorted Fadeev's war novel, *The Young Guard*, by forcing the author to elevate the role of the party in the plot. Well-entrenched conservatives lashed back at those who sought liberalizing change, and the intelligentsia was divided into nostalgic Stalinists and reformers. A spate of literary rehabilitations took place beginning in 1956. The satirical novels of the popular Ilf and Petrov, the authors of *The Twelve Chairs* and *The Golden Calf*, two classics of the 1920s, were republished. Works by Isaac Babel, who perished in the purges, and Iurii Olesha, who survived by being silent, were reissued. The journal *New World* became the vehicle for new stories and novels that pushed the frontier of what was permissible. In 1956 it published *Not by Bread Alone*, a novel by Vladimir Dudintsev that exposed the corruption, immorality, and philistinism of Soviet bureaucrats. Dudintsev's novel stimulated a vigorous debate in Soviet society, and critics soon turned their wrath on his characterization of Soviet officials. Rather than simply collapsing before his opponents, Dudintsev argued at a meeting of writers, "I think that we might be allowed, like beginning swimmers, to try to swim on our own, to take our own chances of drowning. But, alas, I always feel a halter, like the harness that children are sometimes supported by. And it keeps me from swimming."

Younger authors, like the poets Evtushenko and Andrei Voznesenskii, appeared in print, experimenting with form and criticizing remnants of Stalinism. An idealistic search for truth and honesty was explored in Evtushenko's early poem "Zima Station," in which the poet proclaims, "Yes, truth is good, and happiness is better, / But still, without truth there can be no happiness." That sentiment was spoken by the village of Zima, the metaphor for the people, to the lone intellectual who is told to "go into the world" and "love people and you will understand them." The literary scene, particularly in Moscow and Leningrad, blossomed in the mid-1950s. Young people from around the world came to Moscow in 1957 to attend the World Youth Festival, and Soviet young people began to more openly express their own culture and style in dress, taste, and leisure activities. Poetry readings attended by hundreds, then thousands, were held at the monument to Mayakovsky in central Moscow and later at the Luzhniki stadium. Soviet youth rebelled in their own way against the conformity imposed by adult society; some became tough rebels known as *stiliagi*, while others explored the new novels and films coming in from the West. Interest in jazz revived after the long, imposed drought of the Stalin years. With the heavy weight of pervasive fear of the police lifted, people indulged more in private activities and paid less attention to the demands of the officially proclaimed "Communist morality." Whereas official doctrine required subordination of emotion to reason, individual passion to the good of the family or the larger community, more people now considered their own desires in making life choices. The divorce rate soared in the first decade of Khrushchev's rule.

Khrushchev tried to rein in the liberalization in the arts in the late summer of 1957. He warned that "we support writers who maintain the correct position in literature, who write about what is positive in life." He was prepared to forgive those writers, even Dudintsev, who mended their ways with the help of the party. The boundaries of the permissible were demonstrated most vividly in the famous "Pasternak affair." In 1955 the renowned Soviet poet Boris Pasternak submitted his novel *Doctor Zhivago* to three Soviet publishers, all of whom after a year declined to publish the work, which viewed the revolution as an ambivalent, unheroic event. Khrushchev read only selected excerpts of the novel and, relying on the judgments of others, agreed to ban the work. After the novel appeared in foreign editions, Pasternak was awarded the 1958 Nobel Prize for literature. Two days later a Soviet campaign against the novel and the Nobel Prize began. Under enormous pressure at home, Pasternak wrote to the Swedish Academy: "In view of the meaning given to your award by the society to which I belong, I must renounce this undeserved distinction which has been conferred upon me. Please do not take my voluntary renunciation amiss." The media outside the Soviet bloc attacked Soviet censorship, and by its harsh policy toward critical literature the Soviet Union embarrassed itself internationally. Khrushchev himself later regretted the whole affair and proposed that Pasternak be readmitted to the Writers' Union, from which he had been expelled. But he never challenged the notion that there ought to be an orthodox Soviet literature or that the party ought to play a role in determining the limits of expression. His contribution was to broaden but not to abolish what could and could not be written, painted, or said. The party, he told the writers attending the Third Congress of Soviet Writers in May 1959, had deprived them not only of the right to write badly "but above all of the right to write wrongly."

Cultural policy remained inconsistent and variable throughout the Khrushchev years. Khrushchev reduced the role of Stalin in history and promoted what he considered to be a "return to Leninism." But when historians tried to open up discussion on critical aspects of the party's history, censors hit them hard. The freeze of 1957–59 gave way to a second thaw in cultural affairs, which lasted until about 1962. Young poets again emerged with sharply critical verses. In 1961 the flamboyant Evtushenko wrote his attack on covert anti-Semitism, "Babii Yar," which was followed the next year by his powerful poem "Heirs of Stalin," which appeared in *Pravda*. In 1962, after a personal intervention by Khrushchev, Aleksandr Solzhenitsyn's short novel *One Day in the Life of Ivan Denisovitch*, which told the gripping story of a simple, persevering prisoner in a Siberian labor camp, was published.

The early 1960s was a time when intellectuals still possessed a faith in the socialist project and the possibility of fundamental eradication of the Stalinist legacy. In his novels *The First Circle* and *Cancer Ward*, Solzhenitsyn elaborated an intellectual's vision of a humanistic socialism. But this second thaw was already threatened in December 1962 when Khrushchev visited the Manege, the large exhibition hall by the Kremlin, to view the works of contemporary artists. There he fumed against the abstract experimentation, using foul language and bare-knuckled threats. Still, in his last year in power the experimental theater On the Taganka opened in Moscow and soon introduced stirring productions of Bertoldt Brecht to the Soviet public.

In many ways Khrushchev was an idealistic Communist. At the Twenty-First Party Congress early in 1959 he announced that the USSR was entering a new stage of history, "the period of the full-scale building of communism," a period in which state regulation of society would decrease and the role of public organizations, like the soviets, trade unions, komsomols, would increase. Communist morality, rather than state authority, would regulate the relations between people. Two years later his supporters drafted a new party program, the first since 1919. The new program declared that the USSR was no longer a dictatorship of the proletariat but now was to be considered "a state of the whole people." The program made the bold claim that the Soviet Union would surpass the United States in per-capita output by 1971 and in other economic spheres by the 1980s. Under communism, which was now being built, the state would wither away, though not the party.

Farm, Factory, and School

Khrushchev's political fate was tied intimately to his successes and failures in agriculture. Since the early 1930s agriculture had been the poor cousin in the Soviet economy. In 1958 almost fifteen times more investment capital was made available per industrial worker than per able-bodied collective farmer. Khrushchev increased investment in the countryside, raised procurement prices, replaced the system of compulsory deliveries with planned state purchases, and brought collective farmers into the social security system. He constantly fought conservatives, who wanted to maintain greater state control over the farms, and gave the collective farms greater autonomy. Between 1953 and 1958 farm output increased 8.5 percent annually and 51 percent overall. This was due largely to the opening of new lands and the introduction of incentives. By 1958 collective farmers received double the retail price value that they had received in 1953, and they gained greater mobility when they received the internal passports that all other Soviet citizens had had since the mid-1930s. Overall, Khrushchev's agricultural reforms resulted in an increase in agricultural output of 74 percent, in ruble terms, from 1953 to 1964. At the same time, the number of farmers declined by 10 percent. But far too many people were still engaged in agriculture, and the per-capita productivity of farm labor remained low. By the end of the 1950s, agriculture began to suffer. In 1959 the harvest in Kazakhstan fell 17 million tons short of its grain target, the first notable failure of the Virgin Lands program.

When Khrushchev tried to introduce new, more sweeping reforms in December 1959, the Central Committee resisted. Two years later international tensions between the West and the Soviet Union aided the military–industrial group within the party to defend the traditional investment policies in heavy industry and the military. Farm management was put under more bureaucratic control, as ministries of production and procurement were set up in the union republics. Bad weather devastated the 1963 harvest. The long-term consequences of underinvestment in agriculture, the lack of infrastructure such as proper storage facilities and adequate roads to take goods to market, and the chronic low productivity and colossal waste on the collective farms all testified to a permanent crisis in the rural economy. The overexploitation of the Virgin Lands, where spring wheat was planted, eroded soil and promoted weeds. Those lands, which were dry plains appropriate for grazing but not necessarily planting, demanded expensive irrigation and fertilization, which was an enormous burden on the Soviet economy. Here as in much smokestack industry pell-mell productivism was leading to an impending ecological disaster.

Just as he had improved the lot of the collective farmer, Khrushchev raised the standard of living of industrial workers. Average wages increased from 67 rubles a month for workers and employees in 1952 to 91 rubles in 1964. The government repealed the harsh labor laws of the Stalin period and reduced the work week from 48 hours to 46 in 1956 and to 41 in 1960. Yet at the same time Khrushchev was capable of ruthlessly exercising physical force to maintain the system in which he believed. People in the North Caucasian town of Novocherkassk were experiencing shortages of meat and butter in early June 1962, when unexpectedly the government raised prices for meat and dairy. Workers at the local locomotive plant went on strike and demanded that their complaints be conveyed to the government. They organized a march to the party headquarters for the next morning, which was to feature red banners and Lenin's portrait, but before they could act, the leaders of the protest were arrested, and troops moved into town. Tanks appeared, and machine-guns fired into a crowd gathered at the city party committee to demand the release of those arrested. Over twenty people were killed and thirty wounded. The victims were secretly buried, and seven leaders of the strike were executed. A few concessions were made to the strikers, and local food stores were restocked, but no news of the events appeared in the press for nearly thirty years.

Soviet socialism offered the promise that life would improve over time, and the promise of continued growth was widely believed, not only in the USSR but in the West as well. The Soviet leader's boast that "we will bury you" was taken seriously by commentators in the United States, who were impressed by Soviet rates of economic growth and achievements in education, rocketry, and science. When the Soviet Union launched the first space satellite, called sputnik (fellow traveler), on October 4, 1957, a shock passed through the Western nations. When that success was followed by a rocket orbiting the Earth, carrying the dog Laika and later (April 1961) the first human in space, Yurii Gagarin, a deep panic spurred American and West Europeans to invest in rockets and scientific education. In the late 1950s and throughout the 1960s rocket launches were a major spectator sport in the United States, but the public was dismayed by American failures and Soviet successes. Though the Soviets did not televise their launches, their leadership in the "space race" generated enormous pride and support for the system. The Soviets touted any achievement by the Soviet Union, whether in rocket science or Olympic sports, as evidence of the superiority of Soviet socialism.

In the 1950s the Soviet gross national product grew at an annual rate of 7.1 percent, compared to the American rate of growth of 2.9 percent. But because the economic base from which the United States grew was so much larger, the Soviets still lagged far behind. From 1958, however, the Soviet rate of growth slowed down to 5.3 percent per year, where it remained until 1964, the year of Khrushchev's fall. The USSR's rate of economic growth had peaked and would slow down throughout the next several decades. Labor productivity, as well as the productivity of capital, also declined. Inefficiency and waste were rampant in the system, and reformers like Khrushchev (and later Gorbachev) were unable to reverse the slowdown.

Soviet economists tried to find solutions to the chronic problems of the economy. In 1962 Evsei Liberman proposed an innovative approach calling for more autonomy for enterprises, new material rewards for increasing productivity, profit (revenues over costs) as the indicator of economic success, and prices set by the market rather than by planners. The Liberman Plan was widely discussed, as economists tried to reconcile their new enthusiasm for market mechanisms with the Soviet dedication to planning. The bolder thinkers supported the idea of eliminating price-setting by the state and recognizing that markets, albeit "socialist markets," were indispensable. But conservatives in the party leadership blocked these more radical reforms, and managers of enterprises worked around them. Few were implemented before Khrushchev's fall.

Khrushchev was a simple man, even crude at times, and he remained committed to the egalitarianism inherent in Marxist theory and to the special role of workers. As a product of the working class himself, Khrushchev worried about the condescension of intellectuals and professionals toward manual labor. In an effort both to restore prestige and value to ordinary labor and to increase the skill levels of Soviet workers, he introduced a sweeping educational reform in 1958, which attempted to combine academic learning with vocational training. All students were to go through eight years of compulsory schooling, after which they would either go to work, to a special technical school, or to a school that also offered vocational training. Every student was to do some work in a factory or on a farm, and the total number of required school years was raised from ten to eleven. Though the number of elite "magnet" schools for mathematics, languages, and the arts was increased, most Soviet students were

Figure 18.1. Young Soviet women visiting the Central Lenin Museum in Moscow, May 1966. On the wall, Lenin's words: "Our path is true, and this is a path along which sooner or later the rest of the countries will come" (ITAR-TASS/SOVPHOTO).

to go through general education with three years of vocational training. Special efforts were also made to recruit workers and peasants into the educational system.

A second thrust of the educational reform was to elevate the knowledge of Russian among non-Russians. Though all students had been obliged to learn Russian as a second language since 1938, Khrushchev increased emphasis on Russian-language teaching and allowed those living in non-Russian republics who did not wish to study the local language to choose not to. Thus, a double standard for language learning was enforced: everyone had to learn some Russian but Russian-speakers did not have learn another Soviet language, even if they lived in a non-Russian republic.

Khrushchev attempted to deal with some of the more glaring problems of the non-Russian nationalities. He ended the exile of those small peoples of the North Caucasus, such as the Chechens, Ingush, and Balkars, and allowed them to return to their homelands. But he did not restore the autonomous district of the Volga Germans or permit the Crimean Tatars to return to Crimea. He did not take the borders between Soviet republics seriously and in 1954 casually transferred the Russian-populated Crimea from the Russian Federation to Ukraine. By decentralizing power in the USSR and giving greater authority to local and republic leaders, Khrushchev aided the process of rooting many of the non-Russian nationalities in their own homelands, and in so doing consolidated their ethnic and cultural identities, and strengthened the national intelligentsias and Communist elites on the peripheries. Though occasionally he would remove a Communist leader who appeared to be too close to his own people, Khrushchev was not overly concerned about nationality issues. He firmly believed that ultimately the various peoples of the USSR would grow closer together culturally until they blended into a single nation. He promoted Russian language and culture, particularly in the Baltics, Ukraine, and Belorussia, where Russian in-migration diluted the local national culture to some degree, but in the south the major nationalities in the Central Asian and Transcaucasian republics increasingly became dominant in their home republics.

The Arms Race

Despite Soviet successes in rocketry, the strategic balance of power heavily favored the United States in the late 1950s and early 1960s. In the aftermath of the Hungarian Revolution and the simultaneous Suez crisis, the United States announced its intention to place medium-range nuclear weapons, targeted at the Soviet Union, in Turkey, Iran, Japan, and West Germany. Later that year the Americans and West Germans rejected a Soviet plan to create a nuclear-free zone in central Europe. In 1957 the United States had two thousand nuclear bombs to the Soviet Union's several hundred. The Americans were able to humiliate the Soviets by flying high-speed spy planes over Soviet territory with impunity (until the U-2 incident of 1960) and used "spy satellites" beginning in 1960.

Though the Soviets developed the first intercontinental ballistic missile (ICBM) in 1957, their missiles were highly unreliable, and few in number. Between 1959 and 1965, the USSR had 750 medium-range missiles deployed against Europe, but only 4 that could reach the United States. Their bombers were inferior to the Americans' B-52s. Soviet bombers were able to reach the United States but not to return home. Yet ambitious American politicians claimed that Russia had a much greater bomber force than the United States and that large expenditures were needed to bridge the so-called "bomber gap." In 1960 the United States launched its first Polaris submarine, and by the next year it had procured missiles that allowed the government to state publicly that it could attack the USSR without the Soviets being able to retaliate effectively. At the same time the issue of an alleged "missile gap" with the Soviet Union was featured in the 1960 presidential contest between Nixon and Senator John F. Kennedy.

Rift with China

Faced with a nuclear menace in the West, a rearming West Germany, and unruly satellites in the Soviet bloc, the Soviet Union also had to contend late in the 1950s with growing tensions with the Chinese Communist leaders. In the years 1957–61 the two most powerful Communist parties drifted apart. The post-Stalin leadership was anxious to maintain good relations with China. Khrushchev's first trip abroad, in September 1954, was to China. The Chinese leaders wanted to receive more material and military aid from the Soviet Union and have Soviet troops leave the Chinese ports of Dairen and Port Arthur, where they had been stationed since 1945. Khrushchev thought the Chinese requests excessive but agreed to increase aid, evacuate the Soviet bases, and invite thousands of Chinese students to be educated in the USSR.

China was a mammoth state with its own geopolitical and strategic interests. The Chinese leadership developed its own ties with other Asian and African powers at the Bandung Conference in the spring of 1955, emphasizing its willingness to develop peaceful relations with its neighbors. But Mao Zedong was appalled by Khrushchev's denunciations of Stalin, his rapprochement with the West and Yugoslavia, and the growing disunity in the international Communist movement. In an important statement late in 1956, the Chinese Politburo declared, "In our opinion Stalin's mistakes take second place to his achievements." The declaration recognized the USSR as "the center of international proletarian solidarity" but warned against "big power chauvinism." While the Soviet leaders advocated "peaceful coexistence," discouraged local wars that could escalate into larger ones, and claimed that Soviet power was the principal deterrent to the imperialists making war, the Chinese leadership argued that local wars against imperialism should be encouraged and that the imperialists were plotting new wars. More militantly revolutionary than the Soviets, the Chinese believed that Communists should support revolutionary movements around the world. Khrushchev, however, wished to avoid provocations that would antagonize the United States. Mao wanted nuclear technology from the USSR, but Khrushchev was more interested in preventing the United States from spreading nuclear weapons to its allies, particularly West Germany, than in spreading them to his allies, particularly the Chinese. The Soviet Union gave aid worth several billion dollars to China and helped the initial industrialization of the country, but ultimately the Soviet Union reneged on its promise to help the Chinese build atomic weapons. China's only ally among Communist states was Albania, where the Stalin cult lived on under the rule of Enver Hoxha. Hostile to Yugoslavia and critical of the policy of détente, the Albanian leaders joined the Chinese in the view that a world war would lead to the destruction of international imperialism. For Mao Zedong, Western imperialism was a "paper tiger" not to be feared, but Khrushchev feared such a tiger with atomic weapons.

By the summer of 1960 the Sino-Soviet split had divided the international Communist movement into two camps. In Bucharest, Rumania, Khrushchev denounced the hard-line, anti-Western Chinese and Albanian leaders as dogmatic "Left adventurists" willing to unleash war. The Chinese considered the Soviets to be "revisionists," a serious accusation in the Marxist-Leninist lexicon. A month later, in July, the Soviet Central Committee recalled all Soviet experts in China. That fall eighty-one Communist parties met in Moscow to patch up the divisions in their movement. Most parties backed the Soviet position, but the Chinese and the Albanians refused to capitulate. Relations between the USSR and China continued to worsen in the next several years. As the Soviet Union attempted to improve its relations with the United States and restrict nuclear proliferation, China felt threatened by American nuclear power and humiliated by Soviet condescension, and became determined to become a fully sovereign atomic power dependent on no other country.

Crises in the West

In the late 1950s and early 1960s the major source of Soviet-American tension was in central Europe. West Germany was experiencing an "economic miracle," rapidly becoming one of the richest countries in the world, and its government was determined to have nuclear weapons and be a full partner in the Western alliance. East Germany was also developing rapidly, trading primarily with West Germany, and achieved a standard of living higher than the Soviet Union. But its economy lagged far behind West Germany. Convinced that the United States was determined to give Germany nuclear weapons and strengthen its bases around the USSR, Khrushchev persuaded the Presidium that the Soviet Union should act decisively where the West was most vulnerable. On November 27, 1958, Khrushchev held the first formal press conference in the Kremlin and stunned reporters by declaring, "West Berlin has become a kind of malignant tumor" and surgery is required. If the West did not sign a treaty with Germany, the Soviet Union would do so unilaterally and the East Germans would be free to close access to Berlin. That same day an official note was sent to the Western powers and the two Germanys calling for the demilitarization of Berlin and its conversion to a free city. The West was given six months to respond.

Khrushchev's ultimatum was a dangerous bluff. He did not really want to shut off the GDR from the West German economy or sign a separate treaty with the East Germans, which would only have consolidated the division of Europe. But he did want to prevent the rearmament of West Germany. Senator Hubert Humphrey met Khrushchev in the Kremlin, and the Soviet leader, who had little idea what he would do if the West did not respond positively to his demand, boasted that Soviet missiles could hit any place on earth. "What is your home town, Senator?" he asked. Humphrey told him he was from Minneapolis. Khrushchev drew a blue circle around Minneapolis on his wall map: "I will have to remember to have that city spared when the missiles start flying." Humphrey then asked what Khrushchev's home town was. When the Soviet leader answered "Moscow," the Senator said that he was sorry but that they would not be able to spare Moscow. Everyone laughed.

Eisenhower reluctantly invited Khrushchev to visit the United States. In September 1959 the Soviet Union's most enthusiastic tourist traveled from Washington to New York from California to the corn fields of Iowa. His final meeting with Eisenhower took place at the presidential retreat at Camp David, and there Eisenhower convinced Khrushchev to lift his ultimatum. The president agreed to attend a summit conference and to visit the USSR. The first Berlin crisis had passed, and, despite the suspicions on both sides, the Camp David meeting promised a greater degree of negotiation and agreement in the future. Khrushchev returned home euphoric, and a few months later, "in the spirit of Camp David," he proposed to the Supreme Soviet that Soviet armed forces be reduced by one-third within the next two years.

As preparations for the summit conference in Paris neared completion, Khrushchev remained uneasy about Western plans to give nuclear weapons to West Germany. He was gambling for a better relationship with the United States, while at the same time losing China as a close ally. Suddenly, the international order was jolted by the unexpected. As Soviet leaders set out to celebrate May Day 1960, the Soviet military intercepted and shot down a U-2 spy plane near the city of Sverdlovsk in the Urals. The flight had been personally authorized by Eisenhower, who understood that such overflights were a violation of international law and a serious provocation. The interception placed the upcoming summit in jeopardy. The United States officially announced that one of its meteorological research planes was missing. Khrushchev, whose conciliatory line toward the West had strong opponents within the Presidium, announced that a plane had been downed but deliberately did not mention publicly that the pilot had been captured. The United States continued with its cover story until Khrushchev revealed that they had the pilot. The State Department then admitted that the plane had been spying and defended its action: "The necessity for such activities as measure of legitimate national defense is enhanced by the excessive secrecy practiced by the Soviet Union in contrast to the Free World."

As angry as he was, Khrushchev wanted to absolve Eisenhower of any responsibility in the incident in order to continue with the summit, but the president decided to admit that he had authorized the overflights. He told the National Security Council, "Of course, one had to expect that the thing would fail at one time or another. But that it had to be such a boo-boo and that we would be caught with our pants down was rather painful." The American public was disturbed by Eisenhower's admission that the government had publicly lied to the people. On May 16 Khrushchev met with Eisenhower, Charles de Gaulle, and Harold Macmillan in Paris. Eisenhower had hoped that the Soviets would agree to his plans for disarmament, beginning with a limited nuclear test ban treaty. But Khrushchev demanded that the United States officially repudiate such acts of espionage and apologize for the overflight. Eisenhower indicated that the flights had been suspended, but he stopped short of an apology. Khrushchev stormed out of the conference. The fragile spirit of Camp David quickly dissipated, and the brief first period of Soviet-American détente ended.

Khrushchev suffered from his close identification with Eisenhower, never regaining the degree of authority over foreign policy he had enjoyed before the U-2 incident. Those in the Kremlin who believed that a tougher line toward the West was required, gained influence. Khrushchev also suffered from his crude public behavior, his outbursts and rude language. The Soviet people were used to more distant, cool, dignified leaders, and Khrushchev's common touch often degenerated into vulgarity. Those closest to Khrushchev increasingly deferred to him and hesitated to correct him, allowing his mistakes to compound. In September Khrushchev went to New York for the opening of the UN General Assembly. He stayed for a month, needling the Americans, playing to the galleries as friend of the newly independent African and Asian nations, and, most memorably, banging his shoe on the table at the United Nations to protest a speech by Macmillan. The United States was engaged in its presidential campaign, and all talk was about Soviet aggressiveness and the purported missile gap. Cold War rhetoric was used by both Nixon and Kennedy, as each tried to outdo the other as the most dedicated foe of communism.

Kennedy and Khrushchev

In 1961 the United States had a new president, the suave, Harvard-educated scion of a wealthy New England family, John Fitzgerald Kennedy. As much a committed anti-Communist as Nixon, he had spoken of the Cold War as a "struggle for supremacy between two conflicting ideologies: freedom under God versus ruthless godless tyranny." Thanks to his personal charm, the efforts of his aides, and a cooperative press, the Kennedy image of vigor, energy, toughness with grace, gentility, culture, and civility captured the American and foreign publics, among them the Soviets. But Khrushchev's first impression of the new President, formed after the dismal failure of the American-sponsored invasion of Cuba at the Bay of Pigs in April 1961, was that he was incompetent and weak politically. When he met Kennedy two months later in Vienna, he "found Kennedy a pleasant and reasonable man, . . . a flexible President and, unlike Eisenhower, he was his own boss in foreign policy." Khrushchev insisted that the international status quo should be maintained and that there be no violation of existing borders. But Kennedy went further; he proposed that the internal social and political systems of the nations of the world be preserved and challenged Khrushchev to agree to prevent "subversion." Khrushchev, however, refused to be drawn into any "holy alliance" against revolution. The two men failed to agree on Berlin. Kennedy argued that West Berlin should be considered part of West Germany, but Khrushchev suggested that it be made a free city. Khrushchev returned to Moscow with a sense that the new president was inexperienced and inferior to Eisenhower.

The East German economy needed greater assistance as educated and talented people fled across the border to the West. German party chief Walter Ulbricht suggested to Khrushchev that the Soviets build a wall in Berlin to prevent flight to the West. At first Khrushchev was opposed, but then he decided to renew pressure on the United States over Berlin. As he put it in his memoirs, "To put it crudely, the American foot in Europe had a sore blister on it. That was West Berlin. Anytime we wanted to step on the Americans' foot and make them feel the pain, all we had to do was obstruct Western communications with the city across the territory of the German Democratic Republic." On August 13, 1961, Soviet troops occupied positions along the West Berlin boundary, and workers began constructing a wall to seal off that part of the city for the next twenty-eight years. The West protested angrily but decided not to risk war. The fait accompli of building the Berlin Wall was briefly a triumph for Khrushchev—it stopped the flow of educated East Germans to the West—but the wall soon became the most potent symbol in the Cold War of the repression and isolation of the Soviet Bloc. Kennedy made a dramatic trip to the wall and identified himself with the people of the besieged city in his famous phrase "Ich bin ein Berliner."

Khrushchev's Gamble: The Cuban Missile Crisis

The Soviet–American confrontation entered a particularly dangerous phase in 1962. That year the Soviet Union began to deploy ICBMs aimed at the United States, and in response President Kennedy launched a program of rapid buildup of American strategic forces. The United States was still far ahead of the USSR in nuclear warpower, with warheads and nuclear bombs numbering four thousand, more than eight times the number held by the USSR. The Soviets would not reach four thousand warheads and bombs until the late 1970s, when the USA would again have more than doubled its number. Because of the Kennedy buildup, the USSR was surpassed by the United States in missile development and production by 1965. By that time it also faced new nuclear arsenals in France and Great Britain. Khrushchev decided to try to redress the strategic balance of power by placing short-range missiles on the island of Cuba. As a result the world came closer to nuclear war than at any other time during the Cold War.

Fidel Castro had come to power in Cuba in 1959 after leading a successful guerrilla movement against an American-backed dictator. Fidel Castro was not then a Communist, though his brother Raul and his lieutenant, Che Guevara, probably were. But when Castro nationalized American companies, the United States ordered an economic blockade of the island and broke off relations, as the CIA secretly began planning for an invasion of the island by anti-Castro Cuban exiles. The Soviets began to send oil, arms, and other supplies to Cuba, along with military instructors. In April 1961 the exiles launched an invasion at the Bay of Pigs, but President Kennedy, who had agreed to the operation, refused to offer the Cuban exiles the air support they had anticipated. Castro won a decisive victory and humiliated the United States.

Khrushchev's decision to place missiles in Cuba had less to do with the defense of Cuba than with a transformation of the balance of military power between the USSR and the USA. The actual decision came about during a visit to Bulgaria. As Fedor Burlatsky tells it,

> Khrushchev and R. Malinovskii, who was then the Soviet Defense Minister, were strolling along the Black Sea coast. Malinovskii pointed out to sea and said that on the other shore in Turkey there was an American nuclear missile base. In a matter of six or seven minutes missiles launched from that base could devastate major centers in the Ukraine and southern Russia such as Kiev, Kharkov, Chernigov and Krasnodar, not to mention Sevastopol—an important naval base. Khrushchev asked Malinovskii why the Soviet Union should not have the right to do the same as America. Why, for example, should it not deploy missiles in Cuba? America had surrounded the USSR with bases and was holding it between its claws, whereas the Soviet Union's missiles and atom bombs were deployed only on Soviet territory. This was a double inequality of forces: inequality in quantity and in delivery times.

Khrushchev obtained the approval of the Presidium of the party to place missiles in Cuba, and Castro and the Cuban leadership enthusiastically supported the deployment.

Using aerial reconnaissance photographs, American intelligence soon discovered the sudden increase in Soviet ships going to Cuba and the careful unloading by Soviet personnel. By the time of the "missile crisis," the Soviets had delivered almost everything that they intended to Cuba. "We had installed enough missiles already," writes Khrushchev, "to destroy New York, Chicago, and the other huge industrial cities, not to mention a little village like Washington. I don't think America had ever faced such a real threat of destruction as at that moment." Kennedy increased the number of marines at the Guantanamo Naval Base, evacuated families, and ordered a vast military buildup in Florida. The Soviets continued to deny that they had placed offensive weapons in Cuba. On October 22 President Kennedy spoke to the nation on television. He revealed the Soviet buildup in Cuba and announced that the United States was "quarantining" the island. He said that the armed forces are being prepared for any eventuality and that any nuclear attack from Cuba would bring a full retaliatory response on the USSR. The world stood on the brink of nuclear war. Later Secretary of Defense Robert McNamara would confess that he and the president had underestimated the danger of nuclear war at the time. They had not known that Cubans had been given control of the missiles. Soviet ICBMs were fueled for the first time and ready to be launched. Kennedy had given the USSR an ultimatum—withdraw your missiles from Cuba or face nuclear war—without any prior effort to resolve the issue diplomatically.

On October 24, with the Strategic Air Command of the United States on its highest state of alert, flying with hydrogen bombs in their planes, Soviet ships stopped dead in the water. Secretary of State Dean Rusk said, "We've been eyeball to eyeball, and someone just blinked." Khrushchev called the American actions "outright banditry," but he decided not to risk war. On October 25 Kennedy wrote to Khrushchev, accusing him of giving the United States false assurances that there were no offensive weapons on Cuba. As letters were exchanged, the American Navy boarded a Soviet ship to inspect it and found only paper products. Khrushchev agreed to remove the missiles if there was a promise of no invasion of Cuba. In one letter, which the Americans simply ignored, he asked for removal of American missiles in Turkey. On October 27, the same day that an American U-2 pilot was shot down over Cuba, the only casualty of the crisis, Attorney General Robert Kennedy, the president's brother, visited the Soviet Embassy and came to an agreement with the Soviets. The next day Khrushchev publicly announced the dismantling of missiles in Cuba. Though humiliated and forced to back down, the Soviet Union really had no other choice given the overall strategic advantage of the United States. "Imperialism today is no longer what it used to be," Khrushchev told the Supreme Soviet a few weeks later, but it would be a mistake to consider it a paper tiger. "This paper tiger has atomic teeth. It can use them, and it must not be treated lightly."

In the last Kennedy years, both sides in the Cold War made some moves toward a less confrontational policy. Khrushchev backed away from trying to muscle the Americans into agreeing to détente, and Kennedy talked about the common interests of Americans and Soviets: "We all breathe the same air. We all cherish our children's future. And we are all mortal." In Ann Arbor, Michigan, McNamara announced the "no-cities doctrine"; nuclear attacks would avoid cities and target military and industrial targets as much as possible. It was assumed that the "assured destruction" of one-fourth to one-third of the USSR's population was sufficient to deter war. Soon afterwards the United States replaced the doctrine of "massive retaliation" with "flexible response," the use of a variety of weapons and troops in different situations. The newly formed Special Forces, or Green Berets, were to be used against revolutionary insurgencies, conventional weapons would be used in limited wars, and improved missiles were to be built in case of an all-out nuclear confrontation. And on August 5, 1963, the United States and the USSR signed the Limited Test Ban Treaty in Moscow. Khrushchev sensed he could work with Kennedy and was genuinely shaken when he heard of the young president's assassination in November.

The Fall of Khrushchev

By the early 1960s the conservative forces in the party leadership were inhibiting further reforms and tying Khrushchev's hands in foreign policy. Khrushchev's policy of destalinization receded after the Twenty-Second Party Congress in October 1961 decided to remove Stalin's body from Lenin's mausoleum. The Congress dropped some of Khrushchev's supporters from the Presidium of the party, among them Minister of Culture Elena Furtseva, the bland woman who had risen higher in state politics than any woman in Soviet history. The new Presidium was divided between those who backed Khrushchev most often (Mikoyan, Brezhnev, Kuusinen, Polianskii, Shvernik), those who often held out against him (Suslov, Kozlov), and those who wavered (Voroshilov, Kosygin, Podgornyi). Still firmly supported in the Central Committee, Khrushchev flourished for a few more years. A cult of Khrushchev, complete with huge editions of his published works, ubiquitous portraits, and laudatory articles in the press, became widespread through the Soviet Union.

Khrushchev improved his position in 1962 by briefly reviving the destalinization drive. Once again he liberalized cultural policy and tried to reduce the power and privileges of the ruling elite. Though he abolished the monthly bonuses that officials routinely received, he failed to get his comrades to agree to term limits on politicians. In September 1962 he pressured the Presidium to approve his plan of dividing the party into agricultural and industrial sectors, a measure that was very unpopular with party officials. But after the Soviet defeat and humiliation in the Cuban missile crisis, Khrushchev suffered politically and personally. The party rejected the Lieberman proposals and once again took a harder line against artists and writers. Seriously weakened by the disastrous harvest of 1963, Khrushchev was unable early in 1964 to convince the Central Committee to invest heavily in chemicals and fertilizers for agriculture and lost out to the "steel-eaters," who favored heavy industry.

Khrushchev might have bowed out gracefully had he voluntarily retired after his seventieth birthday in April 1964. But he was still vigorous and engaged in reshaping Soviet society. He traveled constantly. In the first eight months of 1964, he was out of Moscow more than half the time. Though he knew there were plots to remove him, he did not take them seriously. From the spring of the year Leonid Brezhnev and Podgornyi initiated discussions with other members of the Presidium. When asked whether he would join, Aleksei Kosygin asked, "Who is the KGB with?" When told that their support had been secured, he answered, "I agree."

Khrushchev was vacationing in Pitsunda on the Black Sea in October when the members of the Presidium met at Brezhnev's apartment and decided to call him back to Moscow. He flew back to Moscow with Mikoyan, one of his closest friends, and was driven directly to the Kremlin. For two days the Presidium debated. Khrushchev did not vigorously defend himself. He said that he was suffering but that he was also happy, because

> a time has arrived when members of the presidium of the Central Committee have begun to control the activity of the First Secretary of the Central Committee and speak with full voice. . . . Today's meeting of the Presidium of the Central Committee is a victory for the party. I thought that it is time for me to go. But life is quarrelsome. I see myself that I am not handling matters well, that I do not meet with any of you. I have cut myself off from you. You have criticized me well today for that, and I have suffered from that. . . . I ask you, write me a declaration and I will sign it. I am ready to do everything in the name of the party's interests.

Once again the Central Committee made the decision. Brezhnev chaired the meeting, and Suslov made the major address against Khrushchev, declaring, "The man has lost all humility; he has lost his conscience." With Khrushchev sitting uncharacteristically passively, his comrades decided to "retire" him and replace him with Brezhnev as first secretary of the party and Kosygin as prime minister. Besides the two top leaders, the new Presidium was made up of powerful career bureaucrats—Podgornyi, Suslov, Kirilenko, Mikoyan, Polianskii, Shvernik, and Voronov—who had risen steadily through party ranks until they edged ever closer to the summit of power.

Though himself a product of Stalinism and a successful party bureaucrat, Nikita Sergeevich Khrushchev made the most far-reaching attempt in Soviet history to dismantle the worst institutions of Stalinism and reform the conservative, entrenched bureaucracy. He was genuinely interested in shifting investment from industry to agriculture, in decentralizing the economy and lessening social stratification. He tried to bridge the chasm between the leaders and the led in the Soviet population. But his reforms were largely superficial and never touched the fundamental social relations and power structure of the Soviet system. He succeeded in making bureaucrats uneasy and wary of losing their positions and privileges, but he never attempted full democratization of the political order. He did achieve a less repressive society and open the USSR to the West. Once his agricultural policies were proven to have failed, he was vulnerable to those in the elite whom his reforms threatened. In retirement he lived as a privileged pensioner outside Moscow. There he secretly dictated his memoirs onto a tape recorder, assisted by his son. On September

11, 1971, Khrushchev died of a heart attack. He was buried, not in the Kremlin wall along with the most honored Soviet heroes, but in Novodevichii Monastery. Above his grave is a black-and-white marble stone, symbolizing the ambiguous legacy he left. It was made by the artist Ernst Neizvestnyi, an avant-garde sculptor whom Khrushchev had once denounced.

Suggestions for Further Reading

For the Khrushchev period after 1956, particularly interesting works include Roy A. Medvedev and Zhores A. Medvedev, *Khrushchev: The Years in Power* (New York, 1975); Alexander Yanov, *The Drama of the Soviet 1960s: A Lost Reform* (Berkeley, Calif., 1984); Carl A. Linden, *Khrushchev and the Soviet Leadership, 1957–1964* (Baltimore, 1966); Martin McCauley (ed.), *Khrushchev and Khrushchevism* (Bloomington, Ind., 1987); Michel Tatu, *Power in the Kremlin from Khrushchev to Kosygin* (New York, 1960); and R. F. Miller and F. Feher (eds.), *Khrushchev and the Communist World* (London and Totowa, N.J., 1984).

On foreign policy, see Michael R. Beschloss, *Mayday: Eisenhower, Khrushchev, and the U-2 Affair* (New York, 1986) and *The Crisis Years: Kennedy and Khrushchev, 1960–1963* (New York, 1991); James G. Blight, *On the Brink: Americans and Soviets Reexamine the Cuban Missile Crisis*, 2nd ed. (New York, 1990); and James G. Blight, B. J. Allyn, and D. A. Welch, *Cuba on the Brink: Castro, the Missile Crisis, and the Soviet Collapse* (New York, 1993).

CHAPTER 19
The Paradoxes of Brezhnev's Long Reign

The Leadership

Leonid Brezhnev was head of the Communist Party of the Soviet Union and the most powerful politician in the USSR from October 1964 until his death in November 1982. His reign, which later would be considered a period of stagnation, was one of deep paradoxes. Brezhnev presided over a highly stable political regime, but one that proved to be the prelude to political instability and the collapse of the system. The society Brezhnev oversaw was at one and the same time highly dynamic and slowly decaying. An articulate and mobile society developed within a political order that was becoming arthritic. The early years of Brezhnev's government were a time of economic growth, but after a decade the Soviet economy underwent a slowdown and eventually stagnated. Destalinization slowed down, and the party leaders pursued a cautious approach to social change with little emphasis on the Communist future. Cultural policies turned more conservative, and the contraction of the universe of permissible expression left thousands of intellectuals outside the law as dissidents. A Russophilic nationalism eliminated all but a few vestiges of internationalism. The restraints placed on an emerging and articulate society by the aging, immovable bureaucratic state and party became increasingly insupportable.

The internal decline was disguised by the external flexing of Soviet muscle, through the most massive buildup of the Soviet military since World War II and the expansion of Soviet influence into Africa, the Mediterranean, and Southeast Asia, as well as the sending of Soviet troops into neighboring Afghanistan. But the distance and disharmony between the stolid, pragmatic policies, on the one hand, and the rhetoric, pomp, and formal display of revolutionary enthusiasm, on the other, grew greater and greater. Any resemblance between the Brezhnev regime and the revolutionary utopia of the Bolsheviks of the revolutionary years was purely coincidental. In the words of Moshe Lewin, Soviet history had come full circle: "It all began with the bulk of society being composed of a rather primitive, not very dynamic peasantry, facing an action-oriented, bureaucratic state, and ended with a complex urban society, pushing for change, facing a stagnating bureaucratic state."

The consensus among Khrushchev's successors was that the "hare-brained scheming," the erratic reforms, should end and emphasis should be on stability and slow progress. Brezhnev and Podgornyi, the architects of the conspiracy against Khrushchev, felt particularly threatened by the seventy-year-old leader's desire to change the organizational structure of the party. The new leadership quickly reversed some of Khrushchev's more radical reforms. The large regional economic administrations called *sovnarkhozy* were abolished, and the division of the party into industrial and agricultural sections was reconsolidated into single party units. The educational reform of 1958 was modified; eleven-year schools were changed back to ten-year schools, and the emphasis on vocational education was reduced somewhat. The emphasis on the transition to communism, Khrushchev's most utopian effort, was abandoned, and Brezhnev now spoke of the "building of a developed socialist society."

The new regime revived the oligarchic principle of "collective rule." Brezhnev, Suslov, Podgornyi, and Kosygin were the most important oligarchs, and this inner core stayed intact until May 1977 when Podgornyi was dropped from the Politburo. Kosygin ran the government until 1980, while the other three remained secretaries of the Central Committee. Brezhnev slowly emerged as the most powerful among the oligarchs, and he remained head of the party longer than anyone in Soviet history except Stalin. Lower-level officials enjoyed long, often unbroken tenures and grew old in office. Khrushchev's constant attacks on the bureaucracy had been replaced by a cozy arrangement in which lifelong bureaucrats stayed in their offices until they were carried out horizontally.

Leonid Ilich Brezhnev (1906–82) was born in Ekaterinoslav province, Ukraine, the son of a Russian family of metalworkers. At fifteen he joined his father in the plant, but after his family returned to Russia he took up agriculture and completed a four-year course in agricultural techniques. Brezhnev joined the Communist Party in 1929 during the collectivization campaign. Living in the city of Dnepropetrovsk, the industrial center of eastern Ukraine, Brezhnev's political rise began in earnest after the Great Purges of 1937 and especially after he gained the attention of Ukraine's new first secretary, Nikita Khrushchev. He served during World War II as a political commissar and reached the rank of major general in 1944. Due to his close association with Khrushchev, Brezhnev rose rapidly after the war, becoming head of the Communist party in Moldavia in 1950 and a member of the Central Committee two years later. Notable as a loyal follower and trusted lieutenant, Brezhnev became party chief in Kazakhstan during the initial years of the Virgin Lands program, stood by Khrushchev during the anti-party plot in June 1957, and reached the Politburo as a full member. Briefly, in 1960–64, he held the chairmanship of the Presidium of the Supreme Soviet, a largely honorary position but one that was considered the closest to being a president of the Soviet Union. "Power," writes Fedor Burlatskii,

> was thrust upon Brezhnev as a gift of fate.... He assumed power as smoothly as if someone had tried the crown of Monomakh on various heads

well in advance and settled on this one. And this crown fitted him so well that he wore it for eighteen years without fears, cataclysms, or conflicts of any kind. And the people closest to him longed for only one thing: for this man to live forever, it would be so good for them.

As a leader Brezhnev was neither cruel nor confrontational. He was as cautious and unwilling to take risks as Khrushchev had been impetuous and bold. Neither very intellectual—he preferred to have documents read to him—nor decisive, he occupied the political center and consulted the powerful party bosses and state barons who contended for his ear. He had no personal political vision or program. The heir to the Leninist revolution was no revolutionary, only a skilled middle-level bureaucrat who had somehow been promoted by his patrons to the top of the apparat. When his prime minister, Kosygin, spoke of economic reform, Brezhnev confided to his closest associates, "What is he thinking of? Reform, reform. Who needs it, and who can understand it? We need to work better, that is the only problem." Brezhnev told his speechwriters to make his speeches simple and direct and to cut out quotations from the Marxist classics. He told them, "Who is ever going to believe that I read Marx?"

Based on their years together under Khrushchev, the Brezhnev team developed a consensus on domestic policy. There would be no more "voluntarism" or "subjectivism"; that is, no more decisions made impulsively or by the leader alone in the Khrushchev manner. Plans now would be guided by "objective economic calculations." Consumer needs would be met, but unrealistic expectations would no longer be raised by rhetoric about "reaching and surpassing America" or "building communism." The government would encourage scientific and technological innovation, borrowing ideas and technologies from the West. Reformers and conservatives marked out their positions, and three major issues became the battlegrounds over which the future course of the Soviet Union was fought: whether to continue the policy of peaceful coexistence or revert to a tougher "anti-imperialist," "class-conscious" foreign policy; whether to rehabilitate Stalin's name or continue the Twentieth Party Congress line of destalinization; and, finally, whether to introduce reforms into the economy or preserve the basic contours of the Stalinist command economy.

Meeting the American Challenge: Vietnam

Ever since their humiliation in the Cuban missile crisis, the Soviet military commanders had been interested in a massive buildup of their military forces. If the USSR intended to meet the perceived American threat, protect its allies such as Communist North Vietnam and Cuba, hold on to its East European empire, while at the same time countering any threat in the East from a belligerent China, it had no choice, it was argued, but to rebuild and expand its army, navy, and nuclear arsenal. Those among the leadership who wanted to limit military spending argued that the low level of economic development within the country required the Soviet Union to attempt to reach arms limitations agreements with the United States and the European powers and to spend less money on arms and more on building industry, creating housing, and producing consumer goods. The debate between hard-liners and soft-liners raged for years, but several factors, some domestic, some foreign, gave the upper hand to the military. First, suspicion of the West was rampant within the military-industrial complex of the Soviet Union, and the military's power and prestige depended on the perception of a threat from the capitalist world. Second, the problem of verifying that both sides were abiding by an arms treaty was a recurrent stumbling block to agreement. Third, Brezhnev himself considered the military as one of the most stable bases of his own power and eventually gave in to their demands. Defense issues were left to the generals, and, as a Brezhnev advisor wrote, "the remaining members of the Politburo simply decided not to interfere in military matters."

About the time the Brezhnev leadership took over in Moscow, the United States began to increase its commitment to the defense of South Vietnam significantly. And the Soviet Union embarked on a more energetic policy in support of revolutionary movements and leftist governments in the Third World. The Soviet military buildup began in the 1960s and continued into the 1980s. The number of tanks increased by 40 percent, tactical air power by 25 percent, and artillery by 60 percent. Strategic forces expanded rapidly, until by the mid-1970s the Soviet Union had over 300 SS-18 medium-range missiles each equipped with ten nuclear warheads. By that time analysts could speak of strategic parity between the two superpowers.

The Soviet Union only very reluctantly became directly involved in the conflict in Vietnam. They were drawn in by the most popular national figure in Vietnam, the head of the Communist movement, Ho Chi Minh, whom Khrushchev called in his memoirs "an apostle of the Revolution." He had woven together a movement that was both Communist and nationalist, which became the major force working against French colonialism, and was the favored candidate to win the elections after the French left. But rather than concede southern Vietnam to the Communist-ruled north, the United States worked to delay the elections and establish a separate non-Communist, pro-Western state in the south. In May 1959 Ho's Vietnam Workers' Party called for armed struggle against the Saigon government and the following year set up the National Liberation Front to carry on the fight for the south. Only with the fall of Khrushchev and the American bombing of North Vietnam in February 1965 (during a visit to Hanoi by Kosygin) did the Soviet Union decide to provide military assistance to a "fraternal socialist country." Ground-to-air missiles were sent to defend the north, but the Soviets insisted that the war in the south was to be Hanoi's affair. Eventually the USSR gave Vietnam over $1.5 billion in military aid, and China gave an additional $670 million, a fraction of the 112 billion dollars that the United States spent in Vietnam. Though hard-liners in the Kremlin spoke of the United States as a global threat "worse than Hitler," Brezhnev, Kosygin, and Podgornyi argued that Vietnam was an isolated case of American aggressiveness and that the Soviet Union could cooperate with the United States in other areas, particularly in matters of strategic arms control.

In 1968 the Communist forces in the south launched the "Tet Offensive," and though they shocked the Americans with their power, they failed to overthrow the Saigon government. Nevertheless, President Lyndon Johnson decided not to increase American ground troops in Southeast Asia and deescalated the American commitment to the south. Hanoi realized that a conventional military defeat of the southern army was possible. At Easter 1972 the Communists launched a conventional attack on the southern forces but failed to overwhelm the enemy, and the Nixon administration responded by bombing Hanoi and mining Haiphong harbor. The following year the United States and North Vietnam signed the Paris Agreements, which led to the withdrawal of American combat forces from the south. The Nixon administration was itself unraveling in the aftermath of the Watergate scandal. Nixon resigned his office in August 1974 and was succeeded by Gerald Ford, who had the dismal honor of presiding over the first significant defeat of Americans in war in almost two hundred years. In April 1975, as the world watched, the last American helicopters escaped from the roof of the American Embassy in Saigon.

The Communists who entered Saigon had begun their struggle as a "people's war" on the Chinese pattern, but they had ended it as a conventional war based on Soviet operational doctrine and powered by Soviet equipment. The war in Vietnam bled the United States and gave the USSR prestige as the defender of a small Third World country attempting to liberate itself from the vestiges of colonialism. Both the Soviets and the Americans chose this distant land to prove that they were credible world powers that would and could defend their interests even very far from home.

The Defeat of Reforms

The Brezhnev leadership had inherited a society quite different from the one left by Stalin. By the mid-1960s the Soviet Union was a primarily urban society, with peasants accounting for less than thirty percent of the population. Workers were the largest single social class. The better-educated, more mobile urban population placed new demands on the state and expected more freedom, recognition of its interests, and improved material prospects. The limits of the hypercentralized Stalinist economic system had long been reached. Crude centralized planning, which worked fairly well for a more primitive economy in which quantity of output of basic products was adequate, was unable to provide for a more advanced industrial economy. As complexity grew in the economy, the inflexibility and lack of responsiveness of the planning system became a glaring problem. The needs of more sophisticated urban consumers were generally disregarded, and the distorted pricing system, which did not correspond to actual supply and demand but was dictated from on top by inadequately informed planners, made it nearly impossible to calculate the real costs of production. Though gross national product grew in the USSR at an annual rate of 5 to 6 percent in 1964–70 and industrial growth rates averaged just above 8 percent per year, there were some unsettling trends. Labor productivity rose very slowly, and the productivity of capital fell. More and more capital had to be invested over time per unit of output. The economy was operating very inefficiently. Static efficiency was about 34 percent of American efficiency; for the same inputs of capital and labor the Soviet Union received a much lower output.

For a few years after the fall of Khrushchev, Prime Minister Kosygin was powerful enough to attempt to implement significant reforms. In October 1964 he declared, "We cannot hope to exceed the high productivity reached by the most developed capitalist countries unless we increase the workers' initiative and freedom of action." By December new emphasis was placed on consumer goods, and the defense budget was reduced by 600 million rubles. Kosygin noted that even the few rights of autonomy granted earlier to industrial enterprises were "still far from being fully exercised." In March 1965 the Central Committee discussed the question of profit incentives in production and agreed to a massive increase in investments in agriculture and greater freedom for farmers. That fall Kosygin made an important speech in favor of energetic reforms in the economy, along the lines of the Liberman proposals. He called for evaluating an enterprise's worth not by its output but by its sales. The Soviet Union had huge inventories of unsold poor-quality goods. Enterprises were to be given a maximum payroll and allowed to hire whom they wanted. Profit was to be an indicator of success, and bonuses were to be given for innovation and the development of new technology. But the reforms did not go any further. Control over prices remained with the State Committee on Prices, though they were supposed to be set to cover costs and allow a small profit. Costs differed greatly, however, and prices were calculated to compensate for average costs plus a small profit. Thus, prices did not reflect true scarcities. In fact, managers were not given much freedom. Planning was always based on last year's plan and tended to be quite conservative. Managers had an incentive to keep the planned targets down, so as to be able to fulfill or overfulfill their plans. They also tended to falsify results in order to preserve their positions and satisfy the higher-ups.

The reformers in the Soviet economy wanted less state control in the economy, but they were greatly outnumbered by the stolid group of managers, who for thirty-five years had run the economy in Stalinist fashion, producing according to one rule: maximum output regardless of quality or cost. They worked in a simple way: direct command with absolute obedience from those below. The statists identified socialism with direct controls everywhere and saw the reformers, particularly those who favored market mechanisms, as antisocialist. The international environment also thwarted the reformers. Though Kosygin and Podgornyi argued in favor of expanded consumer production, emphasizing that the Soviet people had made great sacrifices in the past, they were answered in a speech by Suslov, who blamed "the imperialist powers [that] are pursuing the arms race and unleashing military aggression first in one and then in another region of the world." Such arguments played into the hands of the defense industry, which became an ever more powerful lobby in government circles. By the 1970s fundamental decisions on defense spending were being made by the military with little control from, and often without the knowledge of, the relevant civilian officials.

Unlike Kosygin, Brezhnev steadily responded to the powerful lobbies of party and military officials and was less sensitive to the needs of society. Eventually, Kosygin's reforms drained away into the sand. Instead of transforming the command economy, the Brezhnev coalition banked on science, technology, and trade with the West as the way out of economic sluggishness. Brezhnev called this "an alliance of the working class with science," and as the final humiliation Kosygin himself had to tell the Twenty-Fourth Party Congress in April 1971 that the party had rejected "all erroneous conceptions that substitute market regulation for the leading role of state-centralized planning."

The relatively liberal line of the post-Khrushchevian party leadership shifted steadily toward conservatism from the fall of 1965. Conservatives were placed in positions overseeing the intelligentsia. Rumors spread in Moscow in 1965–66 that Stalin would be restored as a positive Soviet hero, but after some delay Brezhnev decided not to take any firm decision on the Stalin question and to avoid clear evaluation of a historical record that would only divide the leadership and the population. The strategy of the Brezhnev coalition was to woo certain parts of the intelligentsia to work with the moderately modernizing regime while rejecting any radical proposals for a broad political democratization, as favored by dissidents like the physicist Andrei Sakharov and the historian Roy Medvedev, and coming down hard on those who went beyond the narrowing limits of the permissible. The first alarming sign was the arrest in September 1965 of two writers, Andrei Siniavskii and Iulii Daniel, who had published their critical and satirical works abroad under the pseudonyms Abram Terts and Nikolai Arzhak. They were tried in January 1966. Siniavskii had written a devastating critique, *On Socialist Realism*, and Daniel had tried to warn about a return to Stalinism in a satirical tale based on the idea of a national holiday during which people were allowed to murder anyone they chose without penalty. For such writings Siniavskii received a sentence of seven years and Daniel five. The trial was a serious warning that the new regime would not tolerate deviance from their rules. But the most brutal signal that reform and liberalization would be reined in came in 1968 across the Soviet border in Czechoslovakia.

Crushing the Prague Spring

Of all the East European states Czechoslovakia had been the most industrialized and the most successful democracy in the interwar years. Here the Communist Party had enjoyed a higher degree of popularity than in any other state in the region, and the Soviet Union, as the liberator of the country from the Nazis, was held in high regard by many intellectuals and workers. Yet as Soviet Stalinism blocked the moderate national road to socialism after 1948, the Czechoslovak party squandered much of its support. When economic growth began to falter in the early 1960s, political dissatisfaction followed fast behind. In 1967 the party decided on a program of economic reform, and a long discussion ensued at the top of the party that led in early January 1968 to the selection of the reformer Alexander Dubček as party leader.

Almost immediately censorship fell away, and newspapers published revealing articles about the purge trials of the 1950s, stories about discrimination

against Slovaks, and historical and political discussions about formerly forbidden topics, such as Czechoslovak democracy between the wars. The whole
country awoke politically, and hundreds of public meetings were held. The
movement was spearheaded by intellectuals, writers, scholars, and journalists;
workers and farmers were at first hesitant to join in and only later became supporters of reforms. Dubček spoke about the intimate connection of socialism
and democracy and tried to allay the fears of conservative Communists that
the popular movement was antisocialist. In April the party approved an "Action Program" to create a democratic socialist society with a full guarantee of
political freedoms and civil rights. Plans were laid for developing a pluralistic
party system, "market socialism," and a federal relationship between the Czech
lands and Slovakia. Non-Communist political parties began to form, and criticism of the Soviet Union appeared in the press. By May Day Dubček could
march through the streets of Prague and receive the genuine adulation of the
crowds. Some bold marchers carried their own signs: "With the Soviet Union
for all time, but not a day longer!" and "Long live the USSR—but at its own
expense."

Brezhnev and Soviet party conservatives grew more and more suspicious
of the Czech reformers. As "internationalists," he told a gathering of Communists,

> we cannot and never will be indifferent to the fate of socialist construction
> in other countries and to the general cause of socialism and communism on
> earth, [especially at a time when] apologists for bourgeois systems are pre-
> pared to dress up in any pseudo-socialist attire in attempting, behind the
> mask of "national forms," to shake and "soften" socialism . . . and to weaken
> the fraternal ties among the socialist countries.

The Brezhnev Doctrine proclaimed that the USSR had the right to intervene in
Soviet bloc countries to save "socialism." The Czechoslovak Central Committee tried to assure Moscow that there was no danger either to socialism or the
unity of the Warsaw Pact, but the Soviet leaders were particularly annoyed at
the public attacks on the Soviet Union and feared a form of socialism so different from the Soviet model and its effects on other members of the bloc. They
decided to end the Czechoslovak experiment in "socialism with a human face."

During the night of August 20, 1968, about a half million Soviet and Soviet-
bloc troops crossed the border into Czechoslovakia and brought the "Prague
Spring" to an end. There was almost no resistance from the Czechoslovak
Army, but crowds of ordinary citizens taunted the Soviet troops in the streets
of the cities. The Soviets arrested the Czechoslovak Politburo, then agreed to
let them remain in office, but now under Soviet surveillance. From August on,
the Soviets, who occupied the country, backed the conservative, pro-Soviet minority in the Czechoslovak party and gradually eased Dubček and the reformers from power.

The events of 1968 within Czechoslovakia demonstrated that when given
some autonomy Communist parties were able to initiate reform programs that
could win popular support. While the theory of totalitarianism argued that

such systems were incapable of change from within, the Czechoslovak experience testified that impulses for democratic change existed even within Stalinist parties. But the August invasion was stark proof of the limits of reform everywhere in the Soviet bloc as long as the conservative Brezhnev regime held power in Moscow. In the political opening of 1968 a new kind of socialism might have emerged, but the Brezhnev regime panicked at its potential outcome and chose to use military force to reinstate a monopolistic political and economic regime. Not only for Czechoslovakia but for the Soviet Union, however, 1968 was a turning point at which the socialist camp did not turn.

The effects of the August invasion were felt within the USSR most acutely by the intelligentsia. As an advisor to Brezhnev later wrote:

> Unfortunately, 1968 saw a shift to the right, at least in domestic affairs. The events in Czechoslovakia were in this sense a clear landmark, if not one of the important causes. . . . The crackdown in ideology and culture was openly proclaimed [in March], obviously under the influence of the developments in Czechoslovakia. The roots of the dissident phenomenon probably go back to this period. . . . Censorship became harsher. Many books and articles that previously would have been accepted for publication were now barred. . . . As many foresaw, the intervention in Czechoslovakia had a very negative influence on the whole course of our country's political evolution.

Once the intervention took place, in August, despair set in among much of the Soviet intelligentsia, and a significant minority turned away from the regime and into open, illegal opposition. They became the core of what the West would call the "dissident movement."

Public Opinion and Dissent

Through the years of Stalinism (1928–53) Soviet society was nearly completely dominated by the state and party. Autonomous organizations, such as free trade unions, voluntary associations, clubs, and independent political organizations, were strictly forbidden, and all aspects of social activity were controlled by official institutions. Though informal associations of friends, relatives, schoolmates, and colleagues provided refuge from the close watch of the state, there was neither a public sphere of educated discussion nor a civil society of autonomous organizations outside of state control. But in the early post-Stalin years young people and intellectuals began to organize activities outside officially sanctioned organizations. A youth culture emerged with its own styles, though the party condemned their activities as "decadence" and "hooliganism." The earliest roots of the dissident movement can be traced back to the "Secret Speech" of Khrushchev. A future dissident remembered the effect of 1956 on young people:

> Overthrown was the man who had personified the existing system and ideology to such an extent that the very words "Soviet Power" and "Stalin" seemed to have been synonymous. We all, the future rebels, at the dawn of

our youth had been fanatical Stalinists (and) had believed with a truly religious fervor. . . . Khrushchev's speech and the Twentieth Party Congress
destroyed our faith, having extracted from it its very core. The core was
Joseph Stalin, for such had been the propaganda of the preceding two and
one half decades.

Inspired by the events in Poland and Hungary, Soviet students formed radical circles in Moscow Leningrad, and other universities. They discussed current events and what they knew of the revelations of the Stalinist past. Underground journals appeared, most dedicated to ideologies that their authors
considered "true Marxism-Leninism." When the police got wind of what was
happening, they came down hard on the students, and as many as two thousand were disciplined or expelled in Leningrad alone. Sometime in 1957 or 1958
a badly translated typewritten copy of George Orwell's *1984* circulated in
Moscow. This early example of what later became known as *samizdat* (self-pub-
lishing) had a stunning impact on the few Soviet readers lucky enough to get
hold of the text. Orwell's mirror of a society based on lies and double-think
appeared just after Khrushchev's revelations about the crimes of Stalin and
helped to shake further the monolithic faith of many intellectuals. This new environment of doubt and questioning prompted a growing number of people
to begin learning how to think differently. In a real sense the mid-1950s witnessed the resumption of the history of the Russian intelligentsia, which had
been so brutally broken off during the Stalinist purges.

In the beginning the dominant call of the dissenters was for a democratic-
socialist reformism. Party liberals, like the brothers Roy and Zhores Medvedev,
brought like-minded people together in salons, secretly published political and
historical treatises against Stalinism, and nurtured a return to what they regarded as "Leninism." An eclectic collection of personalities, including Sakharov
and the then-unknown Solzhenitsyn, came together under the influence of the
socialists. Brave individuals circulated their own typed journals. In the mid-
1950s and early 1960s public poetry readings provided an alternative forum
for artistic and even political expression. They were barely tolerated by the
regime, and after increasing harassment, the readings were silenced by the police in 1961. Party conservatives defended a single Marxist-Leninist understanding of the truth and the prescribed Socialist Realist approach to art and
tried to hold the line against the new artistic and political culture that tolerated diverse views and was vitally interested in Western life. In early 1964 the
young poet Josef Brodskii was put on trial in Leningrad, accused of "para-
sitism," that is, having no useful work. At the trial the judge asked the defen-
dant, "In general what is your specialty?" Brodskii answered, "I am a poet, a
poet translator," to which the judge asked, "And who said you are a poet? Who
included you among the ranks of the poets?" Brodskii replied, "No one. And
who included me among the ranks of the human race?" He was sentenced to
five years. Years later, after he left the Soviet Union and emigrated to the United
States, Brodskii won the Nobel Prize for literature.

The Brezhnev government was prepared to repress threats to its rule, but
it attempted to use the minimum of violence and often made concessions to

protesters. The arrest and trial of Siniavskii and Daniel in 1965–66 ushered in a prolonged and uneven struggle between the orthodox defenders of official views and the more liberal and radical elements among the intellectuals. Two hundred students from Siniavskii's institute protested his arrest on December 5, 1965, Soviet Constitution Day, with a demonstration on Pushkin Square in the heart of the capital. This was the first demonstration not sanctioned by the state in Moscow since the 1920s. Later this day became the annual occasion for dissident demonstrations, as they moved beyond the limits of Soviet legality. In 1965 a large demonstration was organized by patriotic activists in Erevan, the capital of Soviet Armenia, on the occasion of the fiftieth anniversary of the Armenian genocide. Soon after, Moscow removed the top Armenian party leader, but rather than cracking down hard on Armenian nationalism Moscow conceded the deep wound that Armenians felt, sanctioned official demonstrations on subsequent anniversaries, and eventually allowed construction of a monument to the victims. The Kremlin cracked down harder on Ukrainian nationalists, twenty of whom were jailed in 1965–66, and on organized political groups that claimed to be "true Marxists."

The Soviet smashing of the Czechoslovak experiment in socialism with a human face dealt a blow to the socialist sympathies of many dissidents and divided the movement between liberals and humanists at one pole and nationalists, chauvinists, and even fascists at the other. Dissidents organized a protest on Red Square, unfurling banners that proclaimed "Long live free and independent Czechoslovakia." "Almost immediately," a participant recalled,

> a whistle blew and plainclothes KGB men rushed at us from all corners of the square. . . . They ran up shouting "They're all Jews!" "Beat the anti-Sovietists!" We sat quietly and did not resist. They tore the banners from our hands . . . [and beat us]. They shouted at us, "Disperse, you scum!" But we remained sitting.

One of those arrested later wrote, "All my conscious life I have wanted to be a citizen—that is, a person who proudly and calmly speaks his mind. For ten minutes, I was a citizen."

The dissidents were a small minority of the population. Most professionals and intellectuals, who directed the political, cultural, and economic life of the country, had become a materially privileged subelite just under the top political leaders. The Soviet middle class was generally optimistic about the soundness and the radiant future of the Soviet system in the 1950s and 1960s. Though they complained about shortages and inefficiencies, lack of freedom, and the low quality of material life, they could observe that their own lives improved materially over time. They might blame individual leaders, for example, Khrushchev in the early 1960s, for the inadequacies of the system, but their faith in the basic principles of the system remained firm. Optimism about material achievements went along with a sense of the superiority of the Soviet system to Western capitalism, a patriotic pride in scientific successes like sputnik or the flight of Yuri Gagarin, and a conviction that Soviet leaders had the best interests of the people at heart.

But by the late 1960s intellectuals began to experience pessimism more widely, and the regime found it harder to pressure and manipulate the attitudes of the intelligentsia. Pessimism spread quickly from the intelligentsia to the middle strata of Soviet society, and consumers lost their conviction that their living standard would rise. Food shortages in the mid-1970s seemed to confirm the sense that the country was not going anywhere. The increasing acceptance of a degree of corruption, the need to engage in bribery, and willingness to "rip off the system" was connected with a growing alienation from the regime. "It is a crime not to steal from them," people claimed; "all they do is steal from us." By the 1970s the earlier idealism and humanism of many believers in the system turned perceptibly toward cynicism and frustration and was reflected in apathetic attitudes toward work and a laissez-faire attitude toward the illegal "second economy." Still, many believed in the principles of socialism as identified with the Soviet system and thought it a superior system to immoral, money-dominated capitalism. A faint hope for future improvement and reform remained intact until the last few years of Gorbachev's rule.

Inspired by the Israeli victory over the Arab states in the Six-Day War (1967), some Soviet Jews began to petition the government to emigrate to Israel. Though the great majority of Jews were neither religious nor fervently Zionist, the widespread social anti-Semitism and the pervasive discrimination against Jews, which included quotas for entry into university and restricted access to certain occupations, convinced many that their future was bleak in the Soviet Union. The Brezhnev regime did little to combat the ever more visible manifestations of anti-Semitism in society and the state apparatus. Year by year the number of Jews who opted out of the Soviet system and struggled to emigrate, the so-called refusniks, increased. Responding to pressure from the West, the Soviet government eventually permitted more than 230,000 Jews to emigrate.

Though socialist dissidents, such as the Medvedevs, believed in a purified Leninism, theirs became a minority voice within the movement. Increasingly pronounced were more liberal, conservative, and nationalist views. Solzhenitsyn desired a return to prerevolutionary values, or what he called "ethical socialism." Liberals, like the physicist Andrei Sakharov, opposed the monopoly of power of the Communist Party and favored the rule of law, respect for basic human rights, and intellectual freedom. While the official state ideology constantly droned on about the harmony between the party and the people, dissidents spoke of the possibility, even the need, for tension and conflict between public authority and individual consciousness. The ideal citizen, in their view, was not unconditionally obedient but an active, autonomous participant in political affairs. The liberal and democratic ideas of many intellectuals were tempered by the widespread doubts about the democratic potential of the Soviet masses and their ability to govern themselves. The novelist Vasilii Grossman wrote, "Where is the epoch of the free Russian human soul? When will it at last come? Maybe it will never come, never." While another dissident spoke of the need for "the knout," claiming that "there is no other way with our people," others, like Sakharov, were more optimistic and believed that only freedom would "squeeze the slave out of the Russian people," under the guidance of the intelligentsia. In his fascinating memoirs, the dissident Vladimir Bukovskii, who grew up in a working-class district of Moscow where fists and curses were the currency of exchange between young boys, tells of his doubts about "proletarian culture":

> To us who had grown up in the communal apartments and backyards of this selfsame proletariat, living among them as equals, not masters, the term "proletarian culture" sounded grotesque. For us, it meant no mystical secret, but drunkenness, brawling, knife fights, obscenity, and chewing sunflower seeds. No true proletarian would have called this culture, because the distinguishing feature of the proletariat was a hatred of all culture, combined with a sort of inexplicable envy. Culture was a witch they stoned. "Intellectual" was an insult hissed venomously by your neighbors.

At the end of the 1960s and into the 1970s a dissident critique of the Soviet system from a conservative, neo-Stalinist, and Russian nationalist position began to emerge in some circles. Growing out of a general mood among intellectuals of nostalgia for the Russian past and love for an idealized and lost Russian village, writers sentimentalized the authenticity of the Russian peasant. Short-story writers turned to rural themes, celebrating nature and Siberia. Out of this relatively benign affection for things Russian came more ferocious fears about the loss of what was genuinely Russian at the hands of "alien" elements, which, in their minds, included the Jews, the Bolsheviks, foreigners, and Western influences. The new KGB chief appointed in 1967, Yuri Andropov, tried to manage the dissident problem through a policy that might be called "soft repression." This involved imprisonment or incarceration in mental hospitals of the most recalcitrant dissidents and refusniks and the export abroad of key figures, like Solzhenitsyn. While dissidents were always in danger of arrest and exile, an ominous "official nationalism" began to pervade state-sponsored journals and organizations. Several writers called for a more Russian orientation to state policy and greater distance from the West. The Central Committee itself, particularly its propaganda apparatus, was divided on these issues. In November 1972 the acting head of the Propaganda Department, Aleksandr Yakovlev, published a long article in which he condemned the attempt to bring back the past and castigated evidence of "Russophilism" in intellectual life. Brezhnev personally reprimanded Yakovlev for his strong antinationalist position (even though it was consistent with Lenin's own position) and sent him off for ten years as ambassador to Canada. With confusion at the top and no clear line against nationalism, Russian nationalism continued to grow within the state and party apparatus, as well as among Russian writers and artists.

By the middle of the 1970s the dissident movement was split between the chauvinist right and the liberal left. The West celebrated the human rights movement and the circles formed to monitor the Helsinki Accords of 1975, but such groups were small in number and largely isolated from the broad population. Only the nationalists, particularly among non-Russian peoples, and evangelical sects, like the Pentecostals and Seventh-Day Adventists, could claim broad support. Much of the Soviet population remained indifferent to the dissidents' critiques and to politics in general. By the early 1980s the government's crackdowns had largely dispersed the dissident movement. Many of its leaders lived in foreign exile or were in labor camps. But feeble as many of their efforts must have seemed at times, their voices had managed to crack the great silence that had enveloped Soviet society. A beacon of rationality and humanism, Sakharov managed to defend his fellow dissidents and express a message of democratic renewal from his enforced exile to the Volga city of Gorky. The views of the dissidents would gain a new power with the renewal of reform efforts in the Gorbachev years.

Agriculture

The Brezhnev leadership did not tinker and experiment with agriculture as Khrushchev had, but it maintained his efforts to reclaim land, modernize animal husbandry, and expand the production of chemical fertilizers. The government laid to rest Khrushchev's pet project of growing corn wherever possible and the Virgin Lands Program as well. Attention was directed toward agricultural development in central Russia. Brezhnev had to overcome the antirural biases among many party leaders in order to continue Khrushchev's policy of gradually increasing the percentage of capital investment in agriculture. Because Khrushchev had elevated so many people interested in agriculture into positions of power, Brezhnev was able to forge a stable coalition of party officials in favor of higher agricultural investment. His administration raised material incentives for farmers, and within a few years the costs of production in farming were covered, for the first time since 1928, by the prices set for farm products. By the end of the 1970s, 27 percent of the capital investment budget of the Soviet Union went to agriculture, a figure twice as high as investment in the 1950s, and it continued to grow. In contrast, the United States, with its much higher agricultural yields, put only 5 percent of its total investment into agriculture.

Despite periodic setbacks due to weather, Soviet agricultural output grew from 1951 to 1975 at an annual rate of 3.4 percent, compared to only 1.6 percent for American agricultural output during the same period. Total meat production in the Soviet Union doubled from the early 1950s to the late 1970s. But the rate of agricultural growth was slowing down. With slower population growth agriculture could not grow through expansion, only through intensification. Compared to the United States, Soviet agriculture was unimpressive. American farming was much more mechanized than the labor-intensive Soviet agriculture. In the United States only 4.6 percent of the total labor force worked in agriculture, while in the USSR 25.4 percent were on the farms. Though it absorbed over a quarter of investment and employed one quarter of Soviet labor, and despite its larger area in cultivated land, Soviet agriculture produced one-sixth less in output value than the United States.

The problems of the rural economy were chronic and deeply imbedded in the collective farm system inherited from Stalin. First, it was over-centralized and over-bureaucratized. Orders came from above, from bureaucrats, on what to plant, when to harvest, and what fertilizers to use. Farmers had little discretion and control over their farming operations. Second, the farms were too large, often involving several villages and hundreds of households. Third, labor was poorly organized and largely unskilled. Farmers were organized into brigades or sections that were moved around the farm to do various tasks. Payment for work was based on work completed rather than on the quality of the work or the actual output achieved. Thus, remuneration was not connected to the results of labor, only to time put in. This had a baleful effect on production. Fourth, though there was no shortage of hands in the countryside for field work, there was a chronic shortage of mechanics and operators of complex machines. Equipment was of poor quality, and machines frequently broke down and lay idle. In addition, roads were often impassable during the rainy or snowy seasons. Everywhere there was waste and spoilage. Finally, the pricing system was simply irrational. Prices were set by the government, not by the market, and procurement prices were not related to scarcities or demand. The prices varied regionally and from farm to farm, but the more efficient farms were paid at a lower rate than the less productive farms, thus discouraging improvements in productivity. The world observed as the Soviets were forced to buy grain abroad in early 1972 and for many years thereafter. The severe drought of 1975 led peasants to slaughter their livestock because they had no grain to feed them.

By the early 1980s the collective farm peasantry made up only 12.5 percent of the Soviet population. Working in the over-bureaucratized agricultural economy, with little effective control over agricultural production and output and few incentives, the collective farmers were demoralized and unproductive. Though they had been brought into the social welfare system and were better compensated for their produce in the post-Stalin years, some 10 million left the farms for the cities from 1959 to 1979. Those who remained were in general better educated than their parents had been, but less well schooled than townspeople. Often they worked perfunctorily on the collective farms and directed their energies toward their family farm plots from which fruits, vegetables, and flowers were grown either to be consumed by the family or sold in urban markets for additional income.

Brezhnev Ascendant

At first the collective leadership of the post-Khrushchev Presidium remained relatively balanced. Brezhnev consulted constantly with his colleagues and made no radical proposals. Stability was the watchword of the day. But he managed to edge out all major rivals for supreme power. At the end of 1965 Brezhnev removed Nikolai Podgornyi as Central Committee secretary and kicked him upstairs to replace Mikoyan as the honorary head of state. Twelve years later Brezhnev himself unceremoniously replaced Podgornyi and made himself head of both party and state. Though Kosygin remained prime minister and a member of the Politburo until just before his death at the end of 1980, he had been eclipsed by Brezhnev, and the two men were personally hostile to one another. By the time of the Twenty-Third Party Congress in March–April 1966, Brezhnev was clearly the paramount figure in Soviet politics. There was so little discussion at the Congress that one political analyst called it "the congress of silences." The Stalin question was not reopened, and that silence meant that the neo-Stalinists had not been able to win over the top leadership and that destalinization was to be pushed no further. Practically the only achievement of the Congress was the restoration of the name Politburo for the highest party organ and the title general secretary for Brezhnev.

Brezhnev's longevity as head of the Communist Party can be accounted for by his shrewd policy of rewards to the ruling elite in the Soviet Union. His principal gift to the ruling class was stability and long tenure in office. The leadership aged over the eighteen years of Brezhnev's reign. Most of the top leaders were over seventy by the end of the 1970s and had been in power much of their mature life. Sixty-one percent of the voting members of the Central Committee of 1961 that were still alive in 1971 were reelected to the Central Committee. Eighty-one percent of the living members of the Central Committee in 1966 remained members in 1971, and 89 percent of the Central Committee of 1971 were reelected in 1976. By 1976 the average age of a Central Committee member was sixty years. As for lower-level officials, that is, the factory managers and regional leaders, Brezhnev did not dismiss them as frequently as Khrushchev had for not fulfilling plans or for poor performance; instead, he made it clear that he trusted the "remarkable commanders of production" and understood the difficulties they faced.

As he grew older and more self-satisfied, Brezhnev gave in to his indulgence for medals, prizes, and titles of all sorts. Jokes circulated in the Soviet Union that if Brezhnev received any more medals he would have to have an operation to have his chest expanded. In 1976 he was given the military rank of marshall of the Soviet Union. He happily accepted expensive gifts from his underlings and enjoyed a fleet of Western automobiles. An anecdote tells of Brezhnev's mother visiting her son and worrying about the luxuries and lavish manner in which he lived. "What's the matter, mother?" Brezhnev asked. "But, Lyonya," she asked, "what will you do if the Bolsheviks return?"

Social Changes in the Era of Stagnation

Whatever economic slowdown the Soviet Union was about to suffer in the early 1970s, it gained a reprieve for a number of years with the oil embargo of 1973–74 organized by the oil-producing (OPEC) nations. Both oil and gold prices increased by five fold, and the Soviet Union was rich in both. The negative effect of the sudden riches from exports of natural resources was that reform seemed unnecessary and domestic development of consumer industries could be deflected while finished goods were imported from the West and East and paid for in the newly earned hard currency. In the 1970s Brezhnev's economic policy included cutting back light industry and consumer goods production, and investing more in agriculture while protecting the defense sector. Defense

Figure 19.1. Leonid Brezhnev and German Chancellor Willi Brandt toast each other, May 18, 1973 (BLACK STAR).

spending expanded in 1974–75 as new strategic weapons were deployed. Brezhnev also wanted to develop Siberia and pushed for the construction of a major railroad, the Baikal-Amur Magistral (BAM), a huge project of Stalinist magnitude. Since he needed Western technology to develop the Soviet economy, Brezhnev combined military buildup with a policy of political détente with the West.

The Soviet Union had become a primarily urban society in the early 1960s. Whereas fifty years earlier only 26.3 million people lived in towns, by 1974 six times as many (153 million) were town or city dwellers. Whereas fifty years earlier only two cities, Moscow and Leningrad, had more than 1 million inhabitants, by 1974 there were thirteen such cities. Moreover, Soviet cities were now desirable places to live, with safe streets and more goods and services than in the countryside and smaller towns. Millions flocked from the countryside to enjoy the higher standard of living in the cities. The government restricted spontaneous migration to cities and required that Soviet citizens be registered officially to live there. Though improvements in housing were marked—40 percent of Soviet families shared their apartments or bathrooms with others in the early Brezhnev years, but by 1975 over 70 percent of worker and employee families lived in unshared apartments—housing shortages persisted.

Far poorer than most Western societies, Soviet society was generally more egalitarian. Wage differentials diminished during the post-Stalin period, and economic equality grew. If one compared the ratio of average earnings of the top 10 percent of the population to the bottom 10 percent, in the United States that ratio in 1968 was 6.7 (that is, the income of the top 10 percent was on the average 6.7 times as great as the bottom 10 percent). In Eastern Europe that ratio was 3. In the USSR it was 4.4 in 1956, 3.7 in 1964, and 3.2 in 1970. Though money was far less important than whom you knew and what position you occupied, workers' wages grew much more rapidly than the salaries of managers and professionals, and farmers did best of all in the early Brezhnev years. Significant differences remained, however, between those who enjoyed special privileges (e.g., special stores, hotels, access to goods and information) and those who did not. Still, inequality of wealth was far less than in the United States, where (in 1983) 10 percent of American families (7.5 million households) owned 84 percent of the nation's assets and the top 1 percent alone (840,000 households) owned 50 percent of the country's wealth.

Sitting securely at the top of Soviet society was the dominant political and managerial elite, sometimes referred to as the nomenklatura (meaning that they were appointees selected by the party leaders from special lists of preferred persons). Brezhnev guaranteed these appointed officials long tenure in office, and with less control from the center they often exercised arbitrary power and engaged in extralegal and corrupt practices. Accountable to their superiors rather than to their constituents, this conservative, entrenched, well-educated, and privileged group of top party officials and regional secretaries made up a separate upper class of privilege and power.

In Soviet understanding the urban labor force in the early 1980s was the largest segment of the population (around two-thirds). The well over 80 million people who made up the working class, as defined by Soviet statistics, included some 31 million industrial workers as well as white-collar workers. Soviet workers were poorly paid, except for the highly skilled, but they enjoyed almost complete job security. Stalinism had essentially eliminated unemployment, and the USSR faced instead a permanent shortage of labor. Though not everyone was gainfully employed and thousands were in dead-end jobs—watching the escalators in the subways, for example—once a person had a job it was almost impossible to be fired from it. Embedded in an elaborate social welfare system that promised free education, free medical care, and cheap housing, as well as low taxes, Soviet workers were at the same time faced with inadequate supplies of goods and poor housing, which kept their living standards down. The quality of the services they received was uniformly poor. Labor productivity remained low, and as a familiar Soviet bloc joke told it, the workers "pretended to work and the authorities pretended to pay them." Because people wanted to improve themselves and move out of the working class and the peasantry, many signs of deep job dissatisfaction were evident. Thirty percent of Soviet workers changed jobs every year. Crime increased, along with child abuse, divorce, and alcoholism, and mortality rates rose while life expectancy declined. People's health and diet suffered. The Soviet Union led the world in alcohol consumption per capita.

Part of the bargain struck by the Communist Party in the Stalin and post-Stalin years was that the Soviet regime would eventually deliver the goods and life would become easier. But that bargain could never be fulfilled fast enough, at least not for the entire population. Though it was the second largest economy in the world, the Soviet Union per-capita consumption of food was about one-half to three-quarters of what it was in advanced Western countries. Soviet citizens ate much higher levels of carbohydrates, particularly bread and potatoes, and much less meat, fresh fruit, and vegetables than their counterparts in the West. Hunger was not a problem for most, but the chronic shortages of goods required consumers to stand in endless lines, waste much time in searching out scarce products, and buy in bulk and hoard what they did find. Interested in bettering their lives materially, young people especially spent time and money looking for the latest Western books, records, fashionable clothes, and electronic equipment. Despite the high rates of upward mobility from one class to another in the past, by the Brezhnev years it became more difficult for people to move out of their class. The society was frozen, though parents tried to pass their privileges on to their children. Basically, Stalinism and the post-Stalinist bureaucratic economic system had created an educated, mobile, expectant society. But the possibility of realizing one's ambitions, of fully expressing ones opinions and interests was precluded given the undemocratic political order and the petrified ideology of Marxism-Leninism.

Though the Soviet state was committed to a full program of social security for its citizens, its intentions and its practices did not always coincide. And there was a palpable decline in the delivery of services. The state-controlled trade unions administered many aspects of the welfare system. Male workers were eligible for retirement benefits by age 60, after 25 years of service; women at 55, after 20 years of employment. By the mid-1970s more than 19 million people were receiving old-age pensions, but many of them were abysmally poor. All areas of medicine were part of the state system under the Ministry of Public Health. Everything from prenatal care to doctors' visits to long-term hospitalization was covered. In the post-Stalin period abortions were relegalized, free of cost (or social stigma), and used as the principal means of birth control. With the largest number of physicians in the world, the Soviet Union excelled in its quick responses to medical emergencies and home visits. Mothers were granted pregnancy and maternity leaves, and daycare was provided free of charge to children of working parents. Yet the level of healthcare was generally acknowledged as being below the standards of developed capitalist nations. A hierarchy of medical facilities provided better care for privileged groups and foreigners, and dismal clinics served the ordinary population. Drugs were free but difficult to obtain, and the black market flourished everywhere. Quality medical care, ostensibly free, could often be secured with bribes. Rather than take chances in the public health system, many preferred to pay doctors privately. Daycare facilities were often inadequate, though the availability and quality of the personnel compared favorably with the United States. As the Brezhnev government failed to finance the social welfare system adequately, its decline accelerated.

The most dramatic indicator of both the success and failure of the Soviet medical system can be found in the statistics for life expectancy. Dramatic advances since the revolution had increased life expectancy for women by the mid-1960s from 33 years to 74, and for men from 31 to 66. The Soviet regime had taught peasants who had never heard of the germ theory about simple hygiene. Infant mortality fell from 268.6 per 1,000 infants dying before the age of one to 22.9 by 1971. However, at the end of the 1960s life expectancy, particularly for males, began to decline, and infant mortality began to rise. As a result, the Soviets stopped publishing the relevant statistics. The widespread use of alcohol, the unaddressed damage to the environment, and inadequate food supplies and medical attention all contributed to a reversal of the long-term improvement in Soviet health. By the mid-1980s these figures had improved somewhat. Infant mortality, for example, was at 26 per 1,000 live births by 1985. This compared unfavorably, however, with European averages (24 per 1,000 in 1979) and American (10.6 per 1,000).

Education, which was constitutionally guaranteed as a right of the people, and free through the university years to those qualified, was one of the great successes of the Soviet experiment. One out of three Soviet citizens, more than 100 million people, were enrolled in some kind of educational institution during the Brezhnev period. Illiteracy, a major scourge of tsarist Russia, had effectively been eliminated, and Soviet educators aimed to achieve secondary education for the whole population. Soviet education was traditionally rigorous and emphasized science, mathematics, command of hard information, and memorization. At the same time, at all levels political education in Marxism–Leninism was required, and the social sciences as well as humanistic studies were taught from the official Soviet Marxist perspective. Much learning was by rote, and critics charged that creative and critical thinking was not encouraged. The best students could go on to one of the sixty universities or eight hundred higher technical schools. From these institutions, which were topped by an array of purely research institutions and capped by the Academy of Sciences, emerged the largest scientific-technological intelligentsia in the world.

While private businesses were not officially permitted before 1985, black marketeers stole from the state sector and sold goods at great profit. In order to live a reasonable life, tens of millions of Soviet citizens engaged in activities that were technically illegal; they might, for example, pass on scarce products to friends rather than selling them to the first customers or hire carpenters privately to build an extension on to their apartment or pay bribes to officials for admission to a medical school. The corruption was especially widespread in the Caucasian and Central Asian republics, where local party leaders controlled the patronage system and lived lavishly on payoffs from their underlings. Repeated efforts to break up these ethnic mafias generally failed, but the pervasive nature of the corruption was a major factor in the call for reform after Brezhnev's death.

While family and ethnicity remained primary focuses of identity for Soviet citizens, religion also played a part in the life of many. Some Western estimates hold that as many as one-third of Soviets were practicing believers in the 1980s. Though the official ideology of the state was atheistic, religion was tolerated, and approximately 8,000 churches, 5,400 Protestant communities, 1,200 mosques, and 60 synagogues operated in the USSR during the Brezhnev era. Unadmitted discrimination against Jews continued under Khrushchev and Brezhnev, and a general condescension by the nominally Christian peoples toward Muslims was widespread. Religious feeling remained strong among

Lithuanian Catholics and various evangelical groups that actively resisted restrictions on their practices. For many others religion was intimately tied to ethnic culture. Armenians revered their Catholicos, the head of their national Christian church, more as a leader of the nation than as a religious figure. Muslims who did not attend the mosque regularly nevertheless identified themselves with an Islamic community and way of life. Sometimes the most secular of citizens would observe various religious rituals and rites of passage, such as a ceremony of marriage or burial, which were conducted according to religious traditions and with the participation of clerics.

Just as in peasant Russia, so in the urban Soviet Union the family remained the center of life. In cities families were very small, usually with only one child, because of cramped housing. By the 1980s Russia's birthrate, like that of Estonia and other western republics, was barely replacing the population, while among Muslims in the east and south large families were common. Young married couples very often had to live with their parents and endure all the tensions generated by such multigenerational families. Grandparents acted as baby-sitters while both parents worked. Great respect was generally paid to the elderly in the Soviet Union, particularly in such traditional societies as Abkhazia (in western Georgia) where the most long-lived people reached record ages of well over one hundred. In general families absorbed the burden of caring for the elderly, and relatively few were sent to old-age homes. But many old people who were left without caring relatives received very low pensions from the state and found themselves among the poorest people in the Soviet Union.

Figure 19.2. A Georgian family having a picnic. Photograph by Stephanie Maze, 1985 (SOVFOTO/TASS).

As the state retreated from full control of social activity, informal organizations were formed. Interest in religion, national culture, and folk arts and performance flourished. Many young people turned their focus toward personal development through such diverse activities as yoga and bodybuilding. Private and personal life, friends and relatives, shielded individuals from the constant intrusions of officialdom. Soviet sociologists noted the development of public opinion that shaped attitudes independently of official propaganda. The growing youth culture and artistic movements, along with the dissident movement, were signs of the emergence of a multifaceted public life—some would say civil society— in the Soviet Union, but by the 1980s that society had no place to go. A deep, dull, persistent conflict developed between the stagnant state structure and the society created by the system. Pressure for greater social autonomy and less interference from the state was building up. But the heavy weight of the party and government, reinforced by the ever-present police, muffled the political expression of the desire for more public space and freedom.

By the early 1980s the Brezhnevian system was grinding to a halt. The long years of his reign had been characterized, on the political level, by a deep conservatism, an unwillingness to reform, a remarkable stability in leadership, and a vigorous and confident military and foreign policy. But on a deeper social and economic level the enormous changes that continued to affect Soviet society were also undermining the political system and the economic machine that had pushed the population into ever less satisfying labors. This deep conservatism of the administrative command system was the fundamental legacy of Stalinism that subsequent reforms had been unable to dislodge. A Soviet joke of the period related that Stalin, Khrushchev, and Brezhnev were sitting in a train that suddenly stopped. Nothing seemed able to make it move again. "Shoot the driver," shouted Stalin. Still the train did not move. "Tell the driver's mate that Communism is just around the corner," shouted Khrushchev. Still the train stood still. Brezhnev then suggested: "Let's pull down the blinds and pretend the train is moving."

Détente and the Arms Race

For Westerners suspicious of Soviet peace initiatives, the invasion of Czechoslovakia was proof positive of Communist expansionism. For Soviet hard-liners the American continuation of the Vietnam War in Southeast Asia demonstrated the dangers from the imperialist powers. Relations with China had deteriorated to the point that the Chinese had made territorial claims on Soviet territory, and in March 1969 fighting between the two largest Communist states broke out briefly on the Ussuri River. The fragility of the eastern borders of the Soviet Union made improvements in relations with the West even more imperative, and Brezhnev and his foreign minister, Andrei Gromyko, pushed ahead for high-level contacts with the United States and for lessening of tensions in Europe. On August 12, 1970, the Soviet Union and the Federal Republic of Germany (FRG) signed a Renunciation of Force Treaty, recognizing the inviolability of borders and leaving aside for the moment the question of

Berlin. A year later, on September 3, 1971, the four powers signed an agreement on Berlin, which gave neither Germany sovereignty over the city, kept the Great Powers involved in its overall fate, and normalized access to and from its territory. Essentially the agreement removed Berlin as a flash point in East-West relations. First on the continent and then between the superpowers, the era of détente was opening.

The buildup on both sides of the Cold War continued through the late 1960s into the 1970s but in an atmosphere of considerably reduced tensions. In 1968 the USSR launched a nuclear submarine equivalent to the Polaris, while the United States was already updating the weapons on their submarines. Two years later the Americans introduced the first multiple warheads on their missiles, the so-called MIRVs, while the Soviets took another five years before they deployed their first multiwarhead missile. Though both sides continued to stockpile weapons and spend their treasure on developing and deploying ever more sophisticated and deadly weaponry, the costs of the arms race impressed politicians on both sides enough to begin Strategic Arms Limitation Talks (SALT) in November 1969. Less than three years later, in May 1972, Brezhnev and Nixon signed the SALT I Treaty in Moscow, the first major arms limitation treaty between the superpowers. Though the USSR was left with 2,400 missile launchers and the United States with only 1,700, the Americans still had more accurate and reliable ICBMs, better submarine-launched missiles and submarines, more and heavier bombers, superior MIRV technology, more warheads, and allied bases around the Soviet Union. Understanding that the SALT I gave no particular advantage to the Soviet Union and established strategic parity between the two countries, the U.S. Senate ratified the treaty.

The constant negotiations between the United States and the Soviet Union in the next several years stand in marked contrast to the colder years of the Cold War when negotiations were considered appeasement. Détente meant discussion of outstanding differences and gradually was extended beyond questions of arms control to economic exchanges. Brezhnev and Nixon came to a far-reaching trade agreement in 1972, which promised an increase in East-West commerce. Brezhnev visited the United States that year. In June 1973 the superpowers agreed to consult whenever there was a potential danger of nuclear war. But at the same time, Nixon and his secretary of state, Henry Kissinger, were interested in "opening" China and sought to develop a relationship with the USSR's giant, hostile rival. In the summer of 1971 Kissinger made a secret journey to Beijing that soon resulted in American recognition of the Chinese Communist government. Even after the fall of Nixon in the summer of 1974, however, détente continued with the Ford administration, in which Kissinger remained as secretary of state. In November 1974 Brezhnev met Ford at Vladivostok in the Soviet Far East, and the USSR accepted the principle that both sides should have an equal number of nuclear launchers.

Détente worked well for the USSR. It created a relatively stable international environment in which the Soviets could expand their military power and at the same time attempt to develop their economy without significant reform. Improved relations with the West allowed for scientific, technological, and economic exchange. At the Conference on Security and Cooperation in Europe (CSCE) in Helsinki in August 1975, a moment that might be considered the apogee of international détente, the European states, the Soviet Union, Canada, and the United States agreed to preserve the post-1945 borders in Europe and to protect human rights in the signatory states. But the world had been transformed significantly for the United States in the mid-1970s. After the humiliation in Vietnam, many Americans experienced a crisis of confidence, and support for détente rapidly withered. Even Kissinger, one of its principal architects, abandoned the concept, at least in his public rhetoric. President Jimmy Carter, elected in 1976, was torn between those in his administration, like Secretary of State Cyrus Vance, who hoped to continue détente and solve major international problems such as the Arab-Israeli conflict, and those, like his national security advisor and former sovietologist, Zbigniew Brzezinski, who was far more suspicious of Soviet intentions and believed that the United States had to gain a strategic advantage over the USSR.

While the Cold War, often referred to as "the balance of terror," stabilized relations in Europe, the less-developed Third World became the new arena for Soviet-American confrontation. Nineteen and a half of the 20 million battle deaths in the world from World War II until the end of the Cold War occurred in the Third World. Encouraged by the more radical Cubans, the Soviets airlifted Cuban forces to southern Africa, where they fought alongside local Marxist guerrillas to establish a left-wing regime in Angola. A Marxist-led revolution in Ethiopa overthrew the Emperor Haile Selassie and brought to power an extremely radical government, which the Soviets then supported. In April 1978 Marxists in the military overthrew the government in Afghanistan and forged an alliance with the Soviet Union. In the Middle East the Soviet Union backed the Palestinian cause against the Israelis and became the major supporter of radical Arab states. The United States lost one of its major allies in January 1979 when radical Muslims under the Ayatollah Khomeini defeated the repressive forces of the shah of Iran. Closer to home, in Grenada, El Salvador, and Nicaragua, leftist forces took power or threatened pro-American regimes.

The perception was widespread in the West that the Soviets were gaining the advantage in the era of détente. Americans suffered from what was known as the "post-Vietnam syndrome," a reluctance to commit its armed forces abroad, and, indeed, while Carter was president, no American was killed in hostile foreign combat. Détente limped along until the end of the 1970s. American conservatives warned of the progressive weakening of American military strength, and public concern about Soviet treatment of dissidents and restrictions on Jewish emigration led to the Jackson-Vanik amendment, which linked improvement in trade relations to Soviet emigration policy. Carter and Brezhnev met in Vienna and signed the SALT II agreement, but the president was unable to convince the Senate to ratify the treaty.

Relations between the superpowers deteriorated at the end of the 1970s as the arms race heated up. As Brzezinski's influence over the president waxed and Vance's waned, the United States more forcefully pursued improvement of its relations with China, which under Deng Xiaoping's leadership had begun economic reforms in the direction of a market economy. In 1979 the United States recognized the Communist government as the only government of China, thus ending its support of the two-China policy. When the Soviets deployed a new missile, the SS-20, targeted at Europe, the United States gave in to pressure from its European allies to deploy Pershing II and cruise missiles in Western Europe. But the heaviest blow to Soviet-American relations came on Christmas Eve 1979, when the Soviet Army moved into Afghanistan to shore up the Marxist government, which was threatened internally by division and from without by Muslim resistance.

Two Crises: Afghanistan and Poland

Afghanistan had had generally peaceful and friendly relations with the Soviet Union, ever since King Amanullah concluded agreements with Lenin's government in the early 1920s. In April 1978 leftist army officers seized power and brought a Marxist government to Kabul. The coup was not the result of Soviet initiative, but the USSR backed the new regime. As the Afghans under President Nur Muhammad Taraki attempted reforms that challenged traditional tribal, patriarchal, and Islamic authority, rebellion and resistance spread through the countryside. The Soviets increased their military presence in the country, bringing the number of troops up to about seven thousand. But in September 1979, when Taraki attempted to remove his radical prime minister, Hafizullah Amin, Amin turned the tables on him; he seized power and had Taraki killed. As the Afghan regime became more militant, Brezhnev decided to overthrow Amin and establish a more moderate Marxist regime. Soviet troops entered Afghanistan on December 24. Amin was killed in the fighting, and the Soviet Union was deeply mired in a vicious interethnic and civil war.

The Soviet move into Afghanistan and the American response effectively buried détente. Carter called the crisis over Afghanistan the greatest danger to world peace since World War II and responded by imposing a grain embargo on the USSR and ordering an American boycott of the forthcoming Moscow Olympics. The Soviet Army was unable to crush the Muslim opposition, even with the help of a brutal Afghan police force. One hundred thousand Soviet troops fought in Afghanistan, while the Muslims were aided by the Central Intelligence Agency of the United States in cooperation with China and Pakistan. By the time the last Soviet soldiers were withdrawn from Afghanistan almost ten years later, in February 1989, fifteen thousand Soviet soldiers had been killed, Afghanistan had been devastated, and hundreds of thousands of Afghans were dead, maimed, or living in exile in Pakistan. After the Soviets left, the civil war raged on between moderate and more radical Muslims. In October 1996 a movement known as Taliban, formed by provincial students, took Kabul, executed the last Communist ruler, and proclaimed a strictly Islamic state.

Late in 1980 and early in 1981 the Soviet Union faced a political crisis in Poland, where a massive trade union movement, Solidarity, was challenging the authority of the ruling Communist Party. Soviet leaders threatened to use force if the Polish government could not control the situation. In December 1981 the party leadership cracked down on Solidarity and imposed martial law. The Polish Communists, having lost the support of the broad masses of the population and now facing an independent labor movement, relied on the army and the backing of the USSR to keep power. The Polish crisis revealed to the world the underlying weakness of Soviet power in its East European empire and the fragility of the European Communist regimes outside the USSR. The people of the empire were no longer willing to acquiesce to the unpopular regimes and obey without question. At the same time Communists both in the Soviet-bloc countries and within the USSR were faltering in their rule, losing confidence and conviction in their ideology and right to rule. As Brezhnev himself grew weaker and more incoherent, the Soviet leadership, the system, and the empire all appeared to be suffering from hardening of the arteries. The stage was set for political transformation on both sides of the Soviet border.

Suggestions for Further Reading

The Brezhnev period has been a fertile field for Western political science. Besides Breslauer, *Khrushchev and Brezhnev as Leaders* (1982), see Alexander Dallin and Thomas B. Larson (eds.), *Soviet Politics since Khrushchev* (Engelwood Cliffs, N.J., 1968); Erik P. Hoffman (ed.), *The Soviet Union in the 1980s* (New York, 1984); three works by Seweryn Bialer, *Stalin's Successors: Leadership, Stability, and Change in the Soviet Union* (Cambridge, Mass., 1980), *The Soviet Paradox: External Expansion, Internal Decline* (New York, 1986), and Seweryn Bialer and Thane Gustafson (eds.), *Russia at the Crossroads: The Twenty-Sixth Congress of the CPSU* (London, 1982); and Jerry F. Hough, *The Soviet Prefects: The Local Party Organs in Industrial Decision-Making* (Cambridge, Mass., 1969); and his *The Soviet Union and Social Science Theory* (Cambridge, Mass., 1979). See also the memoir by Fyodor Burlatsky, "Brezhnev and the End of the Thaw: Reflections on the Nature of Political Leadership," in Isaac J. Tarasulo (ed.), *Gorbachev and Glasnost: Viewpoints from the Soviet Press* (Wilmington, Del., 1989), pp. 50–62; and Andrei Sakharov, *Memoirs* (New York, 1990). Among the better journalistic accounts is Hendrik Smith, *The Russians* (New York, 1976).

On the emergence of society and dissent, see Basile Kerblay, *Modern Soviet Society* (New York, 1983); Konstantin Simis, *USSR—The Corrupt Society: The Secret World of Soviet Capitalism* (New York, 1982); John Dunlop, *The Faces of Contemporary Russian Nationalism* (Princeton, N.J., 1983); Alexander Yanov, *The Russian New Right: Right-Wing Ideologies in the Contemporary USSR* (Berkeley, Calif., 1978); Stephen F. Cohen (ed.), *An End to Silence: Uncensored Opinion in the Soviet Union* (New York, 1982); Ludmilla Alexeyeva, *Soviet Dissent: Contemporary Movements for National, Religious, and Human Rights* (Middletown, Conn., 1985); James Millar (ed.), *Politics, Work, and Daily Life in the USSR: A Survey of Former Soviet Citizens* (New York, 1987); and Moshe Lewin, *The Gorbachev Phenomenon: A Historical Interpretation* (Berkeley, Calif., 2nd ed., 1991).

On foreign policy, see David Holloway, *The Soviet Union and the Arms Race* (New Haven, Conn., 1983); Richard D. Anderson, Jr., *Public Politics in an Authoritarian State: Making Foreign Policy during the Brezhnev Years* (Ithaca, N.Y., 1993); and Ted Hopf, *Peripheral Visions: Deterrence Theory and Soviet Foreign Policy in the Third World, 1965–1990* (Ann Arbor, Mich., 1995). On the non-Russian peoples, see Teresa Rakowska-Harmstone, "The Dialectics of Nationalism in the USSR," *Problems of Communism* 23, no. 3 (May–June 1974): 1–22; and Lubomyr Hajda and Mark Beissinger (eds.), *The Nationalities Factor in Soviet Politics and Society* (Boulder, Colo., 1990).

PART V

REFORM
AND
REVOLUTION

CHAPTER 20
Interregnum and the Road to Revolution

The Brief Reign of Iurii Andropov

On November 10, 1982, Brezhnev died. Within a few days Iurii Andropov (1914–84), the former head of the KGB, became leader of the party. He soon emerged as a moderate reformer who promoted other reformers to positions of influence and power. Almost nothing was known about him in the West, but the media quickly invented a full persona for him. Andropov, it was reported with assurance, spoke fluent English, liked Western music, and preferred scotch to vodka while reading the novels of Jacqueline Susann. In fact, Andropov was an authentic and typical product of the Soviet system. Born in 1914, the son of a railroad worker in Stavropol province, he rose rapidly in the party as the older generation of leaders were wiped out in the Great Purges. After Stalin's death, Andropov became a diplomat, eventually serving as ambassador to Hungary (1954–57), where he pleased his superiors in his handling of events in 1956. Elected to the Central Committee in 1961, Andropov became head of the Committee on State Security (KGB) six years later. A man of the party, determined to keep the police under party control, Andropov brought new efficiency and pride into the organization, professionalizing it and making it an instrument in the fight against corruption.

Andropov had a strict, ascetic character, was indifferent to luxury and privilege, and appalled by the corruption of party leaders around him. In the last year of Brezhnev's life he engaged in investigations that touched many close to the Brezhnev family, including an infamous character known as Boris the Gypsy, who was touted to be the lover of Brezhnev's daughter. Andropov secured the respect and support both of the KGB and the military, and these powerful organizations, along with key party leaders, promoted Andropov's candidacy for the highest party position.

In his brief reign as general secretary, Andropov struggled against corruption and tried to improve labor discipline, but his idea of reform was to improve the system without seriously altering its basic contours. Andropov's discipline campaign had the earmarks of a former KGB chief. Young vigilantes with red armbands swooped down on restaurants and hair salons looking for shirkers and slackers. Such measures only angered people and did little to improve productivity. In 1983 a law on "labor collectives" was issued, which ostensibly gave workers greater influence over decisions in the factories. That same year collective farmers were encouraged to form "brigades," small groups of farmers that would decide what to produce and would be paid according to their output. The brigade system was extended to industry, and workers were allowed to organize their own work and to distribute their pay among the brigade members. But in practice the managers and farm bosses continued to decide most of the important questions, and workers were left to discuss issues of workplace safety and labor discipline. After sixty-five years of Soviet power the regime still did not trust its own workers to make fundamental decisions about the labor process.

Andropov's most significant contribution was to promote younger and more vigorous party officials, such as Mikhail Gorbachev, and remove aging Brezhnev holdovers. His long bout with a fatal kidney disease thwarted his efforts at mild change, and the tragic shoot-down of a Korean airliner over Soviet airspace in September 1983 prevented him from realizing his plans for better relations with the United States. As the end drew near for him, he attempted to arrange his succession and pass on his position to the young Gorbachev. Weeks before his death, Andropov asked the Central Committee to entrust the leadership of the Politburo and Secretariat to Gorbachev. But when the memo was distributed to the Central Committee, the old foxes in the Politburo, led by the Brezhnev loyalist Konstantin Chernenko, left his request out. Not ready for a much younger man, they maneuvered to have Gorbachev passed over when Andropov died on February 9, 1984, at the age of 69.

The Briefer Reign of Konstantin Chernenko

Four days after Andropov's death, the Central Committee elected the aged, infirm Konstantin Chernenko (1911–85) as general secretary of the party. A colorless bureaucrat whose only distinction was his fidelity to Brezhnev, Chernenko followed Brezhnev up the party ladder, becoming a member of the Central Committee in 1971 and a full member of the Politburo in 1978. As the last leader from the older generation that came up through the ranks of Stalinism, Chernenko was clearly the last gasp of a political apparatus devoid of ideas and energy. The Politburo was a gerontocracy. Seven members were in their seventies, two in their sixties, and only two, including Gorbachev, the youngest, in their fifties. This group of aging men were the rulers of the Soviet Union in the year 1984, the year that the British novelist George Orwell had chosen in 1948 as his metaphoric warning about a war-rife totalitarian world. But in the USSR 1984 was marked by a high degree of stability and continuity, a kind of calm before the storm. Tense relations continued between the superpowers, symbolized by the Soviet refusal to participate in the Los Angeles Olympics.

The younger leaders promoted by Andropov already played leading roles in policy formation and execution under Chernenko's reign. In December 1984 it was Gorbachev who gave the key address to the Central Committee plenum. Later that month he traveled to Great Britain to meet Prime Minister Margaret Thatcher, who confirmed that "this was a man one could work with." When Chernenko died on March 10, 1985, the Politburo recommended Gorbachev to the Central Committee for election within twenty-four hours. The dean of the older generation, Andrei Gromyko, nominated Gorbachev, whom he referred to as a man with a nice smile but iron teeth.

The Road to Radical Reform

Mikhail Sergeevich Gorbachev became leader of the Soviet Union at the age of 54. His election as general secretary marked a dramatic shift in power from the older to the younger generation of Soviet politicians. Born on March 2, 1931, in the Stavropol region of southern Russia and raised on a collective farm, he saw the destruction of villages and towns during the German invasion of the Soviet Union in World War II. He studied law at Moscow State University, where he joined the Communist Party in 1952. After graduating he returned to Stavropol, rising steadily through the ranks of the Communist Party. He became first secretary of the Stavropol City Communist Party Committee in September 1966 and four years party leader of the entire Stavropol region. Gorbachev's achievements brought him to the attention of Andropov; in 1978 he was called to the capital and placed in charge of agricultural affairs and in October 1980 made a full member of the Politburo.

Gorbachev came to power as a reformer determined to liberalize the Soviet system but without a clear idea of the how far change would have to reach. He was at one and the same time the greatest extender of freedom and democracy in modern history and the gravedigger of the Bolshevik Revolution. His reform became a revolution that failed to save the system, destroyed the Soviet Union, ended the Cold War, and seriously weakened Russia vis-à-vis the West. The first stage of the "Gorbachev revolution" did not foreshadow what was to come. From roughly March 1985 to December 1986, Gorbachev promoted a slow, cautious Andropov-like reform well within the confines of the existing system. In April 1985 he called for "acceleration" in the economy, greater labor discipline, higher labor productivity, and an end to corruption. His first major campaign, which was extremely unpopular, was the unlamented antialcohol campaign.

Though he was cautious at first, as early as April 1985 Gorbachev elaborated his sense that the party and state were not accountable to the people as they should be; the system was too highly centralized, information was constantly being manipulated and falsified, and officials were ignoring the deep, chronic problems of society. He introduced new emphases into the existing official discourse, speaking of the systemic nature of the problems and the need "to speak with people in the language of truth" and to deepen "socialist democ-

racy, the self-government of the people." Convinced that economic development required a more informed population and greater freedom for people to
make decisions on their own, he pushed for opening up the political structure
and the public media. To convince people of the need for radical change, he
raised the specter of a fundamental breakdown of the system.

In order to carry out the changes he contemplated, Gorbachev needed to
form a broad coalition within the Communist Party. Like his predecessors, Gorbachev quickly rid himself of political rivals and assembled a younger team of
leaders. A month after he became general secretary, he added three new members to the Politburo: Egor Ligachev, Nikolai Ryzhkov, and Viktor Chebrikov,
head of the KGB. He named Edward Shevardnadze, the Georgian party chief,
as foreign minister, elevated the aging Gromyko to president, and made
Ryzhkov prime minister. At the end of 1985 Gorbachev brought in Boris Yeltsin,
a fiery party chieftain from the Urals, to become head of the Moscow party organization. But below the new echelon of top leaders, the Communist Party,
which numbered 19 million members, was divided between those who favored
reform (and probably made up a minority) and those fearful of it. Few party
officials agreed with Gorbachev and Shevardnadze, who had met in years past
and agreed that "things could not go on as they were."

Gorbachev's principal political weapon was the traditions and habits of
obedience within the party to the general secretary. Somehow he needed to an-
imate the huge, lethargic body of the party to act in ways it had not for many
decades and to carry out policies that threatened its own power, prestige, and
normal mode of operation. Gorbachev opened the party's Twenty-Seventh
Congress in February 1986 with a five-hour speech about the need for "radical reform" (perestroika) and more "socialist democracy," but he was not specific about what this entailed. He attacked the inertia and apathy of the recent
past and called for a more flexible system of economic management along with
greater input from below by workers, but he made no gesture toward the more
radical market reforms instituted in Hungary and China. Using the rhetoric of
democracy, Gorbachev encouraged greater openness, more publicity about
shortcomings, introducing a second Russian word, glasnost, into the international lexicon. "Communists," he said, "want the truth, always and under all
circumstances." "Government should not be the privilege of a narrow circle of
professionals."

The Congress adopted a new party program, the first since the Khrushchev
program of 1961. Whereas the old program had spoken of a rapid transition
to Communism, to the classless, stateless society promised by Marx, the new
program referred to the "systematic and all-round improvement of socialism,"
which was defined as including "genuine democracy—power exercised for the
people and by the people." But long years of inflated language from Soviet officials made it difficult to give real meaning to talk about socialism. The Congress maintained the same stage-managed form of previous congresses, and
the style of the discussions did not differ much from those during Brezhnev's
life. Several speakers attacked nonconformists, dissident writers, and even
video recorders, which, it was claimed, were used to spread alien ideas, immorality, and a cult of violence. Ligachev, emerging as the leader of the more

conservative forces at the top of the party, took the party newspaper *Pravda* to task for publishing letters that were too critical of the privileges of party leaders. A careful listener could discern differences between the tones of conservatives and reformers, and few could mistake the message in the dynamic speech of Boris Yeltsin when he denounced "time-servers in possession of party cards" and admitted that in the past he had personally "lacked the courage and political experience" to criticize failings in party work.

Having taken power more quickly than any of his predecessors, Gorbachev had considerable strengths as a leader. Impressive was Gorbachev's intelligence, personal charm and graciousness, and his ability to forge broad political coalitions that linked reformers and conservatives. His style of leadership was less confrontational than others, and he tried to find compromises and avoid the use of force and violence, all while prodding the party and society along the road of reform. At first his wife, Raisa, proved to be an asset, at least abroad, though many Soviets, unused to a female presence near the center of power, were upset at her growing visibility. At the same time Gorbachev tended to be long-winded, his speeches often rambling on for hours, and his southern Russian accent annoyed many intellectuals. More importantly, he often postponed decisions and made poor personnel choices. Finally and most decisively, he did not really understand the depth of Soviet structural weaknesses or have a clear vision of where his reforms were leading.

Gorbachev's success or failure depended from the beginning on the ability of his administration to get the stagnant Soviet economy moving again. As Gorbachev began his second year as general secretary, the Soviet economy was buffeted by a series of misfortunes. On April 26, 1986, a surge of power at reactor no. 4 at the Chernobyl nuclear power station in Ukraine produced steam and hydrogen, which led to an explosion and fire with flames ten feet high. Radioactive dust spewed into the air and spread into Belorussia and toward Europe. Forty thousand people were evacuated from the nearby town of Pripyat; at least thirty people died and three hundred were hospitalized. One of the most immediate casualties was the credibility of the Gorbachev regime, which hesitated to release information on the accident for several days after the event. Wild rumors and sensational stories of thousands of deaths filled the Western press. Although after the initial silence the Soviet media were filled with daily reports on the consequences of the accident, the Chernobyl explosion exposed the resistance of officials to dealing openly with problems. Only in the summer were the officials responsible for the disaster removed from their positions. The burden of cleaning up the aftermath of Chernobyl fell on a weakening Soviet economy.

A second blow to Gorbachev's reforms came from the collapse of world oil prices. As the largest producer of oil in the world, the Soviet Union would have benefited from high world oil prices, but when oil prices fell precipitously, the Soviet Union was forced to borrow more money abroad. The economy had no cushion to fall back on and needed to become more productive very quickly. Still, a few positive signs could be noted in the first years of Gorbachev's rule. Industrial output grew 5.6 percent in the first half of 1986, as compared to the same period in 1985, while labor productivity in industry rose 5.2 percent. Even the chronic weak spot in Soviet economic performance, agriculture, showed some improvement. The high prices for wine and vodka were very unpopular, as were the long lines that formed at the reduced number of outlets for alcohol. Nevertheless, when statistics on infant mortality and life expectancy (which earlier had been suppressed) were again published, they showed that infant mortality rates had improved since the high point of 1974 and that deaths from accidents, poisoning, and injuries had declined by 24 percent since 1985.

Glasnost and the Erosion of Authority

In order to weaken the antireformist conservatives in the party and the state economy, Gorbachev desperately needed allies in society. He removed thousands of party and government officials as the press printed critical articles discussing every aspect of Soviet life, past and present, and attempted to mobilize the intelligentsia as the spearhead of the antibureaucratic movement. Gorbachev urged writers to be innovative and bold, and many among the progressive intelligentsia, like the controversial poet Evtushenko, echoed the party leader in the hope that "self-flattery will be forever rejected, and that openness will become the norm of civic behavior." Step by step censorship fell away, and banned works were published or released to movie theaters. In the theater new plays were staged that explored hitherto forbidden themes like the collectivization of the peasantry, the Cuban missile crisis, and the evils of Stalinism. In the summer of 1986 the party appointed liberal editors at several major national periodicals, and Gorbachev met with writers and explained his view that "a ruling stratum lies between the leadership of the country and the people, who wish for change, who dream of change—the apparat of ministers, the apparat of the party, which does not want transformations, which does not intend to lose certain rights tied to privileges." A few months later he met with social scientists and spoke about the opposition he faced within the ruling elites: "The old does not give up without a fight. . . . Some attempts are being made to squeeze the concepts of acceleration and perestroika into the framework of obsolete dogmas and stereotypes, emasculating their novelty and revolutionary essence in the process."

Steadily Gorbachev loosened party controls on Soviet society. He released prominent dissidents from prison and exile, and in December 1986 placed a telephone call to Andrei Sakharov, the Soviet Union's most distinguished dissident, then in exile in the Volga city of Gorky, and invited him to return to Moscow. Sakharov agreed to help Gorbachev in his efforts at reform but as a critic pushing for greater liberalization and democracy. The invitation to Sakharov was the most dramatic attempt at a new relationship between the party and the intelligentsia, but Gorbachev's search for allies unleashed new critical forces without securing the kind of support that the general secretary desired.

The new openness in the media exposed the weaknesses of the Soviet system to a public thirsty for truth about the past and present. Intellectuals and journalists attacked the encrusted ideological orthodoxies that a year earlier

Figure 20.1. Woman's work on the collective farm (Frederique Lengaigne, Liaison International).

had been untouchable. Early in 1987 economists disputed the reliability of Soviet economic statistics, revealed that Soviet labor productivity was among the
lowest in the industrialized world, and stated boldly that the Soviet economy
had been operated "in defiance . . . of the laws of economic life" since the 1920s.
One critic wrote:

> Apathy and indifference, stealing and disrespect for honest work have all
> become commonplace, along with aggressive envy of those who earn a lot,
> even if they earn it honestly. . . . We must call things by their true names:
> stupidity is stupidity, incompetence is incompetence, and active Stalinism
> is active Stalinism.

A serious discussion of the need for markets or a return to the NEP policies of
the 1920s raged in the press. Gorbachev proposed making every enterprise self-
financing. Instead of being governed by a command economy planned from
the top, enterprises would be allowed to conclude contracts with the state and
with each other. Eventually a real price system would be introduced, as well
as systems of finance and credit from which enterprises could borrow for investment.

After a year and a half in office, Gorbachev came to realize that economic
improvements and social development could not occur without the democratization of the political structure. "Some comrades," he told the Central Committee in January 1987, "apparently find it hard to understand that democratization is not just a slogan but the essence of perestroika." "We must not
retreat," he said. "We have nowhere to retreat to." Gorbachev was setting himself and his program against the very people who had put him in power, the
party apparat. He tried, and failed, to convince them that there ought to be
multicandidate elections by secret ballot within the party for secretaries of committees. Though the Central Committee was resistant, in his concluding speech
to the meeting, which was unprecedentedly televised to the nation, Gorbachev
disingenuously claimed that "members of the Central Committee have spoken
in favor" of a party conference to discuss "further democratizing the life of the
party and society as a whole." Without a clear majority in either the Central
Committee or the Politburo for his most far-reaching reforms, the general secretary had appealed to the public, over the heads of the party, to move further
toward a kind of democracy.

The party leadership itself was divided. At one extreme were a few ultra-
reformers, like Yeltsin, who openly attacked the privileges of the party apparatchiki and appealed to the broad, egalitarian sympathies of ordinary Russians. Yeltsin enhanced his popularity by riding the bus to work and frequently
visiting and talking frankly with workers. He was a simple, direct man with
enormous personal appeal, a politician in full color among the grays of the Soviet bureaucracy. Opposed to Yeltsin was Ligachev, who wanted reform of the
Andropov variety and was terrified of the growing mobilization of society and
the weakening of party control. Ligachev lashed out against the "wholesale
disparagement of everything" and the appearance of "elements of mass bourgeois culture" in the USSR. He attacked the liberal editors of the leading jour-

nals as voices of "enemies from abroad." One style of leadership, self-confidently based in a dying political culture, was being pitted against an incoherent, improvised movement toward greater democracy and an uncertain future.

The tension between Yeltsin and Ligachev within the Politburo reached a breaking point by the fall of 1987. Yeltsin wrote to Gorbachev to warn him that "the struggle to maintain political stability can lead to stagnation, to the state of affairs (or something very like it) that we reached before, under Brezhnev." Within a month the Central Committee met to hear Gorbachev's plans for a historic address on the occasion of the seventieth anniversary of the October Revolution. Yeltsin asked to be allowed to address the meeting and immediately launched into a critique of the top party leadership, their failure to carry out perestroika in a determined fashion, and the continued practice of adulating the general secretary. He then abruptly resigned from the Politburo. Though he had warned Gorbachev of his intentions, the general secretary had tried to persuade him to wait until after the seventieth anniversary celebration of the October Revolution. Yeltsin shocked the assembly, which then turned on him. Ligachev bitterly attacked Yeltsin, and others, including more liberal figures such as Aleksandr Yakovlev, characterizing Yeltsin's remarks as "immoral" because "he put his personal ambitions and personal interests ahead of the general interests of the party." Shevardnadze said that Yeltsin's speech was "a betrayal of the party." Gorbachev ended the discussion by damning Yeltsin: "You had to go to such a level of vanity, of self-regard, to put your ambitions higher than the interests of the party, than the interests of our work! And that at a moment when we find ourselves at such an important stage of perestroika. . . . I consider this an irresponsible action." Yeltsin was driven from office officially in mid-November, when he was summoned from his hospital bed by Gorbachev to be subjected to a formal dismissal. Yeltsin suffered a physical collapse and depression and appeared to have been eliminated from politics. But his dismissal turned him into a political martyr, and Muscovites rallied to him. In the new political environment opened by perestroika, Yeltsin, after sixteen months in political disgrace, reemerged as the leader of the opposition to party conservatives and then to Gorbachev himself.

Gorbachev's policies were contradictory and politically dangerous. They attempted to coordinate complex policies of transformation from the center through the instrumentality of the party while actually eroding central state and party power and authority; this in turn permitted regional and republic elites to grow more independent. The Gorbachev reformers both raised new political and material expectations and proved unable to satisfy them. Gorbachev himself wanted to be both Martin Luther and the pope, both revolutionary reformer and defender of the existing power structure. He wavered back and forth, from left to right, for the next few years, alienating both conservatives and more radical reformers. His anniversary speech in November 1987 was a perfect example of his attempt to straddle the two wings of the party (and society) that were pulling further and further apart. He avoided rehabilitating the anti-Stalinist oppositions of the 1920s and instead claimed that "the party's nucleus, headed by J. V. Stalin, upheld Leninism in the ideological struggle." He glorified Stalin's "revolution from above," though he spoke of "real crimes stemming from an abuse of power." The jumbling of critique and praise disappointed the more liberal and radical elements in the party and intelligentsia and left the country without a clear new interpretation of the significance of the Soviet experience. The speech and the Yeltsin affair began to sow serious doubts among the intelligentsia about Gorbachev's sincerity and commitment to reform. Political mobilization far outstripped the glacial pace of economic development, and the party began to lose the ideological conviction of its right to rule. A political space was opened up for economic protests, like those of the Siberian and Donbass miners, and the massive nationalist movements that erupted, first with the Armenians, in early 1988.

The New Thinking and the End of the Cold War

Gorbachev's first and longest-lasting successes were in foreign policy. His "new thinking" held that the Soviet Union had to retreat in order to rebuild. Foreign policy was to be subordinated to domestic needs, rather than the other way round, as had usually been the case since the early Stalin period. Economic development depended on a decrease in international tensions, to create a breathing space for the Soviet Union, and a reduction in the costs of competition with the United States. As Georgii Arbatov told Western visitors, 'We are going to do the worst thing we can do to you. We are going to deprive you of an enemy." From their first days in office Gorbachev and Shevardnadze hammered away at the need for containing the nuclear arms race and restricting development of new weapons in space. In November 1985 Gorbachev went to Geneva to meet with President Ronald Reagan, a conservative anti-Communist who considered the Soviet Union to be an "evil empire." At this first summit conference since 1979, the two leaders issued a joint statement reaffirming the view that nuclear war was unwinnable, a statement that was a significant shift for Reagan. The two men seemed to get along well, but relations between the two superpowers did not immediately realize the promise of the summit. Reagan's defense program, known as the Strategic Defense Initiative (SDI), or "Star Wars," was an expensive and highly advanced technological deployment of a defensive shield to protect against incoming Soviet nuclear missiles. Such a system, some in the West argued, would require an extremely costly Soviet response, which would tax the poorer USSR and hasten its collapse. But Gorbachev did not in fact raise defense spending to meet the American challenge and instead looked for cheap ways to undermine Star Wars while vigorously pursuing the reduction of nuclear arms by both sides. The argument later made that Reagan's policies led to the end of the Cold War and the collapse of the USSR, thus, was not based on any evidence. Credit (or blame) for both must be given to Gorbachev.

In October 1986 the American president and the general secretary met in Reykjavik, Iceland, in closed sessions to discuss arms control. Gorbachev surprised the president with a proposal to cut strategic arms by 50 percent within five years and to ban deployment of space-based weaponry for ten years. Reagan, to the shock of his advisors, at first agreed, but then the talks collapsed over a disagreement on Star Wars. The meeting broke up with both sides blaming the other for the failure to come to agreement. Gorbachev and Shevardnadze had to contend, not only with recalcitrance from the Reagan administration to move ahead on arms control and give up SDI, but with Soviet hard-liners, who continued to see "warlike imperialist forces" in the West. Groping toward a new foreign policy for the USSR, Gorbachev and Shevardnadze encouraged foreign policy experts to develop a whole new conception of Soviet interests. Instead of speaking of the division of the world into rival camps, the new thinking emphasized common human values that transcended class conflicts. It upgraded peaceful coexistence from a "specific form of the class struggle" to a frank assertion that all states had certain objective interests and that differences between socialism and capitalism did not preclude cooperation. International relations were to be conducted in a "civilized" manner, without resort to military force, and with respect for the sovereignty and independence of states, including the states of Eastern Europe. Not only was nuclear war unwinnable, but low-level conflicts, like those in the Third World, were dangerous, for they could easily escalate into more threatening conflicts. The concept of national security was broadened from merely military security to include economic progress and the development of science, technology, and society in general. Gorbachev spoke of closer relations with Europe, of building "a common European home" from the Atlantic to the Urals, which would end the isolation of the USSR while taking into consideration American interests. As a dramatic sign of their new thinking, Soviet leaders now considered winding down and eventually withdrawing from the war in Afghanistan. By the time Gorbachev traveled to the United States in December to sign an agreement with the Americans limiting intermediate-range nuclear forces, he was regarded by the world community as having seized the initiative in trying to end the Cold War. The trip was a great triumph, complete with elaborate state dinners at the White House, but the impressive prestige and power that Gorbachev displayed in foreign policy eluded him at home. As his stature rose abroad, his popularity and power at home began to wither away.

Politics in a New Idiom

By early 1988 Soviet politics could no longer be contained within the corridors of the Central Committee headquarters on Old Square in Moscow. The streets also spoke, both in the center and in the national republics. The conflict within the party now centered on Yakovlev, the most radical reformer, and Ligachev, the champion of slower change. The conservatives issued a manifesto in the form of a letter from a neo-Stalinist chemistry teacher in Leningrad named Nina Andreeva. The letter, entitled "I Cannot Deny My Principles," appeared on March 13 in the stodgy newspaper *Soviet Russia* and had evidently been encouraged by Ligachev, who praised the letter at a meeting with newspaper editors . Andreeva's call for a "balanced" assessment of Stalinism created a sensation among intellectuals, who feared this was a sign that glasnost and perestroika were about to be reversed. At first there was no official response from Gorbachev, who was traveling in Yugoslavia. It was three weeks after his return, on April 5, that *Pravda* published Yakovlev's denunciation of Nina Andreeva's letter. Though "there are no prohibited topics today," he stated, "the Andreeva letter "is an attempt little by little to revise party decisions." The Politburo reprimanded Ligachev, who thereafter declined in influence, and Yakovlev, now the most radical reformer, emerged as the principal party figure in charge of ideology and the media. More importantly, Gorbachev had broken with his more conservative associate and signaled a sharp turn toward a more democratic politics.

Glasnost, the policy of permitting greater freedom of expression, had the effect of liberating the elements of civil society that had been developing during the Khrushchev and Brezhnev periods. From the Soviet media came a barrage of historical documentaries and discussions of the Stalin era, as the party reformers attempted to demonstrate how Stalinism had been a distortion of the original and, in their view, authentic Leninist form of socialism. Every night television shed light on the dark secrets of the Soviet past—the executions of thousands in death camps in Belorussia, the famine of the 1930s in Ukraine, the "secret protocol" attached to the Nazi-Soviet Pact that allowed the annexation of the Baltic republics. The questioning of the most basic tenets of Marxism-Leninism, and even the role of Lenin and the meaning of the October Revolution, shook the confidence of many Communists and opened the way for even more penetrating analyses of the roots of the present social crisis. An economist spoke of the Soviet people as being "like a seriously ill man who, after a long time in bed, takes his first step with the greatest difficulty and finds, to his horror, that he has almost forgotten how to walk." Viewers watched intently in late May 1988 as American president Ronald Reagan made his first visit to the "evil empire" and warmly embraced Gorbachev. The old enemy was gone, the sense of threat from the outside world dissipated, and along with it much of the justification for unquestioning allegiance to the existing regime. The critique and exposure of the past and present operation of the Soviet system wore away at the popular support of the party, its leadership (including Gorbachev eventually), and state authority. With the coming of glasnost the number of unofficial and informal organizations multiplied manyfold. In any large Soviet city dozens, even hundreds, of groups appeared, from democratic socialists to reactionary nationalists, from ethnic fraternities to environmental activists. The official organizations found themselves in an unenviable competition. Membership in the Komsomol, for example, declined by 4 million in the first four years of Gorbachev's rule. The genie of social activism was out of the bottle, never to be put back in again.

Gorbachev pressured the Communist Party to give up its interference in all aspects of social and economic life. He worked out theses to present to the Nineteenth Party Conference, which would "truly include the broad masses of the working people in the management of all state and public affairs, and to complete the creation of a socialist state based on the rule of law." Specifically, party committees were no longer to be permitted to issue instructions to state and economic agencies or public organizations. The party would cease being the administration of the whole country and be turned into a guiding force. At

the same time the party would be democratized on the basis of multiple candidate elections by secret ballot. This meant the end of the nomenklatura system of appointments from above. At the same time the authority of the soviets was to be restored. Still faced by the entrenched conservatism in the party
apparat, Gorbachev watched as the local and regional party committees chose
well-placed officials rather than the more daring supporters of perestroika as
their delegates to the upcoming conference. A mood of pessimism and resignation could be felt in society, and a Western journalist noted that workers in
Moscow "don't believe in anything, and they especially don't believe that
things will get better."

The Nineteenth Party Conference opened in June 1988 and stunned the
public, which for the first time watched internal party discussions on television. Revelations about the depth of the social and economic crises were in-
terspersed with debates that showed real divisions in the party. Speaker after
speaker exposed the grinding poverty of the countryside, the inadequacy of
school buildings, the deterioration in health and healthcare, and the persistent
lying about achievements. Steadily the mythological underpinnings of Communist Party power fell away. Conservatives, however, did not throw in the
towel without a fight. They castigated the press "that destroys, belittles, and
throws in the trash heap our experiences and our past, things sacred to our nation." With enthusiastic applause from the right, one speaker spoke of perestroika as "an airplane that has taken off without knowing if there is a landing strip at its destination." Gorbachev defended his view that the old methods
would not work, that leaders could no longer bang the table and get results:
"If we do not include the people in the processes of management, no administrative apparatus (and ours consists of eighteen million people, and we spend
forty billion rubles a year to support it) will be able to cope with it."

The most dramatic moment at the conference came when a repentant
Yeltsin asked for political rehabilitation. But he again attacked the privileges
of the party elite and called for the removal of those members of the Politburo
who had sat there with Brezhnev and "kept silent" during the years of stagnation. Ligachev rose to oppose Yeltsin and, sarcastically referring to him with
the familiar "Boris" instead of the polite "Boris Nikolaevich," rejected the claim
that top party members enjoyed unwarranted privileges. In the new political
environment that was being shaped by television, however, Ligachev's speech
had a negative effect on public opinion, while Yeltsin increased his popularity
as the most genuine and intransigent of reformers.

At the very end of the conference Gorbachev made his most radical gesture.
He pulled a piece of paper from his pocket and nervously read a resolution to
push ahead with his plan for the election of a Congress of People's Deputies,
which was to be "the country's supreme body of power." He then called for a
vote, and the conference agreed that elections would be held to a new, somewhat democratic structure of soviets and congresses that would exist alongside
the Communist Party. Gorbachev's plan to increase the power of elected state
institutions at the expense of party bodies was nothing short of a political revolution for the Soviet Union. As they sang the Internationale, many delegates
began to wonder what they had done! In fact, they had created a new state struc-

ture, headed by the Congress of People's Deputies, that would be the instrument to bring democracy to the USSR and end the party's monopoly of power.

From this moment until the Congress met almost a year later, Gorbachev was at the height of his power, influence, and popularity. The proposal for the elections to a new parliament had been his initiative, not a response to social pressure from below. He was the inspiration and the catalyst that moved perestroika from liberalization toward democratization of the system. But already in the borderlands of the Soviet Union this reform from above was being answered by a revolution from below.

The Awakening of Nations

From the time of Khrushchev the Communist Party elites in the non-Russian republics had become entrenched as local centers of power that often demonstrated remarkable resistance to the center's dictates. Their long tenure in power through the Brezhnev years had led to great corruption in many republics, particularly in Transcaucasia and Central Asia. Non-Russian leaderships were particularly resistant to change from the center, and though Gorbachev replaced the top leadership in many republics, the old elites remained intact in the infrastructure of the party, government, and economy. In December 1986 Gorbachev removed the long-time leader of Kazakhstan, Dinmukhammed Kunaev, a native Kazakh, and insensitively replaced him with a Russian. Kazakh students marched through the streets of Alma Ata in protest. Troops were called out and order restored, but not before blood had flowed in the streets. The events in Kazakhstan were the first sign that the leadership had little sense of the potent danger presented by the long failure to deal with the accumulating grievances of the non-Russian nationalities.

The Soviet Union was almost evenly divided between 145 million ethnic Russians and 140.6 million non-Russians. The largest non-Russian nationalities were the other Western Slavic peoples, the Ukrainians (over 44 million) and the Belorussians (10 million), and two of the Muslim peoples of Central Asia, the Uzbeks (nearly 17 million) and the Kazakhs (8 million). Altogether the Slavic peoples made up just under 70 percent of the Soviet population, and the traditionally Muslim peoples (approximately 55 million) represented a little less than 20 percent of the USSR. The Baltic peoples—Estonians, Latvians, and Lithuanians—made up only 3 percent, as did the Transcaucasian nationalities—the Armenians, Azerbaijanis, and Georgians. Yet those six small nationalities, along with the Moldavians, were the most vocal and vociferous in demanding enhanced language rights, cultural and political autonomy, and finally independence. The political revolution from above that Gorbachev had hoped would democratize the Soviet state, revive the Soviet economy, and end the international isolation of his country was in a real sense hijacked in 1988 by massive demonstrations of ethnic nationalists, interethnic conflict, and a seemingly irreversible movement toward independence by the non-Russians.

Soviet state policy toward the non-Russians had been deeply contradictory. On the one hand, it promoted national cultures and education in the union republics and autonomous republics and regions; on the other, it favored the teaching of Russian (after 1938) and restricted nationalist expression. On the one hand, new nations were created (notably in Central Asia, where countries such as Uzbekistan, Turkmenistan, Kyrgyzstan, Tajikistan, and Kazakhstan had never existed before); on the other, the settling of Russians, the attacks on religion and national customs, and the policies of industrialization that stimulated social mobility all eroded national traditions for many former villagers. Even policies that favored the so-called titular nationality in a republic (like the Georgians in Georgia) led to disadvantages and even repression of minority peoples within the republic (like the Abkhaz or Osetins in Georgia). As a result of such contradictions, nationalities were more self-conscious and better educated, more consolidated demographically, and more in control of their own capital city and ensconced in the local government after seventy years of Soviet rule than they had been earlier, yet they were unable to express fully their national aspirations and felt threatened by the possibility of assimilation into an amorphous, Russifying Soviet culture. The pull toward greater national cohesion was countered by a pull toward merging into a single Soviet people, which for many years had been the stated goal of Soviet nationality policy. Ironically, despite the aims of Marxism-Leninism to move beyond the era of nationalism, the Soviet federal state, with its ethnic republics and regions, provided a nursery for nations that in turn became the focus of identity and loyalty for much of the Soviet population.

Once Gorbachev permitted greater public expression and legitimized aspirations toward democracy and autonomy, the tensions between more consolidated and self-conscious nations and the limits of Soviet authoritarianism exploded in a series of separate struggles for greater local control and self-determination. As the Soviet past and Marxism-Leninism were questioned, nationalism provided an alternative worldview that promised a new utopia of freedom and progress. In the first phase of the national movements the Soviet-generated ethnic intelligentsias emerged as credible claimants to national leadership, first within the bounds of perestroika, as they called for radical reform but within the Soviet system, and later as potent opponents to Leninism. Nationalism was allied to democracy against the old imperial state.

Four distinct kinds of problems plagued Moscow and the non-Russian republics in the last years of the Soviet Union. The first involved ethnic conflicts between the dominant nationality in the fifteen union republics and the ethnic minorities that lived within them. In late February 1988 Armenians in the mountainous enclave of Karabakh in Azerbaijan began to demonstrate for a merger with the neighboring republic of Armenia. The Karabakh Armenians made up 75 percent of the population of the Mountainous Karabakh Autonomous Region (NKAO), and the Azerbaijanis refused to give up what they considered part of their national homeland. As tens of thousands of Armenians in Erevan, the capital of the Armenian Republic, marched in solemn processions through the streets chanting "Karabakh," angry Azerbaijanis stormed into the streets of the industrial town of Sumgait and butchered Armenians. Similar conflicts between the dominant nationality and minorities in the republic led to violence in Moldavia, where a Turkic people, the Gagauz, and

Slavic peoples feared the growing pro-Rumanian national movement among the majority Moldavians. In Georgia the Abkhaz and Osetin nationalities protested Georgian attempts to reduce their control over their autonomous republics. Though Osetins made up two-thirds of their region, which they declared an independent republic in the USSR (but not part of Georgia), the Abkhaz were but a mere 17 percent of their republic and faced a much larger Georgian presence (over 40 percent). Nationalist Georgians vigorously and sometimes violently protested against the demands of the non-Georgian peoples within Georgia. In Central Asia, where Western specialists had expected a surge of Muslim fundamentalism and Islamic unity, instead of a supranational religious allegiance, national (at the level of republics) and subnational (regional and tribal) loyalties proved far stronger. Uzbeks clashed with Kyrgyz in the border town of Osh. Uzbeks drove out their fellow Muslims, the Meskhetian Turks, who had been exiled to Central Asia from Georgia by Stalin.

The second kind of ethnic problem was resistance of non-Russian national movements to the old form of imperial rule by the Soviet center. At times such movements took on anti-Russian coloration, but in general they expressed themselves in the language of democracy and self-determination. In April 1988 activists in the Baltic republics began forming popular fronts to support the movement for reform and their own national aspirations. Steadily the popular fronts of Estonia, Latvia, and Lithuania extended their demands from cultural and linguistic to political within a year. The movement for separation from the Soviet Union developed more quickly and more radically in the Baltic republics and Transcaucasia than anywhere else in the USSR.

The third major ethnic problem, "the Russian question," was perhaps the least expected. Neither in the Russian empire nor in the Soviet Union had ethnic Russians ever managed to create a Russian national state that protected and promoted specifically Russian ethnic interests. Under the tsars the idea of nation had been diluted by commitments to empire and orthodox religion. Russian nationalism was most often expressed as an imperial mission, sometimes, in its European or Christian variant, aimed at civilizing less-developed peoples, sometimes, in its Pan-Slavic variant, messianic and racist. In the Soviet period the government strictly forbade expressions of Russian nationalism, except in narrowly prescribed official formulations in which they were fused with Soviet patriotism. The Russian Soviet Federated Soviet Republic (RSFSR) was not as complete a state as the other union republics. Its institutions were often merged with all-Soviet institutions and had little independent competence, until the eruption of nationalist movements in the late 1980s. In 1989–90 a new conception of a sovereign Russian Republic emerged, most powerfully under the leadership of Gorbachev's chief rival, Boris Yeltsin. The promotion of the Russian Republic, unlike the independence movements in Transcaucasia or the Baltic, remained an affair of political activists and intellectuals centered in Moscow rather than the expression of a massive nationalist movement. The Russian nationalists, ranging from benign Slavophiles to rabid anti-Semitic chauvinists, usually identified the great Russian state with the Soviet Union and were opposed to the collapse of the USSR. But Yeltsin and the "democrats" began to envision the Russian Republic as an alternative power structure through which to challenge the Communist conservatives and Gorbachev. In response to the Russian move toward sovereignty, the Tatars of the Volga region declared themselves a sovereign Soviet republic, as did other smaller peoples like the Mari and the Yakuts. Yeltsin himself encouraged these movements, telling the non-Russians to take what they could.

A fourth kind of ethnic problem concerned diasporas within the USSR, people who either lived outside their ethnic homeland or had no territory designated for them. Nearly half of them were Russians, but large numbers of Ukrainians, Tatars, Armenians, Jews, and others had made lives for themselves, intermarried, and raised families outside their home republics. As the nationalist ideology of ethnically distinct nation-states gained power, the fears of Russians and other diaspora peoples that they would be exiles in their own former country increased. These people, who numbered some 60 million in 1989, provided the largest constituency in favor of maintaining some form of federated multinational state.

When Gorbachev loosened the hold of the center over the non-Russian peripheries, local elites, aspiring politicians, and nationalist intellectuals used the language of nationalism to stake their claims to greater power and influence in the new Soviet Union. The resonance of the nationalist message was strongest in the Baltic republics, Armenia, Georgia, Moldavia, and western Ukraine. Here nationalism was a form of self-defense used by nationalities that felt endangered by the Russifying aspects of Soviet culture and modernization, as well as a demand for rights, self-determination, and even privileges over their local minorities. But even where nationalism was weakest, as in Belorussia and the Muslim republics, non-Russian elites resisted the reforming center's attempt to reduce the power they had acquired during the long Brezhnev years. In Central Asia the local party leaders adopted a kind of nomenklatura nationalism to defend their privileges. As the center grew weaker, nationalist movements escalated from cultural and linguistic demands to calls for sovereignty and independence. Thus, the empire's disintegration began in Moscow and was initiated from the top, and only after Soviet rulers seemed uncertain about how to rule did non-Russians step confidently into the breach.

From Reform to Revolution

Two centuries earlier the year 1789 marked the beginning of a revolutionary age in France and throughout Europe. The year 1989 witnessed another revolutionary transformation in Europe, a process of radical political democratization, first in the Soviet Union and then throughout Eastern Europe, which brought the Soviet bloc crashing down along with the wall in Berlin that had symbolized its isolation from the rest of Europe. In the USSR a new political era opened with the elections to the Congress of People's Deputies. The Congress was not fully democratically elected, and there was only one organized political party legally permitted to exist. One-third of the 2,250 deputy positions were to be filled by appointment, which meant by Communist Party members. Two-thirds would be nominated by various organizations and chosen in elections by secret ballot. The Communist Party nominated 100 candidates for its 100 slots in order to avoid any embarrassing rejections, but there were intense struggles in other organizations for nominations. In the Academy of Science the conservative establishment rejected the candidacy of Sakharov until liberal members protested and forced his nomination. Rejected by the Communist Party, Yeltsin was nominated as the citywide candidate of Moscow. Both the nominations process and the elections revealed a deep divide in the country between the political establishment and the newly mobilized forces for reform.

The election campaign was a moment of mass mobilization. Thousands of people began working for candidates. Opposition candidates organized massive rallies. Efforts by party officials to discredit their opponents, particularly Yeltsin, backfired, only encouraging thousands to turn out to demonstrate and vote. Given the skewed nominations system, the Congress ended up with 85 percent of its deputies being members of the Communist Party, but a significant and vocal opposition emerged as a legal phenomenon in the USSR for the first time in more than sixty years. Voters turned against bureaucrats and conservatives more than they voted against Communists, but increasingly they saw the Communist Party, despite Gorbachev, Yakovlev, and Yeltsin, as conservative and bureaucratic. The great victor was Yeltsin, who demolished his official party opponent, receiving over 90 percent of the vote. Some party bosses, such as the Leningrad party chief, received more negative than positive votes, thus losing the election despite the fact that no one was running against him. Significantly, the Communists were routed in the Baltic republics by popular fronts of nationalists and reformers. In his *Memoirs*, Gorbachev recounts how "we were in completely unfamiliar territory" as the elections revealed "feelings and attitudes of various social groups—about which, as it turned out, we had quite false impressions."

The March 1989 elections were a turning point in Soviet history, not unlike the calling of the Estates General in France two hundred years earlier. The country now had a somewhat representative body with the power to debate serious social and political issues. The unquestioned authority of the Communist Party no longer existed; its monopoly of power rested on its retention of the instruments of control, the army and the police, not on a legitimate political myth or a sense that it was competent to lead the state. Thanks to Gorbachev and glasnost the people had lost their fear of the regime. Thanks to the elections the people now had a means to be heard.

Though most Communists were badly demoralized by the elections, Gorbachev was buoyant and confident that "the people had spoken out in favor of perestroika, reaffirmed their allegiance to socialism, and supported the party's line aimed at the further renewal of society." Before the Congress opened, he traveled to China, where he had inspired the democracy movement of thousands of students. Two weeks after he left Beijing, the Chinese Communist leaders cracked down viciously on the students, drenching Tiananmen Square with their blood.

On May 25, 1989, the first session of the Congress of People's Deputies opened in Moscow. Gorbachev had agreed to have the proceedings televised, and the whole nation was watching. The TV coverage of the Congress had an electrifying effect on the Soviet population, providing a largely depoliticized population with an animating political education. With more than 87 percent of the delegates members of the party, Gorbachev set aside party discipline and told his party faithful that they were free to express their own views and not obligated to toe his line. Just before the formal business of the Congress could get under way, a delegate rose to protest the killing of nineteen people in a peaceful demonstration in Tbilisi, Georgia, on April 9. Thus, from the first minutes it was clear that the Congress was not fully under control or completely managed by the party leaders. Although the Congress elected Gorbachev its chairman, delegates vented sharp criticism of the general secretary. A truck driver from Kharkov rudely complained about Raisa Gorbacheva's influence on her husband. A worker from Leningrad asked about expensive country houses being built for Gorbachev. Some delegates called for Gorbachev to give up his leadership of the party and head only the state apparatus. The public could see that Gorbachev was no longer politically invulnerable, publicly infallible, or untouchable. Power had been demystified.

Gorbachev proved to be a skilled parliamentary leader, Soviet-style, but even as he held the political center and kept his coalition together, the Moscow intelligentsia and the more radical delegates split off to form their own faction. The majority of the Congress delegates supported the party leadership and were antagonistic to the more liberal and radical delegates like Sakharov. At the end of the twelve-day session Gorbachev himself lost his temper when Sakharov bitterly denounced the meetings as a "failure." Before the millions of television viewers Gorbachev demanded forcefully that the frail dissenter sit down. Outside the Congress hall viewers were sympathetic to the radicals for boldly speaking back to the powerful, and unknown figures became instant television celebrities. Gorbachev closed the Congress by stating that it had been shown that open discussion, disagreement, and compromise were possible "within the framework of the Soviet political system," and he defended the Communist Party's role as "the political vanguard of Soviet society." When the Congress elected the new Supreme Soviet of 542 deputies from its own membership, it largely chose party loyalists, but glasnost and television had created an alternative public space to the monolithic political sphere that the Communists had controlled in the past. As one of the reformist editors remarked, "The people in the country have always been afraid of power. Now, maybe, the powerful are becoming a little afraid of the people."

Gorbachev continued to straddle both party and society, but the two were pulling further and further apart. Like the Mensheviks and Socialist Revolutionaries in 1917, he tried to bind the "vital forces of the nation" into a single mass movement for gradual political and economic change, but society itself was polarizing into an increasingly fearful and reactionary political establishment and an evermore vocally radical opposition. As Yeltsin put it, "On the day the Congress opened, [the Soviet people] were one sort of people; on the day that it closed, they were a different people. . . . Almost the entire population had awakened from its state of lethargy." The Soviet Union was in a revolutionary situation, one that was already moving beyond the ability of its initiator to control. Gorbachev's own call for contested elections had undermined the very instrument that Gorbachev needed to implement his program, the

Communist Party. From that moment on, power flowed away from the party and its leader, into the streets, the national republics, and the meeting rooms of independent political and social organizations.

Suggestions for Further Reading

The literature on the Gorbachev period is already very large. One might begin with the excellent analysis by Archie Brown, *The Gorbachev Factor* (Oxford, 1996). See also Ben Ekloff, *Soviet Briefing: Gorbachev and the Reform Period* (Boulder, Colo., 1989); Isaac J. Tarasulo (ed.), *Perils of Perestroika: Viewpoints from the Soviet Press, 1989–1991* (Wilmington, Del., 1992); Mikhail S. Gorbachev, *Perestroika: New Thinking for Our Country and the World* (New York, 1988); Stephen White, *Gorbachev and After*, 3rd ed. (Cambridge, 1992); Seweryn Bialer (ed.), *Inside Gorbachev's Russia: Politics, Society, and Nationality* (Boulder, Colo., 1989); Richard Sakwa, *Gorbachev and His Reforms 1985–1990* (London, 1990); Harley D. Balzer (ed.), *Five Years that Shook the World: Gorbachev's Unfinished Revolution* (Boulder, Colo., 1991); and Abraham Brumberg (ed.), *Chronicle of a Revolution: A Western-Soviet Inquiry into Perestroika* (New York, 1990).

On Soviet society and economy during the Gorbachev period, see Stephen Kotkin, *Steeltown USSR: Soviet Society in the Gorbachev Era* (Berkeley, Calif., 1991); Mary Buckley (ed.), *Perestroika and Soviet Women* (Cambridge, 1992); R. W. Davies, *Soviet History in the Gorbachev Revolution* (Bloomington, Ind., 1989); Ellen Mickiewicz, *Split Signals: Television and Politics in the Soviet Union* (New York, 1988); Geoffrey Hosking, *The Awakening of the Soviet Union* (London, 1990); Vladimir Shlapentokh, *Soviet Intellectuals and Political Power: The Post-Stalin Era* (Princeton, N.J., 1990); Murray Feshbach and Albert Friendly, Jr., *Ecocide in the USSR* (New York, 1993); Ed A. Hewett, *Reforming the Soviet Economy: Equality versus Efficiency* (Washington, 1988); and Anders Aslund, *Gorbachev's Struggle for Economic Reform* (Ithaca, N.Y., 1989).

On nationalities, see Ronald Grigor Suny, *The Revenge of the Past* (1993); Gail Lapidus and Victor Zaslavsky (eds.), *From Union to Commonwealth: Nationalism and Separatism in the Soviet Republics* (Cambridge, 1992); Anatol Lieven, *The Baltic Revolution* (New Haven, Conn., 1993); John B. Dunlop, *The Rise of Russia and the Fall of the Soviet Empire* (1993); Alexander J. Motyl (ed.), *Sovietology, Rationality, Nationality: Coming to Grips with Nationalism in the USSR* (New York, 1990), and his *Thinking Theoretically about Soviet Nationalities* (New York, 1992); and Bohdan Nahaylo and Victor Swoboda, *Soviet Disunion: A History of the Nationalities Problem in the USSR* (London, 1990)

On foreign policy, see Michael Mandelbaum (ed.), *Gorbachev's Russia and American Foreign Policy* (Boulder, Colo., 1988), *Central Asia and the World* (New York, 1994), and *The Strategic Quadrangle: Russia, China, Japan, and the United States in East Asia* (New York, 1995)

Journalists were perceptive observers of the Gorbachev reform-turned-revolution. See Martin Walker, *The Waking Giant: Gorbachev's Russia* (New York, 1986); Robert G. Kaiser, *Why Gorbachev Happened: His Triumphs and His Failures* (New York, 1991); Jonathan Steele, *Eternal Russia: Yeltsin, Gorbachev and the Mirage of Democracy* (London, 1994); and Hedrick Smith, *The New Russians* (New York, 1990).

CHAPTER 21
The End of the Soviet Union

The revolution from below intensified in 1989. Economic conditions worsened for many. The whole country was called upon to help alleviate the suffering of Armenians, who had been devastated by an earthquake on December 7, 1988, in which twenty-five thousand were killed. The earthquake, along with the Chernobyl cleanup, were additional costs to an economy weakened by falling oil prices, but even greater burdens came with the growing social unrest. In July miners went on strike in the Kuznetsk Basin in Siberia and the Donbass in Ukraine, largely over intolerable material conditions. Even soap was unavailable to clean the coal dust off after a shift. This was the first widespread expression of labor's power since the 1920s. Gorbachev hurriedly made concessions to keep this vital source of energy flowing, and in September the Supreme Soviet recognized the right of workers to strike. Gorbachev had hoped to raise the Soviet economic growth rate, which had fallen to almost zero by the late 1970s, up to the level of the 1960s of 5 to 6 percent per year. But the antialcohol campaign removed 25 billion rubles from the legal economy and shifted much of that into bootlegging. After the initial upsurge in economic indicators in 1986, the economy began a rapid spiral downward.

Gorbachev encouraged the introduction of cooperatives, which were collectively owned, and therefore not quite private enterprises, but operated independently of the state. The bureaucracy frustrated and sabotaged the cooperatives at every opportunity, refusing them supplies, financing, and access to foreign currency. The cooperatives that survived had high costs and therefore set high prices for their services and goods. Disgruntled consumers complained about the cooperatives, accusing them of speculation, and the growing criminal element sometimes set fire to the cooperatives or attempted to shake down their owners, who then required the protection of other sinister forces. Gorbachev proposed that party and state leaders plan less but plan better and give up trying to micromanage the system. But his own team of reformers was not sure how far to go. Prime Minister Ryzhkov opposed any movement "beyond the framework of socialism," and Gorbachev himself moved very slowly toward an understanding that a freer pricing system and financial system were required to move the economy from command toward marketization. The party's economic policies remained contradictory and incomplete. Ministries still set control figures and the norms for production, even as enterprises were theoretically supposed to be free to decide what and how to produce. Later Gorbachev recognized that indecision and hesitation in 1987–88, when political and economic conditions were most favorable for reform, "was a strategic miscalculation."

The stagnating economy ate away at the claims by the Communist Party that it was competent to provide for a prosperous future. An ever greater number of people thought of the party powerful as a self-serving, corrupt, incompetent elite. In various parts of the country people turned on local party officials for their privileged access to special stores and better housing. As prosperity and order gave way to material hardships and growing chaos, Gorbachev's popularity eroded, and his approval rating fell from well over 80 percent at the end of 1989 to 56 percent at the end of 1990.

The Unraveling of the Empire at Home

One by one the nationalist movements in the Soviet Union escalated their demands. In May 1989 Lithuania and Estonia declared themselves sovereign republics and claimed that their laws overruled Soviet laws. In July Latvia followed their example. On the fiftieth anniversary of the Nazi-Soviet Pact, August 23, massive demonstrations were held throughout the Baltic. The central party authorities condemned separatist tendencies, declaring that "things have gone too far" in the Baltic republics, and Gorbachev met with the three Baltic Communist leaders to calm the situation, but he hesitated to initiate a crackdown on the rebellious republics. Two months later, on November 16, the Lithuanian Politburo decided that the party should be independent of the Communist Party of the Soviet Union.

Gorbachev was extremely reluctant to use physical force against the population, which his own policies had awakened. He told a high-level meeting called to discuss the nationality question that "we will not depart from the path of solving all problems by means of political methods, but where the critical nature of the situation dictates it, where there is a threat to people's lives and safety, we will act decisively, using the full force of Soviet laws." In answer to calls by non-Russian party leaders for greater rights for the union republics, national military units, the elevation of autonomous republics to union republics, and changes in boundaries, Gorbachev refused to change the status and borders of national entities. While all across the Union ethnic conflict erupted and nationalist movements grew stronger, the ruling party stood pat.

In Armenia, Azerbaijan, and Georgia, the local Communist parties steadily lost authority to nationalists organized in popular fronts. Under pressure from nationalists, the Supreme Soviet in Baku declared Azerbaijan a sovereign socialist state within the USSR, claiming that that sovereignty extended over Karabakh and Nakhichevan, and spoke of secession from the USSR. Azerbaijani activists marched to the border with Iran, tore down Soviet border posts, and linked up with Azeri compatriots on the other side. In a country where just a few years earlier an airliner had been shot down for violating the Soviet border, now guards were ordered not to resist as ordinary citizens opened the border on their own. Georgians fought with Abkhazians and Osetins, and both minority nationalities eventually declared their desire to secede from Georgia.

Belorussia, Ukraine, and the Muslim republics were slower to develop popular nationalist movements than the Baltic and Caucasian republics, but Western Ukraine, which had never fully acquiesced to Soviet rule, became a center for separatist nationalism. In early September a Ukrainian nationalist organization, Rukh (Movement), was founded in Kiev, but Ukraine, the second most populous Soviet republic, was not united around a nationalist agenda. Russians and Russian-speaking Ukrainians retained an identity with the Soviet Union. In neighboring Moldavia violence broke up the November celebration of the revolution in Kishinev, and both Turkic and Slavic peoples within the republic looked toward the central Soviet government to protect them against the more nationalist Moldavians.

Surrendering Stalin's Empire

Reformers in Eastern Europe watched the events in Moscow attentively. The Soviet Union was the major conservative force in the Soviet bloc, along with East Germany, preventing reform in the Eastern European economies and societies since the Prague Spring of 1968. In his very first days in office, indeed, at the time of Chernenko's funeral in March 1985, Gorbachev had made it clear to the Communist leaders of Eastern Europe that the Brezhnev Doctrine, that the USSR would intervene to save the present regimes in Eastern Europe, was no longer Soviet policy. For the East Germans particularly this shift signaled disaster, for it meant that the USSR was no longer committed as firmly to a separate socialist Germany. With the new political thaw in the USSR, East European Communists began to shift toward reform. In 1988 the Hungarians retired their long-time party boss, Janos Kadar, the heir to the Soviet suppression of the 1956 revolution. At the beginning of 1989 they legalized freedom of assembly and association and a multiparty system, and on March 3 Gorbachev sanctioned the new political system in Hungary. By spring demonstrators in Budapest were calling for free elections and the withdrawal of Soviet troops. In early May the barbed wire that separated Hungary and Austria was removed, and the border was opened for free transit to the West. No reaction came from the Soviet Union as hundreds of East Germans used the Hungarian border crossings as an escape hatch to the West. In Poland military dictator General Wojciech Jaruzelski, who had cracked down on the mass democratic movement, Solidarity, nine years earlier, opened a dialogue with the opposition, and in February 1989 roundtable talks were held between the Communists and Solidarity, which led to free elections on June 4. Solidarity swept the elections, and the Communists were exposed as an unpopular minority party. In August the Soviet Defense Council ordered its troops in Eastern Europe not to interfere in domestic conflicts, and Gorbachev telephoned the leader of the Communist Party in Poland and urged him to join a coalition government with Solidarity. The Communists were basically told to relinquish their power to their political rivals without a fight. Given the stark choice of conceding to the democratization of Eastern Europe or using the military, Gorbachev chose not to use force. The days of the Soviet Union's empire in Eastern Europe were numbered.

The radical shifts in Eastern Europe were officially sanctioned by Gorbachev, first when he visited West Germany in June and answered a question about the possibility of bringing down the Berlin Wall by saying, "Nothing is eternal in this world." But much more dramatic was his visit on October 6 to East Germany for its fortieth anniversary. Even as he embraced the leaders of the socialist Germany, Gorbachev made it clear that the Soviet Union would not back up the German regime with troops. Crowds shouted, "Freedom, freedom! Gorby! Gorby! Help us!" The day after he left, fifty thousand Germans demonstrated in Leipzig against the regime. Soviet troops were ordered to stay in their barracks. Party leader Erich Honecker ordered his troops to fire on the crowds, but the conductor Kurt Masur intervened and prevented violence. By October 18 Honecker had fallen, and on November 9 the Berlin Wall was dismantled by crowds of ordinary people. Gorbachev, who had urged reforms in the GDR that its leaders had been reluctant to implement, was reported to have said, "Life punishes latecomers."

One by one the East European Communist regimes were replaced by coalition or even non-Communist governments. On Christmas Day 1989 the ruthless dictator of Rumania, Nicolae Ceaucescu, was overthrown and executed. The major dividing issue remaining in Europe was the question of the two German states. Gorbachev had long insisted that the West would have to accept the division of Germany, but, according to his foreign policy advisor, the general secretary "was already convinced that without a resolution of the Germany question . . . no reconciliation would occur in Europe or the world." The Soviet leader saw West Germany as its "main partner in the building of a new Europe." Still, it was not until a year after the collapse of the Eastern European Communist governments in the fall of 1989, an event that changed completely the post–World War II political settlement, that Soviet leaders consented to a united Germany.

Gorbachev probably did not anticipate that the East European regimes would collapse so quickly or that socialism would be so rapidly abandoned in favor of Western-style market capitalism. The precipitous rush from the Soviet model was a body blow to the historical justifications for socialism in the Soviet Union. Though many of the original rebels against the Communist dictatorships in Eastern Europe were, in fact, socialists who were seeking some third way between American-style capitalism and Soviet-style state socialism, the enthusiasm for the market economy overwhelmed that alternative in the immediate aftermath of the "velvet revolutions" in Eastern Europe. Only a few years later would more moderate reformers, and even former Communists, be returned to power in Hungary, Poland, and elsewhere as the original bloom of excitement over the market economy faded.

Gorbachev's foreign policy revolution radically changed the nature of the international political system. No longer a superpower, the Soviet Union quickly lost its military and political influence in the world. In the West pundits spoke of the USSR as having lost the Cold War, but in large part the Soviets simply lost in 1989 what they had won in World War II. Their empire in Eastern Europe was gone, and Germany once again a strong, united state in central Europe. Gorbachev withdrew Soviet troops from Afghanistan and restored ties with China in 1989, after more than thirty years of hostility between the two countries. The USSR was no longer able economically or militarily to project its power in the Third World. Its clients in the Middle East had no recourse but to recognize the increased power of the United States or risk isolation or defeat. In his last year in power Gorbachev attempted to mediate the conflict between the United States and Iraq over Iraq's invasion of Kuwait, but by that time Soviet influence was at a low ebb, and the dispute would be settled by a stunning show of American military might in early 1991. Gorbachev's achievements in bringing the Cold War and the division of Europe to an end were recognized when he was rewarded with the Nobel Prize for peace in 1990. There were no prizes, however, for his progressive weakening of the USSR and his ultimate failure to hold together the country he ruled.

Power to the People

Though he could still rely on the traditional loyalty and obedience that party members showed their general secretary, Gorbachev had moved far away from the majority opinion in the party. He and his closest associates represented a radical minority view within the party. By November 1989 he publicly gave

Figure 21.1. Mikhail and Raisa Gorbachev visiting Ronald and Nancy Reagan at the Reagan ranch in Santa Barbara, California (Jerry Mennenga, Liaison International).

up the idea that Marxism held a monopoly on truth. Without abandoning socialism, he said, "We no longer think that we are the best and that we are always right, that those who disagree with us are our enemies." On his way to an audience with Pope John Paul II, he sanctioned the idea of tolerance for religion: "Faith is a matter of conscience for each person and something in which no one should interfere." At a summit of the Warsaw Pact he repudiated the Soviet invasion of Czechoslovakia and put the USSR on record in favor of political rather than military means for dealing with problems in Eastern Europe. He could see that events were overtaking the party and that the apparatchiki were preventing the party from leading the reform movement, but he continued to believe that the party "could be renewed." He was careful not to move too far ahead of the other party leaders, which would have lead to a mutiny in the Central Committee and his dismissal, but at the same time he steadily worked at weakening party power and shifting authority to the new state institutions. Ironically, as his stature and influence grew in the West, Gorbachev became less and less popular at home, and his authority both within and outside the Communist Party withered away.

The election of the Congress of Peoples' Deputies and the Supreme Soviet radically shifted power at the top of the state structure from the party to the state and gave Gorbachev, now chairman of both, a new base of power outside the party. But the old institutions of party control still remained very influential both in the ministries, the army, and the police and outside of Moscow in the regions and republics. The old power structure still had to be dismantled, and resistance to the further reduction of party power grew among party leaders. The prime minister, Ryzhkov, gravitated toward the more conservative Ligachev, while the more radical democratic forces, clustering around Yeltsin, pushed for more rapid reform. By the second half of 1989 the forces favoring radical change within the Soviet Union had far outstripped the more cautious Gorbachev. Desperately trying to hold a centrist position between radicals and conservatives, he swung back and forth from one side to the other, alienating each in turn. The radicals in the party raised the issue of Article 6 of the Soviet constitution, which stated, "The leading and guiding force of Soviet society and the nucleus of its political system, of all state organizations and public organizations, is the Communist Party of the Soviet Union." But Gorbachev, apparently fearful of a reaction from the conservative majority in the Central Committee, hesitated, even though political pluralism already existed in the Soviet Union. Article 6 became a symbolic issue of enormous importance, and Gorbachev's opposition to its removal, which he later defended as necessary maneuvering in the face of the conservative opposition in the party, alienated the liberals. One of his most determined critics, urging radicalization of perestroika, was academician Andrei Sakharov, who was gearing up for a battle with Gorbachev when, on December 14, 1989, he suffered a fatal heart attack. Less than two months later the general secretary came out for eliminating Article 6, moved up the date for the next party congress, and arranged for real elections of officials within the party. On February 7 the Central Committee renounced the party's monopoly on power. A new political arena had been created in which political organizations and parties could freely compete with the Communists for political power, for the first time since the days of the civil war.

By January 1990 Gorbachev was a fireman rushing from one conflagration to the next. Television viewers watched as he stood in the streets of Vilnius, Lithuania, surrounded by a quarter of a million people, and tried, and failed, to convince the Lithuanians that it was to their advantage not to declare independence from the Soviet Union. Before the Lithuanian crisis had settled down, Azerbaijanis in Baku began attacking and killing Armenians. After some hesitation, Gorbachev sent troops to restore order in Baku and to prevent the popular front there from increasing its power. Bloody fighting ensued; hundreds were killed, and Azerbaijanis turned decisively against the central Soviet regime.

Gorbachev was the head of a party-state that was a kind of grand coalition that uneasily included reformers who looked ahead to a multiparty socialist democracy, a multinational federation of republics with greater local control, and a Communist Party that would look more like the social democratic parties out of which Bolshevism grew, and conservatives who wanted preservation of the Communist Party as the unchallenged leading force in the country, a centralized union of subordinate republics, and tighter control over the instruments of information. But unlike the most radical democrats, Gorbachev was not prepared to give up on socialism or the Communist Party or to allow separation of the non-Russian republics from the Soviet Union. "Our ideal is a humane, democratic socialism," he told the Central Committee in February 1990. "We remain committed to the choice made in October 1917." The Communist Party would compete in the new multiparty political arena for the position of ruling party. One emboldened conservative hinted broadly that Gorbachev should be removed: "Someone should answer, comrades, for the breakdown of party unity and for ideological failures; someone should answer, comrades, for the events in Eastern Europe." From the other extreme, Yeltsin attacked Gorbachev for not going far enough fast enough and voted alone against his proposals.

No longer reliable allies for Gorbachev, the self-styled "democratic" forces had moved beyond reform within the system to a call for the abolition of the system itself. They abandoned Gorbachev for Yeltsin, and the democrats and the nationalists together, particularly in the Baltic republics, combined ideas of anti-Communism with support for independence of the republics. On February 25, 1990, demonstrations in support of the democratic opposition were held throughout the country. About one hundred thousand people marched in Moscow, with smaller numbers in Kiev, Tbilisi, Minsk, and Tashkent. As elections to local soviets proceeded throughout the country, Communists were defeated almost everywhere. In Leningrad the opposition won 60 percent of the seats. On March 11 the newly elected parliament of Lithuania, led by the popular front called Sajudis, declared Lithuania an independent state and elected an intransigent nationalist, Vytautas Landsbergis, president of the country. Gorbachev sent KGB troops to Vilnius and imposed economic sanctions, cutting off oil and gas to the republic, but rejected calls from the old-style Communists to use force to overthrow the new government. When the Lithuanian parliament suspended its declaration of independence in June, Moscow lifted the economic embargo. But a nervous stalemate kept tensions high for the next year.

As the Union unraveled, Gorbachev tried to strengthen the new elected institutions in the center. The Congress of People's Deputies elected Gorbachev as the first (and, as it turned out, the last) president of the Soviet Union. Gorbachev chose not to be elected directly by the people of the USSR, though he would probably have won such an election, because of the urgent need for an executive authority. The decision to forego a popular election would later return to haunt the new president, for it meant that he did not gain his legitimacy from the people directly but from a Communist-dominated institution. On May Day, as Kremlin leaders stood on Lenin's mausoleum watching the parade, Gorbachev experienced a humiliating affirmation that people now felt themselves freer in the Soviet Union. Crowds jeered and shouted at those on Lenin's tomb, carried placards equating the Soviet party chiefs with the deposed and murdered Ceausescu of Rumania, and waved portraits of their new heroes, Sakharov and Yeltsin.

As Gorbachev's popularity declined, that of Boris Yeltsin increased. Yeltsin's popular touch, his image as an opponent (and victim) of the Communist conservatives, his commitment to even more radical reform than Gorbachev, and his identification with the Russian republic all served to secure a power base for his political comeback. While Gorbachev was consolidating his formal power in the state institutions at the level of the Soviet Union, Yeltsin gained institutional power at the level of the Russian Federation. Both the all-Soviet and the RSFSR state institutions had been equally formal, symbolic, and ceremonial, the rubber stamps of the Communist Party. Now that Gorbachev's policies had breathed life back into them, state institutions at the republic level became potential competitors of all-union institutions for the mantle and power of the moribund Communist Party. When Gorbachev became president of the Soviet Union, leaders in the union republics demanded that presidencies be created in their republics as well. In their bid for power non-Russian nationalists declared their nation's sovereignty at the expense of the Soviet Union. The governments of the republics, several of which were being reelected in relatively democratic elections, fought a war of laws with the Soviet center. In March 1990 Yeltsin was elected to the RSFSR Congress of People's Deputies, and at the end of May he was narrowly elected its chairman. He declared that Russia would soon declare its "real sovereignty." "If the center does not overthrow us in the next 100 days," he said, challenging the all-Union leaders, "then grounding ourselves on the declaration [of sovereignty] . . . Russia will be independent in everything. Russian laws will be higher than union ones." Yeltsin had shrewdly adopted as his platform the defense of the Russian republic, coopting the more benign forms of Russian nationalism to the democratic cause and providing the democrats with a broader base of support than they had hitherto enjoyed. Two weeks later the Russian parliament overwhelmingly proclaimed the sovereignty of the republic. In June, at the Twenty-Eighth (and last) Congress of the Communist Party of the Soviet Union, Yeltsin dramatically resigned from the severely weakened and divided Communist Party and walked out of the Congress. While Gorbachev cobbled together new institutions to recreate a looser, more democratic Soviet federation and tried to keep the party unified, Yeltsin strode confidently toward another future, still uncharted, but now he was free of identification with the Communist Party or socialism.

In the summer of 1990 the democratic opposition acquired its own program of reform, a plan proposed by Stanislav Shatalin for radical economic reform within 500 days. The Shatalin plan, which aimed at privatizing large parts of the state economy by selling off assets to ordinary Soviet citizens, became the basis for a brief political alliance in late July between Gorbachev and Yeltsin. The billions of rubles hoarded by Soviet consumers, who had little on which to spend them, had for years had an inflationary effect on the economy. Shatalin's plan would have alleviated that pressure both by absorbing savings and by cutting back on government spending. But feeling pressure from conservatives within the government and fearful that he could not convince the Supreme Soviet to pass the Shatalin plan, Gorbachev retreated, moderating the plan by borrowing ideas from an alternative offered by his prime minister, Ryzhkov. The Supreme Soviet, however, was wary of the consequences of the plan for both the managerial elite and the already burdened populace; instead of adopting the Shatalin plan, it granted Gorbachev emergency economic powers. The president, in turn, gutted the 500-day program, continued to rely on the old administrative system, and put forward a much more moderate variant of a market reform. Gorbachev's successful strategy of broad coalition building in his early years in power was no longer appropriate as the country polarized. By siding with the conservatives and breaking with the democrats, he made what was arguably his most fatal political error. His tactical accommodation with the "forces of order" was a blow to the democrats that convinced many of them that compromise with Gorbachev and his socialist program was impossible. The Soviet economy could not simply be reformed; it had to be replaced.

The Final Crisis

Responding to the fears of the army and state officials that the country was disintegrating, Gorbachev brought more conservatives into his inner circle and lost several of his reformist allies, most notably Yakovlev and Shevardnadze. While he had managed progressively to weaken the central party bodies, reducing the number of departments and personnel in the Secretariat and holding less frequent meetings of the Politburo, he was not successful in creating authoritative state institutions to replace them. He formed an advisory body, the President's Council, which began to act effectively, but in December he replaced it with a new Council of the Federation that was to have policymaking powers, along with a Cabinet of Ministers, and a consultative Security Council. But these new structures were little more than cosmetic and could not prevent the rapid erosion of the Kremlin's authority. Presidential decrees were not enforced, young men resisted the draft, and local officials paid less and less attention to Moscow. The Politburo was now made up, not of the most important officials in the center, but of the first secretaries of the various Communist parties in the republics, and the Council of the Federation was likewise made up of the heads of state of the fifteen republics, along with Gorbachev. A vacuum had been created at the center, and both the party and the Union were on their way to becoming de facto confederations.

Two major issues confronted Soviet leaders in 1990–91—reviving the economy and keeping the Union together. Increasingly these two issues were considered closely intertwined. Not only nationalists but many Communists in the republics had come to believe that they could handle economic questions better than the center and that independence would open the way to economic progress. Yeltsin declared, "The so-called revolution from above has ended. The Kremlin is no longer the initiator of the country's renewal or an active champion of the new. The processes of renewal, blocked at the level of the center, have moved to the republics." From the other side Prime Minister Ryzhkov worried that an "undeclared war" against government had been unleashed, which aimed "to strike a blow at the state, at the sociopolitical system, and to crush it once and for all." The war is being waged "under the flag of the market." The government, he went on, is in favor of sovereignty for the republics, but also the sovereignty of the Union as a whole. Gorbachev's strategy for recreating a "firm power" was to propose a popular referendum on a Union of sovereign states, which would have a new division of authority but be "a single state nevertheless."

As he allied himself with the forces suspicious of further reform, Gorbachev lost one of his most dedicated supporters, Foreign Minister Shevardnadze. On December 20 Shevardnadze publicly resigned his post to protest against the "dictatorship" that was coming and the resurgence of the militantly antireformist forces. His prediction that sinister forces were on the march seemed to be confirmed by signs of more aggressive activity by the party conservatives in the Baltic region. On January 8, 1991, workers marched to the Lithuanian parliament to protest price hikes and demand the resignation of the government. Water cannons dispersed the crowds. Gorbachev called on Lithuania to restore the full force of the USSR and Lithuanian SSR constitutions, but President Landsbergis refused to restore what he labeled the "constitution of invaders" and called for civil disobedience. A pro-Soviet minority movement called for direct presidential rule of Lithuania, and on January 11 Soviet MVD troops opened fire on a crowd in Vilnius, killing fourteen people and wounding hundreds. On January 16–17 tensions led to shooting in Riga, Latvia, where five people were killed. In Moscow tens of thousands rallied in the center of the city to protest what looked like a determined attempt to crush the democratic movement in the Baltic republics. Gorbachev responded to the Baltic crisis with regret, but he argued that the clashes were the result of intransigence on the part of the Lithuanians. However, he ordered that no troops engage in unauthorized activity and that no one be allowed to appeal to the armed forces in the political struggle. And again he refused suggestions from party conservatives that he impose presidential rule. Defiantly, the Lithuanians overwhelmingly voted on February 19 for an independent and democratic republic.

Gorbachev's inconsistent and halfhearted crackdowns—sending troops here and there, censoring television programs, ordering soldiers and police to patrol certain cities—not only did not calm the situation but increased popular hostility to his continued rule. Public opinion toward Gorbachev cooled rapidly after the Baltic crisis. More and more open attacks were made on him by the opposition. By March 1991 a stalemate had been reached between those around Yeltsin, who wanted more rapid democratization and marketization; the party conservatives, who wanted a retreat to law and order; and Gorbachev, who wanted gradual, controlled movement forward. Grappling with the two paramount problems, the failing economy and the breakup of the union, Gorbachev tried to achieve consensus on the union treaty as a necessary first step toward economic revival. On March 17 a referendum was held throughout the Soviet Union on the question "Do you consider necessary the preservation of the Union of Soviet Socialist Republics as a renewed federation of equal sovereign republics, in which the rights and freedom of an individual of any nationality will be fully guaranteed?" Over 80 percent of the Soviet adult population voted, and 76.4 percent came out for the Union. In the nine republics that participated in the vote, all returned a large majority in favor of maintaining the Union. Six republics (Armenia, Georgia, Moldavia, and the Baltic republics) refused to participate. Russia and others added other questions to the referendum. Though support for Yeltsin was strong in Russia, where his proposal for an elected presidency passed overwhelmingly (70 percent), Gorbachev could be satisfied with a slightly larger Russian vote for the Union (71 percent). The greatest support for the Union came from the countryside and the more conservative republics in Central Asia, the least from the largest cities—Moscow, Leningrad, and Kiev. But now Gorbachev could argue that he had a mandate for reforming the USSR as a free association of sovereign republics.

The crisis intensified in April. As Yeltsin won new powers in the Russian republic, Gorbachev reconsidered his strategy. His turn to the right had effectively restrained the "forces of order" for five months but had not halted the drift toward independence in the Baltics, Transcaucasia, and Moldavia. A choice had to be made between armed force and a complete break with the democrats, on one hand, and accommodation and negotiation with the popular forces, on the other. Now, with the democrats more popular than ever, Gorbachev shifted once again. On April 23 he met with Yeltsin and the leaders of eight other republics at a dacha at Novo-Ogarevo and hastily worked out an agreement to finalize the draft of the union treaty, prepare a constitution for the union of sovereign states within six months after the signing of the treaty, and carry out new elections for the union political bodies. No overthrow of elected bodies was to be tolerated; the role of union republics was to be radically enhanced, and the center would be reduced to an executive dependent on the wills and revenues of the republics.

Both the drafting of the union treaty and the referendum indicated that the Soviet Union had divided into two parts: the six independence-minded republics for whom no form of union was acceptable and the Muslim–Slavic majority that had voted for union, though the form was yet to be decided. At Novo-Ogarevo

Gorbachev had essentially agreed to recognize the sovereignty of all union republics and the right of those who wished to opt out of the union to do so.
Though he still faced significant opposition from conservatives, who feared that
the union treaty conceded far too much power to the republics, Gorbachev managed to tame resistance to the treaty in the USSR Supreme Soviet and to force
through a social democratic platform in the party's Central Committee.

Ostensibly allies once again, Gorbachev and Yeltsin were in fact rivals for
power with contrasting visions of the new union of republics. While Gorbachev
spoke of strong republics and a strong union, Yeltsin and his allies pushed hard
for stronger republics and a weaker union. On June 12 Yeltsin triumphed in
the popular elections for president of the RSFSR, winning 57 percent of the
vote. Russia now became symbolically linked, along with the Baltic republics,
to more determined democratic and market-oriented reform. The promotion
of Russian statehood was based on a concept of Russia as a multinational federation, rather than on an ethnic Russian nationalism. As the movement for a
sovereign Russian state grew, however, it adopted symbols of the old Russia—
the tricolor flag and the double-headed eagle of the tsarist monarchy. Russian
leaders spoke of bringing Russia back into the mainstream of civilization and
to continue its modernization in a more humane, democratic form. Russian
statehood had displaced the Soviet center as the principal vehicle of democratic reform.

On July 11 the USSR Congress of People's Deputies approved the general
conception of the new Union Treaty. A Union of Soviet Sovereign States made
up of sovereign states and itself sovereign was projected. Even though the word
"socialist" had been voted on as part of the name of the new union in the March
referendum, because many republics had given up the word, it was dropped
in the interests of unity. Five days later, however, the leader of Ukraine, Leonid
Kravchuk, warned that Ukraine would not let this opportunity to establish its
statehood slip by and therefore would delay its decision on signing the Union
Treaty. The treaty, he stated, did not conform to the idea of state sovereignty,
and although 26 million people in Ukraine had voted for preserving the Union,
they did not vote for this treaty. Yeltsin as well continued to ask for changes
to the treaty, escalating his demands from meeting to meeting.

Though some of his closest allies, such as Yakovlev, tried to convince Gorbachev to give up on the Communist Party and the idea of socialism, the general secretary refused. Instead, he convinced the Central Committee in July
1991 to adopt a new program that was essentially social democratic. He now
advocated a notion of "market socialism" and planned in private to push for
a split in the party at the forthcoming party congress scheduled for November. Gorbachev agreed with Yeltsin's order to have Communist cells removed
from economic enterprises—a position that irked party conservatives. Convinced that he had tamed the Communist Party and that a renewed party could
be used as an instrument for the renewal of the country, and certain that he
had saved what he could of the Union, Gorbachev set a date, August 21, for
the formal signing of the union treaty and left for vacation in Crimea. But three
days before that, on Sunday, August 18, a group of conservative Communist

leaders, calling themselves the State Committee for the Emergency (GKChP), ordered Gorbachev's arrest and sent tanks into the streets of Moscow.

Coup and Collapse

The coup against Gorbachev and Yeltsin was led by several of the conservative Communists whom Gorbachev had trusted and appointed to office, including his vice president (Yanaev), the prime minister (Pavlov), the defense minister (Yazov), the interior minister (Pugo), the head of the KGB (Kriuchkov), and his own chief of staff (Boldin). All over the world people watched the broadcasts of the Cable News Network (CNN) for the next three days to follow the fate of the Soviet Union. Tanks were stationed in the center of Moscow, newspapers were disciplined or closed, and the coup leaders went on television to explain that they had been forced to take action because Gorbachev was ill and incapacitated and the country had to be saved. Some leaders in the republics went along with the coup. In Azerbaijan, Belorussia, and Uzbekistan local Communists backed the GKChP. Georgia's president, Zviad Gamsakhurdia, equivocated and made an agreement with the local Soviet commander. But in Armenia Levon Ter Petrosian prepared for resistance, in Kazakhstan Nursultan Nazarbaev declared the coup unconstitutional, and in Kyrgyzstan Askar Akaev said that the republic would follow the path of sovereignty no matter what and took measures against the local Communist Party. Estonia and Latvia declared themselves independent. On the day after the coup failed, the Ukrainian Supreme Soviet voted to hold a referendum on the question of secession. On August 27 Moldova (formerly Moldavia) declared itself an independent state. "The center," Armenia's Ter Petrosian said, "has committed suicide."

In Moscow Yeltsin slipped away from the men sent to detain him, made his way to the White House, the Russian parliament building, in the center of the city, and mounted a bold and courageous defense of democracy. The coup leaders hesitated to attack the crowds around the White House, and the soldiers, even the KGB elite units, declined to fire on the demonstrators. Gorbachev, kept relatively isolated in his Crimean home, refused to capitulate to his captors or sanction the coup. By August 21 the coup leaders had given up, and an exhausted Gorbachev returned to the capital. But the sinister plot of the drunken adventurers had completely transformed the political scene. When Gorbachev emerged in the evening of August 22 to give a press conference, he continued to talk as if the party could be saved and as if socialism were a viable political alternative, apparently without realizing that in the eyes of the public both the Communist Party and its ideology had been completely discredited. When he finally visited the Russian parliament, Yeltsin's stronghold, he was treated with disrespect, humiliated by Yeltsin, and taunted by the deputies. Under pressure from Yeltsin, Gorbachev, who clung to the "socialist choice," agreed reluctantly to the dissolution of the Communist Party. In a stroke he lost one of his principal institutional bases of power.

Figure 21.2. Boris Yeltsin defending the White House during the August 1991 coup attempt by conservative Communists (SOVFOTO/TASS).

Yeltsin, strengthened by his defiant resistance to the coup plotters and by the fact that he was the legitimate and popularly elected president of the RSFSR, emerged as the strongest political figure in the country, while Gorbachev was isolated in the Kremlin. The institutions that had constituted the Soviet center—the Communist Party, the state bureaucracy, the army, and the police—were all suspect, and the victorious democrats swiftly dismantled what they could. Yeltsin declared all property of the Communist Party, worth billions of dollars, to be RSFSR state property, and began taking over the institutions of the moribund Soviet Union. Gorbachev met with Yeltsin and the leaders of ten other union republics the day after his return to Moscow, and they agreed that the Congress of People's Deputies, the supreme legislative body of the Soviet Union, should be dissolved and that supreme power in the country during the transition period would devolve to a State Council made up of the leaders of the union republics and a newly elected Supreme Soviet. Still hoping that the Union of Sovereign States envisioned in the unsigned Union Treaty would come into being, Gorbachev admitted at the last session of the Congress that he had not acted decisively enough to free the country from "the structures of the totalitarian system that we had been holding onto." Both conservatives and reformers protested dissolving the Congress, while the radicals applauded it and looked forward to a looser commonwealth of sovereign states. By dissolving the Congress Gorbachev eliminated one more base of his power. Essentially, on September 5 the old Soviet Union died, but it was not buried for a few months, as Gorbachev tried in vain to create new interconnective tissues among the republics.

The weakness of many of the republics, most importantly in Central Asia and Transcaucasia, and the economic dependence of the periphery on the center slowed the drift to full separation for a time. A statement by Yeltsin's press officer about rethinking the borders between the Russian republic and its neighbors with Russian subpopulations sent a collective shiver through the republics, particularly in Ukraine and Kazakhstan, and forced a retreat to the pragmatic recognition of all existing borders. The newly formed State Council's first decision was to recognize the independence of the three Baltic republics. The republics of Armenia, Kazakhstan, and Ukraine declared independence, or at least the intention of becoming independent. Gorbachev worked tirelessly to rebuild the central institutions of the Union, but each time he seemed to secure an agreement, it soon unraveled.

At the same time Yeltsin was trying to get his house in order. His government intended to carry out radical economic reforms once plans to "finish demolishing" the center had been completed. Step by step Yeltsin abolished or emasculated the union ministries. At the beginning of November the Russian Congress of People's Deputies granted Yeltsin extraordinary powers to create a stronger state and accelerate reforms. Many feared that the centrifugal forces that had pulled the Soviet Union apart would do the same with the Russian Federation.

Yeltsin created his own governing team, led by Gennadii Burbulis, a representative from Yeltsin's hometown, Sverdlovsk; Egor Gaidar, an economist; and the diplomat Andrei Kozyrev, the foreign minister of Russia. Their program was to complete the destruction of the totalitarian state system, to destroy the power of the Communist nomenklatura, and to institute a market economy. This revolutionary course was popular among some intellectuals and the public in the largest Russian cities, though far less widely supported outside of the capitals. Opposition began forming almost immediately, and by December Yeltsin's vice president, Aleksandr Rutskoi, began speaking out against the planned freeing of prices.

From late August to late December 1991, two competing governments existed in Moscow. The one led by Gorbachev slowly evaporated, as the movement for independence in the republics sapped the strength of the center. The other government, led by Yeltsin, swelled with new powers, sucking the sense out of an all-union government. Many in the West, including President George Bush, hoped desperately that some form of union might be preserved. At the same time they identified Yeltsin as the most reliable democratic and market-oriented politician. For most ordinary Russians, however, Yeltsin's appeal came, not from his shift toward democracy and the market, but from his image as a man of the people and his strong will.

The end for the Union came in December. On the first of the month voters in Ukraine elected the former boss of the Communist Party, Leonid Kravchuk, as president of the republic and overwhelmingly approved independence. Kravchuk opposed Gorbachev's plans for a new union, and by this vote the resurrection of the Union became impossible. A week later, at a closed meeting in Khrushchev's old hunting lodge in Belovezhskaia Pushcha, Belorus, Yeltsin and Kravchuk met with the Belorussian leader, Stanislav Shushkevich, and the three heads of state agreed to terminate the USSR and form a Commonwealth of Independent States (CIS). When informed of the decision, Gorbachev was shocked: "They had already decided everything and they had support—they had spoken with [President] Bush. I said, that's a disgrace, an outrage. You've talked with the President of the United States, but you didn't consult the President of the USSR."

The dismantling of the Union was now unstoppable. The Central Asian republics, which had been left out of the decision to form the Commonwealth, agreed to join the CIS, and on December 21 eleven republics (the Baltic states and Georgia did not attend) issued a statement in Alma-Ata: "With the formation of the Commonwealth of Independent States, the USSR ceases to exist." It only remained for Gorbachev to address the television audience on December 25 and formally resign as president of a country that no longer existed. Now triumphant, having vanquished his political foe, Yeltsin spoke of Gorbachev in the past tense: "He thought he could unite the impossible: communism with the market, ownership by the people with private ownership, a multiparty system with the Communist Party of the Soviet Union. These are impossible unions. But he wanted to achieve them, and this was his basic strategic mistake."

The death of the Soviet Union in its seventy-fourth year represented a failure of Gorbachev's attempt to manage a triple reform of democratization, economic transformation, and decolonization of the non-Russian republics. The system was simply not equipped to dismantle all at once, and at a late date, the old practices of command in the economic and political spheres and to construct a democratic multinational federation. Had reform begun earlier, or economic conditions been more fortuitous, or the reforms been carried out sequentially, as in China, with economic changes preceding political changes, rather than happening simultaneously, perhaps perestroika might have had a different outcome. The Soviet system had weathered far worse crises in the past than it faced in the late 1980s, but once a program of liberalization had been initiated from above, it moved quickly out of the control of its initiators. Gorbachev's project of reform from above prompted a series of national movements from below. As several republics went their own way, Gorbachev's "socialist choice" and supranational ideology evaporated—the victim of economic collapse, the dissolution of state authority, and the rise of powerful nationalisms and ambitious local elites.

Suggestions for Further Reading

The collapse of the Soviet Union remains an open topic of investigation by historians and other social scientists. Some of the more interesting analyses of recent years of the USSR include Linda J. Cook, *The Soviet Social Contract and Why It Failed* (Cambridge, Mass., 1993); Philip Roeder, *Red Sunset: The Failure of Soviet Politics* (Princeton, N.J., 1993); Zbigniew Brzezinski, *The Grand Failure* (New York, 1989); Martin Malia, *The Soviet Tragedy: A History of Socialism in the Russia, 1917–1991* (New York, 1994); Ken Jowitt, *New World Disorder: The Leninist Extinction* (Berkeley, Calif., 1992); Manuel Castells and Emma Kiselyova, *The Collapse of Soviet Communism: A View from the Information Society*

(Berkeley, Calif., 1995); Angus Roxburgh, *The Second Russian Revolution* (London, 1991); John Miller, *Mikhail Gorbachev and the End of Soviet Power* (London, 1993); and a prize-winning account by journalist David Remnick, *Lenin's Tomb: The Last Days of the Soviet Empire* (New York, 1994).

Very important collections of articles should be considered: Alexander Dallin and Gail W. Lapidus (eds.), *The Soviet System from Crisis to Collapse* (Boulder, Colo., 1995); Rachel Denber (ed.), *The Soviet Nationality Reader: The Disintegration in Context* (Boulder, Colo., 1992); and Michael Mandelbaum (ed.), *The Rise of Nations in the Soviet Union: American Foreign Policy and the Disintegration of the USSR* (New York, 1991).

Several important memoirs should be read: Mikhail Gorbachev, *Memoirs* (New York, 1995); Yegor Ligachev, *Inside Gorbachev's Kremlin* (New York, 1993); Valery Boldin, *Ten Years that Shook the World: The Gorbachev Era as Witnessed by his Chief of Staff* (New York, 1994); Edward Shevardnadze, *The Future Belongs to Freedom* (London, 1991); and Andrei S. Grachev, *Final Days; The Inside Story of the Collapse of the Soviet Union* (Boulder, Colo., 1995).

CHAPTER 22
The Second Russian Republic and the Near Abroad

For television viewers in the West watching the confusing cascade of events in Russia after the collapse of the Soviet Union, two contrasting images were indelibly etched into their minds: first, the courageous Boris Yeltsin standing on a tank before the massive edifice known as the White House to defend the democratic reforms in August 1991, and second, the scorched remains of the same building after the siege ordered by the Russian president. In the early 1990s Yeltsin was the West's most familiar Russian icon, the recognizable symbol of shared hopes for democracy. As the principal player in a drama to which hundreds of millions of citizens of the Russian Federation and other former Soviet republics and much of the post–Cold War world were spectators, Yeltsin anchored the uncertainties of the move toward democracy and a market economy and seemed to provide a reliable guide to an unknown future.

Boris Yeltsin was born in 1931 in the Sverdlovsk district of the Urals. His father was an enterprising peasant who in 1934 was arrested as a kulak and served a three-year sentence. Young Boris was a boisterous boy, excelling in sports, particularly volleyball, and early on displayed a competitive, combative nature. His education was largely technical, and his early career was in the construction industry. He joined the Communist Party in 1961 and, in his own words, threw himself "into a party career as I had once thrown myself into spiking a volleyball." He advanced rapidly. By 1976 he was first secretary of the Sverdlovsk district committee, and in 1981 he was elevated to the Central Committee. Proposed by Gorbachev's lieutenant, Ligachev, Yeltsin in December 1985 became first secretary of the Moscow city committee of the party, in effect, the all-powerful mayor of the city, and immediately gained a reputation as a plain-talking enthusiast for perestroika. He soon was raised to the position of candidate member of the Politburo, but even as his star was rising, Yeltsin began to have doubts about the sincerity of Gorbachev's reformist impulses. Yeltsin's career seemed to come to a halt in October 1987, when he lashed out at Ligachev and resigned as Moscow city committee secretary. His fondness for alcohol and his heart condition did not bode well for a political future. But then he was hooked by history, as his status as a martyr and his frankness and popular touch endeared him to the radical reformers who wanted to push further and faster toward the pluralistic democracy that Gorbachev had envisioned.

Yeltsin proved to be a talented politician in the public arena that had opened up in the Soviet Union. Tall and broadly built, he displayed a massive physical presence, a sense of confidence and conviction, and honesty and authenticity at a time when Gorbachev appeared hesitant and even devious. Yeltsin's courage was evident early in 1991 during the crisis over the Baltic republics, when he flew to the region to show his support for their independence movements, and again in August during the coup attempt by the conservative Communists. Less attractive were Yeltsin's petty and vindictive treatment of Gorbachev after defeating him, his tendency to be confrontational rather than ready to negotiate with his political opponents, his inability to consolidate alliances, and his willingness to take a tough line and even use military power, all of which compounded the difficulty of solving political issues, as in the struggle with his first parliament in September–October 1993 and in the conflict over Chechnya.

Various analysts have blamed the initial difficulties of the transition to democracy in the former Soviet Union on the legacies of the Communist regime, which had scoured the landscape of democratic traditions and alternative elites and left an enduring economic crisis. Others reach back further and indict Russian political culture with its affinity for authoritarianism. But among the most potent factors in the difficult passage toward democracy was the choice to take a revolutionary rather than a gradualist path from Communist Party rule to a more representative system. Though Gorbachev attempted to maintain a steady reform process through the existing state institutions and within a unified Soviet Union, his opponents who were committed to rapid democratization, led by Yeltsin and the nationalist leaders of the Baltic republics, favored a more radical break with the existing system and the breakup of the USSR. In the revolutionary transition, instead of compromises and agreements within the elites, battlelines hardened into confrontation and a winner-take-all struggle for power. The result was a far more unpredictable and socially costly process of change than Gorbachev and the moderates had contemplated. Those supporting Yeltsin argued that only such a revolutionary course would allow reform to succeed. Any other course would lead to collapse or restoration of the former Communist elite.

The attempt to reverse perestroika in August 1991 by conservative Communists was a desperate gamble by men who understood that Gorbachev had by that time turned decisively toward alliance with the more democratic forces in society. The failure of the ill-planned coup demonstrated how successful Gorbachev had been in undermining the power base of the old Communist elite. Three important consequences were soon apparent. First, the new Russia was deeply divided politically. Hard-line Communists, those who wanted a restoration of the system and the Soviet Union to the nostalgic ideal of Brezhnev's USSR, were largely marginalized after the August coup. The "red-browns," as the hard-liners were called, marched in the streets and issued chilling denunciations of their opponents in the unfettered press but had little popular following. Yet at the same time, according to one opinion poll, 40 percent of the population supported the program of the "putchists" who had carried out the August coup. The so-called democratic forces were themselves split between more moderate elements who favored a gradualist course of reform—keeping the Soviet Union intact as a looser federation and promoting moderate economic changes using both market and state forces—and more radical elements around Yeltsin who proposed the strengthening of the republics, particularly Russia, and a rapid push toward a fully marketized economy. Though there was an upsurge in popular support for reform in late 1991, there was no general consensus in Russia, let alone the Soviet Union, on a political or economic program for the future, and the fractures in the ruling elites that emerged in the late Soviet and early post-Soviet period widened under the impact of Yeltsin's initial policies.

Second, the principal links holding the Soviet Union (and even Russia) together, both as an empire and as a coherent and cohesive state, were being torn apart. The Communist Party, the army, and the police had all been compromised, and their leaders discredited. The decision by Yeltsin to abolish the Communist Party (which Gorbachev opposed at first) removed the very sinews of the old system. Though it ended the possibility of restoring the old order, it also dissolved the musculature that made the country move. Decisions might be taken by the leadership, but there was no guarantee that they would be carried out. Long before the August coup, the command system had been undermined, but after August most of the commanders remained in place, still running the economy and holding many of their offices in the state. With the former Soviet Communist Party treated as an outlaw organization, the Communist parties that emerged after the disbandment of the CPSU were far different from the social democratic organization that Gorbachev had hoped to build. The Communist Party of the Russian Federation and its allied parties were statist nationalist parties, made up of "national Bolsheviks," that bound together conservatives from the old CPSU with national patriots nostalgic for the Soviet Union of Brezhnev's or even Stalin's days.

Though in 1991 Yeltsin publicly maintained that he wanted to preserve some form of union with the other republics, he was increasingly unwilling to share power with Gorbachev and was prepared to assist the centrifugal forces tearing the Union into separate republics. The official dissolution of the Soviet Union in December led to the third major consequence. No shared consensus on the future of Russia and the Commonwealth of Independent States existed among those who had climbed to power, and the breakup of the Union, which few politicians in Russia desired, created one more fracture in leadership circles. At the same time, the overwhelming majority of leaders, most of whom were former members of the Communist Party, faced an ideological abyss. Only a few understood the new language of politics or had much experience with building political consensus through compromise. The vaguely outlined goals—democracy, market economy, national rights—gave little guidance. Russia's democracy was incomplete, unconsolidated, and not yet fully representative, competitive, or pluralist. The constitution was a carryover from Soviet times, amended dozens of times, and was unclear about the division of power between president and parliament. For many of its critics Russian democracy meant simply rule by those who were elected and called themselves democrats. And that understanding was reinforced by Western supporters, particularly the United States, who identified democracy not so much with institutions and practices as with particular individuals.

Yeltsin squandered the enormous popularity he enjoyed at the end of 1991 by acting inconsistently in the political realm. He ignored the advice of some of his advisors to call new elections to the parliament of Russia, the Congress of People's Deputies, and the Supreme Soviet. He also neglected to form his own political party, which might have given his government an institutional base of support in future campaigns. Instead of having regional leaders elected, the president chose to appoint them and left the local soviets in place. He failed to hold elections, which might have assisted the formation of competitive political parties, a necessary element in the transition to a democratic political system. Though embryonic parties had emerged in the last years of the Soviet Union, they were largely elite organizations, often clustered around particular leaders, with unreliable popular support. Without elections they withered away in the first years of the independent Russian Republic. Instead of popular parties, powerful interest groups imbedded in the new economy made their own ad hoc arrangements with state authorities to their own mutual benefit. Politics moved from the street and the electoral arena into the hallways of the bureaucracy and the backrooms of the presidential apparatus.

The first two years of the new Russian Republic, from the August 1991 coup to the September 1993 dismissal of parliament, was marked by a vigorous, even vicious struggle for power between the ruling elites. Because Russia's transition to democracy was at one and the same time a transition to capitalism, that struggle was all the more intense. In the absence of a broad political consensus on what kind of economic system should be established in Russia, those around Yeltsin developed and pushed their own agenda of a rapid transition from a state-run to a market-capitalist economy, a program that became known as "shock therapy." As the old command economy was transformed into a market system, those who held political power were in a position to determine the distribution of massive property and wealth in the greatest giveaway of assets in history. As the pain from the economic transition increased, it became evident that it was impossible for Russia both to impose shock therapy and maintain the existing constitutional order with power uncertainly divided between president and parliament.

The Shock of Therapy

As the fifteen union republics became fifteen independent states, eleven of which were loosely associated in a Commonwealth, the highly centralized and integrated economy of the Soviet Union broke up into separate economies cut off from one another by new borders. Ethnic conflict and warfare in parts of the former USSR further depressed certain regions and divided one area from another. At the same time trade with Eastern Europe fell, as goods had to be purchased at world market prices and paid for in hard currency. Russia, which was the most powerful economy in the region and the source of most of the energy that fueled the industry of the former USSR, turned inward to deal with its declining economic prospects and the growing problem of inflation. Even before the Union had been dissolved, young radical reformers within the circles around Yeltsin, led by Burbulis and Gaidar, pushed an agenda of rapid dismantling of the old political and economic system. Gaidar's conception was that "Russia must have its own monetary and fiscal policy and its own bank" and treat "all other republics as sovereign states." Yeltsin adopted their position and announced, in Gaidar's words, "To make a switch to market prices in one motion is a severe, forced, but necessary measure." The Russian president promised a short period of pain to be followed by prosperity: "Everyone will find life harder for approximately six months, then prices will fall and goods will begin to fill the market. By the autumn of 1992 the economy will have stabilized."

The new year, 1992, began with the launching of Gaidar's radical economic program of "shock therapy." Advised and influenced by Western economists of the monetarist school, the young theorists in Russia's new government wanted to remove the government from the economy and allow the market free rein. They believed that their strategy, which emphasized rapid privatization, marketization, an end of state subsidies to industry, and convertibility of the currency, would remove the ground from under the Communist nomenklatura and render impossible any restoration of the old system. The radical shift to capitalism, like Stalin's abrupt break with NEP, was as much a political as an economic program. Beginning on January 2 prices were freed on 90 percent of goods, excluding bread, vodka, public transport, and energy. Prices soared rapidly, the first day by 250 percent. Within a few months inflation wiped out the savings of millions, while others benefited from their privileged positions, their closeness to people in power, or their willingness to bend the rules to become wealthy. Subsidized credit to industry was to end, and enterprises were supposed to compete in the marketplace. In the first quarter of the new year, Gaidar set out to eliminate Russia's budget deficit, which had amounted to somewhere between 17 and 21 percent of gross domestic product in 1991. In fact, the deficit ran about 8 to 10 percent of GNP in the first quarter of 1992. When faced by opposition in April, the government prudently decided not to tighten credit further, which would have thrown millions of people out of work.

The obstacles to successful reform were formidable. The Soviet economy had been highly monopolistic, with single industries or plants producing a product. Seventy-seven percent of products were made by a single enterprise. Industries were run by state managers who were unwilling to operate in conformity with the rules of the market. The Russian government began to turn industrial enterprises over to new joint-stock companies with shares available to ordinary citizens through a voucher system. Each citizen eventually was given a voucher worth 10,000 rubles (about $22) with which to pursue stock. The vouchers bought little, but many workers invested them in the factories in which they worked. Some plants, about 64 percent in January 1993, were essentially owned by the workers, but the former managers actually controlled the enterprises. These managers, who previously had been supervised by the industrial ministries, the planning agencies, and the party, now were free to take over their plants and industries. Workers in general lost what little influence they had gained in the Andropov and Gorbachev years.

Even as enterprise directors allied with politicians gained from the move toward privatization, they frustrated other parts of Gaidar's program, particularly the move to make enterprises respond to market forces. Holding the levers of industrial production in their hands and threatening the collapse of industry, managers were able to demand subsidized credits from the government. They received the credits, made money from government subsidies rather than profits in the market, and socked their money into Swiss bank accounts and foreign investments. In one notorious case, the president of LUKoil, who had no real assets in 1991, increased his worth to $2.4 billion by 1995. In monopoly conditions managers set prices as they wished, further fueling inflation. Corruption, bribery, and criminality became part of the fabric of daily life in Russia. One report prepared for Yeltsin in January 1994 claimed that criminal mafias controlled in some fashion 70 to 80 percent of all business and banking.

Gaidar was never able to convince Yeltsin of the need to cut off subsidies to industry and interrepublic trade. On this issue he was defeated by the resistance of the industrial managers. Russia's energy industry, headed by the powerful Viktor Chernomyrdin, resisted the shift to world market prices in 1992 and gave gas and oil to Russian industry at about 1 percent of the world price. Middlemen bought up Russian oil at the domestic price and then sold it abroad for up to 100 times that price. The same thing happened with subsidized grain. Russia continued to supply other former Soviet republics with energy at lower than world market prices, though the price of oil and gas began to rise after the collapse of the USSR. Other exports to the Commonwealth states were also given credits, which were subsidized at low interest rates. Russia gave more in credits to Central Asia than it exported to the region. Even so, despite the subsidies, trade between former Soviet republics fell by half from 1990 to 1992. Summarizing the effects of the first year and a half of reform, political scientist Michael McFaul concluded, "By the summer of 1993, insiders had acquired majority shares in two-thirds of Russia's privatized and privatizing firms, state subsidies accounted for 22 percent of Russia's GNP, little if any restructuring (bankruptcies, downsizing, unbundling) had taken place within enterprises, and few market institutions had been created."

Already weakened by the Gorbachev reforms—the national income had declined by 19 percent in 1991—the economy went into a tailspin. In the first six months of 1992 national income fell an additional 20 percent. By 1995 GNP and industrial production were about 50 percent of what they had been in 1991. Though shops were filled with goods and 5 percent of the population had become wealthy, for the bulk of the people poverty had become the norm. Pensioners were hardest hit and could barely survive. In central Moscow whole streets were blocked by people selling off their personal goods to make ends meet. Train stations became hostels for the growing number of homeless and runaway children. Unemployment rose; by mid-1992 almost a million people

lost their jobs, the majority of them women. Salaried workers and even officers and soldiers in the army did not receive their wages month after month.
With prices rising twenty-six-fold in 1992, wages could not keep up with inflation, which by the end of the year was at 2,500 percent. By March 1995 the
average Russian salary was 33 percent lower than it had been a year earlier.
Nearly a third of the population had incomes below the subsistence minimum.
As Russian industrial output spiraled downward, 50 percent of what consumers lived on was imported goods, often sold in small kiosks on the streets
or at the entrances to the subway.

The radicalization of economic policy in the first year of Yeltsin's rule meant
that a strategy based on compromise and brokered consensus was jettisoned
for a rapid advance that further divided public opinion and eventually the leadership of the republic itself. As Russia descended into economic meltdown, the
government was faced by a deepening crisis of political credibility, with the
population growing ever poorer and more disillusioned with politics and political leaders. Yeltsin's popularity, even among his former followers, diminished, and his opponents within the parliament appealed for more gradual
moves toward privatization and greater guarantees of social protection. Rus-
lan Khasbulatov, who had been Yeltsin's ally during the struggles against Gorbachev and his choice for speaker of the parliament, and Rutskoi, who had
stood side by side with Yeltsin during the defense of the White House in 1991
and had been Yeltsin's choice for vice president, turned into leaders of the opposition. In April 1992 the parliament challenged Gaidar's program, and the
prime minister was forced to respond by inviting representatives of powerful
industrial interests, most importantly Chernomyrdin, the leading figure in the
energy industry, into the government. A significant sign of compromise with
the powerfully entrenched economic interests was the appointment of a friend
of the indusrialists as head of the Russian Central Bank. Many commentators
saw these additions to the circles of political power as the effective end to the
program of "shock therapy." On the president's side Yeltsin solidified his own
office by creating a Security Council to coordinate the army and police forces.

The political establishment divided into two broad camps: the presidential
camp, which represented the liberal reformers and technocrats, and the parliamentary, which represented nationalists and populists. In September 1992
Yeltsin angrily confronted the legislature and told them to "desist from pointless activity," but in the next two months, faced by the relentless opposition,
he steadily reduced his support for Gaidar, fired Burbulis, and promoted more
conservative figures. To gain support from the regional governors he formed
a Council of Heads of Republics and a Council of Governors. As the economy
failed to recover, even economic reformers broke with the radical approach of
Gaidar. In December 1992 the economist Shatalin, whose credentials as a reformer were impeccable, rejected the idea that the Gaidar approach was the
only way to reach a market economy and called for combining reform with social welfare. "The liberal approach means going against the will of the majority," he wrote, "and destroying the social welfare guarantees and the material
basis for paying for them which people have managed to reach at such great
sacrifice."

The economic crisis deepened the growing differences between the president's men and the parliament, and the first of a series of political showdowns occurred in December 1992 when the Congress of Peoples' Deputies reduced Yeltsin's power. With confrontation and political breakdown imminent, a compromise was brokered. The Congress agreed to a referendum (desired by Yeltsin) to resolve the question of whether Russia would have a parliamentary or presidential republic. Yeltsin replaced Gaidar with Chernomyrdin, who promised more moderate reforms. Instead of launching a working arrangement, however, the December compromise led to nine months of political squabbling.

Constitutional Crisis

Throughout much of 1993 the popularity and prestige of both the government and the parliament continued to erode. When elected in March 1990, the Congress had had more than 80 percent Communist Party members, and many saw it as representative of the corrupt and power-hungry nomenklatura of the Soviet period. The Supreme Soviet, chosen by the Congress, was divided into fourteen principal factions, from hard-liners to democrats, but the tone and direction of its debates often reflected the arrogance of its chairman, Khasbulatov, and his ally, Rutskoi, both of whom associated with unsavory allies on the political Right such as monarchists, restorationist Communists, and rabid Russian nationalists. They feared that the forthcoming referendum would become a plebiscite against the parliament. A crisis broke out in early spring. Congress scrapped the December agreement, came out against the referendum, and rejected advancing the elections to parliament. On March 20 Yeltsin went on television and issued a decree on "special rule." He ordered the referendum to be held and denounced the actions of the Congress as "revenge . . . by former party nomenklatura." Yeltsin seemed to many to be preparing for a coup against the parliament. The Constitutional Court condemned Yeltsin's speech as a violation of the constitution, and important constituencies, such as the Civic Union, which represented many industrial managers, opposed the decree. Within a few days Yeltsin was forced to back down, and the Congress, at the end of a stormy session, agreed to Yeltsin's referendum.

The referendum, held on April 25, was a victory for Yeltsin: 58 percent expressed confidence in the president, and 53 percent supported his reform policies. But there were ominous aspects. While Yeltsin's greatest support came from Moscow and St. Petersburg, as well as the far eastern regions of Russia (Khabarovsk, Kamchatka), the north, and the Urals, he lost heavily in the non-Russian autonomous republics, the Volga region, and central Russia. While slightly more than two-thirds of the army voted for Yeltsin, nearly a third voted against him. His popularity had slipped in the last year. The clearest message of the referendum was that the vast country was deeply divided about its political leadership and its economic program. Yeltsin was certainly more popular than the parliament, but the parliament represented a significant proportion of the electorate and, more importantly, the political elite, particularly outside Moscow, where local leaders preferred the parliament to the president.

Figure 22.1. Democracy Russian-style. President Yeltsin does the frug while campaigning for reelection, June 1996 (REUTERS/Victor Korotayev/Archive Photos).

As in the last year of Gorbachev's rule, so in the second year of the Yeltsin administration the erosion of power in the center led to fragmentation of the country. Various Russian regions and non-Russian republics declared their laws superior to those of the federation and tried to control their own natural resources and retain the taxes they collected. The government appeared powerless to stop the centrifugal forces in the country, and though it worked out a Federation Treaty for the units of the federation to sign, different arrangements were negotiated with different autonomies. With parliament and the executive in a state of near-permanent gridlock, Yeltsin's advisors began looking for ways to resolve the crisis of power. In the summer the president organized his own constitutional conference, which approved the draft of a new constitution written by his advisors. Yeltsin's constitution was based on a strong presidency to which the government and the bureaucracy were responsible. The president would nominate the members of courts and have the right to dissolve the bicameral legislature in case of emergency. Parliament dug in its heels and stood by its own constitutional draft. No resolution of the crisis appeared possible within the framework of the old constitution. After parliament overturned Yeltsin's veto of an anti-inflationary budget, Yeltsin made a series of visits to military bases, and while inspecting the MVD troops, he announced that Gaidar would return to his government. As one journalist put it, "The president's best ideas come to him when he is, if not on top of a tank, at least in the immediate vicinity of one." On September 21 Yeltsin suspended parliament and announced parliamentary elections for December.

Parliament refused to retire quietly; when its most militant members holed up in the White House, the lines were drawn for confrontation. The Constitutional Court again ruled that Yeltsin had acted unconstitutionally. When on Sunday, October 3, crowds of pro-Soviet demonstrators broke through police lines to rally at the White House, the two-week stalemate exploded into open warfare. Rutskoi incited the armed irregulars to seize city hall and the television center at Ostankino. Khasbulatov told the parliament that it might become necessary to occupy the Kremlin. The government was eerily silent at first. It was not clear for many hours which side the army and police might take. Only after Yeltsin went personally to the Ministry of Defense to assure the high command that the army would not be held responsible for the consequences of an attack on the parliament did the military send specially picked troops to launch its attack on the White House. Yeltsin spoke to the nation of an armed Communist-fascist mutiny. Artillery blasted the building, setting it on fire, and the parliament quickly succumbed. The building that had resisted the coup two years earlier burned for almost a day.

The violence in the streets of Moscow was shocking to most Russians. This was the first use of military force in a massive way in Russian politics since the civil war. After some hesitation Yeltsin acted decisively to quell the crisis he had initiated. He used the military in a way that the coup organizers in August 1991 had balked at doing. Besides further splitting the political forces in the country, the bloodshed and brutality drove many of the democratic intelligentsia and like-minded politicians out of the Yeltsin camp. Russia entered a new and uncertain period after September 21, 1993. The institutions and rules of conduct of perestroika period had been swept away. The kindest reading of the effects of Yeltsin's actions was that the last vestiges of Soviet power had been eliminated, that no alternative to the seizure of power and crushing of resistance existed, and that Russia had embarked on the surest road to democracy. The cruelest reading was that the lurching reforms and gradualist evolutionary dismantling of the old order and the building of a new legal and constitutional order had been summarily replaced by a revolutionary, more authoritarian path to establishing a yet unknown Russian state. Yeltsin's first two years in power had failed to set a firm economic course or to build the broad political coalitions needed to move Russia toward capitalism. He had constructed a political world in which the opposition was demonized as Communist hard-liners and his program was imagined as the only path to civilization.

When elections were held in December, the voters turned away from the pro-Yeltsin forces and the radical market reformers and voted for the nationalists, led by the inflammatory Vladimir Zhirinovskii, and the former Communists. In the elections to the Duma, the lower house, Gaidar's party, Russia's Choice, ended up with only 15.5 percent of the popular vote. Altogether the reformist parties won 27.5 percent, the centrist parties 25 percent, and the anti-Yeltsin opposition parties (the Russian Communist Party; their rural allies, the Agrarians; and Zhirinovskii's misnamed Liberal Democrats) over 43 percent. A volatile and charismatic demagogue, Zhirinovskii had campaigned effectively on television, speaking loosely of nuclear war, restoration of the Russian Empire, expansion to the Indian Ocean, and taking back Alaska from the United States. Officially the Yeltsin constitution was barely approved, and suspicions remained that it had not, in fact, been ratified by a majority. In any case, the votes cast by the followers of the radical nationalists were key to the passage of the constitution. The elections were a repudiation of the Gaidar reform program and a call for order, less disruptive change, and restoration of Russian power.

Russia, the Near Abroad, and Beyond

The dissolution of the Soviet Union and the creation of a new Russian state fundamentally changed international politics. Suddenly, one of the superpowers was gone, replaced by a far weaker cluster of states. The Russian Republic became the successor to the USSR, took over its seat in the United Nations and on the Security Council, and absorbed all the ministries and institutions of the now-defunct Union, but it possessed only a shadow of the power and influence of the old Soviet Union. Most of the former Soviet republics, except the Baltic republics and Georgia, joined the new Commonwealth of Independent States (CIS), a loose arrangement that attempted to maintain some military and economic ties among the republics. Russia's policy in the republics of the former Soviet Union, the so-called Near Abroad, was inconsistent and hesitant. Consumed by its own internal problems and divided between two rival centers of authority—the presidency and the parliament—the Russian government was unable to assert forcefully its authority outside its borders. The result was that various republics looked further afield for new friends, and other powers were able to make influential inroads into the former Soviet periphery: Turkey and Iran in the Caucasus and Central Asia, the Scandinavian countries in the Baltic republics, and Eastern Europe in Belorus and Ukraine. Georgia made appeals to Germany, Ukraine, and the world community in general. Armenia tried to play both the Turkish and Iranian cards, while Azerbaijan, which was ruled briefly by a nationalist government, attempted to bring Turkey directly into Transcaucasian politics. But the fears and dreams of a Pan-Turkish future in the Caucasus proved illusory, a figment not only of Armenian imagination but of Turkish as well.

The post-Soviet world was not a world of equals. Almost all the republics that emerged from the Soviet Union were relatively weak economically and militarily, and Russia loomed over its neighbors as a colossus among pygmies. The reduced former superpower at first attempted to demonstrate that it was prepared to live in peace with its neighbors, use diplomatic rather than military means to solve disputes, and deal with the former Soviet republics as equal and sovereign states. Yeltsin and his foreign minister, Andrei Kozyrev, had made their reputations by supporting the political independence of the non-Russian republics, particularly the rights of the Baltic states. But almost immediately after the breakup of the Soviet Union, the issues of Russian troops on the territory of other republics, treatment of ethnic Russian and Russian-

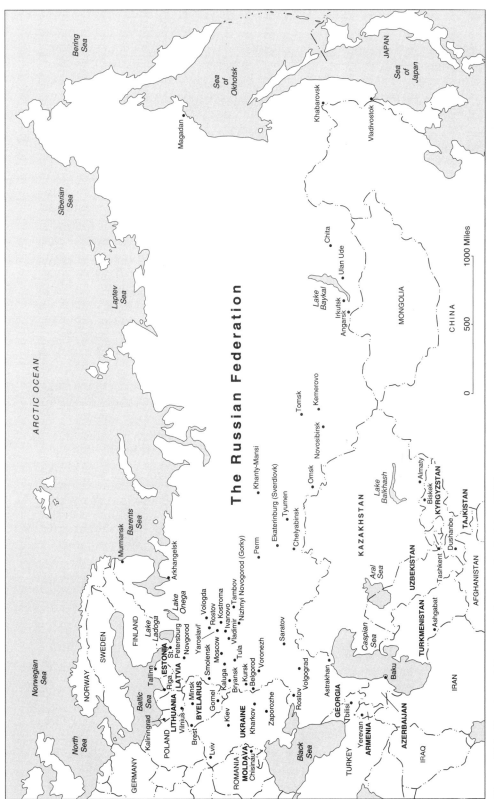

Figure 22.2. Russia and the newly independent states, 1997.

speaking peoples in the newly independent states, and the nature of economic relations created tensions between Russia and the other states. The new Russian state began to reassert its special role in the region, particularly in the states of the southern tier, that is, Central Asia and Transcaucasia, and in Belorus and Moldova.

When the Soviet Union fell apart, it fragmented into fifteen states that corresponded to the fifteen former union republics. However artificial some of those republics might have been at their creation in the 1920s and 1930s, they had become, over the years of Soviet power, something like nation-states. Almost all had majorities of the titular nationality (Kazakhstan was the single exception), and even after independence national Communist political elites remained in power in most of them, in one form or another. At one extreme, in the Central Asian republics of Turkmenistan and Uzbekistan, the old Communist elite remained in power with little change. The leaders of these republics, Saparmurat Niiazov and Islam Karimov, effectively eliminated opposition, preserved much of the old economic system, and kept the monopoly of power in the hands of the old party, now refurbished as a national party. In Kazakhstan Nursultan Nazarbaev, the former party leader and ally of Gorbachev, retained power and was eventually elected president for an extended term. Kazakhstan maintained a policy of ethnic toleration, divided as it was between large Russian and Slavic populations, particularly in the north, and the native Kazakhs and some Uzbeks primarily in the south. Tajikistan tragically dissolved into civil war between regional elites and was pacified only with the intervention of Russian troops. Resource-poor Kyrgyzstan fared better under the leadership of the academic Askar Akaev, who established a relatively democratic political system and reduced the influence of the Communists.

To the west of Russia Belorus remained largely run by the former Communists. Given its relatively weak sense of national identity, leading Belorussian politicians and intellectuals pressed for the merger of their republic with Russia. Moldova suffered from the rebellion of the Slavic people of Transdneistria, and its leaders steadily moved away from earlier interest in merging with neighboring Rumania and toward a clearer sense of Moldovan identity and independent statehood. Ukraine, the second-largest post-Soviet state, was ruled by an old Communist elite that accommodated itself to the new nationalist mood in much of the country. The nationalist forces around Rukh backed Kravchuk as he became the president of the independent state and a defender of Ukrainian interests in the early conflicts with Russia over the division of the Black Sea fleet and Crimea. The Baltic countries made the most rapid and successful transition to democracy and a market economy of any of the former Soviet states. Estonia and Latvia were ruled by anti-Communist nationalists, while in Lithuania the national Communists, transformed into social democrats, returned to power in democratic elections.

The Transcaucasian republics had three distinct post-Soviet experiences. Armenia made the gentlest and most successful transition to democracy under its nationalist president, Levon Ter Petrosian, though eventually his government used the instruments of the state against major oppositional parties and manipulated elections in order to stay in power. Georgia, on the other hand, fragmented into regions and nationalities when a rabidly chauvinistic leader, Zviad Gamsakhurdia, attempted to construct a Georgia exclusively for Georgians. Ethnic war was followed by civil war. Many of Gamsakhuria's supporters turned against him and invited Shevardnadze, the former Communist Party chief, to return to Georgia. Only then were Georgians able to begin the painful process of reintegrating the fractured country. Azerbaijan remained in Communist hands until May 1992, when the nationalist popular front came to power. But the nationalist regime failed to wage effective war against the Armenians in the rebellious region of Mountainous Karabakh, and a military coup brought the former Communist leader, Heidar Aliev, back to Baku. There, as in most post-Soviet states, Communists presented themselves as the transformed leaders of the new nation.

For the fifteen new states in the region, not only state building but construction of a sense of nationhood was on the agenda. To compete in the new discursive and political environment for the available political and economic resources, to gain legitimacy and recognition by the great capitalist democracies and access to the multinational sources of funding, the post-Soviet states had to appear to be creating democratic political systems, establishing market economies, and rejecting state socialism. The difficulty, if not impossibility in the short run, of creating a stable democratic state based on a dominant nationality was compounded by the deep and continuing weakening of state power, which only accelerated after the fall of the USSR. State weakness and the continuous flaring of ethnic and civil strife presented Russia with opportunities to influence, and even intervene, in the states nearest its borders.

In 1993 Russia became more assertive in its claim that the territory of the former Soviet Union was a "a zone of vital interest," in Kozyrev's words. In February Yeltsin indicated that Russia had to defend its interests in the former Soviet Union:

> Russia continues to have a vital interest in the cessation of all armed conflict on the territory of the former USSR. Moreover, the world community is increasingly coming to realize our country's special responsibility in this difficult matter. I believe the time has come for authoritative international organizations, including the UN, to grant Russia special powers as guarantor of peace and stability in this region.

When rogue Russian army officers took action on their own in the Georgian-Abkhaz conflict in Transcaucasia and the Slavic-Moldovan clashes in Transdneistria, their actions appeared to have been sanctioned, and probably were initiated, by elements in the capital. Though it remained more cautious in its dealings with Ukraine and the Baltic states, Russia acted as if it had a freer hand in the southern tier of the CIS.

The question in the Near Abroad was not whether there would be Russian dominance or not but how much dominance and what kind. Once a global power, Russia had become a regional power, as the United States had been in the first half of the nineteenth century, defining its borders and policing its neighborhood to prevent any rivals from establishing influence in its sphere of interest. At the end of 1994 and through 1995 Yeltsin and Kozyrev publicly declared their support for the reintegration of the countries of the former Soviet Union, first economically, but also militarily and possibly politically. But Yeltsin's policy was aimed at voluntary reunion, and he did not respond to the more nationalist voices in Russia who urged the government to carry out an imperial, restorationist policy and "gather" the lands of the former Soviet Union under Moscow's control. Realistically Russia was no longer capable of reconstructing the empire by force. It had neither the military power, the economic capacity, nor the ideological drive to recreate the empire.

With the end of the Cold War and the fall of the Soviet Union, both the Bush and Clinton administrations maintained the same vision of Russia as a partner in the new world order. They invited Yeltsin to the meetings of the G-7, the economic summit of the most powerful and developed capitalist states. Both Russia and Ukraine joined discussions on GATT, the General Agreement on Tariffs and Trade. And all the states of the former Soviet Union joined the Conference on Security and Cooperation in Europe (CSCE, later OSCE). In September 1994 President Bill Clinton met with Yeltsin in a summit meeting in Vancouver and pledged increased economic assistance to Russia. The Clinton administration, however, responded positively to the interest of several East European states in being admitted to NATO. Russian politicians, both in and outside of government, vociferously opposed the expansion of NATO to the east. The United States compromised by inviting the states of the region to join the "Partnership for Peace" program, a solution that partially met the security concerns of East European states but did not actually extend the NATO alliance closer to the borders of Russia. Neither side was completely satisfied, however, and the issue continued to smolder. Supporters of NATO expansion believed that the new democracies of Eastern Europe needed Western security guarantees and that Russia should not be given a veto over their military relations. Critics of NATO expansion, both in Russia and the West, pointed out that further extension of the NATO alliance would not only be unacceptable to Russia but was likely to produce precisely the kind of isolated, confrontational Russian state that the West wanted most to avoid. Reluctantly, Yeltsin signed an accord with NATO in May 1997 that accepted expansion with some concessions to Russian security.

The War in Chechnya

Russia's most unstable border lay in the North Caucasus, where local peoples were barely under the control of Moscow, and Russia was faced with a separatist regime in the Chechen Republic, which the nationalists called Ichkeria. An Islamic people organized into patriarchal clans, the Chechens numbered just under a million in 1989. Active in the anti-Russian resistance led by Imam Shamil in the mid-nineteenth century, they had resisted Soviet power during the Russian Revolution and civil war and fought against the imposition of collective farming in the early 1930s. Ten years later Chechens suffered their greatest tragedy to date when Stalin decided to deport them to Central Asia for their alleged collaboration with the Nazi invaders. In 1956 Khrushchev restored their republic and returned the survivors.

In the last years of the Soviet Union Yeltsin, in a move to secure the support of regional leaders as he campaigned against Gorbachev, publicly advised non-Russian leaders to "seize as much sovereignty as you can handle." This license to gain greater autonomy, even independence, eventually had disastrous effects. At the time of the 1991 coup against Gorbachev a flamboyant officer, Jokhar Dudaev, was elected by a council of elders as leader of Chechnya, and with a small band of armed men he took power from the local party boss. When Dudaev declared Chechnya an independent state, Yeltsin decided to move against the rebels but was restrained by the Russian parliament. After being elected president of the Chechen Republic, in dubious elections, Dudaev defied Russian authority and allowed his republic to become a center for freewheeling economic and criminal activity.

For three years there was a stalemate with Chechnya while Yeltsin successfully negotiated federal relations and treaties with all the other autonomies within the RSFSR. This was one of Yeltsin's more successful efforts at state building and culminated in the Federation Treaty of 1992. The federalists won out against those Russian-nationalists who favored a unitary state. Even Tatarstan, which had claimed to be a sovereign state, agreed to give up its claims to sovereignty for concessions to local authority. Only Chechnya remained a thorn in Yeltsin's side. His agents attempted several times to overthrow Dudaev and set up a puppet government, but all efforts failed. Humiliated and angered, Yeltsin's closest advisors in the Security Council, decided to invade Chechnya without consulting parliament or public opinion.

Russians did not support the Chechnya adventure. On December 8, 1994, the Russian Duma overwhelmingly came out against a state of emergency or a military move against Chechnya. Prominent generals, like the popular Aleksandr Lebed, came out against military action. Even the Communists condemned the president, and their leader, Gennadii Ziuganov, protested, "A year ago they surrounded the House of Soviets, and now they are surrounding a whole republic." On December 11, forty thousand Russian troops were sent into Chechnya. The Russian government was convinced that the victory in Chechnya would come quickly, but its army was ill-prepared. Troops were in disarray, soldiers suffered from low morale, and commanders were unenthusiastic about the war. The storming of the Chechen capital, Groznyi, from late December until early February 1995 left a major city in ruins and tens of thousands of refugees fleeing into the countryside. The war then moved into the hills of Chechnya, and guerrilla bands continued to harass the Russians both inside and outside of Chechnya. For a while negotiators sought a peaceful end to the conflict, but neither side would concede on the issue of independence. Chechnya had been occupied by the Russians but not subdued. In the summer of 1996 the Chechens retook Groznyi from the dispirited Russian troops, and Yeltsin reluctantly gave full powers to General Lebed to negotiate a peace. Lebed won the trust of the rebels and agreed to withdraw Russian troops from the republic, set up a coalition government, and leave the final status of Chechnya undetermined for the next five years. The former superpower had been defeated by guerrillas on its own territory.

Treading Water

Even as the American president visited Moscow in January 1994, proclaiming his support for economic reforms and the Russian president, a new political coalition was being formed. Prime Minister Chernomyrdin dismissed Gaidar and invited representatives of the agrarian and industrial lobbies into the new government. The prime minister told the media that the days of "economic romanticism" were over. A period of much more moderate reform began, and the social polarization between the Yeltsin government and the social forces represented in the parliament diminished somewhat through 1994. Yeltsin became less publicly active and to some degree stood above the political fray. After the bloody denouement of the constitutional crisis of 1993, he tried to appear as a moderate and a centrist, distancing himself from the more radical reformers like Gaidar, the chauvinists around Zhirinovskii, and the Communists led by Ziuganov.

The new Russian state apparatus was centered around the president, whose role had been considerably strengthened by the December 1993 constitution. Under the constitution the president nominated the prime minister, who was then approved by the Duma. In essence the government served at the pleasure of the president, not the parliament. The president was also empowered to legislate by decree. An enormous, unwieldy bureaucracy, employing somewhere between 5,000 and 27,000 people, the presidency looked much like the traditional pattern of Russian rulership. The Russian parliament was made up of two houses: the Federal Council, with two representatives from each of the eighty-nine territorial units in the federation, and the Duma with 550 members, half of them elected from national party lists by proportional representation and half elected from single-member electoral districts. A majority of the Duma deputies elected from party lists were from Moscow, underlining the capital-centric nature of the political parties. Much less confrontational than the first Russian parliament, the Duma leaders worked to create an atmosphere of civil discourse that their predecessors never successfully achieved.

Even as the economy moved toward capitalism, the state failed to construct the legal infrastructure that would protect property, enforce contracts, deal with bankruptcy, and suppress the rising criminality. Corruption was widespread, and political influence colored decisions. The court system remained undeveloped and suspect. The Constitutional Court, which had opposed Yeltsin on occasion in the past, was tamed effectively, and in one of its early rulings agreed that the invasion of Chechnya was constitutional. The rule of law, which had been one of the initial goals of perestroika, continued to elude the Russian political system.

The constitution regularized the relations of the provinces and republics within Russia with the center, reducing the autonomous powers of some that had negotiated greater autonomy in 1992. All eighty-nine "subjects" of the Russian Federation were declared to be equal "in relations with state federal bodies." Federal laws were to be supreme in all fields, and republics within Russia were no longer to be referred to as "sovereign." Several republics, however, maintained constitutions that contradicted the new centralizing moves by Moscow. Tatarstan, Tuva, and Bashkortostan reserved various powers for themselves. Sakha, the former Yakutia, made a lucrative financial deal with the center that allowed it to retain half of its hard currency profits from its diamond mines and all of its tax revenues in 1994. The regions of Russia were at first run by appointed governors , who ruled by decree with little interference from the weak local dumas, but all were to be elected by the end of 1996. Several larger, richer ethnically Russian regions, like Ekaterinburg in the Urals, asserted their wishes for greater local power, and as the economic ties between center and periphery grew weaker, regional economic links were strengthened.

The economic and political crises of 1991 through 1993 had begun a grand process of redistributing wealth and property in Russia and other post-Soviet republics. When the Duma delayed ratifying the government's draft law on privatization and left for its summer 1994 recess, the president enacted the law by decree. Privatization accelerated in 1994–95. By the summer of 1994 over 100,000 enterprises had been privatized. By the summer of 1995 half the country's labor force worked for privatized firms. A social revolution of enormous dimensions took place that in effect created a new property-owning class. This new Russian bourgeoisie was made up of former state-enterprise managers, well-placed politicians, new entrepreneurs and bankers, and criminal elements who managed to accumulate great wealth. Highly concentrated in the center—80 percent of assets were located in Moscow—Russian capital remained, as it had been before the revolution, closely tied to the state. Taking advantage of their positions, high government officials emerged as some of the richest people in the country. While production of manufactured goods collapsed, the most dynamic economic activity was found in banking, export, trade, and services. Indeed, bankers became the new economic tsars as their institutions bought up much of the assets in privatized enterprises. Ominously, the criminal and semicriminal elements played a key role in the new Russian banking community. Along with state officials, regional governors, and managers of state and collective farms, industrialists and bankers made up the sociopolitical elite of the country. Not only did they have access to politicians, with whom they would make deals, but they were influential in the media as well. A multimillionaire banker controlled his own independent television network, NTV. The largest network, ORT, was owned 51 percent by the state and 49 percent by wealthy individuals close to the Yeltsin government. Russia's second network was wholly owned by the state. Newspapers remained free of censorship, though the vagaries of the marketplace made survival difficult for them. *Izvestiia*, once the organ of the Soviet state, became in the Yeltsin years the most consistently pro-government mouthpiece with a national reach.

After four years of some form of capitalism and some kind of democracy, Russians were exhausted, exasperated, increasingly apathetic politically, and often cynical. Poverty and economic uncertainty, the loss of its empire and superpower status, a general sense of humiliation, and fear of the future affected millions of people. Fewer voters turned out for elections. Many were disgusted with the political infighting in parliament; others were appalled at Yeltsin's bloody dismissal of parliament and the invasion of Chechnya. A majority (65 percent), wished that Russia had a strong leader, and only a quarter of the population had a positive opinion about "democracy," a word that was often snarled by politicians and increasingly became identified with the economic and social disasters that had been visited upon Russia. Nostalgia for the old Soviet Union grew, and in 1994 pollsters discovered that 71 percent believed that its breakup had been a mistake. Many of those who desired the paternalistic protections of the old system and hoped to recover the sense that Russia was a great power voted either for the Communists, their allies, the Agrarians, or the nationalistic Zhirinovskii party.

In December 1995 the second Russian parliamentary elections were held. The biggest winner was the Communist Party, which took 22.3 percent of the popular vote. Zhirinovskii's party won 11 percent, while the government and the reform parties, Chernomyrdin's Our Home Is Russia and Grigorii Yavlinskii's Yabloko, won 10 percent and 6.9 percent respectively. The biggest losers were the moderate centrist parties, which did not gain the necessary 5 percent of the popular vote to win seats in the Duma. Many analysts saw the results as a another sign of the political polarization of the Russian electorate between those forces that wanted to continue rapid marketization and those that opposed liberal reform. More than half the voters cast their ballots for parties that were not committed to liberal democracy. The Communists and their allies alone won almost 40 percent of the vote. The only hopeful sign here for the liberals was that the Communist vote was quite geriatric. Over half the party's voters were pensioners.

With the power of the presidency enhanced, the personality, political vision, and health of Boris Yeltsin became a principal concern of observers both in Russia and the West. Yeltsin's popularity was at a historic low a few months before the June 1996 election of the Russian president, and there was widespread anxiety in the West and among Russian democrats that the Communists might win the election. But the Yeltsin forces rallied in the spring; they launched a vigorous campaign in the media, which they monopolized, and managed to paint the Communists as a dangerous throwback to the past. Networks and major newspapers backed Yeltsin and kept Ziuganov out of the public eye. Yeltsin traveled widely in the country, promised to bring the Chechen war to an end, and lavishly bestowed gifts and promises on potential voters. Yeltsin won the first round of the election, with Ziuganov second and Lebed third. In a shrewd tactical move, the president allied himself with Lebed, promising him a powerful post as security chief, and swept to victory in the second round in July. The alliance with Lebed lasted only a few months more before Yeltsin dismissed him as a destructive, uncooperative force within the government. By the end of 1996 Russia's government was a listing ship of state with an ill president barely grasping the wheel and pretenders to power waiting below deck. Factions and competing interest groups kept each other in balance, with no single figure or group able to defeat and eliminate the others.

The lesson of the recent history of Russia (and the other former Soviet republics) is that in order to make a successful social transition from authoritarianism to democracy and from a state economy to a market economy it is essential to have a viable state authority. The state comes first. Without an authoritative state (not necessarily, one hopes, an authoritarian state), the creation of modern democratic institutions based on the rule of law, a market system with protected property and enforcement of contracts, and a minimum of social order is impossible. After more than five years of social and political turmoil the Russian state remained fragile and unable to exercise some of its basic tasks, such as maintaining civil order, collecting taxes, and guarding its borders (the Russian state had not even been able to decide on words to its national anthem). Extrastate forces—entrenched old elites, parvenu criminal mafias, and more legitimate entrepreneurs—filled the space left by the retreat of the state. Russian leaders had seen the old state as the major impediment to the reconstruction of the social order, and in their revolutionary fervor they accelerated the dissolution of state authority left by Gorbachev. Russia's transition was a genuine revolution that brought down a state and an empire. But it had yet to show that it could also create a new state, the essential first condition for establishing the rule of law, a market economy, and a democratic polity.

The great achievement of the Soviet experiment was the rough modernization of a backward, agrarian society. Soviet power industrialized, urbanized, and educated a mass society through the exercise of state power on a mobilized population. But social and economic modernization resulted in an incompletely modern society. The modernity achieved by 1985 did not include democratic institutions, a legally sanctioned civil society, the rule of law, or a consumer-driven economy—all of which had become part of the universal definition of modernity by the end of the twentieth century. Gorbachev's reforms eliminated the most oppressive aspects of the Soviet system, moved the country toward democracy, and ended the Communist monopoly on power. Much of the raw material for creating a liberated society and democratic state was available at the end of the Soviet period, but the great problem was how to do it. Russians and non-Russians proved to be better at tearing down old edifices than building new ones. The blueprints they chose came from the West. In this sense most of the educated and political elite had already turned toward a Western notion of modernity. But the open questions were whether they would successfully use their skills and talents to build a modern democratic society and whether what they built would be for the fortunate few or the great many.

Suggestions for Further Reading

The verdict on the Yeltsin years and the new post-Soviet republics is still not in. For some interim reports, see Stephen Fish, *Democracy from Scratch: Opposition and Regime in the New Russian Revolution* (Princeton, N.J., 1995); Michael McFaul, *Post-Communist Politics: Democratic Prospects in Russia and Eastern Europe* (Washington, D.C., 1993); Michael McFaul and Sergei Markov, *The Troubled Birth of Russian Democracy* (Stanford, Calif., 1993); Gail Lapidus (ed.), *The New Russia* (Boulder, Colo., 1994); Timothy Colton and Robert Legvold (eds.), *After the Soviet Union: From Empire to Nations* (New York,

1992); Michael Urban, Stephen White, Alex Pravda, and Zvi Gitelman (eds.), *Developments in Soviet and Post-Soviet Politics* (Durham, N.C., 1992); James R. Millar and Sharon L. Wolchik (eds.), *The Social Legacy of Communism* (Cambridge, 1994); Karen Dawisha and Bruce Parrott (eds.), *Russia and the New States of Eurasia* (Cambridge, 1994); and Michael Urban, with Vyacheslav Igrunov and Sergei Mitrokhin, *The Rebirth of Politics in Russia* (Cambridge, 1997).

For a biography of Yeltsin, see John Morrison, *Boris Yeltsin: From Bolshevik to Democrat* (New York, 1991). Yeltsin's own (or ghost-written) autobiographies are also worth reading: Boris Yeltsin, *Against the Grain: An Autobiography* (New York, 1990) and *The Struggle for Russia* (New York, 1994). An exceptionally useful volume is Timothy J. Colton and Robert C. Tucker (eds.), *Patterns in Post-Soviet Leadership* (Boulder, Colo., 1995).

On the non-Russian successor states, see Ian Bremmer and Ray Taras (eds.), *New States, New Politics: Building the Post-Soviet Nations* (Cambridge, 1997); William E. Odom and Robert Dujarrie, *Commonwealth or Empire? Russia, Central Asia, and theTranscaucasus* (Indianapolis, Ind., 1995); Ronald Grigor Suny, *Looking toward Ararat: Armenia in Modern History* (Bloomington, Ind., 1993); Jan Zaprudnik, *Belarus at a Crossroads in History* (Boulder, Colo., 1993); and Dilip Hiro, *Between Marx and Muhammad: The Changing Face of Central Asia* (London, 1994).

To understand the influence of media on the new Russian politics, see Ellen Mickiewicz, *Changing Channels: Television and the Struggle for Power in Russia* (New York, 1997).

Chronology

882	Traditional date for the founding of the first Russian state (Kievan Rus).
988	The princes of Kiev adopt Christianity as their official religion.
1237–1240	The Russian lands are conquered by the Mongols.
1533–1584	Reign of Ivan IV "the Terrible," first tsar of Russia.
1613	Beginning of the Romanov dynasty, which lasts until 1917.
1682–1725	Reign of Peter I "the Great."
1762–1796	Reign of Catherine II "the Great."
1855–1881	Reign of Alexander II, "the tsar-liberator."
1861	The Era of the Great Reforms begins with the emancipation of the serfs.
1863	Polish rebellion against Russian authority is crushed by the tsarist state.
1881–1894	Reign of Alexander III.
1883	First Russian Marxist organization, the Liberation of Labor Group is founded.
Late 1880s–Early 1890s	Russia's first industrial "takeoff."
1894–1917	Reign of Nicholas II, the last tsar of Russia.
1898	Russian Social Democratic Workers' Party is founded.
1902	Vladimir Ilich Lenin (1870–1924) writes *What Is to Be Done?*
1903	Split of the Social Democrats into Bolsheviks (later Communists) and Mensheviks.
1904–1905	Russo-Japanese War, which ends in Russia's defeat.
1905–1907	First Russian Revolution leads to a semiconstitutional regime.
1906–1911	Prime ministry of Petr Stolypin, who introduces reforms of the peasant commune.
1914–1918	World War I.

1917
February 23–28 (March 8–13)
The insurrection in Petrograd; the "February Revolution."
February 27 (March 12)
Formation of the Provisional Government and the election of the Soviet of Workers' Deputies. Establishment of "Dual Power."

March 2 (15) Abdication of Nicholas II.
April 3 (16) Lenin returns to Russia from exile in Switzerland.
May 1 (14) After the "April Crisis," the Coalition Government is formed.
June 18 (July 1)
    "Kerensky Offensive" begins.
July 3–5 (16–18)
    The "July Days" lead to a reaction against the Bolsheviks.
July 8 (21) Alexander Kerensky becomes prime minister.
August 24–31 (September 6–13)
    The "mutiny" of General Lavr Kornilov.
October 25 (November 7)
    The "October Revolution" establishes "Soviet Power."
October 26 (November 8)
    Lenin forms the first Council of People's Commissars (Sovnarkom) and issues the decrees on peace and land.
Late November
    Formation of a "left coalition" Soviet government, with a Bolshevik majority and a Left SR minority; elections to the Constituent Assembly.
November 23 (December 6)
    Finland declares its independence from Russia.
December 1 (14)
    Formation of the Supreme Council of National Economy (VSNKh).
December 2 (15)
    Soviet Russia signs an armistice with Germany.
December 7 (20)
    Sovnarkom sets up the Extraordinary Commission to Combat Counterrevolution and Sabotage (Cheka).
December The Taryba in Vilnius declares the independence of Lithuania.

1918
January 5 (18)
    First (and last) session of the Constituent Assembly.
January 12–13 (24–25)
    The Rada in Kiev declares Ukraine's independence from Russia.
February 24 Estonia declares its independence.
March 3 Soviet government signs Treaty of Brest-Litovsk with Central Powers.
March 4 Trotsky beomes People's commissar of war and organizes the Red Army.
March 6 British troops occupy Murmansk.
March 19 The Left SRs resign from the Sovnarkom.
April 5 British and Japanese land at Vladivostok.
April 22 Transcaucasian Federal Republic declares independence from Russia.
May Revolt of the Czechoslovak legions, which seize the Trans-Siberian railroad.
May 26–28 Georgia, Armenia, and Azerbaijan declare independence from Russia.
June 11 Committees of the Poor Peasantry are formed.
June 14 Bolshevik majority expels Mensheviks and Right SRs from the All-Russian Central Executive Committee of Soviets (VTsIK).
July 6 Left SR rebellion against the Soviet government.
July 16–17 Murder by local Bolsheviks of Nicholas II and his family.

July 31	Fall of the Baku Commune.
July	First Constitution of the Russian Soviet Federated Socialist Republic is adopted.
August	Military food brigades begin confiscating peasants' grain.
September 2	Systematic terror launched by the government against its enemies.
October 31	Compulsory labor obligation introduced.
November	White generals overthrow the SR-led Directorate and make Admiral Kolchak "Supreme Ruler" of Russia.
November 11	End of World War I.
November 18	Latvia declares its independence.

1919

March	Eighth Congress of the RKP (b) decides to form a Political Bureau (Politburo), an Organizational Bureau (Orgburo), and a Secretariat with a principal responsible secretary.
March	Formation of the autonomous Bashkir Soviet Republic.
March 2–6	First Congress of the Third International (Comintern).
October	General Denikin's armies come within 200 miles of Moscow.
December 2–4	
	Eighth Conference of the RKP (b).

1920

January	Admiral Kolchak abdicates in favor of Denikin.
January	Establishment of the Tatar Soviet Socialist Republic.
March 29–April 5	
	Ninth Congress of the RSDRP (b).
April 25	Pilsudski's Poland invades Ukraine, beginning the Russo-Polish War.
April 28	The Red Army takes Baku and Azerbaijan becomes a Soviet republic.
July 21–August 6	
	Second Congress of the Comintern.
September 1–7	
	First Congress of the Peoples of the East is held in Baku.
September 22–25	
	Ninth Conference of the RKP (b) discusses the trade union issue.
October	Formation of the All-Russian Association of Proletarian Writers (VAPP).
November 9–10	
	Defeated, General Wrangel abandons Crimea for exile.
December 2	Armenia becomes a Soviet republic.

1921

February 25	The Red Army invades Georgia, which becomes a Soviet republic.
February 28–March 18	
	Revolt of the sailors at Kronstadt.
March 8–16	Tenth Congress of the RKP (b); defeat of the Workers' Opposition and the passing of the resolution against organized factions within the party; introduction of the New Economic Policy (NEP).
March 16	Anglo-Soviet Trade Agreement.
March 18	Treaty of Riga ends the Russo-Polish War.
June 22–July 12	
	Third Congress of the Comintern.
July	The journal *Changing of Signposts* begins publication in Prague.

Summer	Famine spreads throughout Russia (1921–1922).
August 7	Death of the poet Aleksandr Blok.

1922

February 6	The Cheka becomes the GPU.
March 26	Lenin suffers his first stroke.
March 27–April 2	
	Eleventh Congress of the RKP (b); Stalin becomes general secretary of the Communist party.
April 16	Treaty of Rapallo is signed with Germany.
May	Soviet government arrests Patriarch Tikhon, head of the Russian Orthodox church.
June	Trial of the Right SRs.
June 8	Glavlit, the censorship authority, is established.
August	Soviet government decides to deport over 160 intellectuals.
August 4	Red cavalry kills Enver Pasha and puts down the Basmachi rebellion.
September	Stalin introduces his "autonomization" plan.
October	Currency reform.
December 25	Lenin dictates much of his "Testament."
December 30	The USSR is formally inaugurated.

1923

January	Soviet government establishes a state monopoly on alcohol production.
March 9	A stroke incapacitates Lenin, removing him from politics.
April 17–25	Twelfth Congress of the RKP (b).
Summer–Fall	The "Scissors Crisis."
October 15	"Platform of the 46" attacks bureaucratism in the party.
October 21–23	Communist "revolution" fails in Germany.
December 14	Beginning of the campaign against the Opposition.

1924

January 21	Death of Lenin. Triumvirate of Stalin, Zinoviev, and Kamenev.
January 31	Constitution of the USSR is ratified.
February	"Lenin Enrollment" brings more workers into the party.
April–May	Stalin's lectures on *Foundations of Leninism*.
May 22	Party leaders decide not to release Lenin's "Testament."
May 23–31	Thirteenth Congress of the RKP (b).
July 17–July 8	Fifth Congress of the Comintern.
October	Trotsky publishes *Lessons of October*.
December	Stalin promotes idea of "Socialism in One Country," along with Bukharin.

1925

January	Trotsky is replaced as commissar of war by Frunze.
April 17	Bukharin tells the peasants to "enrich themselves."
July 1	Central Committee takes a relatively neutral position in literary matters.
November 28	Suicide of Esenin.
December 18–31	
	The Stalin-Bukharin "centrist" position triumphs over the Opposition at the Fourteenth Congress of the RKP (b).

1926
January   Zinovievists are removed from the Leningrad party leadership.
April   United Opposition formed by Trotsky and Zinoviev.
July 14–23   Central Committee plenum removes Zinoviev from the Politburo.
October 23–26
                  Trotsky and Kamenev from the Politburo. Bukharin replaces Zinoviev
                  as Chairman of the Comintern.
November   The Code on Marriage, Family, and Guardianship is adopted.

1927
April 27   Chiang Kai-Shek attacks Communists in Shanghai.
May   Great Britain breaks off relations with the Soviet Union and sets off a
                  "war scare."
May 25   United Opposition issues its "Declaration of the 84."
Fall   Peasants begin reducing grain sales to the state authorities.
November 15   Trotsky and Zinoviev are expelled from the Communist party.
December 12–19
                  Fifteenth Congress of the VKP (b) calls for a Five-Year Plan of eco-
                  nomic development and voluntary collectivization.

1928
January 16   Trotsky is exiled to Alma Ata, Kazakhstan.
March   The "Cultural Revolution" begins with Stalin's attack on "bourgeois
                  specialists."
April   The Politburo pressures the Academy of Sciences to become more
                  Marxist.
May 18–July 5
                  Shakhty trial.
July 4–12   The "Right" and Stalin argue about collectivization in the Central
                  Committee.
July 17–September 1
                  Sixth Congress of the Comintern adopts the "social fascist" line.
September 30 Bukharin's "Notes of an Economist" published in *Pravda*.
October 18–19 Uglanov and the "Right" are defeated in the Moscow party organiza-
                  tion.
December   The Central Committee calls for publication of more socially useful
                  books.
December 10–24
                  Tomskii and the "Right" lose at the Eighth Trade Union Congress.

1929
February 9–10 The Politburo condemns Bukharin, Rykov, and Tomskii.
February 11   Trotsky is deported from the USSR to Turkey.
April 23–29   Sixteenth Conference of the VKP (b).
July 3   Molotov replaces Bukharin as chairman of the Comintern.
November 10–17
                  Central Committee plenum removes Bukharin from the Politburo.
November 7   Stalin's article "The Year of the Great Breakthrough" appears in
                  Pravda.
December 21   Stalin's 50th birthday; the beginning of the "Stalin Cult."
December 27   Stalin calls for more rapid collectivization and liquidation of the ku-
                  laks.

1930

March 2   Stalin's article "Dizziness from Success" reverses the collectivization drive.

April 14   Suicide of Mayakovskii.

June 26–July 13

Sixteenth Congress of the VKP (b); Tomskii is dropped from the Politburo.

July 1930   Litvinov replaces Chicherin as people's commissar of foreign affairs.

July 30   Peasant communes and village gatherings are officially abolished.

November   Molotov replaces Rykov as chairman of Sovnarkom; Orjonikidze becomes the head of the industrialization drive.

November–December

Trial of the "Industrial Party."

December   The Syrtsov-Lominadze affair.

1931

June 21   Stalin speaks against equalization of wages and attacks on "specialists"; end of the "Cultural Revolution"; beginning of the "Great Retreat."

October   Stalin publishes his letter to *Proletarian Revolution* on writing party history.

1932

January 30–February 4

Seventeenth Conference of the VKP (b).

April   Dissolution of RAPP and other proletarian artists' associations.

October   The Riutin affair.

November   Stalin's wife, Nadezhda Allilueva, commits suicide.

December   Introduction of the internal passport system for urban population. Famine in Ukraine (1932–1933).

1933

January 1   The Second Five-Year Plan (1932–1937) begins.

May   Suicide of Mykola Skypnyk as a result of attacks on Ukrainian "nationalists."

November 16 United States and Soviet Union establish diplomatic relations.

1934

January 26–February 10

Seventeenth Congress of the VKP (b), the "Congress of the Victors."

August   First Congress of Soviet Writers adopts "Socialist Realism" as official style.

June 9   Law on "betrayal of the motherland" prescribes the death penalty.

September 18 USSR enters the League of Nations.

December 1   The assassination of Kirov.

Vasilev brothers' film *Chapaev* is released.

1935

January 1   End of food rationing that began in 1930.

January 15–16

The first trial of Kamenev and Zinoviev.

May   Stalin changes the slogan "Technology decides everything" to "Cadres decide everything."

May 2	Franco-Soviet Treaty of Mutual Assistance.
July–August	Seventh Congress of the Comintern adopts "Popular Front" line.
August 30	Beginning of the Stakhanovism campaign.
October 17	Law against pornography in art or literature is adopted.

1936

June 27	New laws prohibiting abortion and tightening the structure of the family.
July 18	Outbreak of the Spanish Civil War.
August 19–24	Moscow "show trial" of Zinoviev and Kamenev, who are convicted and shot.
August 23	Tomskii commits suicide.
September 25	Stalin replaces Iagoda with Ezhov as head of the security apparatus.
December 5	Constitution of the USSR is adopted.

1937

January 28	Attack on Shostakovich's opera, *Lady Macbeth of Mtsensk.*
January 23–30	
	Moscow "show trial" of Radek, Piatakov, Sokolnikov, and Serebriakov.
February 18	Orjonikidze commits suicide.
February	Central Committee plenum discusses Bukharin's fate.
May–June	Purge of army officers; secret trial and execution of Tukhachevskii and other top military commanders.
	Height of the Great Purges, the "Ezhovshchina."

1938

March	*Anschluss* of Austria by Germany.
March 13	Russian language is made compulsory in all Soviet schools.
March 2–13	Moscow "show trial" of Bukharin and Radek.
July	Clashes with Japanese military forces at Lake Khasan.
September	The *Short Course of the History of the Communist Party* is published.
September 30	Germany, Italy, France, and Great Britain sign the Munich Pact.
December	Beria replaces Ezhov as head of the NKVD.

1939

March 2–13	Eighteenth Congress of the VKP (b).
March 15	German occupation of Czechoslovakia.
May 3	Molotov replaces Litvinov as people's commissar of foreign affairs.
May 11–August 31	
	Soviet clashes with the Japanese at Khalkin-Gol.
August 23	Molotov-Ribbentrop Pact of Non-Aggression between the USSR and Germany.
September 1	Germany invades Poland; beginning of World War II.
September 17	Soviet forces invade Poland.
November 1–2	
	Annexation of western Belorussia and western Ukraine by the USSR.
November 30–March 12, 1940	
	Russo-Finnish War.
December 14	USSR is expelled from the League of Nations.

1940

April 8–11	Soviet secret police murder thousands of Polish officers at Katyn.
June 26	Restrictive labor laws are adopted by Soviet government.

June 28	USSR annexes Bessarabia and northern Bukovina from Rumania.
August 3–6	Lithuania, Latvia, and Estonia are joined to the Soviet Union.
August 20	The assassination of Trotsky in Coyoacan, Mexico.

1941

May 6	Stalin becomes chairman of Sovnarkom.
June 22	Germany invades the Soviet Union.
June 30	Creation of the State Defense Council, headed by Stalin.
June 28	Fall of Minsk.
July 3	Stalin speaks to the Soviet people by radio.
August 25	Soviet and British troops move into Iran.
September 8	Leningrad surrounded; beginning of the 900-day "Seige of Leningrad."
September 18	Fall of Kiev.
September 30–Spring 1942	
	Battle of Moscow.
October 16	The "Great Panic" in Moscow.
December 7	Japanese attack Pearl Harbor; the United States enters World War II.

1942

May 17–28	Red Army is defeated at Kharkov.
June 28	Germans launch "Operation Blue" toward Voronezh and the Don River.
	"Black Summer" of 1942; Germans advance eastward.
July 17–February 2, 1943	
	Battle of Stalingrad.
July 28	Stalin orders "Not one step back!"
August 21	German Army reaches the Great Caucasus Range.
December 27	General Vlasov creates his anti-Soviet Russian Liberation Army.

1943

April 13	Germans announce the discovery of mass graves at Katyn.
April 26	USSR severs relations with the London Poles.
May 23	Dissolution of the Comintern.
July 5–August 23	
	Battle of Kursk.
September	Stalin allows the Russian Orthodox church to elect a new Patriarch.
November	Reduction of the bread ration.
November 28–December 1	
	The Teheran Conference.
November–December	
	Deportation of the Karachais and Kalmyks; later the Chechens, In- gushi, and Balkars (February–March 1944); and the Crimean Tatars (May).

1944

January 1	A new Soviet anthem replaces the "Internationale."
January 27	The Siege of Leningrad ends.
April 8–May 12	
	Soviet Army drives the Germans from Crimea.
June 6	American and British troops land at Normandy.
July 3	Liberation of Minsk.
July 9	Soviet family law re-establishes the concept of illegitimate children.

August 1–October 2
> Warsaw Uprising.

August 31   Soviet Army enters Budapest.

September 16 Soviet Army enters Sofia; leftist Fatherland Front comes to power.

October   Stalin and Churchill conclude the "percentages agreement."

1945

January 12   Stalin orders the Soviet offensive through Poland.

February 4–11 Yalta Conference.

March   Communist-Socialist coalition government formed in Czechoslovakia.

April 12   Roosevelt dies of a brain hemorrhage and is succeeded by Truman.

April 13   Soviet Army enters Vienna.

April 16–May 8
> Final Soviet offensive against Berlin.

May 8–9   The war in Europe ends.

May   Communists win the largest plurality (38 percent) in Czechoslovak
                   elections.

June 28   Coalition government, made up of Lublin and London Poles, is
                   formed in Poland.

July 17–August 2
> Potsdam Conference.

August 6   The United States drops an atomic bomb on Hiroshima.

August 8   USSR declares war on Japan.

August 9–September 2
> Soviet Army fights the Japanese in Manchuria.

September 2   Japan surrenders; end of World War II.

October 24   Founding of the United Nations.

November   Communists receive only 17 percent in Hungarian elections.

1946

February 9   Stalin's "Pre-election Speech."

February 22   George Kennan's "Long Telegram" from Moscow.

March 5   Churchill's "Iron Curtain" speech in Fulton, Missouri.

March   USSR withdraws claims for Armenian (later Georgian) irredenta in
                   Turkey.

April   SDs and Communists merge into Socialist Unity party in East Ger-
                   many.

August 14   Attack on Zoshchenko and Akhmatova; beginning of the
                   Zhdanovshchina.

1947

March 12   Truman Doctrine is declared by the president.

June 5   Marshal Plan is proposed.

September   Founding of the Cominform.

December 14 End of wartime rationing.

1948

January 13   Murder of the Jewish actor Solomon Mikhoels.

February   The Czechoslovak "coup."

March 27   Rupture of relations between Stalin and Tito's Yugoslavia.

June 24–May 5, 1949
> Berlin Blockade.

July 13–August 7
　　　　　Academy of Agricultural Sciences is forced to adopt Lysenkoism.
　　　　　The "Leningrad Affair."

1949
April　　　Formation of the NATO alliance.
October 1　Founding of the People's Republic of China.

1950
June 26　　North Korea invades the south and begins the Korean War.
August 29　USSR explodes its first atomic bomb.

1952
October 5–14 Nineteenth Congress of the VKP (b).
October　　Stalin publishes *Economic Problems of Socialism in the USSR*.

1953
January 13　Announcement of the "Doctors' Plot."
March 5　　Death of Stalin. Malenkov becomes chairman of Council of Ministers.
June　　　Workers' uprising in East Germany.
June 26　　Arrest of Beria.
September　Khrushchev becomes first secretary of the Communist party.

1954
　　　　　Khrushchev transfers Crimea from the Russian Republic to Ukraine.

1955
February 8　Bulganin replaces Malenkov as chairman of the Council of Ministers.
May 14　　Formation of the Warsaw Pact.
July　　　Geneva Summit Conference.

1956
February 14–25
　　　　　Twentieth Congress of the CPSU; Khrushchev's "Secret Speech."
April　　　Dissolution of the Cominform.
October 23–November 4
　　　　　Revolution in Hungary.

1957
June 17–29　"Anti-party Group"(Malenkov, Molotov, and Kaganovich) acts against
　　　　　Khrushchev.
October 4　Soviet Union launches *Sputnik*, the first artificial satellite of the Earth.

1958
March 27　Khrushchev replaces Bulganin as chairman of the Council of Ministers.
October–November
　　　　　Campaign against Nobel Prize winner Boris Pasternak.
November 27 Khrushchev initiates the Berlin Crisis.

1959
September　Khrushchev visits the United States; "Spirit of Camp David."

1960
April　　　Sino-Soviet split comes into the open.
May 1　　American U-2 spy plane is shot down over the Soviet Union.

1961
April 12   Yurii Gagarin becomes the first man in space.
July   Khrushchev and Kennedy meet in Vienna.
August   The Berlin Wall is built.
October 17–31
                 Twenty-Second Congress of the CPSU. Stalin's body is removed from the Lenin Mauseleum.

1962
June 2   Riots in Novocherkassk.
October 22–28 Cuban Missile Crisis.
                 Liberman proposals.

1963
August 5   Nuclear Test Ban Treaty is signed.

1964
October 14   Khrushchev is removed as first secretary by the Central Committee and is replaced by Brezhnev.

1965
                 Kosygin attempts to introduce economic reforms.
April 24   Armenians march in Erevan to mark fiftieth anniversary of genocide.
December 5   First open dissident demonstration in Moscow.

1966
February   President Johnson bombs North Vietnam, escalating the war in Indochina.
February 10–14
                 Trial of Siniavskii and Daniel.

1967
June   Israeli victory in the Six-Day War inspires Soviet "refusniks."

1968
January–August
                 "Prague Spring."
August 20–21
                 Soviet army invades and occupies Czechoslovakia.

1969
October   Solzhenitsyn wins the Nobel Prize for Literature.

1970
August 12   USSR and West Germany sign a Renunciation of Force Treaty.

1971
September 3   Four-Power agreement is signed on status of Berlin.

1972
May 22–30   Brezhnev and Nixon sign SALT I in Moscow. Period of détente.

1975
August 1   Helsinki Accords signed.
December   Sakharov wins the Nobel Prize for Peace.

1977

October 7   Adoption of new Constitution of the USSR.

1979

December 24–26

               Soviet troops move into Afghanistan to back Marxist government.

1980

August   Formation of the independent Polish trade union, Solidarity.

1981

December 13

               Polish government cracks down on Solidarity and declares martial law.

1982

November 10

               Brezhnev dies and is succeeded by Andropov.

1983

September 1   Soviet jet shoots down Korean Air 007.

1984

February 9   Andropov dies and is succeeded by Chernenko.

1985

March 10   Chernenko dies and is succeeded by Gorbachev.

1986

April 26   Chernobyl nuclear accident.
October   Gorbachev and Reagan meet in Reykjavik, Iceland.
December   Gorbachev invites Sakharov to return to Moscow from exile.
December   Kazakhs demonstrate in protest against appointment of a Russian party chief.

1987

October–November

               Yeltsin is demoted after he criticizes the party leadership.

1988

February   Crisis over Nagorno-Karabakh erupts.
March 13   Nina Andreeva's letter, "I Cannot Deny My Principles" is published.
June 28   Nineteenth Conference of the CPSU opens.

1989

April 9   Violent suppression of demonstrators in Tbilisi, Georgia.
May 18   Estonia and Lithuania declare their sovereignty.
May 25   Congress of People's Deputies convenes.
August 24   Non-Communist government comes to power in Poland.
November 9   The Berlin Wall is torn down.

1990

January   Soviet troops move into Azerbaijan to quell riots and restore order.
March 6   Article Six of the Soviet Constitution is removed.
October 15   Gorbachev wins the Nobel Prize for Peace.

December 20 Shevardnadze resigns as foreign minister.

1991
January Soviet troops fire on crowds in Latvia and Lithuania.
March 17 Referendum on the future structure of the USSR.
June 12 Yeltsin is elected president of the Russian Federation.
August 18–21 Attempted coup against Gorbachev fails.
December 25 Gorbachev resigns as president of the Soviet Union.

1992
January 2 Gaidar launches "shock therapy" economic policy.
May Nationalist Popular Front comes to power in Azerbaijan.
December 14 Gaidar is replaced by Chernomyrdin as prime minister.

1993
April 25 Referendum supports Yeltsin's reform policies.
September 21 Yeltsin dissolves the Russian parliament and calls elections to a State Duma.
October 3–4 Clashes between forces backing the parliament and those backing the president.
December 12 Elections to the State Duma reject the radical reformers and support nationalists and former Communists; ratification of the new Constitution.

1994
December 11 Russian troops invade Chechnya.

1995
December 17 Elections to the State Duma; Communists win largest plurality.

1996
June–July Yeltsin wins re-election as president of the Russian Federation.

1997
April 2 Russia and Belarus sign a treaty of union.
May 27 Yeltsin and NATO leaders sign the "Founding Act" of mutual cooperation and security.

Index

Abakumov, V.S., 373
Abkhazia, 114, 441
Abovian, Khachatur, 273
Academy of Sciences, 210, 211, 440, 511
Acheson, Dean, 361, 378
Acmeism, 196
Adriatic, 352
Afghanistan
  Amir Amanullah, 118
  Basmachi rebels, 82, 118, 293, 510
  Soviet activity in, 163, 421, 444–45, 459, 473, 518
  Taliban, 445
Africa, 341, 421, 444
Agrarians, 504
Agriculture
  Academy of Agricultural Sciences, 371, 516
  collectivization, 218–31, 244, 256, 286, 328, 364, 376, 454, 500
  grain requisitions, 89–90, 104, 135, 218, 222, 241, 257–58, 241–42
  harvests, 158, 227, 257, 401, 408, 418, 435
  under Khrushchev, 391–92, 407–08, 418, 419
  land for, 46, 88–89, 349
  nationalization of, 58
  and NEP, 150, 154–59, 178–79
  and peasants, 7–8, 15, 220
  productivity, 240, 323, 365–67, 450
  scissors crisis, 150–51, 510
  subsidies, 137, 426
Akaev, Askar, 481, 498
Akhmatova, Anna, 196, 318, 369, 515
Akhundzada , Mirza Fath Ali (Mirza Fatali Akhundov), 116, 273
Alaska, 496
Albania, 160, 348, 357, 358, 377, 412
Alcohol
  alcoholism, 203, 212, 230, 245, 438, 440
  anti-alcohol campaign, 451, 469
  consumption, 10, 87, 206, 433, 454
  state control over, 3, 510
Aleksandrov, Grigorii
  Circus; Joyful Guys; Radiant Road; Volga, Volga, 276
Alekseev, General Mikhail, 42, 49, 74
Alexander I, 111
Alexander II, 12, 18, 19, 507
Alexander III, 12, 13, 14, 16, 507
Alexandra, Tsaritsa, 27, 33, 70
Aliev, Heidar, 499
Allilueva, Nadezhda, 258, 319, 394, 512
All-Russian Directorate, 80
Alma Ata, 462, 511
Altai Mountains, 3
Alter, Viktor, 373

Altman, Natan, 199
Amanullah, King (Amir), 118, 445
American Relief Administration (ARA), 149
Amin, Hafizullah, 445
Amsterdam, 294
Anarchism
  political program, 61, 63, 136, 298
  repression of, 68, 125
  and terrorism, 71
Anatolia, 99, 101, 102, 352
Andreeva, Nina
  I Cannot Deny My Principles, 459, 518
Andropov, Iurii
  as General Secretary, 449–450, 451, 518
  as KGB chief, 433
Angelina, Praskovia, 279
Angola, 444
Anschluss, 299, 513
Antonov, A.S., 135
Apparatchiki, 267, 456, 474
April Crisis, 508
Arabs, 116, 286, 432, 444
Aral Sea, 239
Arbatov, Georgii, 458
Archives, 266, 267
Arctic Ocean, 3
Arkhangelsk, 77, 81
Armand, Inessa, 186
Armenia 4–5, 19, 66, 116, 463, 475, 499, 508
  Armenian Apostolic Church, 4, 100, 441
  genocide, 82, 100, 102, 431, 517
  independence from Soviet Union, 483, 496, 498
  national consciousness, 97–99, 101, 273, 281, 289, 458, 462, 465, 470
  SFSR, 142–43, 285, 287, 479, 481, 483, 509
Arms race, 338, 378, 395–98, 411, 426, 442–45, 458–59
Arsenal, 36
Art, 15, 430, 433, 513
  and Bolsheviks, 195–207, 212–13, 269–76
  and the Great Retreat, 258
  and the Great Terror, 276–78
  after World War II, 369–72, 404–07, 418, 420
Arteli, 91, 174–75, 243
Assassinations, 512, 514
  attempt on Alexander II, 19
  attempt on Lenin (1918), 70, 191
  of Sergei Kirov (1934), 260–62, 512
  of Minister of Education (1901), 24
  of Minister of Interior (1902), 24
  of Grigorii Rasputin (1916), 33
  of Soviet Ambassador to Poland (1927), 165
  of Petr Stolypin (1911), 26
  of Leon Trotsky (1940), 266, 514